SOCIALIST PARTIES IN POSTWAR JAPAN

VOLUME II OF

STUDIES ON JAPAN'S SOCIAL DEMOCRATIC PARTIES

SOCIALIST PARTIES IN POSTWAR JAPAN

戦後日本社会党論

by

ALLAN B. COLE

GEORGE O. TOTTEN

CECIL H. UYEHARA

with a contributed chapter by

RONALD P. DORE

New Haven and London, Yale University Press, 1966

Designed by John O. C. McCrillis,
set in Baskerville type,
and printed in the United States of America by
Connecticut Printers, Inc., Bloomfield, Connecticut.
Distributed in Canada by McGill University Press.

Library of Congress catalog card number: 66–21511

Published with assistance from the foundation
established in memory of Henry Weldon Barnes of
the Class of 1882, Yale College.

We affectionately dedicate this volume to our wives,

Marjorie Cole, Astrid Totten, and Allie Uyehara

Preface

Since 1947–48, when Japan's Social Democratic Party shared in two successive ruling coalitions, its activists have several times predicted the party would assume power by obtaining a majority after a few more elections. But this hope has repeatedly been dashed; the remarkable political and social changes accompanying recent economic growth have made its attainment more difficult. Since 1958–59, electoral support—reflected by the number of seats in the Diet—has reached a plateau, the "barrier of one third," as referred to by the Socialists themselves. The number of votes and percentage of total votes received by the Socialists and other leftist forces have, however, steadily increased and now exceed 40 per cent of the total votes cast. With approximately one third of the seats in the national legislative bodies they and their allies have been, in some senses, defending aspects of postwar democratization, trying to promote the interests of their allied movements, seeking to strengthen Japanese neutralism in the cold war, striving to reorient Japan toward closer relations with the socialist states, and, since the autumn of 1948, generally acting as the opposition.

Though these parties do not seem to be within easy reach of periodic majorities and power, their role may enable them to reap advantages from shifts which are not yet clearly foreseen. In any case, Japanese socialism, which somewhat unsteadily accepts representative politics, has for more than a generation expressed certain durable interests and traditions in Japan's industrializing society. Earlier in the process of modernization, conditions and tensions in Japan were more like those which gave Marxism some cogency and following in other industrializing, late-developing societies. In the course of time and struggles a veritable socialist ethos developed. Especially in a culture in which militancy, loyalty, sacrifice, patriarchal elitism, and social chasms are prominent, such a philosophy and movement developed persistent traditions. In some senses these are emotional traditions to which activists become devoted. Somewhat as the range of denominational sects in Western Christianity apparently conform to a spectrum of human experience and need, so in secular politics there has developed a variety of traditions, each with its momentum, each combining opportunism and principles while striving to adjust to changing realities. Paradoxically, even a revolutionary cause like Marxist socialism in time has developed a core of orthodoxy and hence its own relative conservatism.

As Japanese modernization developed and matured, new social strata, or classes, emerged; some more than others organized self-consciously to promote their distinct interests. We shall see that Japan's Social Democrats have considered themselves to be the natural allies of organized labor. The white-collar class, students, and many intellectuals have been poorly paid, are highly literate, and are either unionized or otherwise organized. Their inclinations have tended to be more reformist or radical than two other groups which the Socialists have tried to attract: the rural and what some have called the "urban peasantry." Since the postwar land reform, the Social Democratic Party (SDP, also called the Japan Socialist Party, JSP) has tried to win support from farmers more on specific issues than on class and ideological grounds. Voters in the small business sector have mostly been conservative, though a fraction smaller than one third has tended to support Socialist candidates. These interests are becoming better organized and politically less apathetic, but growing prosperity and capital development have filtered to them and strengthened proprietary tendencies. Other interests, such as those of women, youth, and consumers, also receive Socialist attention. We shall discuss how these noncommunist parties on the left have tried to reconcile their ideologically rationalized positions with the political fact that electoral support for all major parties in Japan is cross-stratal.

Especially since 1955 there has been much discussion of whether a two-main-party system is suitable for Japan. While true that the SDP is the pivot of the opposition, and that the two main conservative party lineages have been combined, it is clear that the emergence of two national parties with considerable overlap in common basic policies is unlikely soon to take shape. On the right of the spectrum is a coalition of conservative factions. Observers follow their rivalries and combinations, but the underlying distinction is between traditional conservatives, whose attitudes were mainly formed under the authoritarian Meiji system, and cautiously progressive elements.

The three main sectors in the opposition have been the evolutionary, reformist right-wing Socialists, the revolutionary left-wing Socialists with intramural differences but, under dominant capitalism, favoring parliamentary politics, and the Communists whose principle of proletarian dictatorship is well known. One can distinguish fundamentally between the milder right-wing Socialists (since 1960 called Democratic Socialists) and the more moderate revolutionaries in the SDP "mainstream" groups, on the one hand, and the more drastically radical intraparty opposition plus the Communists, on the other. This does not mean, however, that the two more moderate Socialist groups, or the two more revolutionary forces, are likely to form lasting combinations. The ebb and flow of personal, factional, organizational, and environmental conditions, as well as strategic relationships, give each of these groupings a role to play.

Japan's multiparty pattern has in some ways been simplified but in others has become more complicated since the mid-'fifties. Political movements are afoot which relate to the vast petty middle class, to unorganized industrial workers and clerks—thus to the "floating vote"—to the opportunities for Japanese traditionalism to find channeled expression, and to the participation of those millions who have lived in poverty at the foot of the social ladder. After ten years of organization and political growth, the Sōka Gakkai, a religio-political movement of Buddhist laymen and their converts, in 1964 founded the Komeitō (Clean Government Party). In some ways this new force, though still somewhat obscure as to policies and main direction, may already be stronger than the socialist parties.

The leftist Social Democratic Party is in some respects an anomaly. For a party which receives such sizable support in national elections it has a very small membership and weak regional and local organizations. In these respects and in the circulation of its published organs it is weaker than the Communist Party. It is also weaker in its discipline, clarity of policies, and ability to mobilize campaigns of action. Financially and in programs of action it is seriously dependent on Sōhyō, the principal left-wing federation of labor and its component unions. Moreover, the controversies which beset socialists, since capitalism in the world and in Japan is obviously not moribund, cut right across this party. The perplexities of the "structural reformers" in the SDP, whose views we shall discuss, derive from their attempt to cope with contradictions for socialism which have recently been more troublesome than for regulated and resurgently dynamic capitalism. We shall see that minority socialism in Japan is making contributions toward the development of a welfare state. But the definitive doers are, and may continue to be, the governing Liberal Democrats. Inherent in this situation are socialist frustrations which can be utilized by advocates of direct action in efforts to justify extraparliamentary methods for seizing power and compelling "qualitative" changes. At present it appears that the stage is being set for great struggles over constitutional revision and, in 1970, over the renewal of the military-political alliance with the United States. Foreign observers often become excessively alarmed at such demonstrations of opposition.

Japan's technology and economy are rapidly maturing to a new level capable of keeping ahead of later developing countries and competing to supply many of their needs. Japan is beginning to play a more positive, nonimperialistic role in international affairs. Its productive growth and prosperity are making possible a greater capacity to protect its own security, to provide higher incomes and social security for its people, to shift more families from crowded agriculture into urban occupations, and to come closer to full employment. Middle strata in society are growing in size and confidence, and are attaining higher cultural levels. Professional people and the army of clerical workers are receiving more adequate salaries. Farmers are joining in the consumer boom and are being more fully integrated into the body politic. Even though there has been mild inflation, discontents which tend to foster susceptibility to revolutionary appeals have subsided. Socialism's champions, though more reluctant than their counterparts in Western and Central Europe, have been compelled to cope with the practical and theoretical implications of these changes.

In writing this study of Japan's noncommunist Social Democratic parties since their revival in 1945 to 1960–61, just after the assassination of Inejirō Asanuma, the party's Chairman, the authors have combined the historical method with political description and analysis. The first two chapters provide an historical survey according to phases of party development. The charts depicting party splits and mergers, leadership lineages, as well as successive labor and farmer organizations provide additional guideposts. Topical chapters then can and do assume that the reader has an overview of the party's political history; they refer only briefly to such events and can freely treat their subjects according to analytical and interpretative requirements. Of course, each of these topics is much more complex than we have had space to explain. We have had to select, simplify, and generalize, using a broader background in making judgments. There is, for example, need for more research on the interpretation of socialist thought; and we have had to omit treatment of cultural movements related to the Socialists.

It seemed to us that, although the Socialists have most often emphasized and split over foreign policy issues, the competence and validity of Socialist economic proposals should also be evaluated. We enlisted the assistance of the Kokumin Keizai Kenkyū Kyōkai (National Economic Research Institute), an unofficial and nonpartisan agency, to help us outline and evaluate the policies advocated by right-wing and left-wing Socialists during successive stages of Japan's postwar economic development. Subtopics under foreign policies could be multiplied but we were obliged to select key issues on which major debates have been waged and which continue to be matters of controversy.

The chapters on party organization and leadership have also been distilled from considerably longer manuscript treatments. The special relations between the party and labor unions in policy, finances, organization, and personnel, warranted a careful description and analysis covering both cooperation and confrontation. We are grateful to Professor Ronald P. Dore for contributing to this volume the chapter on "The Socialist Party and the Farmers." The chapter on middle and other strata attempts to find indications from opinion polls as to trends of opinion in relation to policy positions taken by the Socialist Parties. The final chapter pulls threads together, makes some general interpretations, and scans the forward horizon. This study is Volume 2 of "Studies on Japan's Social Democratic Parties," Volume 1 being *The Social Democratic Movement in Prewar Japan* (New Haven, Yale University Press, 1966) by George Oakley Totten, III, which traces the origins of the movement back to the end of the nineteenth century but concentrates on the noncommunist proletarian parties of the 1920s and 1930s and their labor, agrarian, and other organized supporters. An earlier product of this same project is *Leftwing Social*

Movements in Japan: An Annotated Bibliography (Tokyo, Japan, and Rutland, Vermont, The Charles E. Tuttle Company, 1959) by Cecil H. Uyehara, in which may be found the bulk of the Japanese language primary and secondary bibliographical materials then available. The existence of that publication and the fact that full citations have been provided in the footnotes obviate the need for a separate bibliography in this volume.

Our principal consultants in this undertaking have been Professors Masamichi Rōyama, formerly of Tokyo University, then President of Ochanomizu Women's University; Chitoshi Yanaga of the Department of Political Science at Yale University; and Edwin O. Reischauer, formerly Director of the Harvard-Yenching Institute at Harvard University and more recently United States Ambassador to Japan. We are grateful not only to them but also to Mr. and Mrs. Michio Rōyama, Mr. Masao Yoshida, and Mr. Seiichi Izumi, who served as research assistants at various times. To Mr. Hidezō Inaba and the staff of the Kokumin Keizai Kenkyū Kyōkai we are indebted for their economic studies. Leading officers of the SDP, Socialist Party Diet members, the professional staff in the party's national headquarters, numerous SDP-oriented labor union officials in Sōhyō, Zenrō, and other organizations, and very many local party and labor union executives gave most generously of their time in responding to numerous queries from project members when they visited Japan and traveled from Hokkaidō to Kyūshū. We wish especially to thank Messrs. Shimpei Fujimaki, Masamichi Horigome, Tamio Kawakami, and Fusao Yamaguchi. We also wish to thank Miss Ruth L. Davis and Mr. David Horne of the Yale University Press for their editorial advice and other efforts. The Ford Foundation supplied financial support during the research and early writing stages of this project. Tufts University provided a home for and administrative support to the project. The initial encouragement and guidance by Dr. Robert B. Stewart, formerly Dean of The Fletcher School of Law and Diplomacy at Tufts University, in launching the project is remembered with gratitude. We deeply appreciate all the advice, suggestions, and assistance provided to project members individually and to the effort as a whole, but the responsibility for factual material and interpretations appearing in this book is necessarily our own.

ALLAN B. COLE
GEORGE O. TOTTEN
CECIL H. UYEHARA

January 1966

Contents

Tables

Charts

Postwar Party History

1. The Socialist Taste of Power and Decline

REBIRTH OF THE JAPANESE SOCIALIST PARTY

When, in that fateful August of 1945, Suehiro Nishio heard in Osaka the Emperor's broadcast call for his people to lay down their arms and "bear the unbearable," he is said to have straightway boarded an electric train to visit another veteran right-wing socialist, Chōzaburō Mizutani, in Kyoto. There he vigorously expounded the need for reorganization of labor and farmers' unions and for a socialist party to contribute in reconstructing the devastated country. Two days later, with rucksack on his back, Nishio started for Tokyo to confer with another former colleague, the veteran organizer Komakichi Matsuoka, who also favored reviving the trade union movement.

Political consultations in the next few months reflected the physical and spiritual turmoil of a society still suffering from the shock of defeat. Conservative and socialist leaders, who would later be bitterly antagonistic, conferred about policies to meet the national crisis. Some of them had been elected to the Diet in 1942 without Tōjō's blessing and for years had faced the scorn of the militarists in power. Men prominent in most of the prewar proletarian lineages, motivated by a combination of ambition and public responsibility, were again astir and renewing contacts.

Three days after the ceremony of surrender aboard the U.S.S. *Missouri,* thirteen former socialist Diet members decided to form a new party. Despite widespread privation, social and political instability, and economic near-paralysis, more than one hundred persons from many parts of the main islands answered the call for a national conference and selected an inaugural committee of 25 members. Within two months, on November 2, 1945, these champions of the interests of workers, farmers, and the petty middle strata founded Japan's first postwar political party. Having in the past known oppression, and being uncertain about policies to be required by the Allied Occupation authorities, they chose the name Nihon Shakaitō (Socialist Party of Japan) but also were careful to adopt as the official English translation the title Social Democratic Party of Japan (SDP or SDPJ). It seemed safer to announce only a general program of three aims: democracy, socialism, and eternal peace. The convention was chaired by Matsuoka (future Speaker of the Lower House). Tetsu Katayama (who later became Socialist Prime Minister) was elected Secretary-General. Suehiro Nishio, Chōzaburō Mizutani, Rikizō Hirano (future Ministers of State) and the other members of the inaugural committee were installed as the party's first Executive Committee. Amid thunderous applause, Masaru Nomizo (who would soon become Minister of Agriculture), read the Inaugural Declaration, proclaiming that "Japan is about to experience an historical transformation" and calling on the assembled five thousand and the nation to "cooperate in carrying out this historic undertaking. The gates of the Social Democratic Party of Japan are freely open to all."

It was not without traditions and experience that such a large group responded with new hope to the summons of that small band of socialist leaders emerging from forced hibernation. As a precursory volume[1] has explained, movements of peasant protest had multiplied in the later decades of Japan's last feudal era and during the early Meiji period. Such revolts were suppressed and for sixty years after the Imperial Restoration common farmers and industrial workers, without votes, were governed and usually represented by economic magnates and oligarchs or their agents. The molders of the new Japan, though mostly risen from lower ranks of the warrior elite, developed a latently authoritarian regime; the Diet was constitutionally circum-

1. Chapter 1 is intended to serve as a bridge between this volume and George O. Totten's *The Social Democratic Movement in Prewar Japan* (New Haven, Yale University Press, 1966), which is Vol. 1 of "Studies on Japan's Social Democratic Parties."

scribed and rested on a limited and reluctantly expanded electorate. Much from the feudal emphasis on hierarchy and absolutism was transmitted into the new polity and the sharply pyramided new economic structure. The farmers, who had paid disproportionately for the cost of Japan's modernization, were joined among the discontented by urban workers, growing at first slowly, then rapidly, in number. In Japan's capitalist system, the poorer farmers—though no longer serfs with feudal obligations and controls—became tenants. Workers in more modern industries were less encumbered and protected by the old institutions of guild and apprenticeship. Regulative legislation lagged, and in Japan there was an "industrial reign of terror" mitigated mainly by the paternalism of entrepreneurs.

Political awareness and strategies were slow in developing among the underprivileged and powerless. The first tenant and labor unions were organized between the turn of the century and World War I. Liberalism had been rather erratically espoused by opponents of oligarchic governments, especially since the early 1880s, but the various schools of socialism began their precarious existence as the contemporaries, and soon the allies, of the early trade unions. Every modern war stimulated Japan's industrialization, but it was notably economic expansion and inflation during and after the First World War which augmented the numbers of workers and their determination to organize. Marxian socialism had exerted slight influence in Japan since the 1890s, concentrated among a few intellectuals; it was only in the chaos following the global conflict that it established a revolutionary base in the greatest Eurasian state and became a neighboring force greatly feared by the masters of the Meiji system.

Most of the determinative institutions of this conservative regime had been founded before the oligarchy yielded to demands for a constitution and a parliament. Moreover, before their inauguration and before each subsequent extension of suffrage, the Peace Police or Peace Preservation Laws were tightened. Only lack of strict enforcement permitted illegal labor unions to be organized. Even at the height of their interwar development, their members numbered fewer than half a million; the movement was more significant as a portent for the future of an industrialized society than for its then existing influence. However, individuals and associations—whether concerned chiefly with proletarian philosophies, economic bargaining, or strategies for attaining political power—were watched and placed under severe disabilities by agencies of law and control. By the mid-1930s the modified Meiji system had become an atavistic police state reminiscent (in a modern context) of the Tokugawa system and many of its component feudal regimes. This was not all foreordained, but there were certainly built-in reasons why it could happen.

The increased popularity of democracy and the growth of urban middle strata contributed to the ferment which followed the First World War. In the early 1920s, a national federation of labor and one of farmers' unions were formed. The Japan Communist Party (JCP) was also founded, its components usually working through other leftwing movements. Shortly before and after enactment of the universal manhood suffrage law in 1925, the Japan Farmers' Union, and especially leftist elements in the General Federation of Labor (Sōdōmei), became more politically oriented. Their members and prospective constituents would soon be able to vote, and they would consequently have a larger stake in the parliamentary system. Many leftists really doubted that socialism could triumph over bourgeois capitalism and other conservative elements only through electoral campaigns and the Diet, but it was expedient to keep within the pale of legality by avowing at least a degree of respect for this institutionalized form of struggle.

Stronger political emphases in both the labor and farmers' movements caused sharper distinctions and tensions between their left and moderate wings. The General Federation of Labor was split at its convention in 1925, the leftists forming the Council of Japanese Labor Unions (Hyōgikai). Thereafter, the labor movement was plagued by competing organizations, guided by irreconcilable leaders mostly discernible in four groups: social democrats, radical leftists, Communists, and, for a time, anarchists. The first proletarian political party was banned in 1925 as being Communist-influenced. In the following year, four parties were formed: the Labor Farmer Party (Rōdō Nōmintō), the Japan Labor-Farmer Party (Nihon Rōnōtō), the Social Democratic Party (Shakai Minshūtō), and the Japan Farmers' Party (Nihon Nōmintō)—in order of general radicalism from left to right. The resulting factions of leaders have persisted to this day. A succession of Communist-dominated parties on the extreme left, though repeatedly suppressed by police actions, excelled in the disciplined vigor of their leaders and in electoral results. By the spring of 1929, however, such a political organization could no longer operate publicly.

More moderate left-wing groups attracted some of the splinters resulting from the government's hammer blows as well as dissidents from the right-wing Social Democratic Party. While the legal or noncommunist left benefited in one way from official repression, this situation bred a kind of opportunism which made some of its leaders susceptible later to the pressures of chauvinism and national socialism. Moreover, the latitude for legal activities was repeatedly narrowed, especially during and after the Manchurian crisis.

By 1931 there were only two main parties on the left: the intellectually radical National Labor-Farmer Masses' Party (Zenkoku Rōnō Taishūtō) and the more conservative Social Democratic Party mentioned above (but not to be confused with the postwar party). Heightened nationalism caused attrition in both these organizations and their component factions. The latter split in part over the issue of military action in Manchuria but more fundamentally Tetsu Katayama represented those upholding social democratic principles, while Akamatsu led those who inclined toward national socialism and soon bolted the party—with some labor elements—to support military leadership. The former also split over "state socialism." In mid-1932, the two still anti-fascist parties merged to form the Socialist Masses' Party (Shakai Taishūtō). The two main factions in this new party were thereafter known as the "Socio-Democratic" (Shaminkei) and the "Japan-Labor" (Nichirōkei) cliques, from abbreviations of the names of the parties they had originally founded. But the process of yielding to overwhelming pressures was renewed, and by the time clashes led to war in China in 1937, this harassed organization promised to help promote national unity in the face of the crisis. Earlier in that same year dissidents, led by Kanjū Katō and Mosaburō Suzuki, had founded the last of Japan's prewar leftist parties. They called it the Japan Proletarian Party (Nihon Musantō) and tried to make it the vehicle for a united front. But by the end of the year the party was ordered disbanded and its leaders were arrested. Although the Socialist Masses' Party had gained the third largest representation in the House of Representatives, in the elections of 1937, it had no chance for further growth. Its Japan-Laborites, led by Hisashi Asō, tried to ride the bandwagon of total mobilization, but some of the more moderate and politically principled Socio-Democrats under Isoo Abe and Tetsu Katayama left the party in 1940. Later that year the Socialist Masses' Party outdistanced its bourgeois rivals in dissolving all political parties to make way for the Imperial Rule Assistance Association (IRAA) which some of them erroneously thought could help control the military.

A small number of former proletarian party leaders, some with and others without Tōjō's blessing, were elected to the Diet in 1942. Still others, mainly certain Japan-Laborites, served in the IRAA and the Japanese version of a "labor front" during the war in the Pacific. Some established small businesses and cooperated with the war effort while others quietly retired. Despite the national emergency and the dreaded "thought police," the IRAA never became a harmonious single party. Some former proletarian leaders, like conservative politicians, maintained liaison, survived the holocaust, and promptly emerged in September 1945 from strategic retirement.

Japan's military machine had been destroyed; civilian political authority was discredited and confused. The Allied Powers declared that Japan would be completely disarmed and demilitarized. The influence of chauvinistic nationalism was to be totally eliminated. All restrictions on political, civil, and religious liberties were rescinded. Democratic parties with rights of free speech and assembly were to be encouraged. In these sudden and extraordinary circumstances, it was imperative that some organized movement—perhaps a spectrum of them—fill the immediate postwar vacuum. The Social Democratic Party hoped to benefit by the new prestige of "democracy." Its leaders had fought a rearguard action, not without compromises, for many of the ultimate objectives proclaimed by the victorious Allies. Disillusioned by the national leadership that had brought them to the brink of almost total destruction, the Japanese people seemed to have repudiated war and militarism and to be ready for something new. The prewar social democrats of many hues, regrouping themselves in the Social Democratic Party, appeared to be one of the best solutions during the critical period of reconstruction. Professional and academic observers as well as the man on the street expected much of this party. According to one prominent educator, "Our hope for possible escape from the present ruinous chaos and for our possible revival as a nation hinges upon the future of the Party."[2]

The SDP was and still is a controversial organization, or movement, advocating a program based on socialism. In the immediate postwar months, Mitzutani declared that socialists would build a "Japanese-type democratic government in accordance with the Imperial Charter

2. Kisaburō Yokota, "Social Democratic Party," in *Digest Service, 1* (Sept. 8, 1946).

Oath of 1868, by means of a mass party based on socialistic principles."[3] When they began laying the groundwork for a comprehensive coalition, the Socialists soon discovered that years of suppression had neither tempered their respective philosophies nor lessened their factional proclivities. The Emperor system, wartime collaboration by some, and the problem of selecting the supreme party leadership were the first knotty problems. The conservative Nishio group, which was predisposed to uphold the Imperial institution, contended this to be in the interests of the party and to be a correct reflection of the popular will. This view was accepted by the newborn party. Each principal constituent from the prewar movement suggested as a prospective party Chairman some prestigious figure outside of their own members: a prominent member of the former Japanese peerage, or a conservative businessman or politician. The compromise was a headless beginning, with Katayama serving as Secretary-General. The ideological jumble in the party's top leadership was aptly described by a Tokyo daily in 1945 as

> a heterogeneous alliance of all socialist groups . . . There are the intellectual Utopians and the religious idealists, the hardheaded laborites who have come up through the rough and tumble mill of union activities—incidentally divided among themselves between the right-wing and the left-wing factions, the opportunists who swerved from socialism during the war but who are now trying to come back into the fold like repentant prodigals, and the uncompromising and unforgiving orthodox materialistic Marxists who have always been single-mindedly devoted to the "Cause."[4]

THE POLITICS OF PROTEST

When the war ended in August 1945, the Japanese industrial system had almost ground to a halt. Industrial and mineral production in 1945 and the early part of 1946 was about 10 per cent of the 1934–36 average. Not only had human resources been completely overworked during the war years; the industrial plant had also been allowed to deteriorate. The exigencies of war had concentrated all resources on military objectives; consumer goods industries had been largely squeezed out of existence. Air raids had not only demolished

3. *Asahi Shimbun,* Sept. 16, 1945.
4. *Nippon Times,* Nov. 3, 1945.

most of Japan's industrial capacity but had cut off its overseas food supplies and had destroyed much housing. Immediate postwar cabinets made no attempt to carry out a planned conversion of Japan's remaining industrial plant to peacetime production. The government failed to control the distribution of the gigantic supplies of food and materials stockpiled by the Japanese armed forces. An equitable distribution of these commodities could have eased the initial impact of the acute shortages and the uncontrolled inflation after the war ended. Hoarded foods and materials slipped from one black market to another, accelerating each time the spiral of prices. Deliberately or through sheer ineptitude, the government stimulated inflation by releasing enormous military funds, by making peacetime reconversion loans to industry, and by subsidizing industrial production. Barely subsisting on meager diets, sheltered in dilapidated and makeshift dwellings, the people gave vent to long pent-up discontents, thus adding fuel to the crisis. By the end of 1945, just three and a half months after termination of the war, black market prices had risen 93 times above the prewar level.

This desperate situation was the background for a determined bid of the regrouped Social Democratic Party for postwar leadership, a vigorous revival of the legalized Japan Communist Party, and the meteoric rise of labor unions, both numerically and politically. Communist leaders just released from prison in October 1945 repeatedly called upon the SDP for the formation of "a common front of democratic forces in the new Japan." Although the right-wing Socialists were able to dominate the party during the early postwar years, they had also to contend with a persistent and vocal left wing. The relative unity of the Communists at this time contrasted with the divided Social Democrats. In most respects, the former were more aggressive in the immediate postwar period; they held rallies to ferret out and make lists of war criminals, organized demonstrations on a variety of issues, discovered and forced the rationing of hoarded foods and materials. The Socialists were pressed to the wall in justifying their continued and sometimes equivocal rejection of Communist overtures. First, they declined on grounds that neither group had formed a party or drafted policies; that "going one's own way" would be more effective than cooperation; that Socialists could not trust a secret Communist Party; and lastly, the 1946 general elections were used as an excuse. Even right-wing SDP leaders recognized that objective conditions were ripe for a democratic front but that their party had not been sufficiently organized to assure Socialist leadership of it. Significantly, it was always the Communists who approached the Socialists and the latter, at times politely, at times bluntly, demurred.

The 1946 return from China of Sanzō Nozaka, the suave, soft-spoken Communist leader, his appeal for a "lovable" JCP, and left-wing Socialist efforts to force the hand of the SDP by forming their own Democratic People's League (Minshu Jimmin Remmei) under the leadership of the veteran socialist, Hitoshi Yamakawa, embarrassed the party's right wing. The Communists appealed to rank-and-file Socialists, especially on the local level, where they were partially successful. The Socialist national leadership was unable to prevent limited cooperation between Socialists and Communists in outlying areas during elections. The latter tried to coax Socialists into cooperating on specific issues, such as "Food May Day" (May 22, 1946), when increased rice and other rations were demanded. After the elections of April 1946, a right-wing Socialist, Tatsuo Morito, proposed a Democratic League for National Salvation (Kyūkoku Minshu Sensen Remmei), hoping thereby to reestablish SDP leadership among all democratic forces in and out of the Diet. Socialist procrastination in joining or creating its own "common front" was due to the party's internal dissension, especially on the crucial point of participation with the JCP, and the deep suspicion of all leftists harbored by right-wing Socialists. The latter insisted on continued rejection of Communist overtures because they expected the conservative Yoshida Cabinet to reach an impasse in its economic policies and then to call upon the Socialists to help form a national government. Democratic leagues of the Communist or right or left Socialist brands, furthermore, did not arouse public opinion or bring about a union of democratic forces. The National Salvation League was an anticlimactic termination to Socialist–Communist sparring in their bid for left-wing leadership. It was more tactical in nature than sincere in purpose.

Ironically the Diet, which had been elected under the strong guidance of General Tōjō in 1942, was directed by the Allied Occupation to legislate many important democratizing innovations into the Japanese political and electoral systems toward the end of its term in 1945–46. Noteworthy among these changes were the granting of woman suffrage and stronger safeguards to assure honest elections. All restrictions on free speech and association had been removed. Leftists, who had always operated insecurely, had never experienced such an unhampered atmosphere in which to challenge the regime; but the "new forces" in Japan had not recovered from the war and were poorly organized, factious, and plagued by problems of wartime collaboration as well as by competing ideologies. During the long campaign preceding the elections of April 1946, the SDP was initially cautious as to the number of candidates it selected. Its central slogan was simply "socialism or capitalism" with a promise of gradualism in the socialization of banking, and of the coal, iron, fertilizer, electric power, and transportation industries.

On January 4, 1946, a "purge directive" was handed to the Japanese government. All parties except the Communists were affected, conservatives and right-wing Socialists in larger numbers being disqualified from holding public offices. The problem of responsibility for aggressive war had been a source of constant irritation in Socialist ranks. Left-wing factions had repeatedly called for a purification of the party and for removal of wartime collaborators sitting in its highest councils. But they had not been successful. It was only through implementation of the purge that several leaders of the dominant right wing were politically barred. Its advantage was due less to organizational strength than to prewar experience and renown. While only a few Socialists were affected by the purge, Diet delegations of the conservative parties were seriously depleted. This emboldened the Socialists to increase the number of their candidates for the Diet elections in April. But the contest when it came was still far from equal: the intense indoctrination of prewar education, substitution of the henchmen of some purgees in the electoral race, and concentration of governmental authority and prestige in the old guard weighed against the Socialists.

Still, the SDP emerged from the first postwar elections as a major political entity. It became the second largest party with 92 members in the House of Representatives, only 21 of whom had formerly sat in the Diet. A large proportion of the new SDP Diet delegation was composed of freshmen in politics who were attracted to "socialism" as a panacea for the ills of postwar Japan but whose ideas were not based on any solid philosophical convictions. No political party received a clear mandate in this election; a coalition was unavoidable. Similarities in political outlook and historical background and their combined majority naturally placed the two conservative parties in a position to form the next Cabinet. Realizing that the demands of labor—

expressed in successive labor offensives as well as through the SDP and JCP—could not be ignored, the conservatives tried to entice the right-wing Socialists into a coalition. In the post-election negotiations, and later during the peak of the labor offensive in December 1946 to January 1947, many of the right-wing Socialists were willing and eager bargainers for governmental posts. The Socialist position was further strengthened by personality conflicts among conservative politicians, a legacy from prewar years. However, the Socialists themselves were divided in their attitude toward participation in a coalition government; the left wing vehemently opposed any such dilution of socialist principles.

When Shidehara finally resigned on April 22, 1946, he demanded that the next Premier and Cabinet be a "stabilizing force." After protracted negotiations, the initiative to form a Cabinet passed from the Liberals to the SDP and back again. Shigeru Yoshida, the Liberal Party's new president after the purge of Ichirō Hatoyama, formed a Cabinet, but it failed to provide stability. It did not raise production, was forced into modified economic planning, and antagonized labor through derogatory statements and inflationary financial policies. These chaotic conditions encouraged continued Socialist–conservative negotiations, which, though long unsuccessful, whetted right-wing SDP leaders' thirst for ministerial posts and afforded the left wing a chance to exert more influence in party councils.

The advent of the Allied Occupation had freed the labor movement of its shackles. It was soon legally recognized and actively encouraged. A basic labor union law was enacted in December 1945 and became effective in March 1946, giving workers the right to bargain collectively and to strike. Prewar labor leaders, many of whom were affiliated with the former proletarian parties, reemerged and soon became prominent. In less than a year after the surrender, almost 13,000 unions with more than 3.8 million members had come into existence, and this growth continued—usually at an accelerating rate—until March 1949. Prewar unions were reactivated, but more importantly, workers in many new industries were organized. Leaders associated with the prewar Socio-Democratic clique reestablished the General Federation of Labor (Sōdōmei) in August 1946. More radical prewar leaders in the same month created a competing organization along industrial lines; this Congress of Industrial Unions (Sambetsu, or the CIU) came increasingly under the dominance of the JCP.

Food shortages, lack of raw materials, and inflation spurred strikes.

Managements, shaken by a breakdown in social order, acceded to most of labor's demands. Organized workers even adopted "production control" as a strike tactic until this was later declared to be illegal. Instances of irresponsible violence by labor and mob pressures occurred. But this was only natural when the government showed itself totally unable to control prices and wages; it had no food policy and took only weak financial measures. The depreciation of real wages progressively aggravated the already explosive situation. Soon after taking office, Premier Yoshida (in June 1946) issued a statement on the maintenance of social order, in which he said there were certain elements in Japan who, on the pretext of practicing democracy, were apt to ignore order, hold law in contempt, and indulge in inflammatory speeches and actions. This comment only accelerated social unrest and further aroused the hostility of organized labor. In turn, the government, supported by influential capitalists, took a stronger stand and attempted large-scale personnel retrenchment without adequate unemployment insurance, tried to enact a Labor Relations Adjustment Law taking away from governmental workers the right to strike, and blandly ignored the steadily deteriorating economic situation.

Then even the moderate Federation of Labor could no longer stand idly by. The politically oriented labor offensives organized by the CIU were gathering momentum. The first peak was reached on December 17, 1946, with a mass rally of half a million workers mobilized by the General Federation, the CIU, farmers' unions, and independent trade unions, demanding the overthrow of the Yoshida Cabinet and the establishment of a democratic government with SDP control of key ministries. The rally was coordinated with a non-confidence motion presented in the House of Representatives which was, of course, defeated by the conservative majority. While members of the right-wing SDP contented themselves with this motion, left-wingers were more concerned with its being synchronized with the rally. Yoshida's New Year greeting, containing a reference to "those base fellows" (a mild translation), stiffened labor's attitude. The government workers' unions, about 2.6 million strong, thereupon called a general strike for February 1, 1947. In order to prevent the labor offensive from being totally guided by the JCP, the SDP—especially its left wing—reluctantly participated. As a party of the workers, it felt compelled to condone the general strike and to uphold all economic demands. Only a written directive from General MacArthur as Supreme Commander for the Allied Powers (SCAP) prevented the "use of so deadly a social weapon in the present impoverished and emaciated condition of Japan." A week later he wrote to Premier Yoshida requesting "another democratic expression of the people's will."

Because the new Japanese Constitution was soon to come into effect, elections to the House of Councillors, to prefectural legislatures, and to governorships were scheduled for April 1947. The selection of a new House of Representatives was thus added to a multiplicity of elections. All indicators of public opinion showed growing support for the Social Democratic Party. Just before the last Imperial Diet adjourned, however, the ruling conservative parties pushed through a revision of electoral districts, changing them from large prefectural constituencies with plural balloting to medium-sized constituencies with single balloting. The Socialists vigorously opposed this move. It was obvious that this revision would seriously hurt their candidates in the forthcoming contests, but SCAP did not raise a finger to prevent the old guard from consolidating its power through such last-minute schemes.

Disillusionment with bureaucratic ineptitude, popular identification of the conservatives with the discredited wartime regime, the attraction of a new force, and a feeling of desperation on the part of the people—all heaped unreasonable and naïve expectations on the SDP. As a symbol of the new era, and the only party that might be trusted to guide Japan toward democratic aims, the SDP had become the chief beneficiary of the prevailing mood. The ruling conservatives had been slow in enforcing the purge—even overlooking certain cabinet ministers—had maintained a more than friendly relationship with the chief director of the purge, and had crippled the Economic Stabilization Board. The confident SDP rejected a bid from the JCP for electoral cooperation. During the campaign, Socialists emphasized the deficiencies of the retiring Yoshida administration and advocated governmental control of coal mines and the fertilizer industry, taxation of wartime black market profiteers, and suspension of interest payments on wartime government bonds.

To their own surprise the Socialists obtained a plurality with 143 members in the House of Representatives. The two conservative parties, Liberals and Democrats (with factional rearrangements, the Progressive Party having changed its name), obtained 132 and 126, respectively. The People's Cooperative Party had 31 members elected, while the JCP secured only four seats. The extent of discontent was thus indicated. But the tenacity, skill, and determination of conservative politicians was equally apparent.

SHARING POWER: THE KATAYAMA CABINET

"We shall struggle against the conservative reactionary camp and carry out a revolution through the Diet"—so spoke Tetsu Katayama, Chairman of the SDP, immediately after the elections from the balcony of the *Asahi* Newspaper building to crowds assembled below. It proved to be no more than a bold gesture.

Should the SDP, with only a plurality in the Lower House, try to form a cabinet? Tension persisted between its left and right wings on this score. The left opposed participating in the government because of the difficult economic situation, the lack of an absolute majority, and slim hopes for a future Socialist government if it failed the first time. The right wing, on the other hand, felt that the SDP should participate in the government since the people had given the largest support to the Socialists; because the party must not seem to lack in political courage; because it should abide by parliamentary practices as the plurality party; and it was, they argued, the only party that could "save the masses" from postwar economic chaos. The Socialist predicament was accentuated by the overwhelming conservative majority, though split as it was into competing parties and jealous factions.

For a month the four main parties (the SDP, the Democrats, the Liberals, and the People's Cooperative Party) worked toward a national unity government and a four-party policy agreement. The JCP was pointedly omitted. The left-wing Socialist leaders, Mosaburō Suzuki and Kanjū Katō—in order to placate the suspicions of the conservatives on account of their active role in the aforementioned labor offensives, and in a bid for possible participation in the government—made a dramatic anticommunist declaration. Instead of accepting these gestures, however, the Liberals demanded that the SDP be purged of its left wing. This the Socialists refused to do, but they agreed to exclude them from cabinet posts, to reject the extreme left and right, to prevent leakage of state secrets, and to refrain from any action conducive to social unrest. With more concessions from the SDP than from the conservatives, a four-party policy agreement was concluded. The Socialists pledged not to demand a freeze of the "new yen" or suspension of interest payments on war bonds and acceded to a diluted version of their coal nationalization policy. Socialist policies for overcoming chronic inflation were also sacrificed. At the last minute, the Liberal Party declared it would not participate in the government anyway. The Socialists, Democrats, and People's Cooperative Party eventually formed an administration. While they were officially bound by the four-party agreement, the Liberal Party as "friendly" opposition could not be counted on for much cooperation. The ratio of cabinet seats was seven each for the SDP and the Democrats and two for the People's Cooperatives. The Socialists held the portfolios of Education, Agriculture and Forestry, Justice, Commerce and Industry, and in addition the directorship of the Economic Stabilization Board. Thus, for the first time in modern Japanese history, a Socialist (and incidentally a Christian), Tetsu Katayama, headed the government. He was also the first Premier under the new Constitution.

The Katayama cabinet inherited an intolerable crisis from its predecessor: the vicious wage–price spiral, the militant demands of labor, and the food problem. In retrospect, Katayama claims that there was only four days' supply of rice in government warehouses when he took office. The paramount mission of this cabinet was, therefore, the formulation and execution of effective economic policies. The Premier made desperate appeals to the people to bear up under the crisis and to cooperate with the government. The economic measures adopted by the Socialist-led government were in line with the general requirements enumerated in a letter from General MacArthur to the previous Prime Minister, calling for strong economic controls. As a result, Hiroo Wada, Director General of the Economic Stabilization Board (ESB), the chief economic planning agency, wielded considerable power in the cabinet. Under Wada's direction, the ESB compiled the first economic white paper in Japan and devised a wage–price stabilization program pegging wages at 26.8 times those of the 1934–36 level, prices at 65 times, coal at 127 times, and iron at 220 times their levels during that same earlier period. The government tried to enforce the program with penal sanctions but was not successful.

Passage of the bill for state control of the coal mining industry proved to be the only quasi-socialistic policy pushed through by the Socialist–conservative coalition government. As soon as Minister of Commerce and Industry Mizutani had announced his intention to draft such a bill, the Liberal Party had declared it would not be bound by the four-party agreement on the issue. In order to obtain the support of conservative members of the cabinet, the SDP made one concession after another. When the bill was debated in the Diet, it was further diluted by the conservative forces. As finally passed by the House of Representatives on November 25, 1947, perhaps only the title—Temporary Law for the State Control of Coal Mining—closely resembled the original Socialist proposal. Of all the economic measures proposed by the government, this law most epitomized the basic incompatibility within the coalition. In actuality the emasculated bill signified that the obsolescent machinery in Japanese collieries would be modernized at the taxpayers' expense and soon returned with the mines themselves to private hands.

The more positive achievements of the Katayama cabinet included various laws to implement the new Constitution. For these, the Socialists were assured of the backing of SCAP; in fact initiative usually came from General Headquarters. These laws concerned institutional reforms of the government, procedural improvements, and strengthening of the social and economic foundations and procedures for building democracy. The Ministries of War, Navy, and Home Affairs were abolished. The Attorney General's office and a new Ministry of Labor were created, both headed by Socialists. Local government and the police were reorganized. The criminal code was revised, and support for the patriarchal family system was eliminated from the civil code. The first group of Japanese Supreme Court justices was appointed, and a government employees law was enacted. Labor standards, anti-monopoly and economic power deconcentration laws were passed and land reform further implemented. Most of this legislation did not basically affect the size of the powerful bureaucracy in Japan. While being somewhat reduced in numbers, its personnel was usually just reassigned. Even the purges mainly affected the ministries which were to be abolished. The "arrogant" bureaucracy proved to be the most unshatterable institution of the old, centralized system.

Toward the end of 1947, the SDP showed signs of serious internal dissension. In his zealousness to attract agrarian support, the Socialist Minister of Agriculture and Forestry, Rikizō Hirano, began to upset superficial coalition tranquility. He advocated that the government pay the growers higher prices for rice they were obliged to "deliver." If carried out, this would have disrupted not only the government's budgetary plans but also Wada's ESB plans to curb inflation. Hirano's proposal, suddenly made public while he was on a stumping tour, rekindled irritation and dissatisfaction among SDP leaders over his prewar ultranationalistic activities and high-handed role in earlier coalition negotiations. The possibility of his purge was also mentioned, as it had been when the cabinet was formed. Premier Katayama and his chief lieutenant, Nishio, supported Wada against Hirano as did the SDP left wing. Soon Katayama was forced to dismiss Hirano as a "disturber of the coalition peace." That stormy petrel was later officially purged from political life. He had already left the party, followed by 15 of his *kobun* or followers.

The "Hirano incident" consolidated the Socialist left wing into a stiffer attitude toward the right wing and other governmental parties. Its spokesmen demanded unsuccessfully that a member of their group be appointed Minister of Agriculture and Forestry. This was unacceptable to the Democratic and the People's Cooperative Parties because they regarded the SDP left wing as too pro-Communist. When Kanae Hatano, a nonparty university professor with right-wing Socialist connections, was ultimately selected, the left wing formed the May Society (Satsuki-kai), in order to consolidate its forces, declared its opposition within the party, reserved the right to criticize the government, and called for the abrogation of the four-party policy agreement which it regarded as a serious impediment to effective Socialist policies. The left-wing Socialist appeal met with marked success at the party's third national convention in January 1948, which resulted in a "policy victory" for the left and a "personnel victory" for the right. The latter was able to maintain its leadership only after overcoming a serious challenge. It found itself in the anomalous position of having to carry out leftist policies. Katayama was reelected chairman of the Central Executive Committee (CEC) but with many blank votes cast "against" him; abrogation of the four-party policy agreement—the basis of his own cabinet—was endorsed by the convention. In essence, the party had withdrawn the props from under its own shared government.

At the time the Katayama cabinet had been formed, the labor movement had supported the Socialist Party. The conservative Federation of Labor (Sōdōmei) had promised the coalition government its unqualified support, while the Sambetsu (the CIU) had given approval upon condition that socialist policies should continue to be effected. Labor disputes and strikes had temporarily decreased. The

Sōdōmei had proposed a rally to "support the Katayama cabinet" but, at the insistence of the Sambetsu, this was changed to "encourage the SDP." The difference in the attitudes of these two major labor federations was significant. When the government announced its wage–price stabilization program, the Sōdōmei reluctantly gave its support to the government, but Sambetsu demanded the fulfillment of SDP promises and the abandonment of the four-party policy agreement. Although the government had initiated many institutional reforms in favor of labor, it was unable to curb the deteriorating economic situation. Labor became restive; disputes and strikes began to increase again. Because private employers were able to circumvent the government's wage–price stabilization program with impunity, the real wages of government workers began to lag. Negotiations became protracted and bitter. The Central Labor Relations Board urged the adoption of a compromise: the payment of 2.8 months of a government worker's salary to overcome the inflationary deficit. The government paid two months extra wages; only the 0.8 month's pay remained, but this was too great a problem for the SDP and the coalition government.

Since the right wing had monopolized all cabinet posts allotted to the Socialists, the left wing had sought compensation in the form of a number of important party posts and numerous Diet committee chairmanships. The two most important they obtained were the chairmanship of the Budget Committee of the House of Representatives and of the party's Policy Planning Board, both held by Suzuki. When the government decided to raise railway and postal rates to pay for the 0.8 month's pay, he, backed by the May Society and in this case the opposition Liberals, vehemently opposed the plan. The former demanded that the government workers' wage increase be paid for through the sale of cotton goods in government warehouses. The right-wing Socialists and the government refused to accept this proposal. Suzuki allowed a fellow left-winger to submit a motion rejecting the budget. It passed, and the government withdrew its budget. Suzuki resigned his chairmanships. A hue and cry was raised for the expulsion of the recalcitrant leftists, but this was no longer possible without destroying the party. A few days later, on February 10, 1948, after being in office for only a little more than eight months, the Katayama coalition government resigned. It was forced out by intraparty conflict.

"Mr. Katayama and his cabinet have given the country a conscientious and patriotic leadership," declared General MacArthur when the cabinet stepped down. That government has since been criticized as a rubber stamp of the Allied Occupation. This was, of course, steadfastly denied by those in the coalition; but there was undeniably at least a limited meeting of minds between Occupation officials and the government, especially the SDP, concerning numerous measures to promote democratization. Indeed, ever since the beginning of the Occupation, the SDP had often been trying to "catch up" with the Allied program of reforms. There was a naïve, vague impression in Socialist circles that somehow democratization policies would improve the living standards of the people. A harsh lesson was learned in this respect. Socialists had been demanding many of these reforms since before the war with little hope of their realization. Then, after national disaster, they were deluged with one reform after another. Even in such a basic document as the Constitution, the Socialists, who had been regarded as radical, lagged behind Allied policy. The official Socialist position placed sovereignty, under the new Constitution, in the state, which included the Emperor. The left wing argued for having it reside in the people, as was finally provided by the Diet at the insistence of SCAP.

Very few Socialists had had any experience as administrators when their party first participated in this coalition. Their leaders had lacked adequate opportunities to draft national administrative plans and policies. They had made few preparations; they had neither resources nor personnel to create long-range plans which would spark the imagination, enthusiasm, and initiative of a people suffering from manifold disaster. They had no strong, nationwide grass-roots organization to sustain them and no adequate grip on local government, which was essentially conservative. Had the SDP not led the government at that time, however, democratization would not have progressed as far as it did. The immediate results were catastrophic for the party, but it can be argued that long-range benefits accrued to Japan by the participation of the SDP in the government at that time.

Unfortunately, the Katayama cabinet presided over the highest inflation rate yet. It faced an almost unmanageable situation. To raise production and hold down inflation simultaneously seemed impossible. In emphasizing the revival of basic industries, it gave industrial management and capital a breathing spell, and also restrained the demands and pressures of trade unions. It incurred the antipathy of farmers when it ordered compulsory collection of rice quotas to ease the food situation. When prices were controlled, black markets prospered. Taxes rose, unemployment spread, and scarcity prevailed. Efforts of the Socialists had the ironical effect of strengthening the entrenched bureaucracy because of necessary dependence on it for the formulation and enforcement of policies, in spite of their hopes for "socialistic planning and control."

Intertwined with these problems was the harassing experience of a coalition government with two divergent ideologies, capitalism and socialism, bound together by a vague policy statement. Socialist willingness to compromise was based on the illusion that eventually, through a cumulative process, their socialist objectives would be attained—an illusion that was completely shattered. This and the ensuing experience impressed upon the SDP the undesirability of a tenuous coalition with parties bent upon conserving capitalist interests. Furthermore, the SDP should not have expected to initiate a wholly socialistic program under a basically conservative, even though benevolently reformist, occupying power. There is no doubt that factional strife within the party and its coalition partners had its toll on the efficiency of governmental leadership; but after all the criticism has been heaped on the Katayama government and the SDP, it is more than rhetorical to ask whether this tragicomedy was not virtually inevitable in the circumstances, the more so once the party decided to join the coalition. Socialists have since realized that there would be less excuse in the future if history in this regard should ever be repeated.

COALITION RENEWED: THE ASHIDA CABINET

The Liberal Party, as the opposition, insisted that formation of a new cabinet should be its responsibility. Its leaders continued their refusal to participate in negotiations toward a new coalition. The Democrats, weakened by defections to this conservative rival, desired a four-party coalition. Officially, the SDP did not demand the premiership and declared it would support the Democrats if a policy agreement could be reached; but left-wing Socialists stubbornly demanded the redesignation of Katayama as Premier. They feared the Liberals would revert to reactionary policies and call for an election which would result in Socialist defeat. Only after Katayama refused to accept their nomination did they concede and vote for Hitoshi Ashida, President of the Democratic Party, as new Premier.

The left wing in the SDP had expressed its disinterest in and opposition to participation in a revised coalition cabinet. In order to avert a party crisis, Katō and Nomizo, two leading members of the May Society—the very faction which had brought down the Katayama cabinet—consented to join the cabinet as Minister of Labor and Minister without Portfolio, respectively. This switch within the left wing severely strained its factional unity. Suzuki, foremost of the group, gave his tacit approval, but Hisao Kuroda, a doctrinaire Marxist, persisted in his opposition to participation in the cabinet. In addition to the two ministerial posts already mentioned, the Socialists obtained six more: the office of Vice-Premier (going to Nishio), the Attorney Generalship, and the Ministries of Education, Agriculture and Forestry, and Commerce and Communications. The Democrats held seven posts and the People's Cooperatives two.

After a month's negotiations, the three parties concluded a policy agreement. It was more detailed than the previous one, but on such crucial matters as interest payments on war bonds it was exceedingly vague, calling for a "termination-like disposition"; more important was the growing influence of the international situation on Japan. The cold war between the Soviet Union and the United States was being intensified. The Truman Administration had announced the inauguration of the Marshall Plan. Several missions of high-ranking governmental officials visited Japan, and Occupation policies shifted from emphasis on reform to accents on security and on speeding Japanese recovery as the workshop of Asia. Premier Ashida stressed the mission of his cabinet to facilitate the introduction of foreign capital and a substantial improvement of production as the only ways to improve living standards.

From the outset, the Ashida cabinet was beleaguered by labor offensives. The spearhead of these disputes was again the federated government workers' unions. This group had formed a council and, in concert with Sambetsu as well as the coal mining and electric power workers' unions, participated in a March labor offensive, one objective of which was to prevent the dreaded retrogressive revision of major labor laws. The unions were also demanding wage increases, but the union of workers in the Ministry of Communications, the driving force behind these offensives, based its calculation on the income necessary to maintain a diet of 2,400 calories per day. A truce was arranged between the government and its own labor unions in March 1948, but the lull was soon broken over formulation of the national budget, related as that was, and always is, to the wages of governmental employees.

The new labor offensive was checked only in July when the Occupation authorities sent a letter to Premier Ashida recommending that the National Public Service Law be amended to deny the right of government employees to strike. This letter placed the SDP, especially Katō as Minister of Labor, in a very embarrassing position. A week later, on July 31, 1948, the government issued an ordinance implementing the no-strike, no-collective-bargaining request and providing penal measures for violations. The next step was to submit similar legislation to the Diet. At this point the SDP equivocated, for it did not want to be party to any further restrictions on activities of the labor movement. Still, the Socialists finally decided to stay in the Cabinet—instead of calling for a dissolution of the Diet—in an attempt to limit the severity with which the rights of governmental workers would be curtailed. Dissatisfied with Socialist leadership and reacting against the restrictive Occupation policies, the unions became increasingly restive and militant. At the same time, groups within the labor movement which were not in agreement with the more aggressive tactics used in the past, formed "democratization leagues" (Mindō) and began successfully to challenge radical leadership which had led the unions through the abortive strike early in 1947 and the more recent offensives with no gains.

Prior to culmination of the Cabinet's labor troubles, controversies raged again over compilation of the budget. At the same time, the alleged involvement of Nishio in large-scale illegal financial contributions was brought to light. He became an easy target for left-wing attacks and was forced to resign his vice-premiership and leave the party in order to prevent the passage of a personal non-confidence motion in the Diet. In the meantime, the SDP and the Democratic Party agreed to delay interest payments on war bonds for one year, but this resulted in another defection from the Democratic Party. When the budget was finally passed, the Kuroda faction voted against it. Like Nishio, its members were later disciplined and expelled from the SDP. The respite from scandals, expulsions, and budget wrangling soon came to an end when the Shōwa Denkō scandal concerning political subsidies from a fertilizer company was revealed with the arrest of the conservative director-general of the Economic Stabilization Board. Soon thereafter, Nishio was arrested for allegedly having received a million yen to "hush up" the case. The cabinet resigned on October 7, 1948.

The Ashida cabinet had lasted eight months. It had been unable to curb inflation or to achieve any great measure of economic recovery and had been saved from the onslaught of determined labor offensives only by the Supreme Commander's intervention. It had been rent by policy dissensions resulting in expulsions on the left, defections on the right. The gravitation of dissident Democratic splinters toward the newly formed Democratic-Liberal Party had been disruptive. Moreover, Nishio had become vulnerable to left-wing attacks. Ignoble was the denouement.

Shigeru Yoshida formed what was meant to be a caretaker government. Fearing losses, the SDP tried to postpone the elections. The party had grown more factionally fragmented; its organization was shattered. The Kuroda group had revived the tradition of a Worker-Farmer Party, advocating closer cooperation with the Communists. The latter, for obvious reasons, did not propose a united front but ran their own candidates. The elections, held on January 24, 1949, resulted in the most severe electoral setback suffered by the SDP during the entire postwar period. From a plurality of 143 seats in the Lower House, it fell to 48. Many Socialist cabinet ministers, including Katayama, Katō, and Nomizo, were defeated. The SDP polled only 4.1 million votes or 13 per cent of the total cast. On the other hand, the JCP elected 35 Representatives, attaining the peak of its postwar popularity.

In addition to all the aforementioned weaknesses and ills of the Social Democratic Party, the shifting psychology of a defeated, insecure people had marked effects on the first three postwar elections. Voters were more intent on surviving the difficulties and confusion of the postwar period than on absorbing the ideas of a socialist utopia. The rise of the SDP had been as dramatic as was its sudden decline. Faced with an absolute conservative majority, guided by the autocratic hand of their implacable political opponent, Shigeru Yoshida, the Socialists had only one recourse: to rebuild from the shambles and for many years to fight a rearguard defense of gains made during the preceding period of democratization.

GREAT DEBATES IN 1949–51

There ensued a dramatic period in the evolution of the Social Democratic Party. The three years 1949–51 were marked by two historic controversies over the philosophical basis and proper character of the party, and the attitude to be adopted toward the Japanese peace and security treaties. The former problem has never been fully resolved; the latter may be settled by the passage of time, but some of the issues raised by alliance with the United States have continued and again came to the fore in 1958–60 as revision and ratification of the security treaty were negotiated.

The Socialist Party had made a bid for power, though never really convinced that it would succeed. Its sudden prominence had inflated membership rolls and had attracted many nonsocialist Diet members whom the party had felt obliged to accept because of its paucity of effective candidates. Of the 143 SDP candidates returned to the Diet in 1947, no less than 48 have not since been reelected. Thereafter, the number of SDP Diet members who had been elected only once to the House of Representatives was never more than four in any one contest. It seems clear, therefore, that the 1949 election constituted a dividing line between the early postwar party and the organization which had to rejuvenate itself from debacle. To be sure, the upper echelons of leadership remained intact, but a new group of secondary leaders emerged in the SDP Diet delegation and Executive Committee. This group, often working through the older leadership, exerted great influence in councils on all levels.

The Inamura–Morito Controversy

The Socialist convention in 1949 was postponed until after elections in January. To show their sense of responsibility for drastic defeat, the leaders, including members of the CEC, resigned en masse but immediately reconstituted themselves as caretakers of the party. The convention in 1949 is generally referred to as the fourth "reconstruction" convention, though actually this was a misnomer.

The troubles of the Katayama and Ashida cabinets put right-wing Socialists on the defensive; the leftist attack was correspondingly determined. The controversy over the party name during inaugural negotiations illustrated the delicate balance of power which persisted. The right wing advocated changing the official designation to "Shakai Minshutō" (Social Democratic Party); the left wing wanted to retain the name Nihon Shakaitō (Japan Socialist Party) although allowing the official English translation to remain the Social Democratic Party of Japan (SDP or SDPJ). The latter was adopted by a majority of one vote. At almost every turn, such disputes have plagued the party.

In 1949 the leftist attack, which had focused on more basic philosophical problems, reached a new crescendo. In accordance with the usual practice, a special committee to draft the annual action program was established. Significantly, the chairman of this committee was Suzuki, concurrently chairman of the party's Policy Planning Board. In subsequent negotiations among the right, left, and center factions, the left wing demanded thorough self-criticism, pinpointing responsibility for the existing crises, enunciation of a fundamental philosophy based upon "scientific socialism," creation of a class party based on organized workers, utilization of competent leaders from forces outside the party, and the exclusion of wartime collaborators. The right-wing rebuttal, vague and innocuous, called for the dissolution of factions, for the outgoing executives to decline renomination at that year's convention as an expression of collective responsibility, and for the establishment of a theory and party posture to combat both conservatism and communism. Being on the defensive, the moderates hoped to reinforce their dwindling authority by attracting the center factions with a broad and obviously acceptable statement of policy.

Suzuki's chief theoretician, a noncommunist Marxist named Junzō Inamura, drafted the committee's version of an action program, which was immediately countered by another written by Tatsuo Morito, who relied considerably on the philosophical foundations of the British Labour Party. Inamura was a veteran socialist and a prominent member of the prewar noncommunist Marxist Labor-Farmer faction (the Rōnōha). In contrast, Morito, though he had been on the moderate fringe of the prewar social democratic movement, had recently entered politics and had become a leading right-wing theoretician when he justified the creation of the Democratic League for National Salvation in 1946. Later he had become Minister of Education in the Katayama Cabinet. The "reconstruction" convention was to assemble in two or three days, yet the opposing factions adamantly clung to their divergent interpretations. The deadlock was broken only when Seiichi Katsumata, a newcomer to the SDP from the bureaucracy, was instructed to draft a compromise. This he accomplished in one night at the home of his political mentor, Wada, completing the task by seven the next morning. On the same day, the party CEC accepted it as its official draft.

The convention was marked by a debate between the two protagonists, Inamura and Morito. Though inconclusive, it revolved around several points. The right wing maintained that socialism would be attained gradually through effective democratic government, while the left claimed that the change from capitalism to socialism must be by revolution and that the conservatives could be expected to try all means including force to stem the tide. Such a counter-revolution would have to be met by correspondingly great force. The left wing wanted to give workers—principally factory employees—a preferred status in the party and in the guidance of this revolution, producing thus essentially a "class" party. The right wing urged a broadly based party with all social classes on an equal footing—in essence a "national" party. The Katsumata compromise, with typical skill, fused the two conflicting theories (based, respectively, on German social democracy and British socialism) by shifting the frame of reference to the JCP, but this only blurred the real nature of the controversy. Unlike the Communist Party and its revolutionary tactics, the compromise declared that the SDP would carry out constructive policies aimed toward socialism and would also organize the masses to meet any counterattack by the conservatives. The SDP was not to be a vanguard party like the JCP but a "class oriented mass party." In this way, the political "face" of both factions was preserved. The action program, as finally adopted, included several crippling riders which only meant that the final showdown was postponed another year.

Although a crisis over the program of action could thus be temporarily evaded, a struggle over the selection of officers was inevitable. The left wing demanded the resignation of the entire right-wing leadership, the election of Suzuki as Secretary General, and the reelection of Katayama as Chairman. In recognition of the role they were expected to play in reconstructing the party, labor union leaders were encouraged, especially by the left wing, to join en masse and were invited to the convention as special delegates with full voting rights. This group consisted mainly of "democratization leagues" organized in the National Railway Workers Union and in Sambetsu unions in opposition to militant Communists in these bodies and to the conservative labor federation, Sōdōmei. Except for a few leaders, this group was actively wooed by, and supported, the left wing. In contrast, the more conservative faction, lacking the vigorous leadership of such persons as Nishio, failed to maintain liaison with this crucial group of about 65 labor delegates. In the nominating committee Inejirō Asanuma, the right-wing candidate for Secretary General, won over Suzuki, 31 to 30, but when the full convention voted Suzuki was upheld by a wide margin: 390 to 261. After bargaining all through the night, the ratio of factional strength in the CEC was set at ten each for the left and right wings, five each for the center faction and the leftist National Labor Union Congress leaders. Katayama was reelected Chairman. The fourth SDP convention was not constructive; only a patchwork settlement was achieved. The relentless attack by the left wing had been successful. It had demonstrated its superior skill in convention strategy, an advantage which it repeatedly pressed. It had all but overwhelmed the right wing in policy decisions and personnel appointments. The "mainstream" in party authority had shifted decisively to the left.

In preparing for the fifth national convention in 1950, there continued to be friction between the left and right wings. Both sides developed youth departments as rival avenues to party hegemony. Although youthful radicals were more attracted to the left wing, the right—not to be outmaneuvered—created the Independent Youth League in July 1949. Leaders of the SDP right attended its inaugural ceremonies, exposing themselves to charges of factionalism by left-wingers who had already obtained firm control of the party's Youth Department. The left wing was further irritated by Sadachika Nabeyama, the right-wing theorist behind the Independent Youth League. He was a former Communist who had become vehemently opposed to extremism and who regarded the left wing as composed of "pseudo-Marxist-Leninists." Just before the convention in January 1950, the leftist-dominated Youth Department held a national convention at which it decided to demand the expulsion of party members who also had joined the Independent Youth League and to present to the full party convention a motion of non-confidence in Chairman Katayama. The CEC tried to calm the irreconcilables. Internecine struggle became more bitter by the day and hour. Except for a centrist convention president, the left wing captured all important chairmanships at the fifth convention with a greater majority vote than in 1949. Secretary General Suzuki reflected this strength when he declared that those who rejected the principle of a class party would not be tolerated. After three days of hopeless negotiations, even a sudden threat by Katayama to decline further nomination to the chairmanship was not enough to bring about a truce in factional conflict. When, on the final day of the convention, Katayama declined nomination for reelection (and he was never thereafter reelected), the entire right wing walked out of the convention. Thus the postwar SDP experienced its first major schism.

Its leaders in their narrow feuds for posts had lost control of themselves, the convention, the delegates, and the whole trend of events. They were thus swept toward a lasting split. A large proportion of SDP Diet members was uncommitted, however, and formed a centrist group. Through a "Unification Discussion Group" they attempted to reconcile the warring factions. Though the right- and left-wing groups had held their own conventions, they cooperated in the Diet. They were impelled to unite because some labor unions, their main source of support, were in the midst of a spring wage offensive. The National Railway Workers Union even intimated that it would withdraw its support from the SDP unless the party became more effective through unity. The split was widely condemned as irrational and without justifiable political basis. The ensuing House of Councillors election in June 1950, the decline of Prime Minister Yoshida's popularity, and the consequent revival of support for the SDP—indicated by journalists and public opinion polls—gradually forced a reconciliation. After three months of tedious negotiations, the three groups, left, center and right, were reunited on April 3 at the sixth special convention. The right wing failed in its attempt to change the character of the Youth Department but the Marxist tinge in the party's action program since 1949 was modified and accepted without debate. The chairmanship was left vacant. Suzuki retired in favor of Asanuma as Secretary General, but the left wing gained 15 of the 30 CEC seats, the right wing receiving nine and the center faction six.

Between 1949 and 1951, Japanese Socialist attitudes toward the Allied (chiefly American) Occupation's policy changed from oblique criticism to direct attack. Japan could not escape the repercussions of the cold war. Occupation policy no longer emphasized reform but rather recovery and security. The land reform program had been virtually completed, but industrial and financial deconcentration, which had also been regarded as essential to democratization of Japanese economic and political institutions, was brought to a halt; gradual, later marked, reconcentration and revision of antitrust legislation became a contrary trend. SDP disillusionment with the United States was further deepened by the strict enforcement of the so-called "Dodge line," which called for a balanced budget, severe curtailment of credit from governmental banks, a single exchange rate, and retrenchment of personnel in governmental and private industries. The Socialist Party, together with the principal labor unions and federations, grudgingly accepted these measures in principle but lamented what they called the "one-sided" sacrifices being forced on the mass of workers and small entrepreneurs. Recognizing that they had little power to prevent enforcement of this program, the SDP and allied unions did their best to mitigate resultant sacrifices. The right- and left-wing factions supported the unions to varying degrees in their successive offensives. While the left wing generally encouraged more militant tactics pointing toward a general strike, the right rejected any attempt to use this weapon.

When the Communists scored their spectacular electoral gains in 1949, they controlled a large segment of the labor movement, but since the abortive strike intended for February 1, 1947, the challenge to their influence had been gathering momentum. This was centered in the so-called democratization leagues, which were being established in various national unions, and the trend was accelerated by the violent resistance of Communist-dominated unions against the personnel retrenchment prescribed by the "Dodge line." When the JCP was criticized early in January 1950 by the Cominform for its somewhat conciliatory attitude toward the Japanese government and the American Occupation, it shifted to a more "positive" policy of sabotage, violence, and militant strikes. This aroused criticism of Communist leadership in the labor unions and assisted the activities of the democratization leagues.

The American Occupation authorities also took a strong stand against Communist elements in the unions and actively supported their purge. A series of directives in May and June 1950 culminated in drastic reduction of JCP influence in both the Diet and in the labor movement amid charges of grave disregard of civil liberties. On May 3, 1950, the third anniversary of the new Japanese Constitution, General MacArthur suggested outlawing the JCP but, for various reasons, even conservative leaders in the main preferred not to do so. On June 3 and 7, 1950, the Japanese Government at the behest of SCAP purged 24 members of the JCP Central Committee from public office and 17 editors from the party's organ, *Akahata* (Red Flag). On June 27, two days after the Korean War started, this newspaper was suspended. The nearby conflict seemed further to justify a thorough purge of Communist elements from the ranks of organized labor. From 1949 to the end of November 1950, this expulsion—the "Red Purge"—eliminated 11,000 workers in private industry and 1,200 in governmental service. The Socialist Party did not actively oppose the purge, for its leaders realized that, with outside assistance, the way was being cleared for their domination of a large sector of the labor movement. With the blessings and active encouragement of the Occupation, the democratized labor unions began moving toward the establishment of a common organization near the end of 1949. The democratization leagues, formation of the International Confederation of Free Trade Unions, and the labor offensive in March 1950 led to the creation of the General Council of Japanese Trade Unions (Sōhyō) in July 1950. It brought together about 3,000,000 organized Japanese workers many of whom had ousted their Communist leaders. Sōhyō, born of anticommunism, did not directly oppose the purging of labor ranks; rather it regarded this measure as inevitable in the circumstances, and it joined in denouncing the destructive tactics of the JCP.

A month earlier, on June 4, 1950, the SDP had faced its first major national election since 1949. As previously intimated, all indications showed Socialist popularity to be on the rise again after the serious lapse. Party morale was given a boost when a Socialist won the governorship of Kyoto in April. Though barely recovered from its incipient rift earlier that year, the SDP campaigned for a comprehensive peace treaty and against the disinflationary financial policies of the Yoshida government. Virtual elimination of Communist opportunities caused the labor unions to concentrate support behind the SDP. It became the second largest party in the House of Councillors with 61 out of 250 seats. On the prefectural level, Socialist candidates polled more votes than in 1947. The Communists declined, never to rise again during the period under consideration. Only 17 months following their disastrous defeat, the Socialists regained a posture of some strength. They steadily increased their Diet membership until a plateau was reached in 1958–60. But less than three weeks after their electoral rejoicing, they were faced with a serious international crisis, for, on June 25, 1950, the Korean War began.

The Peace Treaty

The SDP condemned the North Koreans for using military force to reunite their country, but gave only moral support to the actions of the United Nations forces. The Socialists were impressed by India's limited compliance with the Security Council decision to aid South

Korea and by neutralist Sweden's support. But they noted that, since Japan was still occupied, it was in no position freely to express its will. They admonished the conservative government to carry out the orders of the Occupation authorities only insofar as the terms of surrender required. They were apparently not in sympathy with any zealous cooperation with the Western powers. Although its position was to change radically at a later date, Sōhyō, which was being organized when the Korean War began, also pointed the finger of accusation at North Korea. Important as the Korean War was for the world, for the Japanese economy, and for Socialist thinking, it was overshadowed for the Socialists in 1950–51 by the decisive controversy over the nature of the expected peace treaty and related security arrangements. The Korean War hastened the conclusion of a peace settlement with Japan.

Official termination of the state of war and of the Occupation had been delayed mainly by Soviet-American differences. American policy toward Japan had become less restrictive, and Chinese Communist victories had forced reconsideration of the whole problem of noncommunist security in Asia. Negotiations, when renewed, bogged down between the Departments of Defense and State on touchy problems of national security and foreign relations. On April 6, 1950, John Foster Dulles was appointed consultant to Dean Acheson, who was then Secretary of State, to make a determined effort to negotiate a peace treaty between Japan and its recent enemies.

The Socialists reacted to each change in Allied policy. The Katayama government, for instance, had made a weak bid to represent the Japanese people at a peace conference; but food, inflation, and other economic matters were then far more pressing both on the Cabinet and on the people. While the United States government was endeavoring to unify its own policies, the SDP began formulating its views regarding a settlement. It had early decided that Japan should (1) conclude one peace treaty with all its former enemies, (2) maintain neutrality, and (3) neither conclude military pacts with any one country, nor give military bases in Japan to any foreign country. It asked that special consideration be given to Japan because of its constitutional prohibition preventing participation in any sanctions against an aggressor. It is significant that these policies, generally referred to as the "three principles of peace," were initially accepted by both wings of the party.

However, as the provisions of the expected treaty gradually became sharper issues both in Japanese national politics and in the SDP itself, the attitude the party should adopt became intimately linked to the question of party control. The seventh convention in 1951 not only reaffirmed the previously formulated three principles of peace but, at the insistence of the left wing, added a fourth opposing the rearmament of Japan. This faction believed that the United States was considering the peace treaty as only a preliminary step to a security treaty which would require Japan to rearm. They were emotionally, theoretically, and strategically opposed to any rearmament proposals. The right wing, however, forced the left into a lengthy debate on the merits of a separate peace and self-defense treaty. The former's position was, no doubt, strengthened in 1951 by General MacArthur's New Year statement to the Japanese people in which he referred to the inherent right of self-defense. A proposition to endorse that right suffered an overwhelming defeat, however, and was followed by the election of Suzuki as party Chairman, although right-wingers were elected Secretary-General and Treasurer. The CEC was divided into fifteen members for the left wing, ten for the right, and five for the center.

The left-wing position was massively reinforced by its labor union supporters. Sōhyō, the Teacher's Union, the National Railway Workers Union, and others in convention all supported leftist policies. Religious leaders of several faiths, together with Sōhyō and other major national labor unions, formed a National Conference for Furthering the Peace. Initially, it excluded Communists but later was extensively infiltrated by them. The labor union front was by no means unanimous, since the Sōdōmei and moderate factions in certain other unions rather ineffectually opposed the movement's left wing. The Sōdōmei regarded a separate or partial peace treaty as inevitable but was relatively inactive in pressing its case.

In tenaciously sustaining its four principles of peace, the left SDP was conscious of compromises in the name of expediency at the time of the Manchurian Incident twenty years previously. Its leaders felt conscience-bound not to surrender to "reaction," this time in the form of the Western "imperialist" camp. They believed, furthermore, that peaceful coexistence was possible between the opposing Communist and free world blocs and that only through general peace could they achieve their program of socialism in Japan. Outright alignment with the West would only jeopardize their position of neutrality. A rearmed nation, they reasoned, would not only offer a pretext for aggression against Japan but could easily involve Japan in highly undesirable foreign wars. Such an armed force would not be a national army but merely a mercenary one which might be used in the suppression of the Japanese working class—a fear not wholly without grounds in the light of historical experience. Left-wing Socialists aimed at achieving "positive" rather than "passive" neutrality, at creating a "third force" in world affairs. They further based their stand on postwar pacifist tendencies among the Japanese people, their revulsion against ultranationalism, and their fear of war in the nuclear age.

The right wing, on the other hand, viewed such policies as idealistic and claimed that, realistically—in the world of power politics—a separate peace was inevitable. So long as Japan sided with the West, strict neutrality was impossible. Communist aggression, direct or indirect, must be countered by some sort of self-defense. The right-wing position was bolstered by the definition of "democratic socialism" adopted by the Socialist International in 1951, by its rejection of dogmatic Marxism, and by its condemnation of the Communist camp as the main source of world tension and the cause for top priority being given to Western military preparedness.

The differences between the left- and right-wing Socialists may be simply stated by reverting for a moment to observations made by the Socialists in 1945 on the unresolved contradictions between dictatorship and democracy and between socialism and capitalism. As viewed by left-wingers, the basic contradiction was between socialism and capitalism; right-wingers, however, observed that the fundamental choice was between democracy and dictatorship. Apart from any theorizing, these choices were colored by definite mental predispositions long nurtured by leaders of the various factions. Notwithstanding their differences, the Socialists did represent a brand of left-wing nationalism aimed at achieving "true national independence."

Unable to agree among themselves, they repeatedly procrastinated. In a speech on March 31, 1951, John Foster Dulles revealed the general contents of the proposed peace treaty. On August 15, the final draft was announced. On September 4, the treaty was signed in San Francisco. It had been negotiated, hotly debated in and outside Japan, and then signed, but the Socialists still could not agree on their attitude. From spring into the fall of 1951, when the treaty was ratified by the Diet, they inched painfully toward a decision. Only the highlights of the intricate maneuvering which led up to the eighth special convention can be recounted here.

The right-wing Socialists demanded a reevaluation of policy at every opportune moment. The relatively poor showing made by the Socialists in the 1951 local elections was blamed on their unrealistic attitudes toward the peace treaty. But the left wing was unmoved. The CEC met frequently; subcommittees were formed and dissolved; groups of three and four discussed the irreconcilable positions; the right wing initially accepted the peace and security treaties but the left wing rejected both. Chairman Suzuki agreed to attend the committee of the Socialist International Conference and possibly to restudy the four principles of peace. But he abstained from voting on the resolution concerning peace and military preparedness presented to that conference, returned to Japan, and reported that he saw no necessity for any reconsideration of party policy. During his absence, the right wing had tried unsuccessfully to change this position. The left wing called for a special convention and strengthened its ties with leftist labor unions. The rival faction countered by organizing more than half of the SDP Diet delegation into an ad hoc committee headed by Kanjū Katō, who had come to be affiliated with the right wing. At last, on October 5, 1951, the CEC adopted by a vote of 16 to 14 a compromise plan for approval by the convention; it provided for acceptance of the peace treaty and rejection of the security treaty.

The right wing feared a convention; the left realized it would be defeated in the two highest party committees—the CEC and the Central Committee—where these decisions were being made. The apparently unavoidable eighth special convention was convened on October 23, 1951. The special session of the Diet called to approve the treaties was already in session. After seventeen hours of confusion, the Socialist convention split in two. The main factions continued their separate conventions in Buddhist temples, each claiming to be the "real" party, so they both used exactly the same name. In the Diet, left-wing Socialists voted against the treaties; the right Socialists voted for the peace treaty and against the security treaty.

2. Frustrations of the Revived but Chronic Opposition

SOCIALIST SCHISM

Factionally and organizationally divided, the Socialists faced the new era of national independence in April 1952 with uncertainty. International events and domestic politics at times deepened the gulf and intensified the competition between the two main factions and then forcibly brought them closer together. The possibility of a conservative merger and recognition that, divided, the Socialists could never achieve a parliamentary majority slowly induced rapprochement.[1]

In the meantime, the most pressing problem for the Socialists was separately to regroup their forces to meet any conservative challenge. Hurriedly both Socialist parties held their conventions in January 1952, only three months after the split. Given a prominent role by the leftists in the reconstruction of their organization, Sōhyō reciprocated significantly with financial subsidies and personnel. In contrast, the Right SDP received only weak support from its labor allies. The Left Socialists at first tempered their policies, calling for a revision of the peace treaty and abrogation of the security pact; but supporting unions obliged these leaders to adopt a stronger stand against the two

1. Hereafter, when reference is made to either of the two Socialist parties in the context of the 1951–55 schism, Right and Left will be capitalized; when referring only to factional affiliation, they will be lower case.

treaties and to champion the four principles of peace. The Right Socialists accused their rivals of being pro-Communist because their criticism of the JCP and the Cominform lacked thoroughness and conviction. They rejected any possibility of reunification while such basic differences persisted and instead pressed for the organization of all "democratic socialist" as distinct from "social democratic" forces. Japan, they asserted, had to rely on collective security and could not subscribe to the leftist notion of no defenses and no resistance. They did not believe, however, that Japan had wholly regained its independence, so they advocated a revision of the peace and especially the security treaties to rectify this inadequacy. The finality of the Socialist cleavage was sealed by the election of separate slates of officers. The Left SDP elected Mosaburō Suzuki as Chairman, Masaru Nomizo as Secretary-General, Hiroo Wada as chairman of the Policy Planning Board, and Hyō Hara as Treasurer. The Right SDP left its chairmanship temporarily vacant and elected Inejirō Asanuma and Kyōhei Shimojō as Secretary-General and Treasurer, respectively.

Reverse Course

The divided Socialists fought their first important legislative battle against the conservative government's Subversive Activities Prevention Bill—the first major measure proposed after the end of Occupation controls. Although the ostensible aim of the bill was to curb Communist activities, Socialists in both main factions and labor unions unanimously opposed it. They were motivated not by compassion for Communists but by a deep-seated distrust of a revived political police. The left wing in Japan is not likely to forget its experiences under the notorious Peace Preservation Law, the interpretation of which had been extended to include all opposition groups. The Socialists labeled the new bill a postwar edition of the former hated law, merely clothed in democratic terminology. Despite their serious numerical handicap in the Diet (48 out of 466 in the House of Representatives), the Socialists carried out a vigorous and partially successful campaign to embarrass the government and to force revisions of the bill. All left-wing elements opposed the measure, but there was considerable difference in the degree of their intensity. Possibly because more left than right Socialists had suffered under the prewar thought police, and also because the campaign against the bill served as a convenient rallying point for lukewarm Socialists, the Left SDP

CHRONOLOGY OF THE SOCIAL DEMOCRATIC PARTY OF JAPAN

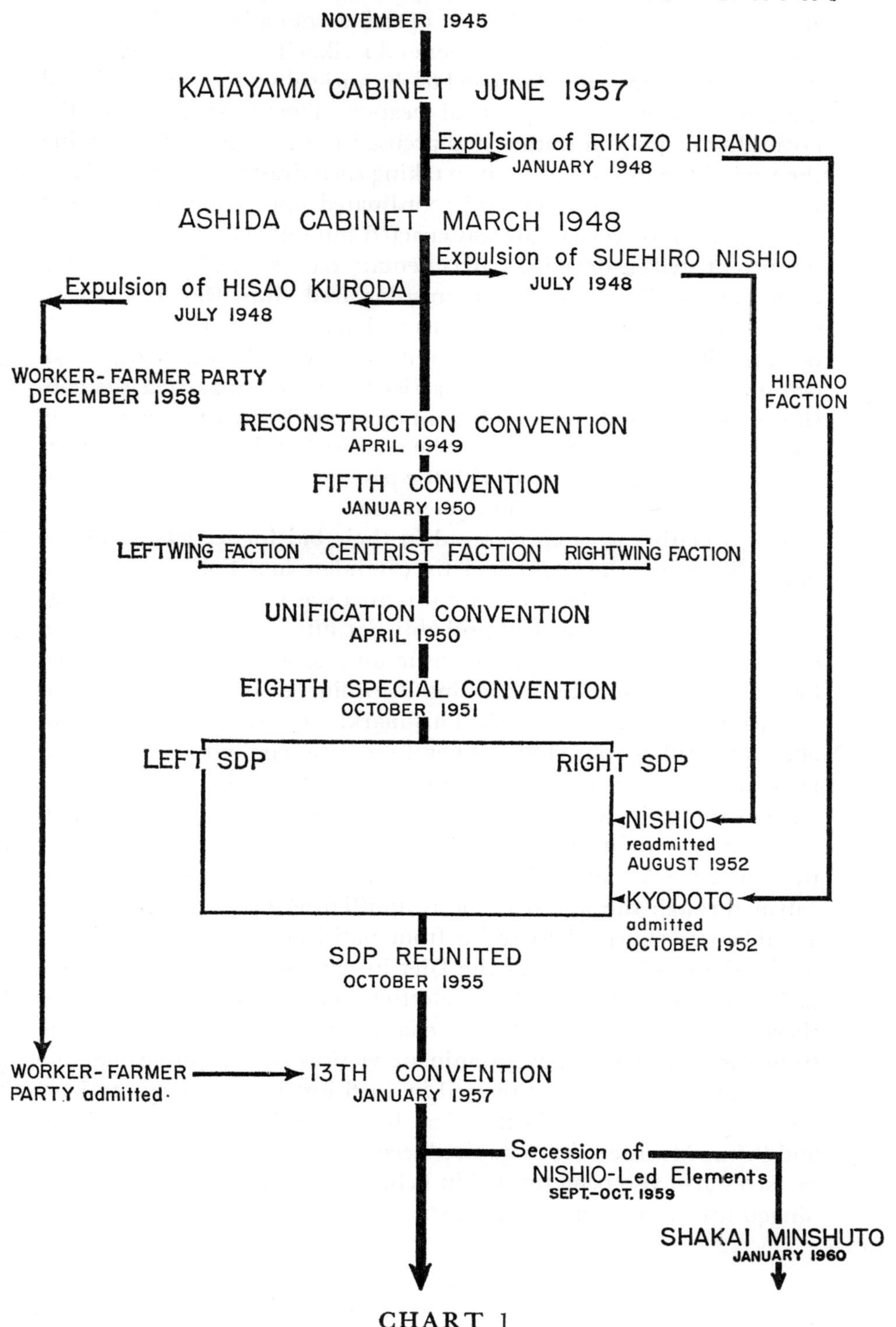

CHART 1

and Sōhyō organized several waves of strikes (not all of them effective) and even threatened resort to a general strike. The Right SDP and its supporting unions, while opposed to the anti-subversive law, criticized the use of the strike as a political weapon. They warned against the possibility of JCP infiltration and accused the government of forcing the Socialists and their allies into taking such drastic measures. These were the most determined and coordinated opposition tactics since 1945. The controversial law was enacted but only after 79 days of intermittent strikes, delaying parliamentary tactics, detailed interpellations, and a disastrous Communist-inspired May Day riot which greatly reinforced the government's rationale. Opposition to the bill not only illustrated essential differences between Left and Right Socialists in political strategy and tactics but also emphasized the continuing lack of confidence and common ground between the majority conservatives and the Socialists. The severity of this confrontation has been only slightly mitigated with the passage of years and has erupted into violence over several subsequent issues.

The Socialists were encouraged in their bid for leadership of the opposition when the Right Socialist candidate in a Tokyo by-election in March 1952 was elected. Since this area was within Right Socialist "territory," the Left SDP had probably not intended to elect its candidate; but his electoral support was more than double that predicted by public opinion polls, suggesting the influence of supporting labor unions, particularly of Sōhyō. This marked the early resumption of effective results from close cooperation between Left Socialists and labor unions and was a harbinger of Socialist revival.

Soon after this election, the peace treaty came into effect, and Japan regained exercise of its sovereignty. After having been Premier since the fall of the Ashida cabinet in 1948, and having successfully guided Japan through the last years of a humiliating Occupation, Shigeru Yoshida was expected to retire from political life. Instead, he dissolved the special session of the Diet in August 1952, even before it had convened, and called for elections on October 1. He hoped thereby to minimize the growing challenge to his authority resulting from the return of many prominent victims of the purge, notably Hatoyama, who had been purged in 1946 just before he was to have become Premier; Yoshida then had become Liberal Party President and Prime Minister. A reorganized second conservative party, the Progressives, had also been formed in February 1952, headed by Mamoru Shigemitsu, also previously purged.

The Right Socialists campaigned for revision of the two treaties and the abolition of the administrative agreement implementing the U.S.-Japan Security Pact, for a planned economy, a stable balance of payments, and the use of foreign exchange accumulated from the Korean War boom to rebuild industry and to raise living standards. The Left Socialists called for a struggle against Japan's "subordinate" position stemming from the two treaties. They opposed rearmament and the "reverse course," urged neutrality independent of both the free world and the communist camp, and rejected any joint struggle offers from the Communists. Sōhyō gave these policies unqualified support.

The electoral judgment was harsh on the Liberals who barely maintained their majority. From 285 returned in 1949, they were reduced to 240 seats. The Progressive Party obtained only 85. The Communists were totally unsuccessful; their leaders were mostly underground or in exile and their association with violent tactics in the public mind did them no good. It is estimated that many of their votes shifted to the Left Socialists, who made the most spectacular advances —from a mere 16 seats, when the SDP had split a year previously, to 54 seats and three and a half million votes, or 9.9 per cent of the total. The Right SDP increased its representation from 30 seats at the time of the schism to 57 elected by four million votes, which comprised 11.4 per cent of the total. An unstable political situation was thus created. The conservatives were not only divided into two parties but the separatist Hatoyama faction in the Liberal Party held the balance. This indication of the popular will convinced the Socialists, especially the Left SDP that their arguments were valid and that they should intensify their opposition. The Socialists maintained their respective election policy committees in full operation. Another characteristic of this election was the large number of depurgees returned to the Diet. Out of 466 members, 140 were in this category. Only 16 were members of the SDP—13 of them, including Chairman Jōtarō Kawakami, being in the Right SDP. This trend reinforced Socialist contentions that the domestic danger was not coming from Communists but from ultranationalists and that it was the mission of the SDP to correct the "reverse course."

This term became popular after General Ridgway, on May 1, 1951, announced that the Japanese government might reconsider Occupation-sponsored laws and institutions. Premier Yoshida promptly formed a committee for this purpose. The conservatives were only too eager to "rectify" key democratization policies which they considered not to be in line with Japanese realities and traditions. They tried to classify all elementary and high school teachers as public officials to prevent strikes and political activities and to centralize controls. The Liberal government wanted particularly to curb the political effectiveness of the powerful Japan Teachers' Union which supported the Socialists. The attempt to increase and strengthen the control of the national police over rural and municipal police forces caused Socialists to risk the use of violence in the chambers of the Diet. Efforts were made to revive control over the press and other media of information. Abolition of the public election of prefectural governors in favor of centralized appointment (as in prewar years) was seriously considered. A law for registration of the citizenry was also passed. The conservatives wanted to enact tighter controls over the labor movement, reinstate the legal sanctions of the old family system, and above all revise the anti-rearmament Constitution. After repeatedly overcoming stiff Socialist resistance, they scored numerous successes in their "reverse course" policies despite much factional bickering.

The administrative agreement was signed by the Japanese and American governments just before the peace and security treaties went into effect. It stipulated that Japan would provide military bases for United States security forces. The Socialists claimed that the agreement was unconstitutional, and they appealed unsuccessfully to the Japanese Supreme Court. The agreement proved to be closely linked to the Japanese national budget as it provided for annual Japanese defense contributions—an aspect of the agreement that later embarrassed the Japanese conservatives and the United States government. Japan's police reserve, created soon after the Korean War started, was to become a "peace preservation force"—another proof, in Socialist eyes, of the trend toward remilitarization.

The Right SDP demanded that the stabilization of the national livelihood should come before any rearmament. Both wings insisted that military expenditures be eliminated from the national budget. The Left was more drastic in proposed budgetary pruning. When, in the spring of 1953, the Japanese and American governments moved to extend United States military bases, as provided in the administrative agreement, the Left Socialists, Sōhyō-affiliated labor unions, and the local populace organized intensive resistance movements. The best known of these were directed against new bases at Uchinada (Ishikawa prefecture), Asama (Nagano), and Myōgi (Gumma). On-the-spot demonstrations were coordinated with political opposition in the Diet. Socialist doggedness and insistence that the availability of military bases for a foreign power on Japanese soil only fostered world tension was encouraged by a growing anti-American feeling among the Japanese people and by the changing international situation.

The Peace Offensive and the Elections of 1953

Efforts toward a truce in Korea led to a trend which soon came to be recognized as a Communist "peace offensive." Premier Malenkov's flexibility after Stalin's death in March 1953, the explosion of a Russian H-bomb, Chou En-lai's peace statement that spring—all added weight to the Socialist demand in Japan for a more independent and neutral foreign policy. Especially the Left SDP became convinced that the Soviets desired peaceful coexistence. By the summer of that year, a truce was concluded in Korea. After Kyūichi Tokuda's statement the previous summer, the JCP had adopted a more conciliatory line. The effect on the Japanese economy of reduced offshore military procurement caused the people to realize the extent of their country's dependence on the United States to balance its international payments. Even with massive special procurement, Japan was not able to achieve a favorable balance of trade in 1953. Personnel retrenchments and wage cutbacks affected workers. Conservative designs to draw closer to the United States and to build Japanese armed forces were regarded as ominous trends by the Socialists and their sympathizers.

Although the Left and Right Socialists each sponsored their own Chairman as a candidate for the premiership after the 1952 elections, they began to develop a close working partnership in other Diet strategy, and utilized conservative dissension to the hilt by cooperating with the Progressive Party and with dissident factions among the Liberals. They succeeded, for example, in passing a motion of non-confidence in Yoshida's Finance Minister. Outside the Diet, however, the two Socialist factions threw acid political epithets at one another. Members of the Right SDP were labeled class traitors and lackeys of native and foreign capitalists. Leftwingers were characterized as pro-Communist, if not Communists in disguise, as solely bent on carrying out destructive class warfare at the risk of mutual destruction. They even took their quarrels abroad and inconclusively contended for support of their respective policies at the first Asian Socialist Conference at Rangoon in January 1953, at the Socialist International Congress at Stockholm in July, and at the Asian Socialist Conference Bureau Meeting immediately afterward.

Conservative wrangling played directly into the hands of the Socialists. In a moment of rashness, Yoshida blurted: *"bakayarō"* ("you stupid fool") to a right-wing Socialist. With the critical abstention of dissident Hatoyama-Liberals, the Socialists and the opposition conservatives promptly passed a non-confidence motion in the Cabinet. Yoshida again dissolved the Diet less than six months after the previous election. Voters returned to the polls on April 19, 1953, only five days before the regular House of Councillors' election. With the conservatives divided and the Communist leaders still mostly underground or in exile, the Socialists were able to gain once more. The conservative Liberal Party further declined from 240 to 199 seats, becoming a mere plurality party. The Hatoyama-Liberal Party remained stationary with 35 seats, the exact additional number necessary for a Liberal majority. The Progressive Party lost 12 seats, leaving them only 76. The JCP gained one seat. The Left Socialists for the first time overtook their rivals, advancing to 72 as compared with 66 seats for the Right.

In elections to the House of Councillors, party affiliation was accentuated by the sudden decline of the independent, though conservative, Ryokufūkai (Green Breeze Society). The Liberals became the plurality party with 93 seats. Combined Socialist strength increased from 61 to 66 seats, but it was the Left Socialists who gained—from 31 to 40 seats; the Right, on the contrary, declined from 30 to 26 seats. These elections dealt Right Socialist prestige a telling blow. Most of the newcomers to the Left Socialist camp were labor union leaders affiliated with Sōhyō unions. The power of the organized vote and perhaps also the emotional appeals of the Left Socialists to women and youths concerning the alternatives of war and peace were demonstrated.

The next problem facing the Socialists was whom to support as Prime Minister. With a total of 138 seats, the two Social Democratic Parties were no longer mere splinters. During the elections, Right SDP leaders proposed that a single Socialist candidate for Premier be selected, but the Left, holding more seats, maintained that its Chairman should be supported. The Right SDP promised to cooperate if it should be possible to form a coalition government with the Progressive Party and the splinter Liberal Party. This arrangement failed partly because the Secretary-General of Sōhyō, Minoru Takano, asked the Left Socialists (though in vain) to support Mamoru Shigemitsu, President of the Progressive Party, as the next Premier. Overthrowing the Yoshida government had become such an obsession with Takano that he ventured to propose another conservative as Premier. His demand, coinciding with Communist support of Shigemitsu, was an illustration of the growing influence of the so-called "peace force theory," particularly among leftist labor unions and at Sōhyō headquarters and in the more extreme factions of the Left SDP. This theory was, of course, synchronized with and stimulated by the international Communist peace offensive beginning in 1953.

The majority of Left Socialist leaders, fearful of the consequences of accepting such popular front tactics, called a special convention to "dispose" of the Takano demand just two days before the Diet was to elect the new Premier. So powerful had extreme left-wing influence become that Left Socialists wavered almost to the moment of balloting in the House of Representatives. Eventually they voted for their own Chairman. After two ballots, Yoshida became Premier for the fifth time. Then the Progressives declared they would no longer cooperate with the Socialists to fight Yoshida and the Liberal Party. With their assistance the Liberals were able to pass the Strike Control Bill which resulted from the prolonged strike conducted by the coal miners and electric power workers in the fall and winter of 1952. The feud between the prevailing Left Socialist groups and the Takano faction in Sōhyō was only one symptom of a gathering storm climaxed within the party by the controversy over a program or basic platform which raged early in 1954.

The Platform Controversy

After adopting a very simple basic platform (*kōryō*) on socialism, democracy, and pacifism in 1945, the Socialist Party had never bothered to draft a more definitive statement of its appraisal of political and economic conditions, or of its character and mission. In view of the party's composition, this was an almost impossible task. Even after the schism in 1951, the two wings still maintained the same program of three principles. The annual action programs adopted by the two national conventions described their parties' positions on immediate issues. Following the decision at the Left SDP's tenth annual convention in January 1953 to draft a new basic platform, a special committee was created with Wada as chairman and Inamura as staff director. About two months before the convention in January 1954, the party announced a draft program and called for mass discussion before final adoption.[2]

Since revival of the Left SDP was so closely related to the development of and support by Sōhyō, the platform controversy must also be considered as affected by changing trends within that labor federation. Sōhyō gradually changed its political orientation from outward condemnation of communism in 1950 to extreme criticism of the United States and to a not uncontested alignment with the "peace force" theory during 1953–55. At its convention in 1952, Sōhyō emphasized Japan's "subordination" to the United States and failed to criticize the Soviet Union. It looked upon the former as the provocateur of war and ignored Soviet stress on heavy armaments. The seeming contrast between the Soviet peace offensive in 1953 and the Korean truce, on the one hand, and the American "roll-back policy" and "unleashing" of Chiang Kai-shek, on the other, only accelerated Sōhyō radicalism. At that federation's fourth convention in the summer of 1953, the factions led by Secretary-General Takano forced the adoption of an action program embodying the "peace force" theory, which advocated alignment of Japan with the allegedly "peaceful" nations, Communist China and the Soviet Union, against the United States. This policy was pushed through the convention against the better judgment of Left SDP leadership and after riding roughshod over the moderate interpretations of four conservative labor unions in Sōhyō. Although the federation's political policies had veered from the "third force" theory of the Left SDP, both organizations pretended that no contradictions existed. But Kaoru Ōta, who was closely associated on a personal basis with the Wada-Katsumata faction in the Left SDP, resigned from his Sōhyō vice-presidency as a result of this change of policy.

Inamura's draft platform was essentially a Marxist interpretation of Japanese political and economic history. As a class party, the principal socialist target was Japanese monopoly capitalism which was asserted to be closely linked with its counterpart in the United States. The

2. A topical arrangement of this platform, as adopted, appears in C. H. Uyehara, M. and S. Rōyama, S. Ogata, trans. and eds., "Comparative Platforms of Japan's Major Parties," Studies on Japan's Social Democratic Parties (Medford, Mass., The Fletcher School, Tufts University, mimeo., 1955), hereafter cited as "Comparative Platforms."

overall socialist strategy was, therefore, a contest between such conservatives (the representatives of monopoly capitalism) and all socialists, particularly those on the Left. In the CEC and party caucus, the opposing "peace force" theory was presented by Shinzō Shimizu, a close associate of Takano's, and a former officer of the Steel Workers Union. In convention, the Osaka and Kyoto prefectural organizations presented a substitute platform based upon Shimizu's "private plan" —supported by a group in the Left SDP known as the "peace force" or "platform" faction—which singled out American monopoly capitalism as the real power manipulating Japan and its weaker plutocratic system. From this theory flowed the argument that the struggle was one of national (or "racial") independence against a distant foe. It called for a popular front for national liberation, alleging that the choice was between subservience and independence. It seemed to many Socialists that this interpretation was embarrassingly close to that of the Communists.

The principal business of the twelfth Left SDP convention in January 1954 was to decide on the basic platform. In typical socialist fashion, an inconclusive political compromise was accepted so that both factions could claim victory. Japanese monopoly capitalism was described as subservient to American monopoly capitalism, and one of the chief objectives of a transitional socialist government would be the struggle for national independence. So preoccupied were delegates with the basic platform that they reaffirmed without debate a foreign policy of independent neutrality, advocating that in international affairs Japan should join a third force.

Although the "platform faction" was sufficiently vocal to force a compromise on the statement of basic policies, the four top elective positions in the party were held by men in favor of third force diplomacy. Suzuki was reelected Chairman. Wada became the new Secretary-General; Kōdō Itō was elected chairman of the Policy Planning Board, and Kōzō Sasaki, chairman of the Control Commission. Outside the party, the first sequel to this struggle for power was the failure of Ōta's bid—with open Socialist support—to replace Takano at Sōhyō's summer convention in 1954.

Although the Right Socialist convention that year received much less publicity than its Left counterpart, and though its inner struggle was much less spectacular, it was significant for its controversies about defense and foreign policy. Since the peace treaty there has been an acute divergence of opinion over self-defense and foreign policy among the conservative Socio-Democratic clique headed by Nishio and Sone, the Japan-Labor faction led by Chairman Kawakami, and a centrist group. At their convention in 1953, the Right Socialists had accepted the necessity of maintaining a police reserve sufficient to guarantee internal security and had called for an allocation of five per cent of the national budget for this purpose. They had declared that Japan should not be required to contribute to a United Nations police force but had recognized that their country had the right of self-defense as a sovereign state. In successive CEC and Central Committee meetings, the Nishio group—through Sone, its chief spokesman—tried to push this policy one step further to the recognition of the present security arrangements with the United States and to acceptance of Japan's right and obligation to participate in a U.N. police force when it might be created. This policy was enthusiastically supported by the Seamen's Union, a component of the Japanese Trade Union Congress (Zenrō Kaigi),[3] for accepting mutual security assistance (under M.S.A.) from the United States, revision of the postwar Constitution, and limited rearmament. The compromise reached at this time, however, urged stabilization of national livelihood before rearmament, which favored the anti-Nishio groups. Kawakami, Asanuma, and Ushirō Itō were reelected as Chairman, Secretary-General, and Treasurer, respectively. Nishio was relegated to the post of adviser. Consequently, by the end of 1954 the Left SDP had a new basic platform, a long-range program, but the Right did not. Controversy was already raging in the Right SDP. The question of the kind of platform continued to be tied to the knotty issue of reunification.

The Elections of 1955

The Yoshida government's position had been slowly crumbling from relentless attack by the minority Socialists and by the second conservative party. In December 1953, the Liberal Party further deteriorated from within; a series of financial scandals reaching up to the party's Secretary-General were uncovered. The Hatoyama Liberals, believing Yoshida could be challenged more effectively from

3. The full name of this moderate labor federation is the All-Japan Trade Union Congress (Zen Nihon Rōdō Kumiai Kaigi). For more information about its formation, composition and policies, see pp. 52–53 later in this chapter and especially pp. 338–44 in Chap. 10.

within the party, had returned to the Liberal fold in November 1953 but again bolted a year later. This time they joined with the Progressives to form the Japan Democratic Party. When they and the Socialists presented a motion of non-confidence in the cabinet on December 7, 1954, Yoshida resigned instead of calling for new elections. Two days later, Hatoyama was designated caretaker Premier with the assistance of the Socialists, after he had promised to hold elections early in the following year.

In reaction to Yoshida's autocracy, his successor's common touch kindled a "Hatoyama boom." Even during Yoshida's decline, the Socialists merely promised a "coalition" Socialist government. To offset the momentum of Hatoyama's popularity, however, they were compelled to become more dynamic. A "unified" Socialist government was their answer. Efforts toward this rapprochement were goaded by the conservative progress toward merger and by rumors that this might lead to an irresistible torrent of retrogressive legislation. For the first time since the 1951 split, the Left and Right Socialists adopted the same election slogans: opposition to rearmament and U.S. mutual security assistance, stabilization of the national livelihood, protection of the democratic Constitution and parliamentary government, the abolition or revision of unequal treaties, complete Japanese independence, restoration of relations with Communist China and the Soviet Union, enlargement of trade, prohibition of nuclear tests, and support for peaceful uses of atomic energy. Since the Hatoyama government was reluctant to make campaign issues of constitutional revision and military conscription, the opposition insistently raised these matters by charging that the conservatives planned to gain sufficient seats to alter the basic nature of the Constitution and to revive the dreaded prewar conscription system. The Socialists aimed to capture at least the one third of the House of Representatives which would enable them and the more extreme leftist splinter groups to block any attempt at constitutional amendment, since a two-thirds majority of both Houses of the Diet had first to pass on any constitutional amendment before submitting it to the people for ratification through majority vote in a special referendum or election. The conciliatory "Geneva spirit" emanating from the summer summit conference in 1954 seemed to underscore the Socialist contention that conservative policies could only augment rather than reduce international tension. Hatoyama's bid to restore Soviet-Japanese relations—originally a Socialist policy—met a favorable response from Moscow. Diplomatic expectations and the future role of the SDP combined to make this election historic.

Ballots were cast on February 27, 1955. Hatoyama's Democratic Party was returned with a plurality of 185; the Liberal Party plummeted to 112 seats. The Socialists secured 156 seats, just a single seat more than one third. They now had more seats and votes (10.8 million votes as compared with 7.1 million) than when they had headed the government in 1947. Left Socialist advances were most spectacular, outstripping the Right wing 89 to 67. This was again due largely to the organizational power of Sōhyō and its affiliated unions. Hatoyama's progressive policies also had apparently attracted many Right Socialist votes.

Whereas Socialist strength had previously been in the large five-man electoral districts, they had begun to win in some three-man constituencies, often gaining there the highest number of votes. Their electoral successes were fraught with future dangers, since a majority of the runners-up were conservative and a slight adverse change in a capricious public opinion would endanger such slender advantages. The Socialists also began making inroads into rural districts which have been traditionally conservative strongholds. This was particularly true of Left Socialist candidates whose national unions—such as those of the railway, electric power, and communications workers—reached into homes where one or more members of farming families commuted to unionized workshops. They became agents relaying Left Socialist appeals to rural voters. As a result, the party in 1955 made greater gains in rural prefectures than in highly unionized urban areas.

Notice was served on the conservatives that the Socialists were no longer a mere minority nuisance but a serious and determined contender for state power, or at least an opposition with which they must carefully reckon. The outcome accelerated further the trends toward conservative amalgamation and Socialist reunification.

Rapprochement

The national party rupture in October 1951 had been personal and bitter, creating wounds that were difficult to heal. Yet many were convinced that the schism was folly. Three Socialist governors had tried to reconcile the two factions. The National Railway Workers

Union and a number of prefectural party branches had called for "unconditional reunification." All efforts were for a time in vain. Animosity and mutual distrust had deepened between Left and Right Socialist leaders and affiliated organizations, although they had not been immediately translated into action on local party levels. It took almost two years for both factions to divide the party organization in every prefecture. Chiba Prefecture, which is adjacent to Tokyo, was the last to split. Even in Hokkaidō, where the Socialists had usually held the governorship since the war, the SDP had not been riven for almost a year, and then over a trivial issue far removed from the peace treaty. While the SDP national leadership and other divisive forces had striven to establish two separate organizations, an uncoordinated pincer movement, impelled by intraparty pressures, domestic politics, and international developments, gradually brought about a rapprochement.

Although the Socialist wings were fiercely competitive with each other outside the Diet, we have noted how Left and Right cooperated on legislative strategy. A notable example was in the joint compilation of alternative budgets to be submitted to the Diet—of course, destined each time to be summarily defeated by overwhelming conservative majorities. Insofar as policy adjustments were imperative if a joint alternative budget was to be proposed, this practice—begun with the 1953 supplementary budget—became one of the processes making for reunification of this opposition party. When, after the elections of 1953, the two conservative parties began to cooperate more closely, the Left and Right Socialists felt obliged to counter with a similar strategy. The year-end labor union struggles, which occurred with monotonous regularity, dulled their differences and antagonism. Left and Right SDP Diet members held joint caucus meetings and participated in joint speechmaking rallies. In July 1953, Suzuki, the Left SDP Chairman, called for reunification of the party. This gesture was not regarded as a genuine desire for unity but rather as a political maneuver to offset the growing influence of "popular front" tendencies in the party, as well as in Sōhyō, and the challenge this presented to his authority. It will be recalled that a lively debate was in progress at that time concerning American pressure on Japan to rearm with mutual security assistance granted under certain conditions. The anti-military-base movement was also in full swing. The Right SDP responded by suggesting that the leftists rid themselves of pro-Communist elements. This was not only an impossible request but was also intended as a temporary damper on the pro-unification group in the Right SDP. That party had become wary of such overtures since it had been exceeded by the Left in Diet strength. Only a few months later, in August and September 1953, the Left and Right each created official party machinery very slowly and cautiously to explore the problems of reunification. Subsequently, the two Chairmen and Secretaries-General conferred on closer future cooperation in the Diet, a single Socialist candidate for Premier, and even agreed to study coordination of activities outside the Diet. It had required almost two years for tempers to cool sufficiently to realize the increasing political necessity for a détente.

When the Left SDP adopted the new Marxist-oriented basic platform in January 1954 and the Right drew up a bill of particulars stressing the differences between the two groups on all essential policies, fervor for reunification markedly abated. But conversely, Yoshida's waning influence, the disclosure of scandals, and the discord in his cabinet soon rekindled Socialist interest in reunification; only thus could there be any hope of a reformist majority and government.

In March 1954, the respective Chairmen, while attending a rally for the protection of the Constitution, declared that their parties were prepared to form a caretaker coalition government. Within less than a month, the two groups drafted a joint statement of policies. On the question of rearmament they expressed determination to prevent the strengthening and enlarging of Japan's self-defense force through U.S. aid. After the joint SDP motion of non-confidence in the Yoshida cabinet was defeated on April 24, 1954 (because the Progressive Party members had absented themselves), the possibility of a Socialist government evaporated and talk of reunification again subsided.

About this time, the creation of the Zenrō Kaigi, or Congress of Japanese Trade Unions, strengthened the dichotomy which had been growing in the labor movement since the fall of 1951. The new labor federation was strongly anti-Communist; its component unions, allied with the Sōdōmei, supported the International Confederation of Free Trade Unions (ICFTU) and the Right SDP. Like the "cautious faction" in that party, it was not outwardly against reunification but wanted it based on a responsible agreement of policies and a moderate common platform. Three months after Zenrō Kaigi was created, Sōhyō held its regular summer convention. It was there that Kaoru Ōta, who favored reconciliatory talks "centered on the Left SDP," was defeated by Minoru Takano, the incumbent Secretary-General, who proposed "unifying all peace forces," meaning the two Socialist Parties and the more leftist Worker-Farmer Party created by Hisao Kuroda when he left the SDP in 1948. In the Right SDP, Nishio, who stemmed from the prewar Socio-Democratic clique, supported cautious reunification but stoutly opposed any "unprincipled" merger which, he declared, was one of the mistakes of the Katayama coalition government. This evoked a minor controversy, for Mitsu Kōno, the Right Socialist theoretician for the Japan-Labor clique, expounded the merits of early reunification. In the leftist camp, Professor Itsurō Sakisaka demanded that any such talks should not deviate from the new Left SDP basic platform. When the parties were apparently about to be reunited, the Matsumoto "platform faction" suddenly echoed Takano's demand for remerger of the "three socialist" parties. Even such strident forces as these were able only occasionally to disrupt the almost inexorable trend toward reconciliation.

The Left and Right SDP extended a bipartisan welcome to a delegation of British Labour Party leaders in September 1954. Cognizant of the factional rivalry among their hosts, the British Labourites skillfully avoided making known their impressions of China and the Soviet Union, which they had just visited, and refrained from commenting on Japan's foreign and defense policies. Instead, Aneurin Bevan called upon both factions speedily to reunite. The Secretary-General of the Burmese Socialist Party similarly exhorted them when he visited Japan in August. As if in anticipation of these admonitions, the Left and Right SDP had each elevated their study groups—created in the previous year—to "committees to stimulate unification." Periodic conferences had been held since May 1954 between top policy planners and foreign policy experts from each side.

On January 18, 1955, the two Socialist parties in separate conventions solemnly pledged to reunite after the general election in February. The public was calling for a reunited SDP and had little patience with the details of relative Socialist power and factional feuding. The two parties adopted identical resolutions to reunite as "a class oriented mass party," to put forward only one candidate for Premier, to overthrow capitalism, to destroy fascism, to reject communism, and to achieve socialism through a democratic and peaceful formula. A motion in the Left SDP convention to include the Worker-Farmer Party in any reunification was defeated, but it received the support of one third of the delegates. The Right SDP convention was equally stormy. In order to present a common front to the people, differences were temporarily suppressed.

In April 1955, two ten-member unification negotiation committees and two five-member subcommittees on policy, organization, and operations were created. These met at least three times a week until September, when they completed a draft program for a unified SDP. In the meantime, the Right SDP, with the assistance of the League for Democratic Socialism (Minshu Shakaishugi Remmei), drafted for the first time its own basic platform. It followed closely in format, reasoning, and even wording the basic declaration of the Socialist International.[4] As anticipated, the foreign and defense policies and the causes of the schism in 1951 proved to be the most difficult to reconcile. The word "neutral" was replaced by "a foreign policy independent (*jishu dokuritsu*) of both blocs." The term "third force" was superseded by "strengthening cooperation with Asian countries not aligned with any bloc." In defense policy the Socialists agreed to be against "present rearmament." Japan was not to be regarded as a subordinate nation, as the Left had been asserting, but as one which was not completely independent since it had to comply with policies of the United States. Communism was recognized as a variant of socialism—a Left-wing contention, but the Soviet Union was characterized as a dictatorship—a Right-wing evaluation. These compromises were reminiscent of the noted Inamura–Morito controversy in 1949.

The basic platform or program for the reunified SDP was hailed as a triumph for the Right SDP by the "bourgeois" press. Platform terminology was such, however, that each wing could easily interpret the formulae to suit its own convenience. The willingness of the cautious Nishio faction to accept the new platform, and the unexpected outbursts of indignation in the Left SDP against it, roughly gauged the degree of concessions by that wing. Unable to quiet these voices without a full convention, the separate Left held its last tense conclave on September 19–20, 1955. Although the new platform was eventually ratified, more than one third supported a resolution demanding its revision. The Right merely convened an enlarged Central Committee

4. This platform also is translated and topically arranged in Uyehara et al., eds., "Comparative Platforms."

meeting on September 27–28 but was faced with an almost equally belligerent resolution to uphold the new platform.

On October 13, a unified convention unanimously adopted the "contractual" platform without debate; but outside the convention hall, supporters of Professor Sakisaka in and out of the party distributed pamphlets demanding revision of the new platform. The "reunited" leaders, each testing his own factional support, kept the disgusted convention spectators, the impatient delegates, the bored press, and the wondering public waiting for fourteen hours before they could agree on apportionment of party posts. The seven top elective positions were distributed four-to-three in favor of the Left wing. Suzuki became Chairman and Asanuma Secretary-General. The Central Executive Committee and Control Commission were divided equally between the two wings. Thus, after ten tempestuous years, the Social Democratic Party of Japan completed another cycle of divorce and reconciliation—this time emerging as the second largest party in the Diet.

When the second Hatoyama cabinet was formed after the general election in February 1955, the Socialists did not immediately oppose the government, since it promised to restore relations with the Soviet Union and to carry out progressive housing, extended social security, and other welfare policies. This unusual situation was soon normalized by a tense confrontation. Japanese-American negotiations on Japan's defense contributions to be included in the national budget were regarded by Socialists as a prime example of blatant American interference in Japanese domestic affairs. The government's decision (in response to American requests) to enlarge five air bases and press forward with rearmament aroused the determined ire of the opposition and their organized labor support. Even though a minority, the Socialists were able to shelve two crucial government bills to create a defense council and another to revise the Constitution. In July 1955 they declared full-scale opposition to the "reactionary" Hatoyama government. When reunified in October, the Socialists by constitutional practice became heirs-apparent to the minority Hatoyama government. The specter of a Socialist government prompted the conservatives to overcome all personality conflicts in order to create the Liberal-Democratic Party on November 14, 1955. This signaled the opening of a new era in Japanese politics. Far from mitigating conservative–socialist antagonisms, development of a two-main-party system sharpened the confrontation, occasionally even to the point of limited violence.[5]

THE NEW SITUATION

After the fall of 1955—for the first time in modern Japan—political parties in the Diet, especially in the House of Representatives, were clearly divided between socialists and conservatives. Although two major parties had emerged, the ratio of power between them was two-to-one in the Lower House in favor of the Conservatives; Socialists were an even smaller minority in the House of Councillors. And there was less common ground between Socialists and Conservatives concerning basic political philosophy, world outlook, and political strategy than existed in Western two-party systems. If these parties were to alternate in office, the swing of the pendulum as regards policies would at first be very great. Furthermore, because of deep mutual distrust the Socialists have not been able to exploit the rampant factionalism among the Liberal Democrats or to combine with LDP dissidents on common goals to any appreciable extent. Their suspicions of conservatives, stemming in part from remembering how many of those leaders had helped to suppress the prewar socialist movement, has occasionally erupted; at other times chronic numerical inferiority has made Socialist leaders lethargic.

The special Diet session, convened in the latter part of 1955, was closely watched as an indication of how the two parties were going to adjust to the new situation. Prime Minister Hatoyama stated that he would respect the opinions of the minority. His Liberal Democrats did not try to push their legislative program through the Diet. But this was only a deceptive calm before storms.

Early in 1956, the SDP selected five points on which to challenge the Conservatives: (1) defense of the postwar Constitution and rejection of the small constituency principle; (2) opposition to military bases; (3) restoration of relations with the Soviet Union and Communist China; (4) action to cause the downfall of the Hatoyama Cabinet; and (5) capture of one third of the House of Councillors in the forthcom-

5. Professor Robert Scalapino has aptly characterized Japan's political situation since 1955 as a "one-and-a-half party system," conservative strength being so preponderant and the Liberal Democrats having the only adequate nationwide web of organization.

ing election. As for the Liberal Democrats, they had voiced diametrically opposed policies described as "rectification of excesses" wrought in the course of Occupation reforms. Aging Premier Hatoyama declared at a mass rally that he would like to revise the Constitution even if he had to "reduce" (*gensatsu*) Socialist strength. Replying on January 30, 1956, former Chairman of the Right SDP Kawakami—a devout Christian and moderate leader—strongly intimated Socialist intentions when he noted that in many countries retrogressive constitutional revision meant riots and disturbances. Any revision of the present Japanese Constitution would be no exception, he warned. Hatoyama became known for his frequent "slips of the tongue," especially regarding his opposition to the existing Constitution, the legal status of Japan's self-defense forces, and the possibility of attacking enemy bases outside Japan in case of a general war. The SDP threatened mass absenteeism of its Diet members in the face of any drive to revise the basic law, tried to turn mass sympathy for the ailing Premier into an image of senility, incompetence, and ill-health, and submitted a motion to censure the Prime Minister. The Socialists believed that their opponents aimed to limit popular sovereignty, restore the absolutist imperial system, limit basic human rights, revive legal buttressing of the patriarchal family system, rearm and reintroduce conscription, and—when expedient—despatch troops overseas. Socialist determination was whetted by public opinion polls which showed that they were gradually growing in popularity.

Two of the numerous bills to revive old laws and to create new institutions particularly aroused Socialist ire in 1956: one to revise all electoral districts into small constituencies and another to make school boards appointive rather than elective. Although the Liberal Democrats denied political motivation, it was obvious that they hoped to reduce Socialist representation in the Diet below the one third mark by adopting the small constituency principle. If a relatively nonpartisan rearrangement of districts had been proposed, the Socialists would have been hard pressed in their opposition, and they would surely have lost many seats in one or more subsequent elections. It was generally accepted by the press and other informed opinion that the small constituency system *might* eventually lead to a more stable two-party system. But the conservatives overplayed their advantage. Their proposed rearrangement involved such blatant gerrymandering that even the press (referred to by left Socialists as "the bourgeois press") and a substantial portion of their own colleagues in and out of the Liberal Democratic Party were dissatisfied. According to Socialist calculations, passage of this revision of the electoral law would nullify most of the opposition party's gains since 1952. To many of its leaders this was a problem of political survival. The gerrymandering would have most affected the younger left-wing SDP Diet members who relied upon labor union support. Many older Socialists, particularly in the right wing, were not against small constituencies but were compelled to oppose such gross manipulation which might at least temporarily shatter their party. The opposition accused the conservatives of attempting a "legalized coup d'état," and of trying to establish a "stable government" at the expense of popular respect for the fairness of the legislative process.

The Socialists utilized every parliamentary trick and tactic short of illegality. Although House Speaker Hidetsugu Masutani was a conservative, he was a member of the "out" group and was apparently not in favor of ramming the small constituency bill through the House. Fearing that public opinion might be repelled, the Socialists were persuaded, after bitter debate in their CEC and in caucus, to accept a modified version of the electoral bill without the appended electoral districts—a compromise suggested by the Speaker. Chairman Suzuki and his followers, together with Secretary-General Asanuma, advocated a fight to the finish but Jusō Miwa, Hiroo Wada, Seiichi Katsumata, and Ushirō Itō persuaded their colleagues to accept the compromise.

In the House of Councillors, the bill immediately became involved with another contest over passage of a measure to make members of school boards subject to appointment by the usually conservative heads of local bodies. This change was aimed at reducing the influence which the politically powerful Japan Teachers Union had gained in these boards during the previous decade; it was also intended to centralize control over education. While SDP leaders thought that public opinion would tolerate "fairly strong" resistance to this bill, they judged that it would be difficult to prevent its ultimate passage. Control by party leadership slipped when Socialist members from the Teachers Union in the Upper House (backed by members from the National Railway Workers Union) dominated floor tactics, threatening violence. Eventually the President of the Upper House called for the assistance of 500 policemen and tried to convene a "surprise" plenary session, with few SDP members present, in order to pass the bill. This precipitated a scene of utter confusion and violence. The next day (June 2, 1956), amid an uncanny silence in the Diet chambers the school board bill was passed but other important measures, such as the small constituency bill, failed of enactment.

Only six weeks after this episode, half of the members of the House of Councillors were to be elected. Of the 68 SDP members in that chamber, 37 were candidates for reelection. Their party would have to elect 53 candidates if it were to constitute more than one third of the Upper House. Even with strong support from labor unions this was a formidable task. Immediately after the Diet adjourned, public opinion polls showed SDP popularity waning, due, it was supposed, to recent violence in the Diet; but it gradually began to rise again toward the end of the campaign. When ballots were counted, the Socialists had elected 49 candidates, making a total of 80 Socialist seats. The number of LDP Councillors remained stationary, while the nonparty Green Breeze conservatives lost 12 seats. Together with splinter groups (including Communists), the opposition controlled one third of that House. It had campaigned with grim determination and improved political techniques, after carefully selecting candidates and placing them so as to avoid intraparty competition and, by "apportioning" prefectural votes, maximized its support. More than half of the SDP candidates had been recommended by labor unions. Sōhyō-sponsored contestants had been much more successful than those supported by Zenrō Kaigi. In the national constituency 72.4 per cent and on the prefectural level 55.7 per cent of SDP candidates were elected. In the former, the SDP received 8.5 million votes (29.8% of the total); on the prefectural level its slates attracted 11.1 million (37.6%). Socialist emphasis on foreign policy issues, such as the Okinawa controversy and appeals to nationalism, was apparently more effective than the single-minded conservative condemnation of SDP violence. This election defeated any hopes to amend the Constitution within the next three years.

The SDP Convention of 1957

The artificial balance of power accepted by both major wings of the SDP at the time of reunification in 1955 was upset at the annual convention in January 1957. As usual, the conflicts there centered on interpretations of foreign and domestic events during the previous year and not directly on socialist policies. Such issues as the suppression of the Hungarian uprising, the Suez crisis, cooperation with the Communists, and the Productivity Center (which had been established with conservative and American support) were focal points of bitter wrangling. The left wing overwhelmingly prevailed in all votes. The ratio in the top seven positions between the two factions remained the same, but composition of the CEC was tilted in favor of the left, 22 to 18. Even though Wada, chairman of the Policy Planning Board, was prohibited from holding posts in the summer of 1957 because of alleged financial irregularities when he had been Secretary-General of the former Left SDP, his chief lieutenant, Katsumata, succeeded him at the 1958 convention, at which time the balance of power changed but slightly. Although the party's International Bureau was headed by a left-winger, chairmanship of the Committee on National Movements—which included special committees for the protection of the Constitution, the restoration of relations with Red China, and the return of Okinawa—was significantly allotted to a right-winger.

The SDP reiterated its determination clearly to differentiate itself from the JCP but modified its total rejection of cooperation with the Communists by advocating Socialist participation in non-exclusive mass movements with the intent to gain leadership over them. This change in Socialist attitudes—particularly in the left wing—stemmed in part from a Communist reevaluation of violence after the Twentieth Party Congress in the Soviet Union. In 1955, the last of the living top JCP leaders had returned to public life from underground activities since the Korean War. In June 1956, the plenary session of the Central Committee of the JCP emphasized the possibility of a peaceful revolution, revising the violent tactics of its 1951 platform. This tactical shift had had immediate effects in Sōhyō's convention that summer. Although the Takano faction had failed to regain leadership, it had been able to force a change in one of Sōhyō's basic policies, the rejection of all joint struggles with the Communists at any time. Sōhyō could thereafter exert such common efforts in certain circumstances. Secretary General Akira Iwai's plan to create conferences of SDP members in labor unions was probably intended to counter this new trend and to minimize Communist infiltration. His idea of "competitive coexistence" with the Communists remained distasteful to right-wing Socialists, particularly to the Nishio faction.

Frequent and blatant pressures by Sōhyō aroused the animosity not only of the right wing but also of a large segment of responsible left-wing leaders. Sōhyō intransigence was obvious during passage of the Law to Assist Small and Medium Businessmen. A compromise measure was jointly sponsored and passed in the Lower House, but in the House of Councillors, Sōhyō–SDP Diet members, revolting against party decisions, refused to accept one aspect of the bill. After three stormy CEC sessions, Chairman Suzuki could only admonish them to vote according to their best judgment. Vacillation of the leadership and its inability to enforce a central tenet of Socialist discipline again highlighted the role of labor unions in party councils as well as the lack of adequate consideration and timely adjustment of policies by the party.

Kishi's Challenge

The Socialist star continued to rise during the winter of 1956. The SDP had achieved two and parts of two others of its five aims mentioned earlier; its leaders apparently felt confident of soon assuming power, but their hopes were dashed when Premier Hatoyama resigned in mid-December after the Diet had ratified the Japanese-Soviet declaration restoring "normal" relations. Tanzan Ishibashi was chosen President of the Liberal Democratic Party and, on December 23, 1956, he formed his Cabinet, promising a ¥100 billion tax reduction and ¥100 billion for expanding the economy. Japan was then experiencing a major boom, and such a positive, expansive financial policy threw the SDP on the defensive. This was in contrast to its attitude toward Ishibashi when, as Minister of Finance in the first Yoshida government ten years earlier, he had been the prime SDP target as the evil genius of runaway inflation. Nine weeks after becoming Premier, however, Ishibashi was forced to resign because of illness. Nobusuke Kishi, who succeeded him on February 25, 1957, appropriated more and more Socialist policies. He openly proclaimed a showdown (*taiketsu*) with the SDP and its supporters, particularly Sōhyō. His emphasis on closer cooperation with the United States was ironic, for he had been Premier Tōjō's Minister of Commerce and later Vice-Minister of Munitions during the Pacific War, and he had paid for this in Sugamo Prison. His aggressiveness and bold tactics at home and his missions abroad won him initial applause, but toward the end of 1957 his popularity and authority began to wane both within and outside his party.

In addition to the SDP, Sōhyō and its component unions had constituted the principal organized forces resisting the "reverse course" away from democratization. The spring labor offensive in 1957 was spearheaded by the National Railway Workers and Coal Miners Unions, both important affiliates of Sōhyō. Chairman Suzuki of the SDP was able to avert one crisis by reaching a compromise with Kishi, which enabled the government and the Railway Union to accept arbitration. But soon afterward the government had a number of employees fired from their jobs including the chairman of the National Railway Workers Union and 22 other leaders of governmental workers' unions. This ignited another series of acrimonious strikes, but the government refused to budge. At union conventions the discharged leaders were reconfirmed in their union posts. In an attempt further to weaken union leadership and financial power, the government by ordinance withdrew from certain categories of civil servants the right to maintain union membership and prohibited automatic withholding of union fees from paychecks. In another attempt to reduce the influence of the Japan Teachers Union, it instituted the "efficiency rating system" for promotion of teachers. The temporary law limiting the right of coal miners and electric power workers to strike was made permanent. Feeling ran high in conservative circles in favor of further circumscribing all types of union activities.

In an attempt to create a Kishi boom, the Premier called on President Eisenhower and in 1957 twice visited Southeast Asia in the interests of expanding trade and investments. Kishi obtained only an American promise to withdraw most ground troops from Japan. This forced the Socialists into a reappraisal of their anti-military-base policy, which had reached the height of violence in October 1956, when more than 1,000 persons were injured in a clash between the police and unionists, students, villagers, and SDP members over the extension of an airfield runway just outside Tokyo. Many American military bases were soon returned to Japan. With the imminent withdrawal of thousands of American troops, the Socialists and others were now confronted with the knotty problem of finding work for more than 100,000 persons who had been employed by the security forces, and of adjusting dislocated local economies around military bases. Under relentless interpellation by the opposition, Kishi admitted that the introduction of nuclear weapons into Japan was unconstitutional. Still, a Japanese government in cooperation with the American government was continuing to expand Japan's armed forces. In March

1958, the Premier declared that an attack on American bases in Japan would be regarded as an attack on Japan, and that Japanese armed forces might be sent overseas, reversing a policy enunciated only four months earlier.

Premier Kishi continued to keep the Socialists on the defensive but his position within his own party was becoming increasingly precarious toward the end of 1957. He carried out Ishibashi's expansive economic policies which soon drained Japan's foreign exchange reserves to a dangerously low point. Hurriedly he then had to resort to stringent economic policies. The Socialists accused him of befriending monopoly business interests at the expense of small and medium enterprises. The Kishi Plan to develop Southeast Asia with Japanese technical knowledge and American capital encountered scepticism both in Washington and in the region to be assisted. How to bolster his leadership as a national election approached was the problem confronting the Premier.

The Election of 1958

Time was fast running out in the spring of 1958 for Premier Kishi to hold a general election under his own conditions. Since the last one in February 1955, Socialist and Conservative forces had achieved mergers; the gavel had passed to four successive Conservative Cabinets without an electoral contest (except the partial Upper House election in 1956); the international climate had changed considerably; and Japan had begun to take a more active role in world affairs. The SDP emphasized its demand for an election in early 1958 by postponing its convention until February; the lobbying and pork barrel scars on the national budget passed by the Diet on March 31 also presaged an election. Only the date remained to be set. In line with his challenge to the Socialists, Kishi had hoped to call a sudden election but by this time all element of surprise had vanished. For the first time in Japanese political history, the Premier and the leader of the opposition together "agreed to dissolve" the Diet and hold a general election: the date set was May 22, 1958.

On the domestic front, the Conservatives had appropriated many SDP demands: increased social security, health insurance, and old age pensions. They were bitterly opposed, however, on labor and educational policies. In the field of foreign relations the Liberal Democrats had passed a Diet resolution (in conjunction with the Socialists) calling for the cessation of nuclear tests, had sent emissaries to the three nuclear powers to press their point, and had supported the Soviet Union's unilateral nuclear test ban on March 31, 1958. Both parties were in favor of world peace, greater independence for Japan, and giving precedence to Japan's relations with Afro-Asian countries. Negotiations with South Korea, which had been broken off since 1953, had recently been resumed; a fisheries agreement with the Soviet Union had been concluded.

Differences in foreign policy were focused on two issues: the recognition of and trade with Communist China, and the appropriate degree of cooperation with the United States. While it had been the steadfast policy of recent conservative governments not to recognize Communist China and only reluctantly to allow limited, slowly expanding trade with the mainland, it had been one of the major objectives of Socialist foreign policy in recent years to foster in every possible way the resumption of commercial and diplomatic relations with the People's Republic of China. Faced with mounting economic difficulties at home, the government was weakening under pressure from its own business supporters and the SDP for a liberalization of this trade. A private mission to Red China headed by a conservative Diet member, but including Socialists, concluded the fourth unofficial barter trade agreement early in 1958 for exchanges worth approximately $196 million. During the electoral campaign, Red China broke off the agreement, declaring unsatisfactory the formula proposed in Tokyo for privileges to be enjoyed by a permanent Communist Chinese commercial office. The Russians played into the Liberals' hands—as the United States had inadvertently helped the Socialist cause in earlier elections—by inquiring whether nuclear weapons were being stored in Japan, and were promptly accused of meddling in Japan's internal affairs.

A Conservative majority was never in doubt; the crux was rather how much the Socialists would increase their representation. In elections to the Upper House in 1956, the SDP had narrowed the margin to three million votes. Could it match or improve on this record?

Although the election was held on a weekday and coincided with a busy farming season, 77 per cent of eligible voters—a postwar record—went to the polls. The Soviet and Chinese Communists had helped to arouse popular interest in an otherwise dull contest. As usual, the Socialists, in contrast to their opponents, suffered from an insufficiency of candidates. The party had hoped to mobilize "intellectual and cultural personages" as candidates but in this it failed. There were more than enough candidates in urban areas but a woeful lack in rural constituencies; 246 candidates ran, only 12 more than a majority in the House of Representatives. The total number of candidates and rate of competition (two to one seat) were the lowest in the postwar period. While the JCP had withdrawn strategically located candidates in favor of Socialists in 1956, it did not scratch any of its 114 candidates in 1958, thereby blunting possible Socialist advances.

Contrary to expectations, the SDP increased its Diet representation by only 8 seats, from 158 to 166. Thirty-five Representatives, including many prominent Socialists elected in 1955, were defeated. The proportion of total votes cast for Socialist candidates was only 2.7 per cent greater than in 1955. The press called on the SDP to reevaluate its policies; the party leadership reluctantly conceded its relative defeat and submitted to perfunctory self-criticism. Nevertheless, in number of votes the SDP had made its largest gains since 1952. While its support had increased by one million votes in each election since then, its most recent gain was by 2.2 million over the 1955 level. For the first time, the Socialists alone obtained 33 per cent of the total vote. By contrast Conservative support had dropped, and the Communists had regained the 2.3 per cent of total vote which they had received in 1947. Furthermore, the Socialists had been able to break the Conservative monopoly in ten of twelve constituencies where they had been totally unsuccessful in the past. This was the first postwar election from which results were approximately the same as when the Diet was dissolved. Had the Liberal Democrats, Communists, and Socialists reached a temporary plateau in their respective strengths? Within the party the left wing slightly increased its factional strength. The Suzuki and Kawakami factions came to equal each other in size and continued to hold the party reins jointly. But intraparty opposition was building up as a result of the disappointing electoral results.

TEACHERS, POLICE, AND FOREIGN AFFAIRS

After the general election of 1958, confrontation between the two main parties gradually became more intense. As the majority party, the Liberal Democrats voted themselves the chairmanships of all committees in the House of Representatives. Previously these posts had been shared with the opposition. For several years the Conservatives had been attacking the political influence of the Japan Teachers' Union—one of the pillars of the SDP. As soon as the second Kishi cabinet was formed in June 1958, the Minister of Education declared that teacher efficiency rating would be instituted throughout the country. Although ostensibly an administrative move, the political intent was obvious: to weaken the Teachers' Union substantially, both as an organization and as a force in elections to the Diet. This change would correspondingly, though indirectly, weaken Socialist strength in the Diet.

The opposition, including leftist labor unions, were determined to do all in their power to challenge this new threat. Unions and students held rallies; demonstrators clashed with the police; the SDP attempted to mobilize members of Parent-Teacher Associations, housewives, and workers into a national joint-struggle organization; teachers and their pupils went on "mass leave."

As a corollary to the efficiency rating, the conservatives rammed through a bill to increase the "supervisory allowance" for grade and high school principals. The SDP and the Japan Teachers' Union regarded this as a deliberate attempt to alienate school principals from the union. In the House of Representatives the Socialists stalled, negotiated, forced votes on motions of non-confidence, but could not prevent passage of the bill. They tried to take advantage of their control over the chairmanship of the educational committee in the House of Councillors, but their rivals forced a vote calling for an interim report and then a final tally. Tension was aggravated when the Liberal Democrats instructed the schools to revive the teaching of "ethics" (*shūshin*). Socialists bitterly denounced this as an effort to reindoctrinate the Japanese people in outworn traditions invalidated by the war. Again and in vain they resorted desperately to defensive tactics which may have hurt them somewhat in elections to the Upper House in 1959.

The thirtieth session of the Diet convened on September 29, 1958. It began innocently enough by passing laws not requiring budgetary authorization. But the parliamentary process was soured when Premier Kishi, after secret preparations, suddenly submitted a drastic revision of the Police Duties Law on October 8 and forced a showdown. With the support of labor, farmer, and other organizations, together with that of intellectuals, the Socialists responded to this challenge with even greater determination.

This revision was one more attempt to tighten internal security laws and to centralize governmental and police authority. SDP resistance to partial centralization of the police had several years earlier resulted in a fight on the Diet floor. And, as we have seen, the Socialists had without success opposed passage of the Subversive Activities Prevention Law in 1952. The objective of the later proposals was to change the emphasis of the police law from protection of individual persons and property to public safety and maintenance of order. Socialists and their allied movements feared that any political or social movement could be obstructed if the police decided it was contrary to the official concept of public safety and order.

In the Diet, the Socialists refused to participate in related deliberations. When the Speaker of the House sent the police bill to committee without debate, they packed the committee room. Outside the Diet, the depth and determination of the opposition was emphasized by the participation even of Zenrō Kaigi in a national conference to oppose revision of the police law. For the first time, this right-wing labor federation earnestly joined in an organization the avowed aim of which was opposition to a political measure with only indirect economic consequences for unions. The SDP, both main labor federations, independent unions, farmers' unions, women's organizations, youth groups, and the like joined in this People's Council. By the end of October 1958, branches of the conference had been formed in every prefecture. The JCP had been excluded at the national level but its components became part of the common front in localities. Many types of religious, academic, artistic, farmer, and student organizations, numbering in all more than 600, had joined the Council by early November. The press and public opinion also vigorously opposed the revision. Rallies were held; some unions struck; and the SDP synchronized these protests with opposition tactics in the Diet.

In desperation, the LDP, on November 4—before all Socialist Representatives had entered the chamber—extended the Diet for 30 days, a tactic similar to those used in 1956. It further enraged the opposition; again the Socialists refused to assemble and vote. By this time, criticism in Kishi's own party demanded the shelving of the revision. In line with Nishio's comment that the Diet extension was legally effective but politically invalid, the second conference between Premier Kishi and Chairman Suzuki, on November 22, resulted in recognition of the "unfinished deliberation"—in other words the defeat—of the bill to revise the police law.

On the positive side, improvement of relations with Communist

China was made a major socialist objective in 1959. The impasse which had become almost total in the previous year continued, however, and repeated efforts of the SDP and Sōhyō to employ "people's diplomacy" encountered intransigent Chinese suspicions of Japanese conservatism and of the military alliance with the United States. Speculation that the retirement of Mao Tse-tung as Chairman of the Central People's Government might ameliorate official policies in Peking proved to be wishful; Premier Chou En-lai and Foreign Minister Ch'en Yi continued to be adamant, although they indicated that in altered circumstances broader, beneficial intercourse should be possible.

There was division within the SDP as to policy toward both Chinas, right-wingers being skeptical about rapprochement with Communist China. But outwardly the most vocal party spokesmen advocated revived bipartisanship on such issues and renewed activity by the Diet Members' League for Promotion of Trade with China. Much of the business community also joined this chorus.

The other major issue in and after the winter of 1958 in regard to Japan's foreign relations was the opposition's desire for "independent neutralism" versus the government's determination to revise the security treaty with the United States in order to achieve "more equal terms" within the framework of a renewed alliance. In this controversy, too, certain right-wing Socialists were closer to the conservative position and, as eight years previously, it was a factor precipitating renewed schism in October 1959.

The one development which gave some marginal support to the Socialist stand, however, was a decision by Judge Akio Date in the Tokyo District Court that the stationing of American troops in Japan was unconstitutional. The case at issue involved arrests of student and labor union demonstrators against the expansion of the military base at Sunakawa in October 1956. Judge Date's decision was reversed by the Supreme Court late in 1959. During the lengthy proceedings, however, the arguments were again much publicized; nationalist sentiments as well as any candid interpretation of the new Constitution favored Socialist views. Debates along these lines raged on, with lulls, until January 1960, when the revised security treaty was signed in Washington. The Socialist position was aided by Soviet initiatives toward summitry and disarmament but not by Liberal Democratic recognition of nationalistic demands in negotiation toward treaty revision, nor by the JCP shift from a strongly pro-Soviet to an avowedly more neutralist policy. It thus became harder for the SDP to publicize a distinctive policy.

Although factionalism complicated the conservatives' conduct of parleys with American diplomats, the opposition was also divided. Leftists who attempted to divert the opposition mobilized against the revised police bill to service against this new target encountered difficulties when they tried to organize in March 1959 a People's Council for Blocking the Security Treaty. This time some Communists occupied strategic posts at national and local levels, while Zenrō Kaigi and the SDP right wing held aloof. The Council organized mass rallies, demonstrations, and short political strikes. In the thick of "people's diplomacy" and of harrying government spokesmen in the Diet, even right Socialist leaders sometimes felt prompted to make rather extreme statements, as in the spring of 1959 when Asanuma in Peking declared American "imperialism" to be the "common enemy" of China and Japan, and in the following June when Katayama, interpellating in the Diet, observed that Japan was more a part of Asia than of the Western World and that Japan's present entangling alliance served to foster suspicions on the part of other Asians.

ELECTIONS AND RENEWED SCHISM IN 1959

Conditions in early 1959 were not smiling on the Social Democrats as they had been in 1956–57. The disadvantages of being in perennial opposition were beginning to take their toll; neutralism was attracting fewer votes since Communist China had become more bellicose; socialism in many countries, including Japan, was being challenged by the obvious capacity of private capitalism to complete reconstruction and advance to spectacular new levels of productivity and national as well as individual income. There were also many lesser reasons why Socialist candidates did poorly in elections to the House of Councillors on June 2, 1959.

They did gain in the April elections to prefectural assemblies, advancing the SDP fraction of the total seats in those bodies to 18.5 per cent. Their most surprising victories occurred in a number of rural prefectures. But they lost most of the gubernatorial contests, even those in Hokkaidō (for the first time in twelve years), Tokyo, and Osaka where they had attempted to concentrate efforts. Only 4.6 per cent of assemblymen on the municipal and district level (906) were

Socialists, and the SDP could claim only 666 (0.6%) of all seats in town and rural hamlet councils. The party was short of candidates with strong popular appeal and delayed in nominating some of its slates for the House of Councillors. Also the Communist Party, since July 1958 when its Seventh Congress had reverted to milder tactics, no longer withdrew its candidates late in the campaign in favor of left Socialist contestants.

As elections to the Upper House approached, the Socialists were worried. Could they add to such adversities for the Kishi government as the defeat of the attempt to revise the Police Duties Law and the Premier's failure in intraparty feuding late in 1958? According to opinion polls, Kishi's popularity had plummeted to a point where normally a change of government would have been expected. His foreign policy was being described caustically as "ryō-gishi" (both shores —a pun on the Premier's name which means "shore" or "bank") diplomacy, implying continued dependence on the United States.

When the votes were tallied, the Socialists were found to have only slightly increased their number of Councillors. In the 1956 contest the SDP had increased by 9 per cent its proportion of the total vote in the national constituency and its share of all votes cast in local constituencies by 13 per cent; but in 1959 its percentage of support in the national constituency dipped from 30.5 (1956) to 26.5, and in local districts from 38.0 to 34.1. Not only had the opposition failed to reduce the conservative majority; its defensive position vis à vis threatened amendment of the Constitution and other retrogressive legislation was weakened, as it came within two seats of losing one third of the Upper House. The tendency to level off in the elections of May 1958 had thus turned into decline. In neither legislative body would the Socialists be strong enough to prevent ratification of the anticipated revision of the security treaty with the United States.

Politicians' self-criticism after elections is seldom candid, but the press and public commented that the SDP had again been underfinanced, despite fairly heavy campaign subsidies from Sōhyō. That labor federation and Zenrō Kaigi had conducted separate supportive activities. The right and left wings of the party had not cooperated as well as three years previously; for example, whereas in Tokyo Metropolitan Prefecture two Socialists and one Communist had been elected in 1956, not one of the three candidates whom intraparty rivalry caused to run had this time been successful. In the national constituency and in most single-member prefectural districts, Socialist candidates trailed their LDP rivals. Another factor, even in some districts which had been considered to be Socialist strongholds, was the astounding performance of contestants blessed by the Sōka Gakkai (Value Creating Study Society), an offshoot of the Nichiren Buddhist sect. It rivaled the Socialist appeal to poorly educated and economically precarious voters in a number of cities and adjacent areas, but also undermined conservative strength in some districts. Even some labor union members and adults in their families were influenced by the tactics used by this movement. Many of them were flagrantly illegal though marked by a kind of religious fervor.

Only the holdover from their rather spectacular gains of 1956 permitted the Socialists to retain one third of the Councillors' seats, and they realized that in 1962 a much larger number of their incumbencies would be at stake. Conservative Councillors of the Green Breeze Society (Ryokufūkai) continued to dwindle, and the LDP versus SDP groups were apparently more drastically juxtaposed than ever. There was a tendency to compare this Social Democratic slump with the more severe one a decade earlier, and somewhat similar recriminations coupled with factional struggles for power developed in preparation for a special party convention scheduled for September.

Other causes of the crisis which followed were complex but can be briefly summarized. Chief among the issues which had been glossed over when the SDP was reunified were: the character of the party, the nature of the socialist revolution, relations with the JCP, and certain controversial foreign policies. Not all factions in the two wings had been as keen as those led by Kawakami and Suzuki, on the right and left, respectively. Reluctant leaders in both wings and in their associated labor federations regarded as heresies some of the compromises made then; subsequent events and trends revived and augmented their suspicions.

Since the convention of 1958, a standing committee had been studying party reorganization, urged particularly by headquarters personnel and by local branches. The leadership was under criticism for preoccupation with reelection and activities in the Diet. From branches came demands for more effective Socialist participation in local struggles. The old guard of each wing was hesitant about such changes; on lower levels the issues meshed with controversies over political strikes and joint efforts with JCP factions—issues bound to exacerbate tensions between left and right in the party.

Moreover, employers had been stiffening in the face of wage offensives. Sōhyō unions became alarmed at Zenrō's organization of more "second unions." Communist infiltration of certain leftist unions had gained, and some younger leaders, who had not experienced JCP domination prior to 1950, were impressed by the determination and organizational skills of such elements. Also, their discontent was sharpened by the blocking of promotions for many juniors, since Socialist defeats had closed the route of advancement to the Diet for many an older labor official. For other reasons, too, veterans in these organizations were aware of smoldering threats to their authority. Takano's pro-Communist faction in Sōhyō reasserted itself, and another leftward shift became apparent in that federation's convention in August 1959.

Two issues—the use of forces earlier mobilized against the Police Duties Bill, and policy in regard to revision of the security treaty with the United States—became preeminent on the left in 1959. These involved most of the basic disputes between wings of the SDP and their allied labor movements. Leftists demanded that groups which had been mobilized against the recent police bill should persist until the Kishi cabinet had been forced to resign or the Diet dissolved. Those who advocated direct action in order to achieve political change or state power raised their pens and voices. But those prevailed (notably the faction led by Nishio) who argued that Socialists should end their boycott of the Diet and resume parliamentary functioning so as not to lose public sympathy which had been gained. This rebuff, plus Socialist electoral defeats and other mentioned trends, caused increasing pressure to be exerted by Sōhyō on left-wing party leaders. In September 1958, Nishio's article, entitled "Let the Executive Establish the Independence of the Party" was published in *Gekkan Shakaitō* (Socialist Monthly). While recognizing the inevitability of union pressures, he contended that a cross-stratal party could better maintain its independent balance and adhere to parliamentary methods. He had been answered in part in December by the prominent Marxist ideologue, Itsurō Sakisaka, in *Shakaishugi* (Socialism), who frankly reiterated that capitalist interests could not be expected to submit peaceably to a socialist revolution and that violent action by the organized masses could be justified as necessary in certain situations. Such debates were thus being reintensified in both the party and the labor movement.

The Nishio faction was also the most outspoken among the Socialists in criticizing militant struggles of Sōhyō and the political left against U.S. military bases and other operational aspects of the security treaty. Nishio branded the idea of a four-power nonaggression pact in lieu of the two hostile alliance systems in Northeast Asia as "theoretical" and called for more concrete proposals. As nationalists, many in the right wing did not want to jeopardize the real gains for Japan which a revised treaty would include; the alternative would be indefinite continuance of the much-criticized current agreements. Most of them admitted the need for some allied shield against Communist power until relaxation of international tensions, effective collective security, or greater Japanese economic and military strength could develop. Ultimately, they agreed, Japan should attain a more independent status. They charged that their rivals were not genuinely neutral but intended to profit politically and otherwise by leaning toward the Red Bloc once the alliance with the United States was broken. They objected strongly to Asanuma's anti-American statement in Peking. Since August 1958, these related controversies had been sharpened as the Foreign Ministry under Prime Minister Kishi prepared for and then began negotiations toward revision of the security treaty, and as provisions of the altered draft agreement were later published.

At the special Socialist convention in September 1959, which was supposed to consider reconstruction of the party, leftist delegates from Sōhyō and the party's Youth Division, aided by the Wada and Matsumoto factions, tried to expel Nishio but their attempt was killed in Steering Committee. They then voted—with the support of the Suzuki faction—for a hearing before the Control Committee for alleged "anti-party actions," especially in regard to prevailing SDP opposition to renegotiation of the security treaty and its championing of relations with Communist China, as well as for fostering the development of "second" (i.e. rival, less militant) unions. Nishio was further accused of favoring rearmament, supporting pro-Taiwan organizations, forming branches with the aim of altering the character of the party, and having misled the SDP into negotiations with the government with regard to the abortive police bill. Leftists denounced him above all for drawing a more decisive line between communism and democracy than between capitalism and socialism.

Nishio, who had recently been acquitted of charges concerning the Shōwa Denkō scandal, reacted with characteristic asperity. On September 14, he denounced "anti-democratic" tendencies and "pro-communist" elements in the party, withdrew from the convention with a number of his clique, including those with executive posts, and threatened to form a new party. This jarred even some members of his own faction and placed the moderate Kawakami group in a dilemma. Following five days of struggle, the convention was recessed for one month, after which it reconvened for two days.

Nishio was by no means alone in castigating what he called the "slavish" yielding of leftist factions to radical pressures by Sōhyō, particularly during and after the convention of 1957. An added incitement to conflict was the rise of a new generation of members lacking strong commitments to prewar leaders and lineages. Rather they tended to align over ideological issues into pro-Zenrō versus pro-Sōhyō elements, the latter being preponderant in the Youth Division. Zenrō Kaigi had never been reconciled to SDP reunification and certain of its highest leaders had been consulting with Nishio before his startling declaration. What he was soon calling the Association for Party Reconstruction declared its support for a brand of "democratic socialism" which would seek support from "the whole nation, not merely the labor unions and farmers' organizations." This transitional body met in Tokyo on October 18, immediately after adjournment of the deadlocked convention. Some 300 right-wing leaders, including 28 Diet members, attended. There the decision to split from the main SDP was definitely announced, and it occurred a week later. By November 1959, the Nishio-led right-wing Socialist Club claimed 12 adherents in the House of Councillors and 21 in the Lower House; the SDP proper was left with 72 in the Upper House and 144 Representatives. Zenrō Kaigi had early transferred its support from the SDP to the prospective new party.

Meanwhile, the Suzuki faction, though under strong leftist pressure, moderated its position. When the Kawakami group saw that secession of the other right-wing faction could not be prevented, it resumed cooperation with the "mainstream," permitting Asanuma to run for office against his mentor, Kawakami, at the regular convention in 1960. Suzuki's faction divided in the voting, and the younger leader won the highest party office by a narrow margin.

Nishio insisted that the new organization, which was founded on January 24, 1960, would be a "genuine" Democratic Socialist Party (Minshu Shakaitō—Minshatō, or DSP for short) promoting gradual reforms, but many commentators began to call it a centrist association. The Nishio faction was reported to favor revisions of the Constitution, but publicly the new group, while dissociating itself from the leftist campaign, continued to defend that basic law. Nishio denied any plan to unite with reputedly somewhat liberal factions of the LDP; instead he promised that the new party would cooperate with the Social Democrats to promote policies on which they could agree, stated that this common ground was greater than with the conservatives, and hoped for later Socialist reunification on a more moderate basis.

The provisional program of the nascent party was drafted by members of the Democratic Socialism Study Group, who adapted the West German Social Democratic Party's platform as a model. As could have been predicted, it advocated a "popular" rather than a "class" party. It declared the DSP to be opposed to dictatorships of left or right and to favor gradual achievement of socialism by peaceful, legal means. It rejected Marxism–Leninism and class struggle as a comprehensive solution and instead upheld the kind of modified socialism which has recently been more current in Western Europe. Rather than proletarianizing all of society, this party was encouraged by the continuing boom to hope ultimately "to place all people in the middle strata." It was hoped in these quarters that the Japanese could "make progress while preserving tradition." The platform supported expansion of welfare programs but warned against narrow class interests. Internationally inspected disarmament was advocated but, until effective, the Democratic Socialists favored "more appropriate measures for our own security."

A "SEASON OF DISRUPTION," THEN MODERATION

In the same month that this moderate party was founded, Premier Kishi flew to Washington where he signed the revised security treaty. Already there had been signs that 1960 would be a troubled year though it was a time of high prosperity. Late in the previous November, the eighth in a series of waves protesting against renewal and revision of the security treaty had culminated in massed students breaking through a police cordon to the inner grounds around the Diet building. There they were assisted by Socialist Diet members in submitting petitions. In the following month, both Socialist Parties had boycotted the Diet in an attempt to prevent passage of a measure which would have controlled such efforts at direct pressure on the legislature.

As will be described more fully in Chapter 6, the conglomerate opposition forces shaped their climax to coincide with the conservative drive to gain Diet approval of the revised treaty. Socialist Representatives again resorted to physical obstruction to prevent a meeting where voting was intended on approval of the treaty and on a 50-day extension of the legislative session. Police were summoned and cleared the building of militant opposers, whereupon the conservative majority rammed through its measures. The Socialists branded these votes as illegal, resorted again to boycott of the parliament, and even contemplated the resignation of their Representatives. Since, according to constitutional provision, the treaty would be automatically ratified one month after approval on May 19, opposing demonstrators sought dissolution of the Diet, the resignation of Kishi's government, and cancellation of the scheduled goodwill visit of President Eisenhower just at the time of impending ratification. In the end, the opposition forces failed in their vital aims but won secondary victories: resignation of Kishi's Cabinet *after* ratification of the treaty and cancellation of the President's visit. Had they won dissolution, elections to the new House of Representatives would have been fought mainly on the treaty issue.

Most Japanese are characterized by love of order, respect for law, and a sense of hospitable obligation; many such had been offended during the demonstrations and strikes by leftist students and labor unionists. Yet there were many, including some of Japan's most articulate intellectuals, who deplored the nation's renewed alignment with one side in the cold war. Resurgent nationalism, accompanying greater economic strength, had also aroused considerable sympathy for the opposition. Although there was widespread condemnation of the limited violence, the government of Kishi had become even more unpopular, its arbitrary tactics severely criticized. In retrospect, people and factions interpreted these events according to their biases—left Socialists and labor leaders exaggerating what had been accomplished by direct action and referring to their "precious experience" —yet, not surprisingly, a contested and uneven trend toward moderation ensued. It would have proceeded further had not Sōhyō and the main leftist SDP won so many seats at the expense of the Democratic Socialists with Zenrō backing in the elections of November 1960.

Concern over leftist threats to parliamentary politics was soon to be followed by anxiety over violence from the ultranationalist right. The Liberal Democrats, as in the past after such episodes, tried to enact restrictive measures; their limited success was partly attributable to prevalent sober reflection not only on leftist excesses but also on what reformers called the "tyranny of the majority." The new government of Premier Ikeda discreetly adopted a "low posture" in the interests of pacification. After the elections, bills to prohibit and control violence were submitted by the three main parties but none were enacted at that time. The Liberal Democrats and Nishio's partisans moved toward a compromise which would restrain violence from either extreme, but the SDP argued that there is a significant difference between *putsches* and individual acts of violence by ultrarightists, on one hand, and, in contrast, mass demonstrations in support of the interests of social classes.[6]

The rival Democratic Socialist Party, even though of minor proportions, provided moderate unions affiliated with Zenrō Kaigi with representation in the Diet and before public opinion. This was keenly felt by Sōhyō and the SDP, which took both internal and public steps to shield themselves from the tactics of these rivals. The offensive to split off union affiliates of Sōhyō and to form "second unions" connected with Zenrō-Sōdōmei was nevertheless accelerated, and these more moderate labor-socialist allies took advantage of both current prosperity, which fostered moderation among the rank-and-file, and wide criticism of excessive labor politicism during and after the antitreaty crisis. National Sōhyō leaders, with their Representatives in the Diet and ability to exert pressures on the dependent SDP, had felt obliged by the effects of economic growth and rising wages to emphasize political issues. Opposition to the security treaty had been especially opportune because it could appeal beyond labor's interests and thus rally a united front.

6. The SDP's draft contained provisions for a "Political Terrorism Punishment Law." The party continued to oppose additional powers for the police and the Public Safety Investigation Agency.

Even groups which had participated in the spring struggle, like the National Liaison Council of Independent Unions (Chūritsu Rōren), had grown increasingly disturbed at JCP and noncommunist radical manipulation of the protesting coalition. Some of the main peace and pro-democratic national councils had been riven and weakened by attempts to divert them into the anti-treaty campaign. Kishi's announcement of his willingness to resign had forestalled further effective mass demonstrations. A few of the more candid post mortems, even by certain left Socialists and Sōhyō leaders, admitted that recent elections and demonstrations had again revealed limited public support for socialism or a united front as such. Issues with appeal to a broad social spectrum were needed for mobilization, but once the achievement of immediate goals had satisfied the nonsocialist majority, the "objective conditions" for mass action became less propitious. Additionally, recriminations, tensions, and splits within the labor and socialist movements tended to impair the "subjective conditions" for socialist revolution.

Parallel with the anti-treaty efforts, a long and bitter strike had been waged by the Miike local of the Coal Miners' Union against the Mitsui Mining Company in northern Kyūshū. Because of the forces involved, this became a symbol, a cause célèbre. The national union was a member of Sōhyō, and both came to the support of the embattled miners, imbuing the struggle with national significance and trying to broaden its class and political implications. The Democratic Socialists and Zenrō leaders successfully encouraged a split in the local and formation of a second union. In the end, the ruling of the National Labor Relations Commission was accepted, and the company was allowed to proceed with the rationalization of personnel which the wider use of oil and diesel engines necessitated. This was just one of several such struggles. Leftist labor and socialist circles commented that high profits and expansion were permitting "monopoly capitalism" to assume a "high posture." They rued their inability to link the Miike and anti-treaty struggles, which would have augmented the capacity for direct mass actions.

Special ideological significance was attached to the Miike strike because the members of that union had long been indoctrinated in the Marxist–Leninist interpretations expounded to them by Professor Itsurō Sakisaka, of late the chief ideologue in and out of the Left SDP. Though he and associates tried to put the best face on events, the fact was that soul-searching was called for both in the SDP and in Sōhyō. There was restiveness in the branches of one and among union locals of the other.

Reevaluation was also prompted by the widely held view that extremist policies and actions of the left had further aroused groups on the ultraright. During the excitement in June, the elderly Kawakami was stabbed by a young fanatic; Premier Kishi was knifed the following month. While television cameras were grinding and leaders of the main parties were participating in a joint campaign program on October 12, another youth assassinated Chairman Asanuma of the SDP. In the following January, an attack intended to kill the editor of the *Chūō Kōron* (Central Review) instead wounded his wife and murdered her maid. Later in 1961, in the Kansai region, a plot aimed at assassination of the Cabinet and seizure of state power was nipped. The press and public reacted to these events with shock and disgust. Although some businessmen had begun to contribute to ultranationalist organizations, opinion was overwhelmingly in favor of restabilizing parliamentary politics. Spokesmen of both main parties apparently yielded to these demands. Yet soon the tactics of confrontation were partially resumed. Some left Socialists agreed with the Communists that, in a country where the conservative majority was perennially kept in power by agrarian traditionalism, the economic power of concentrated capitalist enterprises, and bureaucratic cooperation, parliamentary democracy did not rule out bids for power by direct action "in the interests of the masses." This implied that revolutionary elites could decide better than majority votes what was in the best interests of the people.

Such views expressed the frustration of the chronic opposition. The capitalist system and liberal politics persisted, so "progressive" leaders have redoubled efforts to find ways within this framework to "break through the barrier of one third" in the Diet. Inevitably this has involved reconsideration of whether the SDP is, or should be, essentially a national or a class party—an old issue with direct bearing on how broadly the party can attract support.

During the electoral campaign of October-November 1960, the SDP added to its three basic policies—neutrality, support of democracy, and defense of the Constitution—a number of others. It called for abrogation of the security treaty, for diplomatic relations with Communist China, for reduction of the Self-Defense Forces, for expanded social security, and opposed augmenting veterans' pensions. The Democratic Socialists advocated "gradual abolition" of the security treaty, recognition of both Chinas, and raising the lower classes to middle economic status.[7] They also sought a larger share of the "floating vote." Although the Socialist rivals impaired each other's showing in some districts, there were signs that "intra-reformist confrontation" might result in more attention paid to the plight of the approximately ten million Japanese living in severest penury.

During the campaign, the Social Democrats and their allies charged that the conservatives were fostering ultrarightist violence, but the votes of sympathy they attracted on this issue—despite full exploitation of Asanuma's memory—may have just offset their inability to make the impetus of the anti-treaty mobilization carry over strongly into the elections. Although the majority had turned against Kishi, it had not deserted the Liberal Democrats, who claimed their gain of 13 seats to be a virtual plebiscite approving renewal and revision of the alliance with the United States. The new LDP President and automatically Premier, Hayato Ikeda promised to double the national income in ten years, to cut taxation of small businesses by a total of ¥100 million, to expand social security, and to achieve other benefits for farmers and consumers. This program and Japanese capitalism's "great leap forward," while Chinese socialism was encountering difficulties, constituted part of the challenge facing the opposition.

The reformist parties together polled slightly more than 39 per cent of the total votes, 27.5 per cent of this being for SDP candidates. Fifteen of the party's 23 new seats were won at the expense of Nishio's Democratic Socialists. Thus the SDP advanced from 122 to 145 seats, while its socialist rival declined from 40 to 17. Since 1952, votes for the SDP had mounted from 3.4 to 10.9 million, while for the Right Socialists they had, since 1955, dropped from 5.1 to 3.5 million. Besides having very weak regional and local organization, the new DSP had found it difficult to formulate clear policies which could be sufficiently differentiated from its two main rivals. It gave little evidence of being a genuine socialist party and spent much of its time castigating the SDP and Sōhyō for excesses during the spring crisis. Again there

7. The Democratic Socialists also urged protection of parliamentary government and elimination of violence whether from right or left. They denounced plutocracy, the ultra-right, the LDP, Zengakuren (the leftist student federation with its two wings), and the close ties between Sōhyō and the SDP.

was a greater supply of young left Socialist leaders; nine moderate Socialists had been defeated by SDP "new faces," most of them from labor and prefectural assemblies. There were many criticisms of the new party's campaign: that its policies were vague; that it should have spoken out on other issues such as agricultural needs; that it might be at least inadvertently a tool of the LDP; that it was too much dominated by Nishio; that Zenrō's support had been inadequate; that the DSP had done little to prevent renewal of the security treaty; and that, because of a shortage of attractive leaders, many of its candidates had been tardily selected. Thus the two-main-party pattern continued and a liberal center failed to emerge. Instead the Diet nearly lost a "buffer zone."

Actually a new area of tension within the Social Democratic Party had been developing since the parliamentary crisis in the spring of 1960. Secession of the Nishio faction and its support for Zenrō's offensive had given inordinate bargaining influence to the moderate Kawakami faction. It was for purposes of shielding and compromise that party leftists and Sōhyō leaders favored Kawakami as Chairman in 1961 and at the following convention. Another moderating influence emerged as Suzuki's leadership of the "mainstream" faction was relaxed, permitting fissiparous tendencies. Saburō Eda, one of the best minds and voices, with strong support from the party's Youth Section, and Tomomi Narita, chairman of the Policy Planning Board, had begun to champion a theoretical interpretation and related strategic reformulation—"structural reform"—which for the next few years was debated keenly on the left. Adapted from a treatise that Palmiro Togliatti, the Italian Communist leader (1893–1964) had designed in 1956 for a somewhat similar situation, its Japanese Socialist exponents contended that, as a perennial opposition, the party had become "too negative." Japanese socialism could no longer avoid the reevaluation that its Western European counterparts had been undertaking for years, though conclusions might differ. Serious postwar depressions had not resulted from the inner contradictions of capitalism. Better distributive measures had been developed. Although benefiting unequally, working classes had been sharing unprecedented prosperity. Rates of economic growth were mounting, and profound technological changes were underway. Who would be strengthened more by these swift developments, capitalism or labor? It was necessary to work out a more positive strategy to hem in monopoly capitalism. This could be done, it was asserted, by forming a nationwide front of elements opposed to monopolists and their political allies, by moving in the direction of making the SDP a national party. But the younger proponents had to defend themselves against the Marxian scholastics and their political colleagues, so they argued that by such a strategy socialists could press on past the "barrier of one third" toward power through a parliamentary majority, and by cumulative reforms to "qualitative changes" in the economic structure. Once in power, a socialist system could be introduced and consolidated. The agencies of the state could then be allied with mass organizations to defend the new order.

Was this a genuine course of action or merely rationalization of a moderate tack; or was it ideological revisionism? More will be said about "structural reform" in the next chapter. At an extraordinary SDP convention on the day after Asanuma's assassination, Eda was elected Acting Chairman and the new strategy, with modifications, was adopted. Despite keen debate at the regular convention in March 1961, "structural reform" was again espoused in the action program.

Theory, Tactics, and Policies

3. Principles and Theory

Socialist parties naturally emphasize ideology and theory more than do their bourgeois rivals; their programs for change must rest on persuasive analyses of defects in the status quo and on proposals for new institutions and directions.[1] Marxism–Leninism, which has exerted so much influence on the left wing of Japanese socialism and the labor movement, goes further and asserts its version of eternal, "scientific" truths about social processes, evolution, and transformation. Feudal traditions, the illiberal Meiji system, discontent with low levels of consumption and welfare, and the great chasm between elites and ordinary folk have all provided materials for the development of revolutionary doctrines in Japan.

1. For a comparison between the Japanese Conservative and Socialist platforms, see Uyehara et al., "Comparative Platforms." This compares by topic, in nonannotated juxtaposition, the 1955 platform of the Japan Liberal Democratic Party with the 1955 program of the reunited SDP as well as with those of the latter's two predecessors: the 1954 Left Socialist program and the 1955 Right Socialist program.

The 1955 LDP platform, and those of the Socialists, have been supplemented almost yearly by "action policies," which state goals and ideals. Something of a new departure occurred, however, with the passing at the LDP convention on January 27, 1960, of a resolution labeled "The Political Philosophy of the New Conservatism" (*Shin Hoshushugi no Seiji Tetsugaku*). A careful reading reveals Socialist opposition influences. It proclaimed its goals as "creation of a harmonious middle-class, a welfare state based on civilized moral justice. . . ." It also spoke of "respect for individual personality" as the "highest morality of mankind." It rejected "nineteenth century laissez-faire and monopoly capitalism." Very similar goals, as will be noted below, were proclaimed by the Nishio-led Democratic Socialist Party three days earlier.

From the resumption of the social democratic movement in 1945, it was apparent that the right wing was less impelled by doctrinal imperatives, that its leaders thought of revolution more as a basic evolutionary change than as an overthrow. It is an irony and dilemma of Japanese politics that the more practical revisionist wing is less well rooted in organized movements for the reform of economic and political society. Whether identified with the more radical or moderate wing of the movement, and even though claiming to champion the causes of workers and farmers, there has usually been a gap between the more theoretically oriented politicians and intellectuals, on the one hand, and the common people, on the other.

BACKGROUND OF THE 1955 UNIFIED PROGRAM

The three-sentence program adopted by the SDP at its founding convention in November 1945 described the party as "the national rally of the laboring strata" intent upon a democratic structure through political liberty. Stabilization and improvement of the people's livelihood should be achieved by abolishing capitalism and substituting socialism. The various founding elements declared their opposition to militarism and their desire for permanent peace through international cooperation.[2] At this first convention, and ever since, two main concepts of the party's essential nature were expressed: that it should be based on the working—especially the industrial labor—class, and that it should represent the interests of all revisionist strata. There had been a prewar background for these views.[3] The wording of unified programs in 1945 and a decade later had to be blurred in order to achieve compromises. Tensions always remained. At the start, however, when hope for socialist unity was high, it was agreed that the party should seek support broadly from those elements between the Liberal Party, which Hatoyama and other conservatives were about to form, and the Communists, who were emerging into legality.

No prewar proletarian party had attacked militarism so directly or approached so closely a pacifist position. No legal program had demanded thoroughgoing democracy in the political sphere; the Emperor system had required that such proposals be limited to "political

2. Mosaburō Suzuki tells in the *Shakai Taimuzu,* Nov. 24, 1953, about writing the three-point program. Suzuki, from the prewar left wing, and Mitsu Kōno, who by the late 1930s was of the right wing, collaborated; both were theoretically inclined.

3. A discussion of prewar proletarian class concepts and party programs will be found in Totten *The Social Democratic Movement in Prewar Japan* pp. 180–86, 207–09.

liberty" and "parliamentarism," that is, there had been little or no tolerance for demands or methods looking toward revolutionary goals.

Delegates at this first convention were moved by a manifesto written by Hyō Hara, which elaborated and gave perspective to the terse program. In forceful terms it denounced military groups, the bureaucracy, the *zaibatsu,* and those politicians who had sacrificed the prewar parties. It dedicated the party to restoring the dignity of the Diet, establishing responsible government, and promoting democracy; it declared that through peaceful means the party would strive to transform the economy from capitalism to socialism and to regain international goodwill for Japan. With these two statements and a number of policies approved by the convention, the Social Democratic Party of Japan was launched on a sea of economic troubles over which political freedom, like a new sun, was just beginning to shine.

At the next convention and each year thereafter, a new outline of policies was designed to meet current needs, but the three-point basic program endured for nearly a decade. Rapid growth and its period of shared national administration allowed the party little time for any but immediate issues.

The crushing defeat in the elections of January 1949 impelled Socialist leaders to reconsider the party's philosophy preparatory to reconstruction. The controversy that raged while the action policy was being formulated that year came to be named for its main protagonists, Junzō Inamura for the left wing and Tatsuo Morito for the right. In striving for verbal agreement both groups used similar phrases, but with differing connotations, colored by their divergent philosophical systems. The left wing then and since has seen revolution as a qualitative change which takes place when political power is transferred from the bourgeoisie to the proletariat, after which a socialist reconstruction of society can be realized. This school accepts and seeks to apply Marxist–Leninist concepts of dialectical materialism, class struggle, and the "inevitable" results of capitalist contradictions. On the other hand, what Morito called the "social revolution" was basically an evolutionary but fundamental change in economic relations among people, enabling them to develop a more moral society which he equated with socialism.[4]

While this debate did not result in a conclusively resolved theoret-

4. An actual debate between Morito and Inamura with Katsumata as moderator is recorded in *Shakai Shichō,* No. 24 (July 1949), pp. 30–46. This issue contains the Inamura, Morito, and Katsumata drafts as well as minutes from the Action Policy Committee.

ical position, nor in a new platform which could permanently satisfy both party wings, Seiichi Katsumata of the left wing was able to include compromises in concepts and expression sufficient to reconcile the two main factions for a few more years; this draft also furnished a valuable precedent for formulators of the platform on which reunification of the SDP was accomplished, healing the schism of 1951–55. For example, the phrase "class oriented mass party" (*kaikyūteki taishū seitō*), though unused during the period of division, was revived in the reunified program of 1955.

Electoral gains by the Left Socialists in 1952 and the following year led them to consider the earlier three-point program outmoded. Both parties were under pressure to reunite, and the leftists were eager to clarify their ideological position before entering negotiations. Inamura participated in drafting the Left Socialist program of 1954, though Hiroo Wada (Katsumata's mentor) was chairman of the committee which included the able Kōdō Itō. The non-Communist Marxist scholar, Itsurō Sakisaka, a leader of the Socialist Society (Shakaishugi Kyōkai), served as a consultant. The program was divided into three parts: the first devoted to principles and theory; the second to action policy; and the third to party organization.[5] The first was divided into the following subheadings: (1) the historical tasks of the SDP; (2) the present condition of Japanese capitalism; (3) the prospects of peaceful revolution; (4) conditions for a socialist revolution; (5) struggles under the capitalist system; and (6) government in the transitional stage. While it held that the prospects for a peaceful revolution were good, what disturbed the Right Socialists most was the leftist implication that socialists should aim at permanent power.

While the Right Socialists felt challenged to explain their critique and their own views of the revived issues, they decided to formulate a basis for reunification rather than to widen the gap by publishing their own platform. The resulting position-paper was first drafted by Eki Sone and in final form was approved by the Right Socialist Party on May 7, 1955. The preamble was followed by a section dealing with objectives and principles of socialism, and another defining the character of the party and outlining a formula for peaceful revolution.[6] This program had been strongly influenced by the "Declaration of

5. The Left Socialist program of 1954 was published as a pamphlet: Nihon Shakaitō Shuppan Iinkai, ed., *Kōryō* (Program) (Tokyo, 1955).

6. This Right Socialist draft program of 1955, together with an account of its creation and several essays by right-wing theoreticians on various ideological issues, may be found

the Socialist International" and by the Asian Socialist Conference's statement of "Principles and Objectives of Socialism." It upheld "democratic socialism" as an alternative to capitalism, fascism, or communism. Comparison of the two programs indicates that the Right wing was more interested in limitations on action in accordance with fundamental principles but that the Left stressed theory as a guide to revolutionary action.

From May to August 1955, the bases for reunification were tortuously negotiated by experienced leaders from both sides.[7] The question that had worried the Right Socialists most—the relationship of democracy to socialism—was solved by leftist assurances that the existence of opposition parties would be recognized after taking power and that the reins of government would be relinquished if and when the Socialists lost a majority in a subsequent election. The most difficult problems were the definition of Japan's status vis-à-vis the United States and the degree of opposition that should be expressed toward communism.

The resulting program emphasized four points: (1) the present condition of Japan; (2) peaceful revolution and the struggle for national independence; (3) tasks and character of the party; (4) socialist aims. In addition, a statement entitled "Basic Policies" was appended; the Right-wing Socialists considered this to be as much a part of the program as amendments would be part of a constitution.[8]

Though there has been subsequent significant rethinking and debate, particularly since the summer of 1960, this document is the most

---

in Minshu Shakaishugi Remmei, ed., *Tōitsu Shakaitō Kōryō Sōan to Sono Kaisetsu* (The Reunified Social Democratic Party Program and a Commentary on It) (Tokyo, 1955). The first part (principles and theory) of the Left Socialist program was appended.

Most of the actual writing of the right-wing program was by two younger staff members, Shimpei Fujimaki and Tamio Kawakami (eldest son of the party leader), who were constantly advised by other members, particularly those associated with the Democratic Socialist League.

7. Members of this subcommittee for the Left wing were Katsumata, Itō, Sōji Okada, Tadataka Sata, and Tadashi Yaoita (who substituted upon the death of Inamura); the right-wingers included Kōno, Kanendo Matsuzawa, Chōzaburō Mizutani, Eiichi Nishimura, and Sone.

8. The reunified program of 1955 may be found, among other places, in the following: (1) Nihon Shakaitō, ed., *Yobō ni Kotaete: Nihon Shakaitō Taikai Kettei Shū* (Responding to Expectations: The Collected Resolutions of the Social Democratic Party of Japan) (Tokyo, 1955). (2) Hiroshi Yamazaki, *Nihon Shakaitō Jūnen Shi* (A Ten-Year History of the Social Democratic Party of Japan) (Tokyo, 1956). (3) A not very faithful translation into English may be found in Julius Braunthal, ed., *Yearbook of the International Socialist Labour Movement: 1956–1957* (London, 1956), pp. 338–48. (4) A partial but topically arranged translation may be found in "Comparative Platforms."

official, comprehensive statement of principles and theory of the Social Democratic Party of Japan, and it will serve here as a focus for exposition and analysis. To insure accord, much was deliberately left unsaid in this platform. As a compromise it resembled more the prior leftist platform than the moderates' draft; nevertheless the Left continued to be dissatisfied and to press for revisions, both tacit and explicit.

Since ideology, like strategy and tactics (to be treated in the next chapter), must continually be made to cope with realities, we shall pursue this theme beyond 1955, mentioning the treatments of key issues in the program of the Democratic Socialist Party, founded in January 1960, and in the controversies over "structural reform." Since the SDP convention in 1957, those leftist factions in the party and in Sōhyō which felt that the compromises had jeopardized socialist integrity and that attainment of power under such a platform could only achieve a welfare state had been reemphasizing the class character of the party, political action in alliance with organized labor, and direct action ("parliamentarism-plus") at opportune times. Articles by Sakisaka in 1958 calling for revision of the reunification program were supported by the Wada, Nomizo, and Matsumoto factions on the SDP left; the leadership of Sōhyō also insisted on a leftward tack. Chairman Suzuki therefore appointed a committee to study revision of the platform, but Nishio opposed such pressures.

Doctrinal issues were, of course, involved in the secession of the Nishio faction and its greater critical freedom, and in the labor-socialist controversies stirred by failure of the Miike strike and the anti-treaty demonstrations of 1960. The Democratic Socialist program early in 1960 of course presented right-wing views in more undiluted form than in the reunified platform, and it could reflect events which had transpired in the interim, such as the trend of noncommunist international socialism away from Marxism, as evinced by the West German Social Democratic Party's adoption of the so-called Godesberg Program in November 1959, clearly declaring that it had turned from a party of the working class into a party of the people. The DSP program was largely the work of Professor Yoshihiko Seki, a specialist in Western political thought who studied the Godesberg Program as he prepared the new draft.[9]

9. The DSP program of 1960 was approximately the same length as the reunified program. Its third and fourth sections likewise dealt with "tasks" and "aims," but it discussed

Many factors conduced to socialist debates and to the unevenly moderate trend which ensued. Prosperity was percolating down to workers, making them less inclined toward militancy. Excessive labor politicism always comes under attack by moderates after a surge of mass actions. Encouraged by spectacular economic growth, the Ikeda administration not only publicized its income-doubling plan over the next decade but foresaw major changes in the structure of Japanese agriculture and industry. New industrial zones were envisaged transcending existing principles of labor organization based on workshops and regions. Technological changes and rationalizations of personnel required more than crude, defensive responses. Without aping either the Communists or the Democratic Socialists, SDP leaders sought means by which governmental policies could be changed rather than merely opposed. Alternative economic planning had to be formulated more carefully. Capitalism was growing stronger and bringing benefits; the conservative majority in the Diet had grown; extraparliamentary mass actions—even violence—had neither dislodged conservative power nor prevented ratification of the alliance with capitalist America. The public and press were demanding firmer support for parliamentary processes and more positive, responsible opposition forces. Until the economic boom Japanese socialists could ignore the rethinking of doctrinaire Marxism–Leninism which had produced changes in the programs of the British Labour and the West German and Austrian Social Democratic Parties, but such reconsideration could no longer be postponed.

"Structural reform" was borrowed and shaped to meet these conditions. It was championed by some of the ablest younger leaders who seized this opportunity to challenge the doctrinaire and factional rigidities of veteran Socialist and labor politicos. It provided theoretical justification for a socialist strategy under conditions of an advanced economy and an effective parliamentary system. In so doing it had perforce to cope with the problems of how to break the "barrier of one third" in the Diet as well as the basic character and appeals of the party. The Communist Party in Japan rejected structural reform and expelled dissidents for advocating it; thus elements in the Social Dem-

---

the character of the party only in brief and did not attempt to analyze the "present condition of Japan." It began with a declaration of principles and devoted its second section to a summarized history of socialism. The Japanese text of this program was distributed at the DSP founding convention on January 24, 1960.

ocratic Party felt free to propound this reformulation.[10] Indeed, the Japanese controversy was obviously related to the Sino-Soviet debates; this was noticed, and "structural reform" was officially denounced in Peking. Although in Japan a revisionist wing left the JCP in 1961, leftist factions in the SDP and in Sōhyō were more influential than the Communist mainstream in opposing structural reform. They were the counterparts of Stalinists and Maoists in the Japanese debates. And the reformers were presented with predicaments similar to those which confronted Khrushchevian revisionism: how to maintain socialist solidarity while adjusting policies to realities, how to rationalize modifications in a dogmatic system of theory without seriously endangering the whole edifice. They, too, have had to parry more orthodox criticisms by insisting that revolutionary aims, far from having been abandoned, can be attained by a shrewd new strategy more suited to prevailing conditions.

MAJOR AIMS AND TASKS

According to Article 23 of the 1955 program,

> The fundamental task of our Party is to realize a socialist society by transforming the present capitalist society democratically and peacefully in accordance with the historical conditions of the present stage of Japanese capitalist development, that is, by carrying out the so-called peaceful revolution. At the same time, in view of the post-World War II situation within and outside Japan, our Party must shoulder the important task of recovering and making secure the complete independence of Japan.

On the international plane, other articles mentioned two further tasks: securing world peace and helping to unify the international socialist movement.

10. Saburō Eda and the other proponents of "structural reform" naturally had to be cautious in admitting the degree to which they had been influenced by Togliatti's views on how to achieve socialism by a strategy pursued within capitalist society and through the parliamentary system. However, these Japanese socialists have admitted being influenced by the Italian leader's pamphlet *The Road to Communism in Italy* (published in December 1956), by the Rome Appeal in 1958 to representatives of seventeen Communist parties from Western capitalist countries, and by Togliatti's address to the Italian CP Congress in February 1959. The fullest printed exposition of the program of "structural reform" in Japan is to be found in: Central Party School of the Japan Socialist Party, *Kōzō Kaikaku no Riron* (The Theory of Structural Reform) (Tokyo, Shinji Daisha, 1961).

Leftists argue that the contradictions of capitalism will eventually result in "objective conditions" favorable for socialist revolution and that it is vital for the "subjective conditions" of the working class (class consciousness, ideological indoctrination, organization, leadership, militancy, and experience) to be sufficiently developed to enable the masses to seize and even create opportunities. The concept of the "historic mission" of the working class—that is, the achievement of socialism—was also embodied in the reunified program. Revolution of this kind, the left wing stressed, requires a "qualitative change" marked by the social ownership and operation of the means of production, the elimination of bourgeois dominance, and the end of class conflict. The right wing prefers pragmatic improvement of the existing order, including the perfection of liberal democracy. It distrusts "people's democracies" as involving proletarian dictatorship.

The Right Socialist draft program of early 1955, while not calling for opposition to the security treaty and administrative agreement, recognized that they placed Japan in a "very disadvantageous position." It warned, however, that nationalism and anti-Americanism could be utilized by Communists for subversion in the interests of their international movement. The reunified platform warned against allowing either capitalism or communism to exploit for their own purposes the Japanese struggle for independence. At the Left Socialist convention in 1954, a compromise by contesting factions upheld neutralism rather than identification with the Communist peace offensive. Elements descending from the prewar Worker-Farmer faction insisted that independence would be achieved through realization of a socialist revolution. It described Japan as "subservient to," but not as a colony of, the United States. The Takano faction of Sōhyō, with allies in the SDP, called for a united front—even with "national capitalists"—against American "capitalist imperialism." The Left Socialist platform of 1954 also referred to the two main parallel tasks, the struggles for a socialist revolution and for national independence. Support for neutralism was reiterated by the reunified platform, but was weakened by the concluding sentence: "This idea has many supporters in Socialist ranks." By 1959–61, a sharper controversy had developed over whether the prime target should be U.S. imperialism or Japanese monopoly capitalism.

Though both wings have opposed colonialism, they have diverged in their views of international socialist solidarity. The right wing has advocated association of democratic socialist movements in an influential world movement; but the Socialist International's heated opposition to Communist expansionism has led leftists to argue that any such opposition to socialism will play into the hands of reactionaries.

THE CHARACTER OF THE PARTY

Closely related to the aims and mission of the Japanese Socialist Party is the problem of its proper composition and character. A perennial issue, this has attained renewed prominence from a number of factors. Instead of continuing to gain legislative seats in each election, the Socialists apparently reached a plateau by 1958. The party's one third strength in the Diet came to be regarded as a barrier. How could a breakthrough be achieved, and later a majority be won? Economic prosperity was tending to make workers less militant; middle strata were expanding; technological and other changes obviously portended less social insecurity and increasingly significant changes in the structure of society. The crisis of 1960 again highlighted the question whether Socialists should confine their struggles within parliamentary modes or, utilizing all mobilizing techniques, resort to mass pressures, including violence. Moreover, as Socialists tried to formulate alternative policies more specifically and competently, they became more aware of conflicts of interest, even among some groups which they considered to be natural supporters.

Back in 1954–55, Socialists still were hopeful of advancing rather steadily to majority status, and attempts to heal the cleavage raised questions about the essential character of the party, once reunited. Both wings considered industrial workers, white-collar employees, intellectuals, persons employed in small- and medium-scale enterprises, and farmers as potential if not actual constituents. But while right-wingers tended to regard them primarily as educable citizens and voters, the left, with varying emphasis, also viewed them as exploited strata who would increasingly come to identify themselves with the interests and alleged revolutionary determination of the industrial proletariat. The SDP, they argued, should be a "class party" based upon the vanguard of workers and should promote class consciousness and revolutionary militancy.

The cross-stratal, national perspective and strategy urged by right-wingers was suspect on the left as likely to obscure the class struggle and to induce oppressed classes to settle for reforms rather than genuine revolution. In 1959, Sakisaka argued that the working class constituted 42–46 per cent of the total population, farmers and fishing people about 30 per cent, small and medium enterprisers and their employees 17–19 per cent, and intellectuals 5 per cent.[11] If the Socialists could attract the bulk of their votes, a governing majority would be assured. Leftists have periodically been tempted to seize upon public issues and magnify them into crises, in part to create situations which will tend to bend the interests of other classes into agreement with those of mobilized industrial workers. More moderate Socialists have pointed to the actual cross-stratal composition of both main parties' electoral support and insisted that the way to remain stymied at one third of the Diet's seats is to continue the class emphasis. They advocated efforts to attract a broad, national following; they suspected a link between the left's narrower class emphasis and its reservations about liberal democracy, its threatened resort to violence and "permanent revolution." Moderates argued that such means as redistribution of taxes, regulation of trade and manufacturing, nationalization of key industries, and expanded social security measures could lead to welfare state socialism without a destructive cataclysm.

Not only did the 1955 reunification program espouse the compromise formula of a "class oriented mass party," it further described the socialist movement as "a rally, with the working class as its core, of the various strata of the working people, composed of farmers, fishermen, small and middle traders and industrialists, the intelligentsia, and the rest of the people that comprise the great majority of the nation." The party was to be "open to all who agree with Party objectives" and equality of rights and duties was promised for members regardless of social background.[12] But suspicions and discontent remained.

The "Basic Policies" appended to that platform restated the party's continued cooperation with democratic organizations and movements. The two wings have differed as to the advisable degree of labor politicism; here the principle of mutual independence of the party and friendly unions, with domination by neither, was reiterated. Although it would like to, the SDP cannot insist that it should determine political tasks for organized labor. Right-wing Socialists are critical of Sōhyō's influence on the party, and when the Democratic Socialist Party was launched it preserved more autonomy with respect to its

11. Article in *Asahi Shimbun*, Jan. 29, 1959.

12. See Article 27 of the reunified SDP platform of 1955.

labor ally, Zenrō-Sōdōmei. Members of unions and labor federations —as well as farmers' and consumers' unions, research groups, and the like—are supposed to belong (those who do) to the SDP as individuals, but in reality Sōhyō exerts much influence as a body.

Controversy over the essential character of the party was revived at the convention in 1957 and again in the fall of 1958, latterly in the context of massive protest against the revised Police Duties Bill. Sakisaka and Nishio were the leading exponents of views held by the two wings.[13] The former's Labor-Farmer faction and its leftist allies in the SDP and in Sōhyō demanded revisions of the reunified program and a recovery of revolutionary spirit. They bitterly criticized Nishio for having proposed the formula which shelved the Police Bill, thus short-circuiting the plan of leftist elements to use the united front to obtain dissolution of the Diet. The debate was continued in 1959–60, contributed to the schism by the Nishio faction, and assumed even greater proportions during and after the anti-treaty struggle.

Failure of the long Miike strike and the limited successes of the anti-treaty struggle led to renewed recognition of need to break through the barrier of one third. And, since the public and press clamored for reconsolidation of parliamentary government, criticizing the excesses of direct mass action, arguments for a national rather than class party gained in cogency. The swelling of middle social strata, moreover, indicated an enlarged floating vote. It was in these circumstances that "structural reform" was propounded. A broad coalition of forces opposing monopoly capitalism was proposed, and the strategy for peaceful achievement of socialism by democratic processes, for a time within the existing capitalist system, constituted an attempt to bridge the two schools of thought concerning the Socialist Party's basic nature.

THE PROBLEM OF MEANS

If means should be considered as "aims in embryo," the features and orientation of Socialist tactics stem from concepts of the party's basic character. The Left Socialist platform of 1954 stated: "Power can be transferred from the capitalist class to the workers by peaceful

13. See notably Sakisaka's article, "A Proper Platform and a Proper Organization," in *Shakaishugi,* No. 88 (Dec. 1958); an article by Nishio: "Let the Executive Establish the Independence of the Party," in *Gekkan Shakaitō,* No. 16 (Sept. 1958); and a speech by Nishio on December 13 of that year, reported in *Asahi,* Dec. 14, 1958.

means through the Diet under the influence of strong democratic forces."[14] Both then and in discussions of structural reform since 1960 it has been suggested that, if a socialist majority should once be achieved, it would be defended and consolidated by a much more thorough organization and, if necessary, mobilization of class-conscious groups—perhaps similar to the mass organizations in Communist China. The two stages through which the achievement of socialism has been envisaged by leftists were included in their program of 1954 but not in the compromise of the following year. They have conceived of a transitional socialist government—perhaps even a coalition with the Socialists a leading element—of indeterminate duration, followed by consolidation of a socialist regime and economy. During the earlier phase, there might be changes of parties in power; anticapitalist policies would be pressed; the scope of public ownership would be extended; social security would become more adequate; the struggle for national independence would be completed. Some leftists have feared too long a compromise with capitalism lest potentially revolutionary strata might become content with simply a welfare state instead of insisting on a "qualitative change" in institutions. They have even feared the entrenchment of a rival socialist party during the transitional stage.

Peaceful, parliamentary means are part of the right wing's credo but are viewed as a strategy by leftist rivals. The latter argue that only in a country like the United Kingdom, where democracy is thoroughly legitimized and socialism could conceivably be achieved by constitutional procedures, can the use of revolutionary force be unequivocably forsworn. But social chasms are great in Japan; economic and in some senses political powers are concentrated. It cannot be supposed, they aver, that capitalist elites would yield decisive advantages without a struggle. Paralysis of industries and services by general strikes and mass demonstrations focused on the Diet have to date been the chief countermeasures proposed by radical socialists. Of course, they advocate cooperation between the SDP and a united front of anticapitalist forces. In defending reliance on "parliamentarism-plus," the left wing asserts that existing law and its administration are manifestations of bourgeois domination which must be tested and may be evaded. If it is impossible to block "bad" laws, the organized masses

14. "Comparative Platforms," p. 7, and n. 5 above.

can use extraparliamentary pressure to limit the abuse of such measures.

Moderate Socialists are committed to democratic, peaceful means before and after attainment of state power. They contend that no more civilized and fair means have been developed to resolve conflicting interests within a community than the representative system with its legal agencies. Laws must be obeyed but efforts should be made to insure that they will not be too harsh on any particular group. Moderates exalt individualism and humanitarianism, while collectivistic idealists tend rather to regard humanitarian concerns as secondary to the achievement of a successful socialist revolution; at a prior stage there is danger in being too "sentimental" and of distracting attention from "scientific" imperatives. Evolutionary socialists are not bound by Marxist determinism according to the configuration of economic conditions. They are more patient and rely more on education and persuasion. When the DSP was established, champions of such moderate policies could again be more outspoken and, as we have seen, their strategy in alliance with Zenrō-Sōdōmei gave somewhat surprising leverage to moderates who remained in the SDP.

ATTITUDES TOWARD DEMOCRACY AND TOTALITARIAN SYSTEMS

"Socialism is achieved through democracy, and democracy is consummated in socialism"—so declared the platform of October 1955, reflecting the right wing's commitment to democratic means and the left's conviction that only in an egalitarian system, where bourgeois exploitation and class struggles have been eliminated, can genuine democracy be realized. Moderate Socialists insist that the contest between democracy and totalitarianism is of equal importance to that between socialism and capitalism. Dictatorship results from communism combined with socialism or fascism with capitalism, they note. However imperfect, democracy has existed in postwar Japan, and they do give it priority. Such right-wingers consider liberal parliamentary, electoral, and legal principles to be based on experience and on a revulsion against authoritarian and totalitarian systems. They expect a continued plurality of interests requiring equal opportunities for exerting influence—not that, in resulting fact, they can be equal in power.

The Socialist left, on the other hand, asserts that democracy is basically preserved by the countervailing power of the working class, which is justified in an ultimate resort to force if "abuses" become too great. Rivals to the right insist that force, if used, must be for the preservation of liberal democracy and be used legitimately and justly. Leftists tend to consider policies and tactics democratic if obviously in the interests of the masses, especially of industrial workers. The aged Hitoshi Yamakawa, elder statesman of the Worker-Farmerites until he died in 1958 and was succeeded by Sakisaka, commented that the parliamentary system, though not ideal, was better than any other one yet devised; its defects would be overcome by effectively organizing the people.[15] Right-wing Socialists have envisaged an evolutionary and orderly, if irregular, metamorphosis from capitalist into socialist democracy. Leftists have demanded a "new type" of democracy, not just reforms of the bourgeois system. The former have insisted on preservation of the right of voters to change governments, and have argued that the floating vote tends to recognize and support better policies. Yamakawa countered that to allow the floating vote to function in this way is to give the power of decision to many of the least politically conscious and least responsible elements in society.

These lengthy debates among Social Democrats have related to three stages of their movement: (1) efforts within a capitalist parliamentary order to gain power and gradually to reform the system; (2) after obtaining a majority or by other means gaining control of government, a period of socialist-led transition to socialism; (3) then full inauguration and consolidation of socialist institutions. This is as leftists conceive of the progression; right-wingers envisage socialism as evolving through continuation of the first stage. A crucial debate arose, and has subsequently recurred, over leftist assertions (somewhat obscured by evasive verbiage whenever criticism has become too strong) that, when the socialist revolution culminates, it must be made permanent. The Left Socialist platform of 1954 declared that:

> on the basis of a stabilized absolute majority in the Diet, [the party] will revise the Constitution in accordance with socialist principles . . . and orient the various executive and judicial organs of government, as well as the educational system, the newspapers, the press, the broadcasting networks, etc., in the direction of socialism.[16]

Leftists have explained that such measures would be taken only later,

15. Yamakawa, *Shakaishugi e no Michi: Shakaishugi Seitō Ron* (The Path to Socialism: On a Socialist Party) (Tokyo, 1955), especially pp. 109, 119, 132.

16. See above, n. 5; and "Comparative Platforms," p. 8.

when socialism is well advanced, in order to make institutions suit the new conditions. This would not mean imposition of fascist or dictatorial controls. They have denied that education and the mass media are now truly free. But, they have argued, long-range planning and the proper functioning of socialism will require that power not be allowed to alternate between socialist and capitalist governments. Sakisaka has been quite candid about this.[17] But leftist assurances that a socialist regime would not stoop to undemocratic measures must be viewed in the light of the proletarian bias which pervades their definition of democracy. Kōdō Itō, Chairman of the SDP Policy Planning Board at the time of the last Left Socialist convention in September 1955, said that the conservative press had caused such confusion that people could not distinguish between an SDP government and a socialist regime. He advised that the party should avoid further discussion of Socialist revision of the Constitution, but henceforth it should be assumed that after establishment of a Socialist regime, the Constitution would have to be revised in order to realize the greater democracy possible after public replaces private ownership of the means of production.[18]

The reunified platform, adopted in the following month, stated: "Socialism stands for freedom of speech, assembly, association, faith and conscience, free elections and a representative system, both before and after the socialists attain political power." But an earlier article declared that "if there are some who try to impede or restrain measures of our government, we shall be able to cope with them through legitimate legislation passed by the Diet and through the organized power and influence of the democratic masses supporting these measures."[19] Later the structural reformers seemed to veer toward right-wing moderation for the period before socialism comes to power but to make crucial concessions to the left with respect to the third period. Tomomi Narita, while Chief of the Policy Planning Board, pointed out in March 1961 that once the SDP gained a ruling majority it would then control the bureaucracy, police, and military services. And he observed that the existing democratic Constitution, if fully utilized, could pave the way for "a proletarian constitution." The party's ac-

17. Itsurō Sakisaka, *Shakaishugi: Furukute Atarashii Mono* (Socialism: A Thing Both Old and New) (Tokyo, 1956), pp. 130, 133; and his "Structural Reform Theory and the Socialist Party's Tasks," *Shakaishugi*, February 1961.

18. See statement by Kōdō Itō, *Asahi Shimbun*, Sept. 20, 1955.

19. See Articles 24 and 30 of the reunified 1955 SDP platform.

tion policy in that year tried to reassure the public that the Socialists would not establish a "permanent regime" but would uphold parliamentary politics and recognize opposition parties.[20]

Lively debate also focused on prescriptions of structural reform for the existing era and conditions. In Western Europe, even before the Twentieth Congress of the Communist Party of the Soviet Union, Laborites and Social Democrats had observed that workers need no longer be alienated from the state since, in a number of countries, they exert influence on policy making. Nationalization of all means of production in such countries no longer seemed imperative. Socialist parties could press for fairer distribution of national income, planned economic development, and improved programs of welfare. In part these conditions lay back of the thesis that socialism could be achieved by peaceful, constitutional means. Togliatti accepted this thesis, provided the National Assembly really represents the popular will, that it (or its counterparts elsewhere) operates in a democratic manner, that there are opportunities for the masses to assert their will and defend their interests, and that the people's delegates are sufficiently represented in the legislature.

Leftists in Japan, however, have not been satisfied that these conditions prevail to a sufficient extent. When the structural reformers asserted that, after a period of reforms in the interests of workers and farmers, there can ultimately be a significant shift in the wielding of state power, leftists in the SDP and in Sōhyō's mainstream remained skeptical. The Long-Range Policy Committee of that federation, headed by Shinzō Shimizu—another theorist of the Labor-Farmer faction—drafted seven searching questions concerning structural reform theories for Chairman Ōta to deliver to the SDP. One asked specifically how that party proposed to restrict capitalism to the point

20. As recently as May 3, 1963—the sixteenth anniversary of the inauguration of the present Constitution—an article in the SDP organ, *Shakai Shimpō,* entitled "Socialism and the Constitution Protection Movement in Japan," called for a struggle for "full enforcement" of the present "bourgeois Constitution" to bring about "conditions for winning a socialist Constitution." This new constitution is to be adopted after a transitional period of democratic reforms; it is to follow consolidation of a socialist politico-economic system and be enacted with popular consent.

In view of the impending final report concerning recommended constitutional revisions from the Cabinet's Constitutional Research Council, the press compared this Socialist article to the similar section of the Left Socialist platform of 1954 and called on the SDP to state candidly whether it advocated defense of the present Constitution only with the aim of using democratic rights to betray it and substitute a basic law not liberal but socialistic and probably left-authoritarian.

where a socialist revolution could be achieved peaceably. The party's Central Committee responded that an "anti-monopoly national rally" composed of almost all classes would gradually isolate, restrict, and weaken monopoly capitalism to the point where the SDP could serve as the vehicle for a constitutional government committed to democracy and neutralism. Hemming in capitalism would lead to "objective conditions," and strengthening the "rally" would create "subjective conditions" conducive to the desired transformation. The change should result from majority parliamentary action.[21]

But leftist skeptics in the SDP, Sōhyō, and the JCP have doubted the capacity of the Socialist Party to accomplish anything so ambitious. They have seen no impressively concrete plans. Moreover, they have argued that reforms will be inadequate unless they precipitate a fundamental change in power relations in the productive system and in politics. Any compromises by capitalism, they have insisted, will be only to preserve the core of the present system. Sakisaka has warned that advocates of structural reform will always tend to underestimate objective revolutionary situations and to be lax in developing subjective conditions necessary to create and maximize revolutionary possibilities. Thus they will be inclined toward revisionism and opportunism.[22]

Related to their different views on democracy have been characteristic attitudes in the two Socialist wings regarding relations with the JCP. Right Socialists have opposed any cooperation with communism because they considered it to be totalitarian, destructive, and foreign-controlled. Some elements in the SDP (but not the Kawakami faction), less committed to liberal politics and more alienated from bourgeois institutions, have contended that attacking communism can play into the hands of reaction and injure the cause of socialism. For them anticommunism is not a principle. They have considered democracy in Japan to be more threatened by conservatives in alliance with the United States than by the JCP and any foreign socialist power.

21. See especially question 6 in Kaoru Ōta, "Seven Questions about the Socialist Party's Theory of Structural Reform," *Gekkan Sōhyō,* Jan. 1961; and: "Answering the Seven Questions Presented by Mr. Ōta," *Shakai Shimpō,* January 1961. These two documents were republished in *Kōzō Kaikaku no Riron,* pp. 248–57, 258–69.

22. Itsurō Sakisaka, "The Conditions of the Socialist Revolution and the Theory of Structural Reform," *Shakai Shimpō* (Feb. 1961), pp. 231–34.

CRITIQUES OF CAPITALISM

The three platforms of 1954–55, to which we have referred—and especially that of the Left Socialists—were naturally based not only on envisaged features of a socialist Japan but also on analyses of inherent problems of capitalism, historical and contemporary, in the West and (with more divergence of interpretation) in Japan. The Left Socialist analysis of Japanese capitalism is essentially the result of the Labor-Farmer faction's controversy with the pro-Communist "Monographs" faction (Kōza-ha) in prewar Japan.[23] In brief summary: developing Japanese capitalism enabled the bourgeoisie to extend its power into the bureaucracy and Diet, thus making the state an instrument of its rule. This hegemony was completed around the end of the First World War, despite feudalistic survivals in socioeconomic relations, particularly in the countryside and in the monarchic polity. The rise of fascism and imperialism in Japan corresponded with the "highest stage" of capitalist development. Workers and socialists came to recognize that "monopoly capital" had been the main opponent, struggle for a socialist revolution the necessary strategy. Communist analysis, however, has placed more emphasis on feudalistic vestiges, the alliance of bourgeois and landlord classes, and their roles in the authoritarian imperial system; it has advocated a "bourgeois-democratic revolution" prior to the transformation to socialism. The Labor-Farmer and Communist interpretations have both been Marxist, though they have reached different strategic conclusions.

In reviewing Japanese history, the right wing has considered that, under the threat of Western encroachment, capitalism was fostered by the Meiji leaders as part of their policy to "Enrich the country! Strengthen the defenses!" (*Fukoku, kyōhei*). Thanks to that policy, Japan was able to escape becoming a colony of the West, as had most other Asian nations, and instead became—until recently—the only industrialized nation in Asia. However, Japan went too far in countering Western imperialism and itself resorted to expansion abroad. Furthermore, because of governmental paternalism, Japan was not compelled to eradicate the remnants of feudalism at home and consequently failed to create a free society based on the dignity of the

23. For background on this controversy, see Totten, pp. 194–96, and Cecil H. Uyehara, *Leftwing Social Movements in Japan: An Annotated Bibliography* (Tokyo and Rutland, Vt., Charles E. Tuttle, 1959), pp. 134–62.

individual. These peculiarities of Japanese capitalism made it easy for the military to gain a dictatorial position from which they led Japan into the vortex of international politics and a disastrous world war.[24] While the left wing has assigned the cause of the war to the early rise of monopoly capitalism in Japan, the right wing has ascribed it rather to the failure of capitalism to eradicate remnants of feudalism and to develop genuinely liberal democracy.

With regard to postwar Japanese capitalism, both Socialist wings have agreed that the economic deconcentration policies of the Occupation failed. As the reunified platform asserted: "Japan has returned to the stage of monopoly capitalism, and her ruling class, the monopoly capitalists, along with the other capitalists and the government led by them, have built up a modern structure of highly developed capitalism."

They have called the Occupation-encouraged agrarian policies "reformist" since they were not thoroughgoing but did alleviate some of capitalism's worst evils: un- and under-employment and the existence of the once powerful landlord class. But reconcentration of economic power has been permitted by amendment of the antitrust and related postwar laws and by their laxer administration. Transactions in and partial reconcentration of land tenure have occurred. Small and middle size enterprises during recessions have been absorbed or subordinated by formidable corporations. There has been underlying disagreement as to whether fragmented agricultural holdings and the plethora of small enterprises have been economic survivals from feudalism, as the right wing (and the Communists!) have averred, or are

24. Shimpei Fujimaki, in Minshu Shakaishugi Remmei, ed., *Tōitsu Shakaitō Kōryō Sōan to Sono Kaisetsu* (The Reunified Social Democratic Party, Program and Commentary) (Tokyo, 1955), pp. 34–35, reports that when the Right Socialists were drawing up their draft early in 1955, a dispute arose as to whether or not the policy of the Meiji leaders was right, and it was finally decided just to mention it as a historical fact without evaluation. Despite Fujimaki's statement, evaluation did creep in: the Meiji leadership was considered good in keeping Japan independent but bad in opposing democracy. Fujimaki goes on to say that with regard to Japanese expansionism following the Manchurian incident, some, evidently trying to vindicate their own prewar stand, held that this was based on a popular demand that could not be disregarded and thus the whole country was to blame for the defeat of World War II, while others branded the Manchurian incident as aggression and saw only certain segments of Japanese society as having been responsible. It must be emphasized that, when we mention the opinion of the right or left wing, we generalize in ways which inevitably oversimplify. In actuality, opinion in each wing is always highly subdivided and never static.

only aspects of backwardness in Japanese capitalism that will eventually disappear, as the leftist Labor-Farmer faction have maintained. Both wings have agreed that policies of the Occupation did not solve the structural contradictions in Japanese capitalism.

Both have also agreed that, compared to capitalism in advanced Western countries, that of Japan has always been "fragile." The left-wing platform was orthodox in foreseeing a crisis emerging from contradictions in the existing system. Socialists must be ready to press for renovation when ruling elements lose confidence and many popular sectors become insecure and disaffected; and the program outlined what should be done when such an "explosion" occurs. Right-wingers then alleged, but leftists denied, that they would contribute toward such an emergency as depression or war.[25] The latter pointed to their "reformist" policies which were directed at ameliorating the present situation. Fears concerning radical exploitation of any future national crisis were abated when the two Socialist rivals compromised and reunified in 1955. Furthermore, the spectacular growth of the Japanese economy in the booms of 1956–57 and 1959–64 tended to make moderate Socialists more dubious about collapse of capitalism from its own contradictions. Might this not be a dogmatic conception of orthodox Marxism? Might the progressive reform of capitalism toward welfare statism not be more realistic?

Even within the SDP mainstream by 1960 there came a kind of faltering recognition of capitalism's vitality, that depression can apparently be prevented by such measures as monetary and fiscal regulation and public spending; that nuclear war is to be avoided by all possible means. By implication at least the structural reformers recognized that benefits have been accruing—even though unequally—to workers and consumers, and that the middle strata have been expanding. Some SDP politicians were becoming partly disillusioned and secretly more willing to settle for evolutionary reforms, a mixed economy, more adequate social insurance and welfare programs; but they did not care to say so openly for fear of counterattacks by still orthodox Marxists. Realists have thus been confronted by the moral claims of Marxist–Leninist scholastics and other faithful; in a minority "religious" sect, and in matters of its doctrine, leaders have been able to exercise considerable moral authority. So, when Sōhyō challenged the ideas of

25. See, e.g., Sakisaka, *Shakaishugi: Furukute Atarashii Mono,* p. 134.

structural reform with the seven questions, the SDP Central Committee yielded, rejecting the reformist idea that capitalism in its highest stage can experience a transfiguration which can mitigate or eliminate the need for class struggle. Nevertheless, it upheld structural reform as a strategy for coordinating forces against citadels of monopoly while capitalism still continues. The four cardinal policies of the structural reformers, in brief were: improved levels of consumption and welfare; struggle against the monopoly structure; revision of the pattern of trade, shifting some of the emphasis toward Red Bloc countries; and nationalization of key industries.

As remedies, left Socialists advocate nationalization of key enterprises, while right-wingers prefer the milder term socialization. The compromise platform of 1955 mentioned both. It included the moderates' emphasis on increasing production and productivity. And it called for public ownership of key industries, central planning of economic growth, full employment, more equal distribution of incomes, and expansion of social security and of cooperatives—especially among small and medium-sized enterprises. How bureaucracy is to be "eliminated" while state functions are vastly expanded is not explained. Also one finds there the syndicalist proposal that workers and consumers should be represented in management of enterprises. The public was reassured that, broadly speaking, proprietary rights and freedom of professions would not be denied under a socialist government. Private management would also continue in agriculture, handicraft industries, and in commerce.

In the Democratic Socialist platform of 1960, no analysis of contemporary capitalism was provided. Industrial society was, however, declared to be too complex to be described in terms of a two-class conflict. Nationalization was less emphasized. The new party advocated planning but also allowance for the operation of the price mechanism and of competition. Far from seeking ultimate elimination of bourgeois strata, Nishio's faction urged their expansion.

Another issue arousing dissent among socialists has concerned the impact of American capitalism on Japan. Leftists have asserted that Japanese capitalism has been buttressed by and dependent on its U.S. counterpart. Thus the United States has been an accomplice in exploiting Japanese workers. It has exerted undue influence on Japanese foreign policies, promoting rearmament, the revival of Japanese militarism, and potentially a kind of second-class imperialism. Rearmament has strengthened monopoly capitalism, has tended to distort the national economy, and has drained resources from social services and welfare. American aid and credits have been used toward these aims as well as for productivity campaigns. And there has been dumping of American agricultural surpluses in Japan. Trade liberalization, encouraged from Washington, may have made Japanese production more competitive but it has led to personnel rationalization (i.e., loss of jobs) in many industries.

Both wings have agreed that American influence has been based on political and military considerations. Moderates have described relations between the two countries in terms of mutual dependence. They have pointed out that American investments in Japan have not been alarming. Japan has not been a colony exporting only raw materials. It has not followed foreign directions in tariff and fiscal affairs as did prewar China. Its economic dependence has been gradually declining, and there has been no available alternative to the United States as a market and supplier on such an important scale. Japan's frequent unfavorable balance of trade, they argue, has been caused by economic factors other than domination by American capitalism. Leaders in this wing have been skeptical and guarded about drastically altering the pattern of trade in favor of more exchange with Communist countries.

Among the spectrums of capitalist and socialist thought about problems of modern, largely industrialized societies—specifically that of Japan—we have delineated two on the left, one of them near the center. These have become intellectual traditions with accompanying mental, moral, and emotional attachments. They epitomize ways of observing and interpreting the functioning and effects on human life and institutions of two systems—one operative in Japan and hence capable of concrete evaluation, the other known to Japanese only in theory and in the experience of certain countries where varieties of socialism prevail. These two modes of thought and perception have also to do with concepts of history, of the processes of social change, and of the destiny of society. One is more systematic, the other more pragmatic; the former is revolutionary and reserves the right to invoke violence asserting that a minority can truly represent the best interests of the masses, while the latter insists that too many values are sacrificed in such convulsions and that the new order would be more unjust and oppressive than the existing one, which can be gradually reformed.

Reunification of the two Social Democratic parties in 1955 again brought these two ideological streams into a single political channel, but the resulting coalition of factions was hardly more durable than the uneasy confluence of these currents. Though the common platform then adopted is still recognized, it is increasingly regarded as an out-of-date formulation. From 1957 to 1960, leftist forces were resurgent; both they and the conservatives made of events in May–June–October of the latter year a crucible wherein their views and methods were tested. Assertiveness from the left had caused the rightmost faction of the SDP to resume freer, more critical exponence of gradual reformism through parliamentary means. That DSP members participated in obstructive and boycotting tactics in the Diet during the crisis evinced, at least in part, the pressure they felt to participate in socialist opposition. On the other hand, when the storm had passed, the SDP extremists were widely criticized for extraparliamentary struggles.

Then it was that a rising generation of leaders within the Socialist Party decided that an attempt to consider and deal more adequately with the realities of a more affluent, productive Japan could no longer be postponed. In trying, they encountered the intransigence of more doctrinaire colleagues. Rather than precipitate new rifts within the party, the structural reformers have compromised with radicalism but have stressed a strategy for advancing gradually toward revolutionary ends under existing capitalist, parliamentary, and legal conditions. Their efforts have been welcomed with somewhat suspicious satisfaction by Democratic Socialists and have been denounced as reformist and revisionist by the more leftist factions of the SDP and of Sōhyō. There is no prospect that the Japanese Socialists can resolve the dialectical tension between orthodoxy and realism that distinguishes them in different ways from both the conservatives and the Communists.

4. Political Issues and Tactics

The concept that theory and practice should be inextricably linked is a Marxist heritage that is shared by most socialist parties and yet, because of the nature of politics, must often be honored in the breach. Within the context of striving for a "peaceful revolution" almost any policy that would benefit some group other than "monopoly capital" can be rationalized as in some measure leading toward socialism. Likewise almost any tactic or political maneuver that would embarrass their rivals or bring the Socialists a step closer to wielding power can be justified as related to their ideological goals. Consequently, it would be too facile a generalization to say that, while the "bourgeois" or conservative parties form policies to their immediate advantage on an ad hoc basis regardless of whether they conflict with other policies, the Socialists deduce policies by applying theoretical principles to specific cases regardless of how unpopular the resultant policies might be at the moment. It is more accurate to note that, while the Socialists are more concerned with theoretical consistency than the conservatives, this has not hindered them from adopting somewhat contradictory policies or from attempting to take advantage of what they believe to be popular sentiments.

Ethically, the Socialists have been in their strongest position when defending gains in democratization during the immediate postwar period against conservative attempts at revision. Defense, however, may be a sign of weakness. Politically, the Socialists are strongest when they can present the electorate with more attractive alternative policies.

Formulation of policy is becoming an increasingly important function for political parties. From their nature, socialist parties have traditionally placed more emphasis on party platforms than on "faces" or well known leaders. But as public opinion grows better informed in Japan, the voters are less easily satisfied with generalizations and want more proof of planning and competence for coping with complex problems. Consequently, both the Socialists and the conservatives have taken increasing pains in formulating and publicizing specific policies and long-range plans. As background for our discussion of policies to deal with substantive issues, we shall examine the Socialists' strategy and tactics toward their political rivals or opponents on both the left and the right.

TACTICS TOWARD THE COMMUNISTS

In Japanese parlance, the Socialists and Communists have both been included in what, since prewar decades, have been called "forces of reform," or "progressive forces." The adjective "proletarian," which covered both the communist and social democratic prewar movements, is no longer in frequent use. Opinion polls show that the Japanese public now distinguishes clearly between the SDP and the JCP as parties, but this was by no means the case in the immediate post-surrender period. At that time both were talking about revolution, and they were the only two parties taking an active interest in labor and agrarian organization. Considering the similarities of many of their policies, the evaluation of their past failure, and their weakness in numbers and organization, whether they would cooperate was a theme for much speculation.

Almost invariably the Communists took the initiative in proposing a "democratic united front," making the first such proposal before either party was formally established. On October 19 and 20, 1945, three Communist leaders discussed with the Socialists a proposed united struggle at least on wage increases and opposition to forced delivery of rice, even if the Socialists could not go along on abolition of the emperor system. Mosaburō Suzuki, Chōzaburō Mizutani, and Rikizō Hirano replied for the Socialists that such questions should be postponed until the parties were organized.[1] After the parties' formal conventions, the Communists made two detailed proposals for joint struggle in December 1945, which were rejected by the Socialists. This set the pattern for numerous proposals and rejections of united fronts on the upper level in the political, labor, and agrarian movements, though on lower echelons informal alliances have sometimes occurred. Without approval from Socialist headquarters, however, they have always been ephemeral.[2]

After the elections of April 10, 1946, the Socialists led a Four-Party Committee in the Diet, including the Liberals, People's Cooperatives, and the JCP, which had won five seats in the Lower House. Left Socialists and the Communists tried to make this the center for an SDP-led popular front government, but right-wing Socialists were disinclined; and the Liberals demanded exclusion of both leftist elements from the next government. Mass demonstrations organized by the Communists and their allies to demand a popular front government were of no avail, and the SDP found itself with other opposition forces arrayed against the two conservative parties under the premiership of Shigeru Yoshida.

Before the elections, the Labor-Farmer faction in the SDP, headed by the venerable Hitoshi Yamakawa, led in forming a Democratic People's League. But Socialists, especially those in the right wing of the party and of the labor movement, have always been cautious about such combinations. They have realized that JCP members have

1. With regard to the second time the Communists approached the Socialists, Suehiro Nishio reports that, when JCP leaders Kamiyama, Hakamada and others proposed a common struggle on the food problem on December 26, 1945, he crumpled the paper on which the proposal was written as soon as he received it, saying the SDP did not trust the JCP and therefore there would be no common front. To this Kamiyama reportedly replied that the SDP leaders were disregarding the people and that the JCP with the support of the masses would continue to propose over and over again—even a hundred or two hundred times—a popular front. Suehiro Nishio, *Watakushi no Seiji Techō: Fūseki Rokunen no Nihon o Kaerimiru* (My Political Notebook: Looking Back Over Japan's Six Stormy Years) (Tokyo, Jikyoku Kenkyūkai, 1952), p. 7.

2. For accounts in English of Communist tactics for united fronts see the following: Rodger Swearingen and Paul Langer, *Red Flag in Japan; International Communism in Action 1919–1951* (Cambridge, Harvard University Press, 1952), pp. 68, 105–06, 138–41, and 180–86; and for early attempts at united fronts, see Evelyn S. Colbert, *The Left Wing in Japanese Politics* (New York, Institute of Pacific Relations, 1952), pp. 141–47, 189, 260–63, and 283–84; and Toshio G. Tsukahira, "The Postwar Evolution of Communist Strategy in Japan" (Cambridge, Center for International Studies, Massachusetts Institute of Technology, mimeo., 1954), pp. 6–45.

usually been more able than Socialists in infiltrating labor unions and in carrying out disciplined, dedicated, militant mass actions. They have feared that Communists would attain control of component organizations and be able to bend the whole movement in directions they seek. Moreover, they have predicted that Communist participation would alienate mass support after years of anti-Communist propaganda. And, during the Occupation, there was SCAP's disapproval of radicalism to consider. So the support of the General Federation of Labor (Sōdōmei) was not long retained by the new Association to Promote a Democratic Front. It then veered leftward, pro-Communist Sambetsu leaders calling for a front led by mass organizations of labor and cultural circles whose activities would not be confined to parliamentary struggles.

The Democratic League for National Salvation, under right-wing Tatsuo Morito's formal leadership, was the SDP response to this tension. It was to be composed of two sections, one for the Diet and one for people's movements. Representation in the Diet Section was to accord with party and factional strength in the Diet. This was pleasing to the right wing because the insignificant representation of the Communists in the Diet would insure a minimal Communist influence in this more dominant section. The main objections of the left-wing Socialists were obviated by the existence of the People's Movements Section in which labor unions would be equally represented with the political parties. (The exclusion of cultural organizations would further reduce Communist influence.) The two sections were to be coordinated through a Liaison Committee composed of five members of each section. An additional safeguard was a provision that members of the League would refrain from speech or action in violation of the principles of cooperation, integrity, and friendship, thus forestalling Communist attacks against certain SDP leaders as "war criminals."

Thus a measure of unity among Socialists concerning the idea of a popular front was achieved. Even Yamakawa's Democratic People's League came out in reserved support of it.[3] But the Communists and

3. Although Yamakawa went through with a formal organization of the Democratic People's League on July 21, 1946, it criticized both the Communists and Socialists and gradually faded out of the picture. When reflecting on the causes for its failure, Yamakawa blamed chiefly the self-interest of both the Communists and Socialists but also listed others, including his own lack of skill. See Masamichi Inoki, ed., *Nihon no Ni Daiseitō* (The Two Main Parties of Japan) (Tokyo, Hōritsu Bunka Sha, 1956), pp. 235–38.

the Association to Promote a Democratic Front criticized bitterly the SDP-sponsored League, as it was clearly to their disadvantage. The death blow to the popular front in the sense of Socialist–Communist cooperation came with the decision of the SDP Central Executive Committee, on July 14, 1946, to cease further negotiations with the Communists, though this was adopted over leftist opposition. Labor union unity similarly failed.

The Socialists felt vindicated in their official stand against cooperation with the Communists by results of the elections of April 1947 when they received 143 seats to the Communists' 4. Nevertheless, Socialists had been drawn into association with Communists in the movement for a general strike on February 1, 1947, led by government workers for the purpose of overthrowing the Yoshida cabinet. Although the SDP did not condone this strike or officially sponsor the preceding rallies, it nevertheless sent speakers to pre-strike meetings. This was because such discontent had developed within the ranks of labor that the joint strategy committee, composed of representatives from the disputing unions and the three main labor federations (Sambetsu, Sōdōmei, and the Rōdō Kumiai Kaigi), formally asked both the Socialists and Communists to lend support and participate in the movement. The Communists immediately accepted but the Socialists made an equivocal reply because of their negotiations with the Liberals for a coalition government. SCAP banning of the strike just before February 1 strengthened the hand of anti-Communist unions and of Sōdōmei in preventing a revival of joint efforts with Communist-led unions. A rash of self-criticism broke out among Communist union leaders.

This period also marked a change in the attitude of the two most important leaders of the Socialist left. When Mosaburō Suzuki and Kanjū Katō issued their so-called "left-wing manifesto" of May 15, 1947, "drawing a line" between themselves and the Communists, even a number of right-wing Socialists doubted their sincerity. Nevertheless, they have never reversed their stand that cooperation with the JCP was both impractical and undesirable.

There have always been those in the SDP who looked with favor on cooperation with the Communists on a particular issue or at election time. In almost every electoral campaign, reports have appeared concerning sporadic Communist–Socialist cooperation in one or more localities, seldom with the approval of the central party leadership. Even at national headquarters, however, there have been those who have felt that closer cooperation with the Communists would offset excessive compromises with conservatives. The official reason for the expulsion of Hisao Kuroda and five others from the SDP in July 1948 was their opposition to the budget. Probably the real reason was their support for cooperation with the Communists. Others, like Makoto Hori, who took a similar position, were temporarily prohibited from holding any party office. Some of them later resigned from the party to join Kuroda in forming the Worker-Farmer Party in December 1948, though still others who sympathized with Kuroda remained in the SDP.

Even when the right wing of the SDP had been largely discredited by the failures of the Katayama and Ashida cabinets, the party rejected a Communist offer of "amalgamation" before the election of January 23, 1949, when the SDP's representation sank to 48 in the House of Representatives and the JCP's mounted to 35. Following the election, the SDP refused a "magnanimous" JCP gesture to struggle jointly, while the CIU (Sambetsu) tried vainly to persuade the SDP to join a united front with the JCP and the Worker-Farmerites. At the nadir of its prestige, when its membership was deserting and many former SDP Diet members left office never to return, the Socialist CEC in June 1949 decided on a "two front war" against the Yoshida Cabinet and the JCP. Nevertheless, the issue has never died. On September 6, 1949, the Worker-Farmer Party appealed to both the SDP and the JCP for a joint struggle against the Yoshida Cabinet. Because of their sympathetic response, Umeichi Adachi, Toshiaki Wada, and others were expelled from the SDP three days later.

The party's attitude toward SCAP's attack against the JCP leadership just before and after the outbreak of the Korean war, and toward the industrial "Red Purge," was characterized as "*migoroshi*" ("to look on while someone is being killed"). Some Socialists considered that a rival was being eliminated. There came a point, however, when the SDP began to voice fears that the Red Purge was going too far. Many Socialists feared that if the JCP were outlawed, as suggested by SCAP, the suppression of the SDP might be next. It was a comfort to have the JCP as a kind of contrasting buffer on the left. Therefore they opposed outlawing the Communists. In neither the prewar nor postwar situation can the decline of the Communists be attributed mainly to Socialist opposition.

Despite democratic guarantees in postwar Japan, the Communists at the time of the Red Purge feared a return to harsh methods. Most of the top leaders went underground, and only in 1955, after the Occupation had ended and the Korean War was over, did they resume public activities. Both the Left and Right Socialist parties had in the meantime grown and consolidated their positions. Neither through tactics of attack nor cooperation have the Communists been able to make much headway in recovering their earlier vote and Diet representation. Only through infiltration in organized labor and in national struggle councils have they achieved successes.

During the period 1951–55, when the party was split, the tactics of the Left Socialists toward the Communists differed fundamentally from those of the Right SDP. The Left attempted to undermine the Communists by taking over many of their policies and casting their propaganda in Marxist and revolutionary terminology. In this way they made inroads among students and labor voters who might otherwise have supported the Communists. The Right Socialists looked askance at such tactics. They attacked the Communists in strong terms and sought to discredit the Left SDP by calling it pro-Communist. In attempting to outdo the Communists on the same issues, the Left Socialists took part in the anti-military-base struggles at Uchinada, Asama, and Myōgi in the summer of 1953 along with the JCP and the Worker-Farmerites. Also during the floods later that year in Kyūshū and in the Kinki region the Left Socialists made an attempt to compete with Communist-influenced organizations which were aiding and organizing the victims. In 1955 the Left SDP did not participate as a party in the Congress of Mothers, which Right Socialists branded as "Communist-dominated," but some individual leaders did. In that same year, however, it participated hesitantly in the first World Congress against Atomic and Hydrogen Bombs, while the Right SDP abstained. By the time of the third Congress, which was held in Tokyo in 1957, the united party played a leading role, making that Congress by far the most successful to date.

During the schism from 1951 to 1955, the Left SDP in general refrained from attacking the Communists in official policy statements, such as the party program of 1954, however much individual leaders criticized them in campaign speeches and personal utterances. They reasoned that adding fuel to the "anti-communist hysteria" harmed the left as a whole. At various times the leadership issued directives discouraging party members in mass organizations from cooperating with the Communists, particularly when many were finding the "peace force" arguments attractive in the winter of 1953–54.[4] The Left Socialists claimed that it was unjust to characterize them as approving Communist theory and criticizing only Communist tactics, just because they did not repudiate Marxism. By drawing a line between themselves and the Communists they claimed they were creating their own theoretical position (though somewhat Marxist) which differed from that of the Communists, no matter how much various policies adopted by the Communists resembled their own.[5]

The Right Socialists, who in many respects were so insistent on gradualism that they were indistinguishable from nonsocialist liberal reformers, sought to expose Communist policies for what they were throughout the period of the split and to eliminate pro-Communist influence from all activities in which members of the party were involved.[6]

As reunification neared in October 1955, a compromise of these two approaches to the question of tactics toward the Communists became noticeable. While there was less restraint in attacking both the Japanese Communists and international communism, the party as a whole was less fearful of losing out by taking part in various mass campaigns, such as the "peace movement," independently supported by the Communists.[7] Just before the reunification, the Japanese Communists at their Sixth National Conference in July 1955, as we have seen, revised their policy of attacking the Socialists, in line with the changed

4. In fact so strong were "peace force" pressures from Sōhyō on the Left Socialist leaders at this time that the latter had to develop the idea of a "third force" to combat them. The "peace force," in the arguments of its proponents, included the Communist bloc, whereas the "third force" indicated the neutralist nations that stood between the East and the West and were trying to bring about an end to the cold war. As will be seen in more detail in the chapter on leadership factions below, the Left SDP leaders themselves were divided as to tactics vis à vis the Communists.

5. The Left Socialists claimed that finding similarities between their own and Communist policies did not prove that they were pro-Communist but rather that the Communists, for whatever reasons, were adopting correct policies on certain issues. See, for instance, *Yomiuri*, Nov. 2, 1953.

6. At its convention in January 1954, for instance, the Right SDP made it an immediate task to eliminate "peace force" tendencies from the labor movement, concentrating its attention on Sōhyō. See *Asahi*, Dec. 26, 1953.

7. Nihon Shakaitō Seisaku Shingikai (Policy Planning Committee, Social Democratic Party of Japan), *Shakaitō no Seisaku Mondō Shū* (A Collection of Questions and Answers on Policies of the Social Democratic Party) (Tokyo, Nihon Shakaitō Kyōsen-kyoku Shuppambu, 1956), pp. 19–20.

attitudes expressed at the Twentieth Congress of the CPSU.[8] Even before this they had been wooing the Socialists, notably by withdrawing JCP candidates in favor of Left Socialist candidates in the elections of February 1955, and by calling for a "national front" to include bourgeois elements and to stress independence from policies originating in Washington. Though the Communists took a further step in November 1957 by publishing a draft program to be submitted to their Seventh National Conference, which evinced a more friendly attitude toward the Socialists,[9] they were finding it too costly to continue putting up their own candidates and withdrawing them to support Socialist candidates during elections, since it harmed local CP morale; they therefore reduced this practice.[10] The Socialist attitude remained one of caution on changes in the Communist line in the direction of a popular front for "peaceful revolution" or a broad front for "national liberation."

The leftist resurgence within the Socialist Party, which became more evident during and after the convention in 1957, not only augmented tension with right-wing factions and was interrelated with recriminations between leftward trending Sōhyō and the moderate Zenrō-Sōdōmei alliance; it also produced strains in the many "people's movements." In most of these councils, congresses, or committees, SDP leaders and delegations encountered Communist activists and factions. Just the names of such organizations indicate much about Socialist tactics, for they have stood allegedly *for* peace, defense of the Constitution, solution of the Okinawa problem, restoration of rela-

8. Nihon Kyōsantō Chūō Iinkai, Senden Kyōiku Chōsabu (Propaganda and Education Research Section, Central Committee, Japanese Communist Party), *Nihon Kyōsantō no Seisaku* (Policies of the Japan Communist Party) (Tokyo, Gōdō Shuppansha, 1956), p. 249. Also see Rodger Swearingen, "Japanese Communism and the Moscow-Peking Axis," *The Annals of the American Academy of Political and Social Science, 308* (Nov. 1956), 70.

9. Communist leader Sanzō Nozaka appealed for fair competition when he addressed the SDP convention as a guest speaker on February 24, 1958. The new program adopted by the Communists at the Seventh National Conference stated that it was "desirable that the revolution be carried out by bloodless methods." Although the Communists did not rule out the possibility of violence, their program here, as with regard to the land reform and the relation of Japan to the United States, came closer to that of the Socialists, probably with the intention of facilitating joint action in the future.

10. That lack of Communist support could impede the Socialists was shown in the by-election of January 1, 1956, in the Kyoto constituency for the House of Councillors. The Socialist candidate Tōtarō Fujita refused an election agreement with the JCP so the Communist candidate was not withdrawn and consequently, with the leftist vote divided, the Liberal Democratic candidate won. Fujita won, however, in the next regular election.

tions with Communist China, friendship and cultural exchange with Red China and the Soviet Union, and aimed to provide a leftist channel for "democratic scientists" together with other "people of culture"; they have fulminated *against* A- and H-bombs and American military bases in Japan. An unusually broad movement was developed in 1958 against the Police Duties Revision Bill; it continued and was expanded in the ensuing year and a half to oppose ratification of the revised Japan–United States Security Pact.

During crescendoes in such agitation, these organizations mobilized mass demonstrations in cooperation with opposition parties, some or all main labor federations (depending on the issues), and Zengakuren (All-Japan Federation of Student Self-Governing Federations) factions. These actions were usually timed with SDP tactics in the Diet, and Socialist legislators were usually chosen as media for the submission of petitions. No less than 20 million signatures were claimed for the appeal against renewal of the revised security treaty! Membership in these councils has usually been denied to JCP delegations as such, for fear that their participation would alienate public sympathy and right Socialist-labor elements. Communists—as individuals and groups—have countered by the skill and ardor with which they have infiltrated into executive echelons of certain component organizations. Some of their tactics toward a broad "national front" were supported by leftist SDP factions; and as the crises of 1958 and 1959–60 mounted, the movements were bent leftward, adding to their aims the toppling of pro-capitalist governments, dissolution of the Diet, and new elections on issues which opposition forces sought to emphasize. Despite the functions which the Socialist Party was able to perform for these movements—representation, legislative delays, liaison, and coordination—its deficiencies in organization, in well-placed members, and in finances have always been exposed. These deficiencies and its own inner rifts have made it vulnerable to pressures by Sōhyō and the JCP, both through direct channels and through left Socialist factions.

Though right-wing Socialists participated in physical obstructionism in the Diet during the Police Bill and security treaty crises in the fall of 1958 and in May-June 1960, they tried to limit the duration of boycotts of the House of Representatives for the sake of parliamentary effectiveness. Leftists condemned Nishio for negotiating the formula which shelved the Police Bill and torpedoed the leftist People's Council's effort to induce Prime Minister Kishi's resignation and the holding of fresh elections. Moderate Socialists and labor elements castigated as pro-Communist such excesses as the forcing of the Diet's outer gates by student shock units. Such tensions contributed to the split which occurred in the SDP when the Nishio faction and additional adherents denounced pro-Communism as they left the party. Their new and rather weak splinter was a stimulus to Zenrō's moderation and its schismatic influence among labor unions.

Meanwhile similar tensions were disturbing some of the foremost people's movements. In 1957, leftist elements organized an Association for Safeguarding the Constitution, which in the following year affiliated with the National Federation for Preservation of the Constitution (Kempō Yōgo Kokumin Rengō—abbreviated to Goken Rengō), which was three years older and more broadly supported. The Association's participation in other struggles, against American military bases, nuclear bombs, and the revised security treaty caused dissension in the main body. This increased as Nishio's faction departed from the SDP to form a Democratic Socialist Party. Then Sōhyō moved to reorganize the Federation and have it adopt an expanded action program which would include participation in the campaign against the security treaty. This antagonized the moderates who were mostly interested in protection of the liberal Constitution. When Chairman Katayama's compromise plan was rejected, he resigned.

Similarly Sōhyō, SDP leftists and infiltrated Communists precipitated a crisis in the Japan Council Against A- and H-Bombs (Gensuikyō) when they tried to align it with anti-security treaty forces. Their proposal had to be withdrawn. Contention was revived when, at the world congress of this Council at Hiroshima in 1962, these Japanese leftists and the Communist Chinese delegation tried to condone Soviet nuclear tests while denouncing the American series. Communist domination of the organization and sharp conflict between delegations from Moscow and Peking—JCP representatives mainly supporting the latter's drastic views—caused the SDP to withdraw at the last minute from the Council's convention in 1963, and there continued a desperate struggle for control of the organization. The DSP had earlier split off and formed a second Gensuikyō.[11]

After June 1960, all parties were evaluating experiences in the antitreaty crisis. Communists and other leftists, of course, wanted the

11. See George O. Totten and Tamio Kawakami, "Gensuikyō and the Peace Movement in Japan," *Asian Survey*, *4* (July 1964), 833–41.

comprehensive People's Council continued as a "national front" against "monopoly capitalism" and American influence. Sōhyō hoped it could be utilized for economic struggles as well. While wanting to avoid the onus for dissolving that body, the Socialist mainstream, led by the "structural reformers," backed away from the united front and revived the familiar objections: The JCP was not as significantly represented in the Diet as were its fraternal parties in France and Italy; it was suspect to many people who must be included in "democratic forces," so to ally with it would inhibit the broad appeal which alone could enable the SDP to exceed the parliamentary "barrier of one third." Moreover, there were still complaints about the dogmatic, "only the JCP can do" attitude.

At the party convention in March 1961, Sōhyō and the leftist factions were appeased by approval of joint struggles with the JCP, provided the Socialists could retain leadership of movements. But in formulating guidelines that year for elections to local offices and to the House of Councillors, the Central Committee instructed that support by other parties might be welcomed but without any concessions by Socialists as to policies.[12] In line with its strategy of electoral growth and a broad front to hem in Japanese capitalism, the situationally more moderate mainstream of the SDP has advocated consolidation of certain of the people's movements (including the two discussed immediately above) to strengthen support for such demands as an expanded national annuity system. Thus they too are attempting to extend such organizations beyond their original purposes.

Having described themes and patterns in Socialist relations with a Communist Party, which has often shown more vigor in extraparliamentary politics and usually has had a somewhat larger membership than the SDP, it is fitting now to note how Socialist energies have been concentrated on rivalry with conservative parties and administrations for opportunities to determine national policies.

TACTICS TOWARD THE CONSERVATIVES

Japan's national administrations since 1945 have all been essentially conservative, though they have varied in degree. Even when,

12. *Asahi Shimbun,* March 8, 1961; *Tokyo Shimbun,* March 9, 1961; *Shakaitō no Shin Rosen, Dai Nijukkai Teiki Tō Taikai Kettei Shū* (The New Line of the Socialist Party, A Collection of Decisions Made at the 20th Regular Party Convention) (Tokyo, Nihon Shakaitō Kikanshikyoku, 1961), p. 167.

during the height of democratization in 1947, the Socialist Party coalesced with two conservative parties, very few left-wing Socialists attained positions higher than vice-minister and committee chairmanships. Administrations in power have great natural advantages: command over the bureaucracy and over patronage, subsidies, and the letting of contracts; special access to mass media of communication; control of foreign relations and of public finance; and, moreover, they have political initiative and can implement such restrictive legislation as the Subversive Activities Prevention Law.

As evolutionary reformists, right-wing Socialists have occasionally participated in administration and in composite commissions. Even more commonly they have tended to reach specific compromises with conservative politicians, either those in power or leaders of dissident factions. But, even as they can help to deter left-wingers by criticizing pro-communist tendencies, their own rightward proclivities are checked not only by their liberal commitments but by the need for defense against leftist charges that they are not genuine socialists but conservatives in disguise.

Party leftists rely more on extraparliamentary tactics. By temperament they usually prefer direct opposition. In general, they tend to demand more ideal, less easily realizable policies than do their Socialist rivals. The inherent dilemma for the SDP is that measures on which it compromises are more likely of enactment, but the more concessions it makes the less credit it earns and the less distinct are the alternatives it can present to the voters. Yet one or two of these Socialist parties have had to operate between the Communists and conservative elements (the latter since 1955 within a single dominant party) which, through advocacy of progressive policies, are able to steal reformist thunder. Again, conservative ability to do this and limit changes short of basic threats to their positions has been used by the left to justify its emphasis on necessary qualitative changes if a socialist revolution is to be achieved, and its objection to dilution of policies toward that end.

Especially after becoming the main, chronic opposition, the SDP has tactically utilized the lesser advantages of that role—benefiting when possible from governmental errors, scandals, and any apparent humiliations in foreign affairs. Its politicians have become adept in committees and in Houses of the Diet at interpellations, heckling, non-confidence votes, and a variety of tactics for delay and obstruction. These have often been synchronized with strikes, rallies, and demonstrations in many cities but especially in the capital, converging on the Diet.

For a few months after the national surrender, moderate Socialists and some conservative circles ventured a tentative alliance, both being in search of respectability in the eyes of SCAP and of the electorate.[13] A few SDP leaders were trying to live down their records of collaboration with the wartime regime, but in the main the party gained prestige from having opposed ultranationalist expansionism and for having previously advocated many of the reforms soon to be undertaken.

Negotiations after the elections of April 1946 were as much a question of cooperating with the conservative parties as of forming a popular front. While forming his first cabinet, Yoshida considered Socialist participation; but the strong nationalist backgrounds of Nishio and Hirano were obstacles. During these maneuvers, the left wing argued that the SDP should either demand the premiership or refuse to participate in any coalition. Otherwise, they contended, Socialist policies would be so diluted that participation would bring no benefits. Right-wing leaders, in contrast, were keen for governmental posts and experience, but they felt it was better not to assume prime responsibility until they had gained sufficient strength to promise more success. So it was, when Secretary General Nishio heard about his party's plurality in the election of April 1947, that he is said to have muttered something like "That's terrible!"[14]

The Katayama cabinet, as we have seen, was based on a four-party policy agreement which effectively hampered realization of the SDP's main election promises, including the important bill for state control of coal mining. It was a mutilated compromise when it finally passed on November 25, 1947. Only in the area of government reorganization could the SDP claim accomplishment. Such reforms passed without great difficulty because they were backed by SCAP, did not cost much money, and in effect only redistributed personnel. The downfall of the Katayama government, triggered by the left wing of the SDP, highlighted the tensions in the party, particularly with regard to the left's greater emphasis on policy considerations in contrast to the

13. For instance, in the extraordinary session of the Diet that began on November 26, 1945, the SDP parliamentary group helped pass such important legislation as the revised election laws, the revised Agricultural Land Adjustment Law, and the Labor Union Law. The majority who passed these bills, it must be remembered, was conservative, elected while General Hideki Tōjō was Prime Minister.

14. See Nishio, *Watakushi no Seiji Techō,* p. 32.

right's greater desire for having at least some influence on legislation.

The right-wing view prevailed in the decision of the SDP to remain in the Ashida government. Thus the Liberals could be prevented from entering the government on "reactionary" terms; the danger of being further compromised seemed to be the lesser evil.[15] SDP leaders also thought that by remaining in the government they could more effectively soften the enforcement of anti-labor legislation that might follow in the wake of SCAP's suggestion that it was in the national interest to deprive government workers of the rights to bargain collectively and to strike. Added to the difficulties experienced by the SDP in the Ashida government, its resounding defeat in the election of 1949 rendered the question of cooperation with the conservatives academic, at least for a while.

After the SDP split, some time elapsed before the Right and Left Socialists resumed cooperation. On leftist initiative, just before the 15th special session of the Diet began on October 24, 1952, they agreed to form a common opposition front in the legislature. Though they did not cooperate in nominating a Premier, the Right and Left Socialists, together with the Progressives and the Worker Farmer Party, formed a loose opposing coalition with which they were able to harry the Yoshida government severely throughout the session. Late in November 1952, Minister of International Trade and Industry Hayato Ikeda was maneuvered into virtual repetition of a "slip of the tongue" made nearly two years earlier. It made him sound callous to the fate of small businessmen forced to the wall and even to suicide in times of austerity. This was the first postwar instance of forced resignation of a minister; the tactic has succeeded only rarely since.[16] Another first was scored by the Socialists in the next year, as has been mentioned,

15. Some of the right-wing Socialists, however, were so much in favor of continuing the coalition that it was reported Nishio had considered forming a new "center" party under Ashida that would include right-wing members from the SDP and Liberal left-wingers. *Sekai Nippō*, Feb. 9, 1948. The more moderate right-wing Socialists, without considering the idea of a new party, did want Liberals in the coalition, if their terms were not too harsh. Komakichi Matsuoka, as both an SDP leader close to Katayama and as Speaker of the House, served as liaison between Katayama and Yoshida. Although he failed, it was an interesting tactical use of the Speakership. *Asahi*, Feb. 12, 1948. The left wing opposed this whole inclination. The May Society was set against coalition on any terms, and the Thursday Society demanded that the SDP take no part in the government unless Katayama were made Premier again. *Asahi*, Feb. 17, 1948.

16. For a detailed account of this incident from a Right Socialist viewpoint, see Nihon Shakaitō, *Waga Tō wa Kokkai de Ikani Tatakatta ka* (How Did Our Party Fight in the Diet?) (Tokyo, Nihon Shakaitō, 1953), pp. 7–13.

when they led the opposition in a successful move to impeach Prime Minister Yoshida for an impatient epithet hurled at an interpellating Right Socialist. Their dependence on the cooperation of the Progressives was shown by their failure to oust Foreign Minister Katsuo Okazaki for contradictory statements on defense. Much as the opposition conservatives disliked this minister, they were more out of sympathy with the SDP stand on matters affecting national security.

Early in 1954, the two Socialist parties extended their cooperation by an agreement to "struggle jointly" in extraparliamentary tactics as well. Joint action would enable them to maximize advantages from Yoshida's declining popularity as shown by newspaper opinion polls, particularly because of scandals connected with some of his cabinet ministers whom he refused to reprimand or remove. The Right Socialists set up what they called a "national movement headquarters" run by four top leaders in the central party office; it was dedicated to organizing popular indignation for the overthrow of the "corrupt" Yoshida government, its promoters vowing not to use the movement merely for party aggrandizement. Together with the Left Socialists and the Worker-Farmer Party they held a giant rally in the outer moat park in Yotsuya (Tokyo), reporting an attendance of some 25,000. Speakers from each of the parties plus Tetsu Katayama as head of the National Federation for the Preservation of the Constitution addressed the crowd. This was followed by night meetings throughout Tokyo on April 12, when the issues of international control of atomic weapons and complete compensation for damages from United States nuclear explosions on Bikini were linked with overthrowing the Yoshida cabinet. Finally, on April 22, the Socialists mobilized some 4,000 people to hear speeches from the Shimbashi outdoor stage, calling for the overthrow of the cabinet. This was coordinated with submission of a non-confidence motion in the Diet chamber.[17] Despite external pressure, the motion did not pass because of the conservatives' greater commonality of interests at the time in passing education and police legislation over Socialist protests.

By a continuation of these extraparliamentary tactics and by close liaison with various anti-Yoshida conservatives, the Socialists were able in the next Diet session to work out arrangements with the Dem-

17. For an account of the cooperation, see (right-wing) Nihon Shakaitō, *Tōmu Hōkokusho: Shōwa Sanjū Nendo, Dai Jūsankai Rinji Zenkoku Taikai (*Party Affairs Report: 1955, Thirteenth Special National Convention) ([Tokyo], mimeo., 1955), pp. 15–17.

ocrats for a non-confidence vote in the cabinet, which passed on December 6, 1954. The following day, the Yoshida cabinet resigned en masse, throwing the responsibility for forming a new cabinet to the sponsors of the non-confidence resolution. Throughout the summer and fall the Socialists had been talking about closer cooperation with each other and promising the people that they were ready to form a Right–Left Socialist coalition government, but at this juncture they felt they had more to gain from an election than in taking the premiership—an act that would bring on a conservative merger and insure a subsequent rightist government. Therefore, they supported Hatoyama for Premier with the understanding that he would dissolve the Diet by early March.

While this episode tended to confirm the observation that understandings within the Diet are more effective than extraparliamentary pressure, the Socialists still considered rallies important—not only to exert pressure on the Diet but also to take advantage of antigovernment sentiment and stir up enthusiasm for themselves with a view to the next elections.

This tactical cooperation and Socialist advances in almost every election since 1952 were obviously impelling them toward reunification despite their ideological differences. The more likely it seemed that they might be approaching a position to head a government, the more conciliatory the Right and Left Socialists became toward each other. Coupled with better coordination of tactics came a greater similarity in regard to policies.

After recovery of national sovereignty when the Occupation ended in April 1952, the conservative government—the interests behind it and the majority it wielded in the Diet—enacted the series of measures which together came to be called the "reverse course," away from democratization. There were fears on the left that, especially if the conservative parties should merge (as they did in November 1955), there might come an avalanche, including revisions of the three fundamental labor laws, accelerated rearmament, and amendment of the Constitution.[18] So the Socialist parties made a point of reunifying just a month before their opponents merged. They felt some foreboding

18. What the Socialists called the "reverse course" extended to minor issues as well, as, for example, the Conservative attempts on several occasions to reestablish Empire Day (Kigensetsu), which the Socialists have opposed because it was associated with militarism and ultranationalism in the past.

about the resulting two-main-party system and they feared that, with augmented power, the conservatives might revive and pass the gerrymandered Small Election District Bill, after which they might win a two-thirds majority enabling them to amend the Constitution. The dominant party could then be made virtually unassailable. Determined to block such moves, the reunified Socialists strove to rationalize their finances, combine efforts to enlarge membership, and consolidate slates of candidates.

Emergence of two main parties with such an ideological and programmatic gulf between them naturally suggested a degree of polarization. The Socialists have not been able to sweep into office on any tide of revulsion against the Liberal Democratic Party, nor have there been opportunities to align with a conservative party out of power. Only occasionally, as in 1958 when anti-mainstream conservatives also opposed the revised Police Duties Bill, and in 1960 when Kishi's intraparty rivals maneuvered for his resignation after approval of the security treaty, have the Socialists been able to find tactical allies in the other camp.

As legislative contests mounted in intensity, LDP leadership at times became more overbearing, and the opposition felt more than ever frustrated by perennial conservative majorities. To their arsenal of sharpened tactics Socialist Representatives became more tempted to add boycotts of committee or House sessions and even limited violence to obstruct extension of legislative sessions or to prevent voting on specially controversial bills.

The first "employment of force" in the Lower House occurred on June 3, 1954, the second at the end of a tense session in June 1956, when the Socialists had been unable to prevent passage of bills to reorganize Japan's defense forces in order to qualify for M.S.A. aid. A three-service military establishment had been provided for along with a joint Defense Board. In addition to these bills, which already conjured up for Socialists the nightmare of a remilitarized Japan, the government designated as "must" legislation two education bills and a police recentralization measure. The former seemed to portend the beginning of the government's reassertion of authoritarian indoctrination; the police bill, by ending the autonomous police and recentralizing controls, seemed about to jeopardize civil rights.[19]

19. For discussion of the significance of the education and police bills, see Cecil Brett, "Japan's New Education Law," *Far Eastern Survey, 23* (Nov. 1954), and Kurt Steiner, "Local Government in Japan," ibid., *23* (July 1954).

After passage of the education bills, the Socialists thought they could prevent enactment of the police bill because the third extension of the session was to end on the night of June 3. If the Speaker could be prevented from extending the session again, the police bill would have to wait for the next session. To prevent Speaker Kōjirō Tsutsumi from taking his seat, the Socialists occupied the rostrum. Tsutsumi, a fifth degree judo expert, was then pushed into the chamber by a group of chanting Liberals against resisting Socialists. When he approached the Speaker's seat, he was confronted by Socialist Yoshizō Minabe, who had achieved the even higher seventh degree in judo. The Speaker declined a contest, considering himself bested. Meanwhile Liberal Takeo Ōhashi had called in the Metropolitan Police to quell the disorder. Incensed at police interference, the Diet guards joined the Socialists in the fray.[20] Just before midnight the clock was stopped, according to American practice, but in this case not with the mutual consent of the debating sides. Finally, a door was forced open and Tsutsumi, as Speaker, announced an extension of ten days, thus assuring passage of the bill. The Socialists vainly declared this announcement to be illegal as it was not made from the rostrum, and they boycotted subsequent sessions.[21]

The third incident concerned the Boards of Education Bill. It had been passed by the Lower House but became stuck in committee in the House of Councillors. The conservatives called for an interim report to get the bill out of committee and then tried to pass it on the spot. While the bill would not abolish the boards of education, it would make them appointive rather than elective. As the Japan Teachers Union, which supported the Socialists, had established political bridgeheads in some education boards, the conservatives wanted to acquire the power of appointing members. This would enable the government party to reduce union representation and also to use the boards as a new spoils system for its local stalwarts. Though there were more technical issues involved, this was the political basis. In order to prevent passage of the bill in plenary session, the SDP began submitting votes of non-confidence in all the persons to whom

20. This version is based on an account by an *Asahi* newspaperman. See Kōki Yanada, *Nihon Shakaitō* (The Social Democratic Party of Japan) (Tokyo, Meibun Sha, 1956), pp. 160–61.

21. Ironically enough, after the enactment of this law, the Socialists did not find much to complain about in its application until the whole question was opened up again when the Kishi government introduced the revised Police Duties Bill.

such motions could be applied. According to Diet rules, non-confidence motions have priority over all other bills. The Socialists gave long speeches and indulged in "cow walk" tactics to slow up the voting procedure. The speaker, Tsuruhei Matsuno, declared a rest period and then suddenly reconvened the plenary session and quickly had the doors of the chamber closed. A brief scuffle ensued between SDP members and guards. The bills then were passed by the LDP majority. The SDP was roundly attacked in the newspapers, as this incident came on the heels of much public discussion of the impropriety of Diet members' conduct.[22] Nevertheless, in the House of Councillors elections which followed soon afterward on July 10, 1956, the Socialists increased their total vote and their number of seats; evidently they had not been adversely affected.[23]

In the previous section and in Chapter 7 we have described how the Socialist delegation in the Diet, with the cooperation of the few Communist Representatives, had tried to exploit frictions between the LDP mainstream and rival factions and vainly tried to block approval of the revised security treaty. They used physical obstruction and boycotted meetings of the extended Diet session in unsuccessful efforts to prevent approval. Combining such tactics with encouragement to waves of mass demonstrations, the Socialists as part of the opposition front contributed to cancellation of President Eisenhower's visit and the resignation of Prime Minister Kishi. New elections became a virtual certainty. During this crisis, opposition forces proved their ability to mobilize mass demonstrations and coordinate them with Diet struggles even when current prosperity obviated the factor of economic desperation. Socialist Representatives, both in the Special Committee on the security treaty and on the House floor, outdid their reputation for tactics of delay. Despite their party's failure effectively to lead and control the People's Council and the demonstrations, it did play a role

22. For thoughts on SDP rowdyism in the context of violence in Japanese society, see Shimpei Fujimaki, "Shakaitō no 'Bōryoku' ni Tsuite," (On SDP 'Violence') *Shōwa Dōjin*, 2 (June 10, 1956), 357–60; for an opposite view on the seriousness of the injuries suffered by guards at the hands of Socialist Diet members and secretaries, see Sadaichirō Nojima, "Mahiru no Ankoku: Jūrin Sareta Eiji no Jinken" (Darkness at Noon: The Trampled-on Rights of the Guards), ibid., pp. 355–57.

23. The 26th session (1956–57) of the Diet was characterized by an attempt by both major parties to "normalize" the functioning of the Diet. Frequent meetings between the leaders of the two parties on various levels took place to smooth relations and thereafter to avoid untoward incidents.

in more successful involvement of intellectual circles in the crusade. More than before, the masses and the public were "educated" concerning the significance of the treaty issue for national independence, peace, and democratic causes.

Varied are the lenses through which those events have been viewed in retrospect. Objective observers contend that the conservative majority has not learned to respect minority positions sufficiently to work patiently for compromises; on crucial issues it is apt to ram measures through. On its side, the leftist opposition has talked more than ever about the "tyrannous majority." Radical elements have reservations about the principle of majority rule anyway; they are on the lookout for a "revolutionary situation" in which a Marxist–Leninist solution could be imposed by a determined minority on and through a united front.

The weak Democratic Socialist Party and moderate factions in the SDP were again in a dilemma. Along with most of the press they called for restabilization of parliamentary politics. But the poor DSP showing in the elections of November could not be used as an argument that the public was greatly impressed by its policy of acquiescence to, and gradual, piecemeal revision of, the treaty. The stabbings in June and July 1960 of Jōtarō Kawakami of the SDP and Premier Kishi and the assassination in October of SDP Chairman Asanuma apparently vindicated the warnings of the moderates that extremism on the left would exacerbate response from the ultraright. Far rightists had been counterdemonstrating. A few businessmen had resumed contributions to such organizations, whose academies for indoctrination and training once more were multiplying.[24]

In the electoral campaign following the crisis of 1960, speeches and debates over television were more influential than ever. For leaders of the opposition, the Diet serves mainly as a sounding board to popularize their ideas and personalities. Newspaper headlines are created by legislative proceedings in Japan more often than in the United States. Government-operated and private radio stations broadcast important Diet speeches and interpellations. Since the introduction of television in Japan in 1953, many Diet proceedings have been tele-

24. For the best study of the ultraright in Japan, see Ivan Morris, *Nationalism and the Right Wing in Japan* (London, 1960). This and other books are reviewed in "The Right-Wing Revival in Germany and Japan: A Review," *Journal of Conflict Resolution*, 7 (June 1961), 164–70.

vised, and Socialist leaders try to time their speeches to reach TV screens. Moreover, the opposition has utilized the mass media both directly and from the Diet to expose corruption in government and to create the impression that the Conservatives carry on political negotiations while sitting in tea houses surrounded by geisha girls in what is called "assignation house politics."

In prewar Diets the corruption of the ruling party, exposed by the opposition, had much to do with creating the atmosphere of contempt for parliamentarism. Since World War II, the Socialists have been trying to convince the electorate that they constitute a "clean" alternative to unsavory politics. They, too, have been touched by scandal, but they have taken stronger steps against members of their own party who have been under suspicion in this regard than have the conservatives.

Tensions between moderate and radical Socialists have been augmented since the 1960 crisis, but the SDP mainstream returned to the support of parliamentarism. In line with the party's policy of becoming more positive and responsible, it submitted a plan for amending the government's 1961 budget instead of issuing an alternative budget. It also called for "budget campaigns" at all levels in attempts to shape appropriations according to priorities advocated by the Socialists. Opposition tacticians have been trying to puzzle out methods for consolidating popular movements into such a broad front that capitalist interests and their political exponents can be driven into a corner. This ambition has been linked with new schemes for "breaking the barrier of one third" and advancing toward a Socialist majority in the Diet. So spectacular has been economic growth since 1957, and so challenging have been conservative plans for doubling national income during the 'sixties that the Socialists have been obliged to become more realistic and mature in economic counterplanning. Admitting the gains made under capitalism, they stress the growing inequality of benefits.

Meanwhile, the Sōka Gakkai had grown to claim a membership of 3.4 million households (perhaps 10 million members), chiefly poor, unorganized workers and petty enterprisers, persons with little education and feelings of inferiority. The SDP had to take seriously this movement from below, for, between 1956 and 1963, the Sōka Gakkai contingent in the House of Councillors rose to 15. This "Axiological Society" had become stronger in the Upper House than the DSP, and its social foundations were in some respects firmer than those of any leftist party. For one thing, there was an integration between organization and political action which was lacking in leftist party–union dichotomies.

CONSTITUTIONAL ISSUES AND TACTICS

In order for any party to grow, it must take up certain issues which defend or promote values and interests considered important by a much larger section of the populace than would ordinarily support that party. Along with opposition to rearmament and preservation of peace, one of the most important of such issues has been the Socialists' defense of the new Constitution adopted in 1947 and of civil rights guaranteed by it.

The Socialists can claim a record of support for the new Constitution even before its adoption. Soon after the Occupation began, they became aware that SCAP favored scrapping the Meiji Constitution and writing a new one. The SDP immediately set about drawing up its own proposals for a new constitution and published them in January 1946, shortly before the Liberal and Progressive drafts came out. The Socialist proposals were not only the most detailed but also the closest to the Constitution as it was finally enacted.[25] Within the party, however, the right wing was cautious. Earlier, at the founding convention of the party, when there was much talk as to whether the Emperor should be included among those responsible for the war, the majority of those present, despite some opposition, voted to support retention of the Emperor. Later, when the various drafts were being debated in the Diet, right-wing Socialists were hesitant about pressing for the inclusion of a statement in the new Constitution declaring explicitly that sovereignty resides in the people. They were thus thrown into confusion when the government parties, albeit under SCAP pressure, came out clearly for popular sovereignty in July 1946. Nevertheless, a number of Socialist-sponsored proposals were incorporated into the new Constitution which went into effect on May 3, 1947, and the party was proud that it was able to form the first cabinet under the Constitution.

The question of constitutional revision was raised by the Far East-

25. The Communists made known their views on the proposed new constitution but did not draw up a formal draft until July 1946, after the publication of the government's draft.

ern Commission which directed that the Japanese be given an opportunity to review the Constitution during the second year of its existence. Through a statement by Premier Yoshida on April 29, 1949, the conservatives announced that they had no desire for revision. This attitude was to change. Discussion revolved around whether the new Constitution actually had brought an end to Japan's traditional *kokutai* (national polity) or not, without any clear-cut decision.

The situation changed markedly after the outbreak of the Korean War on June 25, 1950. Shortly thereafter, General MacArthur directed the Japanese government to establish the National Police Reserve Force. This was gradually built up and transformed into what was called the National Safety Force in 1952 and then the Self-Defense Force in 1954. The avowed purpose in the beginning was the maintenance of internal security, but by Article 3 of the Self-Defense Force Law of 1954, the principal duty was declared to be the defense of Japan against either direct or indirect aggression. From the beginning, the Socialists branded the maintenance and development of such forces a violation of the Constitution's Article IX, which forbids the maintenance of "land, sea and air forces, as well as other war potential." Premier Yoshida chose to interpret this article liberally enough to allow the patent beginning of rearmament. With the recovery of independence in 1952, anti-Yoshida conservatives echoed the Socialists' cry of violation but concluded oppositely that the Constitution must be revised to allow Japan the legitimate right of self-defense. To counter this pressure, Yoshida ordered his Cabinet Legislative Bureau in November 1953 to explore possible constitutional revision, but in October 1953 the Bureau reported it saw no need for any immediate amendments to the basic law.

In the meantime, however, the Progressive and Liberal Parties set up their own committees to study revision and they both published complete draft revisions in November 1954,[26] proposing many changes besides those connected with rearmament. Chief among them was the proposal to elevate the Emperor to the status of "Head of State" instead of remaining just the "symbol" as stipulated in the Constitution. Although no proposal was specifically made for restor-

26. Subsequently the Ryokufūkai published a draft in May 1955 and the Liberal Democratic Party in March 1956. These, as well as the "Hirose Draft," may be seen compared in parallel columns in Toshiyoshi Miyasawa et al., *Kempō Kaisei* (Constitutional Revision) (Tokyo, Yūhikaku, 1956), appendix.

ing the Emperor to his sacrosanct position of prewar days, the Socialists feared the drafts were a step in this direction.

They spearheaded opposition to this revisionist trend. Only a few Socialists argued that the Constitution was not pressured by SCAP. All held that in any case its spirit was democratic, that the main phase of democratization had taken place under it, and that defense of the Constitution could be equated with defense of postwar democratic gains. They attempted to include various additional issues with their arguments. Since the United States wanted Japan to rearm and desired the revision of Article IX, they asserted that defense of the Constitution also meant preserving Japan's independence from American interference. They reasoned that, if Japan remained unarmed, it could not be used in the cold war struggle for power; thus, defense of the Constitution meant promotion of peace. In fact, the Socialists have perpetuated the early Occupation propaganda to the effect that Japan's war-renouncing Constitution should be a model for all nations to follow; a number of Japanese now believe that their country has the new world mission of persuading other nations to outlaw war and usher in the era of perpetual peace. A central Socialist slogan since independence has been "Defend the Peace Constitution!"

The Socialists have attempted to arouse and organize public opinion on this issue by various means. In March 1952, Left SDP Chairman Suzuki made the dramatic gesture of filing a suit in the Supreme Court seeking annulment of all acts relating to organization and maintenance of the National Police Reserve Force, since its founding on April 1, 1951, claiming that these acts violated Article IX of the Constitution. On October 8, 1952, the Supreme Court rejected the suit on the grounds that it was not empowered to judge the constitutionality of laws or ordinances in the abstract; it could only make a decision on a concrete dispute between or among particular persons.[27] Suzuki, it appears, did not have much hope of winning this case but felt it would publicize the legal issues involved.[28]

27. See "Kuni tai Suzuki" (The State Versus Suzuki), *Saikō Saibansho Hanreishū* (Supreme Court Decisions), *6* (1952), 783. For an English version, see John M. Maki, *Courts and Constitution in Japan: Selected Supreme Court Decisions, 1948–60* (Seattle, University of Washington Press, 1964), pp. 362–65.

28. *Asahi* (evening), Oct. 8, 1952. The Socialists have since drawn up a bill that would redefine the powers of the Supreme Court so that it could rule on the constitutionality of laws, ordinances, and regulations apart from any concrete legal dispute. For the text of this draft bill, see *Shakai Tsūshin* (Socialist Report), Extra (March 18, 1956), pp. 5–7.

Subsequently the Supreme Court came closer to a dictum about the meaning of Article IX. The most notable instance occurred in the fall of 1959 when it revoked the ruling of Tokyo District Court Judge Akio Date which had held that the stationing of United States forces in Japan was unconstitutional.

The case stemmed from the arrest of seven demonstrators for having trespassed upon the American military base at Sunakawa in the summer of 1957. The judge's ruling on March 30, 1959, had surprised the nation and given a boost to Socialist agitation against the American presence in Japan, because its implication was that the security treaty of September 1951 with the United States was invalid. The Kishi government hastily appealed the decision to the Supreme Court. In the midst of Socialist agitation against the LDP's proposals for revising the treaty, Kōtarō Tanaka, Chief Justice of the Supreme Court, ordered a retrial and declared that Judge Date's opinion that the United States security forces constituted part of Japan's "war potential" was in error, because these forces were not under Japanese command.

In its opinion the Supreme Court held that the United States forces were similar to United Nations troops, since their purpose in Japan was the maintenance of peace and security in and around Japan. Quoting the preamble of the Constitution, the Court declared that Japan was supplementing its own dearth of defensive power by "trusting in the justice and faith of the peace-loving peoples of the world." The Left Socialists were quick to point out, however, that in this decision—which they branded as political—the Court did not rule specifically on whether the Japanese Self-Defense Forces were constitutional.[29]

These constitutional questions clearly had tactical value in Japanese politics. It was widely accepted that the District Court decision had been a victory for the Socialists and the Supreme Court reversal a defeat. The reversal also had tactical intraparty repercussions for the Socialists. Coming at the time the Democratic Socialists under Nishio were being organized, it provided these latter added leverage for splitting the SDP. Nishio's less anti-American tenor was supported by the Supreme Court's equating the United States forces and the West with the "peace-loving peoples of the world."

29. See Alfred C. Oppler, "The Sunakawa Case: Its Legal and Political Implications," *Political Science Quarterly*, 76 (June 1961), 241–63; and Maki, *Courts and Constitution in Japan*, pp. 298–362.

Supreme Court pronouncements in Japan do not command the same degree of respect as in the United States. The new Japanese Constitution itself, having no long tradition behind it, remains a political issue. From the first the Socialists have been keenly aware of the importance of organizing public opinion broadly in defense of the Constitution. As early as January 15, 1954, both the Right and Left Socialists and the Worker-Farmer Party gave active personnel and financial support to formation of the National Federation for Preservation of the Constitution, until 1960 under the chairmanship of Tetsu Katayama, who, though a Socialist, had an appeal that went beyond the party following, especially since he had been Prime Minister.

The Federation secured widespread support from organized labor, scholars and other intellectuals, religious organizations, the main farmer unions, youth and women's organizations, and other groups.[30] Although Sōhyō took some of the initiative in launching the Federation, the support of right-wing labor organizations was also obtained. At first certain Right Socialist leaders, notably Nishio, opposed the Federation but soon others, especially those favoring reunification, won majority backing for it.

Soon after its founding, the Federation registered as a political organization. It quickly moved beyond the minimum program and became involved in opposing a variety of what it branded "unconstitutional" measures sponsored by the Yoshida government. In the 1955 Lower House and 1956 Upper House elections the Federation supported those candidates (mainly Socialists) who promised to oppose constitutional revision. By this time the Federation had the amorphous support of some 110 organizations reported to reach four million persons. Its tactics included: (1) theoretical research—fostering the formation of scholarly study groups and publication of their findings on constitutional questions; (2) litigation concerning the constitutionality of legislation and administrative actions; (3) promoting conventions, meetings and discussion groups; (4) publishing a monthly organ, *Heiwa to Minshushugi* (Peace and Democracy) as well as various pamphlets and books; (5) fostering relations with the various media of mass communication; (6) collecting signatures—their

30. For a partial listing of the many organizations and persons in public and cultural life that support the Federations, see Nihon Shakaitō, *Heiwa no Toride: Kempō Mondōshū* (The Fortress of Peace: A Collection of Questions and Answers on the Constitution) (Tokyo, Nihon Shakaitō Kyōiku Sendenkyoku, 1956), pp. 69–70.

goal was 20 million—for a declaration protective of the Constitution; and (7) asking that people write "Let us preserve the Peace Constitution" at the bottom of all their correspondence. In addition, the Federation has attempted to take part in cultural festivals, political activities, and mass action. It has ventured into the area of international cultural exchange. In early 1956 the SDP set up in party headquarters a special committee to defend the Constitution and ordered similar committees formed in each party branch to work closely with the Federation. We have seen in the first section of this chapter how leftist pressures had weakened the Federation by 1960. In the following year, the "structural reformers" began trying to use the organization against "monopoly capitalism's" alleged use and abuse of the Constitution.

Competition with the conservatives over constitutional revision became especially intense when Hatoyama-led Liberal Democrats won the elections in February 1955. Conservative intellectual leaders, who considered a mass movement necessary for achieving constitutional revision, established the League for an Independent Constitution (Jishu Kempō Kisei Dōmei) on May 21, 1955, on the basis of an earlier organization. By the following year the League had not been as successful as the Federation in gaining support either from intellectuals or from mass organizations.[31] According to a student of the Constitution, Professor Nobushige Ukai, the League's and other conservative proposals would in effect: (1) place the Diet over the people, that is, increase the duties of the people at the expense of their rights; (2) place the Cabinet over the Diet, that is, expand the Cabinet's power of dissolution and suspension of the Diet; and (3) place the Emperor over the Cabinet, that is, give the Emperor the functions of "head of state" with the implication of at least partial restoration of his former ordinance power. They would, moreover, (4) qualify and reduce emphasis on civic rights; (5) possibly establish a special court for constitutional review, and abolish the periodic popular referendum on appointments to the Supreme Court.[32] The Socialists opposed all revision in these directions. While Democratic Socialists might be persuaded to discuss desirable amendments, their leftist rivals have

31. See *Mainichi,* May 3, 1956.

32. Nobushige Ukai, "Constitutional Trends and Development," *The Annals of the American Academy of Political and Social Science, 308* (Nov. 1956), 6 ff. See also *Asahi Shimbun,* Jan. 5, 1961.

preferred not to engage in such public consideration. They have feared that to open the door a crack might lead to a flood tide of conservative revisions. In private, however, some have been willing to admit that certain revisions might be advisable in the light of experience since 1947. And, as mentioned in the preceding chapter, there are recurrent indications that, if ever the leftist SDP could attain a majority and fully control the government, it might revise the Constitution or substitute a new one designed to bulwark a socialist system.

What has been the trend in public opinion on constitutional revision? At the time of the recovery of independence in the spring of 1952, opinion polls indicated a widespread desire for revision of the Constitution on the general grounds of making it more suitable to Japanese conditions.[33] In the neighborhood of 40 per cent of a national sample favored revision whereas some 25 per cent was opposed. With the passage of time, however, opinion has gradually come around to some 40 per cent opposing revision to 27 per cent in favor. With regard to the specific question about amending Article IX, public opinion has from the beginning tended to oppose this. Although the trend moved slightly in the other direction in 1954–55, opposition mounted to over 52 per cent against amendment in 1957 as contrasted with 32 per cent in favor.

How much of this was due to the efforts of the Socialists either directly or through the National Federation for the Preservation of the Constitution is probably impossible to ascertain. They either foresaw the trend correctly or have been effective in their efforts. In any case, they have been wise in placing the emphasis of their anti-rearmament drive on constitutional grounds, because public opinion on rearmament as such has shown a somewhat contradictory trend to those just mentioned. As is shown in Chapter 7 on foreign policies, public opinion polls indicate support for Japan's maintaining and expanding its own military forces as an attribute of its sovereign status and for defensive security. The government's cumulative faits accomplis in the course of gradual rearmament have been supported by a slight major-

33. For this and the following observations on Japanese public opinion see Allan B. Cole and Naomichi Nakanishi, comps. and eds., *Japanese Opinion Polls with Socio-Political Significance, 1947–1957* (Medford, Mass., The Fletcher School of Law and Diplomacy, Tufts University, and Williamstown, Mass., The Roper Public Opinion Research Center, Williams College, 1960), pp. 427–79. Hereafter referred to as *Japanese Opinion Polls.*

ity of respondents. A steady and substantial minority of something like 25 per cent has nevertheless opposed this trend and has provided the Socialists with a basis in public opinion.

Stymied by the one-third bloc against constitutional revision in the Diet, the conservatives have turned to further study of proposed amendments. In 1956 they passed legislation to provide for a Constitutional Research Committee (Kempō Chōsakai) under the cabinet. The Socialists branded this an unconstitutional administrative action, on grounds that the Constitution provides that amendments should originate in the Diet. Appointments to the Committee were not made until after Premier Kishi returned from his trip to the United States in the summer of 1957. In this the Socialists claimed to detect American pressure. Most of the appointees were known revisionists. Some opponents refused seats on the Committee, an exception being Masamaichi Rōyama, a right Socialist who was then President of Ochanomizu University and a member of the National Federation for Preservation of the Constitution. The official SDP position was to boycott the Committee by refusing to fill the ten seats the government had assigned the opposition. Party leaders also refused to appear before the Committee to present their views. By this tactic, however, they lost an opportunity for presenting the anti-revisionist case indirectly to the public, so the party had to consider other countermeasures. Although the majority report of the Commission on the Constitution proposed revision of Article IX and the status of the Emperor, as predicted, by the time it finally appeared in the spring of 1964, public opinion had gradually moved in the other direction. The Satō government therefore shelved constitutional amendment indefinitely, giving Socialists and fellow opposition elements a greater sense of accomplishment.

DEFENSE OF CIVIL RIGHTS AND LOCAL INTERESTS

Socialists are prominent among those desiring effective implementation of the third chapter of the Constitution, which contains 30 articles on the rights and duties of the people. Of course, most of these rights are directly or otherwise significant for movements wishing to oppose or criticize the incumbent government. On constitutional grounds, as well as to defend their own future freedom for maneuver, both SDPs in 1952 allied with many other organizations to oppose the Subversive Activities Prevention Bill, which nevertheless was enacted on July 21 of that year. The nation had never seen a wave of strikes as large as the second one in this politically motivated series; and, if shop meetings and other forms of protest action were considered, the mobilization was still more extensive. The Socialists used almost every possible type of tactic, both within and outside the Diet. Confrontation of such dimensions may have alarmed the conservatives into passing the measure without revising the crucial clause on "agitation"; it may also have helped subsequently to restrain them from applying the law except in rare cases. Only about four applications have occurred, mainly involving Communists. Occasionally there has been conservative talk about further toughening the law.

A later example of an issue related to civil rights was the Kishi administration's attempt in the fall of 1958 to strengthen the powers and organization of the police by the so-called revised Police Duties Bill. The Socialists depicted this as a major step toward reviving the prewar police state. In Chapter 2 we described the indignant campaign waged against this bill. In the Diet the opposition finally resorted to a boycott, and the bill was withdrawn. This victory was possible because of wide public criticism and dissatisfaction within the ranks of Liberal Democrats about the way Kishi handled the affair.

After the crisis in the spring and early summer of 1960, Political Violence Prevention Bills were introduced and hotly debated in two successive sessions of the Diet. In June 1961, such a measure was passed by the Lower House, but conservative factional feuding prevented its completed enactment then. The Democratic Socialists had reached an agreement with the LDP to support this revised bill designed to curb terrorist activities and violent demonstrations near the Diet. But prevailing attitudes in the SDP called mainly for legal restraints against ultrarightists; any laws which might hamper extraparliamentary direct action or pressure from the left were described in these quarters as "fascist attempts to destroy civil liberties." Again the Socialists were accused of reflecting the influence of Sōhyō and other radical elements in the People's Council to Oppose the Security Treaty.

This party—sometimes both wings—has championed many other "basic human rights." Some of them have been purely domestic issues; others have had international implications. An example of the former was the outlawry of prostitution and rehabilitation of such exploited women, a cause promoted by both right and left Socialists. Female public opinion became so aroused over related reforms that even the conservatives were impelled to help enact a comprehensive bill which was supposedly in full force by April 1, 1957.

More often civil rights issues involved freedom of the press and other modes of public expression. For instance, in connection with the Anti-Prostitution Bill, a *Yomiuri* reporter wrote in October 1957 that two LDP Diet members were said to have received bribes for opposing it. The Tokyo High Prosecutor's Office arrested the reporter for not revealing the sources of his account. The SDP protested to the Ministry of Justice that freedom of the press was being violated and, moreover, that the government party had interfered in the Prosecutor's Office in order to divert suspicion from the LDP. The reporter was freed and the case dropped.[34]

There were implications for Japanese-American relations when, soon after the recovery of national sovereignty, Kōzō Inomata of the Left SDP demanded an investigation of the disappearance of Wataru Kaji, left-wing artist who had carried on psychological warfare in China for the Chinese Nationalists during the war and had run unsuccessfully as an independent in a Diet election after his return from China. The case received great publicity when Kaji was allegedly released from custody by United States intelligence authorities early in 1953. Although the American Embassy denied it, Kaji asserted that he had been held against his will and had been pressed to turn informer. The case was complicated by the appearance of Masao Mitsuhashi who claimed he knew Kaji as a Soviet spy. A Diet Committee looked into the case during seven public hearings; but the Diet was dissolved after Premier Yoshida's "slip of the tongue," and then Kaji disappeared again, this time voluntarily because he was in bad health; the case blew over. Without trying to defend Kaji, the Left SDP wanted to use the case to decry what it called American "interference" in Japanese affairs, and to demonstrate that Japan was not really independent.[35]

Another incident which the SDP brought up in the Diet, this time to discredit the Self-Defense Forces as well as to defend civil liberties, was the so-called "Hiroshima death march" in February 1957, when

34. See *Asahi Shimbun*, Oct. 27 and 28, 1957, and *Yomiuri*, Oct. 29, 1957.

35. For a rather complete report of the case written shortly after it exploded, see Noboru Yamamoto, *Kaji-Mitsuhashi Jiken* (The Kaji-Mitsuhashi Incident) (Tokyo, Surugadai Shobō, 1953).

orders reminiscent of prewar training methods resulted in the death of two members of the Ground Self-Defense Force. The press was greatly exercised over this incident, and the SDP tried to channel indignation into lines opposing constitutional revision and favoring a reduction of military forces.[36] The party has taken advantage of public ire for similar ends in a number of cases which have involved United States military personnel. Perhaps the most famous was the "Girard case" in the summer and fall of 1957, when an American serviceman was convicted of carelessly killing a Japanese woman as she picked up empty shells on a firing range. The cleverness of such tactics consists in uniting humanitarian sentiments with nationalist feelings and in finding a *cause célèbre* to augment public feelings against the presence of foreign military bases and to insist upon Japanese criminal jurisdiction.

Yet, if it were not for Socialist championing of civil rights, most of these issues might easily have been monopolized by the Communists. In that case, either the rights might have been seriously infringed by strong conservative reactions, or the JCP might have become stronger politically than has so far been possible. While the SDP has been an opposition party, it has served as a watchdog over the democratic, civil rights, and pacifist features of the Constitution. It has utilized all the parliamentary as well as other tactics available to oblige the conservatives to respect the basic liberties of the people; at the same time the Socialists have utilized each issue to publicize their own political and economic programs.

When the interests of a minority have been involved in Socialist defense of equal rights, the aim has been not only to enhance a reputation as champions of justice and constitutionalism but also to gather the votes of the oppressed group. Japan's "special community" (or hamlet) people, although legally emancipated from "Eta" status in 1871, are still somewhat segregated in subvillage units and subject to various kinds of social and economic discriminations. Insofar as they do not become assimilated in large cities they constitute a kind of vestigial out-caste.

During the 1920s, some of these people, reflecting Marxist influence, organized a freedom movement and sought to link it with the proletarian movement as a whole. At first this so-called "Leveling

36. For other repercussions of this incident, see I. I. Morris, "Significance of the Military in Post-War Japan," *Pacific Affairs, 31* (March 1958), 7–9.

Movement" (Suihei Undō) was mainly directed by Communists, but by the mid-'thirties its support had shifted to the growing Socialist Masses' Party and to parliamentary methods. The foremost leader of the "Leveling Movement" was Jiichirō Matsumoto, whose role in a rather extreme faction of the postwar left wing of the SDP will be described in Chapter 9.

Partial homogenization during wartime and democratization since 1945 have brought improvements for people who stem from or still reside in "special communities." The earlier militancy has been less prevalent; instead the [Segregated] Community Emancipation League and the Institute on the [Segregated] Community Problem have engaged mainly in research and publications. Their officers are normally Socialist or Communist supporters but the SDP has usually avoided special appeals to these people lest they alienate other rural voters. In some 6,000 intravillage hamlets, recognizable members of this minority are almost always just one lesser consideration in local campaigning.

Since the fall of 1957, the growth of attention given to interracial problems in the United States and South Africa has led in Japan as well to heightened awareness of discriminations against its main social minority. The press and radio took up the cause,[37] and the SDP for the first time became remedially active in this field. On October 10 of that year, the party's Policy Planning Board approved a program which it and the Community Emancipation League had been formulating since the SDP convention in January. Solutions were envisaged as possible through basic reforms in socioeconomic relations, that is, through democratization, economic reforms, realization of full employment, further land reform, improved housing, and enforcement of respect for human rights. More concretely they proposed the establishment of a committee in the Prime Minister's Office to study the problem of segregated communities. As the Board viewed this problem, it chiefly required aid to the most economically depressed sections of villages; therefore increased governmental grants were urged to villages with "unemancipated" component hamlets for improving

37. See "Buraku o Kaihō-seyo: Nihon no Naka no Hōkensei" (Emancipate the [Segregated] Communities: A Feudal System in the Midst of Japan), *Shūkan Asahi, 62* (Sept. 29, 1957), 3–15. For a longer treatment in English of "community" discrimination in Japan, see George De Vos and Hiroshi Wagatsuma, eds., *The Invisible Race* (Berkeley and Los Angeles, University of California Press, 1966); political activities are treated in chapters by Wagatsuma and Totten.

irrigation, housing, health, and education, as well as to encourage handicrafts and small business. A major emphasis was on extending the benefits of land reform to these people, many of whom had been too poor even to be tenants before the recent land reform. So the Socialists proposed that farmers with less than three *tan* (about three quarters of an acre) be assisted to purchase more, that they be given preferential access to the purchase of reclaimed land in their vicinities, as well as special rights of entrance into forest lands and fishing areas.

This statement of policy by the SDP was hailed as epochal by leaders of the special community, but they also voiced certain criticisms. Policies should have been explained more adequately on the basis of prior studies, they averred. Moreover, in their opinion the SDP exaggerated the responsibility of capitalism for such injustices, ignoring various sources traceable to feudalistic survivals, especially in rural areas. They warned that to establish a separate category in the national budget for improving conditions in special communities might arouse resentment on the part of other rural people. In order that segregation may not be perpetuated, they have urged that assistance be provided to defined types of needy people regardless of their group identifications.

The Social Democrats, in cooperation with labor and farmer unions, youth groups, and women's organizations, have thus taken the lead, though closely rivaled by the Communists, in developing a nationwide program. Significant results will require time. While the constituents concerned are not impressively numerous as voters, they are rather group-conscious and have come to be of widespread humanitarian concern.

The Liberal Democrats have not been unmoved by this issue and have been in a better position than the Socialists to do something about it in monetary terms. They were instrumental in appropriating special funds in 1958 for public baths and community centers in a number of segregated areas. The Community Emancipation League has been developing its contacts even with the conservatives, not to mention the Communists, as well as with the SDP. But because the Socialists were the first postwar party, aside from the Communists, to develop a program of reform on their behalf, and because their leaders include a number of notables from special communities, the SDP hopes to be favored by these voters at the polls.

Obviously, the tactics of the Socialists are legion, and considerable ingenuity is exerted to devise new schemes to suit changing conditions.[38] But no treatment of the subject can be adequate without some mention of local activities. There are weaknesses of organization and membership, and it is with reason that the SDP and Democratic Socialists are self-critical on this score and frequently exhort their branches to perform more effectively. Efforts are made to champion local causes which will be immediately meaningful to voters. Improvements in education, sanitation, drainage, and housing are typically sought. Local Socialists may find ways of helping individuals with private affairs, with legal matters, in financing projects, or in meeting medical problems. Socialist Representatives are sometimes enlisted as advisors to small business associations. They and their family members are often active in dealing with problems of concern to women and women's organizations. PTA chapters and various organizations for social welfare absorb part of their time. Socialists argue that governmental agencies rather than voluntary relief organizations should assume responsibilities in fields of social welfare. They often propose programs for local self-governing bodies, then launch struggles for their attainment. Reform of local taxation and the strengthening of local finance are common concerns.

The party's weakness at the local level often causes branches to rely excessively on local unions and regional labor federations during actual campaigns of several sorts. They are periodically urged from headquarters to attract local leaders by encouraging them to bring their problems and causes to the party and enlist its support in ways which will be mutually strengthening. Despite some activities by party branches in backward fishing and mountain villages, and in other depressed areas, it was not until the Sōka Gakkai successfully organized millions of the "voiceless voices" with political and nationalistic undertones that the secular parties more keenly felt this challenge.

38. In 1961, the SDP prepared to launch a Society to Protect Human Rights in frank competition with the People's Relief Association sponsored by Communists and pro-Communists. It was to be not so much to promote legislation as to assist victims of mass movements, and especially needy families, and to deal with cases of persecution by town bosses. See *Yomiuri,* March 13, 1961.

5. Economic Policies of the Social Democrats during Recovery and Stabilization

One cannot imagine a socialist party that does not emphasize economic policies and planning. We have noted the deep commitment of Japanese Social Democrats, especially those in the stronger left wing, to Marxist analyses and remedies. Although there are other aspects of their thought—ethical, social, and political—the heart of their program and the acid test of its validity are in the economic sphere of national life. In fairness to the Socialists it should be pointed out that few if any political parties analyze and prescribe policies for national economies with the thorough competence expected of academic and governmental research institutes. Politicians must tack in accordance with current exigencies, which have often focused more attention on political issues. And yet, Japan's postwar economic problems have been particularly urgent. The challenge confronting any government in Japan is how to overcome serious difficulties in striving to raise the standard of living while encouraging capital investment so as to keep improving technical modernity and expanding productivity.[1]

1. One of the authors is of the opinion that other factors limited Socialist economic planning and formulation of economic policies during 1945–60. The SDP had neither the requisite financial resources nor a large staff of highly trained planners to prescribe policies for the national economy. The party's association with many intellectuals, including

LIMITATIONS OF THE JAPANESE ECONOMY

Shapers of public policies and plans in postwar Japan, and their would-be successors in power, have had to consider the limitations which have rather seriously hampered economic recovery and further growth. Particularly was this true before 1960. Japan's population by that year reached nearly 93 million citizen-consumers mostly crowded into limited arable regions of an empire shorn of overseas territories and prewar investments. Large additions have yearly joined the labor force seeking employment. The number of well educated persons has grown, and the problem of their suitable employment has been particularly acute. Tremendous problems of industrial reconstruction, including the rebuilding of a once thriving merchant marine, had to be accomplished after the national disasters. And Japan had even fewer material resources at its own disposal. The high degree of its dependence on foreign supplies of raw materials and on overseas trade is proverbial. Yet rather high tariff walls and quota limitations on Japanese exports have persisted; exchanges have not flowed freely, in particular between Red bloc countries and non-communist nations. Resentments and suspicions left in the wake of Japanese imperialism for years impeded the recovery of normal trade with a number of Asian countries. As it became more possible to trade with the new nations of Asia, some of them continued to suffer from political upheavals, and Japanese goods have met increasingly stiff competition from European firms and from Communist China during its first Five-Year Plan.

---

a number of leading economists, and even access to a limited number of bureaucrats in government economic offices were not adequate for the purpose. Although Japan's postwar economic problems have been particularly urgent, the crucial debates among the political parties during this period have been over political, especially foreign policy, issues. The political necessity for the Japanese Socialists, as the leading opposition party, to develop realistic, rational, feasible, and detailed economic plans was slight after 1949. There was never any real expectation that the party would soon take over the government. Their major contests with the conservatives and even the causes of their own party schisms stemmed from differences over foreign policy and divergences in political philosophy. The political appeal and electoral support of the socialists in Japan were based mainly on their stands on foreign policy, not on the intricacies of economic policy. These factors do not excuse the SDP but it is in this perspective that one must view the economic policies of the SDP, their degree of realism, flexibility, and creativity. (C.H.U.) Another view recognizes that the Socialist parties were not adequately staffed for economic planning but argues that, except at certain points, the more important economic issues were as significant for voters and politicians as debates over foreign policies. (A.B.C.)

A damaged Japan with such an unfavorable ratio of people to resources of course was limited in available capital. Even after the redistribution of land, the pattern of tiny farms remained and was even accentuated. Most agrarian families have required auxiliary employment for their members. And, during most years of recovery, precious foreign exchange had to be paid for imports to meet food deficits. As compared with most industrialized economies in the West, Japan's is marked by congestion both in the countryside and in the massive sector of small-scale enterprises. Of course, Japan also has had assets—an industrious populace with a propensity for cooperation and a goodly quota of innovators, a breakwater position across the face of Eastern Asia, plentiful water power and fishery resources, access to foreign capital—yet its limitations imposed serious tests for rival advocates of reconstruction.

Early in 1959, the Japanese economy, encouraged by improved conditions abroad, overcame its "saucer recession" and made new gains. Japan's balance of international payments improved, and reserves of foreign exchange mounted. The index of urban consumption rose by nearly one quarter by 1959 as compared with 1955, and the wage index increased still more. Another rise in consumer spending promised to exceed that during the "Jimmu boom" of 1955–57 (said to be the greatest since the founding of Japan by Emperor Jimmu). Per capita levels of income and consumption were well above the prewar averages in 1934–36, and rural folk had gained even more proportionately than had residents of cities. These periods of prosperity, and evidence that fiscal administrators had found regulatory means for limiting the severity of troughs in business cycles, posed new theoretical and strategic problems for the Socialist opposition. This chapter, however, is more concerned with economic policies advocated and employed by the SDP before 1956, that is, before the implications of capitalist prosperity called so imperatively for reconsiderations.

Those Socialists who fully accept parliamentary modes of power and who helped to attain a two-main-party situation have come to realize that cross-stratal support for the party entails difficulties in reconciling conflicts of economic interests. Major parties in Japan are often in the crossfire of increasingly well organized and politically aroused pressure groups. Even left Socialists and the still more radical, who stress organized labor as the vanguard of the revolutionary forces (but who periodically advocate popular fronts with other elements), must cope in some ways with a complex web of frequently disparate interests. In this chapter we shall survey economic policies adopted by the Socialists both when they shared power and when they were in opposition.[2]

What has been the response of the SDP to basic problems of Japan's postwar economy? The pronouncement of the party program is that they are mainly evils resulting from monopoly capitalism which socialism can eventually resolve. However, Socialist leaders in private readily admit that such problems are far more complicated. As the party is pledged to pursue revolution-by-evolution, it must plan for a transitional stage of indefinite duration in which the economy is mainly capitalistic. In theory, each step should be directed toward the eventual overcoming of economic limitations. Let us examine the various phases through which the economy has passed since 1945 and note how the party concretely responded to each.

COPING WITH IMMEDIATE POSTWAR INFLATION AND RECONSTRUCTION

World War II had left the Japanese economy in shambles. Only about 34 per cent of what had been the total domestic assets in 1935 remained. Compared to industrial capacities at the end of 1944, before saturation bombing became serious, 32.9 per cent of power generation, 27.9 per cent of machine tools, 21.6 per cent of chemicals, and 14 per cent of the textile industry had been destroyed. Losses in overseas assets, excluding individual properties, amounted to some ¥263 billion at the official evaluation rate immediately after the war.[3] Industry had almost ground to a halt. Both people and machinery were worn out; food was scarce, and the black market flourished. During the post-surrender political vacuum, the government released money that had been earmarked for military purposes such as army mustering-out pay, settling debts to former war industries and compensating them for damages. This caused the wartime inflation to become a postwar spiral.

In such circumstances, the stabilization of the people's livelihood

2. This chapter and the next are based largely on research done by the Kokumin Keizai Kenkyū Kyōkai (National Economic Research Council) of Tokyo with a special contribution by one of its directors, Hidezō Inaba.

3. See Tōyō Keizai Shimpō Sha, ed., *Nihon Keizai Nempō* (Japan Economic Bulletin), No. 4 (1953), pp. 13 ff. The figures are from a report issued by the Economic Stabilization Board.

and the rapid recovery of industrial production undoubtedly constituted the most urgent economic tasks. In addition, Japan had to carry out democratization reforms. Zaibatsu combines were dissolved, land reform was enacted, and labor unions were encouraged. As the Social Democratic Party of Japan was being established, its leaders had to shape their appeals to conform with current privations and changes; they had little time for carefully working out a long-range economic program in terms of concrete steps based on detailed statistics.

During the first year of its existence, the party called for nationalization or state operation of the chemical fertilizer industry as a measure to cope with the food shortage, and nationalization of the coal industry to foster industrial production. Both steps were also designed to help overcome galloping inflation. The first Yoshida government meanwhile, with prodding from SCAP, was attempting to stimulate production of coal and steel in order to quicken the economy. Yoshida rallied the best available brains around him and was not averse to Socialist participation. The party was thus largely bereft of any initiative.

The rise of the SDP was so rapid that it came to head a cabinet before it had had time to work out an economic program;[4] also it was restrained from socialist innovations by the four-party agreement.

THE KATAYAMA CABINET

The first task of the Katayama Cabinet was to avert a threatened collapse of the economy by overcoming inflation and the almost complete stagnation of production. In the first "white paper" ever to be issued in Japan, the Katayama Cabinet appealed to the people to bear up under existing difficulties in order to restore a peacetime economy.[5] The government had earlier announced its intention of con-

4. In April 1947, about the time of the elections, the Shakaishugi Seiji Keizai Kenkyūjo (Socialist Institute of Political Economy), headed by left-wing leader Mosaburō Suzuki, published "An Outline of an Emergency Economic Policy For Dealing With Inflation" (Infurē Shori Keizai Kiki Toppa Taisaku Yōkō). This was significant in the light of the importance subsequently placed on planning, first by the Left SDP and later by the reunified party. The policy called for state control (*kokka kanri*) of financial institutions and important industries. This was the first systematically developed set of economic policies by any of the Japanese socialists.

5. Published in July 1947, the "white paper" was called "Keizai Jissō Hōkokusho" (Report on Economic Conditions). The text may be found in any Japanese economic yearbook covering the period.

tinuing the priority production system emphasizing coal and steel, and the control of maximum commodity prices and wage levels.[6]

The most immediate problem was the shortage of food, especially in urban areas. Rations were being distributed about a month late. To close the gap, the government set aside a day or more at a time when no rations would be issued; these amounted to twenty days between July and October 1947. Restaurants without ration cards were closed from July to December. Farmers' deliveries of rice to the government were strictly enforced, and they were encouraged to sell part of the rice they had saved for family consumption. As these measures proved insufficient for feeding the hungry millions, SCAP was induced to supply about a million tons of food from abroad.

The Katayama Cabinet inherited the assumption of the previous government that stepping up coal production was a prerequisite to general industrial recovery. A production target of 30,000,000 metric tons was set for the year 1947. An official price for coal was set (at ¥956 per ton after July 5, 1947) and based, among other factors, on an estimate of wages (¥579 per ton). But due to wage rises the cost of coal production by the end of the year rose to a point (¥1,617) in excess of the official price.[7] To keep the companies mining coal, the government had to make up the difference. Such governmental subsidies, plus huge "loans" made to coal and other industries through the Reconstruction Finance Bank (which started operations in January 1947) contributed greatly to that very inflation that the increased production was supposed to help cure.

Although production of coal fell three million tons short of the 30,000,000 ton target for 1947, output recovered rapidly during the Katayama administration. By December of that year the production index reached 119.9, as compared with the average for 1931–33. The target therefore was raised to 36 million tons for the following year, of which 34.7 million were actually achieved.

The national control of important industries was the only Socialist plank in the four-party coalition agreement. It was felt that if the

6. "Kiki Toppa Keizai Kinyū Taisaku" (Economic and Financial Policies for Overcoming the Crisis), announced in June 1947. The text may be found in any Japanese economic yearbook covering the period.

7. The figures are from Jerome B. Cohen, *Japan's Economy in War and Reconstruction* (Minneapolis, University of Minnesota Press, 1949), p. 465. This work gives the best detailed analysis in English of Japanese official economic policies during the period being discussed.

party was to have anything to show for having headed the government, it must realize this pledge, at least in part. The four-party agreement had already diluted the original aim of the SDP: "state management as a prerequisite to state ownership." That agreement called for state management to "democratize by abolishing methods of bureaucratic control."[8]

The Socialists chose the coal industry as most appropriate for immediate state management or nationalization. Sharp differences soon arose between the SDP and the Democratic Party over meaning and methods. After three months of discussion in the Cabinet and two and a half in the Diet, the so-called Emergency Coal Industry Control Law (*Rinji Sekitan Kōgyō Kanri Hō*) was finally passed on December 8, 1947 (effective April 1). A child of compromise, it was really satisfactory to no group. Even to get this passed, Premier Katayama had to announce that is was only a temporary measure and that he did not plan to extend similar controls to other industries in the immediate future.

The law divided all coal mines into two categories: general and designated mines. In general mines, the government could only inspect to see that production quotas were met with allotted capital goods and funds. In designated mines, however, the government had the power to intervene in management to insure that each mine would meet production quotas. Each designated mine was headed by a controller, selected by management; he was to consult with a Production Council composed of equal representation from management and labor. Minister of Industry and Commerce Chōzaburō Mizutani placed 42 large mines in the designated category. They were divided into four regions, each of which had a Regional Coal Bureau and a Regional Coal Mine Control Committee. An All-Japan Coal Mine Control Committee was made the highest consultative body. Despite this elaborate superstructure the government had only general powers of control, such as supervision, planning, and financing.

While management had strongly opposed the bill, labor had shown little interest in supporting it. Even in the period before its enforcement, Mizutani did little to insure that it would operate in a positive manner. The Socialists claimed the bill vindicated a main election

8. For a discussion of the meanings of these terms in the Japanese context, see Takeo Suzuki, *Gendai Nihon Zaisei Shi* (A History of Present-Day Japanese Finance) (Tokyo, Tokyo Daigaku Shuppankai, 1956), 2, 30 ff.

promise, but the other government parties claimed, with equal justification, that they had shaped the bill to their liking. As it was only a temporary measure, it died a natural death with its expiration three years later under the Yoshida administration.

The second pillar of the Katayama government's economic policies was the establishment of new official commodity prices and a wage freeze, compulsory for government workers but voluntary for employees in private industry. Prices had been officially established at the time of the "new yen" currency conversion in February 1946, but they were being fast lifted by the surge of inflation. On July 5, 1947, the government set new price ceilings at 65 times the average prices during the period 1934–36. Where costs pushed through those ceilings, it was committed to subsidizing the industries concerned to keep them going. Wages were pegged at ¥1,800 per month, only 27.8 times the 1934–36 averages. The lower wage increase over the base period was officially justified by the fact that average per capita output by industrial workers was only one half to one third of 1934–36 levels. Such reasoning may appear strange for a Socialist-led government, but the Economic Stabilization Board, which made the announcement, had inflation as its primary concern. Such a measure could probably have worked only if labor had been highly motivated to endure sacrifices for the common good. Even so, this action had to be based on the assumption that all essential commodities would be obtainable at official prices, which, due to the short supply, was doubtful.

The black market flourished, despite all governmental measures to curb it. The causes of inflation, though complex, were apparent to the government. Consumer goods of all kinds had been woefully lacking and such industrial production had been wholly inadequate since early in the war; imports of raw materials had been insufficient; price control had been inefficient, and wage controls wanting. Also, the government had not been able to collect taxes until it had been helped by Occupation personnel in the last quarter of 1947. Nevertheless, government spending had mounted, flooding into circulation an ever increasing supply of Bank of Japan notes. Actually the Shidehara new yen issue in February 1946 had been bungled and had little effect in preventing inflation while Yoshida's Finance Minister, Tanzan Ishibashi, consciously encouraged inflationary trends. Because the Katayama government still believed that the main way to check inflation was to increase production, one of the prime measures the government was taking to encourage production was also encouraging inflation. In order to hold prices down to official rates, the government was pouring subsidies and loans into industry. Through wage increases and production leaks, money was running into the black market. There was thus some relation between the fact that the note issue of the Bank of Japan more than doubled in 1947 while black market prices of consumer goods rose almost two and a half times and those of producers' goods three times. The government's budgetary deficit operations were putting the burden directly on the people in the form of spiraling household expenses while wages continued to be pegged.

Perhaps only a "socialist" government could have kept labor as quiet as it was for so long, but after September 1947 the number of disputes mounted. The discrepancy became acute between the fixed public workers' salaries and those of workers in private industry, which had been rising. As earlier mentioned, the government finally agreed to raise the average monthly salaries of government workers to ¥2,920 and to pay two months' salary extra to make up household deficits. The government's proposal to raise railway and postal rates to provide this money further angered the already bitter left wing of the SDP, prodded by organized workers, many of whom were then under Communist influence. The result was the collapse of the Katayama Cabinet.

THE ASHIDA CABINET

Right-wing Socialist opinion continued to favor participation in a coalition cabinet, and the party accepted Hitoshi Ashida of the Democratic Party as Prime Minister. Vowing not to repeat the mistake of the four-party agreement during the Katayama Cabinet, the SDP insisted on incorporating more of its own concrete policies in the new three-party agreement with the conservative Democratic and Cooperative Parties. Still, such policies were much modified. For instance, oil, steel, and fertilizer were to be put under national control "as the needs of the case demand," which meant in effect that nothing would be done. Also, the very concrete demand for an end to interest payments on war bonds was not completely settled but was to be left to later decision by a committee.[9] Here was another decision which was

9. For a copy of the economic section of the three-party agreement, see ibid., pp. 155–56, quoted from *Asahi Keizai Nenshi* (The Asahi Economic Yearly History) (Tokyo, 1948), p. 6.

never made. In fact, the agreement proved to be no more than a rationalization for the SDP to join the coalition. The basic economic policy of the Ashida Cabinet was to continue the priority production system in the hope of increasing production of coal and steel, but in other respects policy veered in different directions.

Instead of relying on rigid price and wage controls to halt inflation, the Ashida Cabinet turned to a policy of inviting foreign investments. It was thought that the resultant increase of commodities in relation to the supply of currency would gradually overcome inflation. This was known as an intermediate stabilization policy and contrasted sharply with the issuing of new yen which the SDP had failed to incorporate into the four-party agreement. Ashida's emphasis on the introduction of foreign capital was in response to the Johnston Report; it incorporated the suggestions and findings of the Draper Mission which visited Japan in March 1948.[10] But this policy also failed, in large part because not enough of the hoped for foreign capital arrived at this time. However, the $60 million cotton import credit through the Export-Import Revolving Fund, a loan which had actually been planned under the Katayama Cabinet, began to operate in June 1948.

The Ashida Cabinet was launched with two handicaps. It was not formed until March 10, almost the end of the fiscal year. The new budget was not passed until July, so the country operated for some time on a temporary budget; this also added to the inflationary cycle. The new budget was unbalanced from the beginning. Government workers fought fiercely for salary raises and were only stopped by an order from GHQ on July 31, 1948. Even without the Nishio (or Shōwa Denkō) scandal, which became the immediate cause for the fall of the Ashida Cabinet, it was already doomed from the point of view of economic policy.

A review of the economic policies of these two cabinets shows what great limitations were imposed on the SDP because of its weak position in the coalitions. It had to compromise its policies so much that it alienated its most overt supporters—organized labor—and when even

10. The so-called Draper Mission was led by William H. Draper, Jr., then Undersecretary of the Army. He was accompanied by a high-level economic advisory group under the chairmanship of Percy H. Johnston (Chairman of the Chemical Bank and Trust Company), which included Paul G. Hoffman (Chairman of Studebaker Corporation and subsequently Economic Cooperation Administrator), Robert F. Loree (Chairman of the National Trade Council), and other businessmen and officials. The report is sometimes called the Draper Report.

these policies failed the SDP became the main target for blame. Nor did the Cabinets survive long enough to realize any possible good results from their policies. In terms of maintaining an unsullied reputation, the left wing was probably correct in insisting that the party should not join the coalition governments. However, the party very likely rendered a service in muting class conflicts both by restraining labor and by moderating conservative policies. The Katayama Cabinet inherited the herculean task of stemming the spiral of inflation that the previous Yoshida Cabinet had actually encouraged. But its price and wage ceilings were only stopgaps, since the real cause lay in the dearth of industrial production, on the one hand, and government expenditures, on the other. The use of governmental subsidies involved in the priority production system did eventually promote industrial recovery but at the expense of labor's livelihood, since wages did not overtake price increases. The SDP's participation in the Ashida Cabinet only added to the growing unpopularity of the party, without giving it any achievements to put before the electorate.

DODGE-LINE DISINFLATION

Once again in opposition, the SDP had to make fundamental revisions in policies because of economic changes in the next phase which lasted until effects of the Korean War began to be felt in the fall of 1950. In the first place, SCAP policies invoked the so-called Dodge Line, a thoroughgoing austerity program aimed at a sound Japanese economy based on a competitive price structure with enterprises deprived of governmental subsidies and compelled to cover costs of production by realistic pricing.[11] It was actually a further extension of the basic change of policy that had resulted from the Draper Mission, a shift of emphasis from demilitarization and democratization to reconstruction. The Dodge Line differed from the Draper recommendations in putting stabilization of the economy before industrial reconstruction rather than relying on increasing industrial production in order to overcome inflationary instability.

The Yoshida government followed the Dodge Line dutifully, if grudgingly, and with considerable success in halting inflation. Since

11. Mr. Joseph M. Dodge, a prominent Detroit banker, was sent to Tokyo in February 1949 to observe and make recommendations concerning rehabilitation of the Japanese economy. He was appointed Special Financial Adviser to SCAP and as such had sweeping powers in formulating and supervising what became known as the Dodge Line.

the deficit budget was considered a major cause of inflation, subsidies for price control were to be financed by taxes. A mission headed by Dr. Carl S. Shoup was invited by SCAP to recommend reforms in Japan's system of taxation, with a view to obtaining the maximum tax revenue without reducing the gross national product.[12] In order to increase exports, a uniform exchange rate of 360 yen to the dollar was established. Together with these deflationary measures, the recession in the United States, and the depreciation of the pound sterling by the United Kingdom (setting in motion measures in other countries) helped to reduce imports relative to exports. Though the latter in 1949 were only some 60 per cent of imports, this was a great improvement over previous years when they were only about 38 per cent. Meanwhile, the United States continued to extend unilateral economic aid to Japan and, in order to insure more responsible expenditure of these funds, instituted the U.S. Counterpart Fund for Japan as recommended by Dodge.

Despite such aid, the abandonment of the multiple exchange rate of the yen for domestic and foreign transactions and the stricture on credit caused much suffering, particularly among the mass of small and medium-sized enterprises, many of which failed. Farmers, too, were hit. The further rationalization of industry, which was also part of the Dodge plan, caused large-scale reductions in employment, a trend which was coupled with the "Red purge." Naturally the SDP tried to strengthen itself by voicing widespread discontent with these policies; insofar as such freedom was allowed, the party increased its criticism both of the ruling conservatives and of United States Occupation policies.

The SDP shift from being "pro-American" during the Katayama government to criticizing the Occupation, especially with regard to the American proposal of a separate peace, was a gradual one. For instance, the opposition party's attitude toward MacArthur's nine-point economic stabilization directive to Prime Minister Yoshida in December 1948 was one of support because it would enable the Japa-

12. The Shoup Mission, consisting of seven financial experts, made a detailed study, four volumes in length, with recommendations that have resulted in a revolution in the tax system in Japan, transforming it from a basically Continental European type to an Anglo-American system in which national and local taxes are separated. For a detailed, if very laudatory, explanation of the Shoup Mission Recommendation, see Saburo Shiomi, *Japan's Finance and Taxation: 1940–1956* (New York, Columbia University Press, 1957), Chaps. 4 to 6.

nese to rebuild their country more independently, but Socialists warned against its being implemented in such a way as to strengthen the old ruling classes at the sacrifice of the working masses.[13] A year later the tone of SDP policies had changed to warn more strenuously against monopoly capital taking advantage of the Dodge Line, an oblique attack on that policy itself.[14] This change of tone reflected the rise of the left wing within the SDP. Also, in its weakened condition after the drastic reduction in Diet representation in the election of January 1949, its economic policies became less concrete and more radical in nature.

The outbreak of war in Korea brought about a new phase of Japanese economic development as well as new political and international problems which were to affect profoundly the Japanese Socialist movement, shattering its unity for a time and reorienting its attitudes, particularly toward relations with the United States. Japan became a strategic base of operations and a logistic source of supply for goods and services needed in prosecuting the war. The latter were paid for by United States special procurement funds, which flowed like a transfusion into the arteries of the economy, enabling production to increase. This growth found ready markets abroad, and the volume of exports rocketed. Not only did Japanese productive capacity expand but the economic structure shifted in the direction of a growth in war industries and especially development of the largest enterprises (in Socialist terms "monopoly capitalism").

The Social Democratic Party was gradually impressed by the magnitude of special procurement which amounted to $646 million in the two years after July 1950. Fear of excessive economic dependence on the United States became a theme in party statements. This was the main tenet of the party's first attempt to frame economic policies in the form of a "plan." On November 20, 1950, the SDP Economic Four-Year Plan was announced. Drawn up with the cooperation of scholars outside the party, it did not go into detail but only indicated the direction of envisaged development: (1) stabilization (through full employment, raised standards of living, and social security); (2) com-

13. See *Shakai Shimbun* (Socialist News), Jan. 13, 1949. Also see Nihon Shakaitō, "Dai Gokai Kokkai Tōsō Hōshin" (Struggle Policy for the Fifth Session of the National Diet).

14. See Nihon Shakaitō, "Dai Rokkai Rinji Taikai ni Okeru Tōmen no Nimmu to Tōsō Mokuhyō" (The Present Tasks and Struggle Aims at the Sixth Emergency Convention) [Tokyo, 1949].

mercial expansion in more "normal" channels; and (3) curbing capitalism to create an independent, peace-loving state. Later these basic ideas were to take on a more anti-American twist, interpreting "normal" trade as including Communist China and "peace-loving" as being opposed to American efforts to rearm Japan.[15]

THE STRUGGLE FOR ECONOMIC AND POLITICAL INDEPENDENCE

Differences in attitude toward the way in which Japan regained political independence by the San Francisco Peace Treaty, signed in September 1951, conduced with other factors to split the SDP in the following month. The resulting two Socialist parties differed on almost all political and ideological issues, and yet an underlying area of agreement on practical economic questions remained to help bridge their cleavage and provide some basis for rapprochement.

Uneasiness characterized the nation's economic outlook as it regained its status as a sovereign state, with many lingering restraints. The Korean War boom petered out when that struggle reached a stalemate and peace negotiations were protracted. The world market tightened up, and many an industry in Japan found itself overexpanded. Imports still far exceeded exports. In order to redress the imbalance, the Yoshida government instituted a sound money policy in the fall of 1953 which reduced industrial production by March 1954 and continued into 1955 before its fundamental success became apparent. Meanwhile, deflation and tight money brought bankruptcy to a large number of small and medium manufacturing and commercial enterprises; unemployment became fairly serious.

Doubt about the future impelled the Socialists to think in terms of the need for long-range economic planning and integration of their various disparate economic policies. Attempts by each Socialist party spurred the other to action. This tendency was later accelerated as, with each electoral advance, the dream of gaining national control (with both wings in coalition or united) became brighter; the Socialists wanted to assure the electorate that they were practical enough to work out detailed, high-level economic policies.

The Right Socialists took the first step, approving a "Five-Year Plan

15. This plan was submitted to the Emergency Convention of the party in 1950 under the title "The Road to Peace and Economic Stability: A New Post-Treaty Economic Outline." See the mimeographed document: "Heiwa to Seikatsu Antei e no Michi: Kōwago no Shin Keizai Yōkō."

for Economic Reconstruction" at their national convention on January 18, 1953.[16] This envisaged greater industrialization, full employment, and an elevated standard of living in five years by tax reforms, planned foreign trade, and national operation of special financial agencies, electricity, steel, coal, and chemical fertilizer industries, as well as labor union participation in management. On October 3, 1953, the same party published an "Economic Policy to Conquer the Recession."[17] This dealt with the current recession, but, being based on a long and detailed analysis of the nation's economic problems, it discerned solutions only in terms of more fundamental, long-term policies. It detected in the high cost of commodities in Japan, compared to international free market prices, the main cause for flagging exports which brought on the recession. It argued that big business, because of the way capitalism had developed in Japan and its dependence on special procurement, was incapable of cutting costs without drastic effects on employees, subcontractors, and domestic purchasing power. It therefore proposed working through the state by nationalization of electricity, the Bank of Japan, and the life insurance business, and state management of coal mining, steel, shipbuilding, and the chemical fertilizer industries. It also advocated emphasis on trade with Southeast Asia rather than predominantly with the United States.

The Left SDP Policy Planning Board, headed by Hiroo Wada, a former confidant of Shigeru Yoshida and chief of the Economic Stabilization Board under the Katayama Cabinet, published, on September 2, 1953, a "Five-Year Plan for the Construction of a Peace Economy," subtitled "Challenging MSA [Mutual Security Aid]."[18] It was not a comprehensive economic plan. As the subtitle intimates, the prime objective of this plan was to free Japan from economic (and politico-military) dependence on the United States in such forms as

16. See *Asahi Shimbun,* January 11, 1953; also (Right) Nihon Shakaitō, *Ikani Shite Keizai Saiken Suru ka: Keizai Saiken Gokanen Keikaku* (How Can Economic Reconstruction Be Done?: A Five-Year Plan for Economic Reconstruction) (Tokyo, Nihon Shakaitō Shuppambu, Feb. 1, 1953).

17. See *Asahi Shimbun,* October 4, 1953; also (Right) Nihon Shakaitō Seisaku Shingikai, *Ikani Shite Fukyō o Kokufuku Suru ka: Nihon Shakaitō Kihon Keizai Seisaku* (How to Conquer the Recession: The Basic Economic Policies of the Social Democratic Party of Japan) (Tokyo, Nihon Shakaitō Shuppambu, Oct. 11, 1953).

18. See *Asahi Shimbun,* Sept. 3, 1953; also (Left) Nihon Shakaitō Seisaku Shingikai, *MSA ni Chōsen Shite: Heiwa Keizai Kensetsu Gokanen Keikaku* (Challenging MSA: A Five-Year Plan for the Construction of a Peace Economy) (Tokyo, Nihon Shakaitō Shuppambu, Sept. 2, 1953).

MSA and special procurement, and it opposed the trend toward partial remilitarization of the economic structure. It supported Sōhyō's call for a "National Conference on a Peaceful Economy." It also sought to achieve full employment, build up social security, raise the standard of living, and reorient the economy toward production of peacetime goods. These things were to be done by the establishment of a minimum wage, nationalization of basic industries and financial institutions (in various forms), modernization through the fostering of co-operatives in agriculture and small and medium industry, and the expansion of trade outside the dollar area, especially with the People's Republic of China and the Soviet Union.

Although these two economic "plans" were in some respects similar, differences of emphasis were apparent. The Left SDP saw the greatest danger in Japan's economic (and politico-military) involvement with American capitalism, which it considered to be expansive, aggressive, basically unstable, and for these reasons apt to precipitate a world war. Its spokesmen estimated that the possibilities of commercial expansion with other capitalistic countries were slight due to the prevalent dollar shortage. Only in greater trade with the Communist bloc did they discern a solution.

The Right Socialists, on the other hand, considered stabilization of the economy possible without such a radical shift in foreign relations, although they strongly urged elimination of the "China differential" between the severely restrictive China Committee (CHINCOM) list of embargoed items in trade with China and the somewhat less restrictive Coordinating Committee (COCOM) list of proscribed items in trade with the Soviet bloc.[19] They stressed an increase of trade with Southeast Asia. The Right wing also placed greater stress on increasing worker productivity, a sore point with the Left because of Sōhyō's opposition to what it termed exploitation by speedup. The recession, in the eyes of the Right SDP, was caused mainly by the high costs of production in comparison with countries which were Japan's competitors in the world market. Although the Right SDP looked forward

19. In July 1957, the Japanese government, following Britain's lead, in effect unilaterally did away with the "differential" by announcing a list of 272 previously banned items whose shipment to Communist China would thereafter be allowed. This was one of many examples of a conservative government in Japan taking an action originally advocated by the Socialists. This does not necessarily mean the Socialists have always been right, because the question of timing is extremely important, but it does indicate a trend of responsible thinking by the Socialists, or at least thinking in terms of realities.

to the eventual elimination of special procurement, it did not advocate immediate withdrawal of it as the Left had. Both factions, however, agreed in opposing any increase in the defense budget in the wake of the official decision to accept Mutual Security Aid. In fact, both called for a reduction of self-defense expenditures, adhering to the slogan "butter before guns."

Another development in the direction of more concrete economic policies was the practice of the Socialists, as opposition parties, of drawing up each spring an alternative national budget to the one proposed by the government. It was ironically the Left SDP, so often criticized for its lack of practicality, that started this in 1953. Until 1961, the parties cooperated in drafting an alternative budget for every regular and supplemental budget submitted by the government. This can be counted as one of the important joint activities which facilitated the reunification of the factions in 1955.

A continuing characteristic of these alternative budgets was the smaller proposed appropriation for defense expenditures than the government earmarked each time. With the money "saved" in this category, the Socialists could "appropriate" more for social security or whatever they considered to be more important. For instance, the joint SDP alternative budget for 1954 proposed allocating only ¥25 billion for the National Safety Board compared with the government's proposal of ¥74 billion.[20]

It was significant that both Socialist parties were beginning to respond to Japan's economic problems after independence in more practical ways and more in liaison with each other. In April 1954 they published an agreement on steps toward reunification and in November an outline of new policies the two would jointly promote if they should be able to form a coalition Socialist government.[21] Other examples of increased cooperation on economic policies included Left

20. On this item a paper agreement had been reached which only served to hide a conflict of opinion. The Right SDP, which approved of maintaining a minimum force about the size of the former Police Reserve, interpreted the ¥25 billion as the cost of supporting a reduced Safety Force. However, the Left SDP interpreted this same item as the cost of disbanding the Safety Force altogether, as that party considered the whole force useless. If the parties had been in power at that time, this could have proved to be a thorny problem.

21. See "Ryōsha Tōitsu Kōshōi Seisaku Kyōtei" (Joint SDP Unification Negotiations Committee Policy Agreement), *Jōhō Tsūshin,* No. 97, and "Ryōsha Kyōdō Seiken-ka no Shin Seisaku Taikō" (An Outline of New Policies for a Joint SDP Coalition Government), ibid., No. 121.

SDP support for Right-wing proposals in the Diet early in 1955 for a Department Store Law and a Subcontractors Payment Adjustment Law, both of which were designed to protect small and medium-scale enterprises against unfair practices by large companies.

AN EXPORT BOOM AND THEN RETRENCHMENT

The recession which had followed the Korean War boom began to fade in the middle of 1954, responding to retrenchment at home and general European recovery. Stockpiles accumulated during, and lowered commodity prices brought about by, that recession enabled Japanese exports to gain markedly in relation to imports during the latter half of 1954, as well as in 1955 and 1956. In the latter year, the Suez incident temporarily gave Japan a great advantage over the West in Asian markets. The result was an industrial boom without undue inflation. In 1955, Japan's international balance of payments achieved a remarkable credit balance of $535 million. This was a far cry from 1953, when Japan's balance of payments had been in the red, even with special procurement. This improvement could not be overlooked by the Socialists.

Like all booms, this one in 1955–56 also came to an end with the deterioration in Japan's external position in 1957–58. If the boom in 1953 had been largely one of domestic consumption, this so-called "Jimmu boom" was characterized by domestic investment. The increase in investments had invited too many imports relative to exports, and the government hastily resumed a policy of retrenchment in 1957. Some observers believe that Japanese policy makers have now come to understand the links between short-term economic stability and long-term economic growth and are determined not to let the rate of investment far outrun the rate of savings, in order to prevent any dangerous deterioration in Japan's external accounts. Nevertheless, the recession continued until early 1959, and Japan's basic economic difficulties remained. In some respects the economy had not yet recovered prewar levels. For instance, the volume of exports in 1956 was only 86 per cent of the 1931–36 average, while the volume of imports surpassed the earlier average by 14 per cent. If population increase and world standards of living are taken into consideration, it could be estimated that Japan had only a little more than half recovered its prewar position in international trade.[22]

22. See Cohen, *Japan's Postwar Economy*, pp. 217–18.

The Japanese Socialists responded to these changes by thinking in terms of longer range, better integrated policies. They achieved organizational reunification on October 13, 1955, only after spending the previous summer not only forging their new ideological program but also hammering out a fifteen-year economic program. This, they claimed, would reorganize the structure of the Japanese economy, enabling it to achieve independence in five years and in the subsequent ten-year span to achieve full employment and a higher national standard of living by means of nationalizing important industries and central banking institutions. In the latter part of 1956, the basic five-year plan based on government statistics, was worked out in detail. It won approval at the 13th party convention in January 1957 and remained the basis of economic policies until 1960, since which time the SDP has had to reconsider policies in the light of a still greater surge of prosperity and growth. While Communist planning and frenetic efforts were encountering serious difficulties in mainland China, a "great leap" was being achieved by Japanese capitalism.

6. Socialist Economic Planning for 1957–1961 and Beyond

The reunited Socialists' five-year plan, as the first component of a fifteen-year program, was their most serious and comprehensive economic effort up to 1957, when it was adopted in convention and printed.[1] Its prospectus explained what was obstructing Japan's economic development, why the government's five-year plan was inadequate, and in general what could be expected if national policies were to conform to this Socialist plan. Also, the SDP appended four specific legislative measures designed to achieve immediate reform of tax structure and incidence, local financial reconstruction, a minimum wage, and protection of domestic labor.

The main body of the scheme was subdivided into four sections: (1) In the first, after explaining that Japan and its surrounding waters

1. Nihon Shakaitō, *Dai Jūsankai Teiki Taikai Kettei Shū: Seisaku Hen* (Resolutions of the Thirteenth Regular Convention: Policies Section) (Tokyo, Nihon Shakaitō Shuppambu, 1957); hereafter called *Kettei Shū*. The core of the plan is presented in pp. 23–190. Slightly more than one eighth of its space is devoted to tables of statistics; most of the figures of the base year 1954 were taken from official sources and corresponded in part with those used in the government's "Five-Year Plan for Economic Independence." See ibid., pp. 141–45, and "Keizai Jiritsu Gokanen Keikaku," published by the Economic Planning Agency in December 1955.

The organization of the SDP plan suggests that one intended use was by campaigners. On a given topic, such as tax proposals, relevant material is to be found in as many as five places, giving rise to some confusion and repetition.

were actually "rich" if advanced scientific means were used to exploit available resources, the point was made that the nation's industrial base could be tremendously expanded if attention were paid not only to giant companies but also to the massive sector of small enterprises. And new possibilities were foreseen in the development of nuclear energy. (2) Emphasis was next placed on expanding trade in order to achieve economic independence and to increase employment. (3) Another section dealt with stabilizing and raising levels of consumption by improvement of laboring conditions, social security, and housing, as well as tax redistribution and cultural development. (4) Such institutional reforms as revision of treaties, democratization of industry, socialization, and the fostering of cooperatives were urged. And finally (5), there was stress on financial policies which could provide credit for economic expansion on all levels.

Four salient spheres of economic policy have been chosen from the SDP plan for exposition and evaluation here. Proposals for labor, agriculture and small business will be reserved for later chapters on those subjects.[2]

FOREIGN TRADE

Even though the expansion of Japan's domestic markets has made that nation dependent on foreign trade to a somewhat lesser extent than is commonly thought, still the viability of its economy depends upon commerce to a degree equaled by few other countries. This holds true whether the ruling regime be socialist or conservative. The Socialists, however, wish to alter greatly the pattern of trade as one means to achieve "independence." In their view Japan should have been freed from special economic ties with the United States, symbolized by such conditions as special procurement, aid from American agricultural surpluses, and a usually unfavorable balance of trade. In the years since the Socialist five-year plan was formulated, a number of related economic gains have indicated that some of the Party's proposed objectives are well on the way to being achieved by other means or by concessive conservative policies. For example, between 1952–53 and 1958, reductions in U.S. military procurement and growth of other earnings brought down the percentage of total exchange receipts accounted for by special procurement from nearly 40 per cent

2. See Chaps. 10–12.

to less than 14 per cent. The SDP, however, called for termination of such military purchasing by 1958. The balance of trade with the United States has grown less unfavorable to Japan, and in the latter half of 1959 it was briefly in balance. To prove their neutrality in the cold war the Socialists advocate trade on both sides of the iron and bamboo curtains.

In bold figures, the SDP plan set the target for exports at $3,280 million and imports at $3,300 million by 1961. Both figures constituted approximately a doubling of values as compared with the base year 1954. Thus, the plan asserted, within five years the balance of international payments, without special procurement, could be attained at the $3,600 million level. This was considerably above the government party's five-year target of $2,964 million. Under conservative governments, Japan has since 1955 much improved its position as regards foreign exchange and balance of payments.

The Socialist plan gave various figures for the redirection of trade so as to reduce Japan's one-sided dependence on the United States. These involved augmenting trade with Communist China and other Asian nations. In simple terms, the targets of redistributed trade called for apportionment of Japan's total commerce as follows: 17 per cent with North America; 23 per cent with Southeast Asia; also 23 per cent with China; and 37 per cent with all others.[3] When the plan was drafted in 1956, Japan's actual disposition of trade by areas was: with North America, exports 24.5 per cent and imports 37.5 per cent; with mainland China, exports 2.7 per cent and imports 2.6 per cent; with Taiwan, exports 3.1 per cent and imports 1.4 per cent.[4] In 1957, all of Asia absorbed 40.1 per cent of Japan's exports and supplied 29.1 per cent of its imports.

In order to achieve this redirection the Socialists advocated setting a ceiling of $850 million for trade with North America. (The actual amount spent on imports from the United States alone in 1956 was $1,064 million.) Since the Socialists demanded disassociation of Japan from the CHINCOM list and also a commercial treaty with China (an endeavor that broke down under the conservatives from 1958 to 1960 chiefly because of political problems), they promised to raise Japan's

3. *Kettei Shū,* p. 62. For these figures in dollars, see ibid., p. 130. (Yet notice the contradiction between the figures on imports from North America on pages 62 and 130!)

4. Figures are from Ministry of Foreign Affairs, *Statistical Survey of Economy of Japan 1957* (n.p., n.d.), p. 31.

annual trade with mainland China to some $600 million by the end of five years. This estimate was based on study of Communist China's second five-year plan, one which proved impossible to achieve. Moreover, the Socialists saw opportunities for Japan in the Soviet plan for the development of Siberia, with which they estimated, in five years' time, a $125 million trade could be carried on. Again, the conservatives have been alert to this opportunity and have succeeded in signing advantageous trade agreements with the Soviet Union.

In trade with Southeast Asian and Arab countries, the Socialists maintained that an increase of $400 million could be expected if Japan would expand its exports of machinery and offer technical assistance. By the creation of an Asian Economic Council the plans of all Asian countries could be organically integrated on the basis of mutual cooperation in agriculture, industry, and science.[5] This has been a long-standing, but still elusive, dream of Socialists in Japan and some other Asian countries. The main obstacles have been the incompatibility of communist and traditional capitalist political economies in such an association.

Domestically, the plan called for an increase of exports especially in machine tools and chemicals, since they are most profitable to Japan in terms of obtaining foreign exchange. Then, to prevent the drain of foreign currency through transportation costs, the merchant marine was to be strengthened by building three million gross tons of ocean-going ships.

This, in short, was the Socialists' scheme for trade by 1961. Was it reasonable or was it unrealistically optimistic? Of course, an answer to the question involves many factors, particularly world political and economic conditions. Certain difficulties would have to be overcome if the plan were to be applied as national policy. For example, it would be much more difficult to outgrow Japan's dependence on the United States than the SDP plan indicated. From 1946 to 1958, Japan was buying about twice as much as it was able to sell to the United

5. This was in accordance with a resolution adopted at the founding Congress of the Asian Socialist Conference in Rangoon, January 1953. See (Right) Nihon Shakaitō, Kokusai Kyoku, *Ajia no Dōkō to Sekai Heiwa: Dai Ikkai Ajia Shakaitō Kaigi no Hōkoku* (Asian Trends and World Peace: A Report of the First Congress of the Asian Socialist Conference) (Tokyo, Nihon Shakaitō Shuppambu, 1954), p. 63. See also *Yearbook of the International Socailist Labor Movement: 1956–1957*, ed. Julius Braunthal, under the auspices of the Socialist International and the Asian Socialist Conference (London, 1956), p. 86.

TABLE 1. U.S.-JAPANESE TRADE BALANCES IN RELATION TO U.S. AID AND SPECIAL PROCUREMENT

(in thousands of dollars)

	Exports[a]	*Imports*[a]	*Balance*	*U.S. Aid*[b]	*Special Procurements*[c]
1946	77,437	297,688	−220,251	192,892[d]	—
1948	65,758	441,381	−375,623	461,003	—
1950	179,297	418,236	−237,939	357,298	148,889[e]
1952	229,167	768,291	−539,124	—	824,168
1954	276,844	846,941	−570,097	—	596,164
1956	543,306	1,064,540	−521,234	—	594,400

a. Based on customs clearance statistics.
b. Sum of aid imports and released military goods.
c. Special procurement in the broader sense.
d. 1945–1946.
e. From July through December.

Source: National Economic Research Institute, supplied especially for "Studies of Japan's Social Democratic Parties."

States. This resulted in large deficits ($570 million in 1954, $323 million in 1955, and $521 million in 1956), which were made up only by abnormal special procurement and by other forms of aid from the United States, as may be seen in Table 1. While Japanese Socialists called for increasing exports to the United States (demanding U.S. tariff reductions), the restoration of convertibility of currency, and even triangular trade among the United States, Southeast Asia and Japan, they placed little hope in any of these. Their main remedy was, and still is, redirection of trade. Actually, however, the balance of Japanese trade has improved in those other respects since 1956, and convertibility was partly inaugurated by the second government under Kishi from July 1, 1960.

The left-wing Socialist view that the key to Japan's economic salvation lies in the vast market of mainland China, dominated the five-year plan. To what degree trade with China can develop has been a topic of keen controversy. It did little good to note that China took about 18 per cent of Japanese exports between 1930 and 1937 and furnished Japan with about 12 per cent of its imports, compared to 1.6 and 3.6 per cent respectively in 1948, because, while these years were somewhat "normal" compared to those immediately after 1938 and after 1949, the earlier trade was largely conditioned by political factors. Before the war, Japanese arms and pressure on the Chinese customs system squeezed out concessions and brought about reactions (boycotts) to such a degree that the free play of economic forces was narrow indeed.

Confining the discussion to political and economic conditions in the early 1960s, there was still great divergence of opinion about the degree to which this trade could develop. Perhaps, influenced by differing political climates, Japanese scholars in general have held a more sanguine view of potential trade with mainland China than have most American experts. The arguments against increasing trade with Communist China have been of two kinds: that it is not desirable and that it is not possible to any great extent. The former argument first has pointed out that China engages in state trading, whereas private Japanese sellers must vie with each other to sell and are therefore at a disadvantage. Furthermore, since China's trade is determined more on political than on economic bases, after Japan became heavily dependent on this trade the Communist authorities could suddenly terminate it or could threaten to do so for further advantages. (Some Japanese have replied that, in that case, at least they could return to the present pattern of markets. In certain industries, however, technological problems would be caused by such drastic shifts.)

Economically, the argument has been that China does not really have the means to pay for imports from Japan. Bootstrap economic development in the People's Republic entails squeezing agriculture, but the amount of foreign exchange from this source is limited; China's trade for a decade was mainly oriented toward the Red bloc, and its burden of payments on past loans has, until 1965, been heavy. Only since its internal crisis and rift with the Soviet Union has its trade begun to be more diversified. Its own industrial development has absorbed most of its coking coal and iron ore. China needs long-term credits, but Japan should be wary of financial entanglement; otherwise the latter might find itself pressured unduly like Ceylon, which has extended credits to China in return for importation of Ceylonese rubber. Finally it has been pointed out that West Germany and Britain could probably outbid Japan for what market has existed in China, while China, showing unexpected vigor during its first five-year plan became at least briefly a rival of Japan in Southeast Asia.[6]

6. Most of these arguments can be found in expanded form, with citations to other works, in Cohen, *Japan's Postwar Economy*, pp. 171–90.

The Socialists have replied by turning some of these arguments inside out. They have said they were aware of the dangers of the political use of trade by the Chinese Communists, but they planned to organize Japanese foreign trade so that it could more easily be redirected and also so that small business would not be at such a disadvantage as at present. According to left-wing Socialists, the very fact that China has a socialist, planned economy would, in the long run, make it a more stable partner than a capitalist economy with its cyclical fluctuations. They have urged political concessions in time for Japan to compete in the China market with West Germany and Britain, and they have argued that the more business Japan has with China, the more Japanese businessmen will know about conditions there and be able to anticipate Chinese competition in Southeast Asia. As for China's ability to pay, they have pointed to the rapid tempo of China's industrialization during the first plan. Failure of Red China's "great leap" and subsequent applications for credits have weakened but not deterred Socialist insistence. The agreements with China which they have helped to arrange have been on a strictly barter basis so that Japan has obtained concurrent deliveries, rather than incurring credits as it has in trade with Indonesia.

Arbitrary cancellation by Communist China in April 1958 of the proposed $196 million fourth trade agreement, over what the Japanese government considered a "trivial" incident, demonstrated that Communist China places national prestige above its necessity to trade with Japan; but trade with Communist China would be a built-in economic necessity had the SDP five-year plan, as formulated, been invoked. Also, the barter system has been used by China to exert pressure on Japan to relax the CHINCOM embargo list. Even in the proposed fourth trade agreement, which stipulated only two instead of three commodity categories, there was to be bartering of strategic and less strategic items for their respective counterparts.[7] This hampered trade flexibility but may have been regarded as only a temporary

7. A copy of the agreement may be found in *Asahi Shimbun,* March 6, 1958. In the first category, exports from China were to include: soya beans, coal, iron ore, manganese, pig iron, and tin; and from Japan: railroad cars and parts, electric generators, ships, several kinds of large refining machinery, various types of manufacturing plants, copper ore, aluminum materials, various types of steel sheets and tubes, tin-plate sheets, and various types of iron sheets. In the second category came everything else: from China, rice and other foodstuffs, wool, pig bristles; and from Japan, general machine tools, chemical fertilizers, medical drugs, textiles, and other consumer goods.

measure, since Southeast Asian nations have been moving away from barter to trade based on clearing payment of monetary balances.

Although the SDP five-year plan aimed at an increase in trade with mainland China amounting to a total value of $600 million after five years,[8] other Japanese scholars put the possible maximum of exports to their larger neighbor at closer to $250 million.[9] Thus, contrary to the SDP plan, the hope of remedying the then existing dollar shortage through trade with Communist China could be only a limited one. It should not be forgotten that U.S. special procurements alone came to $594 million in 1956. The United States has remained an important source of Japan's needs, for only in the case of coking coal did the higher cost of transportation very seriously affect the competitive cost.[10] Nevertheless, aside from the political questions involved, the economic basis for fairly significant increase in trade with mainland China exists and, if Japan could obtain some of the raw materials from China which it now buys from the United States—while at the same time maintaining or increasing its exports to the latter country—Japanese-American trade could approach a more normal balance.

The proportion of trade designated by the SDP for Southeast Asia (23 per cent) had been approximated by 1956. Consequently the opposition has found the issue of increasing trade with that area less appealing. In 1957, Prime Minister Kishi made a tour of the area, and in December a reparations agreement with Indonesia was arranged; one with South Vietnam was later concluded. Overall Socialist goals in this area appeared to be realistic, since there were serious limitations to commercial expansion resulting from such conditions as generally low purchasing power (per capita incomes being far below Japanese standards), the region's continuing reliance on foreign aid and credits, lack of foreign exchange reserves—especially in dollars,

8. In China's second five-year plan, basic investment was intended to amount to $40 billion in five years. Some 40% of this was to be for the importation of capital goods (machinery). Some 30%, or $4.8 billion, was to be spent outside the Communist bloc. The SDP expected that Japan could supply half the non-bloc goods. The value of this trade in the first year would amount to $150 million and after five annual increases a total of $600 million would be reached. This was wishful, because Japan would have had to compete with West Germany and Britain, among others, for China's non-bloc trade. See *Kettei Shū*, p. 63.

9. This is according to Hidezō Inaba, "Nihon Shakaitō no Keizai Seisaku no Hyōka" (An Evaluation of Economic Policies of the Social Democratic Party of Japan), 2, 41, an unpublished report to Studies on Japan's Social Democratic Parties.

10. Cohen, *Japan's Postwar Economy*, p. 183.

ties with former metropolitan countries, lingering anti-Japanese feeling, and the fragmentation of markets. These are some of the problems the Japanese Socialists could well study before proposing ways to overcome the increasing competition in the area from West Germany, Britain, France, and Communist China. The Socialists also may have a role to play in the region in calming fears of resurgent Japanese imperialism. Because of its higher rate of capital accumulation, Japan increased its financial stake in that area through joint enterprises, technical assistance arrangements, loans, and investments.

SDP trade policies derive from socialist insistence that the increase of trade with the Sino-Soviet bloc will bring into balance Japanese-U.S. trade and that the elimination of special procurement and military aid would achieve independence and peace. Clearly the Socialists have needed to give much more thought to the logic as well as to the facts of their position. Because their plan depends on an integrated development of the whole economy, we must consider other important policies before passing judgment.

FISCAL POLICIES

The opposition practice, from 1953 to 1961, of submitting a joint alternative to the government's budget almost every year helped the Socialists to consider fiscal policies in a more concrete manner. In 1957 this tradition was interrupted, however. After the draft alternative budget drawn up by the Policy Planning Board became known, the Council of Government Workers' Unions (Kankōrō) demanded that it include a raise for civil servants' salaries, and the Japan Farmers' Union demanded that it peg the producers' price of rice higher. As such last minute demands would throw the whole budget out of kilter, the party in confusion decided not to introduce an alternative budget at that session of the Diet. This experience was repeated in the spring of 1958. The party's excuse was that the government's budget was so inadequate that it had been impossible to construct an alternative one based upon it!

Such incidents do not augur well for the time when the party might come to power, because they reveal how subject the Policy Planning Board has been to pressure from supporting organizations and how, in national perspective, the interests of pressure groups often present contradictions.

Confusion has also existed as to whether the purpose of the alternative budget was to put through amendments to the government's budget or whether it was to show what the SDP would do if it were in power. Two alternative budgets, one to serve each of these purposes, were actually drawn up in 1957, but due to the incident just mentioned they were both withdrawn. A later tactic designed to overcome this dilemma was for the party to submit to the government, before formulation of its budget, a set of detailed SDP demands, omitting figures, which the party asked to have incorporated into the budget. This was first done for the budget of 1958. Although it is still unclear how much the government took Socialist demands into consideration, such a practice might serve to promote smoother operation of the two-main-party system.

An examination of past SDP alternative budgets reveals certain persistent characteristics. With regard to revenue, they include a reduction of the tax burden on lower income strata by raising the level of exemptions and by making the income tax more progressive, a decrease in corporation taxes on small and medium enterprises and instead an excess profits tax on big business, and a lessening of indirect taxes, except on luxury items. With respect to expenditures, Socialists have repeatedly advocated elimination or drastic reduction of defense outlay, a sharp increase in expenditures for social security, unemployment relief, public works, housing projects, and in providing credit for small businesses.

Attempts to equalize the distribution of wealth by means of fiscal policy can be clearly discerned. Such attempts flow from socialist ideology, as we have seen. Moreover, though there have been especially notable gains in personal incomes and consumer expenditures since 1955, there has also been a growing gap between the gains of people at high and low levels of income. The question arises, however, as to whether such equalization as the Socialists have proposed would slow down overall economic growth in comparison with the conservatives' program. For an answer, we shall have to look at SDP tax policies more closely, because taxes would constitute the main source of revenue for financing any Socialist policies.

The SDP five-year plan proposed to reduce the high ratio of national taxes to revenue from 93 per cent in 1954 to 90 per cent in 1961, as may be seen in Table 2. Similarly, the proportion of local taxes to national income would be reduced from 5.8 to 4.8 per cent in the same period—a smaller decrease favoring local government. Tax exemption

TABLE 2. THE TARGET COMPOSITION OF THE GENERAL ACCOUNT OF THE SDP FIVE-YEAR PLAN BUDGET FOR 1961 COMPARED WITH THE 1954 GOVERNMENT BUDGET

(in millions of yen)

	1954		*1961*	
A. National Income	*6,103,400*	*(100%)*	*10,737,300*	*(176%)*[d]
B. General account revenues	999,800	(100%)	1,567,600	(100%)
Taxes, revenue stamps, and profits from the Japan Monopoly Corporation	934,000	(93%)	1,410,600	(90%)
Other revenues	65,800	(7%)	156,700	(10%)
B/A	*16.3%*		*13.1%*	
C. General account expenditures	999,800	(100%)	1,567,600	(100%)
Social security	95,400	(9%)	392,000 (Social security and Pensions combined)	(25%)
Pensions	83,300[a]	(8%)		
Education	117,200	(11%)	203,800	(13%)
Local finances	137,400	(13%)[b]	225,000	(15%)
Public construction (includes housing)	169,600	(17%)	345,000[c]	(22%)
Defense	132,700	(13%)	30,000	(1.9%)
Defense Board	58,400	Nat. Police	30,000	
Defense cost share	74,200		0	
Reparations	10,000	(1%)	35,000	(2.2%)
Miscellaneous	283,700	(28%)	319,000 (Miscellaneous and Adjustment combined)	(21%)
Adjustment	0			

a. On ibid., p. 137, this figure is 81,300.
b. On ibid., p. 138, this figure is 11%.
c. On ibid., this figure is 245,000.
d. Per cent of 1954 income.

Source: "The SDP Five-Year Plan for Economic Construction" (in Japanese), in Nihon Shakaitō, *Dai Jūsankai Teiki Taikai Kettei Shū: Seiji Hen* (Resolutions of the Thirteenth Regular Convention: Political Section) (Tokyo, Nihon Shakaitō Shuppambu, 1957), pp. 110–11.

would be raised to ¥420 thousand a year for a family of five by 1961. (By the tax reform of 1957, the exemption was actually raised only to ¥270 thousand for a family of five.)[11]

More specifically, for 1957—the first year the five-year plan would have been in operation—it promised an exemption of ¥320 thousand

11. *Asahi Shimbun* (evening), Dec. 15, 1957.

for a family of five, with proportional exemptions all along the line. The special exemptions traditional for large corporations, however, would have been abolished. Taxes on small and medium enterprises, on the other hand, would have been reduced to 30 per cent of an annual profit of up to ¥1 million and to 35 per cent up to a profit of ¥2 million.[12] (The actual corporation tax rates were 35 per cent up to an annual profit of ¥1 million and 40 per cent on profits over that amount.)[13] Finally, taxes on *sake* and similar liquors, which the "common people" drink, would be reduced, but new taxes would be placed on luxury goods. The rich would be further affected in various ways, such as by the elimination of prevailing tax exemptions on interest received.

As for local taxes, the five-year plan called for the reduction and readjustment of the inhabitants' tax (*jūmin zei*) for salary earners, the tax on one-man businesses, taxes on small but necessary properties, and taxes on cheap food. But in order to help local government overcome the loss of this revenue, increases were proposed in the local distributive tax (*chihō kōfu zei*) and the tobacco consumption tax which the national government collected and distributed to local governmental jurisdictions.

The plan would thus have reduced the total income tax by ¥85 billion and the total corporation tax by ¥6 billion. To compensate for this, the abolition of special tax exemptions and the institution of new taxes on rich people and luxury goods were calculated to bring in some ¥68 billion. But how great the final loss in tax income might be was not made clear, because figures were not provided for other proposed tax changes.

It is almost certain that tax policies envisioned by the five-year plan would have encountered difficulties if they had been put into effect. Due mainly to the war and subsequent democratization policies, income had been rather drastically redistributed in postwar Japan. The number of people in the higher income brackets had been reduced, while the number of income earners in the lower brackets had swol-

12. See *Kettei Shū,* p. 83. However, if one turns to the appended proposed tax reform for 1957, one finds somewhat different figures. Here, the corporation tax was to be 35% on the first ¥0.5 million of profits, then 37% from there to ¥1 million, and finally 40% for profits above that. Ibid., p. 152.

13. Again, in 1958, the SDP revised its proposed tax rates to a corporation tax of 30% on profits up to ¥0.5 million. See *Tokyo Shimbun,* Feb. 23, 1958.

len.[14] In such a situation, a bearable increase in income taxes on the relatively small number of wealthy probably would not have made up the loss. The projected SDP tax reform, therefore, probably would have resulted in a reduction of governmental revenue. (After the first quarter of 1959, however, when phenomenal economic growth occurred, the Socialist prescription might have fared better, if it would not instead have discouraged such advances.) This further meant that either public expenditure would have to have been reduced, or an SDP government would have had to resort to some such measure as an increase in the issue of government bonds, which would have been inflationary in effect.

It would have been extremely difficult for a Socialist government to reduce expenditures. It would have been committed to raising government workers' salaries, expanding various social security benefits such as unemployment relief, increasing public works, instituting subsidies for the double pricing system for rice and for promoting industry, and aiding chronically ailing local finances. The only area where a big saving could have been effected would have been in defense, but that could not have paid for all the promises, especially with the reduction in tax revenue.

In order to meet this situation, the SDP might well have had to reconsider its position on indirect taxes. It has been traditional for the Japanese Socialists, even before the war, to oppose indirect taxes on non-luxuries, regarding them as "taxation on the masses" (*taishū-zei*). However, given the income distribution before 1960 and the structure of the tax system plus the Socialist needs for revenue, there may have been a limit to the degree indirect taxes could be avoided.

SDP policies regarding taxes on corporations also present a dilemma, for they affect the very important matter of capital formation. A heavy corporation tax would obviously hamper capital accumulation and slow down economic progress. On the other hand, too rapid capital accumulation leads to overinvestment, inducing inflation and thus depressing real wages. If capital formation could be accurately predicted, corporation taxes might be made proportional and thus control the rate, but unfortunately this has not so far been possible. Because of its complexity, the Socialists apparently shelved the subject temporarily, yet obviously the party needs much more study of the whole question of the tax structure.

14. See table on "Distribution of Income During and After World War II" in Shiomi, *Japan's Finance and Taxation*, p. 163.

Not many of the Socialists appeared to have grasped what a ready instrument for controlling capital accumulation they already had in existing institutions. One of the reasons for Japan's high rate of capital formation in recent years has been the fact that the government has been putting about one third of domestic capital accumulation (or 8 per cent of gross national expenditure) into public works and capital equipment for state enterprises. Furthermore, both public and private funds have been mobilized and channeled where needed by an impressive array of public and quasi-public agencies ranging downward from the Bank of Japan to the Small Business Finance Corporation, in addition to the network of some 12,000 agricultural credit cooperatives.

The largest sources of governmentally administered private funds are the people's postal savings and the postal life insurance funds. They provide the government with one of the largest pools of savings in the world for loans and investments, amounting to as much as one fourth of the funds in the whole commercial banking system. In 1954 they amounted to ¥251 billion, but the SDP plan called for encouraging their increase to ¥404 billion by 1961, in addition to which an SDP regime would float a large number of public bonds. (By 1958 the government increased the scale of these fiscal loans and investments to ¥357 billion in addition to which it floated ¥42 billion in public bonds.)[15] The Socialists planned a wide range of uses for these funds. They intended to coordinate them with private investment in hydroelectric power, housing, roads, land development, credit for small and medium industry, promotion of science and technology, purchasing local bonds, and providing subsidies for newly renovated industries. According to opinion within the party, investment for basic industries should be left to private sources whenever possible.[16] The party did, however, advocate the establishment of a central Investment Planning Committee for the purpose of rationalizing investment—in other words to prevent overinvestment in strong industries that needed it least. Party planners considered the democratically administered and

15. *Asahi Shimbun,* Jan. 20, 1958.

16. *Kettei Shū,* p. 111. Later, however, contrary to the five-year plan, the party has advocated the use of these governmental loans and investment funds for the socialization of key industries. See Nihon Shakaitō, *Chōki Keizai Keikaku: Sono Gutaika ni Tsuite* (The Long-Term Economic Plan: With Reference to Making It Concrete) (Tokyo, Nihon Shakaitō Shuppambu, 1957), p. 37. This source also describes more detailed Socialist thinking on the socialization of the Bank of Japan and other financial policies. Ibid., pp. 32–37.

comprehensively planned investment by these means *constituted the core of economic planning.*[17] Apparently the party—at least until the recession of 1958–59—actually had been thinking more in terms of British Labour Party methods than ever before. Nevertheless, judging from the vagueness of SDP policies on investments, it was clear that it had a long way to go in deciding on concrete fiscal policies, especially with regard to relations between public and private enterprise.

Finally, with regard to possible funds available to an SDP government, the controversial question of reducing defense costs could not be avoided. In a later chapter we shall consider it in the foreign policy context; at this point we shall be concerned only with the economic consequences, assuming that reduction might become politically feasible. In such a case, the SDP would face two problems.

First, the saving would not be great. In 1954 only ¥132 billion, or about 2 per cent of the national income, was spent on defense. It constituted about 13 per cent of the national budget in 1959. The SDP plan called for a reduction of this outlay by about ¥100 billion in the five-year period. The right-wing view has prevailed that defense forces would not be entirely eliminated but rather would be reduced to about the size of the former Police Reserve—approximately 75,000 men—which would require some ¥30 billion per year. The plan also foresaw the departure of U.S. security forces (which, with respect to land garrisons, has largely taken place since 1957) and the consequent reduction or elimination of this expense. In any case, since the SDP has planned to reduce the size of the defense force gradually, if and when it attains power, the money saved each year would not be great. Such savings could certainly be diverted to social security and other useful purposes, but even when added to all other sources it could not provide nearly the amount of revenue needed to pay for the planned expenditures.

Secondly, the problem of reemployment for discharged members of the defense force would arise. (In fact, the departure of U.S. land forces has already raised this problem of unemployment with regard to Japanese formerly employed at U.S. barracks and bases.) The five-year plan provided a solution in the proposal for a Peaceful Land Construction Corps (Heiwa Kokudo Kensetsu-tai), an organization

17. See Nihon Shakaitō Hombu, *Yobō ni Kotaete: Nihon Shakaitō Taikai Kettei Shū* (Responding to the People's Trust: Resolutions of the SDP Convention) (Tokyo, Nihon Shakaitō Shuppambu, 1955), pp. 166–67.

that would be roughly like the Civilian Conservation Corps of the early New Deal era in America. It would consist of some 150,000 men who would engage in reforestation, recovery of cultivable land, construction of dams, roads, and harbors, and help in emergencies as well as disasters. However, the estimated cost would come to ¥165 billion, which is ¥33 billion more than the total defense cost in 1954.[18] There can be no doubt that such an organization would be wealth-producing for the country, rather than an economic drain—as most military expenditures are in economic terms—but the initial outlays for this Corps might well eat up the money the SDP plan counted on using for other purposes. (Another question would be whether the kind of people who would be recruited into the Self-Defense Force would agree to be transferred to reconstruction work.)

Not a very bright picture has been painted of planned revenues for a Socialist government. It appears that the defense savings would quickly be absorbed, the various tax cuts would not be offset by other tax impositions, and funds for investment would only be redirected. In these circumstances, nothing less than a large increase in the gross national product would make planned Socialist expenditures possible. Redirection of trade could offer only moderate improvement of the international balance of payments situation, while imports cannot long be allowed to outrun exports. Therefore, the main hope for increasing production (and thus trade and revenue) under a hypothetical Socialist administration would seem to lie in reorganizing and developing the domestic economy. Unprecedented prosperity since late 1959 has challenged the Socialists in many ways, raising the question whether such rapid growth could have been achieved according to their formulae. Their usual reply is that, under socialism, the widening discrepancies of wealth and income would be avoided; this obviously pertains mainly to distributive patterns.

BASIC INDUSTRIES

Ever since the founding of the SDP, and indeed since the days of its precursors, nationalization of key industries has been a basic policy. Recently, however, outright nationalization has been pushed more into the background in favor of preliminary forms of "socialization." This is due partly to the doubts raised by the ineffectiveness of British

18. See: *Chōki Keizai Keikaku,* p. 87.

Labour Party nationalization after the war in the United Kingdom and also to trends in Japan. As a result of national defeat and Occupation policies, the public sector of the Japanese economy has shrunk until now it is smaller than that of any industrialized country except the United States.[19] Not until the mid-'fifties did the Socialists overcome their loss of confidence from the Katayama coal nationalization fiasco sufficiently to draw up more concrete plans for governmental control of basic industries.

Specifically, the five-year plan advocated the socialization of six key industries: electricity, coal, iron and steel, chemical fertilizers, principal means of land and sea transportation, and cement. Three more categories were later added to this list: other energy fuels (gas, oil, and atomic power), air transportation, and the new industries made possible by scientific advances. According to the plan, industry would be regulated by a separate act which would enable the government to determine what the level of production should be as well as to fix factory, wholesale, and retail prices, give permission for expansion or contraction of facilities, and like controls. A supreme planning committee would be established, composed of representatives of management, labor, related industries, the government, and the public, to advise the government with regard to annual production plans. Each enterprise would have its own management council, but the composition of these councils was not specified.[20]

What did the SDP mean by "socialization" of these key industries? As indicated earlier, much confusion still attends this and similar terms. Nevertheless, the "Outline of the Socialization of Important Industries," passed at the party convention in February 1958, described socialization as a gradual process that would ultimately lead to public ownership of the means of production and to the democratization of industry.[21] Fair compensation would be paid to the former

19. For interesting implications of this statement, see William W. Lockwood, "'The Socialistic Society': India and Japan," *Foreign Affairs, 37* (Oct. 1958), 117–30. Despite this and the capitalistic ideology of the Japanese government, Professor Lockwood suggests that in terms of supplying credit, supporting rice prices, aiding capital accumulation, and providing welfare, Japan is more "socialistic" today than India.

20. *Kettei Shū,* pp. 32–33.

21. "Jūyō Sangyō Shakaika no Kōsō," which may be found in *Chōki Keizai Keikaku,* pp. 21–23. As indicated, this was subsequently passed on by the February convention and may therefore also be found in Nihon Shakaitō, *Heiwa to Shakaishugi no Tame ni: Dai Jūyonkai Zenkoku Taikai Kettei Shū* (For Peace and Socialism: Resolutions of the Fourteenth National Convention) (Tokyo, Nihon Shakaitō Shuppan Sendembu, 1958), pp. 202–05.

owners. Ownership would be either by the central government or by local public bodies. Democratization, it was implied, would entail making management responsible to the popular will, which, under the Socialists, would be expressed in national economic planning. That was why the plan called for democratization of the present public corporations: the Japan Monopoly Corporation (which handles tobacco, salt, and camphor), the Japan Telegraph and Telephone Public Corporation, the Japanese National Railways, the Postal Services, the Broadcasting Corporation of Japan (NHK), and the national finance agencies (such as the People's Finance Corporation, the Housing Loan Corporation, and the Small Enterprise Loan Corporation). A system would be established to supervise and regulate these corporations to make them function more in line with the public interest.

By the party convention of 1958, concrete plans for the socialization of only two of the above-mentioned industries, electricity and coal, had been drawn up.[22] Both plans were approved by the convention. The "Outline of Electric Enterprise Socialization" would place all electric power generation and distribution (except that for self-consumption) under central management in the form of a public corporation.[23] The liabilities of the private companies would be transferred to the national government, and the shareholders would receive "electricity bonds" from the government in return for their holdings in these companies. A Ministry of Power would be set up to administer centrally all forms of motive power; under this an Electric Power Corporation, among others, would be created. For the purpose of "democratizing" management, a central electric power control committee would be formed under the Ministry, and electricity consumers' committees would be set up in each locality.

The "Outline of Coal Mining Socialization" was based on the assumption that all underground resources belong to the people as a whole. Coal, like electricity, would be placed under the supervision of the central government for the purpose of determining production targets, prices, degrees of rationalization of operations, distribution of labor, and other matters related to national planning. The government would aid small- and medium-scale mines to merge into larger

22. *Chōki Keizai Keikaku,* pp. 24–32.

23. This would include the nine big electric power companies, organize them on a regional basis, and also include prefectural public utilities as well as all other electrical enterprises. The nine companies produce about 85% of the electric power generated in Japan.

cooperatives for the sake of efficiency. Financed by the Ministry of Power, a Coal Development Corporation would be created to open up new mining sites and develop backward mines; a Coal Delivery Corporation would centrally handle all purchasing, importing, and selling of coal. For democratic supervision, a central coal control committee would be formed in the Ministry of Power and under it there would be local coal control committees. At the lowest level, each mine would have its own management committee.

Plans for socializing other industries were left for the future. It is significant, however, that the first two to be adopted were for power industries. Part of the impetus for emphasizing these two sources of energy arose from the predicted shortage of electric power relative to demand by rapidly developing industries and from depression and adjustments of the coal industry as many fuel users turn to oil.[24] Apart from immediate considerations, however, the priority system is basic in Socialist economic thinking, because its proponents want to concentrate their efforts in order to be effective. Apparently they have no intention of across-the-board measures for socialization. Even the priority system and socialization itself are thought of only as means to the goal of a comprehensively planned economy.

Would the socialization of key industries actually spur the growth of the Japanese economy? The Socialists' unequivocal answer has been that, if they can effectuate their plan, including industrialization, they could double the output of manufacturing and mining in five years' time. Despite this boast, however, a great many obstacles would stand in the way of achieving their goals. An examination of Socialist plans leaves the impression that they are based more on doctrinaire principles than on careful consideration as to whether socialization would promote greater efficiency.

To make socialization mean more than a paper reform, and also more than the mystical transference of ownership from "private" hands to the "people," would require integration of socialized industries into the economy as a whole in a more rational manner than obtains at present. This would involve expertise not only in specific

24. By the early 'sixties it had become apparent that heavy investments in the development of atomic energy would be required and that production at commercially competitive rates was some way off. Development so far has been by a governmental Atomic Energy Development Corporation cooperating with the three leading electrical corporations.

industries but also with respect to their relations to fiscal policy, labor, the consumers' market, and the economy as a whole. Such competence already exists (at least to a fairly high degree) in major industries. The new planners, however, would have to be more motivated in the public interest and also more powerful in having their influence felt throughout the economy.

This has raised the question among planners: would this mean merely an expansion of the present Japanese bureaucracy? Officialdom has been a prime target of criticism by Japanese intellectuals because of its authoritarianism, rigidity, and conservatism. Its expansion might only mean a heavier burden of taxes on the people and even a decrease in the efficiency of the "socialized" industries. Although the capitalist economy may in some respects be "anarchic" and inefficient in terms of social goals, the price mechanism,[25] where it has some play, helps to do away with uneconomic plant operations. With the disappearance of the play of competitive pressures, inefficiency might hide in the recesses of the giant Japanese bureaucracy. A Socialist government, lacking administrative experience, would be especially dependent upon the specialized knowledge of bureaucrats in order to carry out its policies. It would be difficult for such a government to take drastic measures against bureaucratic inefficiency. A weak SDP government might tend to bargain with bureaucracy, labor unions, and small business groups, promising to raise salaries and postponing the advocated rationalization of the civil services and of certain industries. Unless that party has within its own ranks experts able to deal with the bureaucrats on equal terms of knowledge and experience—hardly the situation at present—and unless it has shown the ability to withstand inflationary demands by pressure groups, it could easily be outmaneuvered, especially in economic policies.

SOCIAL SECURITY

It was chiefly after Japan had formally regained its sovereignty that both the Right and Left Socialists began to be more concerned about integrating welfare policies into a social security system. Their advocacy of more constructive uses for money expended for rearmament reinforced this interest. Another factor was the first report of the So-

25. Related to this term, of course, are calculated profits, interest rates, and rather free operation of the forces of supply and demand.

cial Security System Investigation Board which was published early in 1951. It revealed how small a percentage of the whole population benefited from the various types of public welfare and how unequal and spotty the coverage was. Even at the beginning of 1957, all types of medical and health insurance gave some coverage to only 69.7 per cent of the total population. Government annuity and pension systems of various kinds covered not more than 65 per cent of the total employed, or 29 per cent of the total working population. At the same time, only 5 per cent of the national income was being spent on social security in Japan, compared with 9 per cent for the United Kingdom and 13 per cent for West Germany.[26] In short, Socialist criticism has been correct in characterizing the social security system in Japan as "complete in form but not in content." The test of Socialist constructiveness will partly consist in what they propose by way of content and how realistic their financing plans are.

Through a social security program, the Socialists want to achieve a redistribution of income and to reform the social structure in the direction of economic equality. By eliminating the individual's reliance on the extended family system and other "feudalistic" relationships and by preventing destitution, neglect in sickness, and abandonment in old age, the Socialists hope to render Japanese society more humane, efficient, and productive in the modern sense. Thus, social security is seen not only as relief but as an investment which should result in future increased per capita productivity. Their aim is not only a welfare state but a socialist commonwealth.

The five-year plan called for concentrating efforts on three categories of social security measures, aiming to systematize them in three years' time: medical security, a national system of annuities for the aged, the disabled, widows and children, etc., and a national welfare system for the relief of indigency and disability in various forms.[27]

The Socialists proposed to consolidate the various types of medical security into two main programs. The first would be simple health insurance. It would be extended to all employees, including those of petty enterprises which employ less than five workers, who are not

26. *Asahi Shimbun,* Dec. 15, 1957. The figures are from Kōseishō Daijin Kambō Kikakushitsu (Planning Section, Secretariat, Ministry of Welfare), ed., *Kōsei Hakusho: Shōwa Sanjūni Nendo Ban* (Welfare White Paper) (Tokyo, Tōyō Keisai Shimpō Sha, 1957).

27. *Kettei Shū,* pp. 71–77.

included in existing programs. The second would be national health insurance. This would be extended to cover self-employed farmers, fishermen and others, and would be made compulsory. Since employers do not contribute to it, the government's contributions would be greatly increased. Benefits would be raised so as more nearly to cover medical costs, and inequalities among hospitals would be eliminated by improving the poorer ones.

Special stress would be given to the prevention and treatment of tuberculosis. This single disease is such a scourge in Japan that it absorbed 36.7 per cent of the total benefits paid out by the government health insurance program in 1955. The Socialists wanted existing benefits increased to cover, at government expense, the full costs of care, convalescence, and prevention. The plan foresaw the accomplishment of this reform within three years and the total elimination of tuberculosis in five, thus enabling a reduction in the cost of the health insurance program. While tuberculosis has not been entirely eliminated, it has in fact been much reduced since that time, in large part as a result of the efforts of conservative governments and medical services.

Much attention in the press has focused on the proposed national system of annuities, which would cover the most backward areas in Japan with respect to social security. The importance the party has placed on this program was illustrated in the statement of Seiichi Katsumata, chairman of the Policy Planning Board, when he asserted that, if he had to make a choice as to the most urgent among all party economic policies, he would choose the proposal for a national system of annuities.[28] This urgency, however, was also sensed by the Liberal Democrats who promised soon to submit a proposal to the Diet based on a plan drawn up by the Social Security System Investigation Board.[29] Thus, competition with the conservatives on social security issues has become keen. As all indices of economic growth have advanced markedly since 1959, Japan has become able to afford wider coverage and more adequate insurance and compensatory benefits.

28. *Nihon Keizai Shimbun,* April 30, 1958.

29. On the request of the government, the Social Security System Investigation Board drafted a national system of annuities, made public on June 7, 1958. That some Socialist ideas were incorporated into this proposal may be surmised by the fact that the chairman of the Board was a Socialist sympathizer of long standing, the eminent Professor Hyōe Ōuchi, then President of Hōsei University. See *Asahi Shimbun,* June 8, 1958.

Although the five-year plan did not elaborate a scheme for a national system of annuities, the Socialists did approve a plan at their party convention in February 1958.[30] The SDP plan was more ambitious than the Social Security Board's recommendations. It sought to unify all existing annuities and pensions and expand their scope to cover the whole population. It even promised a sliding scale of benefit payments to accord with price fluctuations. All workers between the ages of 20 and 54—that is, for a period of 35 years—would be obliged to contribute annual insurance premiums. ¥84,000 annual insurance pensions would be given to all over 60 years of age; retired employees would receive additional payments based on the level of their earnings. The figure ¥84,000 was probably taken from the per capita consumption rate forecast for 1962.[31] It was twice the amount proposed by the Board at the request of the government.[32] According to Socialist plans, the government's share of payments toward employees' pensions would be 20 per cent and toward all others' pensions 50 per cent. As with social security in the United States, employees' contributions would vary according to the amount of wages; contributions would be based on a combination of earnings and assets. Employers would be obliged to pay 50 per cent of the contributions for employees' annuities.

Actually the Socialists did not call for the full realization of this national system of annuities before the end of 35 years. During the transition, people would receive gradually larger amounts, depending on the length of time they had contributed toward annuity funds.

For immediate benefits the SDP proposed noncontributory annuities of ¥12,000 annually for those between ages 60 and 65, if they had not been covered by contributory annuity plans. Those older than 65 would receive ¥24,000 annually. The Board also recommended noncontributory annuities, but a much lower figure: ¥12,000 payments annually for those over 70 years of age. Also as noncontributory annuities the Socialists proposed an annual ¥36,000 for widows with children and the same amount for disabled persons in general. According to a rough estimate made by the SDP, these noncontributory annuities would have cost the state about ¥113.6 billion if put into

30. See *Chōki Keizai Keikaku,* pp. 37–48.

31. Actually the figure forecast by the government was ¥83,000. See *Asahi Shimbun,* Feb. 14, 1958.

32. The Board proposed annual payments of ¥42,000. *Asahi Shimbun,* June 8, 1958.

effect in 1958.[33] This was almost twice the ¥66 billion annual estimated cost of the national annuity plan recommended by the Board.

The problem of pensions for former military personnel and their families has posed difficulties for the Socialists. This issue came to a head when the Kishi government yielded to the organized pressure of former servicemen and, in the course of formulating the budget for 1958, decided to increase their pensions by an amount that would total about ¥110 billion or 10 per cent of the total budget by the year 1961![34] Since most Socialists regarded this as an impetus to rearmament in Japan, they tended to oppose it on ideological grounds. Faced with a general election for the House of Representatives, however, SDP Diet members and candidates were hesitant about alienating voters. After much internal bickering, the party announced in February 1958 its own policy with regard to military pensions.[35]

It decided to oppose the government's proposed increase in pensions demanding rather that they be adjusted with the national system of annuities. At the same time, the party took cognizance of the special rights of former military personnel by proposing both higher annuities for them and compensation for loss of their former military pensions in the form of commutation bonds. The size of these bonds would depend on a number of variables including the life expectancy of the recipient and the capacity of the national treasury. By this scheme, the SDP claimed it could reduce the costs in this category to only ¥55 billion annually. As to the feasibility of the plan, opinions vary, but the intent was clear: the SDP was willing to pay compensations for ending the system, even at the expense of leaving special categories in an overall annuity system.

Special emphasis on adequate social security has continued as a Socialist theme and has come at a time when other problems have for the time being appeared less urgent. It also has brought SDP policies more in line with those of socialist and labor parties in other countries, especially in the more affluent Western nations. Given the industrious character of the Japanese people and the modesty of benefits proposed by the Socialists in comparison with Western standards, the charge that their social security plans would lead to laziness and loss of incentive in the Japanese economy was not convincing. In fact, the

33. *Nihon Keizai Shimbun,* April 30, 1958.
34. *Asahi Shimbun,* Jan. 26, 1958.
35. *Asahi Shimbun,* Feb. 22, 1958.

Socialists justified the program on the assumption that it would raise productivity in the long run and thus save money. The real problems henceforth will be the enactment of periodic further extensions of social security coverage and increases of benefits in proportion to general economic growth, and the relation of such improvements to sources and types of public revenue.

UNPRECEDENTED PEACETIME ECONOMIC GROWTH AND SOCIALIST RESPONSES

By 1957, two years of the so-called Jimmu boom had encouraged estimates, accepted by conservatives and Socialists, that Japan was about to experience a period of spectacular material growth.[36] The Socialists forecast that, even if taxes were reduced, national revenue could by the end of fiscal 1961 be raised by ¥500 billion. The ruling Liberal Democrats argued, as do conservatives in all capitalist countries, that whatever benefits accrued to business and industries—especially large-scale, modern, efficient enterprises—would trickle down to improve the incomes and welfare of earner-consumers. Socialists, however, worried that augmented wealth and power would entrench capitalism the more, that still more unequally shared profits would proportionally widen the chasms in Japanese society, that economic power would become more concentrated, and that the diffusion of benefits would satisfy the masses to the extent that the existing pattern would become more fixed, less mutable. Probably they sensed that not only would the conservatives claim credit for prosperity and be able to enrich their party coffers but also that expanded revenues would enable the governing party to usurp such welfare state programs as extended social security and to reap electoral rewards. Changes as well as growth have characterized the Japanese economy, especially since 1959. There can be no doubt that capitalism and the middle strata have been strengthened and that the attitudes of workers have become more pragmatic, less inclined to doctrinaire confrontation. Many small enterprisers have been able to attain new levels of technical and managerial efficiency, thus strengthening their proprietary outlook.

Such trends have presented to Socialists a variety of challenges unprecedented either in kind or degree. While a Common Market emerged in Western Europe and a number of capitalist economies,

36. The Socialist Party's five-year plan (1957–61) assumed an annual growth rate of 8%, producing an increase of 76% in national income within that period.

most notably Japan's, were enjoying rapid rates of growth, the two leading socialist countries were experiencing serious difficulties. Japanese Marxists, like their Chinese and some other counterparts, continued to underestimate the efficacy of monetary and fiscal measures by which capitalist governments have succeeded in limiting cyclical troughs to recessions instead of depressions. Some of them continued to warn of an American depression which would remove the buttressing of Japanese capitalism. But gradually others are admitting that the "wait-for-panic" strategy is no longer valid. On the contrary, they wax eloquent when predicting how—as the American-Soviet détente and coexistence develop—socialist economies will constitute two thirds of world industrial production; neutral countries will grow in leverage; and the United States will not be able to deny Red China its rightful place in world affairs. During Japan's recessions and balance-of-payment problems (late 1957 to early 1959, and the milder one from late 1961 into 1962), the political opposition emphasized American tariff and quota restrictions and argued the more vigorously for reorientation of the nation's commercial pattern to give more emphasis to trade with communist countries.

Other dimensions of change and challenge have ironically tended to place the Socialists, as champions of labor interests, in a conservative stance. Automation and other technical advances, as well as the relative decline of certain industries, are causing shifts in the labor force, labor shortages in some sectors and unemployment in others, and necessitating expanded retraining and employment services. In fighting rationalization because of personnel cutbacks in certain adjusting industries the SDP can hardly be regarded as a herald of progress. It can and does try to attract the support of enterprisers hurt by liberalization of trade, but if the total horizon for Japanese trade is much expanded by a truly reciprocal process of tariff reduction, then it is parochial to defend those who must readjust.[37] Socialists can foresee significant implications for their cause from changes in the structure of industry and agriculture which the more flexible and progressive capitalist exponents are seeking. The shift of families from the

37. Some Socialists argued that trade liberalization could be avoided if emphasis were to be shifted to trade with the Red Bloc. See Shuji Ohashi, "Analysis and Criticism of the Economic White Paper," reprinted in Central Party School of the Japan Socialist Party, *Kōzō Kaikaku no Riron* (The Theory of Structural Reform) (Tokyo, Shūji Daisha, 1961), pp. 48–52.

land into other occupations and the consequent approach to more economic scales of farming has recently accelerated in response to conditions which apparently do not require central socialistic planning and collectivism. Of course, Socialists still contend that the trend could be more systematic, efficient, and equitable under their guidance.

Moreover, the rate of labor organization has not kept pace with the growth of the labor force, and industrial dynamism has recently been particularly strong in the private sector of the economy where leftist unions have been weaker. The Democratic Socialists and Zenrō have taken advantage of new opportunities and have continued to foster splits and disintegration in leftist unions. The development of new industrial belts or zones and a more modern transportation system portend changes for labor and anything but a capitalism about to collapse from its inherent contradictions. The powers and functions of the state are bound to grow; the Socialists want this power to be implemented in ways which will favor labor and the public at large rather than "monopolistic" interests. Stated more positively, they would like to be able to guide and utilize this great surge to promote a still more centrally planned, egalitarian order.

Instead it was a conservative party and government which planned and promised that in the 'sixties the income of the nation would double and average individual earnings would approach the Austrian level. Not only the level but also the structure of Japan's economy is expected to approach European patterns. According to the ten-year plan approved by the LDP Cabinet under Hayato Ikeda late in 1960, there would be an average annual gain in gross product of 9 per cent and a tripling of exports.[38] The number of people engaged in farming

38. By 1962 Japan as an industrial power stood fifth in the world. Its gross national product in real (or adjusted) terms gained by 18.3% in 1959, 13% in 1960, 16.1% in 1961, and 5.7% in 1962. This was one of the highest rates of growth in the world. The manufacturing and mining index by May 1961 was 169% higher than in 1955. In some years investments in equipment by small and medium industries were proportionately even greater than by large enterprises. Trade in most commodities was notably expanding. Agriculture was prosperous. Employment was at a high level. Inflation was mild, and on the average wages were gaining more rapidly than prices. Consumption, particularly of durable goods, was high, and so was the rate of saving. Household economies were improving, and amounts spent on education and entertainment were increasing. Despite the general improvement, there were still depressed groups; and inequalities of wealth, though not as marked as before World War II, were again growing.

had declined by 8.2 per cent during 1955–60, and it was predicted that in the next decade one quarter of the peasants would leave the fields. The farm unit would expand, and the emphasis would shift to stock raising and fruit growing. Marginal producers would tend to be eliminated, and further mechanization would be possible. After 1963–64 the technological revolution and the slowing of population growth would induce a shrinkage of the labor force. The conservatives saw new opportunities to strengthen social security and to reduce the gap between wages and productivity in small as compared to large enterprises. Both main parties now advocated "elimination of the dual structure" of Japanese industry. Ikeda's ministers advocated the growth of medium-sized enterprises. Socialists had urged these reforms for decades, but were being challenged by the fact that the conservatives were in a position to accomplish many of them within a changing capitalist context. More adequate low-cost housing has long been a Socialist demand: more recently it has become an LDP promise, along with improved drainage and sanitation systems, communications, transportation, public services, education, hospitals, welfare centers, and parks.

The Socialists criticized what they considered "excessive capital accumulation"; their phrase "economic growth from the top" implied that it would be otherwise under socialism. But where in socialist countries is it so? However, there is some truth in their observation that Japan is "a first-rate power in productivity with a third-rate standard of living." Imbalances are what they stress. From 1956 to 1961, they noted, the GNP rose 1.7 times, but consumption 1.5 and governmental spending nearly 1.7 times. People's monthly earnings rose by little more than 30 per cent, and consumer percentage of total demand has gradually fallen. Socialist planning, they alleged, would avoid excessive, duplicative investment in private manufacturing.

Despite the gains which small and medium enterprises have made and the augmented budgetary provisions for their assistance, the Socialists remain convinced that the "dual economic structure" is being inadequately rectified. They argue that although loans by governmental and private banks are chiefly drawn from the phenomenal savings of the masses, in 1957 one per cent of Japan's enterprises obtained more than 60 per cent of the credit. While corporate profits, reserves, and depreciation allowances have increased, the rate of profit-sharing with workers has gradually declined during the last decade. Some have contended much too pessimistically that inflation will deprive gains in income of real meaning.[39] Aside from extension of social security programs, the Socialists maintain that nothing concrete has been done to assist people in the lowest strata.

Again, referring to the gap between large and smaller enterprises, the Socialists have charged that the government has been vague as to how it would implement technological modernization and tax relief. They have predicted that liberalization of trade would hurt many small businesses while large, modern enterprises would be able to compete and achieve even stronger relative positions. The implications of their own views of policy under a consolidated socialist regime, however, would require elimination of many submarginal businesses in favor of more productive, competitive industries.

The opposition also has warned that urban–rural disparities would grow, in part because, under the LDP income-doubling plan, only one sixteenth of investment would be in agriculture, forestry, and fishing. Trade liberalization and the importation of American surpluses would hurt Japanese farmers, and so would indirect control of the rice market. And Socialists have noted the absence of adequate rural employment services, farm income guarantees, housing programs, and technical education.

In regard to trade, the SDP has doubted that aims of the LDP ten-year plan could be attained. Governmental planners have been accused of exaggerating commercial opportunities in North America and Western Europe. The SDP has argued that United States efforts to conserve dollars required it to maximize its exports to Japan and curtail im-

39. From 1952 to 1960, there was inflation amounting to 23.3%; and in the next three years it rose by about the same percentage. However, the incomes of urban workers' families adjusted for inflation still showed gains of 7.7% in 1960, 4.0% in 1961, and 5.1% in 1962. The gross per capita income in 1962 reached the equivalent of $452. The cash earnings of regular workers increased 33.1% from 1955 to September 1961. By 1960, employment was nearly 65% higher than five years previously; there were further gains in 1960 (11.4%) and 1961 (8.7%). Labor shortages in many smaller industries were mainly accounting for disproportionately large wage gains in that sector, and wage differentials between small to medium and large industries had been reduced by 1962. During 1955–60, labor productivity advanced 47% in manufacturing and 31.2% in mining.

Not only were savings sharply increasing in these prosperous years, but consumer spending soared. In 1960, for example, the consumer index was 29% higher in cities than in 1955 and the rural consumer level in January 1961 was nearly 50% higher than in 1951. Even allowing for a rise of 6.2% in consumer prices in 1961, family spending expanded by 7%. Department store sales and savings in that year both advanced more than 24%. That was a banner year, but all since 1958 had been high in these respects.

portation of Japanese products. For this reason it has pressed Japan to liberalize tariffs, and by so doing the conservative government has shown its subordination. The government has relied on liberalization and lowered costs of production to expand exports, but this has called on labor for undue sacrifices in the form of restraints on wage increases and rationalization of personnel. Only by abandoning one-sided cooperation with the U.S. and emphasizing trade with developing and socialist countries could this situation be corrected.[40] When recurrently it has been necessary for the government to take regulatory steps to keep the balance of payments from threatening operative exchange reserves, the Socialists have charged that this, too, has stemmed from over-dependence on the United States, that small and medium-sized businesses are more affected by the stringency of credit, while major enterprises are able to continue modernization in preparation for tariff liberalization. Rather than see a dip in prices during such a deflationary phase, the Socialists assert that policymakers in industry and business will cut back production with consequent unemployment particularly of older workers. Finally they have warned that after such a boom there is apt to be a depression, and that special measures taken to limit it to a recession will only prolong it.[41]

40. Socialists have been critical that only about 6% of Japan's exports during the decade were to be to the Communist bloc. In recent years (from this writing in 1963), the U.S. has supplied about 38% of Japan's imports and has purchased about 32% of Japan's exports. Except for fiscal 1959, the balance in this bilateral trade has been in favor of the U.S. In 1959 there was a spurt of Japanese exports to the U.S., but for a year beginning in the fall of 1960 there was a decline, while continued heavy Japanese purchases of producers' materials and machinery from the U.S. and European countries would have endangered Japan's exchange reserves but for fiscal and monetary restraints. It was at this time that the Socialists pressed their criticisms with more effect. The nation's export earnings mounted by nearly 20% in 1962, and although there have been chronic annual deficits in the Japanese total trade balances, they have been reduced since fiscal 1961. Normally Japan's overall balance of payments is a plus figure, the trade imbalance being more than made up by so-called "invisible receipts" (e.g., foreign travel, freight earnings, insurance, international investments, foreign military expenditures, and the like). There was an overall negative balance of $338 million in 1961, but in the next fiscal year the normal pattern was resumed with a credit balance of $355 million. Contrary to the impression that some opposition politicians convey, U.S. special procurements (military purchases) in Japan have constituted a declining factor in this overall balance, having been reduced from $481.56 million in 1958 to $376.09 million in 1962.

41. For critiques of the LDP income-doubling plan and reform of the economic structure, see "The Long-Term Political and Economic Plan," in *Shakaitō no Shin Rosen, Dai 20 Kai Teiki Tō Taikai Kettei Shū* (The New Line of the Socialist Party, Decisions of the 20th Regular Party Convention) (Tokyo, Nihon Shakaitō Kikanshi-kyoku, 1961), Economic Growth Starts Crumbling," *Shakai Shimpō*, Nov. 5, 1961; and Ichiji Nagasu,

RECENT SOCIALIST PLANS AND PROPOSALS

Early in 1961, the SDP in convention recalled its three previous economic plans and adopted a new "Long-Term Political and Economic Plan," aimed at phased reform of politics, the economy, society, and culture. It bore the strong imprint of the theories and strategies of "structural reform." It conceived of three economic phases congruent with the stages of transition to socialism envisaged by that faction. But by far the most emphasis was on the last stage, when a "qualitative" transformation would be wrought and a full socialist system be consolidated.

While the economy was being gradually reformed, the Socialists hoped to advance toward a parliamentary majority. There was an intimation that this might be achieved in about four years! More positive and responsible policies were to be consistent with the fundamental party tenets: defense of the Constitution, support of democratic politics, and neutralist foreign policies. For 1961–64 the party outdid the LDP plan by envisaging a leap in production of 8 per cent in the first year and of 10 per cent in each of the next three, but reality outdid both.[42] According to this estimate, average per capita income could by 1964 be half again as large, or approximately ¥70,000; for lower wage earners it should increase fourfold. Every family should be enabled to own a residence, and the consumption of food should increase three to five times. The advocated minimum wage was ¥15,000 for workers aged 18 or more. If trade with communist countries were to be promoted, it was asserted that exports could expand by 18 per cent within four years.

The "Long-Term Plan" repeated the party's general aims: to rectify contradictions in Japanese capitalism and to democratize the economy. Development of a comprehensive program of social security was expected to foster conditions and public attitudes conducive to

"Secret of 'High Economic Growth' and Structural Reform." *Gekkan Shakaitō,* November 1961. These two articles are reprinted in English translation in *Japan Socialist Review,* No. 2 (Nov. 16, 1961), pp. 6–14, 15–26, 62.

42. The Conservatives' income-doubling plan foresaw average annual gains in GNP of 9% during 1960–70. Between 1959 and 1962 the actual average increase was 12%. It may be doubted how much party policies explained such growth, but inasmuch as the Japanese government has important economic functions, and the LDP has exercised administrative power, policies of the ruling party are not insignificant.

later achievement of socialism. The domestic market would be enlarged; reactionary forces would be isolated; people would become convinced that only under socialism could gaps in the dual economic structure be eliminated.

To critics who have accused the Socialists of conservatism because of their opposition to liberalization of tariffs and industrial rationalization in order to make Japanese enterprises more competitive in world markets, the Socialists have contended that they have not opposed innovation and technological change as such, but that under their government rationalization would be compatible with improvements such as a shorter work week, high employment, and other progressive policies. They have demanded immediate democratization of the Ministry of International Trade and Industry's Industrial Rationalization Deliberative Council. Both the SDP and DSP have called for more labor participation in management, in part to deal more effectively with the effects of technological changes.

Both parties have further urged democratization of public enterprises so as to lower the prices of public utilities and services. The left wing has called for rationalization of distribution of fresh foods and reduction of the role of middlemen. In the field of housing, the Socialists have demanded the ending of speculative investments, a governmentally subsidized program to benefit workers, more labor representation in the management of the Housing Corporation, democratic control of the prices of building supplies, and larger appropriations to the Housing Loan Bank as well as credit at lower rates of interest.

The left Socialists have demanded restraints on concentrated economic powers by governmental control of credit, measures for redistribution of income, prevention of monopolistic price-fixing, and centrally planned investment. Reform of taxation should be used as an egalitarian regulator: the income tax should be more steeply graduated; special exemptions should be abolished but the exemptions for lower income groups should be liberalized. Both direct and indirect taxes which fell disproportionately on consumers and low income strata should be reduced. In December 1961 the SDP advocated that all corporate annual incomes over ¥5 million be subject to a 40 per cent tax.

What the Democratic Socialists have proposed for the national economy since their party was founded in 1960 can be seen in their initial platform, their action program adopted in 1961, and their

Eight-Year Plan (1960–68).[43] They envisaged a gradually more democratic and socialistic order through "improving the quality of the present capitalist system." They would retain competition within the price and market mechanism but strengthen central planning and regulation. They advocated less extensive nationalization but stronger public regulation, varying in degree, of a wider range of enterprises. They listed the Bank of Japan, atomic power and electric generation for later nationalization but recommended the "socialization" of coal, steel, gas, fertilizer manufacture, airlines, and railroads. Possible adverse consequences of nationalization were to be anticipated and avoided. Private enterprise was to be permitted in other fields subject, however, to coordinated planning of investments and other legal regulations. Major enterprises should cease to receive special administrative favors and the state should regulate their relations with financial agencies. Investment and credit should conform to governmental plans, and over-concentration of private economic power should be prevented. The production and distribution of foodstuffs should also be nationally planned. Efforts should be exerted to keep abreast of technological advances and to modernize industries.

Like their SDP rivals, the Democratic Socialists favored cooperative management in agriculture and special assistance to the modernization of small and medium-scale enterprises. They, too, proposed progressive taxation but—as in most respects—they were less extreme and specific than was the SDP. Moreover, they warned against narrow labor union pressures.

In its own version of how institutions and the structure of the economy should be reformed in the course of spectacular growth the DSP stressed "balance and equality." Having rejected Marxism and the class struggle as touchstones of social development, it eagerly sought enlargement of middle strata and thereby the strengthening of parliamentary politics. Attention was called to the need for a long-range welfare plan and for budgets in keeping with its successive stages.

In matters of trade, the Democratic Socialists were less sanguine than the Liberal Democrats and, although they also favored unfettered trade with Communist China, they were less emphatic that exchanges with the Red bloc would be a major factor affecting commercial growth. One can see reflections in such economic proposals of the

43. "Provisional Platform of the Japan Democratic Socialist Party," Tokyo, Jan. 24, 1960 (mimeo.); *Asahi Shimbun*, Jan. 16, 1961; Jan. 19, 1961.

moderate, medial position of this party and its consequent difficulty in dramatizing its appeals to voters.

The SDP's "Long-Term Plan" was brief and vague about the second phase of socialist development. Once enjoying a majority in the Diet and in command of national administration, the first of two five-year plans would be launched. Agencies of government would be prepared to administer socialist programs, and systematic central planning of the economy would commence, along with socialization of major enterprises.

The Plan provided considerably more detail about the Socialist vision of how the economy would be managed if and when the new order was consolidated. This was a leap into an idealized future, and policies and agencies were described without any careful economic—particularly financial—analysis. Perhaps it was to please more doctrinaire leftist factions that this, the most specific program for full Japanese socialism yet published as party policy, was included. For anyone acquainted with previous Japanese socialist thought and with practices in other socialist countries, there were no surprises in this program.[44]

Socialist prescriptions for raising the national economic level by increasing production and expanding the domestic market and exports would depend on three basic policies: the importation of cheaper raw materials by redirecting the present pattern of foreign trade; nationalization of key industries and strong governmental control of financial institutions, especially in regard to long-term investment; and winning the enthusiastic cooperation of organized labor in restraining its wage demands and voluntarily increasing per capita productivity.

Administrative execution of such policies would require strong leadership. The SDP would have to be sturdy enough internationally to withstand possible obstructions by the United States, the Nationalist Chinese on Taiwan, and South Korea without, on the other hand, becoming dependent on Communist China. Internally it would have to overcome opposition from powerful conservative groups and, furthermore, masterfully to control the bureaucracy in the interests of efficiency as well as to prevent subtle official obstructions.

Even though it is unrealistic to expect party politicians to conduct

44. *Shakaitō no Shin Rosen*, pp. 145–50.

the exacting analyses and estimates which can be required of professional economists, it is reasonable to expect that the basic economic arguments for a proposed new order should be more thoroughly studied and convincingly demonstrated. We know from actual observation that even socialist planners and implementers have to cope with such problems as capital formation, depreciation, incentives, and efficiency of production, the cost of labor as an ingredient of production, and the characteristics of bureaucracy which proliferates—it has never diminished—in socialist states. The reconciliation of full employment with technological advances and efficient productivity is not achieved by sheer virtue of central planning and public ownership. There is much evidence that socialism provides a milieu conducive to disguised inefficiencies uncorrected by competition and the requirements of a relatively free market. Japan has the choice between applying standards of efficiency which, in many lines of production, can be competitive internationally even though tariffs are further reduced, or of protecting less competitive producers to the detriment of export expansion, or perhaps joining a relatively closed trading system like the Red bloc. But someone pays the bill for inefficiency and, however indirectly, these unadmitted contradictions are reflected in the standard of living. Under capitalism, Socialist ideology and opposition tactics conduce to the argument that the vast programs of state spending which are advocated can be financed by restructuring taxation so as to "soak the rich." That this might destroy entrepreneurial incentives worries left Socialists not in the least, since they hold that bourgeois interests are to be denied.

While Japan's spectacular economic growth makes possible ambitious programs of public works and social overhead, there can still be reasonable doubt that Japanese socialism could more effectively achieve these gains. In any case, the experts employed by Socialist planners have not yet analyzed soundly enough to be convincing on these points; the SDP Plan adopted in 1961 was more doctrinaire, less analytical than that of 1957.

7. Socialist Foreign Policies

Although Social Democrats before the war had not consistently been champions of liberalism and moderation, they emerged from the national disaster in relatively good repute and with improved opportunities. Tides of idealism, including pacifism, for a time ran high; the revived Socialist Party sought leadership in reconstructing a nation which would live down its predatory reputation and regain international confidence. Japan's aggressiveness in the past was ascribed by the Socialists mainly to denial of democratic rights and processes by conservative oligarchs, to monopolistic capitalism, and to the mobilization of petty middle classes while "the masses" had been suppressed.

Until late in the period of recovery, the foreign relations of the shrunken empire consisted chiefly in cooperation with Occupation policies and agencies. While recognizing the limitations of a capitalist United States as a guide through reforms, Japanese Socialists joined in promoting democratization because such renovations were obviously related to the building of a peaceful nation. But, as the cold war developed and communism swept to power in China, Japan's Socialists became critical of the swing of American policies away from disarmament and democratization toward rearmament and involvement of Japan in an anticommunist—and therefore conservative—orbit.

THE DESIRE FOR NEUTRALISM

No sooner had the SDP assumed the chronic opposition stance than its fourth convention, in April 1949, declared that neutralism expressed the ethos of the new, peace-oriented Japan, that ideologically it was in keeping with the distinct position of social democracy vis à vis either capitalism or communism, that it was necessary on constitutional grounds, and that it would be more likely to win the confidence and trade of uncommitted Asian countries. Moreover—and this was henceforth subscribed to by both wings of the party—neutralism offered Japan the possibility of achieving a fuller independence. In terms of propaganda appeal, this factor was to trouble the right wing when it felt compelled to qualify its stand.

As it became apparent that the United States was firmly pressing for conclusion of a peace treaty and that the problem of future national security was involved, the party at its January 1950 convention, as mentioned in Chapter 1, adopted the "three principles of peace": (1) conclusion of a comprehensive peace treaty with the countries which were legally still in a state of war with Japan (even though some of them belonged to mutually hostile alignments); (2) neutrality in accordance with the Constitution; and (3) opposition to the use of Japanese military bases by any foreign forces. In the following year at the seventh convention, a fourth principle, opposition to rearmament, was added. As mentioned earlier, right Socialists had major reservations on these points, while the left wing promoted them rather consistently. Slogans were promptly coined to rally laborers, housewives, white-collar workers, students, intellectuals, and others.

What attitudes to adopt concerning Japan's relation to the Korean War confronted the Foreign Affairs subcommittee of the party's Policy Planning Board. Its formulation of policies was discussed with the Central Executive Committee, and the result was published as a pamphlet entitled *Theory and Practice for Peace*.[1] Right-wing leaders and some from the left were inclined to support the United Nations and the democratic nations, even if led by the capitalistic United States, while others—mostly leftists—favored neutralism. A middle group in the CEC inclined toward those in the right wing who argued that in such a situation Japan needed a defensive military force, but some on

1. Policy Planning Board, ed., *Heiwa no riron to jissen* (Tokyo, July 25, 1950).

the left thought that this would be inconsistent with neutrality and would open the door to fascism.

Since the party had been temporarily riven in the previous April, there was a strong desire for compromise. The upshot was a pamphlet with sections on "Why We Demand an All-Around Peace," "Our Party's Attitude toward the Korean Situation," and "Outline for Developing a Peace Movement." The second division was far more vague than would have been required if Japan had recovered sovereignty and if the SDP had been in power. The party would "defend international peace based on justice." It rejected military aggression and gave "moral support" to the maintenance of law and order under the United Nations, the ultimate guarantor of Japan's security. The use of force by the People's Democratic Republic of (North) Korea in an attempt to unify the peninsula was recognized as having precipitated the conflict. However, the Yoshida government was critized for going further than Japan's status as an occupied country required. Without freedom to express the national will, an outright decision could have been avoided simply by compliance with the orders of Occupation authorities. The SDP would be on guard against capitalist provocateurs of war and, on the other hand, against JCP efforts to foment struggles by organized labor against war-related industries and services in the guise of a peace offensive. The party adhered to neutralism and pacifism and was criticized by public and press for inconsistency between its "three principles" and its policies evoked by the Korean War.[2]

Indeed, controversy continued between the two main party factions and between labor leaders in their respective orbits. Those in the right wing have since argued that, because Stalinism is not genuinely socialistic, conflicts such as those in Korea, Vietnam, and Laos have been predominantly between democracy and totalitarianism rather then between socialism and capitalism. Informed right-wing Socialists have admitted that the governments of Syngman Rhee in South Korea, of Bao Dai with French support, and Ngo Dinh Diem with American assistance in South Vietnam, and of the monarchists in Laos have not been viable democracies. But they have maintained that they have more prospect of democratization than do "people's dictator-

2. *Theory and Practice for Peace,* pp. 25–26.

ships," and that the nations supporting them are interested in the triumph of liberal political systems. They favored contributions to the United Nations cause in Korea by party and union members in order to build a system of collective security. Gradually they receded from strict neutralism toward closer cooperation with the democracies.

Leftists like Katsumata, then chairman of the Policy Planning Board, adhered to thorough renunciation of military power and insisted that the principal reason for supporting the U.N. should be to avoid alliances with any nations or the formation of regional security arrangements. They argued that Socialists should not repeat the prewar mistake of surrendering to militarism, that American democracy was mostly formal and of domestic significance, and that right-wingers were capitulating to the imperialist camp and to conservatism under the pretense of defending democracy. Japan should, they urged, mitigate rather than exacerbate conflicts between the two main camps. The compromise accepted by the Central Committee approved moral and economic support of the U.N. cause but opposed military aid, asked for recognition of Japanese demilitarization, and insisted that foreign forces not use Japan's bases or transport troops across its soil except to defend that country.

Such differences of opinion within the SDP help to explain the crisis which developed in the fall of 1951 from many factors but immediately over policies toward the peace and security treaties. Foreign policies adopted by the separate SDP conventions in January 1952 revealed more clearly their divergence. The Left criticized internal aspects and foreign policies of both the United States and the Soviet Union. It identified neutralism as a "third force" consonant with the attitudes of workers, farmers, intellectuals, and "national capital" in noncommunist countries. It reasserted the "four principles of peace" and favored the five principles of coexistence (the Pancha Shila) which the People's Republic of China (PRC) and India had recently affirmed. The Left SDP was sanguine that the neutralism espoused by numerous Afro-Asian countries and by some nations of Europe would come to exercise key influence.[3]

3. Policy Planning Board of the [Left] SDP, ed., *1952-nen no Zenshin: Nihon Shakaitō Undō Hōshin Sho narabini Shin Gaikō Hōshin to Heiwa Undō* (Advance in 1952: SDP Action Policy, New Foreign Policy, and Peace Movement) (Tokyo, SDP Publishing Dept., 1952), esp. pp. 3–8, 10, 68, 91. An interesting definition of the "third force" was given on pp. 5–7.

Right Socialists, however, charged that a "third force" position ignored certain real dangers in the international scene. They called for a "dauntless attitude" toward communism without "positive anti-Soviet diplomacy." Their party advocated peaceful struggles along lines approved by the Socialist International. It urged cooperation with the United Nations toward ultimate collective security, and meanwhile contributions to the defense of the free world.[4]

Neutralism appeared a more valid position during 1953 for a number of reasons. The H-bomb test over Bikini and the furore raised over fallout injury to the crew of the "Lucky Dragon" augmented popular fear of nuclear war. Japan's potential power was further shrunken in relative terms. The truce in Korea contributed to reduced tensions, which in turn were conducive to more frequent expressions of intermediate national positions. The Soviet Union seemed to be more responsive to the Indian brand of neutralism, and Communist China recognized the possibility of cooperation with Japan if it should become truly neutral and independent. Nevertheless, the difference of views concerning neutralism persisted in the parties' foreign policy platforms of 1954[5] and were again evident in conferences between the chairmen of their Policy Planning Boards and Bureaus of International Affairs during April to June of that year. Right-wingers had become alarmed at the advocacy of a "peace force" which official Sōhyō policy and an extreme faction in the Left SDP asserted should include not only neutralist countries and Japan, but also the U.S.S.R. and China. They charged that the Left unduly minimized the aggressiveness of the main communist powers, that its brand of neutralism might mean pacifism toward the "new imperialism" of those neighbors. And they warned that democratic socialism could not exist under any such totalitarian hegemony.

Leftist leaders replied that the communist giants were preoccupied with economic development, that, since the Korean truce and the spread of the "peace offensive" in Asia, the United States was more belligerent and might even run the risk of a third world war. Furthermore, they averred, ridding Japan of the American capitalist, imperialistic incubus should be the first task. This was described as a men-

4. *Jōhō Tsūshin,* No. 39 (Jan. 1, 1952), pp. 4–7 (draft).

5. "Foreign Policy of the [Right] SDP" (Tokyo, mimeo., 1954); "[Left] SDP Foreign Policy for the Fiscal Year 1954," *Tōkatsudō,* Special Issue, No. 71, pp. 12–14. See also translations on pp. 18–24 in "Comparative Platforms."

ace in being; social democracy could not be attained in Japan as long as this influence predominated.[6] But right-wingers countered that anti-American struggles played into the hands of communism. In subsequent bipartisan meetings they further argued that it was feasible for Austria and Switzerland to obtain international observance of their neutrality, but a populous, productive country in Japan's geographical position would affect the balance of power and perhaps endanger peace by shifting to neutrality. There were other continuing disagreements, but Japanese politicians intent upon a task such as reunifying parties are past masters at glossing over differences if they cannot be altogether reconciled.

Thus, the foreign policy section of the "Fundamental Principles of Policies" which formed the basis for reunification in mid-October 1955 was sketchy. The strengthened party stood for complete national independence and neutralism. It would seek friendly relations with all countries and restoration of normal exchanges with the Soviet Union and Red China. It urged more cooperation with nonaligned countries, efforts toward collective guarantees for Japanese security, and membership in the United Nations. Both the "peace force" position and the right-wing preference for association with the free world were by implication rejected.[7]

Since party reunification there have been a number of further developments in policies related to neutralism. Left-wing pressure in 1957 led to SDP abandonment of the "two Chinas" policy and recognition of Red China's claim to Taiwan. Was this consistent with neutralism? Regarding policies toward mainland China we shall see that the SDP was increasingly "leaning to one side." There was a distinct relationship between sympathy for Peking and emphasis on the "class character" of the party.

Other factional struggles within the party also fostered neutralism.

6. *Tōkatsudō,* No. 91 (Sept. 10, 1954); *Jōhō Tsūshin,* No. 110 (Aug. 25, 1954): "The Interim Report of the Conversations on Policy between Four Members of the Two Socialist Parties" (Tokyo, SDP, mimeo., 1954).

7. "Foreign Policy" in "Independence, Peace and Security," Pt. I of "The Fundamental Principles of Policies," approved at the convention on October 13, 1955, and published in *Nihon Shakai Shimbun,* No. 551. See also "Comparative Platforms," pp. 25–26; Eki Sone, "Foreign Policy of the Japan Socialist Party," in Hitoshi Ashida and Eki Sone, "Japan's Foreign Policy: Conservative and Socialist Views," Japanese Paper No. 2, Thirteenth Conference, Institute of Pacific Relations (Tokyo, 1958), Appendix I, pp. 27–28 (mimeo.).

It was not so difficult to reconcile views and to criticize British and French imperialism in the Suez Canal crisis of 1956, and American troop landings in Lebanon and Jordan, but there was much less unity, and a resort to vague language, in enunciating reactions to the Soviet intervention in Hungary, Chinese suppression of the revolt in Tibet in March 1959, and intrusions into Himalayan borderlands in 1962. The campaign against renewal of the revised security treaty was waged by the Socialists allied with other opposition forces advocating a national position independent of the U.S. alliance system and not provocative to the Communist bloc. However, the simultaneous call for elimination of American bases and forces, a multilateral non-aggression pact, a nuclear free zone in the Pacific, as well as diplomatic relations with China and expanded trade with communist countries might, if realized, have placed a relatively weak Japan in a sphere of Sino-Soviet influence with only a treaty to protect it. The anti-Americanism exhibited during opposition to renewal of the security treaty was explained by SDP leaders as not unfriendly to the American people and democracy. The moderate trends which ensued, under the leadership of the structural reform group within the mainstream faction, included a policy of friendship "toward the U.S., the Soviet Union, and China," though leftists complained that this "offset achievements of the anti-security treaty struggle." In preparing new missions to both camps there was more expected of those despatched to communist countries; Suzuki, whose position was to the left of the structural reformers, remarked during a visit to bloc countries in October 1960 that he favored the Yugoslav rather than the Austrian brand of neutralism for Japan.

THE QUEST FOR SECURITY WITHOUT ALLIANCE OR REARMAMENT

Of course, the policy of neutralism has been closely related to the party's criticism of the three basic agreements with the United States: (1) the multilateral peace treaty signed at San Francisco; (2) the bilateral security treaty; and (3) the administrative agreement. Other corollaries are its opposition to rearmament, to nuclear weapons preparations in Japan or Okinawa, to the manufacture and testing of A- and H-bombs, as well as the quest for a denuclearized zone which would include Japan and provide security either by strengthening the effectiveness of the United Nations or by collective and/or bilateral guarantees.

Right Socialists approved the treaty of peace as a means of obtaining early independence, though both party wings would have preferred an "all-around" settlement, including the two main communist powers and India as signatories. Both factions urged normalization of relations with these states; both criticized territorial provisions in the peace treaty. Especially the left wing denounced the implication of Japanese rearmament and the provision for "stationing or retention of foreign armed forces on Japanese territory" according to subsequent agreements. As we have seen, the left wing refused to approve ratification of this treaty, precipitating party schism.

With differing emphases, both wings of the SDP opposed the security treaty with the United States. They protested that it was concluded before Japan recovered full sovereignty, that it contained no provisions for termination or revision on Japanese initiative, and that it did not establish an alliance of equals. Left Socialists, much more strongly than the Right (which recognized that at least some temporary arrangement was required for national security), denounced American pressure which continued Japan in the American orbit, seemed to offer a choice between the protracted stay of American forces or formidable Japanese rearmament, and might invite retaliation by the communist powers. Left Socialists have been bitterly against such ties to the most powerful capitalist state, which could in many ways fortify their economic, ideological, and political adversaries in Japan. Both SDP wings protested against the provision in Article I that American forces would give assistance "at the express request of the Japanese Government to put down large-scale internal riots and disturbances in Japan, caused through instigation or intervention by an outside power or powers." No sovereign state could long tolerate such an interventionary clause, and among both Socialists and organized labor it has deepened distrust of military forces as agents of conservatism. Nationalism and socialism, coinciding as they have in regard to aspects of this treaty, the leftists' consistent demand for its abrogation has had considerable appeal. Even the conservative party came to advocate revision.

The administrative agreement, which gave legal implementation to the treaty, also became a target of socialists, whatever their tinge. One objection was against negotiations which circumvented the Diet, constitutionally the highest organ of state. Indeed, there was general discontent with the extraterritoriality extended to American military personnel in Japan. This was amended in 1953 to accord with practice in NATO countries, but as late as 1957, in the "Girard case" involving a noncommissioned officer who killed a Japanese woman on a firing range, Left Socialists and Sōhyō were prepared for vigorous demonstrations if the U.S. Supreme Court had not decided that the case should be tried in a Japanese court. These same two forces, sometimes with parallel Communist cooperation and with the aid of farmers' unions when available, conducted a series of well publicized, militant demonstrations against American military bases, particularly from 1953 until the withdrawal of most U.S. ground forces in 1957.[8]

Discussion of these issues naturally required the Socialists to develop alternative proposals for security. The two party wings have expressed hope for ultimate collective security effectively supervised and guaranteed by a strengthened United Nations. Both were eager for Japan to be represented in that organization, and since the truce in Korea they have agreed that Red China and certain other nonmembers should also be admitted. However, by 1952—after passage of the "uniting for peace resolution," the branding of China as an "aggressor" in Korea, and the embargo imposed against the Chinese mainland—Japan's Left Socialists came to regard the U.N., in the main, as a vehicle for United States policies. Its restoration as an organization representing and operating for one world was urged. We have noted divisions in the party over what policy to adopt concerning the U.N. military effort in Korea and over the estimation of the source of the greatest dangers to Japan's security.

8. There were many other Socialist objections to the security treaty and its auxiliary agreement on such points as compulsory requisitioning of lands, military secrecy and its effects on civil rights, the difficulties of applying protective labor laws to the employees of the garrison forces and contracting factories, the annual financial contributions required of Japan for the expenses of American forces, and the economic influence which American military purchasing would continue to exert. In wartime such powers might become formidable, and in any case they would make a transition to socialism and planning of the economy difficult. There was also fear that nuclear weapons would be based in Japan, that Japanese troops might be sent abroad, or that Japan might be made a base for military operations without any real power of sovereign decision. Until it was officially denied, Socialists even charged that there was a secret understanding according to which American advisors would be assigned to each Japanese ministry. Thus, they feared, Japan might become a second Manchukuo. See "Gyōsei Kyōtei narabi ni Himitsu Ryōkai Jikō no taisuru Waga Tō no Taido" (Our Party's Attitude toward the Administrative Agreement and Items of Secret Understanding), *Tōkatsudō Shiryō,* No. 12 (Feb. 20, 1952), pp. 1–2; and right-wing articles in a somewhat similar vein in *Jōhō Tsūshin,* No. 44 (April 1952), pp. 4–10.

The right wing has shown more interest in the U.N., advocating the granting of more power to the General Assembly to counteract big power control, the growth of U.N. capacity to provide collective security step-by-step through development of permanent U.N. military forces, and the control and later inspected prohibition of nuclear weapons, as well as conventional disarmament.

Even before the Occupation ended and the peace treaty came into effect the separate Social Democratic parties each recognized that collective security, at least for Northeast Asia, by bilateral or multilateral nonaggression agreements, would be next in order of preference. Both factions realized that prerequisites would include lessening of tensions in the area along with improved relations with Japan's powerful communist neighbors and with other countries of Asia. They differed about some of the interim steps toward regional security. During negotiations toward party reunification in 1954–55, it became apparent that the Leftists proposed a prior nonaggression pact with China based on the "five principles of coexistence"; this should be expanded by bilateral agreements with other powers, including the Soviet Union. Then the security treaty and administrative agreement with the United States should be abrogated. Right-wing leaders argued that, although negotiations toward this objective could proceed for a while bilaterally, it would be safer to have a multilateral nonaggression agreement in order to have the new system go into effect with simultaneous guarantees. Especially since Communist China became overtly aggressive in Tibet and along the Indian and Nepalese borders in 1959–62, distrust has grown concerning Red China's promise of nonaggression.

In the autumn of 1954, right-wing leaders sounded out Chinese Communists about such a nonaggression pact, and the main Socialist mission to China in 1957 was encouraged by Mao Tse-tung to hope that, if Russia approved, the anti-Japanese military clauses in the existing Sino-Soviet Treaty of Friendship and Alliance could be revised, even before the U.S.-Japan security treaty would be terminated. If relations between Japan and its communist neighbors continue toward normality, pressures on conservative governments to reorient policies toward a Locarno type of regional security will probably increase. This would permit Japan greater freedom of action and comport with resurgent nationalism there but would probably be accepted by the United States only if there were no practicable alternative. Some observers surmise that this kind of reorientation may require two or three decades. Still, Japan's Social Democrats persisted, making an appeal to the leaders of 59 nations in February 1958 to convene the long-delayed summit conference and (in addition to suggestions regarding disarmament and the control of nuclear weapons) proposing eight lines of action to develop a system of collective security in Eastern Asia. These included a web of nonaggression pacts, a zone from which nuclear weapons would be banned, and an international conference on economic aid to Asian countries without political strings.

REARMAMENT: BLIGHT OR NECESSITY?

When the cold war—and then a nearby hot conflict—developed, the socialist parties and factions within them confronted a knotty dilemma. Was continued disarmament consistent with national security, and what should be done about the actual rearmament undertaken by conservative governments? Opposition strategy and a class-party emphasis have made it rather simple for left-wing Socialists to appear consistent with socialist theory, popular aspirations, and even morality in adhering to a contrary course. A dilemma always involves another case, however, and it is this which has troubled the right wing and others.

All varieties of Socialists tend to be suspicious of militarism, particularly in Japan, which in the not so distant past had a feudal military caste and martial traditions and later a system dominated by capitalistic and military oligarchies marked by increasing political intervention of the Army, ending in the complete frustration and discrediting of the old order and its imperialism. Unless and until the Socialists come to power it will be nearly impossible to persuade Japanese leftists that their nation could safely permit moderate, defensive rearmament controlled by civilians and by a liberal, constitutional government. Their skepticism boils down to the fact that Japan is not Switzerland or the United States. They cannot forget the oppressive police state; they know something about Japanese attitudes toward violence. And, as the left-wing theorist, Itsurō Sakisaka, wrote in 1951: a small defense force is futile if a great power does invade, but even a small army suffices to suppress the labor movement.[9]

In January 1951 the seventh national convention adopted a "Reso-

9. "Shakaishugi to Shinryaku" (Socialism and Aggression), *Shakaishugi*, No. 2 (July 1951), pp. 51–52. This journal has been an organ of the Shakaishugi Kyōkai (Socialist Society), composed chiefly of Left Socialist intellectuals.

lution Opposing Rearmament" which was mainly of left-wing origin. By cleaving rather dogmatically to the "principles of peace" those elements encountered another dilemma: how could Japan play an effective role in collective security without at least modest defense forces? And there was a further question: in the light of existing tensions, had not Japanese pacifism been possible because of American ability to balance communist power—and this without much of a Japanese contribution? The stock reply has been that Japan might consider contributing to collective security—not to an alliance—when a genuine United Nations peace force is in being; meanwhile, and even thereafter, Japan should serve as a neutral bridge without incurring avoidable hostile suspicions.

Right-wing footwork has had to be more complicated. Although some in these factions have favored moderate, deterrent military power so that the nation could protect itself minimally, become independent of the United States, and contribute to a U.N. security system,[10] they have had to be cognizant of leftist criticisms that rearmament is unconstitutional, plays into the hands of reactionary forces, and yields to U.S. imperialistic pressures. So they have opposed rearmament in its conservative form. Rather they have advocated maintenance of a police force capable of preventing "indirect aggression," that is, subversion and antidemocratic revolution. Before the first post-Occupation elections, the Right Socialists recognized Japan's right of self-defense and declared unarmed neutrality to be a fallacy. They continued to argue that the essence of national security lay in a sound economy and in the adequacy of public welfare to prevent shifts toward fascism or communism. They did not demand unconditional withdrawal of U.S. forces, but did call for revision of unequal features of the security treaty and the administrative agreement.[11]

10. See the statement by Sone in *Jōhō Tsūshin,* No. 39 (Jan. 1, 1952), pp. 4–7. He also urged that the SDP work through the Socialist International and the International Confederation of Free Trade Unions (ICFTU) to help prevent anticommunist nations from adopting the policy of preventive war. This was followed in March by a statement of views of Right Socialist intellectuals in the Democratic Socialist League. See: Research Department, Secretariat of Minshu Shakaishugi Remmei, ed., *Minshu Shakaishugi no Shiryō-hen* (Source Materials on Democratic Socialism), from January to July 1952. *Minshu Shakaishugi Bunko* (August 1952), pp. 4–9, 124.

11. The statement of the Special Committee for Election Policies in August 1952 is in *Dokuritsu Nihon no Dōhyō* (Guidepost of an Independent Japan) (Tokyo, 1952), pp. 27–28, 34–35. A more definitive statement of January 1953, "Our Party's Policy toward Peace, Security, and Self-Defense," is available in: [Right] SDP Election Policy Committee,

Activities as well as pronouncements evinced the divergent policies toward rearmament during the four-year party schism and in 1954 when the officials responsible for formulating foreign policies conferred in preparation for reunification. The Left SDP, in cooperation with labor and farmer organizations and the radical student federation, waged struggles against U.S. military bases. It demanded abrogation of the security treaty and the administrative agreement. By every available device it demonstrated opposition to the Mutual Security Agreement (M.S.A.) which nevertheless was concluded with the United States in March 1954. Its basic platform adopted in that year demanded withdrawal of foreign garrisons; it advocated dissolution of the National Security and Maritime Safety Forces and in their stead inauguration of a national construction corps for projects of conservation and economic development.[12] And leftists were shrill in warning against alleged conservative plots ultimately to restore conscription and, if urged by the U.S., to dispatch Japanese forces abroad. Repeatedly the charge that Japanese units would in all likelihood be used as "mercenary forces," the pawn of a superpower, was voiced as a genuine fear and to appeal to nationalist sentiment.

Especially after the truce in Korea and the Soviet peace offensive following the death of Stalin, the two Socialist wings also differed as to the principal threat to national security. Right-wingers argued that the communist powers, with their ideology and strategy of world revolution, constituted the major menace and that they were restrained chiefly by the balance of power mainly sustained by the U.S. They criticized anti-American struggles as playing into the hands of the new communist imperialism. Leftists sometimes admitted that the U.S.S.R. bore more than half the responsibility for precipitating the cold war but insisted that, in the current phase of international affairs, the United States was most powerful and most likely to bring on World War III.

Compromise and stress on means for collective security were evident in the formula which became the basis for party reunification. Japan's political, economic, and military dependence on the United States was deplored; American economic pressures were declared to

ed., *Social Democratic Party and the Rearmament Question,* Policy Series No. 1 (Tokyo, SDP Publication Department, 1953). It was approved by the party's convention in January 1953.

12. See "Comparative Platforms," p. 39.

have developed a military emphasis; and negotiations regarding the division of military expenditures were said to have led to American interference with Japanese budget-making. The party opposed rearmament in its existing form and demanded reduction instead of expansion of the Self-Defense Forces. It advocated a U.N. police force and, domestically, a "democratic police organization."[13]

The American willingness to withdraw ground forces from Japan in 1957 was ascribed to the developing nuclear stalemate and the imminent availability of intercontinental ballistic missiles (ICBM). The SDP accentuated public fears that the United States might obtain conservative compliance in establishing missile bases and storing bombs and nuclear warheads in Japan. Socialists expressed anxiety about a new Japanese-American Committee on Security for discussion of military and related matters. It was this committee which negotiated a revised security treaty and administrative agreement. The SDP pressed for a Diet resolution against nuclear testing and hailed the Soviet offer to suspend such tests if the United States and Great Britain would do likewise.[14] Premier Kishi had to qualify earlier comments—to the effect that nuclear weapons might have to be readied in Japan for use in a limited area—so as to reassure the anxious public. The Diet resolution passed with conservative support, and Kishi could not afford to accept President Eisenhower's invitation to send observers to view the thermonuclear tests around Eniwetok in the summer of 1958.

Socialist participation in the Japan Council Against Atomic and Hydrogen Bombs was becoming even more active. Moderates, however, were increasingly uneasy about radical pressures from Sōhyō delegates, the JCP, and left Socialists. Growing bias in the tone of the Council's organ and annual conferences was discernible. In August 1961, Communist elements led in placing the Seventh World Conference Against A- and H-Bombs on record as denouncing in advance

13. The "Foreign Policy" section in "Independence, Peace, and Security," Part I of "The Fundamental Principles of Policies," approved at the Unification Convention on October 13, 1955, and published in *Nihon Shakai Shimbun,* No. 551. See also: "Comparative Platforms," pp. 25–26, 40; Ashida and Sone, "Japan's Foreign Policy," pp. 21–23, 26, Appendix I.

14. Late in March and again in early April 1958, Chairman Suzuki appealed to the Kremlin to prohibit production and testing and for general disarmament. Bulganin replied that the Soviet Union was willing; it was up to the U.S. and Britain. This kind of exchange could also be used for domestic politics.

any nation which tested or used nuclear weapons. When, a fortnight later, the Soviet Union began a new series of tests, the JCP reversed itself, but the Socialist Party criticized both the Soviet Union and soon the United States for testing. Some left Socialists excused the former, explaining that Soviet tests were necessitated by varied American military preparations, that Russian proposals for disarmament and coexistence persisted. The crux of the issue became whether *all* testing by any nation should be denounced or only testing by other than the so-called "peace forces" which included the Soviet Union and China.

The weak Democratic Socialist Party, with cooperation from Zenrō, had that year organized a separate Committee for a People's Rally for the Establishment of Peace and against Nuclear Arms (sometimes called the Second Gensuikyō). This party, and many Japanese at large, were becoming anxious lest Communist China soon develop nuclear weapons, so they favored inclusion of the PRC in discussions aimed at control of armaments. The growing rift between the Soviet Union and Red China affected the Conference Against A- and H-Bombs the following year. In 1963, the historic test-ban treaty was signed by the United States, Great Britain, and the Soviet Union. Both Socialist parties hailed this event, but the Japanese Communists denounced it as only partial and as likely to lull into apathy the world peace movement. Fearing Communist domination of the Ninth World Conference in 1963, the Socialists and Sōhyō withdrew at the last moment and prepared for a showdown on this issue in the coming years against the pro-Chinese JCP. The Chinese delegates to the Congress condemned both the Soviet delegates and the Japanese Socialists in 1963.[15]

Occasionally since World War II, the Socialist Party had argued that a defeated Japan, stripped of empire, could never again hope to compete with the superpowers—that the choice was between neutrality and manipulation as a dependent. As swiftly developing military technology has grown more expensive and destructive, the cogency of this rationale has increased. Soon after the Soviet Union launched its first astral satellites and announced that it had succeeded in producing an ICBM, Socialist spokesmen in both houses of the Diet declared that to expand Japan's land forces to 180,000 was futile and that to suc-

15. See Totten and Kawakami, "Gensuikyō and the Peace Movement in Japan," pp. 833–41.

cumb to increased pressure from the U.S. for missile bases and nuclear weapons would endanger Japan's security.

In partial justification of such forebodings Assistant Secretary of Defense Donald A. Quarles, on April 8, 1958, remarked during a radio interview that the U.S. might seek missile bases in Eastern Asia. Premier Kishi and the director of the Self-Defense Agency, replying to the opposition, stated that conventional forces were still needed against the contingency of limited, regional hostilities. Japan's two main parties differed as to whether it would be possible for another conflict like those in Korea and Indo-China to be limited. In any case, the government promised to develop Japan's own missiles and not to import American nuclear weapons. Left Socialists and Sōhyō unionists continued to demand the withdrawal of all U.S. military bases. They agitated against establishment of an American missile base on Niijima, and later against visits by American nuclear submarines. Leaders in both Socialist parties observed the developing stalemate in nuclear armament and predicted transference of emphasis in the main international struggle to the economic plane. They continued to urge negotiated controls of nuclear weaponry, comprehensive arms limitation, and the strengthening of coexistence.

CRITICISM OF THE UNITED STATES AND OPPOSITION TO RENEWAL OF THE SECURITY TREATY

After American emphasis shifted from democratization to the containment of communism, no one should have been surprised that the stronger, leftist factions in Japan's SDP became more critical of the United States than of Soviet and Chinese Communist policies. While they have led opposition to capitalism, and public sentiment has been so strong against communism, Soviet and mainland Chinese leaders have, rather unevenly, encouraged and cultivated them. In contrast they have been treated with coolness and some suspicion by American officials and public opinion.

Depending on various factional tendencies, adherents of the SDP support Marxist theories and some of Lenin's emphases, including anti-imperialism. They have a common analysis and critique of capitalism, a similar vision of a revolutionized future, however they may differ as to means, stages, and political institutions. The United States, as the leader of capitalism, has been buttressing its political and economic allies in Japan and elsewhere. It therefore stands behind "monopoly capitalism," the often caricatured but deeply feared "enemy" of the socialist opposition. Intellectual orientations, ethical choices, and emotional commitments are involved in these matters.

With such predispositions, plus what might be called opposition nationalism, Japanese Socialists understandably criticize American "imperialism" more than examples of Communist expansionism. The U.S. has tended to back regimes in Eastern Asia much more conservative and authoritarian than its own: those of Syngman Rhee, Ngo Dinh Diem, Chiang Kai-shek, and other dictatorial or monarchical regimes. When dictators are overthrown, the U.S. often recognizes and aids military juntas. McCarthyism, right-wing Republicanism, racial prejudice, growing military influence in politics, and writings about oligarchic tendencies in the United States have led many Japanese to doubt the genuineness and durability of "capitalist democracy" under internal and external pressures, even in the U.S.

The fact that the United States had required Japan to join its system of military-political containment as a price for recovery of national sovereignty, the presence of American bases and forces, American pressures for Japanese rearmament—all fitted the left Socialist image of American imperialism as the most immediate threat to world peace. Right-wing Socialists did not view the situation this way; we have seen that they were neutralists with generally pro-Western leanings.

Few issues have illustrated more clearly the SDP severity in criticizing American as compared with Soviet expansion than the contrasting degrees of agitation for return of insular territories to the northeast and to the southeast and southwest. The left wing was much more vociferous in condemning American retention of and policies in the Ryūkyūs and Bonins, while the right more temperately keeps requesting the return of these archipelagoes as well as the recovery of the Kuriles and Southern Sakhalin.

Although in 1956 the SDP pressed the government to recover from Russia the maximum of lost territories, it accepted disappointment with restraint. In contrast, during the next two years it militantly cooperated with Sōhyō in demanding return of Okinawa to Japanese administration, no further expansion of American bases there, prohibition of the storage of missiles and nuclear warheads, free political processes and abolition of the military governor's veto, and freedom of communication and transportation between Japan and the Ryūkyūs.[16] The right wing was inclined to favor continued U.S. facilities in that archipelago for the sake of security, but both main factions have demanded that the government abandon "subservience" and negotiate successfully for the resumption of Japanese administration. Japanese Communists, fellow travelers, and left Socialists have tried to exert pressures on the United States through a variety of international organizations, including the United Nations. In vain they tried to encourage a radical united front organization in Okinawa called the Liaison Council for the Protection of Democracy, but both it and the pro-American Democrats were defeated in 1958 by the indigenous Socialist Masses' Party.

For some years after the truce in Korea, the Communist peace offensive and emphasis on coexistence met a significant response from socialist circles. Since Chinese intrusions into Himalayan borderlands and the sharpening of the Sino-Soviet debate over coexistence versus support for militant "patriotic wars of national liberation," the SDP has regained better balance. At a special party convention on the day after Asanuma's assassination (October 13, 1960), the Socialists pulled back from the slain leader's earlier statement. In the following March, Tomomi Narita, a "structural reformer" who was then chief of the SDP Policy Planning Board, commented that, while "American imperialism is undoubtedly an 'enemy,' . . . the immediate target of attack is Japan's monopoly capitalism."[17] In November his colleague, Eda, had stated during a pre-election televised debate that his party was not anti-American just because it opposed certain U.S. policies; and, he added, the Soviet Union—like the United States—being a major protagonist in power politics, could not be considered as a force for peace.[18]

Soon, when it became necessary for the United States to reduce its dollar outflow, the Socialists not only opposed repayment of part of

16. A poll on June 27, 1957, conducted by the Public Opinion Science Association, found that nearly two thirds of the respondents in the Tokyo area were critical of the U.S. for unwillingness to return the Ryūkyūs to Japan soon. Those especially dissatisfied included students, professional people, laborers, the salaried, youth, and men distinctly more than women.

17. *Mainichi,* March 8, 1961.

18. See also *Shakai Shimpō,* Dec. 18, 1960.

the American economic assistance extended during the Occupation,[19] but predicted that weakening of U.S. military commitments abroad would impede the LDP program for economic growth, increase pressures for revision of the Japanese Constitution, and make more imperative improvement of relations with Communist China.

Revision and renewal of national alignment with the United States, involving as it did most of the crucial internal and external issues of Japan's orientation, was bound to be challenged by and to test the leftist opposition. A series of diplomatic steps—the Kishi-Eisenhower talks in June 1957, discussions by the Japanese-American Committee on Security during the ensuing year, Foreign Minister Aiichirō Fujiyama's talks with Secretary John Foster Dulles and others in Washington in September 1958, and his sixteen later sessions with Ambassabor MacArthur in Tokyo—led to availability of the new security treaty draft early in October, just as the battle against the Police Duties Revision Bill was beginning. Quite consciously, this confrontation was a dress rehearsal for, and developed some features of, the looming struggle over whether the alliance should be renewed. Dominant factions in the Liberal Democratic Party and in the Socialist Party were committed to their positions a year before the new security treaty was submitted to the Japanese House of Representatives for approval; their polarity meant that one side was likely to suffer complete defeat, hence that parliamentarianism might be in some jeopardy.[20]

After the elections in May 1958, support for the SDP had lost momentum and then declined absolutely, causing leftists again to express their doubts that socialism could be achieved by parliamentary means alone and to reassert both the working class basis of the party and the need for direct mass action against what was viewed as the reactionary aims and the misrepresentative hegemony of the perennial, conserva-

19. In January 1962, the Diet voted to repay $490,000,000 of more than two billion dollars in commodity assistance granted by the United States between September 2, 1945, and April 28, 1952, under programs known as Government Appropriation for Relief in Occupied Areas, and Economic Rehabilitation in Occupied Areas. Leaders of the SDP argued that Japan had not thereby incurred debts; that their government had paid part of the costs of the Occupation; and that, since the commodities imported had been sold to the people, later repayment from tax revenues would constitute twofold payment by the people.

20. Revision and renewal of the security treaty was negotiated in a partisan manner, and it was ruled that there could be no amendment by the Diet. The issue was crucial for both main parties, with Prime Minister Kishi's political future at stake.

tive majority.[21] This leftward trend led to a new split in the SDP and was influenced by a growth of radicalism in the General Council of Trade Unions (Sōhyō), where a policy of cooperation with the Communist Party as well as with the Socialists was advocated with increasing vigor and adopted at its convention in August 1959. Meanwhile, since the July following Khrushchev's de-Stalinization speech at the CPSU's Twentieth Congress in 1956, the JCP had agreed that socialism could be attained by peaceful means and had been calling for a "united democratic front of national liberation." Thus, differences between the three main leftist forces dwindled, and conditions were leading to their cooperation in a common struggle. Still their interests were not identical; suspicions and differences of emphasis persisted.

Another major component of opposition to Japan's alliance with the U.S. was the student federation, Zengakuren; it was the most drastically radical, especially its so-called mainstream which—increasingly in and after 1958—parted company from the pro-JCP wing to stress immediate overthrow not only of the Kishi administration but of conservative power and the existing system. Its invasion of the Diet compound on November 27, 1958, and use of Socialist Diet members for the submission of petitions was a harbinger of demonstrations and other independent actions to come.

But the People's Council to Oppose the Revised Police Duties Law was broader in composition than the People's Council to Prevent Revision of the Security Treaty (hereafter called the People's Council). The 134 original member organizations of the latter did not include such anticommunist and pro-parliamentary groups as the labor federations Zenrō and Shin Sambetsu (the "new" National Federation of Industrial Organizations, an anticommunist offshoot of Sambetsu, formed in 1949). The earlier coalition could be more comprehensive since it was for defense of internal democracy; greater differences appeared when it came to policies for peace.[22] While the united front for

21. Leftist factions on the Central Committee of the SDP during 1958–59 had a majority of 17 to 13.

22. The People's Council to Prevent Revision of the Security Treaty was formally inaugurated on March 28, 1959. Its thirteen initial sponsors included the SDP, Sōhyō, Gensuikyō (The Japan Council against A- and H-Bombs), the Japan Peace Committee, the People's Council for Restoration of Japan-China Relations, the Japan-China Friendship Association, the National Federation for Safeguarding the Constitution, the National Liaison Council against Military Bases, the Joint Struggle Council of Youths and Stu-

protest was being shaped, the SDP was largely paralyzed by inner tensions; it lost the initiative to Sōhyō and the JCP, which mainly determined the campaign's tone and direction. The Socialists were unable to gain control, though in the policymaking bodies of the People's Council they did oppose certain Communist positions and compelled compromises. This anti-treaty Council was organized on national, prefectural, metropolitan, district, and local levels. Communists were very active in nearly two thirds of what came to number 1,686 district councils, whereas the weakness of Socialist local organization was again manifest. Headquarters were established in Socialist rooms in the House of Councillors Annex; a Socialist was made director, and the two assistant directors were from the SDP and Sōhyō. Both organizations were represented on the Board and on the Strategy Committee formed in April 1960. Communist influence in these two bodies was considerably greater than was indicated by the "observer" status of its delegates. The JCP also controlled some of the other represented organizations and had members on the Council's secretariat.

Here we shall summarize main features of Socialist participation in the anti-treaty campaign.[23] Although cooperation with the JCP had been rejected at the party convention in November 1958, this reluctance was overcome by pressure from Sōhyō and other leftist organizations. Their victory and that of leftist factions in the SDP presaged the split of the Nishio group and some defections from the Kawakami faction in the fall of that same year, 1959. As the Socialist Party became increasingly involved in mass demonstrations, it became more reliant on Sōhyō's strength in mobilizing numbers and once more was

dents, the Women's Council for Safeguarding Human Rights, the National Federation of Neutral Labor Unions (Chūritsu Rōren) and the Tokyo Joint Struggle Council for Safeguarding Peace and Democracy. The three principal stated aims of the People's Council were: prevention of renewal of the revised security treaty, neutralism in foreign relations, and abolition of the security system. The last, especially, paralleled Communist aims.

After the climax of the treaty crisis in May-June 1960, there were controversies between such organizations and their inner factions over interpretation of the recent experience and about future policies. The Council mentioned above was dissolved just two years after its formation. Its successor, with much the same primary membership, has been the National Council for Opposition to the Security Treaty and for Safeguarding Peace and Democracy. The Socialist Party increased its reservations regarding this organization, while JCP influence in it gained.

23. A detailed study of the anti-treaty campaign is George R. Packard, III, *Protest in Tokyo, The Security Treaty Crisis of 1960* (Princeton, Princeton University Press, 1966). It forms the basis for the following summary.

impressed by superior Communist revolutionary skills, discipline, and determination. Yielding to pressure from the left increased tension between the two main Socialist wings, though the Kawakami faction was willing to go further than Nishio's adherents in the obstruction of parliamentary procedures. Secession of the Nishio faction removed a brake on radicalism within the party but, once established as the Democratic Socialist Party, this group in alliance with Zenrō forced both the SDP and Sōhyō to shield themselves and to allow Kawakami's faction disproportionate influence in the process. Moreover, the opposition needed the cooperation of the DSP in the Diet in order to demonstrate that the LDP, in pushing through approval of the treaty, was indeed abusing its majority.

Nevertheless, Asanuma (who had been cultivating the leftist factions) was elected Chairman by a narrow margin at an extraordinary party convention on March 25, 1960, and the composition of the Central Executive Committee during the rest of the crisis included only two adherents of the defeated Kawakami and thirteen ranged on the left, the strongest representation being of the Suzuki and Wada factions. Another sign of the party's leftward trend was the growing assertiveness of the Sakisaka clique in both the anti-treaty struggle and the bitter Miike coal miners' strike. They represented the Marxist-Leninist views of the Worker-Farmer school: that revolutionary conditions were fast ripening, could be accelerated, and that socialism could not be achieved without the use of proletarian force at some crucial point.

"Absolute opposition" to the treaty was expressed by Socialists both within and outside the Diet. They obstructed and delayed proceedings, hoping that the session of the Lower House would close without voting approval of the treaty. In debates they launched some telling, well publicized attacks on the treaty text and its implications. As we have seen, they forcibly blocked the Speaker's access to the rostrum to prevent extension of the session and on May 19–20 they were expelled by police. Finally, as a desperate gesture, nearly all of the SDP Representatives submitted their resignations to Chairman Asanuma, who was restrained from submitting them because of the futility of such a move and for fear that the LDP might seize the opportunity to revise the Constitution.

After Kishi's supporters imposed their will early on May 20, Sōhyō launched three nationwide strikes. The SDP and Communists sharply disagreed on the Strategy Committee and Board of Directors of the People's Council. The former insisted that emphasis be on Kishi's resignation, cancellation of President Eisenhower's visit, and new elections followed by legislative action on the treaty. The JCP gave priority to actions opposing American "imperialism." Asanuma personally delivered a letter to the American Embassy asking that President Eisenhower not visit during the crisis, and 30 to 40 Socialist Diet members were at Haneda Airport on June 10, when Press Secretary James C. Hagerty, Ambassador MacArthur, and a presidential appointments secretary were delayed and their car mauled, mainly by Communists and by members of the allied anti-mainstream faction of Zengakuren. This proved to be a turning point in the attitudes of the press and public. All parties were soon obliged to show more concern for restoration of parliamentary processes. The opposition could claim that it had forced Kishi to resign and to cancel the President's visit, but it proved impossible for socialists to block ratification of the treaty or to build electoral strength from the anti-treaty campaign. This process had aroused ultrarightist organizations, and a series of violent incidents ensued.

PARTISAN VIEWS ON RELATIONS WITH THE SOVIET UNION

We have noted how the left Socialists especially objected to the "one-sided" peace treaty, which was unacceptable to neighboring communist powers, and to an alliance that bound Japan to one of the mutually hostile orbits. Because of "communist aggression" in Korea, however, the right wing favored a temporary policy of limited cooperation with efforts to contain those powers. Both factions agreed with the Afro-Asian states and others in opposing extension of that conflict and in urging a truce even though it would leave the nearby peninsula still partitioned. More recently SDP policy has been closer to that of the People's Republic of China: that foreign troops should be withdrawn from Korea, after which "free" elections should be held preparatory to reunification.

After the truce at Panmunjom in July 1953, the Communist peace offensive found the Left Socialists more responsive than those of the Right who were on guard against playing into the hands of pro-Communist elements in the rival SDP. During the winter of 1953–54, the Right SDP denounced any form of neutralism which would jeopardize collective security. It favored improved relations with the U.S.S.R.

and Red China so long as they would not impair cooperation with "free world" democracies and the organization of international democratic socialism.[24]

The Left SDP came out more forthrightly for restoration of normal relations with the communist colossi, hoping that if Japan concluded a series of bilateral nonaggression pacts, the military clause relevant to Japan would be omitted from the Sino-Soviet Treaty of Friendship, Alliance, and Mutual Assistance.[25] Later that year (1954), however, in talks between the four policy leaders from both wings, Mizutani and Sone stated the Right's preference that nonaggression assurances be negotiated between the two alliance systems. That was the summer when the Soviet Union decided not to be deterred much longer by the obstacles to improved Sino-Japanese relations but, when advantageous, to negotiate without its intransigent ally to end the legal state of war with Japan. In September, Molotov indicated to a Japanese editor his government's willingness to "normalize relations," and a month later a Sino-Soviet communiqué declared that this would depend upon Japan becoming independent of security arrangements with the United States.

In December, Foreign Ministers Shigemitsu and Molotov exchanged views, and when Hatoyama became Prime Minister he indicated willingness to be somewhat more independent of American warnings. While Right Socialists continued to be cautious, the Left became more active in the National Conference for the Restoration of Relations with Communist China and the Soviet Union which was organized in January-February 1955 and included numerous conservatives. In negotiations which did begin in June in London, the Soviet plenipotentiary intimated that his government might even be willing to recognize Japanese rearmament and the alliance with the U.S. But the parley foundered. Socialist leaders realized that the Soviet Union was using fishery rights in Russian-controlled northern waters as bargaining pressure. Even though the main conversations were at an impasse they favored continued talks about fishing.

After adoption of the formula for "Peace, Independence, and

24. "Foreign Policies of the Japan Socialist Party," mimeographed draft dated November 26, 1953, and adopted at the Right-wing convention in January 1954. Also, "Comparative Platforms," pp. 18–21.

25. "[Left] SDP Foreign Policies for the Fiscal Year 1954," *Tōkatsudō*, No. 71, Part 2, pp. 12–14; also, "Comparative Platforms," pp. 22–24.

Security," which constituted part of the basis for party reunification, a kind of limited bipartisanship in dealing with the Russians was facilitated by the opposition. Using the "Adenauer formula," the SDP Bureau of International Affairs summarized party views in a draft statement in early December 1955. Restoration of peace by simple declaration and resumption of diplomatic relations were upheld as prime objectives. Shikotan and the Habomai islands, being so close to Hokkaidō, should certainly be returned; but Japan's claims to the Kurile (Chishima) archipelago and to Southern Sakhalin (Karafuto) could be considered later along with claims to the American-held Ryūkyū and Ogasawara (Bōnin) groups. No restrictions should be permitted on use of the Japan Sea by foreign ships, nor should straits leading thereto be closed to vessels of third countries. Japanese war criminals and other prisoners held in China should be repatriated immediately after a declaration of peace. Japan should reject the Soviet demand that it remain aloof from any alliance system and should maintain freedom of decision in this regard. Moreover, renunciation of interference in each other's internal affairs should be written into the later peace treaty as a safeguard against international communist subversion. Principles with respect to fishing and trade should be mentioned in the later, more comprehensive peace treaty; thereafter agreements could be specifically negotiated. Cultural relations could be similarly arranged.[26]

These proposals were not particularly original, since they accorded with a fairly general consensus which had emerged, despite different factional opinions in the Liberal Democratic Party. As talks with Soviet diplomats were resumed in January 1956, they drew the spotlight of attention and held it through much of the year. During the earlier talks in London, the SDP had been somewhat critical of conservative diplomacy. Why was it willing in a preliminary way to settle for less, as indicated by its CEC on February 10? Its strategists recognized that the United States could more easily exert pressures on Japan as long as the state of war continued. The coming of peace and the continuing communist adherence to peaceful coexistence would probably induce the U.S. to change its military policies. The strain in Japan's relations with Afro-Asian as well as communist countries would abate. Russo-Japanese trade and northern fisheries were considerations. And, of

26. Mimeographed draft statement of policies, Dec. 5, 1955.

course, they fully expected that renewal of intercourse with the Soviet Union would soon be followed by similar settlements with the People's Republic of China.

For these reasons, and quite in contrast to its attitude toward relations with the United States, the Socialist Party continued in the bipartisan effort. Certain Socialist leaders were able to relay information from the head of the Soviet fisheries mission in Tokyo to the Prime Minister, the Foreign Ministry, and the Economic Planning Board. Thus the party was engaging in a sort of unofficial diplomacy. But it declined to add one of its members to Hatoyama's delegation to Moscow. After Foreign Ministers Shigemitsu and Shepilov had failed to conclude a comprehensive peace treaty, the SDP maintained pressure on the Hatoyama and Kōno factions to attempt the Adenauer-type of limited agreement. The CEC warned that failure to do so would jeopardize the annual fisheries agreements, would delay Japan's entry into the United Nations, and might cause loss of the Habomais and Shikotan. The party hailed the declaration of peace and the trade protocol signed on October 19, 1956, for the former included the five desiderata which it had specially stressed.[27] But it expressed disappointment that the Habomais and Shikotan were not immediately to be returned and that there had been no statement in favor of prohibiting nuclear tests. Sone criticized the government for not obtaining an agreement for continued talks about territorial questions. Conservative diplomacy was described as having been clumsy and beset by factional feuding.

During and continuing for a while after these events, the Suez and Hungarian crises threw into relief the divergent attitudes of Japan's right and left Socialists toward Western and Soviet imperialisms. Nationalization of the Suez Canal was quickly approved by the SDP Bureau of International Affairs as an expression of Egyptian sovereignty and because unrestricted use was still guaranteed. (Nothing was said

27. An English translation of these two documents can be found in *Current History*, *32* (Jan. 1957), 49–50. The Declaration of Peace stipulated: an end to the state of war, renewal of diplomatic and consular relations, renunciation of force in the relations of the signatories, recognition of each other's right to individual or collective self-defense, assurance against intervention in each other's domestic affairs for economic, political, or ideological reasons, the U.S.S.R. to support Japan's admission to membership in the U.N., repatriation of Japanese prisoners to be completed, Soviet renunciation of reparations claims, and the return of the Habomais and Shikotan to Japan after negotiation of a comprehensive peace treaty.

about denial of access to Israeli ships.) Anglo-French military action was condemned as another example of Western imperialism, and the invasion by Israeli forces was termed a violation of the United Nations Charter. A resolution passed by the second congress of the Asian Socialist Conference condemned these as aggressions and called upon the invaders to withdraw. At the SDP convention in January 1957 some left-wingers charged that the United States refrained from joining the intervention because it wished to replace British and French influence in their erstwhile Middle Eastern colonies, and that the U.S. was doing its utmost to make that region into a great military base against the Soviet Union.

The Soviet intervention to crush a revolt in Hungary, coinciding as it did with the Middle Eastern conflict, caused much sharper debates between the two wings of the SDP and the two main labor federations. The SDP debate came to a climax at the convention in January 1957 when party executives, headed by the right-winger Mitsu Kōno, submitted to the Action Policy Committee a draft which said in part: "In Hungary, the political program of the Nagy government was unacceptable to the Soviet Union and that nation suffered a terrible armed oppression." This was heatedly debated by left and right. Right-wingers led by Nishio and allied with Zenrō submitted a revision which was defeated 13 to 55. It stated that the Nagy government had gone beyond national communism to advocate coalition with the Hungarian Social Democratic Party and in foreign affairs abrogation of adherence to the Warsaw Pact in favor of neutralism. It agreed with a resolution of the recent Asian Socialist Conference session which declared the revolutionary action to have been liberal, not reactionary, and had condemned the Soviet Union. To balance the picture, the statement castigated the British and French for setting a bad example which would affect adversely the efforts of Eastern European nations to recover independence.

Meanwhile, representatives of the leftist Wada, Nomizo, and Matsumoto factions—backed by Sōhyō and later joined by Suzuki's "mainstream" group—combined to pass (by 41 out of 68 votes) their own preferred version. On the main point at issue it read: "In Hungary, the Nagy regime yielded to the pressure of capitalist and landlord forces and brought confusion which led to the demand of the Kadar government for Russian armed intervention."

On the third day of the convention, debate was resumed in the

Action Policy Committee. Kōno and Nishio led the attack against the radical revision. At length it was decided to have the final version drafted by a new eight-man subcommittee composed of representatives of various factions. The diluted result read: "The liberalization movements in Poland and Hungary were developments stemming from the Twentieth Congress of the Communist Party of the Soviet Union and although the subsequent de-Stalinization and liberalization were somewhat taken advantage of by reactionary forces, the armed intervention of the Soviet Union cannot be condoned."[28]

As these crises were subsiding, and after the preliminary agreements with the Soviet Union, Socialist leaders redoubled efforts to augment Russo-Japanese trade and to hasten a formal treaty of peace. One policy adopted by the party convention in February 1958 was to "strengthen the effort it has been making in the field of nongovernmental diplomacy." This referred to the SDP mission to Communist China sent in the previous April; although, in order to obtain passports, its members had pledged not to conclude an agreement with the government in Peking, as we shall see in the next section it could not entirely resist Chinese enticements. Also, Katayama led a nine-man delegation to Peking, Moscow, and Warsaw in September-October 1957. It conducted party-to-party discussions and talks with state planning officials about how Japanese producers and merchants could cooperate with the economic development of China and Siberia, as well as how joint efforts could be made to assist even less developed economies in Asia. The mission furthermore exchanged views concerning North Pacific fishing, cultural relations, a Soviet-Japanese airline, repatriations, territorial questions and a peace treaty, disarmament, and a ban on nuclear testing. Of course, the Socialist emphasis on neutrality, independence from the U.S., reorientation of trade, and recovery of territory from the United States as well as from the Soviet Union in one sense placed that party in a better position for such parleys. But Russian realists must have reminded themselves, if not their guests, that theirs was a minority party hardly as yet within reach of power.

Toward the end of March 1958, Chairman Suzuki wrote Khrushchev congratulating him on becoming Premier and asking for more favorable terms in the annual negotiations about northern fisheries.

28. Sources include: *Asahi,* Jan. 19, 1957; *Mainichi,* Jan. 19, 20, 1957; *Nihon Keizai Shimbun,* Jan. 20, 1957; *Shakai Tsūshin,* No. 233 (Feb. 10, 1957).

The wily Russian timed his reply so that it arrived just a month before the Japanese general elections and immediately after cancellation of the fourth unofficial Sino-Japanese commercial agreement. He asserted that Japan's conservative government, by "artificially hampering" conclusion of a peace treaty, was solely responsible for "material damage" to the Japanese fishing industry. The electoral results, however, indicated that this kind of pressure attempted by both communist governments, probably in part to favor the SDP, not only failed but may have boomeranged.

EFFORTS TO RESTORE RELATIONS WITH MAINLAND CHINA

Qualified success in restoring diplomatic and commercial relations with the U.S.S.R. naturally spurred similar efforts in the direction of Red China. This had been a Socialist policy since the revolution culminated in mainland China, but the problems involved and right-wing reservations made this a barometer of factional influences and of trends in party policy.

After the party schism in 1951, the Left had advocated renewal of diplomatic and commercial relations with the People's Republic of China regardless of Chinese ideology. It had always tried to link policies toward China and the Soviet Union with the peace movement. Its 1954 platform also urged conclusion of peace and nonaggression treaties with Communist China. Taiwan was declared to belong to the People's Republic, but it hoped that acquisition would be achieved "autonomously and peacefully."[29]

This more revolutionary wing has also been active in a series of pressure groups which have included conservatives pragmatically interested in trade with China. Among these organizations were the Diet Members League for the Promotion of Sino-Japanese Trade, the Japan–China Friendship Association, the People's Council for Restoration of Relations with Red China and Russia, and a number of commercial associations.[30]

Policies adopted by the Right wing in 1952 and 1954 had contrasted with those of their leftist rivals. Diplomatic relations with Red China?

29. "[Left] SDP Foreign Policy for the Fiscal Year 1954," *Tōkatsudō*, Special Issue, No. 71, Part 2, pp. 12–14; "Comparative Platforms," pp. 22–24.

30. For a broader discussion of Japanese groups and their thinking about relations with Red China, see: Shao-chuan Leng, "Japanese Attitudes toward Communist China," *Far Eastern Survey*, 27 (June 1958), 81–89; and by the same author, *Japan and Communist China* (Kyoto, Dōshisha University Press, 1958), Chap. 6.

Yes, as long as they would not jeopardize Japan's independence and security. And trade? Again yes—on the same basis as with other Asian and Western nations, except that, until general disarmament could be achieved, Japan should conform with the anti-P.R.C. embargo of the most patently military commodities, not however with the entire CHINCOM list. Until after the Katayama-led mission to China late in 1955, Right Socialists had usually been skeptical about the potential value of Sino-Japanese trade.

While the Korean War lasted, the Right wing had thought neither Chinese regime should be recognized. The Left's idea of a nonaggression treaty had been dubbed "an illusion." Improved relations with China should be accomplished without impairing cooperation with the free world, including democratic socialist forces. The policies molded in 1953–54 had rejected continued disarmament of Japan with its neutrality guaranteed only by the two potent communist neighbors. The party had acquiesced to representation of the P.R.C. in the United Nations if the two communist powers would agree to the peaceful reunification of Korea and if Communist China's accession did not precede Japan's. It had favored temporary U.N. control over Taiwan and an ultimate status for that island in accordance with the free will of its inhabitants. Shortly before the general elections of February 1955, the Socialists had admitted that in one sense this issue of Taiwan was domestic and in another sense international in nature.[31]

By the fall of 1955, the lessening of international tensions and early improvement in actual relations between Japan and Communist China had facilitated the rapprochement of the separate Socialist parties. A Sino-Soviet peace offensive had been launched after the truce in Korea and the "five principles of coexistence" soon were being publicized. During September-October 1954, five from each Social Democratic wing had toured mainland China as part of a composite Diet members' mission.[32] After discussing specific improvements in relations between the two neighboring countries with Chinese offi-

31. Ōhara Shakai Mondai Kenkyūjo, *Nihon Rōdō Nenkan, 1954* (Tokyo, Hōsei University, 1955), p. 670; "Foreign Policy of the Japan Socialist Party [Right]," dated Nov. 26, 1953 (mimeo.), and later submitted to the party convention; also: "Comparative Platforms," pp. 18–21.

32. The Left sent Chairman Suzuki, Sata, Shikaichi Ashika, Kōzō Sasaki, and Yoshio Nakada; the Right nominated Motojirō Sugiyama, Mitsu Kōno, Eki Sone, Seiichi Matsumura, and Tadahisa Matsudaira.

cials, including Chairman Mao and Foreign Minister (and Premier) Chou En-lai, there had been substantial agreement between the two Socialist groups that the Communist regime, although a dictatorship, would be in power for a long time; that it had unified the nation and was effectively answering the needs of the socioeconomy, receiving the support of most mainland Chinese. It was applying Marxist-Leninist principles, but much of its support derived from nationalist appeals. So rapid had been its economic strides that Japan must look to its own industrial development. China was neither Titoist nor a satellite but rather a junior partner advancing toward increasing equality. Moreover, China had become a leader in Asian affairs. Right-wingers had added that China's labor movement was not free, and they had hoped that China would convince its neighbors that it intended no aggressions. While in Peking, they had conceded that Taiwan belonged to mainland China, but they had urged that it be obtained peaceably and not be used subsequently for aggressive purposes. Both groups apparently agreed that Chinese aggression was unlikely and that the Nationalists had no practical hope of recovering the mainland.[33]

When, in June 1955, two leaders from each of the Socialist parties discussed policies toward China, the chief disagreement was over the future of Taiwan. The leftists virtually rejected the idea of a temporary U.N. trusteeship, and, by advocating decision by a plebiscite on the mainland as well as on Taiwan, actually recognized the Communist claim. They were willing for Japan to have only temporary, de facto relations with the regime of Chiang Kai-shek, insisting that the government in Peking was the only legitimate one to recognize. This —and the joint conclusion that, after Chou's promises of peaceful settlements during the Bandung Conference, China was unlikely to invade Taiwan—comprised the rather slim area of agreement on this question.[34] The foreign policy formula which served as a partial basis for party reunification optimistically emphasized Red China's inclusion in a new system of mutually guaranteed nonaggression but left until later the details of SDP proposals on Sino-Japanese relations. The leftists were soon actively trying to push the right toward their own position.

A telling step in this direction seems to have been the 16-man dele-

33. *Tōkatsudō,* No. 97 (Nov. 10, 1954); *Jōhō Tsūshin,* No. 118 (Nov. 15, 1954).
34. *Jōhō Tsūshin,* No. 142 (Aug. 5, 1955); *Tōkatsudō,* Special No. (July 5, 1955).

gation from the National Federation to Protect the Constitution, led by Katayama, which visited Red China in November of that year. The former Japanese Socialist Premier discussed peaceful coexistence and the restoring of normal relations with Chairman Mao, who promised soon to repatriate some hundreds of Japanese prisoners. An agreement for cultural exchanges was made.

In the following month, while on a speaking tour of Shikoku, Suzuki for the first time publicly declared that the time had come for Japan to recognize the People's Republic as the legitimate government of China. This and related problems were straightway discussed at a meeting of party executives, where Nishio argued that the Chinese Nationalist government was more viable than most of his colleagues thought. Searching discussions ensued in the reunified party's Bureau of International Affairs, whose conclusions were cleared with the Policy Planning Board's subcommittee on foreign policies and then were affirmed, in May 1956, by the CEC. As negotiations with the Soviet Union were about to be resumed, the Socialists declared that a treaty of peace with China could not wait for solution of the complex Taiwan question. For the time being, Japan's existing relations with that island's regime should be continued, but Taiwan should be recognized as part of China proper. Rather idealistically the SDP proposed reducing tensions by withdrawal of the U.S. Seventh Fleet, a Communist guarantee of the status quo in Taiwan, and disarmament of the Nationalists.[35]

The practicability of this formula grew dimmer as Premier Chou insisted on rejection of the "two Chinas plot" as a prerequisite of a Sino-Japanese peace settlement. One facet of left Socialist resurgence at the second reunified party convention in January 1957 was incorporation of this demand into voted policy. Creation of the first of what came to be a series of "Special Committees on Sino-Japanese Relations" was another leftist ploy. Instead of letting such policies be formulated by the two regular organs, in which right-wingers were influential, leftists advocated and prevailingly staffed these special

35. Mimeographed statement by the SDP Bureau of International Affairs, March 6, 1956; *Nippon Times,* May 23, 1956. See also the explanation by the Bureau attached to the CEC policy decision on May 31, in *Shakai Tsūshin,* No. 234 (Feb. 15, 1957), which—inter alia—rejected unofficial Anglo-American suggestions of a U.N. trusteeship over or a plebiscite on Taiwan.

committees which were usually placed under the Bureau on Popular Movements.[36]

Thus, a new leftward phase in Japanese Socialist politics preceded the more drastic shift in the Chinese Communist Party (CCP) which occurred in the summer of that same year, after the brief "hundred flowers" episode. It soon became obvious, later admitted by Peking, that coexistence was regarded as a tactic chiefly applicable to weaker neutralist countries, to states like Japan that were beyond Communist control and indeed within the containing perimeter, and for internationally directed propaganda. The attitude of the P.R.C. toward the Kishi government hardened. By the fall of 1957 and into the following spring there emerged a dual Red Chinese strategy of trying to influence the LDP as well and to create conditions favorable to anti-Kishi factions who would be more friendly to establishment of an official Chinese trade mission in Tokyo with diplomatic immunity and banking facilities for trade. Before the Japanese elections in May 1958, Peking tried to convince the Japanese electorate that the SDP was the party which could really improve relations with China; but after that tactic failed, the main Communist interest in the Socialist Party was as a leading element in a united front to block renewal of the security treaty with the United States. Of course, Peking also had liaison with the JCP.

Between April 1957 and January 1962, the Japanese Socialists sent to Red China three major missions, and a number of lesser ones, as

36. Chairman of the first Special Committee on Sino-Japanese Relations was Seiichi Katsumata, a left Socialist; the vice-chairmen were Tadashi Kodaira, Hideo Yamahana, and Hōsei Yoshida; the secretary general was Ryōsaku Sasaki. In all, there were 21 members.

Policies evolved by these organs and the CEC during February culminated in a statement by the CEC on March 2. It upheld Communist China's "right" of representation in the U.N. and repeated the demand for prompt restoration of diplomatic, commercial, and cultural relations between Japan and mainland China. The policy of "two Chinas" was rejected as was a U.N. trusteeship over Taiwan. Then it walked a tightrope: the future of that island should be settled by the P.R.C. and the Nationalist regime directly, as a domestic Chinese problem without foreign interference. Yet (somehow) international tensions over this issue were to be assuaged by peaceful Sino-American and Sino-Japanese negotiations. Until Red China could extend control over Taiwan, Japan should continue existing relations with the latter on a de facto basis. Proposals for a comprehensive peace treaty were summarized; they included nuclear and conventional disarmament as well as the pet idea of a Locarno-type nonaggression framework to replace the existing alliance systems.

agents of "people's diplomacy." During the first of these, Premier Chou En-lai called for resumption of normal relations on the basis of the "five principles of coexistence." He made it clear that his government did not consider Japan to be yet fully independent, but "the Japanese people who have a several-thousand-year-old tradition of independence will surely regain their independence." Chou denounced the "two Chinas" idea, urged that Japan break relations with the Nationalists and establish them with the P.R.C.; he indicated that China could be patient about asserting its claim to Taiwan and about representation in the U.N. There remained a partial gap between the two points of view, as was indicated when Asanuma suggested that, even though Taiwan was a domestic Chinese affair, it was appropriate for Japan to have de facto relations with that island in the interim before P.R.C. hegemony could be extended to it.

Chou gave the impression of favoring an all-inclusive security arrangement for Eastern Asia, and Mao is reported to have promised efforts toward an early nonaggression treaty, including his conditional request that the Soviet Union delete reference to Japan from the Sino-Soviet alliance. There were also lengthy discussions of commercial possibilities in the light of the second Chinese five-year plan, the capacity of the Japanese economy, and the recent SDP five-year plan.

Though the Socialists had assured the government in Tokyo that they would not conclude any formal agreements in Peking, Asanuma and Chairman Chang Hsi-jo of the Chinese People's Institute for Foreign Affairs did sign a joint communiqué which conceded almost all points sought by the hosts. At that time—before Soviet ICBM demonstrations, Sputnik, and Mao's reappraisal of the relative velocities of East and West winds—the statement also called for general reduction of armaments, including prohibition of the production, storage, and use of nuclear weapons. The testing of such weapons should be renounced by the three nuclear powers.[37] When the Socialists returned home, they talked with Premier Kishi and tried to give the public the impression that only their party could accomplish the needed rapprochement. Certain American tariffs and the developing economic recession seemed to lend urgency to these proposals.

In June 1957, the SDP urged termination of the embargo against Communist China. The British and Japanese governments success-

37. *Nitchū no Kokkō Kaifuku e* (Toward the Restoration of Relations between Japan and China) (Tokyo, 1957), pp. 143–47; *Mainichi* (English), April 23, 1957.

fully pressed for significant reduction of such restraints, and a fourth Sino-Japanese trade agreement provided for exchanges totaling more than the value of Red China's trade with any other noncommunist country, greater in value than Japan's trade with Taiwan during the previous year. But this agreement was abruptly canceled by the Chinese when, early in 1958, the Kishi administration, under Nationalist Chinese and U.S. pressure, refused diplomatic status to the prospective P.R.C. trade mission in Tokyo and declined to permit financial transactions to be processed through the quasi-governmental Bank of Tokyo. (The Chinese also took umbrage when their flag was hauled down from a Nagasaki department store display by a young Japanese rightist.) Mainland officials soon denied that they were trying to influence the imminent Japanese elections, declaring that the Japanese would have to decide more basically what their policy toward Communist China should be. The door for resumption of trade with Japan on a significant scale was not reopened until August 1960—after failure of the anti-security treaty struggle, failure also of the "Great Leap Forward," and as Peking's deepening rift with the Soviet Union began to have more serious economic effects.

Japan's Socialists tried to turn the Chinese tactics to their own advantage during the campaign leading to elections in May 1958. They called for "full enforcement" of the recent trade agreement and, in a radio-television debate with Prime Minister Kishi, Chairman Suzuki accused the government of subordination to U.S. policies. The party promised to send another delegation to China to heal the breach. Its special envoy returned from Peking in August with what came to be known as the Chinese government's "three principles," i.e., conditions for the renewal of trade: (1) the Japanese government must suspend statements and actions hostile to the P.R.C.; (2) it must immediately desist from the "plot" to create two Chinas; and (3) it must cease to prevent normalization of bilateral relations.[38]

38. The Chinese Communists also stipulated "three conditions": punishment of the person who had shown disrespect to their five-starred flag, the raising of a similar flag in the same place, and an official visit of apology to Peking. Moreover, the Deputy Director of the Institute for Foreign Affairs asked that the Japanese government subscribe to his dictated statement as follows: "The Japanese Government heartily desires a restoration of normal relations with the Chinese People's Republic and will strive for it." Then an official delegation might be sent for negotiations in Peking. See: Tadataka Sata, "Chūgoku wa dō Kangaete Iruka?" (What Is China Thinking?) *Chūō Kōron* (Oct. 1958), pp. 46–55; and the same author's "Sata Hōkoku o Kiku" (Listening to the Sata Report), *Tairiku Mondai* (Oct. 1958), pp. 8–22.

On September 11, 1958, the SDP issued its "Fundamental Policy Regarding the Revision of Sino-Japanese Relations"; it mainly repeated the contents of the previous Chang-Asanuma communiqué and reiterated the party's determination to push a nationwide movement for normalizing relations with China.[39] Two Socialists joined the Japanese delegation sent to celebrate the eighth anniversary of the founding of the P.R.C., one of them acting as its leader. When, that same fall, Communist China precipitated the second Quemoy crisis, the SDP increased pressure on the government to deny use of Japanese bases for American staging operations in support of Nationalist Chinese positions. It called on the United States to "cease political and military intervention" in the Chinese conflict and urged the government in Peking to seek solutions by negotiation rather than by force. Chinese statements stressed the paramountcy of political decisions before trade with Japan could be improved. They called for "adjustment of internal (Japanese) conditions" and emphasized the need for a united front capable of resisting the renewal of a revised security treaty with the United States.

A number of leftist groups returned from further visits to Peking with suggestions for another official Socialist mission. The party responded in March 1959 with one again led by Secretary-General Asanuma. Discussions with Premier Chou, Foreign Minister Ch'en Yi, Institute Chairman Chang, and other officials followed lines of Chinese policy already mentioned. The Chinese demanded a shift of diplomatic relations from Nationalist to Communist China, abrogation of the alliance with the U.S., and a policy of anti-imperialism. While still hailing the SDP as the leader of reformist forces in Japan, Chou and others insisted that most types of intercourse advocated by the visitors must wait for successful negotiations between the two governments. While the Chinese listened again to the Socialists' explanation of "positive neutralism," only meager fruits of this unofficial diplomacy were offered. The new Chang-Asanuma communiqué comprised an even more sweeping SDP acceptance of Chinese positions. What made the burly Asanuma an overnight hero in the P.R.C. and a controversial figure throughout the noncommunist world was his comment on March 12 that "American imperialism is the common enemy of China and Japan."[40]

39. *Aschi Shimbun,* Sept. 12, 1958.

40. For the text of this joint communiqué, as broadcast by the New China News Agency, see: "Survey of the China Mainland Press," No. 1977 (March 20, 1959), pp. 22–25.

The Liberal Democrats promptly charged that the SDP, and especially leaders in its more aggressive left wing, had become "spokesmen" for the Red Chinese government. Despite much wider criticism, the Socialist Party's CEC supported Asanuma; Chairman Suzuki hailed the "complete agreement of views" reached in Peking, including, he averred, P.R.C. acceptance of his party's "active neutralism." Leftist factions in the SDP were of course pleased with these events, but moderate elements were perturbed. The Nishio faction denounced Asanuma's pronouncements as capitulation to Chinese Communism and as a violation of the intraparty agreement made in advance as a basis for the mission. This was a grievance which contributed to the decision of this faction to secede from the party later that year. Although the party took such a strong stand against American "imperialism," its CEC decided that same year to take a wait-and-see attitude toward Red China's actions in Tibet and in borderlands claimed by India.

Internal feuding and Communist Chinese insistence on reaffirmation of the Asanuma statement delayed the next major Socialist mission to Peking. Tension between "mainstream" moderates and "antimainstream" leftists in the party in part took the form of rivalry between Saburō Eda and Kōzō Sasaki for the Secretary-Generalship. Just before Suzuki, who backed the latter, left for Peking in December 1961 at the head of another mission, he published an article criticizing "structural reform." The CCP was by this time deep in its ideological conflict with the Soviet Union and Titoism. In sessions

---

According to *The Japan Times* (March 18, 1959), the communiqué was drafted by Katsumata (Chairman of the SDP Policy Planning Board) and Liao Cheng-chih (Deputy Director of the Chinese People's Institute for Foreign Affairs).

Another report (*Asahi Shimbun*, April 28, 1959) told how Asanuma made the "common enemy" statement in a speech before a large audience on March 12; during a press conference the following day he explained that it is natural for a socialist party to fight capitalism at home and imperialism in international affairs. According to the transcript of his address on the 12th, as taken down by a Japanese reporter (see ibid.), Asanuma declared:

> American military bases are located in Taiwan which is part of your country; likewise, in my country and in Okinawa there are also American military bases. Furthermore, these bases are being strengthened by nuclear weapons of various sizes. In this regard, the peoples of Communist China and Japan have an important task to fight for: we have to struggle for a nuclear disarmament in Asia, and the removal of foreign military bases. Taiwan is part of China, and Okinawa is part of Japan. Yet these islands are separated from the main country because of American imperialism. American imperialism is the common enemy of China and Japan.

See also, "Survey of the China Mainland Press" (March 18, 1959), pp. 42–45.

with the Japanese Socialists, the Chinese leaders therefore openly denounced "structural reform," identifying it with revisionism; by so doing they were intentionally or by implication affecting internal SDP politics. In Peking, Suzuki reiterated the Asanuma formula, a fait accompli which, though publicly acquiesced in by his party, added fuel to its raging inner controversies.[41] Eda, however, won the contest in the party elections.

Of course, the Democratic Socialist Party, composed of those who had followed Nishio out of the SDP as the anti-treaty struggle was being shaped, was critical of any such extreme positions. Since 1961 this party has urged that the government gradually yet positively overcome obstacles to diplomatic recognition of and relations with the P.R.C. It agreed with the SDP in favoring representation of Communist China in the U.N. and an intergovernmental Sino-Japanese commercial agreement. It maintained that Japan should not intervene in the Taiwan issue but should leave it to the two Chinas, possibly assisted by the United Nations. Before official relations can be renewed with Mainland China, the DSP advocates the exchange of semiofficial commercial agencies.

The main Socialist Party has naturally been more disturbed by Sino-Soviet ideological and political conflicts. In 1963, as we have seen, the Socialists approved the partial nuclear test-ban treaty, thus taking a stand approved by the West and the Soviet Union but condemned by the P.R.C. In October, Hiroo Wada as chief of the International Bureau of the Party wrote that he discerned more latitude for neutralism with the development of communist polycentrism, international shifts in power, and advancing pluralism. He criticized Red China for striving to make nuclear weapons while advocating a zone free of such dangers. But he excused Chinese support for national struggles against American "imperialism" and stated that India and China shared responsibility for violations of coexistence along their common frontiers. He further urged breaking through U.S.-led barriers of containment and advocated aid to China's Socialist construction.[42]

In addition to these main issues of foreign policy, the SDP formulated policies regarding a number of other problems. Its hope that

41. *The Japan Times,* Jan. 13, 20, 1962; for the text of the joint communiqué, see *Peking Review,* No. 3 (Jan. 19, 1962), pp. 11–14.

42. "The Sino-Soviet Controversy and the SDP's Position," *Jiyū,* Oct. 1963.

The Katayama Cabinet, May 24, 1947 to March 10, 1948

(not all members of this Cabinet were in this photograph)

Left to right: Sadayoshi Hitotsumatsu (Welfare); Junzō Sasamori (Director, Reparations Agency and Minister without Portfolio); Takeo Kurusu (Finance); Tatsuo Morito (Education); Chōzaburō Mizutani (Commerce and Industry); Tetsu Katayama (Premier); Suehiro Nishio (without portfolio); Hiroo Wada (Director, Economic Stabilization Board); Kozaemon Kimura (Home, and after abolition of that ministry, without portfolio). (*Copyright Asahi Shimbun. Reproduced by permission.*)

Socialist Chairman Asanuma shakes hands with Chang Hsi-jo, President of the Chinese People's Association for Foreign Affairs, after an exchange of statements regarding normalization of Sino-Japanese Relations, Peking, April 23, 1957.

Socialist Chairman Asanuma at the SDPJ Meeting to Petition the National Diet Not To Approve the Security Treaty, April 26, 1960.

The assassination of Socialist Chairman Inejirō Asanuma by a young fanatic, October 12, 1960.

Sōhyō President Kaoru Ōta speaking at a Sōhyō National Convention, July 24, 1958.

Sōhyō Secretary General Minoru Takano, delivering a speech after being reelected to his post, July 11, 1953.

SDPJ Chairman Mosaburō Suzuki addressing the 13th Regular Party Convention at Shinagawa Public Hall, Tokyo, January 17, 1957. Party notables sit in the front. Slogans on the wall: "Re-establish Sino-Japanese Relations. Push for an Independent Foreign Policy. Oppose Military Bases. Return Okinawa to Japan. Protect the Peace Constitution. Abolish the Unequal Treaty. Promote Scientific Technology. Use Atomic Energy for Peaceful Purposes. Strengthen Ourselves Organizationally. Create a New Party Spirit. Dissolve the House of Representatives. Set Up a Socialist Party Government."

SDPJ leaders in the waiting room for party officers at the 13th Regular Party Convention, January 17, 1957.

Posters being painted for the 25th May Day in Japan, 1952.

The Ōi Local of Kokutetsu (the national railway workers' union) in front of the National Diet. The two large signs in the front together say "Peace."

The 12th National Convention of the Left SDPJ.

Chairman Kawakami and Secretary General Asanuma listening to election returns at the Right SDPJ Headquarters.

The 13th Regular Convention of the SDPJ, January 17, 1957. Signs in the background: Zenrō Kaigi (JTUC) and Sōhyō (GCTUJ).

Hisao Kuroda delivering his final speech at the 6th National Convention of the Worker Farmer Party on January 16, 1957, when it was dissolved to make way for its merger with the Social Democratic Party of Japan.

Leaflets being dropped on the 16th Party Convention in 1959, which considered the "anti-party" activities of Suehiro Nishio. (*Copyright Asahi Shimbun. Reproduced by permission.*)

The Ashida Cabinet, March 10 to October 15, 1948

(not all members of this Cabinet were in this photograph)

Left to right, first row: Chōzaburō Mizutani (Commerce and Industry); Giichi Takeda (Welfare); Suehiro Nishio (Deputy Premier); Hitoshi Ashida (Premier); Sadayoshi Hitotsumatsu (without portfolio, later Minister of Construction); Gizō Tomabechi (Deputy Premier); Tokutarō Kitamura (Finance). *Second row:* Eiji Tomiyoshi (Communications); Kanjū Katō (Labor); Seiichi Okada (Transportation); Kazuo Nagae (Agriculture and Forestry); Takeo Kurusu (Director, Economic Stabilization Board); Masaru Nomizo (Chairman, Local Finance Committee); Tatsuo Morito (Education); Yoshio Suzuki (Attorney General).

expansion of trade could accord with plans made at a series of conferences of Asian socialist states has been obstructed by differences between communist and noncommunist countries. Japanese Socialists have warned against disguised revival of a Greater East Asia Co-prosperity Sphere to promote the interests of native and American capitalists. Left-wingers have wanted Japan to develop relations with North Korea and North Vietnam. They have branded as fascistic the junta which has ruled South Korea since 1961 and have joined the communist chorus against anything like a Northeast Asian Treaty Organization. In 1965 they vociferously opposed the conclusion of a comprehensive treaty and associated agreements with the government in Seoul. In general, leftists interpret American involvement in Laos and South Vietnam as imperialistic and prefer the reunification of these countries under socialist regimes.

If the Socialist Party were to have suddenly come to power in 1965, it would have been faced with the problem of drastically reorienting Japan's foreign policy. It would have begun to work for the abrogation of the Security Treaty with the United States by 1970 at the latest. It would have tried to follow France's lead in recognizing the People's Republic of China but would have had to pay for this by the abrogation of diplomatic and commercial relations with the Nationalist government of China on Taiwan. It might also have attempted to help mediate the war in Vietnam. With regard to Korea, it would probably have tried to convince South Korea to consider the northern regime's proposal of a joint North-South committee on trade and other matters. At the same time, such a hypothetical Socialist government would probably have tried to retain the valuable trade with the United States. How far it would have succeeded in any or all of these efforts would in part have depended on the summoning of able leaders, more than had appeared at the time. But such speculation is not wholly realistic, because in the very process of coming to power through obtaining a parliamentary majority, even more if by coalition with conservative elements which favored trade with mainland China, the party would have had to moderate its posture.

Organization and Leadership

8. Organization and Processes

As a revolutionary party the SDP has stressed the need for effective organization and activities, but it has had to remain self-critical of efforts and results. During its initial surge in postwar popularity the number and size of its agencies grew, then dwindled as the party's access to power faded. The schism in 1951 left its structure in a shambles, and, for the ensuing four years, rival Socialist parties conducted competitive reorganization. After reunification, herculean tasks were undertaken with still anemic organs.

Realizing that efficient organization must precede the regaining of power by electoral progress to majority status, an excellent plan was developed on paper. Some aspects of this were partially instituted; others have been frustrated by financial difficulties, factionalism, the dragging of feet by the old guard, widespread lethargy, and lack of discipline. When electoral growth began to falter in 1957–58, the left wing resumed the call for rejuvenated organization. This time various proposals had some grass-roots support and positive backing by younger Diet members; moreover, full-time members of the party staff—particularly at national headquarters—insisted that reforms were urgent. Still, some older stalwarts were unenthusiastic.

The plan involved changes in the number and method of electing officers to the Central Executive Committee, limiting the prerogatives of Diet members as convention delegates, and consolidating the administrative influence of regular party workers. Sudden implementation was virtually impossible, for the blueprint portended a renovation of top leadership which, with modifications, had persisted since its prewar emergence. For a while decision was postponed, first because of the difficult elections approaching, then by preoccupation with struggles against renewal of the security treaty and the controversy which led to secession of the Nishio faction. However, when, at the 14th national convention in 1958, a Council for Structural Reform was established, its study was consciously related to the problem of transcending the parliamentary "barrier of one third" strength. After relative defeat in the House of Councillors elections in 1959, a "party reconstruction controversy" led to approval of the Council's report and formal adoption of the "Plan for Reform of Party Structure" by the 16th regular convention in September. Some resulting changes, such as reduction of the CEC to one third of its former size, were straightway—though perhaps not all permanently—achieved; others have been more difficult and are occurring gradually through the 'sixties.

BASIC TENETS

The constitution and basic platform adopted by the reunified Socialist Party in 1955 have been the fundamental references in matters of organization. They prescribe equality of membership and inner party democracy. The principle of democratic centralism, though probably borrowed from the Communists, is interpreted with less authoritarian discipline from above. Members and leaders on all levels are said to be free to criticize and participate in the formulation of policies. They may elect officers and be elected to party posts. Party decisions, once made, are to be promptly implemented. Although members are supposed to put "party life" ahead of private affairs, they tend to observe this directive much less rigorously than do many Communists.

Centralism is embodied in the three main party organs: the national convention, the Central Executive Committee and the Control Commission. Their relationships and functions are comparable with the threefold division of many governments. Those who stress organization have striven to emphasize offices rather than the incumbents. This has been particularly applied to the role of Diet members. The left wing wishes to relegate Diet members to a department of party

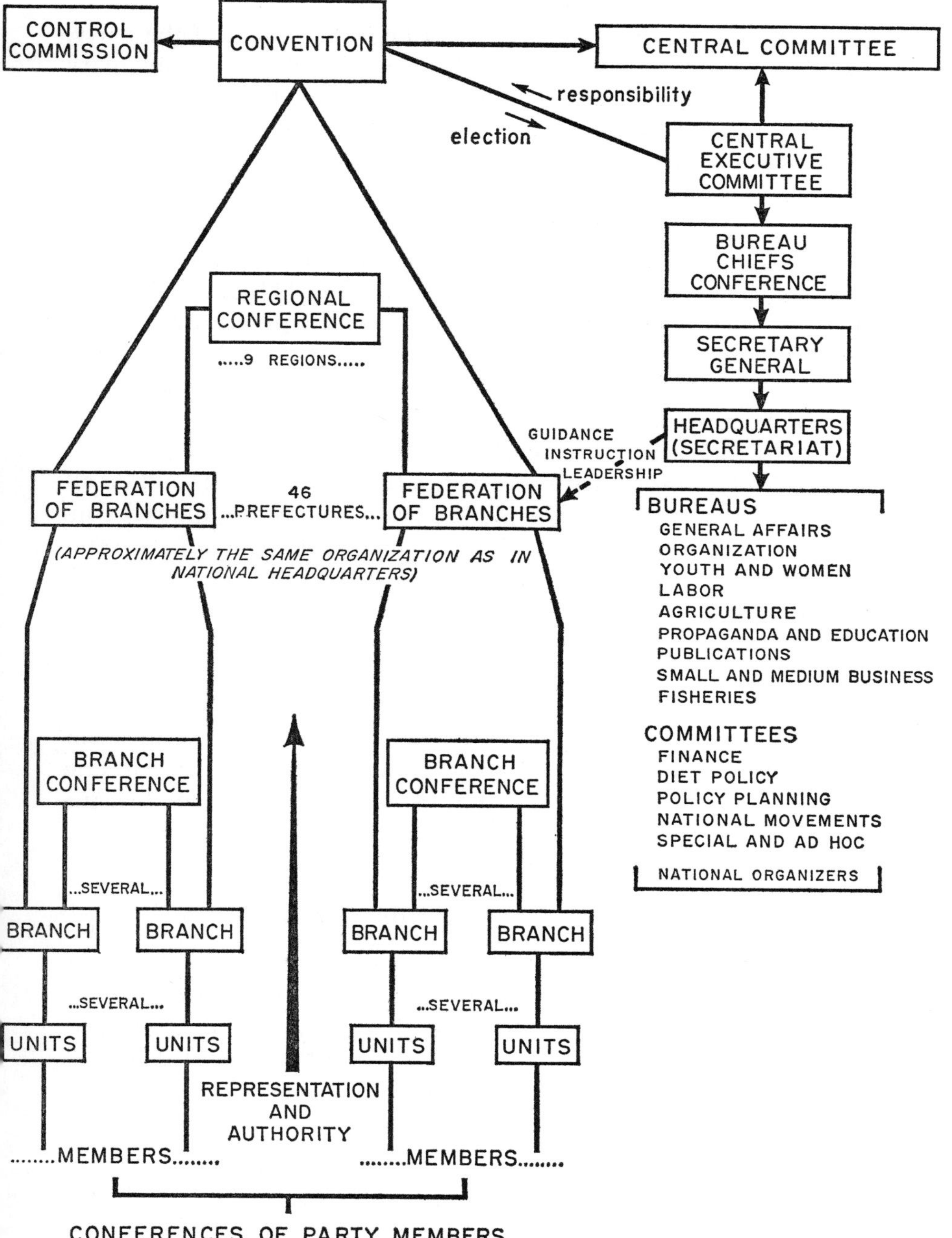

SOCIALIST PARTY ORGANIZATION
CONTROL COMMISSION
CONVENTION
CENTRAL COMMITTEE
responsibility
election
CENTRAL EXECUTIVE COMMITTEE
BUREAU CHIEFS CONFERENCE
SECRETARY GENERAL
HEADQUARTERS (SECRETARIAT)
GUIDANCE
INSTRUCTION
LEADERSHIP
REGIONAL CONFERENCE
.....9 REGIONS.....
FEDERATION OF BRANCHES
46
...PREFECTURES...
FEDERATION OF BRANCHES
(APPROXIMATELY THE SAME ORGANIZATION AS IN NATIONAL HEADQUARTERS)
BUREAUS
GENERAL AFFAIRS
ORGANIZATION
YOUTH AND WOMEN
LABOR
AGRICULTURE
PROPAGANDA AND EDUCATION
PUBLICATIONS
SMALL AND MEDIUM BUSINESS
FISHERIES
COMMITTEES
FINANCE
DIET POLICY
POLICY PLANNING
NATIONAL MOVEMENTS
SPECIAL AND AD HOC
NATIONAL ORGANIZERS
BRANCH CONFERENCE
BRANCH CONFERENCE
...SEVERAL...
...SEVERAL...
BRANCH
BRANCH
BRANCH
BRANCH
...SEVERAL...
...SEVERAL...
UNITS
UNITS
UNITS
UNITS
REPRESENTATION AND AUTHORITY
........MEMBERS........
........MEMBERS........
CONFERENCES OF PARTY MEMBERS INDEPENDENT AND MAINLY IN LABOR UNIONS

CHART 2

organization, claiming they should not be independent of the party, much less dominate it. Even the right wing, for which parliamentary politics is of more central significance, warns that the party must not exist merely for the sake of its legislators. The legislature is viewed as only one theater of struggle toward a new society. Especially left Socialists hope to separate political policymaking, tactics, and strategy from administrative party affairs on all levels of organization; they even envisage separate staffs for these purposes. Hitherto these latter activities have been performed by a party elite led chiefly by Diet members. Even most of these leaders, however, frequently deplore the "inverted pyramid" of party structure, a reference to the concentration of effort and resources to win one third or more of the seats in the national Diet while neglect is reflected in weakness which increases inversely at each descending level of party government.

A relatively uniform table of organization in all regions and on all levels has been another principle. Lower echelons are allowed considerable operational latitude but are expected to observe certain standards such as support of central policies, filling the usual positions, and payment of dues.

Underlying many of these tenets is the desire to assert the "identity" (*shutaisei*) of the party. This concept, probably borrowed from German philosophy, has become a cliché that is invoked in a variety of contexts, including efforts at independence of pressure groups, particularly labor unions. This chapter will analyze the implementation of these principles and the function of each organ as related to the struggle for party control but with minimal reference to ideology and programs of action.[1]

THE SIZE AND COMPOSITION OF MEMBERSHIP

Individuals, not organizations such as labor and farmers' unions, are the basic components of Socialist Party membership. In applying, a prospective member submits a form giving his name, address, age, occupation, and the names of two sponsors. The party is then supposed to investigate the applicant's qualifications; headquarters grants permission to join. Left Socialists regard the role of employed workers

1. Socialist Party organization has been more fully treated in an unpublished monograph written by Cecil H. Uyehara in 1958 and entitled: "The Social Democratic Party of Japan: A Study of Its Organization and Power Structure." Some of the figures mentioned in this chapter are based on detailed statistics included in that study.

as primary, though they accord perfunctory recognition to the equality of all members. In Marxist fashion they view other elements in the party as components of a kind of united front centering on laborers and, to a lesser extent, on farmers. The right wing advocates a national party with members of quite equal status and influence from all social strata.

Without trying to estimate the degree of padding in party claims, let us note that, during the Katayama government, there may have been more than 95,000 SDP members. In February 1958 the total may have been over 56,000, but in the early 'sixties it has probably been between 42,000 and 47,000. In January 1966, the party claimed 53,000 nominal members, only 2,000 of them women. So, recently the number of registered Socialists has been about half the Communist Party total and less than one sixth that of the LDP. Continuously maintained membership rolls date from party reunification in 1955; prior to that there were periodic re-registration drives to which even some Diet members failed to respond. But there has tended to be an upswing of renewals before each national convention; allocation of representation in conventions is according to distribution of dues-paying members. Membership has always been a tiny fraction of Socialist electoral support, as is true of most parties. The discrepancy is far greater in the case of the Japanese than of almost all other social democratic or labor parties. Aside from the large shifting vote in Japan, most Japanese citizens, even most industrial workers, prefer not to be publicly identified with political parties.

Although Socialist leaders would like to believe that all members are ardent believers, informally they distinguish between activists, ordinary members, friends, and supporters of the Party.[2] Activists include national, regional, and local organizers, full-time officers, and secretaries. Some others are only perfunctory members, while still others are duly registered and pay dues. Friends of the party constitute a second class of members with no voting rights, no expectation that they will register, and only a nominal fee to pay.

In 1957, the Planning Bureau of the national headquarters made the first statistical analysis of party membership. It showed that about three quarters of 48,763 members at the time were under age 50; thus

2. Nihon Shakaitō, "Dai Jūsankai Teiki Taikai Kettei Shū" (Resolutions of the Thirteenth Regular Convention) (Tokyo, 1957), p. 54.

most members could not have participated in the prewar socialist movement. While unusually high percentages of new voters and young respondents surveyed by opinion polls are known to support reformist parties, Socialist leaders have been concerned that only 22 per cent of their members are in their twenties. This seems to have improved somewhat during the anti-security treaty campaign in 1960. The percentages are higher for the next two decennial groups. As might be expected, an overwhelming proportion are elementary and junior high school graduates; only 3 per cent have studied in institutions of higher learning.

More than three quarters of all SDP members were classified as workers (52.7%) or farmers (22.9%).[3] Although teachers and engineers constituted only 0.55 per cent, they too were counted as workers. Medium and small businessmen comprised just over 10 per cent, fishermen half of one per cent, people in professions a shade less than one per cent, and students only 0.05 per cent. The left wing tends to have more laboring members, while the right wing has proportionately larger components from small and medium enterprises.

Losses from dropouts also cause the leaders worry. In 1961 it was estimated that if it had not suffered such losses, party membership would be three times its actual size. The national convention early in 1961 tried to launch a drive to raise total membership to 100,000 within the ensuing three years, but in the next six months only 363 new members joined. Each Socialist Diet member has a mailing list of personal followers—said to average 10,000—to whom he sends messages, but requests to turn these over to headquarters for membership drives always fail. In multimember constituencies candidates fear that they might have to share supporters with other aspirants (and other factions) from their own party!

The concept of mass membership is nevertheless deeply embedded in socialist thinking, and no one discusses openly the real elite char-

3. So SDP membership must include less than 22,000 workers and not many more than 1,200 farmers. Identical or similar figures were supplied by the Report of the 14th Convention of the SDP published in *Heiwa to Shakaishugi no tame* (For the Sake of Peace and Socialism) (Tokyo, 1958), pp. 64–72, and in *Sekai,* No. 165 (Sept. 1959), p. 160.

According to the National Public Safety Investigation Agency, in the fall of 1962 nearly 37% of JCP members—a considerably smaller proportion than in the Socialist Party—were workers. These were divided as follows: 13.5% of the total membership were factory workers, 12.7% were public employees, and 10.5% were general laborers. See: *Christian Science Monitor,* Oct. 2, 1962.

acter of SDP membership. It can be described as a militant minority in the body politic.

PARTY ORGANS

The National Convention

As the supreme decision-making organ of the Socialist Party, the national convention decides broad policies and selects top executives, members of the Central Executive Committee, the Control Commission and the Central Committee. These officers, the highest officials and the CEC in particular, are responsible for the execution of party policy. This relationship between leaders and the convention is the main basis of the Socialist claim to inner democracy and the legitimacy of its leadership. The convention is also the final tribunal for adjudication of disciplinary problems. There has, however, never been an appeal to it to reverse a decision of the party's national Control Commission, which is supposed to check any excesses in which the executives may indulge.

When the convention is not in session, the Central Committee is supposed to be the governing organ. It has largely abdicated its responsibilities, however, and has become a mere national liaison conference of party militants, meeting usually not more than three times yearly.

Types of delegates are defined by the party constitution, but the ratio of representation is decided by the CEC. The largest group of delegates has been chosen according to a specified ratio by federations of branches, which are two or three echelons from the ordinary member. There has been a recent move to facilitate the sending of representatives directly from branch organizations, and the number so sent is increasing. They tend to be less affected by factional considerations. Each delegate usually represents between 50 and 150 members, depending on the method of calculation and the number of so-called "convention members." Each prefectural federation of branches is allowed one delegate, which means a total of 46 of this type.

The practice of qualifying all Socialist Diet members as convention delegates has been subjected to increasing criticism. Two hundred and thirty-two of them were accredited to the convention of 1957, and only ten fewer to that of 1961. Reformers argue that Diet members should be recognized as delegates only if elected from local branches. This practice was actually begun with the convention of 1962.

Any organization whose executive organ has decided to support the SDP and pay the requisite dues in keeping with the size of its membership may send to a convention a specified number of delegates, who must be party members. In actuality this has been mostly limited to labor unions. In the convention of 1957 there were only 11 such delegates; by 1961 their number had grown to 62. It has been estimated that at times as many as 45 per cent of regular delegates have been union officials sent as ordinary delegates representing members. Many unions support the SDP (and some the DSP) in elections, but few become supporting organizations.

At most conventions the action program is the most debated statement. As an analysis of international and domestic events in the past year, it is second in importance only to the party's basic platform. It also contains a frequently evasive or perfunctory self-criticism of past activities as well as proposed courses of action for the year ahead. The chairmen of the Policy Planning Board and of the Organization Bureau preside over the special committees created by the CEC to draft the action program and the statement on organizational policy, respectively.[4] Membership on these committees is scrupulously divided between the left and right wings, but attendance is usually poor. The statements are ordinarily drafted by the chairmen and are supposed to be sent to local organizations at least a fortnight before the convention; however, it is doubtful that this is carefully observed.

Reading of draft statements to the convention is the signal for labor and farmers' unions to press for revisions. High ranking officers of Sōhyō frequently meet with party leaders to urge their Federation's views. They further dramatize demands by organizing meetings of Sōhyō-affiliated delegates to the convention. Zenrō, being less politically inclined, has tended to exert less pressure—whether on the SDP before the split in 1959 or on the Democratic Socialist Party since then.

Just before a convention opens, the Chairman of the CEC—who is considered to be Chairman also of the party—calls meetings of the chairmen of local people's movements and of leaders from local and prefectural federations of branches. The latter group usually nomi-

4. An unusually frank appraisal of the party's organizational development is given in "1958-Nendo Soshiki Katsudō Hōshin (An)" (Draft of the 1958 Organizational Policy) in *Shakai Shimpō,* Dec. 26, 1957. This was submitted to the SDP convention held in February 1958.

nates candidates for convention steering, credentials, and other committees. Presiding officers and convention managers are chosen from right- and left-wing factions. These officers all hold rather important positions in such bodies as the Diet, the CEC, and local executive committees or prefectural assemblies.

At the first plenary session, the Party Chairman delivers a short, hortatory address, followed by the Secretary-General's lengthy report on party activities. Then come reports by the Finance and Control Commissions. It is the Secretary-General's statement which evokes the keenest interpellations from the floor; formalized replies are characteristically given by the official in question and at times by the Party Chairman. When the presiding officer calls for unanimous approval of the report, it is always given.

The action program and other statements of policy for the future, such as those on organization and on an economic five-year plan, are explained, interpellated, and defended in plenary session but are quickly referred to committees. Again the action program committee becomes the center of boisterous debate. It is by far the largest committee, during the convention of 1957 having 82 members. That members on it from leftist factions outnumbered those from the right wing by three to one reflected the preponderance of influence on composition of the committee. Its chairman was then head of the Political Affairs Department of Sōhyō, who was representing his home prefecture as an ordinary delegate.[5]

Top party leaders commonly have to call for moderation during committee proceedings. In the heat of debate, executive authority may be ignored, as during the convention of 1957 when factional views were almost deadlocked over interpretation of recent international events. Compromise agreements are usually reached after leaders huddle in ad hoc committees.

Crucial in determining relative factional power—therefore usually decided late during a national convention—is the allocation of what were the three (later the seven) highest positions and distribution of representation on the CEC. Of course, much maneuvering and bargaining precedes these selections. Rather than risk a recorded vote, a standing ovation of unanimity is given to a prearranged slate of prime officers: (1) the Chairman of the CEC, (2) the Secretary-General, and

5. He had formerly been chief party secretary in his home prefecture.

the chairmen of the (3) Finance, (4) Policy Planning, (5) Diet Policy, and (6) Election Policy committees and of (7) the Control Commission. Members of the CEC are usually elected by three-vote plural balloting. There are no electoral districts; candidates seek votes from their own prefectural delegation, their factions, on the basis of their popularity in the party, and by shrewd bargaining. A prospective CEC member in the past has had to mobilize 30 to 50 votes. But once nominations and support have been determined in the smoke-filled rooms and on the floor, the composition of the Central Executive Committee is seldom changed by a convention at large.

Plenary sessions and committee meetings provide sounding boards and valves for the escape of considerable accumulated steam. But, as in virtually all parties, the convention is a very imperfect instrument for either generating policies or holding leadership accountable for past performance. Nomination procedures, the pre-drafting of policies and programs, the scant and perfunctory attention normally given to proposals from local organizations, all mean that only endorsement and discussion remain as the main functions of the convention. It also provides a framework for the struggle for national party power and, if we may mix metaphors, a mirror more for differing views among the elite than for those of the membership. The left wing, being more numerous and adept at maneuvering and organizing delegates, has often utilized the convention for aggressive demonstrations of strength. Proceedings have rarely risen above controversies between advocates of a class versus a national party to the conduct of energetic debates on the content and future direction of Socialist economic planning.

The Central Executive Committee

The Central Executive Committee (CEC) is the supreme executive organ of the party. It is the symbol of party authority and leadership, the epitome of structured power. Constitutionally it is responsible not only to the convention but also to the Central Committee between sessions of the convention. Noncommunist parties of the left in Japan have emphasized the peak position and decisive functions of the CEC, probably to prevent the concentration of inordinate power in the party Chairman. Japanese Socialists often express the wish to emulate the organization and administrative efficiency of the British Labour Party, but the CEC as an institution was modeled before World War II, probably on comparable organs of continental European socialist parties, especially Germany's. Proposals have been made repeatedly to alter the composition of the CEC, but no one has suggested a basic change in its functions and responsibilities, nor in those of its chairman.[6]

There are no regulations governing the recent composition of the CEC, but in practice it has been a near monopoly of Diet members. In times of organizational crisis, as in 1949 and 1951, the SDP has invited a few others—principally national labor union leaders who have not served as legislators—to become members of this body. Local organizations have repeatedly criticized Diet members and the CEC for overconcern with national politics and neglect of downward-reaching organization and procedure. The financial and physical burdens on local representatives would be too heavy if they were to attend regularly the rather frequent meetings of the CEC. But this is only one reason why several attempts to seat such representatives in that committee have failed.

During the first fifteen years after the war, the size of the CEC grew from 25 to 40 members. When the so-called top positions were added, the total reached 47, making it an unwieldy body. In 1957–58 numerous plans were proposed for drastic revision of its structure, size, and selection processes. Such renovation became for a time the main issue, but after the party and national distractions of 1959–60, the accepted compromise was merely to limit the size of the CEC to 15 members without changing the structure and mode of electing officers. In the early 'sixties there were proposals, especially from the left, again urging enlargement. However, a degree of change at the top is indicated by the fact that, before the partial reforms of 1958–60, only 5 of the 80 posts in the CEC and as heads of bureaus and headquarters divisions were held by non-Diet members, whereas by 1961 one third (21 out of 63) of such offices were held by Socialists from outside the Diet. Changes in the age composition of leaders were affecting all levels of the party.[7]

The Central Executive Committee is not only the chief agency for

6. In 1957 for the first time, demands for a thorough reappraisal of the party's organization, particularly the composition of the CEC and the structure of the national headquarters, became so great that the leaders, without enthusiasm, acceded to local insistence. As mentioned early in this chapter, in 1958 a special council was instructed to study party organization and report to the national convention in 1959.

7. Nobuyuki Katō, "Party Renovation Now on the Right Track," *Japan Socialist Review*, No. 2 (Nov. 16, 1961), pp. 84–85.

formulating policies; it also is expected to explain policies to the membership, the convention and the wider public. Energy in party activities can flow upward from localities, but insofar as it is exerted from the top its principal source is the CEC. Much vigor is dissipated, however, in factional contention. It is this committee which can create bureaus, departments, and special committees as necessary. It appoints headquarters personnel and sets standards for the nomination of candidates for national elections. When it makes a decision of special importance, it is supposed to summon a convention, but such extraordinary conventions have usually been called rather to help formulate policies at some crucial juncture.

All CEC decisions are by majority vote, though unanimity is preferred. Rarely and reluctantly has the Committee resorted to a recorded vote. But, for example, when the left and right factions could not agree on a candidate for Premier in 1948, the vote of the CEC went on record. Again in 1951, when there was a controversy over the peace treaty, a vote was taken. The party prefers to foster the image of unity instead of obliging the losing side to expose the dimension of its defeat. This typical Japanese feeling is more fully accepted by the right wing which stresses the value of "concurrence through consultation" (*hanashiai*). The left wing, though not wholly rejecting this philosophy, more readily accepts the practice of voting. This difference is partly explained by the more traditional modes of reaching decisions that characterize moderate middle-aged Socialists, while the younger leftists claim to be more "modern."

Unlike some social democratic parties, the SDPJ does not preclude simultaneous holding of several positions in its own organization. All offices are nonremunerative; indeed, as we shall see, the highest posts entail financial burdens for incumbents. A national leader may hold as many as five party positions. To some degree this overlapping reflects the scarcity of competent personnel and the chronic insufficiency of finances.

The Chairman of the Central Executive Committee and of the Party

As mentioned, the Chairman of the CEC is also nominal head of the party, elected by the convention, normally—but with notable exceptions—in plenary session by unanimous approval. Not only does he represent the party on varied occasions, but he is also responsible for deftly coordinating the views of colleagues and for deciding with them from day to day the party's position on public issues and on parliamentary tactics. Perhaps because the SDP had such a short postwar experience in power and has since not been within likely reach of it, the role of Leader as institutionalized in the British Labour Party has no left of center Japanese equivalent. Leftist elements have tended to be particularly suspicious of concentrated personal authority, in part because of the necessity of compromises with the right wing. Also, as earlier mentioned, the left had been excluded from portfolios in the Katayama administration. Both factionalism and the expectation that the Chairman will remain close to the people, shunning the airs of a "president," make him the symbol of collective leadership but without much opportunity for opinionated expression.

Since 1945, the SDP has had five Chairmen: Tetsu Katayama, Mosaburō Suzuki, Inejirō Asanuma, Jōtarō Kawakami, and Kōzō Sasaki. For a short time in 1960–61, Saburō Eda served as acting Chairman following the assassination of Asanuma. Each was nominated and elected not principally because of his stature in or out of the organization but because he led an important faction, was further strengthened as a candidate by combination with other groups or sub-cliques, and in some cases because he could rather effectively mitigate and compromise factional differences. Katayama became Chairman when the Socio-Democratic clique was dominant in early postwar years. This group never recovered from Socialist failure at governing and the electoral debacle of 1949. When the SDP was divided, the Right Japan-Labor faction elected its depurged leader, Kawakami, as Chairman. Suzuki attained office in 1950 and continued as Chairman of the Left Socialist Party, then of the reunified organization until 1960. As the party adjusted to the secession of the Nishio faction; supporters of Asanuma narrowly defeated those favoring Kawakami; the Suzuki "mainstream" was developing fissures at the time of that convention. Following the assassination of Asanuma, Kawakami succeeded as a compromise candidate who would assist in shielding the SDP, and indirectly the "mainstream" faction of Sōhyō, from DSP-Zenrō pressures. Age and ill health caused his retirement in 1965, and Sasaki, a leftist, was elected in his stead.

These leaders have been identified with different traditions and schools of thought in the Socialist movement. Katayama has maintained a conservative socialist position since the 1920s. Kawakami, though oriented toward Marxism early in his career, belonged to a conciliatory group that ultimately collaborated with prewar and wartime Japanese governments. Suzuki, consistently a noncommunist Marxist, hovered on the verge between legality and illegality before the war. As Chairman of the postwar party for a decade, he was criticized for indecisiveness and lack of political courage. Asanuma was a pragmatic compromiser, though he assumed something of an ideological tinge, especially when latterly catering to the left. Sasaki is noted for being a militant Marxist (though often mild in party negotiations), for his provincial dialect, and for the strong support he receives from many local branches.

The role played by the Chairman in the formulation of policy is obscure. In matters of appointments he has no direct authority but appears to follow decisions by the CEC. It is clear that if and when the SDP can attain a majority in the House of Representatives, the party Chairman will become Premier. Even though defeats have been certain, at appropriate times during their period of continuous opposition the Social Democrats have nominated their chairmen to head administrations. If they should in the future attain and hold national power for a significant length of time, particularly after the fuller emergence of the postwar generation of leaders, the chairmanship might become more fully endowed with powers.

The Conference of Bureau Chiefs

Apathy among members, the inexperience of many local functionaries, and the limitations of most Socialist Diet members have caused a rather small number of party officials to shoulder the main responsibilities. There seemed to be more reliance on the CEC and Central Committee during early postwar years. Since the elections of 1949, the CEC has averaged less than three meetings per month. Most sessions have been attended by two thirds of its members, the most faithful of course being the Chairman and Secretary-General.

During the first twelve years, 1945–57, 156 persons occupied 634 seats on the CEC, an average of three terms per person. Closer examination shows that 29 leaders (about 20%) held 44 per cent of all CEC seats. The average number of terms for this more select and recurrent group was 7.5. Although no one had served continuously for the twelve years in any one capacity, Suzuki and Asanuma had been re-elected to high positions eleven times each. All others of the foremost

29 had been elected six or more times. During the first two years after party reunification, almost all of the seven highest officers and most bureau chiefs were selected from these 29. However, such leaders as Suehiro Nishio, Jōtarō Kawakami, and Jiichirō Matsumoto—who have all been advisers to the party—have exerted greater influence than their ability to attract votes in convention would indicate.

After the schism of 1951, oligarchic tendencies became more pronounced. Both Left and Right Socialists had their informal inner councils, known in each case as the "conference of highest leaders" (*saikō kambu kaigi*) or the "bureau chiefs' and chairmen's conference." These were only consultative organs, since the constitution gave all executive authority to the CEC. The Right SDP partially formalized this practice in 1953, telling its convention that the management of party affairs would thereby be streamlined. When the party was reunited in 1955, the Bureau Chiefs' Conference was institutionalized as part of the decision-making process. It consists of the seven top officers and seven bureau chiefs. This Conference is supposed to meet only when the CEC cannot be convened; in actuality it has often determined policies. During 1955–56 it met 103 times, while the full CEC held only 34 sessions. Thus, from extralegal status the Conference has become the most decisive workaday group, and the CEC has tended to acquiesce to its formulations. Rumblings of dissatisfaction with its role and its cooperation with Sōhyō have elicited demands for the reassertion of the constitutional authority of the Central Executive Committee.[8] On the other hand, proliferation of party organization and some uneven increase in responsible behavior as the parliamentary opposition have led to the suggestion that a "shadow cabinet," like that of the British Labour Party, be created.

The Control Commission

Since its creation in 1946, the Control Commission has functioned as a somewhat circumscribed supreme court of the party. According to the constitution, it is also empowered to inspect and disband party organizations and to discipline members. Theoretically it can approve or deny the admittance or readmittance of all applicants for membership. If it were thoroughly to fulfill its mandate, it would effec-

8. The movement for party reorganization in 1957–59 aimed at abolition of the Bureau Chiefs' Conference and at substitution of a standing CEC with approximately the same responsibilities, but this came to naught.

tively police the conduct of all party affairs and members. From its establishment, however, it has been overshadowed by the CEC, which apparently chose its members until 1949, when this prerogative was transferred to the national convention. After the schism in 1951, the Left Socialists made the chairman of the Control Commission one of the four highest officers of their party, chosen by the convention. More formally than in actuality, their Commission could screen candidates for the posts of city mayor, governor, and prefectural and national legislators. When the two wings were reunited in 1955, the chairman of this Commission became one of the seven chief officials elected by convention. Kanjū Katō, a veteran leader who had moved from left to right, then became chairman of the invigorated Control Commission.

From 1945 to 1957, 83 persons held a total of 162 positions on the Control Commission, serving an average of two terms each. The members of this body change much more often than do those of the CEC, but the former is not a major channel of recruitment for top leadership. It can instead be a plum for patronage. Thus the Commission is not likely to become a truly autonomous judicial organ of the party. Depending on conditions and exigencies within the party, it may investigate and judge whether any member or party agency has violated regulations, whether there has been conduct inimical to the party's prestige, whether adopted lines of legislative action have been departed from, or whether payments of dues are in arrears. Although there are a number of kinds of disciplinary measures the Commission can impose, most decisions concern expulsion from membership and sometimes from offices. Individual members can initiate cases, but most have been introduced by federations of branches. All cases initiated by or referred to the CEC come under the jurisdiction of the national Control Commission. That body usually upholds decisions made by lower commissions.

The authority of the Commission was first tested when, in 1947–48, Nishio, then Vice-Premier in the Ashida cabinet, received large sums from construction companies—the Shōwa Denkō scandal mentioned earlier. He had failed to report these political contributions to the government and later claimed that they had been given to him "as an individual" rather than as party Secretary-General. Though he resigned from the cabinet, the left wing still clamored for his expulsion. The national Control Commission was not allowed to handle the case alone. The CEC formed a special committee, including the Commission, which recommended that Nishio be allowed voluntarily to leave the party. But when Nishio was arrested in October 1948, the Central Committee promptly expelled him. In 1952 he was readmitted into the Right SDP.

In part parallel with this episode, the same special committee recommended various degrees of disciplinary action against Hisao Kuroda and his band of doctrinaire Marxists for voting against the national budget sponsored by his own party as a member of the governing coalition. Refusing to accept the decision, the disaffected group withdrew. Their splinter party never flourished, and they were readmitted into the SDP in 1957.

The Socialist Party is reluctant to discipline an entire unit in its organization, especially on the prefectural level. When the Okayama federation persistently cooperated with the expelled Kuroda clique, however, it was ordered to disband. When the party split in 1951, the Left SDP expelled right-wing members and ordered various agencies to be superseded by newly created units. Sanctions applied in such abnormal circumstances tend to be formalities, invoked only to satisfy inflamed passions. Four years later the same men and organs were reunited.

Since reunification of the two party wings, there have been only a few notable disciplinary cases. One concerned the impropriety of receiving funds from semigovernmental agencies and not properly channeling them through the party's Finance Committee. This was a moral rather than a legal case and the government was not concerned. Those chiefly involved were Hiroo Wada and Masaru Nomizo, who had received the funds in question when they had served as Secretaries-General of the Left SDP. By 1957, the former was chairman of the Policy Planning Board, the latter a party adviser. In contrast to the earlier Nishio case, the Control Commission independently considered the case, rejected all overtures to discuss it informally with the executive, and handed down a relatively severe penalty: one-year suspension of all rights to hold any party office. When, in 1959, resurgent leftists demanded the "trial" of Nishio for a variety of activities described as obstructive in the fields of foreign and labor policies, factional tensions and party unity were immediately involved. Executive organs and mediating elements preferred that a special committee conduct hearings, but Nishio repeatedly denounced extremism in the mentioned policy-areas and in pro-Communist leanings; he chose to bolt the party. The Control Commission has unevenly asserted greater autonomy since 1955, but its deliberations have become involved in, and have sometimes been frustrated by, factional struggles.

The National Headquarters

SDP headquarters, though the nerve center of party activities, was at first rudimentary in organization. Gradually it developed and by 1958 included seven bureaus, 22 departments, four commissions, committees, and boards, and seven ad hoc committees. In recent years all these agencies have made reports to the party convention. While its general role has changed little, the headquarters has grown larger and more bureaucratic, trends often criticized in convention.

Creation of a professional staff, known as the "headquarters secretariat," has long been an aim. Its personnel has fluctuated in number according to party unity or fissions, financial conditions, and efforts toward reorganization and greater efficiency. In 1947–48, when the party shared national administrative power, the secretariat consisted of 53 persons. When both party and secretariat were divided three years later, effectiveness was drastically reduced. Since reunification, personnel at headquarters has totaled about 100. Though much better developed than prefectural office staffs, this germinal bureaucracy in Tokyo has not yet become a strong force within the party hierarchy. It has remained under the control of the CEC and the Socialist Diet delegation, whose members are conscious of its potentialities and limitations.

Party leaders were challenged by members of the secretariat for the first time in 1958, when organizational reforms were being drafted for presentation to the convention. A combination of headquarters staff and younger, second-bench leaders in the SDP Diet delegation almost forced major reorganization of the central party establishment for the purposes of increasing efficiency and surmounting factionalism. The prestige of the leaders, though somewhat tarnished, and their appeal not to rock the boat on the eve of difficult general elections, blunted this demand.

Until 1959, most Diet members were given some title in national headquarters. Bureau chiefs have always been members of the CEC. Seven of the 26 department chiefs in 1957 were concurrently members of that body, including the heads of such important departments as those for organization, labor, agriculture, and small and medium business affairs. Distribution of appointees between left- and right-wing factions is always carefully considered. The professional staff has grown exasperated with the do-nothing attitude of many Diet member appointees, and, as we have seen, their prominence and number has been reduced at headquarters since 1959.

To reward faithful service and create incentive for the future several professional party secretaries have been appointed departmental chiefs and assistant chiefs. As yet, only a few departments are so led, but the increasing influence of career party secretaries is significant.

The Policy Planning Board

As the Socialist Party proposes fundamental reorientation of the socio-economy, it is natural that its Policy Planning Board should occupy a special position at headquarters. It has long been a semi-autonomous agency, the only one in the headquarters to maintain its own secretaries. For a while after World War II, the Board was reserved for high-level policy debates by interested Diet members. Administrative duties were performed by the now-defunct Political Affairs Research Department of the Political Bureau. The resulting confusion has now been largely remedied. The Board is responsible for initial formulation of policy; other departments then publicize and implement specific action and programs. The head of an operative department is commonly appointed staff director of a special board or committee to draft a particular policy.

The Chairman of the Policy Planning Board is one of the seven highest officers elected annually by the convention. In 1958, there were six vice-chairmen divided equally between left- and right-wing factions. In 1957, the director was a left-wing Diet member; his deputy was a professional secretary, formerly with the right wing. The CEC appoints advisers and counselors to the Board representing various schools of thought in the party. The Board's secretariat is the largest in the headquarters, having about 20 persons, and it is the only one able to allow specialization as to spheres of policy among its members. The Board is assisted by a large number of special committees, mostly headed by Diet members. Action or lethargy depends on these chairmen.

The Board's operations are twofold: the drafting of basic policies and of derivative or more detailed policy aspects of Diet activities. It has compiled alternative budgets for submission to the Diet; it handles all administrative matters concerning Socialist Diet operations; it prepares reports, policy explanations, and interpellations, and drafts election slogans. Staff members of the Board, at one time, compiled the *Kokkai Nippō* (Diet Daily) for party use. It also cooperates with many departments at headquarters in planning radio broadcasts and special studies and in supplying material for the party weekly journal, *Shakai Shimpō* (Socialist News Report), and *Gekkan Shakaitō* (Socialist Party Monthly). The board often invites governmental officials, labor union leaders, and academic specialists to lecture and advise on particular policies.

Diet Operations and the Election Policy Committee

The SDP has always maintained a Diet Policy Committee and caucuses of its Diet members. In early postwar years the latter appeared to be consulted and the members' approval sought more frequently than in later years. Party caucuses in each House elect their own officers, who seldom hold other important party posts. These officers act as intermediaries between Diet members and the Diet Policy Committee. Discipline is strict, and casting a vote contrary to a party decision means almost certain expulsion. When the Diet is in session, caucus meetings are frequent; they are apt to generate heat when members vent their dissatisfaction with the conduct of operations.

Tactics are formulated and directed by the Diet Policy Committee, an executive organ responsible to the CEC and composed of about 20 members, a majority of whom are selected from the House of Representatives. About one third of the committee members are concurrently members of the CEC. The chairman represents the party in most negotiations with the government and other political parties. Despite the pivotal position of this committee and the political stature of its chairman, parliamentary deadlocks have recently been resolved by conferences between the two top officers of the government and of the socialist parties.

Accepting as it does the parliamentary process (though with certain reservations on the part of leftists), the Socialist Party's Election Policy Committee has been continuously important. Of course, it and cooperating similar committees in lower echelons are particularly active before and during major campaigns. The national committee's crucial role was emphasized when its chairman was made one of the seven highest party officers. Formerly he had been appointed by the

CEC, which still appoints four vice-chairmen, the administrative director, and the 16 committee members. One half of the committee's members have seats on the CEC as well. During campaigns, election policy committees on prefectural and lower levels are usually, though temporarily, supplanted for guidance and in authority by executive committees.

The national Election Policy Committee has the delicate task of selectively recognizing all candidates for the Diet, for governorships, and for the five principal mayoralties. Normally the committee accepts prefectural nominations but reserves the right to overrule the decisions of lower echelons. Because of its vulnerability in arbitrating between competing factions and personalities in electoral districts, the committee has often been accused in convention of dictatorial methods and bureaucratism.

Political Education and Propaganda

A high priority has been given to vigorous educational and propaganda activities both within the party and among the electorate. For this purpose, the party has steadily maintained a Propaganda and Education Bureau. In 1958 it consisted of departments for speech-making campaigns, party organs, educational-cultural affairs, and publications.[9] After reunification of the two Socialist wings, a new Research and Planning Bureau was created, more to find appointments for certain influential politicians than to clarify departmental functions.

Grandiose plans for educating the membership are always approved by the convention. But in reality only a small fraction of the members is reached. Unlike the Communist Party, applicants are not required to go through any training before becoming members; there is little evidence of individual study after they have joined. Of course, much of the party's political education is beamed at the wider public, especially at groups like students, labor union members and their families, women, and professional people.

"Political central schools" are periodically held by the party for members of the headquarters staff, student leaders, women members, labor union secretaries, and secretaries to SDP legislators, as well as for

9. *Shakaitō no Shin Rosen* (The New Line of the SDP). (Hereafter referred to as: *The New Line of the SDP, 1961.*) A statement of policies in 1961 mentioned recent establishment of a Cultural Bureau in national party headquarters.

members of supporting organizations and of legislative assemblies on all levels. These schools are also held in localities during summers after the Diet has adjourned and when universities have recessed. The party has tried to have texts written for these courses, but differing political interpretations among the lecturers make this virtually impossible. Since 1954, the SDP has maintained a "Labor University," putting the educational program on a much firmer foundation with longer sessions, a sizable student body, but still limited facilities. It has been managed in conjunction with Sōhyō and about 30 other labor unions. Those enrolled are therefore not limited to Socialist Party members as in the political schools. During its first four years, the Labor University "graduated" more than 500 students recruited from among junior union officials, party members, and the general citizenry—especially small and medium enterprisers. In 1958, the party decided to establish a special school to improve the political and theoretical preparation of its members, particularly its own prospective workers.

The SDP publishes a gazette, the *Shakai Tsūshin* (Socialist Communication) mainly for its own functionaries. Several other publications are issued irregularly by various departments for specialized party workers. More recently the party started the *Gekkan Shakaitō,* devoted principally to theory and explanations of policy. Cultural policies were discussed at one time, in a now defunct quarterly magazine, *Shakaishugi Bungaku* (Socialist Literature), published by intellectuals close to the party. Socialist pamphleteering has never been as spectacular and vigorous as that of the Communists.

Unlike the JCP, the Socialists have never been able to publish a daily newspaper. The present party journal, *Shakai Shimpō* (Socialist News Report), which became an official organ in 1955, was issued every ten days until September 1959, when it became a weekly. It was formerly intended mainly for labor unionists, members of prefectural labor federations, peace organizations, women's associations, and youth groups. Since March 1960 its stated aim has been to serve as a "political newspaper for the masses." Whether its circulation has indeed climbed, as claimed, from 45,000 in 1958 to 84,000 in 1960 may be doubted, but probably it has grown. Three fifths of its distribution reportedly is to nonmembers of the party.

The *Shakai Taimusu* (Socialist Times) and the *Nihon Shakai Shimbun* (Japan Socialist Newspaper) were published by leaders and supporters of the Left and Right wings, respectively, until reunification in 1955. The former was the only daily newspaper jointly attempted by the Socialists and Sōhyō. It lasted for only two years after its launching in 1953. It was revived for a time as a tabloid paper bearing the same name after the party was reunited. The *Nihon Shakai Shimbun* has a longer history, going back to 1951 when it was incorporated, with right-wing leaders constituting most of its shareholders. Editorial offices of these papers have been located in party headquarters, though the partisan sheets castigate each other for procommunism or softness toward capitalism, as the case may be. The latter of the two was reorganized in September 1959 as the organ of what was to become the Democratic Socialist Party. Later its name was changed to *Minsha Shimbun* (Democratic Socialist Newspaper) issued weekly.

In order to project its views abroad, the SDP founded an English language organ, *The Japan Socialist Review,* on November 1, 1962. It is published twice monthly and carries translations of full texts or excerpts of party documents, resolutions, and news from the Japanese-language party organs and other sources, as well as, increasingly, pieces written especially for it. It appears to be aimed at foreign correspondents, diplomats, and the international socialist movement.

Elections are regarded as one of the principal means of mass education, but between campaigns the party relies heavily on political speeches and mass rallies, and by now it has had much experience with radio and television programs. There is no realizable master plan according to which all programs of mass communication can be mobilized and coordinated by the party. In any case, the Socialists simply do not have the funds and sufficient trained staff members for an ambitious, sustained program of information. They are as active in disseminating the spoken and written word as resources permit.

PREFECTURAL AND LOCAL ORGANIZATIONS

"Japanese political parties are like ghosts," Tamon Maeda, a *quondam* Minister of Education, once remarked, "they have heads but no feet." From top to bottom Socialists have also been critical of their inverted pyramidal structure. Attention and resources are concentrated on the national level—to retain at least one third strength in the Diet for the opposition and, if possible, to forge ahead toward majority control. At conventions and in their press, leaders verbally flagellate themselves for neglect of organization and active programs at humbler levels; but only a beginning has been made in remedying the situation, despite the much stronger national web which the Liberal Democratic Party has developed and is extending. A Socialist report in 1961 admitted that more than 80 per cent of all local organizations in the country—consumers' units, district welfare commissions, PTA chapters, block associations, and village groups—were under conservative control. Both revolutionary and evolutionary Socialists realize that probably they can never break the barrier of one third in the Diet unless the lag in party development at prefectural and local levels can be rectified.

Weakness of lower party echelons is reflected in electoral results at corresponding levels. Despite its rather impressive showing in the national Diet, its percentages of lower offices in 1961 offered a contrasting picture: less than 17 per cent of the members of metropolitan, prefectural, and Hokkaidō assemblies; only 25 mayors (4.5%); less than 13 per cent of seats in special ward assemblies; 7.4 per cent of those in municipal assemblies; 0.4 per cent of all town and village headmen; and 1.4 per cent of town and village council members.[10] Much time and effort will be required to build sound and vigorous organs from the ground up, for the party is caught in something of a vicious cycle, requiring now the funds and trained personnel which are more characteristic of an organization already further along with its program of development. Japan's Socialists have been impressed by the success in these respects of the British Labour Party[11] and to a lesser degree of the West German Social Democrats.

The basic units of the SDP are local branches, to one of which every member is supposed to be affiliated. Presumably thirty members are required before the CEC recognizes a new branch, but in 1959 some 36 per cent of all branches had fewer than 20 members. Both territorial and factory units are approved, but the former type is preferred. Such branches are usually formed in cities, towns, wards, and villages, but when the party is unable to recruit the requisite number of members it allows a mixed county–city or combined county branch to be

10. Ibid., pp. 167–69.

11. The SDP translated in summary form the so-called "Wilson Report" on British Labour Party organization in 1955. It also published in its theoretical journal, *Gekkan Shakaitō,* a translation of a special 60-page Labour Party pamphlet on organization which it described as useful.

established. Late in 1957 there were 1,320 branches of the Socialist Party, and the total had grown by only 150 by 1961, located in only one quarter of the country's municipalities. In the latter year, only 619 SDP branches and smaller preparatory committees existed in towns and villages, so the rural "grass roots" were being barely touched in any sustained way. As of November 1964 there were 3,319 of the smaller, local units (*shibu*). Many local units are merely groups without programs of activity, and some are just societies for the support of a single Diet member. Small wonder that at these levels the Socialists have usually been eclipsed by conservative organizations and in recent years even by the politically oriented Nichiren Buddhist Sōka Gakkai. In 1961 the party admitted that its local units had not been strengthened by the main mass movements of the previous year: the anti-security treaty struggle and the Miike coal mine strike. Downward-percolating benefits of phenomenal economic growth, tending to improve the welfare and consumption of workers and farmers, seem to be complicating the task for Socialist organizers even though the party also is gaining in prosperity.

Factory branches are more closely knit organizations concentrated in single working areas, normally in one factory or business concern. They were first organized by Socialists to counter Communist infiltration of labor unions in the early postwar years. Party leaders have always entertained certain misgivings about such branches and have tried to induce them to amalgamate with nearby territorial branches. In any case, factory units are expected to coordinate their political programs with local territorial branches. The selection of Socialist candidates for public elections is often a knotty problem in view of the organized strength of workshop branches. When Communist strength in labor unions wanes, the SDP sees less reason for maintaining its own separate units in workshops, but an attempt in 1957 to abolish them was successfully opposed by unionized members.

On paper, branches may have an elaborate array of officers and functions resembling those of prefectural and national organizations. Although local executive officers may be fairly active, ordinary members seldom do more than post announcements when a legislator is to speak to a public meeting. They rarely try to advocate the socialist cause among the people. The local executive meets about once a month, more as a friendly group than as an executive body. The party journal is not necessarily read by most members. Pamphlets on party policies sometimes have to be obtained through personal connections instead of being automatically distributed from headquarters. In recent years, party headquarters has been selling much more elegant pamphlets and claims it reaches more people in this way than when it gave the pamphlets away to anyone on request.

In some districts, Diet members are responsible for the impotence of Socialist branches. Some of them have been elected from constituencies which include less than 100 SDP members. Some have weakened local branches by forming their own groups of supporters who may or may not work within the party structure. A privately financed committee for a certain candidate may be formed independently of the party. Its members may not even be Socialist sympathizers; indeed they may be in general critical of that party. They may back the candidate not for his political views but because of his status in the community, his personal or business connections. Not only are certain right-wing Socialists involved in this pattern; a number of prominent left-wingers, who often make a show of demanding party "modernization," receive substantial support in this manner.

Local branches commonly reflect the attitude of party leaders in not inviting the "masses" to join but rather by trying to attract "respectable" and "key" elements. From above they are urged to join in promoting struggles for the improvement of conditions in communities, to link with leaders of functionally organized movements and to try to interest them in the SDP.[12] Assemblymen are advised to establish complaint and struggle centers in their homes. Branches are supposed to cooperate with labor unions and use their personnel effectively in campaigns, but to become less dependent on the unions as organizations. And, while becoming more responsive to directives from party headquarters, it is hoped that they will become more autonomous in the development of local resources.

Branch conferences coordinate the activities of components in electoral districts for the House of Representatives. However, the Socialists have not been able to establish a conference in each such district. These conferences lack clearly delegated authority; they usually fulfill

12. Among such "struggles," party communications have mentioned efforts to improve administration of the National Pension Law, oppose increase of the national health insurance fee, reform taxation and strengthen local finance, oppose special taxes and fees, improve public works, abolish community chests and substitute more adequate public social welfare programs, and improve conditions in backward villages.

some consultative and liaison functions but their usefulness varies greatly according to regional party development and local conditions.

Conferences of party members, informal groups which are regarded as outside the regular organization, may be formed in labor unions, schools, and workshops. An ordinary conference of this type is under the jurisdiction of a territorial branch. The most numerous and active ones are found in labor unions. Their objectives are to bring more workers into the SDP, to invigorate the party's activities in workshops, and to increase the "theoretical armament" of union members through political education. They are also used for competition with the Communists and to unify distinct labor union influence within the Socialist Party, whose leaders are alert against attempts by such conferences of union–party members to impose their will upon other conferences at prefectural and national levels. Conferences organized on a regional or industrial base could cut across party organization and become powerful pressure groups within and outside the party. Not all the anxiety is on this side, however; there are also apprehensions among labor unions that Socialist factional strife may spread into union affairs, or that political influence may become dominant.

Federations of branches, identified with prefectural regions, had developed before the war and were the main bases for reviving the Socialist Party during early postwar years. According to the constitution, such a federation is formed whenever there are two or more branches in a prefecture, but only one federation is recognized by the CEC in a given prefecture. Such organizations were founded in each case by a few leaders, then were joined by branches which had formed around Diet members or other legislators. These origins explain why vested interests in the federations resist any reforms which threaten cherished autonomy.

The organization of a federation of branches closely resembles that of national headquarters. It is supposed to hold an annual convention, but this does not always occur. Each is headed by a president or chairman assisted by a roster of departmental chiefs who are usually the sole members of their divisions. In January 1957, 33 of the 46 chairmen were members of the Diet. Routine operations are controlled by the chief secretary. Each federation is required to have an office; most can now afford their own offices, but some still use the home of a Diet member, share the space of a labor federation, or occupy a corner of the party's common room in a prefectural assembly. More than half the federations have less than three full-time paid workers. In all 46 organizations there were, in 1957–58, only 142 full-time functionaries. By 1964 there were 125 in this category, 146 secretaries, and some organizers.

With only a few activists and numerous unpaid officers, local Socialist organizations are not able to undertake ambitious, independent programs. Perforce they have relied on close cooperation with labor unions. A limited interlocking membership exists on all important party-and-union councils. Some union officers may not be party members because of political conditions in their unions, but many cooperate fully with Socialist activities. Most federations allied with unions in their regions expend effort organizing anti-military-base demonstrations, peace campaigns, and the like. Few of them publish their own journals or can develop adequate economic policies for their areas. Few keep national headquarters sufficiently informed about their activities. In most prefectures, the main party apparatus concentrates so much on nationally oriented politics that the vital processes of building local and regional strength are neglected.

National and local organizers for the SDP usually lack both the disciplined zeal of Communist cadres and the prestige which Liberal Democratic Party workers gain from their connections with affluent business interests and the ruling party. Militant activists are a tiny fraction of the entire Socialist Party personnel. To accelerate the formation of branches during the Socialist schism, the Left SDP in 1953 launched a system of national and local organizers. At first, Diet members were called "national organizers"; later young, full-time workers in headquarters were assigned this task. The Right wing, during the rift, was even weaker in its regional and local organizations.[13]

13. When the Nishio faction and a few others from the right wing seceded in 1959 and founded the Democratic Socialist Party, it was more a clique with moderate labor union allies than a genuine party organization. Its group of Diet members managed political affairs, while its new CEC directed party affairs. After a severe electoral defeat in November 1960, its provisional regulations were revised and its Diet members' group was abolished. Younger leaders have also been rising to challenge the domination of the old guard around Nishio. Still, this new party is widely criticized for its topheavy structure. Matters of policy are decided by the CEC and its national convention; executive operations are supervised by the CEC. Nishio and other leaders talk wishfully about establishing a chapter in each district for elections to prefectural assemblies, and of "livelihood consultation" offices in the homes of leaders, but such plans are far from adequate realization. Under the Organization Committee new committees have been created for work on the problems of women, youth and students, labor, small and medium

Appointment of national organizers—one of the most dedicated groups in the party—is approved by the CEC; they receive instructions from the chiefs of the Organization Bureau and the department concerned. They are expected to work mainly at the prefectural level for two thirds of each month and to be in Tokyo for the remainder. At headquarters they are members of various bureaus, boards, and committees. Though few in number, they were probably partially responsible for the demand in 1953–54 for reunification and drastic reorganization of the party; as participants in more recent efforts of this sort, they called for a rotation of professional staff members between headquarters and the localities. They are expected to cooperate with their national counterparts and to be thoroughly acquainted with all aspects of local situations. To them should be ascribed much of the drive behind such activities as agitation against military bases. Since reunification, the party has been increasing the number of such organizers as finances permit. Although it is difficult to assess their effectiveness, they seem to have been at least partly responsible for the party's modest gains in certain city and prefectural assemblies.

PARTY FINANCES

The Socialist Party is financed by monthly dues, supporting dues, contributions, and donations. The Treasurer, one of the seven chief officers selected by the convention, is responsible for collection and administration of funds. He is chairman of a Finance Committee generally composed of former Treasurers, advisers, respected elders of the party, and others who have "broad" connections. Administrative departments under the Committee, headed by permanent secretaries, prepare the annual account submitted to the convention, compile a new budget, and—in accordance with law—keep the government informed of contributions received. As will be indicated, probably a candid analysis of private and public financial reports by the party would reveal more of the submerged nine tenths of the financial iceberg.

The financial base of the postwar Socialist Party increased more

enterprises, agriculture–forestry–fisheries, and people's reform movements. By early 1961, the DSP planned its own movements against inflation and revision of the Constitution, for control of nuclear weapons, a Peace Problem Study Council, special committees to promote normalization of Sino-Japanese relations, and for recovery of Okinawa. A Liaison Council for National Movements was also instituted.

than thirty-fold during the first decade, from 2.1 million yen in 1946 to 72.5 million in 1956.[14] Of course, still further growth in recent years has reflected to some degree the nation's economic prosperity. By 1960, the monthly working budget was approximately ¥7,800,000 (about $21,666) and the annual deficit somewhat more than this amount.[15] The outlay by national headquarters in 1956 amounted to more than the combined financial expenditures by all 46 federations of branches. However, the scale of Socialist financial operations at and reaching out from headquarters is modest compared with those of a local government, a large business corporation, or even a major national labor union.

Dues collected provide frail support to the party's hope of becoming a mass organization. Headquarters' payments are the constant element in party revenues; branch and prefectural dues are autonomously determined and vary widely. They may range from ¥50 to ¥100 per member each month, but ¥15 per capita is sent to Tokyo. The amount of dues paid in this manner is crucial at convention time; both membership and dues show a phenomenal rise during months immediately preceding these annual conclaves. During 1955–56, only 5.8 per cent of total party income came from dues, and in 1960 the proportion had grown only to 9.5 per cent. So it is a farce that payment of dues should play such a pivotal role in allocating convention seats.

Becoming a Socialist legislator and an elected or appointed officer in the party entails acceptance of a serious financial burden. Approximately 20–25 per cent of an SDP Diet member's official salary is paid to various levels of the party to satisfy numerous assessments. In 1955–56, this central "party tax" was the second largest source of income, constituting more than one third of the declared total revenue, but this proportion apparently has declined in recent years. The more important the office held, the heavier the "tax." The ordinary Diet member was then required to pay ¥3,000 monthly and a special headquarters' dues 33 times larger than the ordinary party member. He also paid at election time approximately one month's salary as a "recognition fee,"

14. This financial analysis of headquarters operations is based on seven financial statements from 1946 to 1956. The detailed charts have been included in the monograph mentioned in note 1 above.

15. See: Mosaburō Suzuki, "The Path I Have Followed," *Tokyo Shimbun,* May 27, 1960.

and was usually reassessed to defray year-end and summer bonuses for workers at headquarters. These burdens and the dependence of the party on them tend to limit its control over its own legislators at all levels.[16]

The legislative reference allowance of ¥10,000 to each Diet member since 1953 has become another financial pillar of the SDP. This combined sum is sent directly to national headquarters and pays the salaries of most of its personnel. In fiscal 1964–65, this allowance comprised 50 per cent of total regular party income. Thus, ironically, proceeds from the people's taxes have become a financial cornerstone of the first socialist bureaucracy in Japan.

In 1948, the SDP received only one tenth of all political contributions reported in Japan; the proportion doubled in the next eight years.[17] Whereas it relied on smaller contributions in the early years, it has recently come to depend more on large gifts. In 1956, however, single donations of at least one million yen apiece constituted 70 per cent of the SDP's receipts. Just before and during the House of Councillors elections of July 1965, such gifts comprised 25 per cent of party campaign funds. The largest contributors have been Sōhyō, a number of national labor unions, and certain large corporations. Such unions as the National Railway Workers, teachers, coal miners, and express workers form special political committees to dispense these funds. Usually union members who have been elected to the Diet serve on such committees. Additional funds are often separately given by the same unions to their own candidates on the Socialist slate and to other selected aspirants, particularly ones from favored factions. Moreover, union members and officers devote countless hours to electioneering which if paid for would run into large sums, but these are never counted. When the party was divided during 1951–55, most unions gave more generously to the Left. In the election of 1956, after reunification, contributions from unions accounted for two fifths of total Socialist receipts. During elections to the Upper House in 1965, half of all SDP campaign funds came from labor sources.

16. According to Nobuyuki Katō, in 1954–55 the party was dependent on contributions from Diet members to the extent of 59% of total income; by 1960 this had been reduced to 43.7%. See his article: "Party Renovation Now on Right Track," *Japan Socialist Review,* No. 2 (Nov. 16, 1961), p. 84.

17. The analysis of political contributions is based on party reports to the government in accordance with the Political Funds Control Law. These reports reveal only some of the sources tapped.

Ironically, the rest of the party's income for the campaign in 1956 was from businesses. During the campaign for seats in the House of Representatives in the previous year, 65 per cent of all political gifts reported by the Right Socialists were from companies, while for the more radical Left the proportion was only 30 per cent. As is well known, some corporate donors divide their contributions among principal parties, usually decreasing the amounts as they move leftward and usually proceeding no further than the Left Socialists. Some of the principal subsidizers have been: Yawata Steel Works, Japan Sugar Refinery Association, Japan Light Metals, and the Department Stores Association. Some of these donations are, no doubt, made to counter the influence of strong labor unions, consumers' groups, and associations of small business; or they may be designed to help pave the way for certain types of legislation. Critical convention delegates have been told that acceptance of funds from capitalist sources has been at least temporarily imperative in view of chronic deficits and the need for survival. Sōhyō on occasion assails the SDP for inability to control its Diet members. But what can the party do when it is acknowledged that the unreported expenditures by Diet members are more than double the party's prefectural budgets? The scramble for funds has intensified factional strife; it has warped the party's structure, has limited its performance as an instrument of the masses, and has been somewhat inconsistent with its idealistic philosophy.

9. Leaders and Factions

A respect for senior figures and a sense of group loyalty have been nearly as prevalent within Japan's postwar Social Democratic parties as among their conservative rivals. On the left of the general spectrum, however, factional cohesion and policy orientations are determined more—though not exclusively—by ideological commitment. Like the two main wings of the SDP, when united, most of these factions hark back to prewar lineages.[1] Some observers prefer to regard Japan's two major parties since 1955 as factional federations. From 1955 to 1959, the SDP included no less than seven cliques. The Nishio group, accompanied by a number of Kawakami's adherents, seceded to form the minor Democratic Socialist Party in 1959, but in the very next year a continuing rift began to develop in the most numerous Suzuki faction. Insofar as factions tend to have perennial identifications as to leaders, philosophies, connections, and opponents, they impart a measure of stability to politics; but they are fraught with instabilities, too, because of individual and group opportunism in jockeying for candidacies, party posts, and influence in forming action policies. Such alignments tend to fade in significance on lower levels of party life,

1. For an analysis of prewar socialist leadership, see Totten, *The Social Democratic Movement in Prewar Japan,* Chaps. 5–7; also his treatment of postwar leadership: "Problems of Japanese Socialist Leadership," *Pacific Affairs, 28* (June 1955), 160–69; and, with Tamio Kawakami, "The Functions of Factionalism in Japanese Politics," ibid., *38* (Summer 1965), 109–22.

MAIN SOCIALIST LEADERSHIP FACTIONS

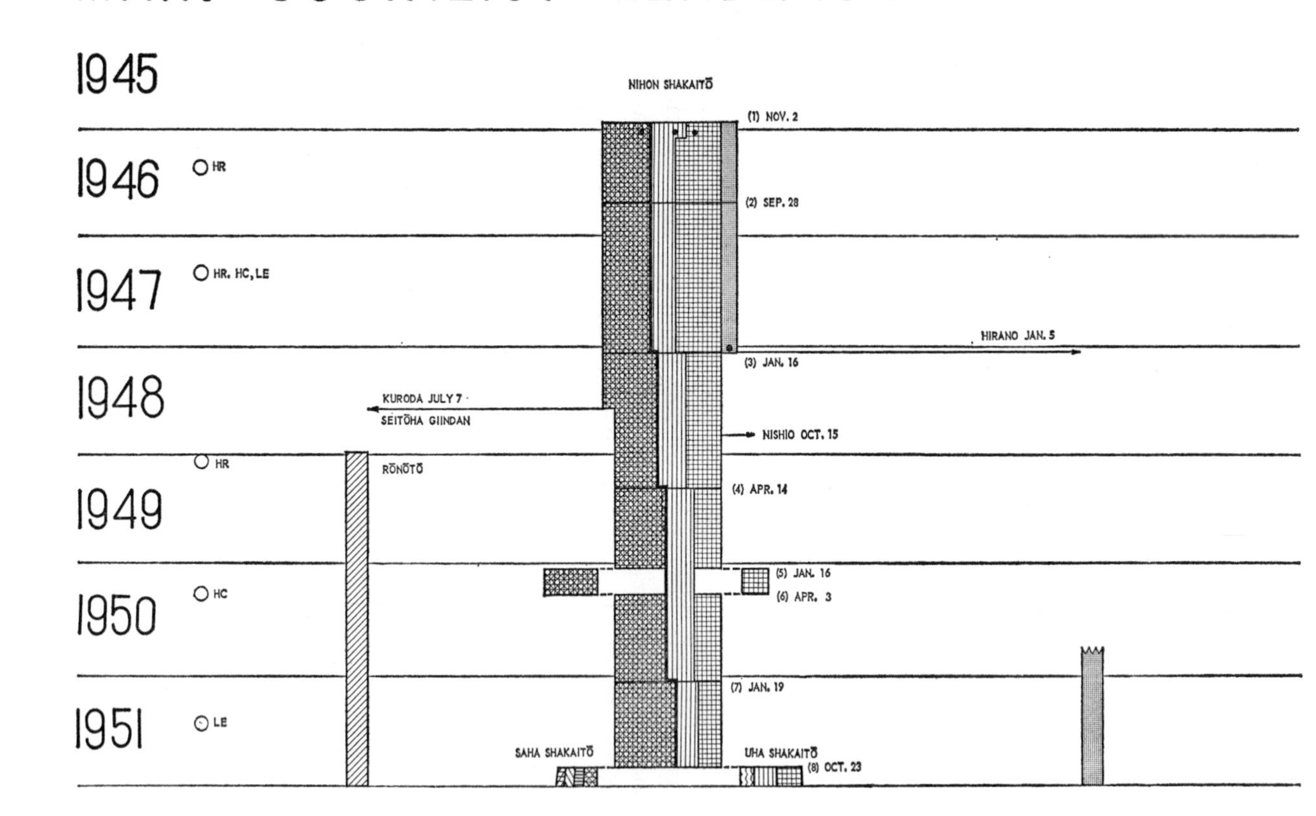

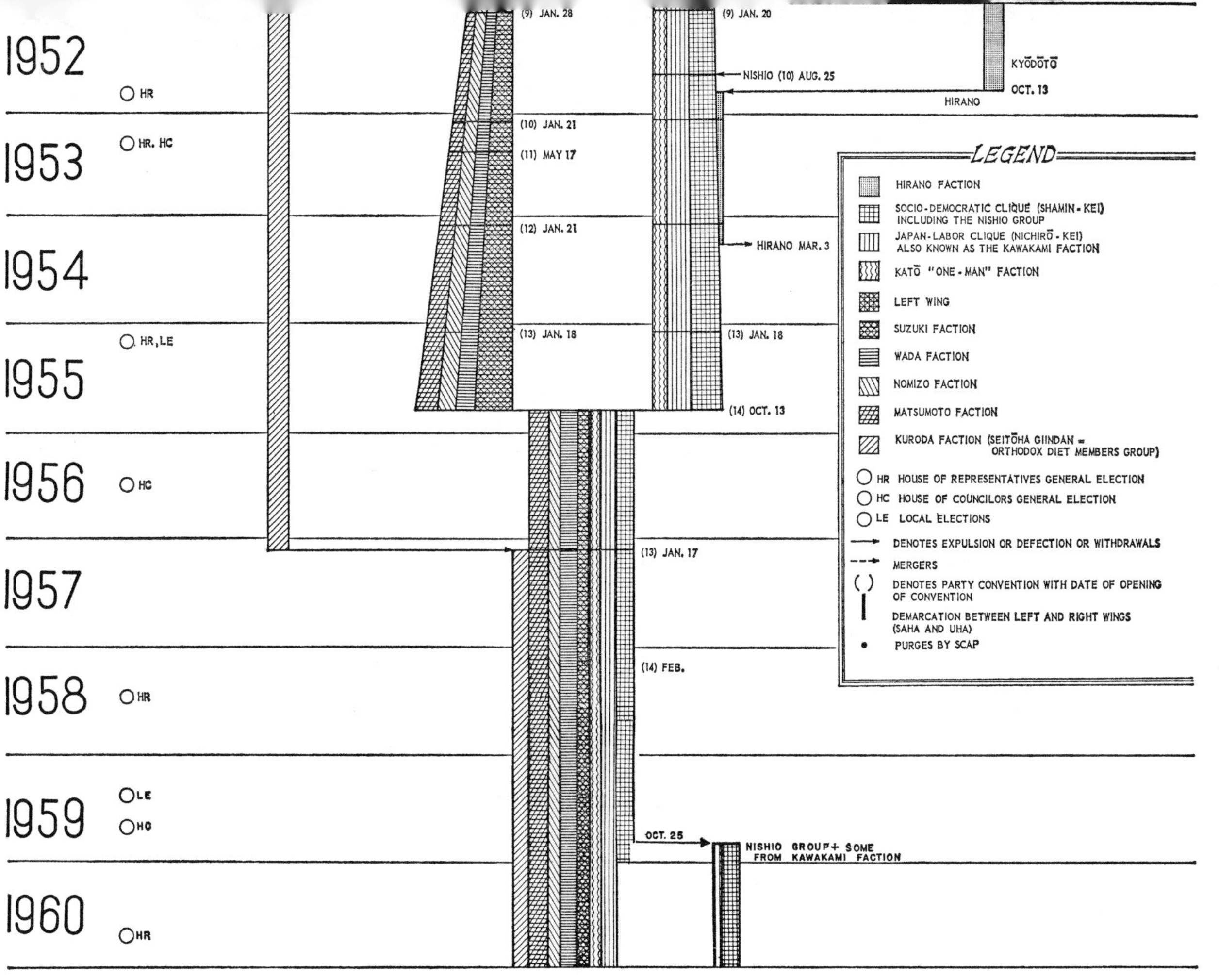
1952
HR
1953
HR, HC
1954
1955
HR, LE
1956
HC
1957
1958
HR
1959
LE
HC
1960
HR
(9) JAN. 28
(10) JAN. 21
(11) MAY 17
(12) JAN. 21
(13) JAN. 18
(9) JAN. 20
NISHIO (10) AUG. 25
HIRANO
KYŌDŌTŌ
OCT. 13
HIRANO MAR. 3
(13) JAN. 18
(14) OCT. 13
(13) JAN. 17
(14) FEB.
OCT. 25
NISHIO GROUP + SOME FROM KAWAKAMI FACTION
LEGEND
HIRANO FACTION
SOCIO-DEMOCRATIC CLIQUE (SHAMIN-KEI) INCLUDING THE NISHIO GROUP
JAPAN-LABOR CLIQUE (NICHIRŌ-KEI) ALSO KNOWN AS THE KAWAKAMI FACTION
KATŌ "ONE-MAN" FACTION
LEFT WING
SUZUKI FACTION
WADA FACTION
NOMIZO FACTION
MATSUMOTO FACTION
KURODA FACTION (SEITŌHA GIINDAN = ORTHODOX DIET MEMBERS GROUP)
HR HOUSE OF REPRESENTATIVES GENERAL ELECTION
HC HOUSE OF COUNCILORS GENERAL ELECTION
LE LOCAL ELECTIONS
DENOTES EXPULSION OR DEFECTION OR WITHDRAWALS
MERGERS
( ) DENOTES PARTY CONVENTION WITH DATE OF OPENING OF CONVENTION
DEMARCATION BETWEEN LEFT AND RIGHT WINGS (SAHA AND UHA)
PURGES BY SCAP

CHART 3

and factionalism is often a target of criticism by delegates from local units at the national convention.

Like other parties, the SDP—and more recently the lesser DSP—have tended to develop a dominant but in time changing alliance of factions harried by "anti-mainstream" elements.[2] During early postwar years, the more conservative Socialists led by Nishio were prominent. Especially after the depurging, their alliance with Kawakami's faction was strengthened, and these two were the main components of the Right Socialist Party from 1951 to 1955.[3] Four leftist factions and their party became stronger in the House of Representatives in and after 1953, however; between SDP reunification in 1955 and the critical year 1960, the Suzuki and Kawakami cliques comprised the "mainstream," being contested by the Nishio group on the right and on the other flank by the more leftist Wada, Nomizo, Matsumoto, and Kuroda factions. Since more conservative leaders followed Nishio out of the SDP in 1959, intensified doctrinal and tactical controversies have raged with a much more even division of strength between a "main current" composed of the more moderate "structural reformers" from the fissioning Suzuki faction allied with Kawakami followers and with Wada's group. The inner opposition is composed of the more leftist part of the Suzuki group (led by the younger Kōzō Sasaki backed by the elderly former party Chairman) plus the three smaller and more extreme cliques. Sōhyō and its major affiliated national federations, whose leaders are the main intrusive force in Socialist politics, have themselves been affected by these debates—controversies which reflect such undeniable realities as the nation's phenomenal economic growth with its implications, technological changes and consequent further rationalization of industries, and repercussions of liberalizing the tariff structure.

There has been fluctuation in the factional identification of Socialists in the House of Representatives; sources vary in estimating factional strength there at almost any specific time, but the following approximations give an idea of recent comparative numbers. The fig-

2. The Democratic Socialist Party is too young, small, and dominated by Nishio to permit a full proliferation of factions. But a group of younger progressives, critical of the old guard, has already emerged, and there are also medial elements and neutrals.

3. Nishio's clique can be traced back to the Socio-Democratic (Shamin-kei) and Kawakami's to the Japan-Labor (Nichirō-kei) clique, both dating from the 1920s.

ures for these factions in both houses in 1959, in order from the right, were:[4]

TABLE 3. SOCIALIST FACTIONAL REPRESENTATION IN THE DIET, 1959

Faction	*Representatives*	*Councillors*
Nishio	27	17
Kawakami	29	10
Suzuki	39	20
Wada	29	10
Matsumoto	12	
Nomizo	5	15
Kuroda	6	

That fall, after the secession of Nishio's group and moderate sympathizers, the number of that faction's Representatives had grown to 33 or 35.[5] It reached 40 by the time the Democratic Socialist Party was inaugurated in January 1960. Another gauge of relative influence is to note factional representation on the Central Executive Committee of the SDP before and after its reduction in size and the 19th party convention in March 1960:[6]

TABLE 4. FACTIONAL REPRESENTATION IN THE CENTRAL EXECUTIVE COMMITTEE OF THE SOCIALIST PARTY, BEFORE AND AFTER MARCH 1960

Faction	*Before*	*After*
Kawakami	2	2
Suzuki	15	7
Wada	3	3
Nomizo	2	2
Matsumoto	1	1

4. Figures for Socialists in the House of Representatives are cited from *Tokyo Shimbun* by Robert A. Scalapino and Junnosuke Masumi, *Parties and Politics in Contemporary Japan* (Berkeley, University of California Press, 1962), pp. 173–74; those for Socialists in the House of Councillors are from the *Japan Times*, Sept. 16, 1959.

5. Estimated figures on SDP (and DSP) factional strengths in the Lower House before and after the secession of Nishio and his adherents in October 1959 are given by Scalapino and Masumi, pp. 173–74. As indicated, this chart also correlates factional groups with background administrative and political experience, higher education, as well as connections with business, agricultural producers' organizations, farmers' unions, and labor unions.

6. See: *Asahi Shimbun*, Feb. 22, 1961; *Tokyo Shimbun*, Feb. 28, 1961.

The distribution and changes indicate the relative strength of leftist cliques—accentuated after the split-off—and the relative decline of the Suzuki group.

Candidates nominated by the Democratic Socialists for the elections of November 1963 were divided as follows: Nishio's "mainstream," 26; the Katayama-led "anti-mainstream," 12; medial elements, 13; others (all "new faces"), 10. After those elections, seats in the Lower House were distributed as follows among SDP factions: Kawakami, 26; Eda–Narita group, 11; Wada, 34; Suzuki–Sasaki, 41; Nomizo (Nōmin Dōshikai), 5; Matsumoto (Heiwa Dōshikai), 11; unaffiliated, 16.[7] Thus the mainstream had only 14 more seats than the inner opposition, and the non-factional Representatives would have held the balance if there had been a vote within the delegation.

After surveying the main Socialist factions, their respective policies, and the careers of certain of their foremost leaders, we shall with the aid of statistics delineate salient characteristics of Socialist leadership in the House of Representatives and conclude this chapter with the main patterns of factional struggles since 1960.

THE LEFT WING

The Suzuki Faction

This largest of the Socialist cliques has been the pivot of the "main current" since party reunification. In point of view its leaders are Marxist but noncommunist. They can be traced back to the prewar Labor-Farmer faction (Rōnōha) which in the late 1920s and early 1930s continuously debated theoretical questions with the Communist-oriented Monographs faction (Kōzaha). In postwar Japan they accept parliamentarianism but also insist on the use of mass actions such as strikes and demonstrations to achieve political goals. Until the general elections of May 1958, the top leaders of this faction in the Diet were all prewar socialists,[8] though not then part of a mainstream.

7. Hans Baerwald, citing *Sankei Shimbun,* Nov. 23, 1963, gives SDP factional distribution of seats in the Lower House before and after the elections of November 22, 1963. His post-election figures give Suzuki 45, four in excess of the total SDP delegation; he must have overlapped in some identifications. See his "Japan at Election Time," *Asian Survey, 4* (Jan. 1964), 648–49, and his "Factional Politics in Japan," *Current History, 46* (April 1964), 222–29, 243–44.

8. They are Mosaburō Suzuki, Isamu Akamatsu, Kōzō Sasaki, Zengorō Shimagami, Shikaichi Yasuhira, Sōji Okada, Toshiharu Shigemori, and the late Junzō Inamura and Kōdō Itō.

Their tendencies had bordered on illegality according to the tightly drawn regulations of prewar days. Though the smaller Eda–Narita, "structural reform" subgroup has, since 1960, differed with the Labor-Farmer Marxist ideologues (and with their doctrinal leader, Sakisaka), the larger, more radical section continues the affinity with that school's doctrines in its prolonged polemic with the Communists over interpreting the development of Japanese capitalism and correct revolutionary tactics.

Soon after World War II, Suzuki and associates formed the Socialist Political and Economic Research Institute (Shakaishugi Seiji Keizai Kenkyūjo) and led the party in economic planning. During the Katayama government, Suzuki, as chairman of the SDP Policy Planning Board, cooperated with the Economic Stabilization Board directed by Wada. Until his death in 1956, Kōdō Itō, a close comrade of Suzuki and like him a former economic journalist, was the party's chief economic planner. He was one of the primary architects of the Left Socialist five-year "peace economy" plan of 1953.

Junzō Inamura, an agricultural specialist before his death in 1955, was Tatsuo Morito's antagonist in the classic debate over the nature of the party and revolutionary versus evolutionary methods in 1949; as principal theoretician for the Suzuki faction he drafted the Left Socialist platform in 1954.

The rise of the Suzuki faction can also be attributed to its close cooperation with democratization within the labor union movement during 1949–50. Isamu Akamatsu worked toward SDP reconstruction with these groups in Sōdōmei (particularly with Minoru Takano), in the Sambetsu democratization movement (with Matsuta Hosoya), and in the National Railway Workers Union. He later became chairman of the Socialists' Party-Labor Union Cooperation Conference. The Secretary-General and President in the early years of Sōhyō were members of the Suzuki faction. Close liaison was maintained between this group and Minoru Takano after he became Secretary-General of Sōhyō. The common bond dating from the Popular Front incident of 1937 was again at work. But when Takano began to shift more and more to the left by embracing the pro-Communist "peace force policy" in 1953, a distinct coolness—and finally hostility—developed between him and the Suzuki faction.

Sensing that reunification of the Left and Right SDP was unavoidable, the Suzuki faction pushed these negotiations in 1954–55, disregarding opposition from other left-wing groups. The isolation of the mainstream was increased when it took too many of the top seven positions at the time of reunification. It flirted with the Japan-Labor clique to maintain its dominant position and returned to the left-wing fold under Sōhyō pressure. The general elections of 1958 dealt the Suzuki faction a telling blow: it failed to reelect a number of important secondary leaders who were replaced by six newcomers from Sōhyō unions, a clergyman, a teacher, and others. Kōzō Sasaki, the chairman of the party's Election Policy Committee for several years, was the sole remaining member of the faction's original top leadership.

In 1958, Saburō Eda emerged as the party's chief organizer. He has been popular among youth and has revitalized their role in the party. But above all, he has dared to face, and serve as spokesman for, the need to rethink the theories and tactics of Japanese socialism.

Eda's principal coadjutor in pressing for greater moderation and realism has been Tomomi Narita, who—after Kōdō Itō—has been the party's leading economic expert. In this function he has worked with Seiichi Katsumata (Wada faction) and Mitsu Kōno (Kawakami-ite). From prior experience with a Mitsui chemical company Narita brought prized administrative experience into the party's service; he has in part made up for lack of a longer "fighting record" by helping to organize unions in his native Kagawa prefecture. Continuously reelected to the Lower House since 1947, he has been affiliated with the Suzuki faction since the early 1950s and chaired the Policy Planning Board during 1955–57 and again from 1960 to 1962. Between these terms he directed the Bureau of General Affairs. He succeeded Eda as Secretary-General in November 1962.

Mosaburō Suzuki, prime leader of this faction and for nine years Chairman successively of the Left Socialists and then the united SDP, is a veteran whose position has been somewhat to the left of the center of his own party. Since 1960 he, like some others of the old guard, has been passing the baton to younger leaders. In the process he has sharply favored the more leftist sector in his own group, headed by Sasaki.

Suzuki was born in Aichi prefecture in 1893, the third son of a poor family. While majoring in political economy at Waseda University, he worked at what the Japanese call "*arubaito*" (part-time work for students, from the German *Arbeit*). After graduation, he became a newspaper reporter, covering the Siberian Expedition between 1917 and 1918. Coming to the United States in 1919, he briefly came under the tutelage of the already well-known Sen Katayama and Tsunao Inomata who by then were convinced Leninists. He left New York in 1921 for the Soviet Union via Europe as a correspondent for the *Yomiuri Shimbun,* arriving back in Japan in 1922. While in Russia he was apparently repelled by the effects of excessive revolutionary violence, though he had long discussions abroad with Japanese Communists who were to become famous. Back in Japan he tried his hand at organizing miners in Kyūshū, but his health could not stand the rigors. Left-wing journalism proved to be his early forte, and it was while thus employed that he participated in forming the first proletarian parties in the 'twenties.

During those years he was active in the Labor-Farmer school (Rōnōha) of applied theory and wrote several treatises on monopoly capitalism. He met Sōji Okada, Minoru Takano, Hisao Kuroda, and others who have played leading roles in postwar leftist political, agrarian, and labor union movements. But Suzuki became known as a socialist intellectual, and later a politician, rather than as an organizer. Soon after the outbreak of war in China in 1937, he was one of those leftists convicted and imprisoned for violating the Peace Preservation Law by activities in the Popular Front. He refused to cooperate with national expansionists, however, and spent the remaining war years operating a small bookstore.[9]

After the nation's catastrophe, Suzuki was among those who rebuilt a Socialist Party closely allied with the labor movement. As Secretary-General in 1950–51, however, he was ineffectual in dealing with the developing party schism. Indeed, Suzuki has a reputation for indecisiveness and for repeatedly declining to take positions on crucial, controversial issues at their climax. As Left Socialist Chairman after 1951, he helped his wing's representation in the House of Representatives grow from 16 to 89 seats in the next four years.

Suzuki continued as Chairman of the reunified party until 1960, when his faction was obliged to support Asanuma, a long-time rival of the incumbent for that post. This burly politico was famed as an intraparty mediator but not as an ideologue; this helps to account for his later radicalism in attempts to woo the more leftist and doc-

9. Suzuki has written two autobiographies: *Ai to Tōsō* (Love and Struggle) (Tokyo, Rōdō Bunka-sha, 1949); and *Aru Shakaishugisha no Hansei* (The Life of a Socialist) (Tokyo, Bungei Shunjū-sha, 1958).

trinaire factions. In that year of crisis, there seemed to be no other candidate emergent in the Suzuki orbit who could satisfy elements on the Left and in Sōhyō; they had been growing more hostile to Suzuki's mainstream and more aroused by public events. After the Nishio faction's secession, the failures of the anti-treaty struggle as well as the Miike strike, and the rightist assassination of Asanuma, the trend toward moderation encouraged a rift in the Suzuki group between the Eda–Narita Socialist reformers and the more revolutionary Suzuki–Sasaki leftists. The structural reformers have received support from a number of national Sōhyō affiliates, but most of the Ōta–Iwai mainstream, and of course Takano's more radical "Progressive Alliance" (Kakushin Dōmei) have opposed the party's new main current combination led by Eda and Narita.

The Wada Faction

This, one of two SDP factions of postwar vintage—the other being the Heiwa Dōshikai—is sometimes called the bureaucratic element in the party; but most of its members have had no administrative experience. Its three prime leaders: Hiroo Wada, Seiichi Katsumata, and Tadataka Sata, have had governmental experience and still have personal connections with numerous bureaucrats. They have attracted a younger generation of adherents, including a number of labor union leaders. They have close connections with the Mindō-Left of Sōhyō and also with some of Takano's "Progressive Alliance."

Wada's political following in the party dates from 1954, when he became Secretary-General of the Left SDP. Unlike Asanuma, his counterpart in the rival wing, he bluntly declined to ingratiate himself with the rank-and-file and tour the country to strengthen local organization. Though criticized as a snob, he has participated vigorously in management of party affairs mainly from Tokyo.

During early schooling in Okayama, which still includes his constituent district—and, more recently, that of Saburō Eda—Wada earned a reputation for brilliance. He was later graduated from the Law Faculty of Tokyo Imperial University, entered the civil service, and rose rapidly. Had it not been for the Planning Board incident in 1940, Wada might have attained a high imperial appointment, but in that case probably would have been purged for some years from postwar political life. With Katsumata, Sata, and several others he was arrested for allegedly trying to utilize existing governmental controls for communist purposes.[10] That experience created a group esprit somewhat like that which exists among veterans of the Suzuki faction who were implicated in the Popular Front incident. Wada and his associates were imprisoned for several years; only after the war was he reinstated as Chief of the Bureau of Agricultural Administration in the Ministry of Agriculture and Forestry.

When, in 1946, Shigeru Yoshida formed his cabinet of fellow bureaucrats, he chose Wada as Minister of Agriculture, despite some objections from conservatives. Wada was thus able to make the unusual leap from bureau chief to minister of state. The Katayama-led coalition government found it needed him as Director-General of the Economic Stabilization Board. A bureaucrat who could be trusted by the Socialists was a great help in providing liaison with the generally more conservative administrative agencies. Wada and his associates in the Economic Stabilization Board made it one of the centers of political authority in the government. In fact, Nishio, the real power behind the Katayama cabinet, came to rely on the former Minister of Agriculture almost to excess. (His current Minister of Agriculture, Rikizō Hirano, objected and this was the root of the fierce quarrel between Hirano and Nishio.)

Wada joined the SDP in February 1949, and less than a year later the broad connections of his colleagues with financial and corporate circles led to his appointment as party Treasurer. In 1957, as we have noted, Wada was criticized for using allegedly questionable methods in obtaining funds and after a party hearing was suspended from office for one year. He has also been active in the planning of policies, particularly in economic fields, and since before the first crisis over the

10. Those implicated in the Planning Board incident are regarded as having been victims of ultranationalist suspicions and of a power struggle. After formation of the first Konoe cabinet (June 1937), national socialism was fostered as part of a "new system" (*shin taisei*). A new group of bureaucrats was formed in the Planning Board to act as the guiding force in this new economic movement to separate capital from management. But certain groups in the Army, particularly the Kōdō faction, and the capitalists were not in favor of this adventure and planned to overthrow the second Konoe cabinet. When the Sorge spy case was dramatically disclosed, the government bore down on the Planning Board. At that time, Wada and others among his colleagues who had been transferred from the Ministry of Agriculture had organized groups to study the rights and problems of tenant farmers, desirable changes of land tenure, and the position of industrial organization in the national economy. He and his associates were imprisoned for several years and claim that they signed confessions of their communist guilt under police duress.

peace and security treaties he has turned his considerable ability to criticism of conservative foreign policies and to alternative proposals. More recently he has directed his party's International Bureau. Indeed, the other name of his clique is the "policy study group." One of the reasons for tension between the Wada and the Suzuki factions was growing recognition of Wada as a contender for the party chairmanship. It is thought that one explanation of his group's moderation toward "structural reform" and support of the new mainstream since 1960 has been its ambition to lift Wada into the top party office after Kawakami retired.

Although there has been some interchange of adherents between the Wada faction and Suzuki's sector (and to a lesser extent the Matsumoto group on the other flank), the former's electoral strength has been rather clearly discernible. After the elections of 1958, its members numbered 28 or 29; after the elections of 1963 its total in the Lower House was 34.[11] Many of these in both Houses have been vigorous postwar leaders from Sōhyō-affiliated unions. Half of its members in the House of Councillors have been from the Japan Teachers' Union. Although main leaders in this faction do not stem from the labor movement, they have assiduously cultivated relations with leaders of large industrial and government workers' unions in the Sōhyō orbit. They broke with Takano's group over its pro-Communist "peace force" position and, in cooperation with other SDP leftists, helped to oust that would-be labor commissar. Wada's relations with Sōhyō were reinforced when Kaoru Ōta, his classmate in the Sixth Higher School, became its Chairman; he is also on good terms with Akira Iwai, Sōhyō's Secretary-General.

Seiichi Katsumata is Wada's chief lieutenant and heir-apparent. He was graduated from Kyoto Imperial University as a specialist in agriculture and, like Wada, spent a few wartime years in prison for im-

11. Members of the Wada faction include: Hiroo Wada himself, Seiichi Katsumata, Hōmei Ogawa, Setsuo Yokomichi, Yoshizō Minabe, Kanjirō Satō, Hidekazu Yanagida, Hiroichi Tsujihara, Motoo Yamazaki, Yoshitaka Takii, Masatsugu Ishibashi, Noboru Yagi, Tomiyuki Takada, and Kenji Sano. According to various identifications, the following are placed in either the Wada or Suzuki factions: Mitsugu Haga, Katsujirō Nagai, Keio Sakurai, Tamotsu Hasegawa, Toshiaki Yokoyama, Torao Gotō, Takeo Tanaka, Gorō Abe, Shinnen Tagaya, Kan Komatsu, Minato Katashima, Susumu Kagata, Hiroshi Yamanaka, and Yoshio Katsuzawa. Airō Kitayama, Yūzen Ishida, and Shichirō Matsumoto have also at times been associated with the Matsumoto faction. In the general election of 1958 the Wada faction lost from its contingent in the Diet Shigeharu Shimura, Terutake Arima, and Kaku Nohara.

plication in the Planning Board incident. During early postwar years he served as Wada's secretary when the latter headed the Economic Stabilization Board. At first Katsumata, from a center stance, tried to devise compromises which could prevent party schism but, during the debate over the peace and security treaties in 1951, he became the foremost left-wing advocate of rejecting both agreements. He played a major role in negotiations toward party reunification and has been influential in the formulation of SDP policies, including those concerned with foreign affairs. He has strongly urged the improvement of relations with Communist China and in 1957 chaired a special committee for this purpose.

Katsumata is an able administrator, shrewd negotiator, and vigorous politician. He has held most of his party's important posts except the topmost two. It was under his strategic leadership that the SDP foiled conservative attempts in 1956 to ram through the Diet a gerrymandered revision of electoral districts designed to reduce the Socialists to impotence. In his Shizuoka constituency, Katsumata is supported by a wide gamut of groups, ranging from labor unions to proprietary interests. He is able to tap sizable financial resources to aid the party and his factional associates.

Ever since tension with the Suzuki faction over party reunification[12] and debates in the process of drafting the basic Left Socialist platform in 1953–54, the Wada clique has been on friendly terms with left-wing academicians[13] and with the leftist Socialist Society (Shakaishugi Kyōkai). The faction has been popular among younger Socialist Diet members, who have frequently met in serious study groups under its auspices. In the CEC, the Wada faction is usually represented by Katsumata, Sata, and sometimes Shigeru Hara, who have also been prominent on the party's Policy Planning and Diet Policy Boards. Their intellectualism is widely respected but at times can lead to adverse reactions by some elements in the party and in laterally connected organizations.

As the Socialist Party works toward becoming a more responsible opposition force, and as it inevitably and increasingly confronts the

12. Many in Suzuki's faction were working for reunification during 1954–55, but the Wada group argued that at the rate Left SDP strength had been growing it could later oblige the rival wing to reunite largely on the Left's terms.

13. They include Itsurō Sakisaka, Masao Takahashi, the late Hitoshi Yamakawa, and Hyōe Ouchi.

implications of economic growth under regulated capitalism as well as improved levels of popular consumption and welfare, the experience and theoretical training of the Wada faction are likely to become even more influential. Especially before 1960–61, Wada and his associates often cooperated with the smaller SDP factions farther to the left, and it is to them that we now turn.

The Nomizo Faction

The declining Nomizo faction, one of the two smallest in the Socialist left wing, centers around a few Diet members affiliated with the Japan Farmers' Union or associated with agricultural cooperatives. This group usually has four or five members in the House of Representatives[14] and three or four in the Upper House.[15] Nomizo himself has at different times had several terms in both Houses. Most of these leaders championed the prewar farmers' movement, and some were jailed for their activities. They have a better than average education, some being university graduates. They have had diverse specialties: law, agricultural engineering, farming, veterinary medicine, and writing. This group attempts to represent agricultural interests in the party but has no monopoly on the allegiance of Socialist Diet members elected from rural districts. They have frequently, and sometimes with success, demanded that a higher rice subsidy be included in party policies. In vain they decry the undue emphasis on the interests of industrial workers in SDP programs and statements of policy. Distinctive principles and policies have not been clearly enunciated by them, however. Although the faction can bargain for party offices, its adherents often fail to gain chairmanships of the subcommittees on agricultural policies under the Policy Planning Board.

Masaru Nomizo is a one-time veterinarian who has long been interested in movements for agrarian reform and for cooperation between farmers' and labor unions. He has not been a Marxist, and before the war was originally associated with the more conservative Socio-Democratic clique, but in 1930 he switched to the then more

14. Members of the Nomizo group who have recently served in the House of Representatives include: Yoichirō Kambayashi, Tadashi Yaoita, Saburō Kuribayashi, Toshio Kurihara, and Kiyoyuki Sanekawa. At different times, Kaku Ashika, Kōichi Yamamoto, Yūzō Awaya, and Tokuji Kameda have been included.

15. Those of the same faction who have recently won seats in the House of Councillors included: Sanshichi Hanyū, Saburō Oka, Teiji Miwa, and Hachijirō Mitsuhashi. As usual, not all these members were always closely identified with the Nomizo faction.

militant Japan-Labor clique. He served as a member of the Central Committee when the Social Democratic Party was organized in 1926. During the war he worked in a peripheral organization of the Ministry of Agriculture and Forestry.

In 1947 Nomizo first became prominent in national politics. Katayama bypassed him for the agricultural portfolio after the dismissal of Hirano, but he was one of the two leftists to gain posts in the Ashida cabinet. He had become Vice-Chairman of the Japan Farmers' Union, which was reorganized after the war; Hisao Kuroda was Chairman. Because of his moderate views, he was chosen Chairman of the Permanent Committee on Agriculture and Forestry in the House of Representatives.

When the SDP split in the fall of 1951, Nomizo became the first Secretary-General of the leftist organization. By cooperating closely with Takano, when the latter was Secretary-General of Sōhyō, he helped to attain that spectacular rise in Left Socialist representation in the Lower House during the early 'fifties. By 1953 he had drawn a significant number of rural Socialists to his clique and carried weight in the central headquarters secretariat and in the Youth Department. His skill as a compromiser and fund-raiser and his conscientiousness were most appreciated. Then his faction's influence waned. The leftist farmers' movement, weakened by the effects of land reform, became seriously divided. The Nomizo group for a while was somewhat isolated from other party factions. Nomizo and some of his colleagues from the Japan Farmers' Union were traveling in the Soviet Union and Communist China when the SDP was reunified and offices were allocated. He helped to achieve reunification of the Japan Farmers' Union in 1958, and a younger member of his faction, Yoichirō Kambayashi, became its new Secretary-General. Until Suzuki's retirement from the party chairmanship, Nomizo's faction joined other far leftist cliques in criticism; it is still aligned with opponents of the recoalesced mainstream, but—with slightly stronger backing—may at times continue to play a mediatory role.

The Matsumoto (or Heiwa Dōshikai) Faction

Besides being a factional leader of considerable skill, Jiichirō Matsumoto has struggled for over half a century for the emancipation of the "*tokushu burakumin*" (special community people), the euphemism for the former *eta* or outcastes who lived for centuries in segregated communities until officially freed in 1871. Unfortunately, social discrimination has continued and Matsumoto's vigorous fight against it has won him the unabating support of many in this indigenous minority group. In 1922 he helped found the Zenkoku Suiheisha (National Leveling Society) dedicated to the social emancipation of all those Japanese who suffer because of their "special" background, and he remained the leader of this movement through many prewar vicissitudes.

Although he is considered very much of a typical "boss" (*oyabun*) over his own followers in the party, he is not an office-seeker as such. The position of adviser is the only party office he has been willing to assume. Yet this does not nearly indicate his influence in SDP affairs. He has a respected ability to mediate personality disputes, and yet this dignified elder has refused to bow even to the Emperor or ever to wear a necktie until discrimination ends. In postwar Japan he has voiced pan-Asian views, has had good words for Communist China and the Soviet Union, and has roundly denounced Japan's ruling classes and Western imperialism.

This faction usually has about a dozen members in the House of Representatives[16] and about five or six in the House of Councillors.[17] It is essentially a postwar creation, only about five of its members having participated in earlier proletarian parties. It was first organized into the Platform Study Group (Kōryō Kenkyūkai) when the Left Socialists worked out their basic platform in 1953–54. Except for Matsumoto most of this group are well educated but diverse in professional background; and ideologically they are hardly unified or committed to any one particular school of Marxism. They have nevertheless consistently allied with other leftists to oppose policies promoted by right-wing factions but have shifted tactics repeatedly with respect to the party's mainstream and its changing components. Strongly allied with the Takano pro-Communist faction in Sōhyō, Matsumoto and others in the group vociferously advocated the "peace

16. They are: Rikiya Nishimura, Ichio Asukada, Kōzō Inomata, Shichirō Hozumi, Orinoshin Tanaka, Hideo Ishimura, Toshio Tanaka, Tsuyoshi Kihara, Taira Sakamoto, and Tōru Ōhara. Yūzen Ishida, Shichirō Matsumoto, Airō Kitayama, and Hideo Yamahana are sometimes included in this faction. In the general election of 1958 the Matsumoto faction lost Masako Fukuda, Kanemitsu Hososeko, Sadao Furuya, and Buichi Aono.

17. In the House of Councillors they are: Jiichirō Matsumoto, Hōsei Yoshida, Seiji Uchimura, Naoko Takada, and Kimiko Abe. When Gengo Kinoshita was in this House he was one of the leaders of this faction.

force" orientation at the Left party convention in 1954. They were cautious about Socialist reunification unless Kuroda's Worker-Farmer Party also joined the merger. When reunification did take place without that splinter party, they formed the Heiwa Dōshikai (Peace Comrades) to counter right-wing influence. A member of this faction has often chaired the national Control Commission, one of the seven top positions. Usually two to four members sit on the Central Executive Committee. Since 1955 the Heiwa Dōshikai name has come to supersede that of Matsumoto to designate this faction. It has continued to collaborate with the Takano group in Sōhyō and has in effect absorbed the group we shall consider next.

The Kuroda Faction

More theoretical in their leftism were those led by Hisao Kuroda. In 1948 he and some of his followers were expelled from the SDP, as we have seen, and for more than eight years maintained a separate existence as the Worker Farmer Party (Rōdōsha Nōmintō, often abbreviated as Rōnōtō).

Like his more moderate rival, Masaru Nomizo, Kuroda has been one of the few Socialists still active after the war in the agrarian movement. He led the pro-communist Unification faction in the Japan Farmers' Union and contributed to its fissiparous turmoil, as explained in Chapter 11. The agrarian movement in Okayama Prefecture has provided the strongest reservoir of organized and electoral support for this faction, usually enabling Kuroda and one or two others to be elected to the House of Representatives—sometimes in competition with Wada and more recently, Eda. Other pockets of their strength lie in Hokkaidō, Mie, Ishikawa, and Shizuoka prefectures, in the last of which they compete with Katsumata.

Despite his radicalism, Kuroda himself stems from a rich landowning family in Okayama and his wife is a highly successful ophthalmologist there. After being converted to Marxism-Leninism and becoming interested in the agrarian movement during student years at Tokyo Imperial University, he devoted his training as a lawyer to the defense of tenant farmers. Before World War II, he was active in a succession of leftist parties whose tactics bordered on the illegal. He, too, was implicated in the Popular Front incident and was imprisoned. His long association with Mosaburō Suzuki ended over the budgetary crisis of 1948 but his friendship with Ikuo Ōyama, which had begun with his proletarian party work in the 1920s and spanned the long period of the latter's exile, was resumed after the war and continued until Ōyama, who never became active in the SDP as such, died in 1955.

Although right-wing Socialists have often considered them as Communists in disguise, the Kuroda faction people always shunned merger with the JCP. They have repeatedly urged at least pragmatic united fronts with all those on the left including the Communists. In the House of Councillors the Worker Farmer Party had three or four members or sympathizers, all of whom had either died or were defeated by the elections of 1956.[18] After rejoining the SDP in 1957, the faction experienced a resurgence; Kuroda and five others were elected to the Lower House in the elections of 1958.[19] But since 1960 it has usually been counted as part of the Peace Comrades.

THE RIGHT WING

More moderate Socialists began the postwar era with advantages both as to leadership and support from organized labor, but after their brief participation in governmental administration the vigor and appeal of their two factions waned. Within four years after the refounding of the SDP, the right wing had crumbled, and the tide of labor unionism was running strongly toward the left. It was not only that policies of the Occupation played into the hands of noncommunist left-wing leaders; the evolutionary Socialists have never recovered from their failure to make a determined, progressive bid for labor union support during the crucial years 1948–51.

Right-wing Socialists, while lacking the cohesion and disciplined direction that an accepted doctrinal corpus can sometimes provide, tend to define positions in regard to issues. In principle they usually support parliamentarianism and legal tactics—the Nishio faction more than that of Kawakami. The former has more organized labor allies than does the Kawakami group, but believes neither in the intrusion of unionism into parties nor in excessive union politicism. The Nishio clique is more aggressive in criticizing Sōhyō influences on the SDP and pro-communist tendencies of that party's more leftist elements. Though Kawakami's faction has only slender roots in the labor move-

18. They were Kihachirō Kimura, Ikuo Ōyama, Makoto Hori, and Gorō Hani.

19. They are Hisao Kuroda, Haruo Okada, Hisao Ishina, Yutaka Kubota, Kenji Nakahara, and Shunzō Tate.

ment, it has been more imbued with Marxist concepts and has tended to be more "idealistic." Since 1959–60, one of these groups has preferred to become a double opposition—against both the LDP and the main Socialist Party; the other has performed a moderating role within the SDP.

The Kawakami Faction

Between the World Wars, leaders in this circle were associated with the Japan-Labor clique (Nichirō-kei), whose prime leader was—until his death in 1940—Hisashi Asō. Finding the way toward socialism blocked first by concentrations of conservative power, then by rising tides of ultranationalism and militarism, leaders of what came to be the Socialist Masses' Party allowed themselves to be persuaded that somehow strong state control over the economy might open a way for genuine socialism. In the postwar scene, some have carried a burden of guilt for having supported the National General Mobilization Act of 1938 and for having in other ways joined trends which were not only inconsistent with their previously championed aims but, as they eventuated, brought national catastrophe. Determination never again to be so opportunistic has imparted special emotion to their postwar socialism and to defense of such gains as the democratic "peace" Constitution.

Of all Socialist factions, this one suffered most from the Occupation-inspired political purge.[20] The bending of Jōtarō Kawakami to nationalist imperialism and his formal acceptance of a director's office in the Imperial Rule Assistance Association had certainly not been in keeping with his record as a Christian socialist, and for this he was willing to atone. After being depurged, he declined an office in his party until he could be elected to the Diet.

Kawakami had been graduated from Tokyo Imperial University in 1915 and had passed the state bar examination. But instead of practicing law he lectured first at St. Paul's University in Tokyo, then for a decade at Kansei Gakuin. During the latter period he had become involved in Japan's youthful labor movement, had helped with some of Toyohiko Kagawa's social projects, and had participated in the

20. Temporarily removed from public life in this clique were such politicos as Jōtarō Kawakami, Mitsu Kōno, Jusō Miwa, Takaichi Nakamura, and Haruji Tahara. Others of their closer colleagues, such as Shōichi Miyake and Inejirō Asanuma, continued to be active.

Political Study Group (Seiji Kenkyūkai), that precursor of several proletarian political parties. As one of the first eight Socialists elected to the Diet after enactment of the manhood suffrage law, Kawakami had devoted himself fully to left-wing politics.

After national defeat and toward the end of the Occupation period, Kawakami became Chairman of the Right Socialist Party; later he worked for reunification of the two Socialist wings and won respect for restraining the demands of his faction for major party offices. There was talk of his soon becoming Chairman of the united party, but the sudden death in 1957 of Jusō Miwa, his friendly adviser and fund-raiser, lessened the likelihood. Early in 1960, this aged politician was drafted as a candidate for Chairman by his own group allied with anti-Suzuki leftist factions. He lost the convention election then but attained that office the following year, after the assassination of Asanuma, retaining it until he died at the age of 79 in December 1965.[21]

That stalwart had been more or less an adherent of Kawakami's circle for some thirty years, and there was some shaking of heads when he ran against his patron just before the anti-treaty campaign came to a head. He had been Secretary-General of the party, and of the Right wing during the schism of the early 'fifties, for almost the whole span from 1947 to his promotion in 1960.

During student days at Waseda University he had assisted a dispute of copper miners, had resisted the introduction of military training on campuses, and—with others who were to become colleagues in the socialist movement—had created the Founders' Federation (Kensetsusha Dōmei). After graduation, he had plunged into the farmers' and labor union movements. It was through his association with the Japan Farmers' Union that he became Secretary-General of the Farmer Labor Party formed after the passage of manhood suffrage in 1925 but lasting only a day because of suppression. He reappeared as a leader time and again through the further splits and mergers of leftist parties. After several attempts, he was elected to the Tokyo municipal assembly in 1933 and became its vice-speaker. Three years later he was elected to the House of Representatives from Tokyo's first district,

21. Kawakami was born in 1889 in Atago, Tokyo, the son of a lumberman. He has been elected ten times from the first district in Hyōgo prefecture. For some years recently he was a party adviser, and from 1961–65 he was Party Chairman. His wife, Sueko, is the daughter of Tsuneyasu Hiraiwa, a leader of the Japanese Methodist Church. His son, Tamio, has edited a short selection of his father's works and published them privately as *Kawakami Jōtarō Enzetsu-shū* (Jōtarō Kawakami, Collected Speeches) (Tokyo, 1966).

and—except for the election of 1942, which Premier Tōjō largely manipulated—was continuously re-elected. Right after World War II he was embarrassed but not purged for having joined a Diet members' league to prosecute the "sacred war" and an East Asia League of Dietmen.

Asanuma was never noted for his grasp and articulation of Socialist theories and policies. Rather he was a veteran who often had helped devise compromises both among Socialist factions and between his own party and the conservatives. Moreover, he was in some respects a colorful figure—massive, energetic, gravel-voiced. Although he tried to subordinate his personal views to those of his faction and party, a rift developed between him and the Kawakami clique during the latter part of his secretary-generalship. After secession of the Nishio group made inevitable a change of offices and committee chairmanships, Chairman Suzuki embarrassed the Kawakami faction by resigning in favor of Asanuma. The latter's rather uncharacteristic extremist utterances, particularly after his controversial denunciation of American "imperialism" in Peking in March 1959, may have been designed to ingratiate himself not only with the Chinese Communists but also with leftists in his own party. During the height of the anti-treaty campaign, Asanuma as party Chairman played a militant and at times clearly anti-American role. It may have been this sharpened radicalism, as well as his position, which made him the target of a fanatic rightist youth.[22]

Doubtless the adherents of the Kawakami faction—as it became known after 1951—have varied in number. A survey of 60 Socialist Representatives after the elections of 1958 indicated about 36 in this camp (including a few unsuccessful candidates) and approximately 11 whose identification was blurred as between the two right-wing cliques.[23] The number of actual incumbents of this stripe was prob-

22. As a memorial and *Festschrift* for Asanuma after his assassination, the SDP supported a publication by the Asanuma Tsuitō Shuppan Henshū Iinkai (Asanuma Memorial Publication Editorial Committee) of the beautifully illustrated *Bakushin: Ningen Kikansha Numa-San no Kiroku Asanuma Inejirō Tsuitō Shuppan* (Dashing Forward: A Record of the Human Locomotive, Mr. Asanuma) (Tokyo, Nihon Shakaitō Kikanshi-kyoku, 1961).

23. See *Tokyo Shimbun*, May 31, 1958; and (with less emphasis) *Yomiuri Shimbun*, May 24, 1958; Scalapino and Masumi, *Parties and Politics*, p. 173. Those generally recognized as adherents or sympathizers of the Kawakami faction include: Jōtarō Kawakami, Inejirō Asanuma, Mitsu Kōno, Eiji Yamashita, Takaichi Nakamura, Shōichi Miyake, Yōnosuke Kikuchi, Yoshio Hino, Daisaku Kanda, Shizue Yamaguchi, Seiichi Ii, Ryōichi

ably about 29. Some of the waverers followed Nishio out of the SDP in 1959–60; after the elections of November 1963 the Kawakami followers in that House were estimated at 26.[24]

The relatively high levels of education which mark this group, and their degree of theoretical emphasis, are among the few attractions it has for promising young leaders. Our survey in 1958 indicated that about one third of the clique's leaders had participated in the prewar social democratic movement; the rest were later adherents. About one quarter of the total had connections with business firms or associations; an equal number claimed to be lawyers or journalists; and there were a few doctors, teachers, two former government officials, a Buddhist priest-turned-teacher, and a union leader. There is almost a complete lack of active labor union officials; less than half a dozen prewar members were labor leaders, but even they now have only tenuous relations with that movement. Only a few Kawakami followers have affiliations with agricultural cooperatives and farmers' unions. In the House of Councillors where, in 1958 as more recently, there was a concentration of former labor leaders, the Kawakami faction had only four members: a bicycle manufacturer, a former local government official, a journalist, and a professor. Thus, features and weaknesses which had characterized the Japan-Labor clique have endured. At each of the first three conventions after SDP reunification, seven members of this faction were elected to the CEC,[25] but since the reduction of that body the Kawakami component has numbered only two.

Oka, Yoshio Dōmori, Motojirō Sugiyama, Masamichi Ōnishi, Hideo Nakamura, Isamu Imazumi, Shinkichi Ukeda, Hirofumi Taman, Tokio Nakamura, Shigeyoshi Matsumae, Tetsu Kinoshita, Tsuguo Komaki, Jūjirō Shimaguchi, Daihachi Onuki, Yuriko Motojima, Kanjū Katō, Shintarō Komatsu, Kanemitsu Yoshikawa, Satoko Togano, Chūjirō Hiraoka, Susumu Kobayashi, Tadahisa Matsudaira, Masao Hori, Hidekazu Hōjō, and Kimiko Kikukawa.

The following are sometimes associated with the Nishio faction: Ikkō Kasuga, Ryō Moji, Tokujirō Nakai, Ikusaburō Tanaka, Kisaburō Yao, Tsuruyo Tsutsumi, Shōzō Ōya, Ryōsaku Sasaki, Toshi Nakazaki, Kōichi Ōno, Katsukuni Hirose. The following were not elected to the House in 1958: Terutake Arima, Eitarō Nakai, Haruji Tahara, Masakichi Matsui, Seion Kawamata, Tsunakichi Hosoda. Three others had died during the previous five years.

24. Baerwald, "Japan at Election Time," p. 659, citing *Sankei Shimbun*, Nov. 23, 1963.

25. They were Masakichi Matsui, Mitsu Kōno, Takaichi Nakamura, Shōichi Miyake, Toshi Nakazaki, Isamu Imazumi, Shigeyoshi Matsumae. Two others, Kisaburō Yao and Seion Kawamata, were elected twice. Eiji Yamashita, Yoshio Hino, Kenjin Matsuzawa, and Jusō Miwa were elected only once.

Kawakami's group hoped that, after party reunification, some labor support—especially from certain Sōhyō affiliates—could be won; instead Sōhyō strategists since 1960 seem to have been more successful in using these Socialists to lessen the effects of competition from right-wing labor organizations and the Democratic Socialists.

During the party crisis in 1959–60, the Kawakami men tried in vain to mediate. At first that fall they declined to accept any posts and demanded the expulsion of Communists from the People's Council Against the Security Treaty. Most of this group resisted pressures to secede with Nishio and preserve right-wing unity but, as we have seen, some members splintered off in that direction. The future of Kawakami's once strong circle looked doubtful, but strategically it was at least temporarily reinforced by a rather unexpected combination of circumstances.

The Nishio Faction

The other right-wing Socialist faction represents moderation bordering on conservatism. The emotional attitudes and behavior of its leaders and active adherents are more traditional than is true of Socialists in groups farther left. These veterans of the prewar Socio-Democratic clique (Shamin-kei) and the later recruits have continued to advocate reform rather than drastic revolution. They have been the philosophical associates and descendants of such liberals as Sakuzō Yoshino, Toyohiko Kagawa, Kiichi Horie, Isoo Abe, and Eijirō Kawaii. Before the war they had advocated the defense and promotion of workers' and farmers' interests within the severe legal restraints imposed by an authoritarian establishment. That issue of legality has paled in the freer postwar situation, taking rather the form of the Nishio-led faction's insistence on parliamentary methods rather than resort to various types of direct action in opposition to policies of conservative governments. As mentioned, this faction has also emphasized as proper an economic rather than political orientation of organized labor. It cooperated with the resurrected Sōdōmei and added special liaisons with Zenrō Kaigi from 1954 and with the Japan Confederation of Labor (Dōmei Kaigi) from its founding in 1962. Though labor's right wing is less politically directed, one has only to contrast the Kawakami faction's lack of significant alliance with labor unions to recognize more clearly that the associations of Nishio's men in labor circles do have political implications.

The rather different reactions of this group to the threatened general strike of February 1, 1947, and the Subversive Activities Prevention Bill (1952) on the one hand, and to the Revised Police Duties Bill (1958), on the other, are revealing. The first fell increasingly under Communist influence and, building on economic grievances, advocated toppling the first Yoshida cabinet. The faction led by Katayama and Nishio supported the movement tardily and with misgivings about a political strike. Nishio and his colleagues, somewhat worried about "indirect aggression," have in the Diet successfully insisted on inclusion in the Subversive Activities Prevention Bill of safeguards against the misuse of the law, once enacted, to curtail the rights and activities of citizens and interest groups. Their labor union allies were slower than Sōhyō's affiliates in staging walkouts and demonstrations. But in 1958, when Premier Kishi sponsored a revision of the police law which contained no assurances about rights to be protected in the processes of enforcement, the Nishio clique and conservative unions were prompt and forthright in the national council of opposing organizations. In many legislative crises, this clique has been more prone to seek compromises which can break deadlocks; in 1958 their efforts resulted in shelving the obnoxious police bill.

The Nishio faction's anticommunism is also expressed in its views about foreign affairs. It suspects the genuineness of the brand of neutralism advocated by factions farther left and, with some strategic blurring, tends to favor a moderate Japanese deterrent capacity under controls which would prevent military resurgence in domestic affairs. It is less responsive to blandishments from Peking; on the contrary, Nishio displayed an interest in the Nationalist government in Taiwan partly in an attempt to balance SDP tendencies. This circle also favors the moderate revisionism of Western European Socialists away from Marxism-Leninism and cooperation with the International Confederation of Free Trade Unions.

Some of these attitudes and policies, and a number of others, led to Nishio's decision to leave rather than be expelled in the fall of 1959. His critics charged that some conservative party leaders and financial tycoons had attended a reception celebrating Nishio's acquittal from charges of having been embroiled in financial scandals in 1948. With characteristic asperity and acumen, he had been championing the concept of a national rather than a class party. He was accused of personally approving the revised security treaty. He had been encouraging Zenrō leaders in the formation of "second unions"—schismatic new organizations in certain industries where Sōhyō radicalism and politicism had become excessive. Since leftist factions in the SDP wanted to turn the committee hearing into a trial, Nishio and company decided to bolt. In so doing they weakened the right wing of Japanese socialism and seriously isolated themselves. Since then they have barely retained their status as a national party.

Suehiro Nishio is a politician with intelligence, agility, thrust. He was born in 1891 on an island in Kagawa prefecture off the coast of Shikoku. His family operated a small shop but had to farm on the side. In the prefectural capital he completed two years beyond elementary school and went to work in Osaka, first as an apprentice for an elder brother-in-law, then at the Taniguchi Iron Works. There in the Kansai area, he became interested in workers' movements and in 1919 was persuaded by Komakichi Matsuoka to join the Yūaikai (Friendly Society). In the next year he became one of its directors. He came to be regarded as a radical and led several strikes, but his socialism stemmed not from Marxism but from "idealistic humanism." Throughout his public career he has shown flexibility and sometimes opportunism; his more doctrinaire acquaintances have at times called him a "social fascist," a "class traitor," and a "decadent" socialist.

Nishio was one of the first Socialists elected to the Diet and has been reelected a dozen times since. We have seen how he served successively as a member of his party's CEC and as Secretary-General, later as a party adviser and more recently as Chairman of the DSP. That he was a minister without portfolio in the Katayama cabinet and became Deputy Premier in the Ashida cabinet has also been noted. But since his resignation under suspicion of implication in financial irregularities, he has never fully regained his former political influence. He returned to the Right Socialist Party fold in 1952 and became one of its elder statesmen; as such he has often negotiated with conservatives to avert or overcome crises in the Diet. In 1950 and again in 1955, his faction was wary about SDP reunification, for its members realized that their labor allies were weaker and that their own role in an enlarged party would inevitably be reduced. The Nishio faction remained the chief guardian of moderate principles and the main critic when the party veered leftward again in and after 1957.

Eki Sone, a bureaucrat from the Foreign Office, a dapper man who married the daughter of a railroad magnate, and a loyal lieutenant of

Nishio, was one of the principal negotiators toward party reunification. Sone is commonly thought to be not a socialist at heart. He joined the SDP after being invited by Nishio to become Deputy Chief Secretary of the Katayama cabinet. He quickly became one of the Right Socialists' foremost experts on foreign policy, and he has been prominent in the debates over the peace and security treaties. In the course of time he developed a broad ability to draft and rationalize policies. Sone's upper-class background and austerity lessen his appeal to rank-and-file workers, but he has been repeatedly elected to the House of Councillors. In 1960 he became Secretary-General of the newly formed Democratic Socialist Party.

Before the split in 1959, there were from 13 to about 30 pro-Nishio adherents in the House of Representatives and 15 to 16 in the House of Councillors—exact figures are impossible because of differing identifications of politicians with the Nishio and Kawakami factions; when the DSP was formed, its members at first held 38 seats there and 16 in the Upper House.[26] The level of education attained by Representatives in this group is higher than among the prewar Socio-Democrats; in 1959, nearly half of this contingent were university graduates. Because of their age and experience, members of this faction often serve on Diet steering committees, while younger, more radical left-wingers have been more influential in the Party's Diet Policy Committee, one stage removed from the hour-to-hour tactics on the floor. The old guard was formerly more active than now in the labor and farmer movements and its leaders still have connections in those circles. Of the ten labor leaders identified with this clique and having seats in the Lower House, most were younger men. Nearly half of these pro-Nishio Representatives were former national and local officials and

26. In November 1959, the following Diet members comprised most of those who supported Nishio: (House of Representatives) Ushirō Itō, Teiji Ikeda, Hitoshi Imamura, Kiyoshi Utsumi, Shōzō Ōya, Ryōzō Katō, Ikkō Kasuga, Tadashi Kodaira, Shintarō Komatsu, Ryōsaku Sasaki, Hajime Suzuki, Gentarō Takeya, Saburō Tsukamoto, Mrs. Tsuruyo Tsutsumi, Naosaku Doi, Eiichi Nishimura, Katsukuni Hirose, Mrs. Toshiko Matsuo, Chōzaburō Mizutani, Takeo Mutō, Isamu Imazumi, Shinkichi Ukeda, Kōichi Ōno, Mrs. Kimiko Kikukawa, Tetsu Kinoshita, Ikusaburō Tanaka, Tokio Nakamura, Shūichi Hōjō, Ryō Moji, Mrs. Yuriko Motojima, Tetsu Katayama, Tsuguo Komaki, Hirofumi Taman, Satoshi Nakazaki, Daihachi Onuki, Daisaku Kanda, Eiji Yamashita, and Sadataka Ozawa. (House of Councillors) Takashi Azuma, Mrs. Tsuneko Akamatsu, Katsumasa Amada, Eki Sone, Kotora Tanahashi, Kanemitsu Tabata, Matsue Tagami, Masao Nakamura, Seiichi Matsuura, Nagatoshi Mukai, Masashichi Motoi, Eiichi Nagasue, Kiyoshi Shima, Sukeharu Sōma, and Setsuo Yamada.

prefectural assemblymen. About one fourth had active business connections, chiefly with small- and medium-scale enterprises.

As for representation of the Nishio clique in SDP posts, in the years 1955–58, Sone, Eiichi Nishimura, and Haruki Satake were three times elected to the CEC. Ryōji Inoue and Teiji Ikeda were elected twice. During the same period, Ushirō Itō, a veteran labor leader, was repeatedly elected Treasurer. Sone was appointed chairman of the National Movements Committee in 1958.

Two main problems continue for this group, especially now that it has become a separate party: how to play a distinctive role between the LDP and the main Socialist Party, and how to grow and gain more vitality through the recruitment of younger leaders. Coupled with the latter is a third problem: the restlessness of younger leaders under the dominance of Nishio and his closer adherents. If the DSP could gain significantly in progressive practical vigor, it might become more attractive to voters. It has not lacked distinguished intellectual support from older scholars, like Masamichi Rōyama and Masamichi Inoki, and from younger men of learning such as Professor Yoshihiko Seki and the younger Michio Rōyama. Men like these are seriously constructive and moderate in their views and activities; they tend to be less ardent and sustained in their political participation than intellectuals of leftist temper and convictions. The size of the "floating vote" and the effects of marked economic growth and prosperity on the size and strength of medial social strata seem to offer great opportunities to such a moderate party, but so far the Democratic Socialists have not found a successful formula. They admit that their local and regional organizations are still seriously weak.

MEDIAL ELEMENTS IN THE PARTY

Unlike other political groupings in the SDP, the centrist "faction" (*chūkan-ha*) has been changeable in composition and objectives, in response to the political problem at hand and the existing balance of power in the party. With each recurring crisis in the SDP, the existence and value of the centrist group has been accentuated. The lack of a strong middle group can, as we shall see, also be serious for the SDP. In the early postwar period, the Kawakami clique (then known as the Japan-Labor clique) was often referred to as centrist. As mentioned previously, this group has always tried, at times opportunistically, to enhance its influence in the party by conciliating the left and right wings. However, it was an important pillar undergirding the Nishio–Katayama control of the party during 1947–49. The influence of the Japan-Labor clique was repeatedly brought to bear in policy and personnel problems before, during, and after the unsuccessful Socialist participation in the government. Centrist elements, consisting mainly of this faction, were among the chief agents facilitating the early reunification of the SDP after its preliminary schism in 1950. The ideological flexibility of the centrist group was illustrated when most of them were claimed by the right and left wings at their respective conventions immediately after that early schism in January 1950.

When the peace treaty issue came into sharp Socialist focus, the centrists at first performed their traditional function as mediators. At the time this group was divided into three schools, and their compromise proposal was presented to the CEC as the Kenjin Matsuzawa plan.[27] But when the left Socialists, in June 1951, showed their strength and adamancy in the Central Committee, opposing ratification of the peace treaty, the centrist and right-wing factions merged forces, the latter accepting the compromise proposals of the centrist group. Kawakami and Kōno were depurged in time to bring their prestige to bear as mediators, but the drift of events and the gradual hardening of determination by Inejirō Asanuma, Shōichi Miyake, and Kyōhei Shimojō (who were regarded as centrists at that time) to oppose the left wing removed the centrist buffer and only accelerated the more lasting split later that year.

This schism temporarily deprived centrist elements of scope for maneuvering. Contrary to the preliminary rift, this break forced all SDP Diet members to choose sides; most of the centrists sided with the right wing. There were some who joined the left for completely nonideological reasons, principally electoral considerations. This was at once a basic weakness of the centrist group and an incentive to reunification. By 1953 the center had changed character; it was no longer dominated by the prewar Japan-Labor faction, the dominant clique in the Right SDP. The new moderate centrists formed the Shakaishugi Seisaku Kenkyūkai (Socialist Policy Study Group),[28]

27. One school was headed by Jusō Miwa; Kanjū Katō, a maverick in postwar SDP factions, headed another; and Chōzaburō Mizutani (prewar) and Isamu Imazumi (postwar) sponsored still another. In the Upper House, Sukeharu Sōma, Hajime Tanaka, and Junichirō Nagai represented the moderates at that time. *Asahi Shimbun*, June 11, 1951.

28. This study group was formed around Isamu Imazumi, Kinji Kawashima, Kisaburō

hoping to reach the restless borderline leftists with the ultimate objective of reunifying the SDP.[29] Asanuma was strongly supported by them. But when the Right SDP "lost" the general elections in April 1953 to the Left, and Asanuma was unable to prevent the Nishio faction from forcing a reconsideration of SDP military policy, the centrists turned from him and looked to Kawakami. Asanuma's threat to resign prevented them from successfully persuading Kawakami to support Suzuki as a united Socialist candidate for Premier in 1953. These maneuvers reflected centrist vulnerability in public elections, the lack of a recognized leader, and their sympathy for left-wing views on defense, national security, and the revision of the Constitution. They have been given additional support by the movement for the protection of the Constitution, until 1960 headed by former Premier Katayama.

Between party reunification and the Nishio faction's secession in 1959–60, the centrists, still without a leader, began to demand a revamping of party organization and, by implication, the retirement of old-timers and a change in the center of political authority. These demands have been made cautiously. Although there is still some opportunity for understandings between younger leaders in the Democratic Socialist Party and the Kawakami faction in the SDP, the split in 1959–60 obstructed the effectiveness of these groups as mediators.

STATISTICS ON SDP CHARACTERISTICS

In addition to examining the factions within which Japanese Socialist leaders have functioned, we can turn to statistical surveys from which emerge general characteristics, trends in, and sources of postwar leadership.[30]

Yao, and Kenjin Matsuzawa. Others include Yoshinobu Yamashita, Ryōichi Oka, Shinichi Satake, Eiichi Yamashita, and Hajime Tanaka. They hoped to attract the support of Tetsu Katayama, Yoshio Suzuki, Kanjū Katō, and Motojirō Sugiyama, veteran leaders of the SDP. It should be noted that many of these members are mentioned elsewhere in connection with other factions, emphasizing the overlapping character of this group.

29. The right-wing centrists hoped to reach such politicos as Kiyoshi Masaki, Sōzō Watanabe, and Mikiji Mori (all from Hokkaidō where the SDP did not immediately split into two parts), Shikaichi Yasuhira (a former follower of Kanjū Katō), and Kanjirō Satō, a former editor of the liberal magazine, *Chūō Kōron*.

30. Figures given and patterns described in this section were obtained from a study of numerous statistical tables prepared for our research project in 1956–57 and also as a result of trips to several parts of Japan in 1955 by Cecil H. Uyehara. More data for the period 1947–58 have been published by Scalapino and Masumi, *Parties and Politics*, pp. 59–60, 66–67, 70–71, 77, and Charts 13–15, pp. 173–76.

In regard to age, the SDP is a relatively young party—its leftist factions more than its moderates. The average age of all Socialist Diet members in the Lower House has been consistently lower than that of the entire House. Even so, the Socialist Representatives as a whole have been growing older, and again this has been more marked in their right wing. The Nishio and Kawakami groups have been conscious of this trend but have made no vigorous and sustained moves to counter it. It is also significant that senior notables recognized as advisers are in the right wing about ten times as numerous as on the Left.[31] As is natural where more experience is needed, the average age of Socialists in the House of Councillors and in the party CEC is older. One advantage of the SDP left is its younger, more vigorous leaders—many of them from the labor movement.

Over the past two decades, the composition of the Socialist delegation in the House of Representatives has tended to become more stabilized. The election of January 1949, which resulted disastrously for the SDP, was in part a watershed. Forty-eight members elected in 1947 were never again returned. Thereafter very few Socialists were elected only once; in the elections of 1955, for instance, more than two thirds of all SDP Representatives had served previous terms. Membership in the SDP delegation in the House of Councillors seems to be more changeable; more than half of those elected in 1956 were new members.

Though the SDP claims to be a "mass party with a class character," more than 60 per cent of its delegation in the Lower House in 1958 had had education beyond the elementary level. Throughout the postwar period the proportion of university graduates among Socialist Representatives has been more than half. Nearly one third in 1958 were graduates of national universities, particularly Tokyo (Imperial) University, and about the same proportion came from private alma maters, notably Waseda, Nihon, and Chūō. Probably fewer than 20 per cent of these Representatives had finished only grade school. Many of the postwar labor union leaders elected to the Diet have completed high school or college. Similar patterns with respect to the education of Socialists apply to members of the House of Councillors. The

31. As a matter of fact, the average age of right-wing Socialist Representatives was older than the average of those associated with the Democratic–Progressive lineage before the merger of the two main conservative parties in the fall of 1955.

party's CEC is clearly dominated by leaders with higher education; in 1958 they composed almost two thirds of that body. A majority of the leaders most frequently elected to the CEC are also university graduates. Here is further evidence of the influence of intellectuals in the labor, farmer, and socialist movements, contributing to their Marxist, theoretical, and political tendencies and their ambivalence toward parliamentarism.

On the other hand, very few officers of local party organizations surveyed had been to college. Many local officers were "company employees" (probably union officers) or small shopkeepers, indicating the inability of the Socialist organization on lower levels to attract better educated persons into effective party work, though many such people do vote for SDP candidates. In view of the emphasis on economic planning by the Socialists, persons with advanced education will probably continue to play leading roles in the party.

We have already remarked on the dearth of Socialist leaders with experience in national administration. In 1959 there were only seven Socialists but 79 LDP members of the Lower House with that kind of experience. Very few have been mayors of cities and small towns. Many more Socialist Diet members—usually between one third and two fifths—have previously served in municipal and prefectural assemblies and in local offices. Men of such experience are particularly numerous among Representatives associated with right Socialist factions; nearly half of those identified with the Nishio and Kawakami factions have such backgrounds.[32] However, this pattern holds mainly for less important members of the party's Diet delegation. Most of the postwar leaders have been directly elected to the Diet.

Only 18 per cent of Socialist Representatives in 1959 were specifically connected with business firms. Those who had been or were still business executives on the side (26, or 14%) were particularly evident in the Nishio, Kawakami, Wada, and Matsumoto cliques. There seems to have been some decline of this pattern, for, in 1955, almost one third of the Socialists in the Lower House had had business connections—mostly with small- and medium-scale enterprises—and in the following year one tenth of the Socialist Councillors were so engaged.

32. In 1959, 45 SDP Representatives (27%) had been prefectural assemblymen; 49 (29%) had been elected to local offices. See: Scalapino and Masumi, *Parties and Politics,* Chart 13, pp. 174–75.

In the last two decades, SDP Diet members have engaged in more than 70 different types of business: apple growing, the producing of chopsticks, engine manufacturing, hotel management, mining, pharmaceuticals, securities, and taxi companies being but a few. In the election of 1955 there were more postwar newcomers than prewar stalwarts engaged in businesses. Twenty Socialist Representatives in that year were connected with 30 companies and associations in manufacturing and services. As usual, they were proprietors, presidents, vice-presidents, and directors. Such interests are sources of personal income but not of heavy contributions to SDP coffers. In numbers, business-connected leaders on the party CEC have at times been nearly comparable with those having trade union backgrounds, but their influence has not been as great.

During 1947–58, nearly one third of the Socialist Representatives were either labor leaders or union officials.[33] Naturally they were more numerous and usually younger in the left than in the right wing. In other words, Zenrō- and Sōdōmei-connected Representatives tended to be older and characteristically "pure worker" types as compared with those affiliated with Sōhyō unions. Of the 98 Socialist Representatives having such connections in 1958, 42 (one quarter of the whole delegation) had had close relations with the prewar labor movement,[34] while 56 (one third of the delegation) were connected with postwar labor unions; the latter pattern was especially marked for the Suzuki, Wada, Kuroda, and Nomizo factions. Most of these Dietmen are, or have been, chairmen of their unions. These same elected union officials are often officers (most of them directors) of prefectural labor banks and credit unions. This increases their influence on union finances, for their organizations have deposited funds in such banks on a cooperative basis. On the party CEC, labor leaders and officials constitute the largest occupational group. And among Socialist Councillors this group predominates, many of them having been elected from the

33. Labor leaders are here defined as those who were once (mostly before World War II) closely connected with the active labor union movement but recently have come to be related to it chiefly insofar as they are able to influence certain unions or federations. Union officials, of course, are leaders actually holding offices.

34. A background of close relations with the prewar labor movement is more marked for the Nishio, Kuroda, Nomizo, and to a lesser extent the Kawakami, factions than for the Suzuki, Wada, and Matsumoto cliques. In 1959, more than half of the Suzuki faction's legislators in the Lower House had reached the Diet from trade unions.

national constituency mainly because of various kinds of labor union support.

The problems encountered by the Socialists in developing rural support since the postwar agrarian reforms are, not accurately but to some degree, reflected in the paucity of SDP Diet members with farm backgrounds and connections. While the proportion of labor-connected Diet members has increased, the number with agrarian relations has declined; in 1958, they constituted one fifth of the party's delegation in the Lower House and most belonged to the small Nomizo and Kuroda groups.

Professional people—notably teachers, lawyers, journalists, and physicians—have played disproportionately important roles in the social democratic movement from its early years. In 1958, 40 per cent of the Socialist legislators in the House of Representatives came from such backgrounds, the most numerous being former teachers; lawyers and journalists were about equal in number. A few of the lawyers had been officials in city, prefectural, or national bar associations. In contrast to some of the lawyers and journalists, most of the Representatives who formerly were secondary school teachers, university professors, and educational administrators have joined the party since the war. In 1958 they were more numerous on the CEC than were lawyers. The SDP delegation also included a few medical doctors and dentists, writers, engineers, social workers, and a former judge. Though the survey on which these and some other data in this chapter rest was made in 1958, these have been persistent patterns.

On the local level, biographical information is very difficult to obtain.[35] Labor unions have the largest representation in party membership with the National Railway Workers, Public Corporation Workers, Electric Power Workers, Japan Express Workers, Private Railway Workers, and mining unions constituting almost half the labor contingent. Unlike the situation in the national party, persons claiming agriculture as their occupation constitute almost one third of the local

35. An occupational breakdown of local SDP leadership was calculated from a list of governors, mayors, and members of prefectural, city, town, and village assemblies given in *Shakai Tsūshin*. No. 254 (July 30, 1957), pp. 2–60. Out of a total of a little more than 3,000 names, the occupations of slightly under one half were given. The occupations of local leaders in Hokkaidō, Fukuoka, Saitama, Tokyo, Kanagawa, Nagano, Ishikawa, Kyoto, Osaka, Okayama, and part of Kumamoto prefectures were not given.

SDP leadership. Businesses, usually very small, are a poor third. If Shizuoka prefecture is at all representative, local SDP leadership consists almost entirely of persons who have emerged since 1945.

RECENT SHIFTS IN FACTIONAL RIVALRY AND PARTY ORIENTATION

Since the anti-treaty crisis of 1960, the maneuvering of groups within the SDP has quickened; the motives behind tactics pursued have continued to be complex; the struggle between Sōhyō-Socialist radicals and somewhat newly aligned moderates became more closely joined and more dramatic. In the face of some unavoidable and persisting realities—the lengthening plateau of one third strength in the Diet, the capacity of capitalism for self-reform and revitalization, the belated and inevitable need to rethink socialist theories, the provocation of the ultra-right and partial loss of public approval after excesses of the anti-treaty mobilizations, new threats to leftist positions by the Nishio–Zenrō–Sōdōmei axis, and the failure of Sakisaka tactics in the bitter Miike coal mine strike—the party's orientation has been hotly and revealingly debated. Factional contention has been the dominant mode of continuing inner controversies.

The retirement of Suzuki from the party chairmanship in March 1960, when added to the deaths of a number of veterans and the failure of others to be reelected, signaled the accelerated fading of a generation of leaders whose careers straddled the two world wars. Another generation of Socialist leaders is already middle-aged and increasingly assertive. This thrust of younger leaders has already been related to the promotion of "structural reform" by the Eda–Narita group, at first still within the formerly more unified Suzuki faction. Along the fault-line of the ensuing polemic the factions, or their dividing blocs, have been ranged in attempts to determine the direction of policies. It has been a tortuous debate, epitomized tactically in the question whether party policies should be predicated on a preference for moderation and gradualism—even though a socialist revolution remains the ultimate aim—or should continue, as in 1960, to be radically revolutionary. Younger leaders, moving from within the Suzuki "mainstream," have been able intellectually to rationalize an altered strategy which they claim holds more promise. Like their more leftist rivals, they have utilized an ideological position for factional and personal advantage; but they are more than opportunists.

Tomomi Narita, Tadataka Sata, and Shigeo Tsubaki are among the leading structural reformers; their foremost spokesman and theorist is Saburō Eda. He was born in Okayama prefecture in 1907, and this has been his political constituency. His father was earlier a minor Minseitō leader. The younger Eda was graduated before World War II from the Tokyo University of Commerce (precursor of Hitotsubashi University, famous for its Faculty of Economics), and gained experience in both the farmers' and labor movements. He was elected to the Okayama Prefectural Assembly in 1937 but was then imprisoned for two and a half years as a result of the Popular Front incident in 1937. From 1943 to 1946 he worked in China (presumably for the government), at one point carrying on negotiations with the Communist Eighth Route Army. After returning to Japan, he joined the Socialist Party and led in a regional farmers' movement. Though he had been close to the Kuroda faction, he did not secede with it in 1948, perhaps in part because he was a member of the Socialist Party's CEC.

Eda is famous in Japan as a handsome, intellectual, persuasive leader. His performances on television might be compared with those of John F. Kennedy. While usually mild, he can be quick-tempered and decisive. Apparently he is criticized as an inner party strategist, and some say that he has lacked persistence in promoting policies. Eda has been head of the party's central Organization Bureau and was Secretary-General at the time of Asanuma's assassination; he was named acting Chairman until the 20th convention in March 1961.[36]

The Wada faction, as rivals of Suzuki's "mainstream," supported the structural reformers, who criticized the sterility of strict Marxism and advocated abandoning "defensive radicalism" and instead the launching of "positive struggles for social reforms." After party reunification in 1955, Wada's group had failed in attempts to coalesce with the Nomizo and Matsumoto cliques against the Suzuki–Kawakami main current. From August 1958 it wooed Asanuma, which partly accounted for his swing to the left. The Nishio faction for a while boosted Asanuma as the next Chairman but lost interest when, in early 1959, he began obviously moving leftward. After the secession of the Nishio clique, Wada's men favored in successive convention elections the candidacy of Kawakami for party Chairman. Thus a revised mainstream came to be composed of Kawakami men, the Eda–Narita minority in the Suzuki faction, and the Wada group. Kawa-

36. Yukio Takatsu and Gosuke Endō, "Saburō Eda and His Environment," *Asahi Jānaru,* Jan. 22, 1961.

kami's election to the chairmanship in 1961 was the result of a compromise between the Wada and Suzuki–Sasaki factions. The altered mainstream has been closely challenged by the more leftist factions who have been influenced by Sakisaka's polemical writings and have received stronger support from both the Ōta-Iwai "mainstream" of Sōhyō (the earlier Mindō Left) and Takano's still more radical "Progressive Alliance." Some younger Sōhyō leaders have tended to support the Eda–Narita line, and in January 1962 ten labor federations affiliated with the General Council declared their support of structural reform. Sōhyō's main current has been divided on the issue of reconsidered socialism in recent years, but partly for strategic reasons.

Wada, Sasaki, and Eda were the leading aspirants to the top party office after Kawakami's retirement on May 6, 1965. This was reported to be a main reason for the willingness of Wada's faction, which until that point had been farther left in position, to support the more moderate coalition. Kawakami's election in 1961 followed meetings among all the factions including and to the right of Matsumoto's Heiwa Dōshikai. This latter group cooperated reluctantly and warned that it would oppose the new Chairman's policies if they should become conservative. At that same convention, the Suzuki faction attained an absolute majority on the party's CEC; one of its eight members was Sasaki. It also won the chairmanships of the Policy Planning Board, the Diet Policy Committee, and the National Organization Committee. Kawakami's clique became weaker. Mitsu Kōno, its chief policymaker, was crowded out electorally by a member of Nomizo's entourage.

In January 1962, the contest between supporters of Eda and Sasaki for the secretary-generalship became a trial of strength between the new SDP mainstream and the opponents of structural reform. Eda had not only the support of certain unions in Sōhyō but also many in the party's Youth Department. His allies were said to control some other party organs, certain labor schools, and to have the loyalty of many local SDP activists. But Sasaki, too, had strong support from leaders at lower organizational levels. Eda remained Secretary-General after a convention vote of 323 to 260 in his favor.[37]

This time his tenure was short, however. Prior to the 22nd conven-

37. Before the crucial convention vote for Eda versus Kōzō Sasaki as Secretary-General in January 1962, it was roughly estimated that about 40 of the Suzuki group supported the latter; approximately 20 supported Eda.

tion in November 1962, he published an article in *Economisuto* under the title "A New Vision for Socialism."[38] Idealistically he advocated that Japan should ultimately have a standard of living comparable to that of the United States, a thorough system of social security like that of the Soviet Union, a British-style parliamentary system, and its own peace Constitution. Whether by critics or in the course of popularization, these four points came to be referred to as "Eda-vision." During the convention a resolution stating that such views would divide the leadership and confuse socialist theory was passed by a majority of only 21 votes.[39] Eda resigned and resumed his earlier post at the head of the Organization Bureau. Narita received a margin of 93 votes and in effect exchanged posts with his colleague.[40] Two years later, following Kawakami's retirement, the election of Sasaki as Chairman was a victory for the left. As usual, however, the winner had to make some concessions to rival factions for the sake of party cohesion.

Degrees of tension between leaders of pre- and postwar vintage have also affected the contest between these principal coalitions: old guard types tending to be among those who favor the Sasaki-led doctrinal revolutionaries; younger leaders, who can be more realistic in rethinking socialism, favoring Eda's combination. Yet there are younger leaders on both sides. Many of the same vigorous elements who have been demanding reorganization of the party and its procedures—some of them supported by trade unions or themselves formerly union leaders—are having to decide between more pragmatic reformism, which is indeed revisionist, and the Labor-Farmer brand of Marxist orthodoxy.

38. His article has been translated and reprinted in the *Journal of Social and Political Ideas in Japan, I* (Aug. 1963), 48–50.

39. From the vote on this resolution, 102 delegates abstained, 37 of them being Sōhyō delegates. Immediately thereafter, the "mainstream" groups launched a counteroffensive which not only elected Narita to the office of Secretary-General but also won other important positions.

40. Narita and Kawakami were reelected to their posts at the next party convention which did not take place until February 1964, and "structural reform" was reaffirmed, though barely.

Electoral and Organized Support

10. The Articulation of Organized Labor with Social Democratic Parties

Democratization fostered in the early postwar years was, of course, not wholly an alien importation. There were dammed up forces within Japan intent upon greater social justice if not thoroughgoing social revolution. The labor movement became the most powerful and militant as well as the best organized of these. Its elite lineages and political orientations were in part revived from prewar experiences, but patterns of activity responded to new conditions. We shall note some political effects of the unionizing of more than half of the wage earners by 1949, the curbs and cleavages which caused a temporary decline in numbers and dynamism, followed by new waves of workers' political action allied overwhelmingly with the Social Democratic parties or factions. Attempting to be more analytical than historical, however, let us first scrutinize basic principles and realities of union–party relationships and ascertain why most Japanese unionists, however they may differ as to implementation, agree that political action by organized workers is imperative.

UNION–PARTY TENSIONS, COOPERATION, AND LABOR POLITICISM

Two principles regarding union–party relations have been most widely accepted and abused in postwar Japan. In theory, labor organizations and leftist parties are supposed to be independent of each

LINEAGES OF JAPANESE LABOR FEDERATIONS

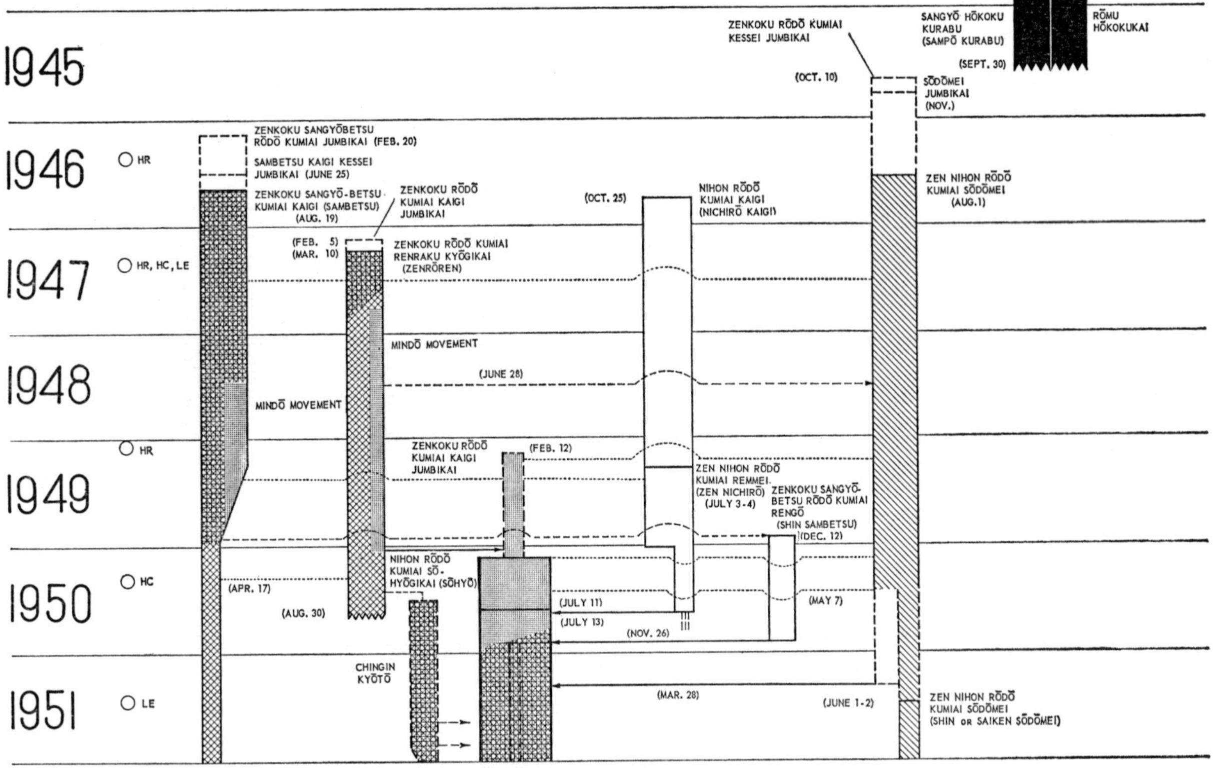

1945
1946 ○ HR
1947 ○ HR, HC, LE
1948
○ HR
1949
1950 ○ HC
1951 ○ LE

RŌMU HŌKOKUKAI
SANGYŌ HŌKOKU KURABU (SAMPŌ KURABU)
(SEPT. 30)
ZENKOKU RŌDŌ KUMIAI KESSEI JUMBIKAI
(OCT. 10)
SŌDŌMEI JUMBIKAI (NOV.)
ZEN NIHON RŌDŌ KUMIAI SŌDŌMEI (AUG.1)
ZENKOKU SANGYŌBETSU RŌDŌ KUMIAI JUMBIKAI (FEB. 20)
SAMBETSU KAIGI KESSEI JUMBIKAI (JUNE 25)
ZENKOKU SANGYŌ-BETSU KUMIAI KAIGI (SAMBETSU) (AUG. 19)
ZENKOKU RŌDŌ KUMIAI KAIGI JUMBIKAI
(FEB. 5)
(MAR. 10)
ZENKOKU RŌDŌ KUMIAI RENRAKU KYŌGIKAI (ZENRŌREN)
(OCT. 25)
NIHON RŌDŌ KUMIAI KAIGI (NICHIRŌ KAIGI)
MINDŌ MOVEMENT
(JUNE 28)
MINDŌ MOVEMENT
ZENKOKU RŌDŌ KUMIAI KAIGI JUMBIKAI
(FEB. 12)
ZEN NIHON RŌDŌ KUMIAI REMMEI. (ZEN NICHIRŌ) (JULY 3-4)
ZENKOKU SANGYŌ-BETSU RŌDŌ KUMIAI RENGŌ (SHIN SAMBETSU) (DEC. 12)
NIHON RŌDŌ KUMIAI SŌ-HYŌGIKAI (SŌHYŌ)
(APR. 17)
(AUG. 30)
(JULY 11)
(JULY 13)
(NOV. 26)
(MAY 7)
CHINGIN KYŌTŌ
(MAR. 28)
(JUNE 1-2)
ZEN NIHON RŌDŌ KUMIAI SŌDŌMEI (SHIN or SAIKEN SŌDŌMEI)

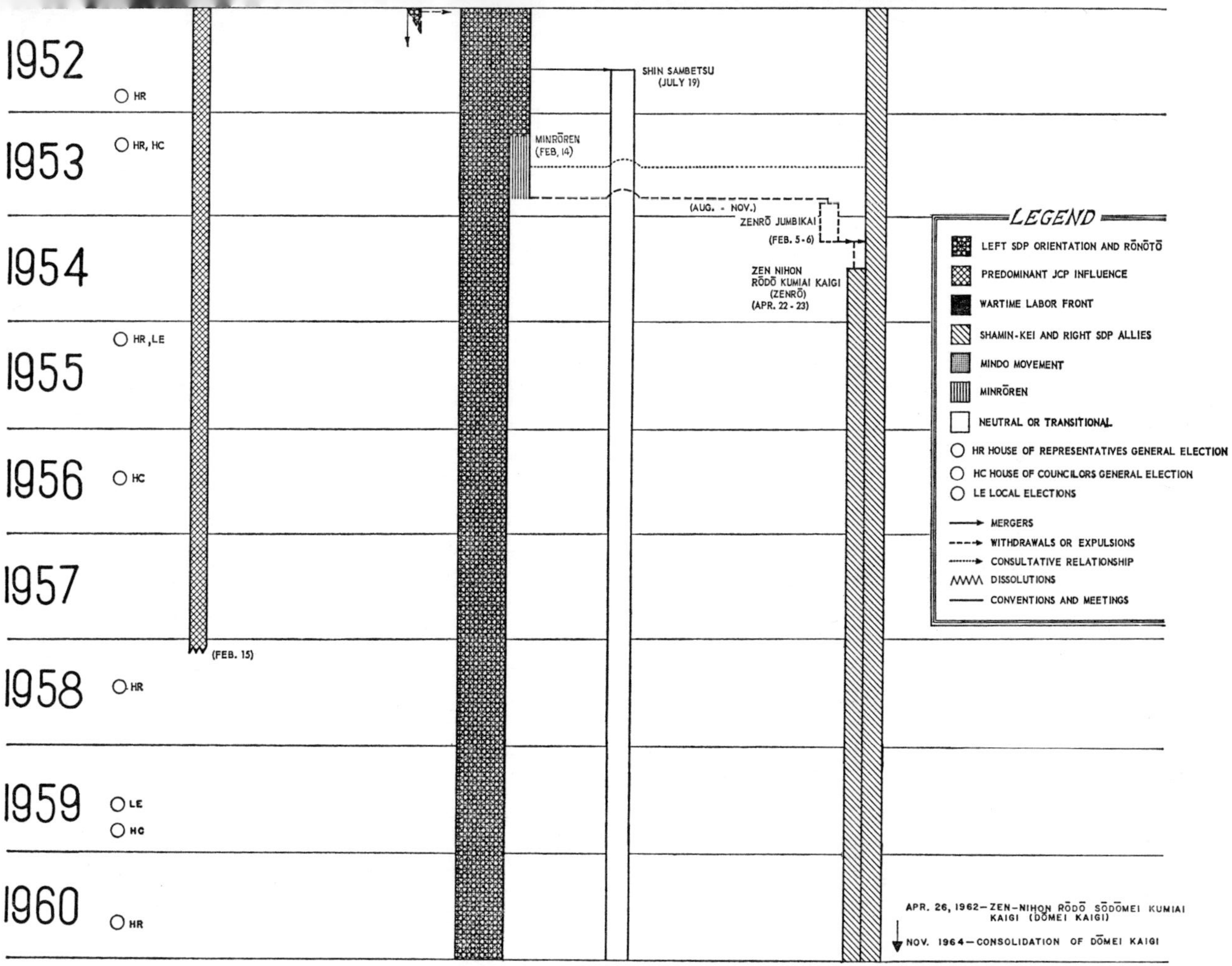

1952
HR
SHIN SAMBETSU
(JULY 19)
1953
HR, HC
MINRŌREN
(FEB. 14)
(AUG. - NOV.)
ZENRŌ JUMBIKAI
(FEB. 5-6)
1954
ZEN NIHON
RŌDŌ KUMIAI KAIGI
(ZENRŌ)
(APR. 22 - 23)
1955
HR, LE
1956
HC
1957
(FEB. 15)
1958
HR
1959
LE
HC
1960
HR
APR. 26, 1962—ZEN-NIHON RŌDŌ SŌDŌMEI KUMIAI KAIGI (DŌMEI KAIGI)
NOV. 1964—CONSOLIDATION OF DŌMEI KAIGI

LEGEND
LEFT SDP ORIENTATION AND RŌNŌTŌ
PREDOMINANT JCP INFLUENCE
WARTIME LABOR FRONT
SHAMIN-KEI AND RIGHT SDP ALLIES
MINDO MOVEMENT
MINRŌREN
NEUTRAL OR TRANSITIONAL
HR HOUSE OF REPRESENTATIVES GENERAL ELECTION
HC HOUSE OF COUNCILORS GENERAL ELECTION
LE LOCAL ELECTIONS
MERGERS
WITHDRAWALS OR EXPULSIONS
CONSULTATIVE RELATIONSHIP
DISSOLUTIONS
CONVENTIONS AND MEETINGS

CHART 4

other; they should cooperate, but neither should seek domination over the other. And the corollary has been that union members, in voting and other political activities, should be free to support parties according to individual choice. In contrast, Communists have used the principle of individual choice to keep open the door for the activities of their fractions within unions when, as after 1948–50 and since the crisis of 1959–60, they have lost ascendancy. But when riding high, they soft-pedal both these principles and advocate a united labor front behind working class political parties, various pressures on the individual unionist being used to induce support of his organization's position.

The Social Democratic Party, having a tiny membership and shallow rootage in union locals, depending on labor organizations for mobilizing voters and financial support, is susceptible to union pressures. Moreover, the main leftist labor federations have often managed political struggles which have carried them deeply into party activities. Since 1947, labor leaders have been the largest special interest group among SDP Diet members in both Houses. Labor leaders, particularly those of a more conservative stripe, have reacted against divisive Communist manipulation of the early postwar labor movement, and party (SDP or JCP) attempts to control unions. On the other hand, national leadership of the leftist Sōhyō has, since SDP unification in 1955, more frequently called for expansion of Socialist Party membership in unionized shops. The National Liaison Council for Socialist Party members in Sōhyō, founded by party and union leaders in August 1961, coordinated ten such councils in industrial unions.[1] Although many members are reluctant to be publicly labeled as to party, a marked majority of leaders of labor federations connected with Sōhyō tend to be SDP members. At the 17th Sōhyō convention in August 1961, more than 60 per cent of the delegates were politically

1. Through such local councils within unions, the SDP hopes also to recruit members and electoral support, explain its policies more widely, help resolve contradictions between the party and friendly unions, expand subscriptions to the party organ, and improve the focus of the party's policies in regard to workers' interests. These local councils are regarded as possible channels for young labor leaders to gain experience in party politics. They are, moreover, intended to help diminish "enterprise-centered" attitudes and contribute in the more serious effort to develop centralized industrial unions. Some expect these councils to fend off the "second union" splitting encouraged by the right wing of the socialist-labor movement. There are also vaguer, more idealistic hopes, such as "enriching theory and practice" and cultivating the desire to "serve the masses."

so identified, but SDP party members among the rank-and-file are few.[2] On the other hand, about half of the executives of local SDP federations are from unions.[3] These party–union members' councils never thrived, however, due perhaps to certain qualms among union officials about such campaigns.

Whether the aims of labor politicians be self-promotion, economic improvement, or to raise the class and political consciousness of workers against alleged exploiters, excessive pressure for a certain political alignment and associated policies has tended to weaken unions by inducing controversies and schisms. During and after unification negotiations in 1954–55, leaders of the main right- and left-wing labor federations reemphasized the principle of union autonomy to protect their structures and organs from policy compromises on the political plane, and to shield themselves against continued factional strife within the party. Nevertheless, most of the large national unions and federations at their annual conventions usually have supported a socialist party and have urged members, as well as their voting relatives, to do likewise.

In brief, then, cooperation and interaction between labor unions and socialist parties is natural and inevitable unless blocked by laws which some conservative forces would like to enact. But the union–party comradeship is also marked by tensions, which frequently result in alliances and counter-combinations of party–union factions, the pendulum tending to swing unsteadily between party or union ascendancy. For example, the Left Social Democrats became increasingly dependent on Sōhyō during 1951–53, while Communists and crypto-Marxists infiltrated the organs of that labor federation, pressing its official policies leftward. A crisis smoldered between the party and its

2. A 1947 survey of 3,856 labor leaders in the Keihin industrial region between Tokyo and Yokohama showed that two thirds of those whose unions were affiliated with one of the three main labor federations belonged to no party, and similarly in the case of nearly three fourths of the leaders of independent unions. A large percentage of those mentioning party membership had chosen the SDP. See: Tokyo University, Shakai Kagaku Kenkyūjo, *Sengo Rōdō Kumiai no Jittai* (The Conditions of Postwar Labor Unions) (Tokyo, 1950), II, Sect. V, No. 1.

3. Of 367 responding members of regional Left Socialist Executive Committees surveyed in June 1955, 144 were also active union leaders. In the same areas, of 73 responding Right Socialist counterparts, 21 were union activists simultaneously. See Soukup, "Labor and Politics in Postwar Japan, A Study of the Political Attitudes and Activities of Selected Japanese Labor Organizations" (Ph.D dissertation, University of Michigan, 1957), pp. 243–44, and n. 66.

ally especially during 1953–55. At the fourth convention of Sōhyō in July 1953, the Communist peace offensive prompted the Takano faction to press successfully for its concept of Japan as part of the self-styled "peace force" in world affairs, while a minority composed of groups allied with the Left SDP preferred a "third force" policy. Sōdōmei was opposing the politicism and pro-communist policies of Sōhyō's radical wing, led by Secretary-General Minoru Takano; and four moderate unions decided to split from that federation. Left Socialist politicians, smarting from charges that they were becoming "errand boys" of Sōhyō, stiffened their stand.

Two further controversies were with difficulty blurred and kept behind the scenes during 1953–54. A Sōhyō contingent within the Left Socialist committee drafting an action program for the party's 1954 convention tried unsuccessfully to secure acceptance of its Marxist version, known as the Shimizu platform,[4] though, in the process, it was able to force some verbal compromises. There was a dispute regarding how far the Left SDP might go in disciplining party members within unions for local infractions of the Central Committee's injunction against cooperation with JCP fractions. In this case it was the party which was politely told of its limitations.[5]

4. It criticized the party CEC's draft platform of November 1953 as being "academic, opportunistic, and smacking of progressivism." Instead, it called for a revolution for national independence against U.S. capitalistic imperialism and a "national independence government" which would abrogate the San Francisco Peace Treaty, the Security Pact, and the Administrative Agreement. It would, moreover, accomplish the withdrawal of U.S. military bases and would conclude an overall peace including as signatories the U.S.S.R. and the People's Republic of China.

It further advocated calling a Diet representative of all classes to revise the Constitution, establish a unicameral legislature, reform drastically the electoral system, prohibit the Emperor from acting in matters of state, and permit the Diet to determine succession to the throne. Still more extreme was its proposal of a plebiscite with respect to adoption of a republican form of government. Nothing is clearer evidence than this of Communist or Rōnōha inspiration, for in the national opinion polls only these groups in Japan were overwhelmingly in favor of such a change, though it should be added that Jiichirō Matsumoto and many of his followers are staunch republicans.

Hegemony of the Sōhyō Left over its political ally was implied by the suggestion that the Party's Secretary-General and half of its CEC should be elected from among non-Diet members. A united front extending from the Right Socialists to the JCP was urged. See: *Yomiuri,* Jan. 21, 1954.

5. At a meeting of Sōhyō and Left Socialist leaders on November 11, 1953, it was reluctantly agreed that the party could control its members within unions after consulting with the labor organizations affected. However, this could not be carried out very effectively, for the party's practical influence on labor organizations was less than that of Sōhyō. See: *Asahi,* July 19, 1953, Nov. 12, 1953; *Mainichi,* Nov. 9, 12, 1953; *Tokyo Taimusu,* Jan. 12, 1954.

At the Sōhyō convention in 1955, a majority of delegates allied with Left Socialist opponents of Takano replaced him with Akira Iwai as Secretary-General of Sōhyō; his colleague, Kaoru Ōta, was elected Chairman in 1958. This team, leading Sōhyō's mainstream, had emerged from the Mindō Left. Though revolutionary Marxists, such leaders have advocated strengthening the SDP as a political vehicle for working class interests. The Takano-led anti-mainstream faction, however, has scorned the weakness of the Socialist Party and has argued that Sōhyō and its affiliates should themselves become in effect a major political force relying more on an alliance with the JCP. At times of crisis, as during 1959–60, the Takano faction has called for the same kind of anti-capitalist and anti-imperialist united front as the Communists. As labor radicals they have been allied with the Matsumoto and Kuroda factions on the Socialist Party's extreme left. They have also cooperated with certain more radical members of the Suzuki-led Socialist mainstream.

What at first appeared to be a moderate reaction in the coordinate labor and socialist movements to the third round of radical politicism in the early 'fifties soon headed into a new cycle of extremism, extraparliamentary demonstrations, and violence, precipitating again much loss of public sympathy, new legislative restrictions, dissension among Left Socialists and unionists, renewed splits in both movements, gains by right-wing labor federations, and protective maneuvers by combined leftist rivals. This cycle culminated in the struggle against proposed revisions of the police duties law, and a fifth reached a crisis in the anti-security treaty struggle and the Socialist-labor polemic over structural reform in the early 'sixties.

During 1955–58, labor politicians from Sōhyō, including Diet members and other sympathizers in the reunited party, continued to operate as a potent pressure group. They had successfully insisted on delayed inclusion of the Worker Farmer Party in the Socialist merger. Real alarm on the part of the right-wing labor–party entente was stirred when these same combined leftist forces at the party convention in 1957 pushed the action policy distinctly leftward of the basis on which reunification had been achieved fifteen months earlier.

Differences between left and right Socialists on the one hand and Sōhyō and Sōdōmei-Zenrō on the other concerning necessary political action boiled down to the degree to which such activities should be limited to tactics to promote the economic ends of organized workers. Leftists insisted that against the focused political influence of monopoly capitalism there would be only amorphous national opinion unless the labor movement mobilized purposeful numbers to offset those forces and, hopefully, to achieve a socialist order. This turned into a vicious cycle with the conservative interests of organized employers interreacting with labor's tendencies to transform economic into political struggles.

The decisive prize, of course, has been control of the regulative and once oppressive state. Its policies affect not only the rights which can protect or break the labor movement; they can also exert decisive influence toward inflation or deflation, with consequences for the real income and job security of workers; the state determines the distribution of tax incidence as well as policies like rearmament and the liberalization of tariffs which have significance for workers' interests. This outlook had considerable appeal as long as Japanese society provided workers with little stake except subsistence employment in the capitalist system.

Profound changes, especially since 1957–59, have been affecting Japan's industrial relations and the environment of proletarian politics. Technological innovations and spectacular economic growth have impelled industrial shifts affecting employment. They have accentuated rewards and new semi-managerial statuses available for those with recent specialized training, so that new professionalization is expanding in larger factories. Labor–management relations are being modernized, and paternalism as well as the seniority system are being modified, the latter by increasing distinction in wages according to type of work. The productivity of labor is being greatly increased. More representatives of labor have been added to governmental commissions. Drastic liberalization of the tariff structure has further affected business organizations and job security. Retraining and reemployment services for workers have received more emphasis. There have even been scattered labor shortages.

Though Socialists maintain correctly that profits from economic growth have not been equally shared, still, the incomes, consumption, and welfare of most workers have been significantly improved. Of course, analogies with the conditions and attitudes of workers in the United States and Western Europe could be misleading, but, as we shall see, there are many recent signs that in Japan, too, better levels of living and the proven fact that regulated capitalism need not cause continual shrinkage of purchasing power and chronically expanding productive surpluses have tended to moderate the temper of workers. Japanese union leaders and Socialist politicians have noted the very practical impact of these changes and have had to develop responses.

Another causal dimension of labor politicism in Japan is to be found in the structure of union organizations. In the sector of large private industries, populous national labor federations have been constructed of enterprise union components which tenaciously control their own bargaining with management. Mobilization for political struggles as extensions of economic demands often constitutes the principal self-justifying strategy for national leadership and central organs. Thus, among leftist unions a premium is placed on militancy, and a tradition with emotional and philosophic implications has developed. Furthermore, during the early postwar chaos, the weaknesses of industries imposed objective limitations to feasible bargaining demands of unions, while after 1950 the relative power of unions dwindled in the face of resurgent managerial strength. Thus many unionists have preferred political activism to the apparent alternatives: lethargy and company union docility.[6]

The other more vigorous sector of the labor movement is composed of unionized workers in governmental services and monopoly corporations. Their loss of strike and, on the part of the former, collective bargaining rights has left them little but political demonstrations and limited dispute tactics. Of course, the employer toward whom their struggles are directed is the government and for this reason successive councils of national and local government workers' unions have found it useful to ally with Sōhyō and the left Socialists. It was, however, chiefly Communist leadership which tried to mold these unions into a striking force in 1947–48 to attain a so-called "people's government." Indeed, it has been observed that almost any widespread strike is bound to assume political significance, and short strikes are usually used to reinforce any extraordinary political demonstration.

Finally there are views and interests of union leaders and the rank-and-file which induce politicism. Among veteran leaders are some who, as intellectuals-turned-labor-elite between the world wars, were imbued with Marxist doctrines and became accustomed to combina-

6. For further discussion of these patterns, see: Solomon B. Levine, *Industrial Relations in Postwar Japan* (Urbana, University of Illinois Press, 1958), Chaps. 3, 4; Kazuo Ōkochi, *Labor in Modern Japan*. Economic Series No. 18 (Tokyo, The Science Council of Japan, 1958), Chap. 3 and supplement.

tions of unions being in most respects, except electoral numbers, congruent with prewar parties. Even more numerous are leaders of the younger and now often more boldly radical postwar generation. It is difficult for such men to return to industrial jobs and union offices after a term in the national Diet. Other aspirants crowd up the union ladder, and labor–SDP legislators with the support of their organizations usually try to be reelected. One of their perpetual problems is to keep in close touch with labor constituents. Some but not all labor Diet members have behaved as though they were aware that they represented more interests among their complex constituencies than just those of organized workers.

Though there is such a natural entente between trade unions and the Socialist parties, organized workers comprise a minority of the electorate, even if industrial and service employees are added to white collar and governmental functionaries. The proportion of those organized has slipped with the faster growth of the labor force to less than 35 per cent. Labor leaders confess that the party receiving official union support cannot depend on a tight discipline binding its members as the conservative parties can rely on traditional prestige and sanctions wielded by rural patriarchal bosses. Many of the urban leaders as well as the rank-and-file have become somewhat disillusioned with politicians and the ballot box, while others feel that, lacking the massive, disciplined union membership of its British counterpart, the party alone cannot conduct effective struggles outside the Diet. Thus, and especially when economic grievances were acute, members often responded to the political strategies urged by leaders of national industrial and general federations. At both union and Socialist Party conventions criticisms are often heard to the effect that party–union relations are confined to elites of party and union national headquarters. This is somewhat less true in prefectural and municipal politics.

DURING DEMOCRATIZATION AND WHILE THE SOCIALISTS SHARED POWER

Promotion of democratization and of pacific policies during the Occupation and, later, defense of liberal gains against the conservative "reverse course" have constituted two further reasons for workers' participation in political activities. However, experience in the wartime Industrial Patriotic Association (Sangyō Hōkokukai, or Sampō) movement had augmented bureaucratic elitism among labor leaders and had perpetuated the low political consciousness of workers. Communist labor factions as well as other union and Socialist leaders did strive to exploit trends toward democratic change, but masses of workers shared the national confusion and temporary despair, being more aware of immediate privations than of political goals. Japanese observers agree that in those circumstances workers could be easily swayed by leaders, and that the policies of the Labor Division, Economic and Scientific Section of the Occupation, were ultimately decisive.

Almost immediately after SCAP ordered the abolition of repressive state agencies and the removal of curbs on civil liberties, groups of Socialist labor leaders from the prewar legal left were first to convene a Conference for Formation of a National Union. Right-wing Socialists were predominant in this movement, though there were also leftists and leaders from the pre-1940 Worker-Farmer faction. On the day this conference met (October 10, 1945), Communist leaders were released from prison and with remarkable energy and discipline launched unionizing campaigns. From the beginning of these revivals there were hopes in all leftist quarters that a united labor front, cooperating with newly formed socialist parties, could be achieved. But only the Communists were specifically clear about their ultimate politico-economic aims.

Passage of the Trade Union Law in December 1945 gave further impetus to the organization of labor, which proceeded unevenly but at a phenomenal rate until a peak was reached in March 1949, when total union membership was officially reported to have reached more than 6,896,000. Socialists of various stripes were quick to sense in this movement at least one formidable political force.

Efforts to unify or even loosely to federate the burgeoning movement failed; though supported by left Socialists, they foundered on the suspicions of moderate labor and Socialist leaders that Communists would seek to dominate a united front. So two main labor organizations emerged between October 1946 and the following August—Sōdōmei on the right and the National Congress of Industrial Unions (Zenkoku Sangyō-betsu Kumiai Kaigi, or Sambetsu) on the left.[7] The

7. A group of 208 neutral unions with 115,000 members organized the Japan Labor Union Congress (Nihon Rōdō Kumiai Kaigi, or Nichirō Kaigi) in October 1946, but it was not very active and failed to unify the entire movement. See Figure 4: "Lineages of Japanese Labor Federations."

former was a consultative and advisory federation based on 33 prefectural councils revived, in the main, by prewar veteran leaders. Many of them were somewhat "boss-type" and were used to bargaining on behalf of their union members in ways which also had been found convenient by employers.

To these councils were added, at first, five vertically organized national unions in which younger, more radical, and for the most part *après guerre* leaders became assertive. Sōdōmei claimed about 900,000 members, slightly more than 18 per cent of the total. The mainstays of Sambetsu were 21 national industrial unions (at its beginning), each of whose enterprise unions was connected directly with its national headquarters. It was much easier for centralized leadership to be exerted in and by such unions coordinated under Sambetsu. Accordingly it was simpler for Communists to extend their influence working behind leaders on both levels. Sambetsu boasted a total membership of approximately 1.5 million, which constituted nearly one quarter of all organized workers. Governmental workers' unions claimed 1,837,000 members by October 1948. One of these, the Communist-dominated Communications Workers Union, belonged to Sambetsu, while the two largest unions—of railroad workers and teachers—were leftist but independent even of the governmental workers' labor council.

Left-wing Socialists were active in both of the main rival, though sometimes cooperating, labor camps. While they were influential in some unions, until 1950–51 they failed to develop predominant political leadership in coordination with either of these two federations. They failed similarly in the student movement, and such a consistent "second fiddle" position made their strategy appear to be pro-communist, particularly since (except during 1950–55) the JCP has also "recognized" the parliamentary system as a main field of struggle for power.

The newly formed but factious Social Democratic Party, then, provided only weak assistance to the developing federations. Because of more unity, discipline, and effective planning, together with the ardor of labor fractions conferring horizontally with each other and vertically up to the JCP Central Committee, the Communists assumed far more initiative. The Socialists established a few labor schools in Tokyo, Osaka, Kanagawa, and Ishikawa prefectures, but they were no match for those operated by Communists in almost every prefecture. The SDP contributed little even to Sōdōmei development and refrained from open concentration on that alliance for fear of antagonizing its own leftist elements as well as the larger and stronger Sambetsu. Socialist leaders tended to take for granted the support of workers and to view them as just so many voters to be cultivated during electoral campaigns.

The first joint political action in which the SDP cooperated with labor unions and the Communists was a "people's meeting" convened on April 7, 1946, to demand the resignation of the conservative Shidehara cabinet. That same spring the party responded, with right-wing reserve, to calls for a "democratic people's front." Moderate Socialists proposed a Democratic League for National Salvation to keep the mass movement within parliamentary channels and to counteract JCP pressures. Leftist leaders were trying to form a united labor front and extend it to achieve a "democratic" political front. But the preparatory organization for Sōdōmei withdrew support.

In the fall of 1946, a labor offensive was launched centering on six nationwide disputes. At that time, inflation was rampant, food shortages chronic, and workers were clamoring for wage increases, tax relief, job security, and other improvements. After a lull in December, Communists and other leftists in some of the largest governmental workers' unions led in forming the first of what was to be a series of ad hoc labor joint struggle committees. At first Sōdōmei joined these committees and was encouraged by the SDP. Although the moderates became alarmed when a general strike was planned for February 1, 1947, with the "establishment of a democratic government" as one declared objective, the SDP reluctantly condoned it. Some of its left-wing members were prepared to participate to prevent it from being totally guided by the JCP. Certain party moderates, however, opposed the proposed direct action and encouraged Sōdōmei's withdrawal from the joint struggle committee. It soon became clear that the Communists had overplayed their hand. SCAP not only prohibited the general strike but also began to consider other curbs on labor extremism. Rifts, which multiplied and widened in the next three years, began to develop in many of the politically more active unions.

Nevertheless, a number of economic concessions were made to labor, and within a week of the strike ban General MacArthur advised a new election before inauguration of the democratic Constitution in May. In what proved to be a lasting rejection of a united front with the JCP, the Socialists cited their fundamental criticism of the abuse of political strikes. During the electoral campaign, many labor unions supported independent candidates; Sambetsu also backed certain SDP and JCP aspirants, while Sōdōmei favored only the SDP. About 32 known union leaders were successful for the SDP in the Lower House, while about a dozen others identified with labor unions were returned by leftist parties to the House of Councillors. The Socialists won a plurality in the Diet but felt obliged to enter a coalition.

On grounds of both principles and opportunism the tide of labor leadership began to turn against the Communists and in favor of Left Socialists during the Katayama and Ashida governments and in the years of leftist decline which immediately followed. This was true even in Sambetsu and in a number of the largest and most leftist of the governmental workers' unions. However, the Democratization Leagues (Minshuka Dōmei, or Mindō), which were organized within labor unions and gradually generated a movement beneficial for the Social Democrats, was initiated in the main autonomously by anti-Communist union forces and soon with SCAP encouragement. As usual, Socialist politicians were eager to maximize such advantages; thus, in a Left Socialist manifesto in mid-May 1947, Mosaburō Suzuki and Kanjū Katō, who led a sizable group of left-wing Socialist Representatives, boasted that the SDP had become the chief political influence in about 70 per cent of the unions. Among these Diet members the Labor-Farmer faction was farthest left; later, in July 1948, its members were partly expelled and some resigned from the SDP.

Following the prohibited general strike effort and in order to continue the snowballed unity, a National Labor Union Liaison Council (Zenkoku Rōdō Kumiai Renraku Kyōgikai, or Zenrōren) had been founded in February-March 1947. Even though its national union and federation affiliates were autonomous, Sōdōmei's membership in it was uneasy; the Communist-inspired militancy of Zenrōren activities in the fall of 1947 and the spring of 1948 led to Sōdōmei's secession in June. Rivalry between Communist- and left-wing SDP-oriented labor groups was also reflected in this Council. At the acme of its strength, however, Zenrōren claimed the adherence of unions totalling more than five million members.

Much of Japan's basic democratizing legislation was enacted during the eighteen months when the Socialists shared power with two conservative parties. Some of these measures affecting the labor movement—the Labor Standards Act, the Unemployment Insurance Law, and establishment of the first Japanese Labor Ministry (September 1, 1947)—were enacted during the premiership of Tetsu Katayama. Sōdōmei, except for certain of its left-wing dissidents, backed the right Socialists staunchly, if sometimes with misgivings, in this period. Mitsusuke Yonekubo, a veteran labor leader in this orbit, became a minister without portfolio until the new ministry was inaugurated.

The Economic Stabilization Board also had among its advisers a few labor leaders; and labor was represented on the Payroll Commission which dealt with the wage problems of governmental workers, on the national and regional committees which temporarily regulated coal mining, and on production committees at mines.

Leftist Socialists and labor leaders had reluctantly accepted SDP participation in a predominantly conservative government, but as concessions had repeatedly to be made, they gradually criticized more vehemently the basic agreements on which the coalition rested. By the fall of 1947, labor and party discontent was coming to a head. Sambetsu unions, in cooperation with Zenrōren and the more militant components of the council of governmental workers' unions, challenged the official wage–price formula. Eventually it was the left-wing Socialist, Mosaburō Suzuki, who, as chairman of the House budget committee, allowed his party's coalition government to fall.[8]

Yet, when the Ashida government was formed, it had become clear that the conservative parties really needed Socialist participation as a hedge against labor offensives which might otherwise be controllable only with SCAP intervention. Communists and fellow travelers were making the most of the suffering caused by the lag of wages behind prices. In later years, the SDP could join the clamor for higher wages as an opposition party, but this strategic advantage was denied while it shared governmental responsibility. In the circumstances, it was a corollary that at least the larger and more vigorous leftist components of the labor movement would gradually conclude that the SDP was betraying their interests.

The political trend which affected labor interests most seriously during the Ashida government was revision of the National Public

8. For a more detailed treatment in English of events and trends during these periods, see relevant chapters in Evelyn S. Colbert, *The Left Wing in Japanese Politics* (New York, Institute of Pacific Relations, 1952), and Miriam S. Farley, *Aspects of Japan's Labor Problems* (New York, John Day and Institute of Pacific Relations, 1950).

Service Law, which deprived about one third of Japan's unions and about the same proportion of organized workers of their right to strike.[9] Before concentrating on labor–SDP relations in that connection, however, we should discern changes in the distribution of power in the labor movement, tensions and shifts which were fraught with political significance.

Democratization in Sambetsu and in certain hitherto and still predominantly leftist unions—such as the main federations of railway workers and miners—became a real movement during November-February 1947–48. Incipient splits were developing, and Socialist influence tended to gain unevenly at Communist expense; but the latter reacted vigorously and was able to exploit the definite evidences of a conservative counteroffensive to press for a united labor front, to depict the SDP as traitorous to the cause of labor, and to attract the Labor-Farmer faction on the extreme left of the SDP, as well as a number of labor-connected Councillors in the Upper House. Democratization was a two-edged weapon. Sōdōmei, which in December-January, began creating the Democratization Leagues (Mindō), and its right-wing Socialist ally were widely suspected in labor circles. Later, in October 1948, the left wing of Sōdōmei began to assert itself against the old guard. At the federation's convention in that month, Minoru Takano won the secretary-generalship, while Zengorō Shimagami became treasurer. Sōdōmei had to promise its own democratization and cooperation with other democratic unions, many of which, as mentioned, were gravitating toward the left-wing Socialists.

Inflation and the wage lag, together with fear of drastic reductions of governmental and probably private industrial personnel, caused militant protests and demands far exceeding in scope the effects of Communist influence; yet JCP fractions were the chief motive agents in the offensives of the past autumn and the spring of 1948. The wave of intensive and diverse dispute tactics brought three interventions by SCAP in late March and early April. All strikes in communications were banned, as was "any systematic or coordinated series of related

9. Unions of national railway workers and employees of the salt, camphor, and tobacco monopolies did not lose all bargaining rights, but the Public Corporations Labor Relations Law provided for arbitration by a special board, which might make recommendations to the government. Also special conciliation and mediation procedures were provided for public corporation workers. The National Public Service Law is more drastic than the Public Corporation and National Enterprise Law in limiting dispute tactics. There was in 1948 a total of about 2.7 million governmental employees.

work stoppages on the part of members of affiliated labor unions in a single industry or group of industries." Actually the latter ban was not fully enforced.

Activities short of a strike, especially by government workers' unions, continued, pressing for higher wages and trying to dissuade the government from revising the National Public Service Law, as the Ashida cabinet had threatened to do almost from its inauguration. The Occupation's GHQ had preferred that nonclerical civil servants not be permitted to strike when that law was enacted in the previous October, but right-wing Socialist and Sōdōmei leaders had differed and won their point. Less than a year later, the excessive politicism of certain Communist-dominated unions, such as the communications workers, led some of these same leaders to change their opinions—but not Socialists farther left. Interaction was thus accelerated between those who suspected that economic grievances were being exploited to exert political pressures toward truly revolutionary aims, and those who detected that conservatism was beginning to resurge and must be impressed by labor's power. These alignments cut across the Social Democratic Party, though efforts were made to evade or compromise on decisions which would split it.

When, on July 22, 1948, General MacArthur directed the Ashida government to proceed with revision of the controversial law, the SDP as well as Mindō leadership of some major unions were put in a dilemma, while the Communists were given political ammunition. Representatives of the Council of National and Local Government Workers' Unions (Zenkankō) called on Inejirō Asanuma, then a right-wing Socialist leader, and urged that the SDP secede from the coalition and lead the struggle against revision. But Asanuma explained that, in such a case, the next government would be even more conservative, that the best strategy was to remain in the government and do everything possible to limit the extent of revision.[10] This was the embarrassing task of the right-wing Socialists, especially of Labor Minister Katō who had been repeatedly promising no revision of basic labor laws. No wonder, then, that criticism from the party's left wing grew more intense, and that part of the Labor-Farmer faction withdrew. The Social Democrats, whose participation in the coalition had not succeeded in controlling the labor movement, were able in consulta-

10. *Shiryō, Rōdō Undō Shi, Shōwa Nijū-san Nen* (Sources, History of the Labor Movement, 1948) (Tokyo, 1952), p. 1164.

tion with leaders of Sōdōmei, Sambetsu Mindō, Kokutetsu (railway workers), and other unions, to mitigate somewhat the revision of the National Public Service Law.

Manifold changes were afoot in Japan and abroad. Chinese Communists were sweeping the Nationalists off the continent. The Occupation's emphasis was shifting from demilitarization and reforms to stabilization and economic recovery by the fastest possible capitalist methods. The reconcentration of business, industry, and finance was beginning. The Dodge plan of economic stabilization, or disinflation, was announced with all it signified for management and labor. Both organized labor and the related Social Democratic Party suffered decline, bitter divisions, and general readjustments. By the time they began to recover in 1951–52, the separate Left Socialists and Sōhyō were outstripping the influence of their right-wing rivals, having replaced the JCP and Sambetsu as the most militantly effective champions of labor interests.

DECLINE, SCHISM, AND RECOVERY OF LABOR AND SOCIALIST ORGANIZATIONS

Disinflation and the "Red purge" were the two trends during 1949–50 that threw the labor movement into confusion and retreat, with repercussions also on the temporarily discredited Social Democratic Party. At SCAP insistence, governmental credit to enable deficit financing of industries was to cease; the Japanese economy was to be prepared to stand independently and to enter the competitive international market. This entailed indirect wage stabilization and reductions of both governmental and private industrial personnel. Occupation authorities tried to insist on a distinction between this painful readjustment, which affected more than 400,000 workers, and the political as well as labor purge of Communists plus extremist sympathizers, which gained momentum after General MacArthur's Constitution Day speech in May 1950. But when SCAP opened the door to conservative renovationists, there was no adequate screening process before dismissals. By the end of that year, at least 11,000 labor leftists had been fired from more than 20 industries; more than 1,000 lost jobs in governmental services and enterprises which had experienced the most militant labor activities, while similarly inclined unions in key private industries were also weakened. The process undoubtedly involved widespread disregard of basic civil and human rights.

Not only Communists but also other activists on the "struggle committees" of unions were dismissed, and usually this involved loss of their union membership. After the outbreak of the Korean War in June, "security risks" were fired from companies with "special procurement" contracts. Conservative bureaucrats and such organizations as the Japanese Federation of Employer Associations (Nikkeiren) tried to convert these trends into a full union-busting movement, but SCAP's Labor Division applied brakes. During the year beginning in June 1949, Japanese unions declined in number by more than 5,500 and in membership by 880,000. The retreat slowed by the first half of 1951, and in the following twelve months mild recovery began. In fact, Japanese capitalism was by 1950 able to launch its first postwar offensive; SCAP held and tipped the balance decisively. The Occupation had directed the purge of rightist nationalists in 1947–49, and now the pendulum swung against the other extreme.

These trends accelerated the Mindō movement, the accentuation of factions within unions, a series of secessions, and the founding of new organizations. Sambetsu had, by June 1950, dwindled to slightly more than one quarter of its former membership, and after the inauguration of Sōhyō it was reduced further to less than 47,000 members.[11]

Opportunity and policies of the Occupation's Labor Division favored the Mindō leaders who soon came to support mainly the left-wing Socialists. Moreover, the same division and its field representatives strongly supported the principle of national industrial unions, despite their susceptibility to centralized control. Probably this was in order to offset Communist influence more effectively and to help consolidate a new federation before the Occupation ended. Right-wing Socialists and Sōdōmei leaders, both of whom were having difficulties with the left wings of their organizations, were bitter about being unable to maximize advantages from the Mindō movement which they had helped to develop.

Instead, Sōdōmei insurgent leftists, who harked back to the prewar legal left and who were critical of the nexus between labor bosses—or at least old-type union leaders—and right-wing Socialist leaders of the Socio-Democratic clique, had been gaining since the Federation's third convention in 1948. At the next convention in the following

11. Sambetsu further declined in membership to 27,000 in 1952, and to 13,000 in 1953. It was dissolved on February 15, 1958.

year, the veteran Socio-Democratic leader, Komakichi Matsuoka, was re-elected but left-wingers won predominance in other top positions. Motions were passed for Sōdōmei's adherence to the newly organized International Confederation of Free Trade Unions (ICFTU) and for participation of moderate unions with this connection in the conference which was preparing to launch a federation intended for virtually all noncommunist unions. The Sōdōmei right wanted this to be a loose liaison body under which its own autonomy could be preserved, though ultimately it might see fit to release its components for direct affiliation. The left wing of Sōdōmei, however, insisted on reorganization of the rest of their federation's unions along national industrial lines, dissolution of Sōdōmei, and immediate direct affiliation with the imminent Sōhyō.

Chiefly over these issues, most right-wing delegates walked out of the fifth convention on November 30, 1950, and in the following March the left had its way. Early in May 1951 the erstwhile Sōdōmei leftists carried perhaps five eighths of the membership into Sōhyō; three weeks later, Matsuoka, Tadao Kikukawa, and other right-wing stalwarts denied that their federation had been dissolved and reorganized the shrunken rump into what for a while was called the "New Sōdōmei" but later resumed its old name. Its representatives agreed somewhat cautiously to cooperate with Sōhyō affiliates in wage struggles and, when advisable, to conduct joint struggles with the SDP, especially its right wing, in the Diet.[12] The national unions from Sōdōmei became prominent allies of the left Socialists within the recently founded General Council of Trade Unions (Sōhyō). Meanwhile, the Mindō faction in the crumbling Sambetsu under the recent Communist, Matsuta Hosoya, was preparing to secede and to join with the leftist Takano faction of Sōdōmei, together with major governmental

12. Although most membership claims of Japanese trade unions are grossly exaggerated, the proportion of Sōdōmei claimed by the Left wing was probably more nearly accurate; its figures were: 530,000 who went into Sōhyō, 300,000 remaining in New Sōdōmei. A labor expert informed the writer later that the second figure had probably been nearer 80,000.

The National Federation of Textile Industry Workers Unions (Zensen Dōmei) with about 300,000 members, though remaining friendly to Sōdōmei, decided to become independent. It later joined the moderate wing of Sōhyō but subsequently seceded with the Minrōren group of unions. Thereafter and to date it has remained independent but friendly to Sōdōmei-Zenrō Kaigi, later to the moderate Dōmei Kaigi, and to the Democratic Socialists.

workers' unions and neutral organizations under the Labor Union Federation[13] to form a vigorous General Council.[14]

Sōhyō was officially inaugurated a month after the outbreak of war in Korea. Its immediate labor background was an offensive which had again verged on general strike tactics, only to be checked by SCAP rulings. Again the wage demands of strikers and demonstrators had been supported in the Diet by the Socialists. The Communist Party had largely gone underground, and the Social Democratic Party had become the main vehicle for political reformism and protest. Communists were soon directed to infiltrate the new federation and its component unions and to push for a "united front from below." A year previously the more extreme elements of the left-wing Socialists, neutralized as they were by the "democratization trend," had resolved on a somewhat similar strategy, working from the party structure. The new General Council not only pressed toward economic objectives but also allied itself with leftist labor unions in supporting the Socialists, chiefly the left-wing Social Democrats. Many of these labor leaders became members of the SDP and in so doing strengthened the demand that it become a class party. Sōhyō even formed a Joint Diet Struggle Committee with the SDP for its "base-up" wage offensive and reconstruction of the labor movement.

From its inception Sōhyō was by far the strongest of Japan's labor

13. The Zen Nihon Rōdō Kumiai Remmei (Zen Nichirō), which, in July 1949, had continued the lineage of the Nihon Rōdō Kumiai Kaigi (Nichirō Kaigi). Some of these unions did not join Sōhyō until July 1950. See Figure 4.

14. Just after the schism in Sōdōmei, Hosoya did lead his Mindō group out of Sambetsu, but it did not join Sōhyō until November 1950, and even thereafter it retained its identity, being suspended and seceding in July 1951 to form a small bloc (as can be seen in Figure 4) ideologically and politically between Sōhyō and Sōdōmei. In general, however, its unions continued to favor leftist parties, especially the Left Socialists. Hosoya advocated labor reorganization by lower echelons upward to form Sōhyō, but during the delay caused by such problems as the strife within Sōdōmei, Takano and his colleagues formed another preparatory council which forged the new federation through topflight leadership and by means of the nationally federated union structures. This was a harbinger of the kind of guidance-from-above which Sōhyō has since exercised in both economic and political struggles.

At the time of its inauguration, Shin (New) Sambetsu included three national unions, one industrial trade union, one regional federation, and 13 directly affiliated local unions. Its claim to nearly 55,000 members was probably excessive, for subsequent official reports usually have given figures between 35,000 and 40,000.

Its initial program called for a united front of democratic unions and cooperation with "socialistic and democratic political parties." Shin Sambetsu leaders such as Hosoya and Eiichi Ochiai have served as influential advisers to the SDP.

federations, and it still claims more than half of all unionized workers. It grew from 15 unions to 21 unions of government and public workers and 17 national unions in private industries in the fall of 1954. The railway workers' and teachers' unions were the largest components and they had also been among the leaders of the Mindō movement. The pro-right Socialist faction in the National Railway Workers' Union (Kokutetsu or Kokurō) had, until late 1960, been weaker than the Marxist Worker-Farmer group. The claimed total membership of Sōhyō grew by 1962 to 3.7 million, at least 70 per cent of them employees of the national and local governments and state corporations.

As a Mindō product, Sōhyō at first evinced moderate tendencies, inclining toward affiliation with the new International Confederation of Free Trade Unions. Many of its unions were critical of the Communist invasion of South Korea and favored United Nations resistance. They reaffirmed the fundamental principles of union autonomy from party influences together with the political independence of members. Though the primacy of labor's economic objectives was emphasized, class struggle and rigorous collective bargaining received more stress than cooperation between management and labor. Unions were to struggle jointly with socialist parties and to influence the Diet in favor of measures to promote mass movements, raise public workers' wages, revise economic stabilization policies, and cause the fall of the Yoshida Cabinet.

But an ambivalence as to objectives and tactics persisted. This problem and other current issues eventually pushed Sōhyō again toward militant leftism—sometimes barely within the pale of parliamentarism. The continuing conflict of economic interests—the exigencies of collective bargaining and dispute activities—confronted labor leaders with the problem of how to attain by moderate means enough of their unions' objectives to satisfy the rank-and-file. Many leaders rued having acquiesced so far in the "Red purge" and observed that capitalists had taken unfair advantage of lessened labor militancy. Labor was anxious to have its share in the Korean War boom, though some extreme leftists were willing to intensify strikes for economic aims to hamper anticommunist military deliveries.

As conclusion of a peace treaty and related agreements approached, it appeared to politically conscious workers that the Occupation authorities were swiftly bolstering conservative power in Japan and that the security treaty with the United States was both unequal and dangerous, as it aligned Japan with one of the two hostile camps. They naturally observed that such a connection would strengthen Japanese capitalism; indeed, those more to the left charged that American "capitalist imperialism" was the ultimate foe, having subordinated its Japanese partner. As conservative nationalists were depurged, many re-entering politics, organized labor feared retrogressive revision of the basic protective labor laws, if not of the democratic Constitution itself. The rearmament issue came to incorporate many aspects of these questions and fears; for this had become a main U.S. objective, and Japanese conservatives were the most eager to cooperate. Part of labor's vociferous objection to such trends was an expression of nationalist reaction to humiliations of the Occupation period.

Disagreements over these matters appeared within Mindō unions, and the rifts were carried into Sōhyō when it was formed. They were paralleled by left and right factional positions in the Social Democratic Party. From mid-September 1950 until the following spring, the Socialists again cooperated with one of the series of Sōhyō sponsored "democratic" joint struggle committees which coordinated the autumn offensive under Mindō leadership. SDP cooperation was sought not only in support of wage demands but also to oppose efforts to deprive teachers of their rights to engage in political activities, as well as to promote peace and the revision of the tax structure.

Over the protest of Sōdōmei together with the seamen's and textile workers' unions, the second Sōhyō convention in March 1951 adopted the "Four Principles of Peace," just after their passage by the sharply divided Socialist Party convention. The controversy over whether to adhere to the ICFTU served as a barometer of left-right tendencies in both the labor and Socialist movements. At this time, Sōhyō made a decision which still holds: that member unions might affiliate with that international body, but the central Sōhyō organization would remain neutral. Some leaders of component unions and of Sōhyō have shown a greater affinity for the pro-communist World Federation of Trade Unions (WFTU) and the national labor federation in Red China. A neutralist tendency toward the Korean War developed. The convention also resolved to cooperate with socialist parties in the coming local elections and to coordinate the spring economic offensive with political campaigns. Schism of the SDP in October accentuated the main rift in Sōhyō; the Left Socialists as a working class party thereafter teamed up even more closely with Sōhyō leftists, while the latter managed the fall offensive to maximize pressure on the Diet in its abortive attempt to block labor law revision and ratification of the treaties. Early in November, Chairman Mutō of Sōhyō declared a "state of emergency" caused by the accelerating "reverse course," including a law to regulate organizations.

Opposition to retrogressive legislation, along with economic demands, continued to be emphasized in the labor offensive of the spring and summer of 1952. The military portion of the budget, the General Strike Prohibition Law, and especially the Subversive Activities Prevention Law were targets of both Sōhyō and Left Socialists; Sōdōmei and Right Socialists also opposed them more discreetly. No less than five waves of strikes were mounted between March and June; extremists infiltrated a section of the May Day demonstrations, causing violence. This and prolonged public suffering in the cold of November and December, during a bitter strike of coal and electric workers for exorbitant demands advised by Sōhyō, drew public criticism which the conservatives were quick to use for passage of more restrictive legislation.

At the third Sōhyō convention in July 1953, leftists pushed through a decision to redirect the Mindō anticommunist emphasis and its implications. "Complete independence of the Japanese nation" became a slogan, and anti-American actions, chiefly against military bases and aid, became more prominent. On the other hand, charges of excessive politicism were again hurled not only by Sōdōmei but also by moderate unions within Sōhyō, involving, as usual, the two Socialist parties. Thus, the third in a series of labor-political cycles had again reached a point of dénouement. In 1947, 1948, and 1952, conditions had conduced to labor militancy; this had been exploited politically by left extremists whose excesses had provoked governmental restrictions and fissions within numerous labor unions and federations. The convictions and psychology of "confrontation" were being driven ever more deeply into the consciousness and habits of the labor partisans and their political allies.

LABOR'S ROLE IN THE SCHISM AND REUNIFICATION OF THE SDP

The leftward turn of Sōhyō coincided with the Socialist Party's split and was marked by the accentuation of factions within the former. These were chiefly three in number: the Worker Comrades Society

(Rōdōsha Dōshikai) allied with the Left Socialists; the Unification faction (Tōitsuha) which first rose to power in the organization under the leadership of Takano and was pro-Communist in the Worker-Farmer (Rōnōha) manner; and a weaker element of moderate union leaders—the Democratic Labor Movement Study Group (Minrōken)—whose orientation was toward political neutralism or toward Sōdōmei and the Right Socialists.

The Rōdōsha Dōshikai was established in the spring of 1951 and during August-September, prompted by formation of the rival Minrōken, agreed upon its own policy principles. Its leaders were class-conscious; they supported the "Four Principles of Peace" and probably persuaded the left-wing Socialists to insist upon them in the party's convention in 1951, thereby contributing to the split. These unions were independently critical of the ICFTU; they advocated a unified labor front and preservation of democracy against either extreme of totalitarianism. Seven Sōhyō unions—especially the dominant pro-Left Socialist factions of the railway, teachers, communications workers, and synthetic chemical workers' unions—formed the nucleus of this group, and a number of outside organizations, including the Shin Sambetsu, were also influential. Their leaders had close connections with the Wada and Suzuki factions of the Left Socialists. Takano is reported to have sought a compromise with this group, but he was adamant against permitting Left Socialist domination of Sōhyō. Eventually such efforts failed, and by the fourth convention of Sōhyō in 1953 the Unification faction's flirtation with the Communist-sponsored "national salvation front" and advocacy of the "peace force" policy deepened the combined hostility of the Dōshikai and its friends in the Left SDP. Kaoru Ōta (from the Synthetic Chemical Workers' Union), their candidate for the Sōhyō secretary-generalship, was defeated in 1954, but at the next convention Akira Iwai (from the National Railway Workers Union) narrowly defeated Takano for the same office.[15]

More extreme leftists continued to operate both within Sōhyō and the Left Socialist faction, but Socialist-labor Diet members began to adjust to the preeminence of what came to be called the Ōta–Iwai

15. Another policy difference between these two leftist factions was that the Takano-led group emphasized the importance of mass movements and activities outside as well as in the Diet, while Dōshikai leaders at that time stressed the parliamentary process. Their emphasis changed by 1959.

main current group. The Dōshikai as such lapsed after 1955, but a loosely identifiable group of radical left-wing SDP Diet members, dissatisfied with the compromise with the Right Socialists, that year formed the Heiwa Dōshikai (Peace Comrades). Some of them were connected with the Sōhyō left. These Sōhyō-related Socialists encouraged the three more leftist factions of the party's radical wing to dissuade the Suzuki group from compromising with the right wing. Thus, as previously explained (pp. 59–60, 71–74, 288–89), the leftist factions were able to modify certain key action policies in a radical direction.

Parallel with these leftward developments, a counteractive coalition of 13 moderate unions in Sōhyō, known as the Democratic Labor Movement Study Group (Minshu Rōdō Undō Kenkyūkai, or Minrōken), also began to take shape one month before the SDP cleavage.[16] Some of these unions withdrew from the second wave of strikes in 1952, which were becoming more politically focused against the Subversive Activities Prevention Bill; their criticism was further aroused by the disastrous coal and electric strikes which Sōhyō's Takano faction in part directed according to its excessive "market basket" wage formula. Fissures broke open in those unions, and immediately after failure in their disputes, four conservative unions in Sōhyō blasted out their criticisms of the Sōhyō Left.[17] These agreed with the views of Sōdōmei and Right Socialist leaders, who had been encouraging this discontent from its start. In mid-January 1953, representatives from an enlarged group of protesting unions adopted a constitution and set of principles intended as a basis for the Liaison Council for a Democratic Labor Movement (Minshushugi Rōdō Undō Renraku Kyōgikai, or Minrōren), inaugurated a month later. Some of these unions seceded from Sōhyō in the fall of 1953, and founded the All-Japan Trade Union Congress (Zen Nihon Rōdō Kumiai Kaigi, or Zenrō Kaigi) in April 1954.[18] Sōdōmei hampered the effectiveness of this right-wing

16. One of the chief segments of the so-called Minrōken within Sōhyō was a pro-Right Socialist group of moderate railroad union leaders of Kokutetsu, known as the Regenerated Democratic League (Shinsei Mindō). In addition, such Sōdōmei (and Right Socialist) leaders as Matsuoka, Kikukawa, Shigeeda Takami, Shigeo Ihori, and Torazō Kumamoto—together with Chairman Minoru Takita of the Textile Industry W.U.—helped to launch the Minrōken and its successors, Minrōren and Zenrō Kaigi.

17. The four unions were the Federation of Textile Workers, the Japan Broadcasting Workers, the National Movie and Theater Workers, and the All-Japan Seamen's Union.

18. Since 1954, "second unions" have been formed in a number of industries, especially in those whose extremism led to unsuccessful strikes and sometimes to govern-

labor coalition by insisting on autonomy within it and regarding it merely as a convenient liaison mechanism. Rivalry between these two and the need to augment support of the Nishio-led Right Socialists led them and other anti-Sōhyō unions, including the National Council of Government and Public Workers' Unions (Zenkankō), in 1962 to form a rather loose General Confederation of Japanese Labor Organizations (Dōmei Kaigi). It soon was expanding more rapidly than Sōhyō, and achieved consolidation in the fall of 1964.

A brief résumé of principles upheld in Zenrō and then Dōmei Kaigi unions will indicate how nearly identical they were with those of Sōdōmei and the Right Socialists. While defending the basic rights and economic interests of labor, they have criticized the ultra-leftist trend of Sōhyō and the latter's conducting itself in many respects as a political party. They tried to reassert the founding principles and program of the anti-communist Mindō and of Sōhyō. Excessive use of strikes was denounced as injurious to labor and to the national economy. Socialism should be the aim of parliamentary efforts, and could not be democratically achieved by direct action. United fronts with the Communists were regarded as anathema; instead democratic unions were urged to cooperate and to affiliate with the ICFTU.

Thus, both the socialist and labor movements were riven into roughly congruent, mutually distrustful wings. One charged the other with pro-communist fellow traveling and undemocratic power ambitions, and was in turn accused as the dupe if not the accomplice of capitalist divisive tactics. Therefore, one camp was encouraged to continue as the barely legal left, while the other was restrained from being too compliant with conservative governments and managements.

We have seen how divisions between conservative and radical factions within both general federations of Japanese labor immediately preceded and contributed to the more enduring Socialist Party schism of October 1951. In addition to their views on domestic issues, predominant elements in Sōhyō and Shin Sambetsu strongly opposed

mental interference and even restrictive legislation—as in the coal and electric industries. Numbers of the more moderate off-split unions have adhered to Zenrō Kaigi, augmenting its strength. However, the combined claim of Zenrō and Sōdōmei to 850,000 members in the spring of 1954 was an exaggeration by perhaps 35–40%. In 1959 these federations were still claiming 770,000 and, by 1963, 1.5 million members. Sōhyō has remained far stronger. Four unions of workers in the textile industry, seamen, movie and theater workers, and garrison forces employees were charter members of Zenrō along with the Sōdōmei en bloc.

ratification of the recently signed Peace and Security Treaties. They induced the Left Socialists to insist upon the Four Principles of Peace, and some observers thought that these leftists were among the chief impellers of the split.

After the schism, Takano hailed the Left Socialists as a class party which had sloughed off "bourgeois remnants" from immature prewar socialism. In the next seven national elections, Sōhyō nominally supported the campaigns of the three socialist parties, but overwhelmingly it aided the Left Socialists. The demand for reunification of the related labor and socialist movements persisted, however, and extended beyond organized workers. Leaders in each of the two main labor–party orbits wavered, weighing comparative advantages, between advocating that their particular party and federation should absorb their rivals and, on the other hand, realizing that neither wing could alone attain a Diet majority. During maneuvers concerning possible SDP reunification, each side expressed willingness, provided the other would alter some of its basic principles. During the campaigns in March-April 1953, Sōhyō warned its political partner against reunification unless the Right Socialists agreed to oppose the peace and security treaties, to favor trade with Communist China, and to adopt independent, neutral foreign policies. Suzuki soon repeated similar terms. Later, Takano added that the Left Socialists would have to become the "central force" if there was to be reunification; moreover, certain more conservative right-wingers, such as Nishio and Yagi, would have to be expelled, and the Right Socialists should cease backing Minrōren and trying to split Sōhyō.

Nevertheless, many neutral and industrial unions in the private sector continued to urge SDP reunification. Legislators on the national and prefectural levels, some with labor backgrounds, hoped that their support from workers would increase if the Socialist Party could be reunited, and some feared that long postponement might lose them many labor votes. Probably several factors induced Takano to shift early in 1954 and to begin advocating—as at the responsive fifth Sōhyō convention—reunification of the three noncommunist "labor political parties." International tensions were subsiding, and Communist neighbors had adopted a softer line, urging Japan to become more independent. The JCP had veered once more, calling for a national front led by labor but embracing all other strata who could be mobilized against the arch-enemy: American capitalist "imperialism."

Doubtless Takano was affected by this change either directly from Communists in Sōhyō or via the Worker-Farmerites.

He also reacted, as the Socialists did, to the growing indications of forthcoming conservative party mergers. Even if SDP reunification might not soon produce a Socialist majority in the Diet, failure to reunite might enable a stronger conservative coalition to revise the "Peace Constitution" and the basic labor laws, also to accelerate rearmament. Moreover, there is evidence that leaders of Sōhyō sought to minimize the effects of the Minrōren secessions and the subsequent organization of Zenrō Kaigi. Sōhyō's convention in 1954 pledged financial and electoral support to the three "labor political parties," proposed to improve relations with Zenrō and Shin Sambetsu, and to conduct joint struggles with various elements in the National League for Protection of the Peace Constitution. Defeat of the Takano faction in the Sōhyō convention in 1955 seemed to promise milder policies and thus enhanced the possibility of party reunification.[19]

But could the Ōta–Iwai type of basically Marxist leadership, teamed with men of similar outlook among the left Socialists and later with the still more radical Worker-Farmer group, cooperate effectively with evolutionary Socialists? The former Dōshikai faction was opposed to Communist-led united fronts, favored Japanese neutralism in foreign relations, gave more emphasis to legal parliamentarism, and was at first somewhat less militant in labor disputes—especially in those with small companies. But fundamentally it still advocated revolution led by a working class party, not a national, cross-stratal party; its leaders have been committed to "confrontation" rather than compromise and cooperation for the sake of improved productivity and the economy viewed broadly according to the interests of all classes. Despite misgivings on such points, Socialist labor and party groups on the right increasingly recognized the urgency of reunification and considered that it might tend to block the spread of Communist influence in the twin movements.

Reunification of the Social Democratic Party late in 1955, while differences between the two main labor wings remained unreconciled,

19. When personnel decisions were made on August 17, 1955, by the Executive Committee of Sōhyō—after the Sixth Convention—Ryōji Koyama was appointed to head the Political Department. This was interpreted as an attempt of the now dominant Ōta–Iwai group to smooth relations with the Left SDP, for Koyama was a leader of the National Railways Union who had formerly been chief secretary of the Left Socialist organization in Aichi Prefecture.

was evidence that the Socialist Parties were not completely dominated by labor union considerations. Still, continuing division in the latter movement—unlike the main farmers' unions, which were helped by the Socialist example to reunite by March 1958—remained one of the chief factors of instability in the recombined SDP. During the long negotiations of 1955 between the two party groups, Left Socialist leaders and intellectuals urged Sōhyō to press resolutely for unification of the labor federations. And after Socialist reunification, party leaders were introduced at a conference with officials of labor federations, one implication being that a united front in that related sector would be desirable.

The major labor lineages had differed in their policies toward Socialist reunification when that was in the making. Sōhyō had urged such a move before the general elections in February; when only partial steps could then be taken, the General Council had decided to postpone its pressure for inclusion of the Worker-Farmer element in the merger until after the two Social Democratic wings had succeeded. Shin Sambetsu as well as Sōdōmei and Zenrō Kaigi strongly opposed such a Marxist addition. Probably, at least the left wing of Sōhyō was influenced by the Communist Party's shift to a more moderate line early in 1955, returning to operations within the parliamentary system and advocating multiclass combination against alleged American imperialism.[20] According to one interpretation, in these circumstances a factor conducing the Left Socialists toward reunification was fear of a JCP–Sōhyō combination, but, in view of the Takano faction's decline, this was probably not such a serious anxiety.

While Zenrō Kaigi and Sōdōmei continued to urge their members to support the SDP and did not actively oppose party reunification, they observed that it was accomplished on the basis of expediency rather than by genuine compromises and agreements. They called attention to indications during the Left Socialist special convention,

20. Such Communist policies have been further developed. On September 30, 1957, following Khrushchev's famous speech at the C.P.S.U. 20th congress in the previous year, the party's Central Committee decided to present to the next convention an amendment of the theory of workers' control through revolution. It recognized that democratic government could be a transitional stage leading toward complete revolution. Kenji Miyamoto explained that the new program "laid the foundation for future party activities" and that the JCP should seek public confidence. The Committee promised that the party would support "Japan's present democratic [meaning Socialist] parties and trade unions." Such a change facilitated infiltration of leftist parties and unions.

held in September to discuss and ratify the negotiated common policy, that controversial compromises were being only nominally accepted with the intention of reasserting leftist policies in the drafting of the action programs to be submitted to subsequent party conventions. And they insisted that the "democratic socialists" oppose communism in all its guises and that parliamentary democracy be supported. Procommunism was discerned by conservative labor leaders in the Left Socialists' continued anti-Americanism and opposition to U.S. military bases in Japan. The leftists seemed to have made concessions with respect to their Four Peace Principles, but would this prove to be more apparent than real? Zenrō Kaigi in particular feared that, in a reunified SDP, its influence might be swamped by that of Sōhyō, that Sōhyō radicalism would—with this expanded scope—pervade more widely not only the socialist but also the labor movement. Its very raison d'être being thus menaced, Zenrō reemphasized the principle of union autonomy.

During the autumn of 1955, a subcommittee of the bipartisan group of Socialists, which was drafting the common program, formulated a so-called "Attitude toward the Internal and International Labor Movement." After reaffirming the liberal principles of party–union relationships, this statement promised close cooperation between the two toward attainment of a socialist society; it urged unification of a labor front and declared that the SDP expected union orientation toward the ICFTU, "joining hands with workers of the world." While Zenrō Kaigi leaders worked through Right Socialists to obtain a more forthright anticommunist policy—to specify what kind of a labor movement the reunified SDP would promote, and to clarify the decision in favor of the ICFTU—top officials of Sōhyō urged Left Socialist Chairman Suzuki to correct the definition of socialist revolution, to strengthen the party's position on Japan's independence of U.S. policies, and not to stipulate union affiliation with the ICFTU. That clause in the SDP joint statement was nevertheless ratified by both special party conventions, but Sōhyō protesters were assured that this policy of international labor affiliation would not be emphasized in the near future.

Sōhyō conventions and officials continued their appeals for labor unification and looked to the SDP for support and to provide liaison agencies. A roundtable of neutral union leaders also tried to mediate between the major federations. The main impeding issues, in addition to the ICFTU vs. WFTU questions, have been: whether organized labor should cooperate with the Japan Productivity Center established in February 1955;[21] whether the advocated statutory minimum wage should be fixed generally or be adjusted according to conditions in various industries; the left's greater penchant for radical political activities; and Sōhyō's greater concern for the interests of governmental workers. Zenrō and Sōdōmei uneasily continued membership in a revised Joint Diet Struggles Council but avoided relations with the Worker-Farmer radical faction. After its own reunification, the SDP naturally increased its support for unification of both the main farmers' and workers' federated unions. Right-wing objections, however, caused leftist party and Sōhyō factions to assay the building of greater unity pragmatically by piecemeal joint activities, including pressures on the Diet.

MOUNTING CRISES, 1958–61

Organized labor and the Socialists have been challenged in recent years by manifold changes to which we have already alluded. In responding, the two allied movements have continued to interact on each other. The unsuccessful dispute waged by the Railway Workers' Union over personnel dismissed in Niigata late in 1957 marked a sustained stiffening of governmental and private administration of labor affairs. Prosperity and bumper crops had prevailed since 1955, with two "saucer recessions," the latter from mid-1958 into 1959. During such lulls, employers were more resistant to wage offensives. However, the filtering down of gains in income evinced a broader distribution

21. This program and center were instituted in mid-February 1955 with funds supplied in part by the United States government's Foreign Operations Administration and the support of Japanese official and business circles, including the Labor Ministry. Even Sōdōmei and Zenrō Kaigi have been cautious about overtures for the cooperation of organized labor, in part because these invitations came somewhat belatedly. However, in September 1955, the former joined on unilaterally stipulated terms. Zenrō would probably have adhered, but the reluctance of the friendly Union of Textile Industry Workers' Unions caused it merely to free its member unions to cooperate. In 1957, these federations criticized the draft SDP program for dodging the productivity issue.

Of course, the proposition that workers' incomes can best be improved by raising productivity cannot be logically gainsaid. Dominant elements in Sōhyō, however, argued that labor could only cooperate safely in such programs if they could be conducted within a socialist framework so that, possessing decisive political power, workers could assure that the state would safeguard their interests. Under capitalism, it asserted, such efforts will result in intensification of labor, reduction of personnel and consequent job insecurity, the unfair distribution of profits, the hastening of rearmament, the strengthening of Japanese capitalism, and continued subservience to American designs.

of profits, which tended to have a moderating effect on rank-and-file workers and contributed to fission in union politics. The revisionist trends in British, West German, and Italian socialism began to have their counterpart in Japan. In certain years Japan was able to balance payments, and prospects were good that undue economic dependence on the United States could be outgrown. But it would require higher levels of productivity and rationalization of personnel. Job security again became a major objective of labor action, and in firing workers some employers did not overlook the opportunity again to rid their companies of active Socialist and Communist party members.

Moreover, since mid-1957 it had been clear that the second government under Premier Nobusuke Kishi was intent upon renewing the security treaty with the United States on more equal terms. In preparation for this, Kishi announced his determination to clip the political wings of Sōhyō and of the teachers' and other unions of government employees.

The significance for Japanese socialism of international trends has been explained in Chapter 7. Tensions and temporary relaxations caused by the Khrushchevian "thaw," and the 1960 summit failure, for example, had repercussions in Japan and indeed throughout the world. At this point we are more concerned with them as factors conditioning the maneuvers of interrelated radical versus moderate elements in Japan's labor and socialist organizations. In general it can be observed that political radicalism in Japan was resurgent in these rather prosperous years, that radical minorities felt challenged both by conditions unfavorable to labor and by the moderation induced in their own organizations when the environment grew more favorable. Obstacles encountered in collective bargaining encouraged leaders to stress political issues.

Sōhyō's leftist Mindō leadership under Ōta and Iwai felt threatened not only by employers and the government but also from within by the Takano faction and by the pressure of middle-ranking activists. Industrial changes were impairing the controls which the Mindō group had exerted mainly through foremen, and the rising new leaders felt frustrated by slower advancement and by growing bureaucratism.[22] Nearly half the delegates to Sōhyō's convention in July 1958 were anti-mainstream advocates, critical of the "low tone" of recent

22. For a more detailed and interpretative account, see David C. S. Sissons, "Recent Developments in Japan's Socialist Movement (I)," *Far Eastern Survey, 29* (March 1960), 40–47.

offensives. Policies were adopted to promote trade with Communist China and to strengthen the SDP as a class party. In accordance with another decision, Sōhyō in the ensuing fall threw its weight behind the teachers' union struggle against enactment of an efficiency rating system for instructors. Despite noisy demonstrations, coordinated again with opposition by Socialists in the Diet, this resistance obtained only a few legislative compromises.

Suddenly, on October 8, the campaign shifted when Kishi's party introduced the Police Duties Revision Bill in the Lower House. The Socialist Party declared a state of emergency and staged a preliminary boycott of the House of Representatives. Sōhyō called a special conference, and for the first time all labor federations cooperated in a non-economic struggle. (Zenrō-Sōdōmei joined with the proviso that the labor front should abandon the policy of class struggle.) Another national council was quickly established and was supported by the National Farmers' Union and by numerous academic, cultural, and women's organizations. When Communist China precipitated another Quemoy crisis and, in the midst of the furor in Japan, Premier Kishi remarked that Japan must prepare to play its full part in restraining Red aggression and make ready for this by amending the Constitution, opposition to the "blitz bill" was accentuated.

When the Socialists failed to prevent the conservative government from extending the Diet session for thiry days in November 1958, the exasperated Socialist Secretary-General, Asanuma (formerly a stickler for parliamentary procedures), was quoted as having exclaimed: "There is no other way to gain the reins of government but violent revolution."[23] The opposition party declared that enactments during the absence of its Representatives would be illegal. Sōhyō had been planning to lead a series of short, general strikes; and, the day after these stormy events, four million workers in various parts of the country left their jobs to demonstrate. That evening 10,000 students and unionists marched and shouted in front of the Diet building, and a few hundred broke in even as their more orderly delegation was about to present a statement to Socialist Representatives. The public temper was rising and, as we shall see, radical leftists were trying to gain advantages.

As explained in Chapter 2, Kishi was persuaded to negotiate. The

23. *Japan Times*, Nov. 5, 1958.

ensuing talks resulted in compromises according to which, among other things, the objectionable police bill was withdrawn; the Conservatives intimated that more heed would be paid to the need for prior discussions and compromises with the minority; the Socialists agreed to resume their legislative seats and their observance of legal procedures. Both sides promised "mutual trust," but the violence that had occurred was to reappear in the spring of 1960, when the Kishi administration prepared to ram through ratification of the controversial revised security treaty.

Sōhyō leaders were glad to have this political diversion from their otherwise rather unsuccessful autumn offensive. Like the Communist Party and the more extreme left-wing Socialists, they called for a "people's front" not only against the police bill but also to topple the government. Though the SDP acted as the political spearhead for resistance, its executive declined cooperation with the JCP on the national level. In about a score of prefectures, however, Socialists did participate with Communists in joint efforts; and denunciatory demonstrations flared in most of Japan's major centers.

In November 1958, while the crisis was still rife, a "Group to Strengthen the Socialist Party" was formed within Sōhyō. It was partly composed of former Rōdōsha Dōshikai members and was connected with the Shakaishugi Kyōkai (Socialist Society), the theoretical mainstay of the left-wing Socialists. By January 1959, the objective of the new group in Sōhyō was a reformed coalition of leftists emphasizing the class nature of the SDP and imbued with the doctrine of achieving socialist revolution by peaceful means if possible but by force in certain circumstances. Ōta, now Sōhyō's Chairman, and the Wada Socialist faction were connected with these plans.[24] It should be noted that the pro-communism of the Rōnōha extremists was the philosophy of the Takano faction in Sōhyō, indicating that the Mindō leadership was again being pressed well to the left of its earlier position.

Despite the blame which more pronounced leftists placed on the Nishio faction and allied Zenrō-Sōdōmei unions for swinging the SDP back toward parliamentary participation before the Kishi government could be overthrown, Sōhyō and Zenrō leaders again considered re-

24. Iwai showed more ambivalence and favored the "Platform Study Group," which advocated close bonds between the SDP and unionized workshops, stronger Socialist leadership of workshop activities, better discipline in the party, and clear SDP devotion to a socialist revolution with its own theory embodied in its platform.

unification early in 1959. But these efforts failed because of Zenrō's continued demands that it must be on an anticommunist basis and must include abandonment of the doctrine of "class struggle first" as well as affiliation with the ICFTU. Moreover, Zenrō was willing to accept the conservative minimum wage bill, hoping for later revisions, and it opposed admission of the JCP into the National Council Against the Security Treaty. Leftists in and allied with Sōhyō were trying to perpetuate forces which had been mobilized against the police bill and to direct them against the revised treaty. At its fifteenth convention, the Socialist Party that year called for a continuing joint struggle structure for which it proposed the name: "People's Council for Protection of Democracy." Ōta called for increased political action by organized labor, a united front, and sharper class consciousness in struggles ahead.

Socialist disappointment in elections to the House of Councillors in June 1959 was followed by dissatisfaction among union members against both SDP and Sōhyō leadership. Ōta and Iwai soon issued a statement favoring qualified cooperation with the Communists, accusing the Socialists of weakness, and suggesting the resignation of Suzuki and Asanuma. Obviously Sōhyō was pushing for a leftist combination against the security treaty. Four days later, the Sōhyō executive published an analysis of the election which accused the SDP of failing to make clear its working class basis and of not outlining plainly its program for a socialist revolution. "A party which does not base itself on the organized power and action of organized labor is not a socialist party," it declared. Since problems of the party could no longer be solved by dividing posts among factions, the center of power must be shifted from Diet members to activists related with the labor-farmer van. And Sōhyō warned that the Socialists should not necessarily count on its continued exclusive support, especially since the JCP had moderated its policies. During Sōhyō's convention in August 1959, the Takano forces failed to pass a resolution advocating political support of the Communist Party but succeeded in blocking a proposal to renew exclusive support of the SDP.

While the leftward trend within Sōhyō was progressing, in June the Suzuki faction abandoned its efforts to reconcile views in the right and left wings as to the essential nature of the Socialist Party. Even the Kawakami group declined to join the more militantly moderate position of Nishio and his colleagues, clinging instead to the compromise formula of 1955. After the Sōhyō statements, Suzuki's mainstream faction called for a class party orientation and replacement of the two highest party officers. Demands by Sōhyō's "Group to Strengthen the Socialist Party" could not be ignored, because of the party's weakness and dependence. These developments constituted the background for leftist charges against Nishio when the so-called "reconstruction convention" of the party met in September; they explain why Nishio and his group decided to make a stand and if necessary to secede. They also contribute to an understanding of the greater vehemence of the attack in the spring of 1960 against ratification of the revised security treaty. Further, we have seen that the new Democratic Socialist Party, inaugurated in January 1960, was promptly supported by Zenrō-Sōdōmei, a long-time ally of the Nishio faction. Although still reluctant, these labor leaders and unions were thus put under pressure to become more active politically.

The Japanese labor movement during those years had reached another turning point in its history. While, for the variety of reasons given, the Mindō leadership of Sōhyō was to a considerable extent emulating the Takano position—nearly completing another cycle of the Japanese labor movement—some of the same economic and political trends had given rise to factions and splits in a number of major unions as well as in a number of cause-supporting movements. Moderate minorities had split from the Sōhyō-affiliated federated unions of forestry and chemical workers, teachers, electric workers, post office and postal service employees, those in the tax agency, and railway craft workers. Some of these major federations were vital for the strength of Sōhyō. Again, as a decade previously when Communists and fellow travelers had carried labor tactics to extremes, factionalism and secessions continued. Formation of "second unions," begun in 1954, was accelerated during this period. In 1961, a moderate group seceded from the council of government workers' unions, and Sōdōmei-Zenrō-Dōmei continued to grow. Zenrō's president called the trend a "second Mindō movement."

In the spring of 1960, the attention of the SDP and the country was attracted to a bitter struggle at the rich Miike colliery of the Mitsui Mining Company located in Kyūshū. The Miike union belonged to a federation of Mitsui enterprise unions, which in turn was a component of Tanrō, one of the bastions of Sōhyō. In cutting back personnel at Miike (because industries and transportation had been switching from coal to oil), the management fired 120 members of the local Socialist Party branch and 31 Communists, among others. A considerable number of the Miike union's members had been indoctrinated by Sakisaka and associates in a long series of lectures in a labor school conducted by members of the institute where that professor was employed. So this became a *cause célèbre,* involving the validity of the militant leftism of the Rōnō faction and the current trend in Sōhyō. Not only did the enterprise federation reject instructions from Sōhyō to join a sympathetic strike, but the National Labor Relations Commission made a mediatory decision mainly favoring the company, and about one third of the membership of the original union formed a "second union." Zenrō and the new Democratic Socialist Party hurried to succor the dissident unionists, who returned to work. The company brought in goon squads to protect them, and violence followed. The SDP sent a delegation to observe, and soon Jiichirō Matsumoto was despatched to try to pacify matters in his familiar bailiwick. Of course, the Social Democrats and the Democratic Socialists took opposite views of the NLRC's decision, though the former left Tanrō free to accept it. This was just the most dramatic of a series of such incidents, and it illustrated attitudes and behavior of the two general labor federations and their allied Socialist parties.

The Ōta–Iwai leadership of Sōhyō was thus in a multiple dilemma; besides dealing with the many opposed interests already mentioned, it had to return at least in part to pursue economic aims and perhaps even to selective compromises with the SDP, much to the Takano faction's disgust. One reason why many Sōhyō delegates at the Socialist convention in 1960 voted for Kawakami as compromise candidate for party Chairman was to protect the solidarity of Sōhyō affiliates. These dilemmas help to explain why resistance to the widely unpopular security treaty again offered welcome relief to these leaders—it provided a common ground and distraction from the failure of several prominent disputes.

Since the political and labor crises of 1960, moderation has gained in both the Socialist Party and its main allied labor council. Both organizations have backed away from collaboration with the JCP, while leaving doors ajar for cooperation in certain campaigns. But moderation and Sōhyō's economic emphasis, dubbed "Japanese unionism" by its mainstream, have been stoutly challenged. In both that federation and the SDP, the dominant factions have accepted revisions, and their margins over the strength of their more radical critics have been rather slim.

Not only did structural reform precipitate collisions between major Socialist alignments (Kawakami followers, the Eda–Narita wing of the fading Suzuki mainstream, and Wada's factions versus the Suzuki–Sasaki radicals) but it became a gauge of the status of moderate policies in Sōhyō as well. We have noted how Ōta and the Heiwa Dōshikai in the SDP challenged structural reform when first publicly expounded in Japan. In Socialist conventions and in formulating action platforms the Sōhyō mainstream has itself been divided. While making concessions in their own sphere, some elements have combined with still more radical leaders to abet the Suzuki–Sasaki group in blunting the influence of the revisionists. Narita was able to retain the Party's secretary-generalship in February 1964, but had to endure further dilution of structural reform. Yet when Iwai proposed that the office of party vice-chairman be newly created with Sasaki as first incumbent, he was obliged to withdraw the proposal under the frown of a new power center which, in formulating high policy, has gained influence at the partial expense of Sōhyō's secretariat. This was the Meeting of Affiliated Trade Union Chairmen (Tōsan Iinchō Kaigi), more than half of whose members supported structural reform and its party proponents. They and majorities in their unions have reacted against excessive political action in view of economic changes and improvements, and to counter union-splitting offensives by right-wing labor–Socialist rivals. Some of their central committees have changed in personnel to favor greater moderation.

Meanwhile, more radical elements in the SDP, and especially in Sōhyō, had been weakened. Takano was no longer on the central committee of even his own union. However, it is much too early to hail as stable the degree of harassed moderation which these less extreme Marxist forces have attained. While it was clear that the Japanese economy had become one of the most advanced in the world, and that a new level of institutional development was being sought, consonant with the altered conditions, responses from organized workers and Socialists were likely to continue along a tortuous course.

FUNCTIONAL PARTY–UNION RELATIONS, LEFT AND RIGHT

We have noted, particularly on the left, the affinity and recognized needs of socialists and labor organizations for cooperation. They have striven jointly to mobilize voters during electoral campaigns. Both have encouraged Sōhyō affiliates and their locals to form election committees and joint struggle councils, hold meetings of workers and intellectuals in their districts, approach other labor and farmer unions, send youth teams to lead discussions in villages, and raise funds. Major labor federations are among the strongest organizations for attracting votes, especially for candidates in the national constituency for the House of Councillors. The teachers' union has been particularly influential, not only because of its access to youth in classrooms but also because of the social prestige of teachers and their influence in relations with parents.[25]

Politicians watch the national conventions of major industrial federations and of such general federations as Sōhyō and Zenrō (more recently Dōmei Kaigi) to see what parties and candidates are recommended for support by members. These actions, of course, reflect the relative strength of internal factions just before elections. Reliance of Socialist candidates on union backing has grown. As already indicated, these parties have usually suffered from a shortage of good candidates, and labor unions have been active in the nomination process. No quota for union candidates is set by the party, however. "Recommendation" of a candidate by a union has two meanings: (1) The party headquarters invites unions to recommend nominees from their districts, and, after candidacies have been approved by the party, the federation and its component unions recommend candidates to their members for support. (2) Unions and prefectural federations may take the initiative in making recommendations to the party; if there is already another strong candidate in a given district, or if the party has some objection to a proposal, discussions and adjustments are required. Usually recommendations are made through Sōhyō headquarters to the party, though the assistance of local politicians may also be solicited. The continuing low level of class and political consciousness, and the pervasiveness of traditional attitudes even among

25. The Japan Teachers' Union organized the Japan Democratic Education Political League. All of its candidates in 1956 belonged to this organization. The JTU contributed ¥10 million to the SDP campaign chest in that year. In 1958, 8% of the SDP representation in the Lower House and 19% of this group in the House of Councillors were composed of former JTU leaders. Certain other labor unions, notably the National Railway Workers' Union, the Federation of Coal Miners' Union, and the Postal Workers' Union have been politically very active.

workers are evinced by frequent electoral appeals to "support and show our gratitude to our chairman."[26]

On the national and district levels, especially the left Socialist election policy committees have included representatives from friendly unions. Since local labor organizations are usually stronger than party branches, the election committees of the two are commonly almost synonymous. Sometimes the local candidate is chosen only after long discussions, and campaign strategy—how to convince fellow union members, relatives, school friends, neighbors, etc.—is carefully planned. Both members of paid union staffs and volunteers can be mobilized for campaign activities. Labor candidates sometimes receive funds from the enterprises with which they and their unions are identified. But excessive resort to these party–union practices can reach the point of diminishing returns and can result in members feeling that their union has grown too partisan and has made excessive demands on them.

Two kinds of labor–party joint committees in Tokyo, sometimes with counterparts on lower levels, coordinate activities in and outside of the Diet. Leftist elements tend to predominate in both the Labor Liaison Committee and in the Joint Diet Struggles Committee, which is organized for each legislative session. The former is supposed to convene at least twice monthly and usually is attended by the Socialist Party's Secretary-General, its chiefs of the Labor and Diet Activities Sections, and the chief of its Policy Planning Board. Sōhyō is repre-

26. For an example of a union paper's advice to members telling how to rally others to the support of the SDP, see *Shitetsu Shimbun,* June 23, 1956; and for a hortatory article entitled: "Let Us Elect Our Chairman Ichikawa to the House of Councillors," see *Zenchūrō,* June 25, 1965.

In addition to distributing newspapers, pamphlets, and fliers telling members and their families the names and views of favored socialist candidates, in some towns jointly sponsored workers' conferences hear socialist candidates speak. "Table talks" are led by some union leaders during factory rest periods, and sometimes invited candidates give short speeches during noon recesses. Political discussion meetings are sometimes held in company dormitories. A few unions sponsor "continuous" political discussion groups. Door-to-door canvassing, though illegal, is done to some extent, particularly to the homes of union members. Most electioneering is still promoted inside the union, though inter-union cooperation has grown, and—especially under Takano's leadership—attempts have been made by union members to persuade "outside" elements to vote for "progressive" candidates. Sōhyō headquarters often exhort campaign personnel to be as militant as the rather severe Public Election Law permits. Some features of this measure apparently were designed to curb labor's campaign tactics. See Soukup, "Labor and Politics," pp. 185, 187, 193–96, 201–02.

sented by its Chairman and certain Vice-Chairmen, its Secretary-General, picked members of its Central Executive Committee, and the chief of its Political Department. Selected intellectuals and SDP Diet members with labor union connections are also invited. These committees have attempted to coordinate economic struggles with political strategy, especially with the advocacy of, and opposition to, controversial legislation; but they can make no binding decisions. They also have sought to combine the efforts of private and governmental workers' unions with those of farmers' unions. Often conservative budget-making has borne the brunt of their attack, and they also have made concerted attempts to overthrow a cabinet, dissolve the Diet, block renewal of the security treaty, opposite revision of labor laws, pass a minimum wage bill, and push through a "base-up" wage adjustment for governmental employees.

Representation on these committees is usually extensive, including chairmen of the Diet Activities Committees of the Socialist parties and other such political leaders, plus delegates from the major labor federations of left and right, from Kankōrō, Zenrō, Shin Sambetsu, and important independent unions. Right Socialist, Zenrō, and Shin Sambetsu representatives usually have as little as possible to do with the Marxist Labor-Farmer element in these groups; representatives of independent unions are not regarded as continuing members. The chairman is usually the chief of Sōhyō's Political Department, and the committee's Secretary-General is usually from the Council of National and Local Governmental Workers' Unions. It is natural that joint struggle committees are most active in promoting the wage demands of governmental employees. The confidence of workers in private industrial unions in these successive committees has declined since the failure of efforts in 1952 to prevent the enactment of legislation to control strikes and the Subversive Activities Prevention Law.

Already we have noted the interpenetration of top Socialist Party and labor federation personnel and the influence they exert in each other's central and local organs, as well as on each other's national conventions. Many special ad hoc committees have also been formed to hammer out common strategies and propaganda for specific political objectives. In the Diet and in press conferences, SDP leaders have tried to rationalize labor aims and tactics.

Outside the Diet there have been, of course, numerous other modes of cooperation between Social Democrats and their labor allies, for example, conferences designed chiefly to direct the thinking of labor activists and socialists. In addition, however, a number of national councils for various causes, while including Sōhyō and left-wing Socialists among their most energetic components, have been designed to attract groups and leaders from the whole political spectrum. If, in these, Communists have been working behind certain labor and socialist elements, the latter have also tried to influence other groups to give mass reinforcement to SDP policies. The hope is that such movements, labor offensives, and electoral campaigns will stimulate and influence each other.

When the Occupation terminated and Prime Minister Yoshida appointed Nobusuke Kishi to chair a committee to study revisions of the Constitution, labor and socialist leaders shared the anxieties of many others; in November 1953, a Conference to Safeguard the Peace Constitution was sponsored by Sōhyō and attended by representatives of the Socialist parties among others. Sōhyō and its closest Socialist ally were the backbone of the National Federation for Defense of the Constitution which was soon launched, and Katayama became its chairman until after the Nishio schism in 1960. Foremost among its 150 affiliates were the three socialist factions and some 64 labor organizations, including all of the major federations.

A more militant series of anti-American movements were mounted mainly by Sōhyō with left Socialists in secondary roles. Both organizations sent representatives to rallies opposing Mutual Security Aid in 1953. Protest demonstrations against U.S. military bases were carried out at Uchinada, Asamayama, and Myōgisan; and these were extended and intensified elsewhere until in 1957 it was announced that most American ground forces would soon be withdrawn. This plus the defeat of the Takano faction caused Sōhyō to cease direct leadership and to fall back on cooperation with the Anti-Military Base Liaison Council, formed in September 1955, and centered on the left-wing Socialists. To keep inciting hostility against the United States, a National Movement Liaison Board for Solution of the Okinawa Problem was organized after 1956. We have already noted the national council formed to oppose signing and ratifying the revised security treaty in 1959–60. Since 1962 there have been repeated demonstrations against allowing United States nuclear submarines (without nuclear warheads) to use Japanese bases.

In a somewhat different pattern, the Japan-China and Japan-Soviet

Friendship Associations are guided by labor and party leftists, well known pro-communists, and a few outright JCP members. They attract and use as a partial façade more conservative business people and politicians who, motivated by other kinds of opportunism, also desire renewal of diplomatic and commercial (if not cultural) relations with the Communist states. Sōhyō and all the leftist parties, as well as numerous business and veterans' organizations, sent congratulations to the National Council for Resumption of Diplomatic Relations with Soviet Russia and Communist China when it was inaugurated in the spring of 1955. Sōhyō joined it in November. Leftists in these movements are, of course, eager for Japan to move out of the American orbit; some, but not right-wing Socialists, would probably then move further toward the opposing bloc of "peace-loving nations."

Even this summary does not exhaust the list of efforts in which Sōhyō and leftist Socialist factions have cooperated. During 1953–55, they jointly made a daily of the *Shakai Taimuzu* (Socialist Times), hoping to rival the Communists' *Akahata* (Red Flag). Their Educational Sections have operated a modest number of "labor universities" for the indoctrination and training of young trade union leaders. Also, in July 1955, they led in forming a National Cultural Congress the aims of which were, in part, to imbue youth and intellectuals with nationalism and a determination to make Japan independent of the United States, and to coordinate their defense of the Constitution.

In the right wing of labor–party activities such factors as Fabian moderation, perhaps more traditional modes of thought and behavior, greater emphasis on autonomy of the two types of organization and on the economic objectives of workers explain the less militant nature of cooperation between labor and Democratic Socialists. Furthermore, affiliates of moderate federations like Sōdōmei and—since their successive inauguration in 1954 and 1962—of Zenrō and Dōmei Kaigi, insist that union tactics must consider the general condition of the nation's economy and of specific industries.[27] Veterans in both these

27. The Democratic Socialist Party is as far left as most businesses of sizable capitalization are willing to contribute to; its share of such grants is smaller than those of conservative parties.

Soukup ("Labor and Politics," pp. 209–10 and n. 47) cites *Asahi Shimbun* (Jan. 27, 1955) as reporting that Sōdōmei expected to contribute ¥7 million to the Right Socialist campaign and ¥1 million to the Left. However, Sōdōmei donations have often been made locally except for candidates in the national constituency for the House of Councillors. The Seamen's Union is an important contributor, but Zenrō as a whole was rather weak in this respect.

right-wing spheres mostly belonged to the prewar legal left; they still deplore "direct action" and tendencies toward illegal methods. They point out, for example, how the excesses of 1960 led to passage by 1964 of an act outlawing the use of politically motivated violence in the capital region. They insist that the Diet should be the only arena where organized workers seek to attain political aims; that they should work through the Democratic Socialist Party; and that, though labor federations may try to influence the Socialist Party, they should not attempt to impose their policies on it by "organizational pressure." Such unions have discouraged the diversion of their best leaders into the party organization.

With some local exceptions, however, moderate labor unions and federations do not provide their political allies with as strong electoral support as do leftist organizations, and for a number of reasons. Small enterprise unions federated on a regional basis are not as centralized structurally for such action. The electioneering methods and discipline of these unions are less vigorous; therefore, and because their leaders may be more careful to respect the freedom of union members to vote as individuals, the proportion of workers who follow union recommendations tends to be smaller. Moreover, workers in some of the industries in which these unions are located are more susceptible to managerial influence.

Like the Left SDP–Sōhyō combination, the Right Socialists before party reunification participated at first with Sōdōmei in a liaison council which sometimes met almost weekly. After the organization of Zenrō, and later of Dōmei Kaigi, it has met nearly every month to discuss such matters as planned and pending legislation, disputes, joint electoral campaign strategy, (in 1954–55) SDP reunification, and (in 1959–60) organization of the separate Democratic Socialist Party. Zenrō had a Political Action Committee, and cooperation was close between the Research Section of Sōdōmei and the Right Socialist Policy Planning Board. After SDP reunification, right-wing federations had in part to adjust to relations with bodies which included representatives from leftist party factions and unions, but we have seen that the moderate labor federations continued to reject reunification of the labor movement. And when Nishio and his adherents bolted the SDP in 1959, he could count on support from Sōdōmei-Zenrō.

The extent of such political assistance was next tested and found inadequate in the fall elections of 1960, following which the new Democratic Socialist Party was in danger of ceasing to exist on the national level. Although there still were principled misgivings in these labor circles, energetic measures were required. Need was also felt for a context which would reconcile the rivalry that had developed between Sōdōmei and Zenrō in matters of local organization and the forming of new regional federations of unions. Therefore, the confederation Dōmei Kaigi was launched in 1962, two more years being required for its consolidation. It was to integrate the two existing right-wing labor federations together with Zenkankō and a number of independent unions which were critical of Sōhyō. In cooperation with the Dōmei Kaigi, Zenrō earlier had formed a Committee for Political Action to promote educational work and intensive electioneering. Support for the DSP had thus improved in the elections of November 1963.

SOCIALIST LABOR POLICIES

The proposals of left and right Socialists on behalf of workers are mainly to be found in annual action programs adopted by conventions, in five-year or longer term plans, in a somewhat similar set of three fundamental platforms, in speeches in the Diet, and in statements issued by the parties' Central Committees and by individual leaders. Here we shall indicate phases of Socialist thinking about labor problems and some persistent issues between the left and right wings; a number of further policies will be given succinct, topical treatment.

During the early years of reconstruction and democratization, Social Democrats eagerly supported reforms already mentioned. They advocated democratic workshop and management committees, training institutes for young workers, health centers and birth control information, as well as improved social security. During periods of unemployment, and increasingly with the intensification of this problem before 1955, the Socialists urged expanded public works and natural resource development schemes as well as more efficient employment information services. Then and since they have called for more adequate unemployment insurance, the elimination of unfair treatment of temporary workers, reduction of working hours and extension of the shift system, retraining of the technologically unemployed, and emphasis on specific sectors most affected by unemployment.

During the party's participation in two successive governments, the right wing particularly had to face realistically the inflationary force of wage raises. By the time the "Dodge line" disinflationary program was inaugurated, however, both main factions, and especially the left, could revert to the less responsible tactics of opposition politicos trying to reap advantages from every aggrieved group, notably labor.

Reduction of taxes on lower incomes and a minimum wage have been perennial emphases. Right-wingers are agreeable to wage floors varying according to industry, while most leftists will compromise no further than to approve "equal pay for equal work." Sōhyō and the leftist Socialists long demanded a state-guaranteed minimum of ¥8,000 per month for workers 18 or more years of age, but recent booms and inflation have required revisions in this demand.

During party cleavages, divergence in the two SDP approaches to labor problems has been even more marked. This has stemmed chiefly from differences in their views of capitalism and of relations with employers and labor federations. It has also reflected differing emphases on economic as compared with political objectives. Semantic, ideological, and emotional differences in regard to the meaning and application of democracy have been accentuated. Open rivalry has encouraged policy divergence and recrimination. These have been years that saw opportunities for projecting domestic controversies into the somewhat similar issues agitating international labor and socialist movements.

Nevertheless, both parties were agreed (as Suzuki declared in the Diet in 1952) that it was unsound for 20 per cent of the national budget to be spent for armaments while only 8 per cent was devoted to social security. Both regarded the army as an agency for conservative indoctrination, paternalistic exploitation, and potentially for control of the labor movement. Since unprecedented economic growth became possible after 1957, moderate armaments and considerably improved social security under conservative auspices obliged socialists to dispute mainly the levels of both.

After a conference of leaders from both parties in mid-November 1954, there were increasing signs of compromises toward a new joint platform as a basis for reunification. The labor section of this bipartisan formula, as it emerged from negotiations by September 1955, contained five brief points, the repercussions of which in labor circles we have already noted. Close cooperation between the SDP and labor organizations was again pledged toward "peaceful realization" of a socialist society. And a "united front of free democratic unions"—free, that is, from governmental or company controls—was declared to be an aim.[28]

The vicious cycle of "confrontation," marked by conservative revisionism taking advantage of any loss by labor of public sympathy because of its extreme tactics, has resulted in a series of restrictive measures. Since 1948, especially leftist unions and Socialists have been attempting to restore to local and national government employees the competence to bargain collectively and to strike. In vain the SDP in 1949 opposed revision of the Labor Union Law to ban the use of violence, enlarge the definition of unfair labor union practices, clarify the responsibilities of unions, and strengthen arbitral commissions. Basically it was the increase of governmental supervision which evoked opposition. Also the Socialists and labor federations tried to defeat partial amendment of the Labor Relations Adjustment Law which was enacted to restrict strikes in public corporations. Such efforts reached an apex in 1952, when these same forces were mobilized against the Subversive Activities Prevention Bill and a law to prohibit general strikes. They also tried unsuccessfully to block amendments of the Labor Standards Law and changes in the Labor Relations Adjustment Law which would permit the Minister of Labor to intervene in public utility strikes. Moreover, it made individuals liable to penalty for illegal labor dispute activities.

Opposition against the expansion and strengthening of police forces began in 1949 and became intensified when the outbreak of the Korean War stimulated SCAP encouragement of Japanese rearmament and buttressed public security. In 1952, an amendment to the police law which permitted centralization of military and police powers under the Prime Minister during emergencies was opposed in vain. Socialists and laborites argued that the Law Concerning Maintenance of Order in Mass Demonstrations would violate constitutional rights

28. Many other measures have been urged by the SDP on behalf of workers. The left-wingers have advocated abolition of the widespread practice of hiring temporary workers. They have pressed more ardently for governmental spending programs and have denounced deflationary policies. And they have proposed application of the Labor Standards Law even to small enterprises, as well as new legislation to protect domestic workers. The Socialists have promoted bills to protect industrial workers from silicosis and another measure on behalf of waterfront laborers. They have advocated an ambitious program of housing for workers. Both wings have favored expansion and strengthening of labor banks.

of expression and assembly, for the police rather than Public Safety Commissions would be likely to impose restraints. The actual intent, they averred, was to suppress mass movements by declaring them to impair the public welfare. The SDP and Sōhyō fought determinedly, after the demonstrations and violence in 1960, to prevent enactment of a law which would prohibit such methods of direct pressure on the Diet, but again, by 1964, they failed.

The recovery of confidence and power on the part of large capitalist interests by 1953, the deflationary policies adopted after the Korean War boom, and the rather automatic operation of conservative majorities in the Diet discouraged the opposition forces, yet they kept struggling. By March 1954—despite remonstrance from Socialists, labor leaders, and some intellectuals—two bills were passed which placed teachers under the financial control of the Ministry of Education and attempted to restrict their political activities. Right-wing Socialists upheld the principle of the political neutralism of public school instruction but were critical of these laws as enacted.

With increased vigor after the fall of 1954, the conservatives have proposed further revision of the Labor Standards and Labor Relations Adjustment Laws and have confronted the same opponents. Slowdowns and other short-of-strike dispute tactics by national railway workers and employees of certain other public corporations led, in 1956, to renewed controversy about further proposals for changes in the Public Corporations Labor Relations Law and the National Public Service Law.

Accelerating economic and technological dynamism since the late 'fifties has not only challenged or belied certain cherished themes of the labor-socialist alliance; it has whetted the desire—particularly on the left—to press on toward the long-discussed reorganization of union structure: from individual enterprise units to centralized, industry-wide unions. The more syndicalistically inclined talk about organized labor developing its own system of social security as an inducement toward this goal. The conservative elites recognize that new industrial zones and a new plane of industrialization will outmode labor organizations based on regions and workshops; indeed they have already become somewhat anachronistic. But serious obstacles persist.[29]

29. Some of the impediments to reorganizing labor unions along industry-wide lines stem from the loyalty that middle-rank labor leaders feel both to their unions and to their modernizing companies. They consciously prize their responsible positions. Their

Socialists and labor leaders continue to advocate the recovery of "fundamental rights" by workers, and in this connection have championed Japan's adherence to I.L.O. Convention No. 87, a basic document defining and supporting such rights, even for unions of governmental employees. By the fall of 1964, bills to accomplish this had been submitted to the Diet no less than six times, until at last—during formal I.L.O. hearings in Japan—Premier Ikeda impelled the LDP to introduce and enact the needed legislation.

Sōhyō and the SDP have usually reacted negatively to the personnel rationalization entailed in some of the booming economic growth and adjustment. Right-wingers stress the need for prior consultations and for shock-absorbing measures to which unions, management, and government should contribute. Leaders in both orbits argue that such growth should achieve for workers price benefits and improved conditions of labor. Demand for a 40-hour work week has spread. Part of the agitation for much more adequate social insurance has been coupled with renewed calls for better workers' housing.

Neither wing is satisfied with the mild Minimum Wage Law which went into effect in mid-April 1959. The measure had been sponsored by the Liberal Democrats, but only after long promotion of the cause from left of center. Such wage minima have thus come to be encouraged in the form of agreements among a majority of employers in a given field of production, nationally or regionally. The government will help to administer and enforce uniform application of such agreements within their intended scope. In other fields, where managements do not take the initiative, the government will make studies and recommendations. A Minimum Wage Council has been established to cooperate with the Ministry of Labor and prefectural Labor Standards Offices.

---

statuses in unions are commonly related to their positions and functions in workshops. Many of the changes now in progress tend either to advance the vigorous worker-leaders, bringing them closer to management, or to promote younger workers with new skills. Older workers who have to meet competition from the younger tend to advance less rapidly and even to be crowded out. This, of course, affects their union positions. There is visible a growing gap between workers in their forties—who have been more politically ardent—and younger workers, who have been educated since the war, are more rational in their evaluations and hence are more matter-of-fact regarding both enterprises and unions, and tend to be less interested in liberation of their class than in improved income and working conditions. Kiyoshi Ebata, "The Labor Unions Today," *Japan Quarterly, 10* (July-Sept. 1963), 322–23.

Another perennial and ambitious aim of both evolutionary and revolutionary labor-socialists is to eliminate the dual structure in industry and labor organizations. This, of course, refers to the scale, prosperity, and relatively high wage levels of large as compared with small and medium-scale enterprises. Actually, however, economic forces in recent years have been accomplishing more than all previously organized efforts with regard to wages. The shortage of skilled labor has obliged many small employers to pay slightly higher initial wages than do some larger firms!

Though the structural reform of socialism has been both advocated and opposed, it has had a revisionist effect on the policies of the SDP and a number of its allied unions. Emphasis has come to be placed more on realizable reforms than on precipitating revolution. And the need to ally more practically and durably with those nonproletarian elements which also criticize concentrated capitalist power is more clearly recognized. Both wings of the Social Democratic and labor movements insist that workers must be accorded their share in the gains of advancing technology and economic growth, and that further progress should not be at the expense of employment and good conditions of labor.

Spokesmen in the right wing of these twin movements refer to "workers" in a broader sense. They are willing to face the prospect that, in a high-level and still expanding socio-economy, workers may move toward hitherto middle-class styles of living and thinking. At the present stage, they tolerate regulated capitalism and urge welfare state policies. They avoid excessive stress on ideology, oppose communist influence and proletarian dictatorship, and reject class struggle—as well as the Hegelian dualistic collision-synthesis as a touchstone of social history. Moderate Socialist and labor leaders favor more democracy in industry and, at least avowedly, in unions. They both encourage the trend toward more modern labor–management relations and improved personnel policies. By being more adjustable in the face of manifold economic and social changes, they hope to strengthen their movements and to expand at the expense of their more inflexible rivals.

TO WHAT DEGREE DO WORKERS SUPPORT THE SDP?

Elections by secret ballots in complex societies always elude complete analysis, yet much can be understood by consideration of current issues and the public temper; party events, characteristics, and policies which may attract and repel various interest-sectors; special relations between organized groups and parties; and the recent history of nomination and campaign methods. Having described and illustrated most of these related factors, we now examine the main data which indicate how workers, both unionized and unorganized, have responded electorally to efforts of the Social Democratic Parties.

Especially in the left wing there is unmistakable emphasis on a class party reliant chiefly on industrial labor support. Of 81 successful SDP candidates for the House of Representatives who replied to a questionnaire immediately after the elections of February 1955, 66 mentioned labor unions as their foremost supporting organizations. Weighting revealed almost twice as much emphasis on this support by leftists as compared with the impressions of right-wing candidates. Only 11 right Socialist respondents, but 35 leftists, reported support from Sōhyō and local federations; 31 right-wingers and 60 leftists mentioned support by Sōhyō component unions; 7 right Socialists and only 2 on the left reported support by Sōdōmei and affiliated unions; 14 right-wingers and only 3 leftists mentioned support by Zenrō and related unions; 13 of the former and 33 of the latter reported support by local unions. When asked to rank in order of importance their support by various types of organized interest groups, all left Socialist respondents mentioned labor unions and 44 gave them first place; 41 of the 43 right-wing respondents mentioned labor unions, and 28 gave them primary stress. Analysis of occupational groups among this sample of Socialist Representatives revealed that all except those from agrarian backgrounds emphasized support by organized workers.[30] The salience of Sōhyō, weaker support by right-wing labor federations, and the considerable importance of local unions were thus indicated.

These, however, were the impressions of Socialist politicians when replying for indirect publication. Other data indicate that Socialist leaders may exaggerate this kind of support both from theoretical bias and because obviously labor organizations do provide the *best organized* sector of their support. Just after that election of 1955, Haruo Wada, Secretary-General of Zenrō, estimated that only half of the

30. Cole et al., "Support for Japanese Social Democrats in 1955," pp. 7–8, 10, 18.

13 million votes for the SDP had been cast by "pure workers" (while others estimated that about 7.3 million unionists and members of their families supported the Socialists). Liberally totaling the number of unionized workers at 6.5 million, and calculating that there were some 15 million unorganized workers and their families, Wada was puzzled as to where the other labor votes had gone.[31] Newspaper analysts estimate that from 30 to 40 per cent of Japan's labor voters usually support conservative parties, and this is borne out by national opinion polls. The "don't know" and other columns indicating indifference or indecision would suggest that some workers abstain.

Nevertheless, the degree of organized labor's influence has been impressive. After the Upper House elections in 1956, there were 26 Sōhyō-affiliated Representatives and 38 such Councillors in the Diet, together constituting one fifth of the Socialist Party's delegation. In the general elections of May 1958, Sōhyō recommended 182, while Zenrō approved 127, SDP candidates (with some overlapping); the former federation promised to contribute ¥150 million and the latter ¥70 million to the Socialist campaign. After the polls closed it was found that, whereas 35 Socialist incumbents had lost their seats, 34 freshmen Sōhyō candidates had won. In that year it was estimated that less than 28,000 (well over one third) of the entire SDP membership was composed of workers, most of them organized, but that only three to five thousand of these could be considered activists. In elections to the House of Councillors in June 1959, Sōhyō recommended 16 Socialists in the national constituency and about 36 in local districts; 18 of the Socialist candidates in that campaign were union leaders. Since 1959, former labor leaders have comprised 56 per cent of the SDP contingent in the Lower House and nearly two thirds of its Councillors in the Upper Chamber.

If one maps the distribution of right and left labor federation memberships by prefectures and compares them with pro-Socialist votes in each of the postwar national elections, one is struck by the correspondence of distribution. If, further, the prefectures are arranged in five groupings in order of the strength of organized labor, it is found that the distribution of Socialist votes can be similarly arranged. But, especially in urban areas, how do we know that the official policies of

31. Soukup, "Labor and Politics in Postwar Japan," p. 186.

unions are persuading their members, that many union members are not voting conservatively, and that other social sectors may not be fully as important as labor in support of the Social Democrats?[32]

Opinion polls—41 nationwide and 17 in the Tokyo area between January 1948 and March 1957—indicated that students and the salariat were proportionately heavier supporters of the SDP than were workers, if unorganized workers are included.[33] And, although certain national unions have actively campaigned in rural areas, more than half of all Socialist legislators are elected from agrarian and mixed districts, where labor unions are less influential. Small wonder that party strategists sometimes, though usually in private, advise their colleagues during campaigns to exert as much as 70 per cent of their efforts in attracting non-union support.

Only a few national polls by *Asahi Shimbun* distinguish between the political preferences of organized and unorganized labor. As might be expected, support of the SDP by unorganized workers is markedly weaker. In mid-October 1948, 40 per cent of the interviewed organized workers favored the Social Democrats, while only 18 per cent of those outside unions did so; nearly a year later the comparable figures were 39 and 28 per cent. In mid-April 1950, 37 per cent of sampled union members and 19 per cent of adults in their families were pro-SDP, while 26 per cent of unorganized workers and 13 per cent of their adult family members were similarly inclined. Of the 81 successful Social Democratic candidates who responded after the elections of 1955 to questions about support from unorganized social strata, 47 leftist Representatives mentioned unorganized labor and of these 31 considered its support to be of preeminent importance. Among the right-wing respondents, 33 mentioned this sector, 15 recognizing its foremost significance.

Before looking further into what news service polls indicate about

32. When the headquarters even of some Sōhyō-affiliated industrial unions decide officially to support left Socialist candidates, some local branches may divide the votes of members between the two Socialist wings, and even among other parties. In 1953, a poll of members of the radical Automobile Workers' Union at the Koyasu plant of the Nissan Company found that 28% of them supported the right Socialists. A survey of 300 factory workers compared with the responses of 400 citizens at large in the Jōtō area of Tokyo's sixth electoral district (in October 1952) indicated that twice as many workers as others intended to vote as their unions or other associations advised. Nevertheless, only 27% responded to this effect. The latter results are taken from a manuscript report of the survey conducted by the Senkyō Jittai Chōsakai (Society for Research on Electoral Conditions) led by Professors Masamichi Rōyama and Nobushige Ukai.

33. Cole and Nakanishi, *Japanese Opinion Polls*, pp. 1–278.

the electoral tendencies of laborers, it is interesting to note the stronger support of socialist parties by workers in a sample of 899 males of voting age in Japan's six largest cities. Their political opinions were correlated with occupational and class identifications by a research committee of the Japan Sociological Association in 1952. Sixty-three per cent of the white-collar workers, police, and firemen supported reformist parties, while the same preference was shown by 61.7 per cent of industrial, craft, and transport workers.[34]

Numerous polls as to political preference and support show some fluctuation on the part of labor voters, but usually 25 to 33 per cent favored the SDP; sometimes support fell as low as 21 per cent, and at others it rose as high as 43 per cent. Labor support for conservative parties was often higher than for the SDP, but after the emergence of the two-main-party system the proportion of workers preferring the reunified Social Democratic Party seemed to be greater, usually more than 40 per cent being of this persuasion. From one fifth to one third of the labor respondents have been in noncommittal or indecisive political categories.

After the party split late in 1951, the polls indicate that most pro-Socialist labor supporters chose between the two wings. Studies of electoral results during 1951–55 show that, despite considerable rivalry, the two parties were usually strong in different districts or their candidates appealed to somewhat different elements in the same areas, so that after reunification they could be at least partially complementary. Labor support seems to have been most influential in the industrialized and mining districts of Hokkaidō, in Tokyo, Kanagawa, and in the urban parts of Aiichi, Osaka, Hyōgo, and Fukuoka. Probably because of the conservatism of workers in small and medium enterprises (less than 6 per cent of whom were then unionized), general samples of labor between April 1952 and December 1954 almost invariably showed a preference for the Right over the Left Socialists. But the relative advantage seems to have been mildly reversed after the latter date.[35] Fragmentary evidence indicates that the labor fol-

34. "Report of a Sample Survey of Social Stratification and Mobility in the Six Large Cities of Japan" (Tokyo, mimeo., Dec. 1952); also, Allan B. Cole, *Japanese Society and Politics: The Impact of Social Stratification and Mobility on Politics* (Boston, Department of Government, Boston University, 1956), pp. 64–65.

35. Soukup ("Labor and Politics in Postwar Japan," Table 6, pp. 190–92) asked leaders of leftist, right-wing, and neutral unions to estimate the political proclivities of their members. It was estimated that 65–70% of the members of the Electrical Workers' Union

lowing of the Right Socialists may have been somewhat steadier than that of the rival wing.

Still considering workers in and out of unions, it may be surprising to find that, judging from the polls, the Social Democrats actually elicited disappointingly slight support for two of their sustained and most publicized policies: opposition to rearmament and to revision of the Constitution, especially of Article IX which bans war-making power. The responses of 550 labor *leaders* to a questionnaire in 1953 showed much higher interest in these problems than did the newspaper polls of workers at large. The latter indicated that even before the Korean War, and until international tensions relaxed in and after 1953, a majority of workers favored defensive rearmament and were on the whole satisfied with the existing police establishment. However, if questions were posed in terms of choice between rearmament and stabilization of livelihood—as the Socialists tried to describe the issue—most laborers emphasized the latter.

In and after 1953 there has been a more even division between workers who favored and those who opposed rearmament. Growth of labor nationalism was indicated by the greater opposition to U.S. military aid and bases than to rearmament after 1953. Before that year, the polls showed that a consistent plurality of workers preferred to have American forces stay in Japan for a limited period of time. Some nine polls indicated massive ignorance among workers concerning the Constitution and proposed amendments. Modest pluralities have usually opposed revision, probably not so much to safeguard Article IX as because amendments might threaten important guarantees of workers' rights.

We can justifiably conclude that not only do industrial workers constitute a minority in Japanese society but also that the Socialist parties do not yet attract a majority of their votes—only a plurality. Political ignorance and apathy are still widespread in this sector, but more recently rational moderation has been growing. However, the counter-elite of labor is highly class-conscious and politically aware,

---

preferred the Left Socialist Party (1954–55) and 15% the Right Socialists. The respective figures for the other unions were: National Railway Workers' Union: 61% and 23%; Coal Mine Workers' Union: 70% and 10%; the Electrical Workers' Federation (independent): 40% and 50%; about 70–80% of the members of five regional branches of the Seamen's Union favored the Right SDP, while about 10% of three of them inclined toward the Left wing.

and the activism of labor organizations provides the Socialists with support which exceeds in significance the votes which can be mobilized. Unionized labor, with political allies, can to some extent exact a price for its cooperation in essential services and productive processes.

11. The Socialist Party and the Farmers

By 1962 the proportion of employed Japanese relying partly or wholly on agriculture for livelihoods had declined to about 30 per cent, but as late as 1955 it was still around 40 per cent. Without significant support from this large sector, no party can hope to gain or keep power.

Japanese peasants have long been noted for their conservatism, tenacious attachment to the soil, and an ingrained attitude which has seen tradition as the truest guide to conduct and has often shown deep prejudice against all forms of urban intellectualism. But by 1945, when the Socialist Party began to seek support from the countryside, these farmers were no longer a mere "sack of rice." The great rise in agricultural productivity in the last century—still continuing—has provided evidence that traditions can yield to technical innovations. Rural areas have shared with towns and cities a system of universal education well established by the beginning of this century. Conscription, accompanied by intensive political indoctrination of military personnel for nearly a century, along with widespread diffusion of the national press, and (more recently) broadcasting, have contributed to a development of national consciousness and an awareness of, as well as a sense of involvement in, national political issues. The

---

This chapter was basically written by Ronald P. Dore. It has been slightly condensed and updated by members of this project.

party, moreover, had an established tradition of prewar left-wing activity in rural areas on which to base its approaches to farmers. The origins and nature of these previous movements have been described in the companion to this volume.[1]

The prewar "problem of the villages" was compounded of two distinguishable strains of protest. There was the protest of the tenants directed against the landlords, demanding reduction of rents and improvement in conditions of tenancy, and there was the protest of rural classes as a whole, demanding a greater share for agriculture in the distribution of national income.

Events of the early 'thirties changed the character of the movement. The agricultural depression intensified the second voice of protest from the villages—the demand for policies favoring the agricultural classes as a whole—and in it the sectional protest of the tenants began to be submerged. It was, moreover, the Communists and leftist Rōnōha leaders who were more inclined to foster the divisive class antagonism of the tenants; with their arrest and disappearance, the Japan-Labor (Nichirōkei) and Socio-Democratic (Shaminkei) leaders who remained were more inclined, for reasons of ideology as well as of expediency, to shift emphasis from *tenant* demands to *farmer* demands, which had the support also of the army and could claim as their justification not the promptings of alien ideologies but the need to preserve the integrity of the countryside as the guardian of truly Japanese virtues.

As we shall see, many elements of the prewar history of the farmers' movement have recurred since the war. Land reform, by largely solving the particular grievances of the tenants, has changed the expression of the original leftist impulse to champion the underdog without, however, destroying that impulse. At the same time, the definition of the main enemy as capitalism has provided a theoretical justification for a Socialist appeal to *all* farmers, while an increasing concern with the capture of power, as distinct from agitation in perpetual opposition, has added a tactical incentive for such a policy.

THE IMMEDIATE POSTWAR PERIOD

The formation of the Social Democratic Party in 1945 brought together men with a great diversity of experience in political activity in

1. See Totten, *The Social Democratic Movement in Prewar Japan.*

LINEAGES OF JAPANESE FARMERS' UNIONS

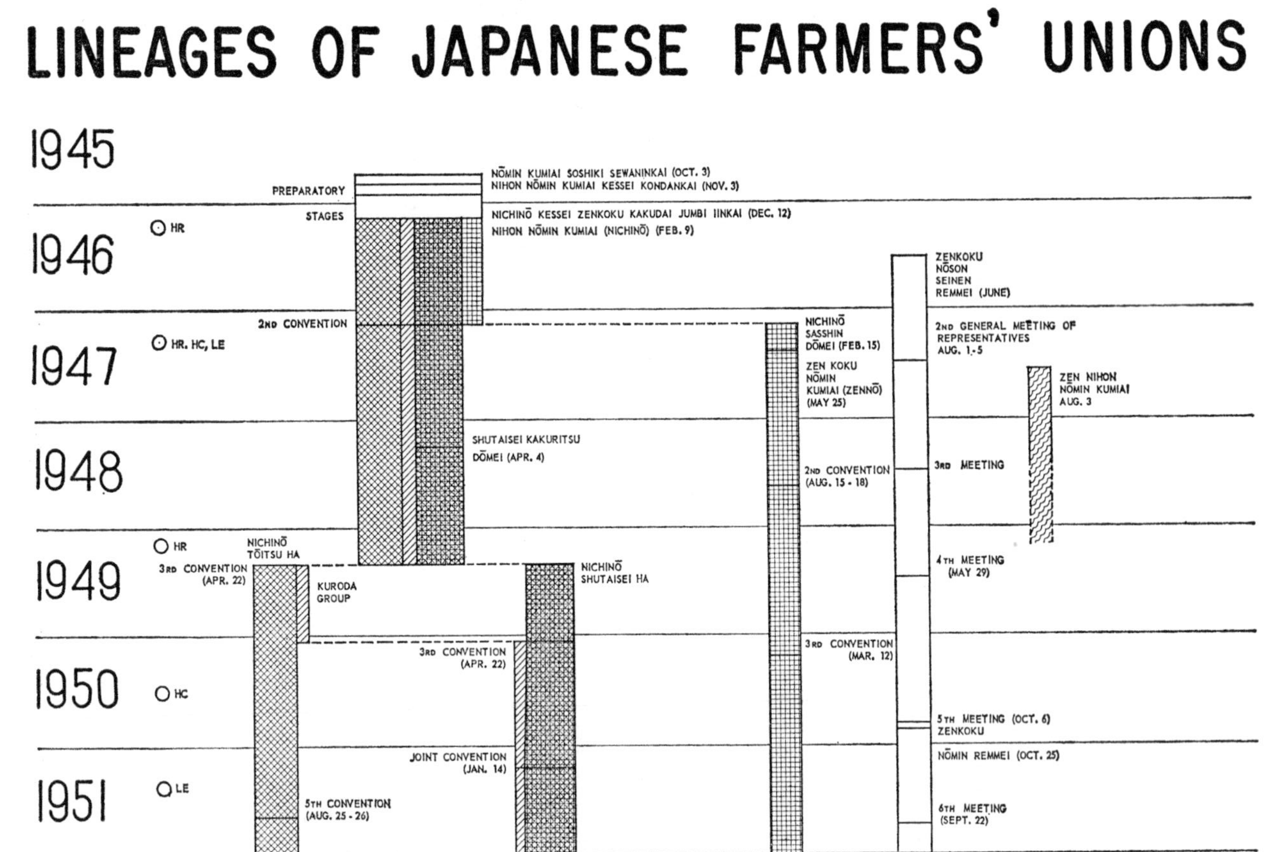

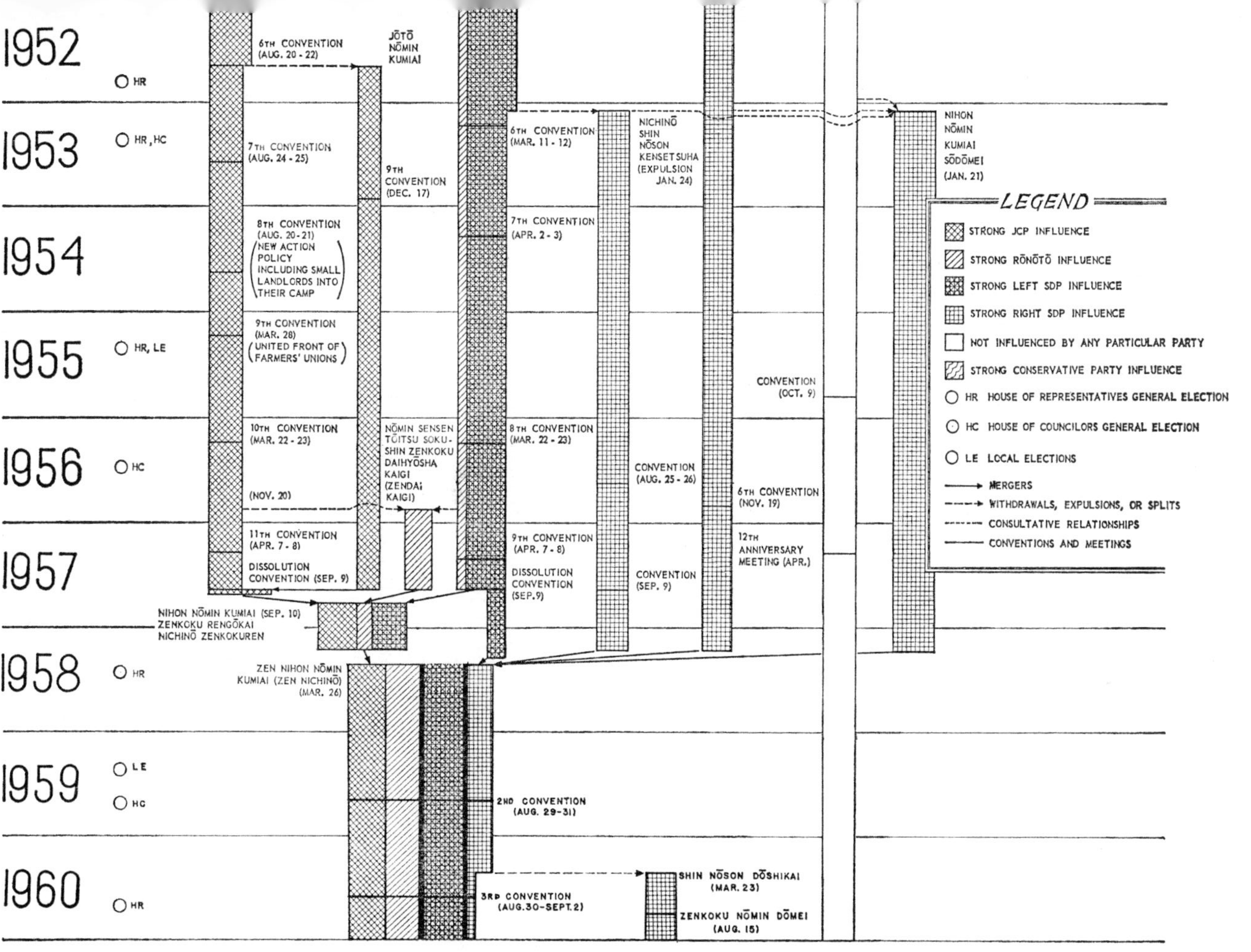
1952
HR
6TH CONVENTION (AUG. 20 - 22)
JŌTŌ NŌMIN KUMIAI
1953
HR, HC
7TH CONVENTION (AUG. 24 - 25)
9TH CONVENTION (DEC. 17)
6TH CONVENTION (MAR. 11 - 12)
NICHINŌ SHIN NŌSON KENSETSUHA (EXPULSION JAN. 24)
NIHON NŌMIN KUMIAI SŌDŌMEI (JAN. 21)
1954
8TH CONVENTION (AUG. 20-21) (NEW ACTION POLICY INCLUDING SMALL LANDLORDS INTO THEIR CAMP)
7TH CONVENTION (APR. 2 - 3)
1955
HR, LE
9TH CONVENTION (MAR. 28) (UNITED FRONT OF FARMERS' UNIONS)
CONVENTION (OCT. 9)
1956
HC
10TH CONVENTION (MAR. 22 - 23)
(NOV. 20)
NŌMIN SENSEN TŌITSU SOKUSHIN ZENKOKU DAIHYŌSHA KAIGI (ZENDAI KAIGI)
8TH CONVENTION (MAR. 22 - 23)
CONVENTION (AUG. 25 - 26)
6TH CONVENTION (NOV. 19)
1957
11TH CONVENTION (APR. 7 - 8)
DISSOLUTION CONVENTION (SEP. 9)
9TH CONVENTION (APR. 7 - 8)
DISSOLUTION CONVENTION (SEP.9)
CONVENTION (SEP. 9)
12TH ANNIVERSARY MEETING (APR.)
NIHON NŌMIN KUMIAI (SEP. 10)
ZENKOKU RENGŌKAI
NICHINŌ ZENKOKUREN
1958
HR
ZEN NIHON NŌMIN KUMIAI (ZEN NICHINŌ) (MAR. 26)
1959
LE
HC
2ND CONVENTION (AUG. 29-31)
1960
HR
3RD CONVENTION (AUG.30-SEPT.2)
SHIN NŌSON DŌSHIKAI (MAR. 23)
ZENKOKU NŌMIN DŌMEI (AUG. 15)
LEGEND
STRONG JCP INFLUENCE
STRONG RŌNŌTŌ INFLUENCE
STRONG LEFT SDP INFLUENCE
STRONG RIGHT SDP INFLUENCE
NOT INFLUENCED BY ANY PARTICULAR PARTY
STRONG CONSERVATIVE PARTY INFLUENCE
HR HOUSE OF REPRESENTATIVES GENERAL ELECTION
HC HOUSE OF COUNCILORS GENERAL ELECTION
LE LOCAL ELECTIONS
MERGERS
WITHDRAWALS, EXPULSIONS, OR SPLITS
CONSULTATIVE RELATIONSHIPS
CONVENTIONS AND MEETINGS

CHART 5

rural areas. At one extreme were men like Rikizō Hirano and Takato Inatomi, who from the first had combined with support for the tenant underdog all the characteristic anti-urbanism and blood-and-soil mysticism of agrarian fascism and had soon found their spiritual home in the 'thirties in the chauvinistic national socialist parties of the radical right.[2] The two largest groups were, firstly, the Labor-Farmer faction of those, like Sōji Okada, Masamichi Takatsu, Chōji Yamada, Hisao Kuroda, and Junzō Inamura, who, basically Marxist in their inspiration, had sailed as close to the wind of illegality as was possible in the early 'thirties. As the left wing of the legal proletarian parties they had tempered their class consciousness and anti-imperialism with a modicum of lip service to accepted nationalist doctrines until the arrests of 1937 put them out of active politics.

Secondly, there were those of the Socio-Democratic and Japan-Labor cliques, men like Motojirō Sugiyama, Masaru Nomizo, Yoshio Matsunaga, Yōnosuke Kikuchi, Shōichi Miyake, Takaichi Nakamura, Seion Kawamata, Kō Sunaga, and Eiji Tomiyoshi. Their agrarian activities had been less "ideological" in inspiration and had displayed, in varying degrees, a greater willingness to compromise with established authority, some from a sense of patriotism which made alienation from the nation-family at a time of stress emotionally insupportable, some from a reluctance to relinquish the pleasures of office. Most of them, particularly those of the Japan-Labor clique, had played an active part in the wartime organization of patriotic farmers, and some were purged for this soon after the war.[3]

With some changes, these groupings have maintained their factional cohesion throughout the postwar history of the Socialist Party and its related farmers' union activities. In planning the policy and strategy of the new party at its inception, however, there was no immediate cause for dissension. The removal of police repression meant that there was no dispute over the desirability of tactical compromise. There was, moreover, every reason for giving tenant demands priority, for the rural situation had changed. With the cities ravaged by fire and on the verge of famine, farmers as a whole, now able to exact high

2. There was at least one with a colorful record of extreme political oscillation—Kanemitsu Hososako, who began as an uncompromising Marxist, underwent a jail "conversion," emerged as a patriotic, unsubversive, but still energetic citizen, became wartime mayor of his native city, and was soon to be found again on the postwar Socialist Party's left wing.

3. For these groupings see the work by Totten mentioned in note 1.

prices for black market sales of food to foraging city dwellers, no longer had cause for envy and resentment of the towns. At the same time, the wartime differential price system for deliveries of staple crops to the government had already brought a considerable amelioration of the tenant's position, and, in an atmosphere by now favorable to radical change, it seemed that no government would be able to resist pressure for some solution of the long-standing problems of the tenancy system.

Accordingly, when on October 20, 1945, the Party Preparatory Committee announced its program, the list of agricultural policy objectives—which included such perennials from the platforms of prewar parties as nationalization of the fertilizer industry, establishment of agricultural insurance, development of cooperatives, and increased mechanization and diversification—was headed by the demand for "a fundamental reform of the land tenure system, the rational distribution of land, and the reduction of rents."[4]

By the time the Emergency Diet Session was convened on November 26, plans for a "fundamental reform of the land tenure system" had already been published in the form of a draft bill to be presented to the Diet by the Shidehara government. During the Diet discussions on the bill, Socialist spokesmen, who as wartime Diet members were necessarily representatives of the party's right wing, criticized its contents on the grounds that it did not go far enough. They did not, however, take up a position of uncompromising opposition such as that adopted by the newly formed Communist Party which was already advocating the confiscation, without compensation, of all leased and all reclaimable land. They voted for the bill.

The first few months of 1946, during which the Socialist Party began its preparation of the forthcoming elections, saw two new developments which greatly affected Socialist thinking on agricultural matters and its approach to the rural electors. In the first place, it became clear that the Occupation authorities were dissatisfied with the land reform measure enacted in December and would demand a radical revision. Secondly, a new organization of leftist activists came into being with the formation, in February 1946, of the Japan Farmers' Union (Nihon Nōmin Kumiai, or Nichinō).

Historically, the formation of farmers' unions has preceded the

4. Rōdōshō (Ministry of Labor), ed., (*Shiryō*) *Rōdō Undō Shi 1945–46* (Materials on Labor History 1945–46) (Tokyo, 1951), p. 893.

organization of left-wing political parties. Some of their leaders—men like Hisao Kuroda and Rikizō Hirano—even though participants in founding the Socialist Party in 1945, had always been more closely associated with the farmers' movement proper than with central party activity. As soon as the war ended and police controls were lifted, many of them had actively begun to revive farmers' organizations in their prewar stamping grounds. In many other districts, in the closing months of 1945, local leaders revived prewar tenant unions and some considerable successes were reported in collective bargaining with landlords for the reduction of rental rates.[5] The creation of a central organization linking all these provincial unions was the obvious next step. Preliminary discussions began in October 1945. A month later some three hundred delegates met in Tokyo, the day after the inaugural convention of the SDP, to lay plans for the formation of a new farmers' union. By the time of the inaugural convention of the resulting Japan Farmers' Union in the following February, the Socialist farmer-leader factions identified in an earlier paragraph were joined by yet a further group, the Communists.

Before the war, the active Marxists in the farmers' movement had consistently viewed the organization of farmers' unions as a means to eventual revolution in which the farmers were destined to play a role subordinate to that of the industrial workers. This, too, was the attitude adopted by the Communist Party at the time of its re-formation after the war. Farmers' committees were to be established as subsections of the "people's committees" which were to organize a revolutionary takeover of power. Accordingly there could be no association with the farmers' organizations inspired by more gradualist democratic ideas.

With the return of Sanzō Nozaka from China, however, and the switch to popular front tactics, the Communist line changed. As a result of approaches by Nozaka and Ritsu Itō to Hirano and Nomizo, it was agreed that Communist-influenced unions should take part in the new farmers' organization.[6] The Japan Farmers' Union which came

5. For an Ibaragi example see Kōzō Uno et al., *Nihon Nōgyō Nempō* (Japan Agricultural Annual), *5* (1956), 53.

6. Sōji Okada, "Nichinō to Kyōsantō to no Kankei" (The Relations between the Japan Farmers' Union and the Communist Party), in *Zenshin* (Dec. 4, 1945), pp. 28–29. Quoted in Junzō Inamura, Shinichirō Ōmori, and Sōji Okada, *Nōmin Undō Ron* (On the Farmers' Movement) (Tokyo, Sangen-sha, 1949), p. 85. Okada himself gives a slightly different and vaguer version of these circumstances in ibid., p. 206.

into being on February 9, 1946, was to be an association of all farmers, directed toward the promotion of the farmers' economic interests and the democratization of the villages. Members were to be free to associate with any party. Thus, out of a desire for unity, understandable after the prewar experience of bitter factional division, the fiction was established that the aims and functions of the Japan Farmers' Union, though political, were somehow nonparty.

At no time, however, during the popular front period before the Japan Farmers' Union split in 1949, did Communists manage to secure any great influence in the union's national leadership. These national leaders were predominantly Socialist Party members, and after the elections of 1946 most of them became Socialist Diet members. Equally, the agrarian experts of the Socialist Party were almost without exception prominent leaders of the Japan Farmers' Union. Hence, in the next few years there was a close integration of policy and tactics between the two organizations. Insofar as a distinction can be made, it was the Farmers' Union which took the lead. Inasmuch as the leaders worked out their strategy and policies in response to the temper and criticism of lower echelons, it was mostly in their Farmers' Union hats that they did so, since it was the union, rather than the party, which had large and active local organizations.

As might be expected from the diversity of their backgrounds, however, these leaders were by no means unanimous in outlook, and in the first few months of 1946 different balances of power between the factions in the party and in the union, respectively, resulted in some differences in the declared policies of the two organizations. The left wing, which had the support of the bulk of the delegates to the inaugural congress of the union, was much more sharply critical of the government's land reform legislation than the Socialist Party's right-wing spokesmen had been in the Diet. A further point of dispute concerned the government's announcement in January of its intention to take strong measures to enforce its system of food requisitioning from farmers. The Socialist Party, which was as concerned as the government that food should get to the towns, could not be as heartily critical of this "arbitrary despotism" as the union, concerned only with the interests of the farmers, some of whom, indeed, might be under pressure to surrender rice their own families needed, but some of whom were profiting on the black market with rice which should have been surrendered. The party contented itself with demanding a more democratic procedure for the apportionment of delivery quotas. The union went further in its opposition to all use of legal sanctions.[7]

Nevertheless, there was little more than a difference of emphasis on these two central issues between the policy adopted at the Japan Farmers' Union inaugural convention and the electoral policy announced by the Socialist Party for the elections of April 1946.[8] Neither was very explicit about the directions in which land reform should be extended. Both, revealing the prewar suspicion of land redistribution measures as an inadequate substitute for the improvement of the tenants' position as tenants, stressed the lowering of rents and the guarantee of security of tenure against widespread landlord attempts to repossess land which the law threatened soon to take away from them. Both statements were mild compared with the confiscatory program advocated by the Communist Party, a fact explained by the influence which the right wing, led by Hirano, still exercised in the leadership of the union as well as of the party.

Once established, the Japan Farmers' Union grew rapidly. Democracy was in the air; land reform was promised; and farmers throughout the country hastened to put themselves on the side of the angels. Within two months of its inception, the union could claim over two thousand branches and more than a quarter of a million members.

The union organization was doubtless important in securing many votes for Socialist candidates in the elections of April 1946, though whether the votes cast for the Socialist Party in rural areas were indeed votes for its policy, votes mobilized by the Farmers' Union, votes for old-time leaders of local tenants' movements, or votes cast for, or at the instigation of, local bosses who saw prospects of future gain in jumping onto the Socialist bandwagon,[9] it is impossible to say. At any rate, the returns showed that the Socialists had found a good deal of support in rural areas. In a number of predominantly agricultural constituencies such as Tochigi, Gumma, Yamanashi, Shiga, Kagawa, and Shimane prefectures, Socialist candidates secured more than one

7. Hisao Kuroda and Tsuneo Ikeda, *Nihon Nōmin Kumiai Undō Shi* (A History of the Japan Farmers' Union) (Tokyo, Shinchi Shobō, 1949), p. 244.

8. For the former, see ibid., p. 244. For the latter, Rōdōshō, (*Shiryō*) *Rōdō 1945–46*, p. 923.

9. For an example of such a temporary Socialist—a local politician of the type who operates by bullying and graft on the fringe of legality—see Paul S. Dull, "A Japanese Political Boss," in Center for Japanese Studies, University of Michigan, *Occasional Papers*, 7 (1957), p. 19.

fifth of the total votes cast. It is perhaps not without significance that Yamanashi prefecture, which in 1935–36 had the highest number of tenancy disputes per acre of tenanted land, gave 31.5 per cent of its votes to Socialists, a proportion exceeded only in the prewar proletarian strongholds of Tokyo and Fukuoka.[10] But the continuation of a prewar radical tradition was not the only factor involved. Even in Iwate, where tenant unions had never made much headway and where the proletarian parties had not even bothered to put up a candidate in 1937, two Socialist candidates were elected with 15 per cent of the total votes.

An important effect of this election was to give left-wing members of the party the influence of Diet positions and so strengthen their position vis-à-vis the right. This was particularly the case in the party's rural segment. Five of the seven executive members of the Japan Farmers' Union were elected, including left-wing leaders Hisao Kuroda and Masaru Nomizo; the latter, under the influence of the union, was to begin his journey to the left from the ambiance of the prewar Japan-Labor faction.

The role of the Japan Farmers' Union in forming policy for the Socialist Party became clearer in the months after the election. A law to give it legal status was drafted by the union and presented to the Diet in the name of the Socialist Party by the union's Secretary-General, Nomizo.[11] On the central agricultural policy issue of the day—the form to be taken by the revised land reform measure—there was little discussion until the measure was presented to the Diet. Until then the matter had been removed to the authoritarian realms of Occupation decision. As soon as the bills were before the Diet, however, the union issued a critical statement which was echoed in the Diet by its President, Kō Sunaga, speaking for the Socialist Party. In a speech cut short by a heart attack from which he died in a few hours, he presented the Socialist amendments which called for deletion of the clause permitting landlords to retain up to one *chō* of tenanted land,

10. In the 11 prefectures which in 1935–36 recorded more than eight disputes per thousand *chō* of tenanted land, the average Socialist share of the total vote was 16.9%. In the 13 prefectures which recorded less than three disputes per thousand *chō* the comparable figure was 12.5%. For figures for disputes see Teikoku Nōkai (Imperial Agricultural Association), ed., *Nōgyō Nenkan 1938* (Agricultural Yearbook 1938), pp. 85–86, 122–23.

11. Keiichirō Aoki, *Nihon Nōmin Kumiai Undō Shi* (A History of the Japan Farmers' Movement) (Tokyo, Kyōseikaku, 1947), pp. 452–53.

and of the bonus compensation payment to landlords, and a change in the composition of land committees to increase the tenants' representation. After these amendments were defeated, however, the Socialists, unlike the Communists, voted for the bills. The Japan Farmers' Union supported their position.[12]

These matters were not the chief concern of the union's activists in the countryside, however. The organizers of the rapidly multiplying union branches were often young firebrands whose chief emotional impulse was revolt against established authority. The governmental system of food requisitioning was an instrument shaped to their hands. By denouncing it they were able to appeal to a wholly nonideological sense of self-interest in the farmers, and their appeal was often successful. Thus, although in some districts the union branch was organized chiefly around tenants who sought mutual support in resisting landlord attempts to evict them from land which the reform promised to make their own, in many others, "down with forced food requisitions" was the major slogan to which farmers of all classes and persuasions rallied. So common was this, in fact, that the first annual report of the union gives the requisitioning issue pride of place.[13] It also, significantly, contains a reflective passage on the frequent "hundred per cent village membership" branches formed in response to anti-requisitioning slogans. While such solidarity was admirable, universal membership implied a danger that leadership in these branches would slip into the hands of "the conservative forces of landlords and middling farmers."[14]

On this matter, at least, there was friction between the union and the party. When the government, in August 1946, sought retroactive approval for its ordinance which authorized requisitioning by force and provided legal sanctions against noncompliance with the system, the Socialist Party, after the government had accepted some modifications, gave its support. The union, on the other hand, aware of the feelings of its lower echelons, had to register uncompromising opposition to the ordinances. Its statement, indicated, however, that it did not wish to bind the "Japan Farmers' Union Diet Members Group" who would "submit" to the Socialist Party's decision.[15]

12. Ibid., p. 452.
13. Ibid., p. 444.
14. Ibid., p. 457.
15. Ibid., p. 451.

THE PERIOD OF LAND REFORM AND A SOCIALIST GOVERNMENT

Conflicts on the requisitioning issue flared again at the union's second convention in February 1947 and provided one motive for Rikizō Hirano's break with the union. It was symptomatic of a natural incompatibility between the role of a national party, which, even in opposition, must to some extent base its policy on a broad conception of the national interest, and that of a union organization which is basically founded on a sectional economic interest laced with a strong impulse to revolt against all manifestations of authority. This incompatibility resulted in even sharper conflict when the Socialist Party headed a government coalition in 1947, a conflict intensified by the fact that its first Minister of Agriculture was Rikizō Hirano, who, as leader of the extreme right wing of the farmers' movement, had by that time already been driven from the Farmers' Union.

Meanwhile, however, the expanding local branches of the union provided an organizational framework for the Socialist Party's attempts to increase its support in the elections of April 1947. Of the 143 Socialists returned in the Lower House election, 31 were officers, either at the national or prefectural level, of the Japan Farmers' Union,[16] and eight more were members of Hirano's schismatic union. Perhaps the national constituency section of the Upper House elections provides the best measure of the organizational strength of the Farmers' Union as such. The union officially sponsored two candidates, Sōji Okada, who ran as a Socialist, and Toshio Ōnishi, an independent. Together they received 280,000 votes, of which Okada's share, but not Ōnishi's, was enough to secure election. This was by no means a large number compared with the claimed union membership at that time of over a million households, and, although this figure cannot properly be taken as a measure of the extent to which, in the more immediate local situation, Socialist candidates succeeded in working through Farmers' Union branches in their electoral campaigns, it seems probable that the Farmers' Union was not the major factor in prompting the big swing of votes to the Socialists in rural constituencies at this election. There was a significant number of voters in rural areas (and this was especially the case immediately after the war, after the bombing evacuations) who were aware of national political issues and voted on the basis of their assessment of a

16. For a list of officers, see Kuroda and Ikeda, *Nihon Nōmin,* pp. 291–301.

government's record or of an opposition's apparent potentialities. It was probably a widespread feeling among such voters, as it apppears to have been throughout the country, that the time had come for a change, which explains the increase in the Socialist vote in rural, as in urban, areas.

Such influence as the Japan Farmers' Union did exert on behalf of the Socialist Party was, however, to be seriously impaired by the factional divisions which developed after the 1947 elections. At the local level, union branches continued forceful and often successful activity in dealing with local issues; the three dominant motifs were the "struggle" against governmental requisition quotas deemed to be excessive, the "struggle" against taxation which was beginning to bear more heavily on farmers as agriculture—then the only successful branch of the economy—was taxed to provide funds for industrial reconstruction, and the "struggle" to enforce land reform and prevent any evasion of the law by landlord-dominated land committees. But national coordination and central political direction of the movement were vitiated by the struggle between the Socialists, who dominated the national leadership, and Communists who became increasingly influential in the lower echelons.

The first incident of overt dissension, as mentioned, came before the elections at the time of the union's second convention in February 1947. Hirano, who had never felt much at home in the atmosphere of revolutionary enthusiasm which pervaded the union's meetings, as chief of the Political Section had had to bear the brunt of attacks by Communists and left-wing Socialists on his and the Socialist Party's attitudes, first, toward enforced requisitioning, and second, toward the negotiations (in which he had personally played a leading part) for a Socialist–Liberal coalition. The tension culminated in a near-riot when one of Hirano's supporters was overruled on a point of order. The Hirano faction withdrew from the meeting, declaring that they could no longer work with Communists; they were expelled from the union the next day. Carrying with them an estimated 15 per cent of the total membership of the Japan Farmers' Union, they formed the League for Revivifying the Japan Farmers' Union (Nichinō Sasshin Dōmei), to be renamed some six months later the All-Japan Farmers' Union (Zen-Nihon Nōmin Kumiai, or Zennō).[17]

17. For accounts of these incidents see Aoki, *Nihon Nōmin,* pp. 473–78 and Uno, *Nihon Nōgyō,* pp. 63–64.

Most of the Socialist Diet members who remained in the Japan Farmers' Union had no particular love for Hirano and were happy to see him go. But within six months their sympathy for the revolutionary ardors of the Communist group had been dissipated. The elections themselves were one factor in this process, showing the fundamental contradictions of a movement which was political, and led by politicians, but in theory nonparty. In constituencies where Socialists ran in competition with Communist candidates, the local Farmers' Union branch was divided in support. The long policy statement adopted at the union's second convention abounds with warnings against tendencies to "make union branches into political party branches or use them as electioneering bases . . . thus leading to disunity and factionalism in union ranks."[18] But these were unrealistic though earnest counsels of perfection. From the Socialist point of view it was chiefly the Communists who were to blame. It was suspected that they had not abandoned their original policy of forming "farmer's committees" as party cells, subordinate to party organs and destined to prepare for a takeover of power after revolution. The policy statement of the second convention remarks, in guarded terms, that "the Communist Party has changed [this policy] . . . and, reforming the farmers' organizations under its guidance into branches of the Japan Farmers' Union, has merged its Federation of Farmers' Organizations into the Union. It is, however, extremely regrettable, that in its operational policy it has caused splits in the organization of the Japan Farmers' Union and hindered its development."[19]

Six months later the Socialist Diet members who led the union decided to be more explicit. At the end of May 1947, when the Socialist Party was preparing to head a coalition of four parties in an atmosphere (a few months after the announcement of the Truman Doctrine) of growing Occupation and right-wing hostility to Communism, the left-wing leaders Suzuki and Katō, issued, as we have seen, a statement proclaiming their determination to eschew all association with Communists. Thereafter the Farmers' Union, as the one farmers' organization in which left-wing Socialists cooperated with Communists, became something of an anomaly. Tension was increased when the Katayama government announced its economic plans on June 11 and was sharply criticized by the Communists on grounds, among

18. Aoki, p. 496. See also pp. 504, 505.
19. Ibid., pp. 468–69.

others, that the announcement contained no reference to a "third land reform" or to the democratization of the food requisitioning procedures—two of the main items in the policy statement of the Japan Farmers' Union agreed on at its second convention in February.[20] The Diet member leaders of the Farmers' Union, torn between their loyalty to the party and the government on the one hand and pressure, led by Communists within the union, for more radical policies on the other, issued statements on August 29 and October 3 denouncing Communist factional activities within the union. The Socialists, however, were divided among themselves. A small left-wing group under the leadership of Hisao Kuroda refused in the name of farmer unity to be associated with the statement. It was not until Kuroda was expelled from the SDP in July 1948, for refusing to vote for the Ashida government's budget, that some semblance of unity was achieved even among the Socialist agrarian leaders.

The latter had further cause for wishing to dissociate themselves from the Communists when, at the end of 1947, their leader, Nomizo, failed to secure appointment as Minister of Agriculture after Hirano's dismissal and expulsion from the party. Katayama was forced to reject the strong demand within the party for his appointment when the conservative coalition parties objected that Nomizo, as chairman of the Farmers' Union, was committed to fellow-traveling with the Communists.[21] The hardening of the factions within the union was exacerbated by a statement by Kyūichi Tokuda at the sixth Communist Party convention in December which was interpreted to mean that Communists should seek to turn farmers' union branches into party cells.[22]

All this time, with the Socialist leaders of the Japan Farmers' Union held prisoner by their loyalty to the government, Communist influence in the union's local organizations seemed to be increasing. As members of the government party, the Socialist leaders voted for the Emergency Food Procurement Law which was denounced in the villages as oppression of the farmer. The gulf between the national leadership of the union and its lower echelons became clear when, in February 1948, Chairman Nomizo was expelled by the Farmers' Union Federation in his own prefecture. The Standing Executive Commit-

20. Rōdōshō, ed., (*Shiryō*) *Rōdō Undōshi 1947*, p. 1005.
21. Ibid., p. 1014.
22. Inamura, Ōmori, and Okada, *Nōmin Undō Ron*, p. 77.

tee of the union only demonstrated its own impotence when it replied by ordering this and other federations to dissolve themselves.[23] Disunity was so intense that no national convention could be held in 1948. A Central Committee meeting in 1947 and a National Delegates, Conference in 1948 both ended in fiasco when the leaders refused to allow votes to be taken, sensing that their opponents were in a majority.

Gradually the factions hardened. In April 1948, Socialist leaders established within the union an organization called the League for the Establishment of Independence (i.e., from Communist Party influence); Kuroda and the Communists formed a counter organization called the Unity Discussion Group. In July and August, Socialist Party organs published secret orders by the Communist Party to its rural members instructing them to capture control of Farmers' Union branches and turn them into "farmers' committees" on the original Communist model, to which the Communist Party replied by denying the authenticity of the documents and accusing the Socialists of deceitful forgery.[24] The division was finally formalized on April 22, 1949, when two Japan Farmers' Union national conventions were held simultaneously and two separate organizations came into being: the Independence Group (Shutaiseiha) of Socialist supporters, and the Unity Group (Tōitsuha) headed by Kuroda, but, after his defection a year later, almost exclusively in the hands of Communists. Of the two it appears certain that the latter group carried with it the bulk of the provincial membership.[25]

From this time onward the Socialist Party had its own Farmers' Union organization, but it was already a sadly fragmented and weakened one. Left-wing activists had been alienated by the "weak-kneed" attitudes of the Socialist agrarian leaders toward the Katayama and Ashida coalitions; at the end of 1948 there were in many districts wholesale defections of rural Socialists to the Communist camp,[26] and a good many of the votes which in the Lower House elections of 1949 helped to elect nine Communist members in predominantly rural districts probably came from former Socialist voters. Other less politi-

23. Uno, *Nihon Nōgyō,* pp. 70–71.

24. Kuroda and Ikeda, pp. 280–84.

25. Ibid., p. 290, and Ie no Hikari Kyōkai, *1950 Nihon Nōgyō Nenkan* (The 1950 Agricultural Yearbook), pp. 380–81.

26. Uno, p. 70.

cally minded farmers were alienated from the movement by the viciousness of the power struggles between its factions. Some felt they had been betrayed by organizers who had carried their revolutionary enthusiasm too far. (In Akita prefecture a decline in the farmers' movement is said to have set in when an "anti-requisition struggle" led by a fiery leader was followed by police searches, arrests, and eventually the suicide of law-abiding farmers suddenly shocked to find what they had done.)[27] Many of the immediate postwar leaders of local farmers' union branches—and this was a potent factor in the union's decline[28]—had by then been elected to positions of administrative responsibility in land committees and village assemblies and had lost interest in the mere organization of movements of protest. Moreover, the immediate issues which had provided a powerful impetus to the organization of local "struggles" had lost some of their urgency. With an easing of the food situation, the government's requisitioning program began to press less heavily on the farmer; smaller delivery quotas were imposed for the harvest of 1948 than for the year before, despite a considerably larger yield. By the end of 1948 the land reform program was well under way. Landlords' efforts to repossess land as an attempt to evade the reform were largely an immediate postwar phenomenon which had later ceased to provide a common motif for struggles. The demands for democratization of the agricultural associations had been answered with the establishment of a new system of agricultural cooperatives. Only demonstrations against heavy tax assessments remained as the chief staple of local activity.

These latter factors generally, and their effect in weakening the Farmers' Union specifically, may have contributed to the Socialists' loss of support in rural areas in the elections of 1949. There is some evidence, at any rate, that the swing away from the Socialists was greater in rural than in urban areas. In 1947, 50 per cent of the Socialists elected to the Lower House had come from 69 of the most rural constituencies. In 1949 these constituencies provided only 44 per cent of the much smaller total of Socialists elected.[29] However, it was probable that the Socialist rural losses again stemmed from other more general factors, not specifically from the rural situation: the

27. *Shakai Tsūshin, 181* (May 20, 1956), 2.

28. *Jōhō Tsūshin, 28–29* (March 31, 1951), 1.

29. These 69 constituencies are those which, at the time of the 1950 census, had less than 30% of their population in urban (*shibu*) areas.

feeling that the Socialists were not of the caliber required for government, disappointment at their factional disunity and indecision and at the revelation that their claim to be "purer" in money matters than conservative politicians had little foundation.

FROM THE 1949 ELECTIONS TO THE MAJOR PARTY SPLIT

Agrarian leaders of the Socialist Party, though some had lost their Diet seats, were in a somewhat happier position as the party began to salvage what it could from its electoral defeat and rebuild its strength in rural areas. They had made their break with the Communists and now had their own farmers' organization. Secure in the irresponsible position of a small opposition party, they were able to give rein to their natural impulse to struggle, protest, and oppose. As party theorist Hitoshi Yamakawa wrote at the time: "The Socialist Party has now cut its unsavory connections with the bourgeois capitalist parties and is now in a position to say freely what it thinks."[30] In good conscience the leaders of the Independence Group could now open the executive's general report to the convention of February 1949 with the paragraph:

> The land reform program is drawing to a close. The Agricultural Cooperatives are established and the food requisitioning system has been fundamentally reorganized. Now, as the weight of taxation begins to bear ever more heavily on the farmer and as the rapidly reintegrated forces of monopoly capital begin to stretch their evil claws relentlessly over the farmer, the villages face the critical threat of total destruction. . . . The reactionary government, seeking to solve the crisis of Japanese capitalism by plundering and sacrificing the workers and farmers, is using its whole armory of violent repression against the toiling masses.[31]

Here was foreshadowed the main theme of the Socialist—at least of the left-wing—appeal to the farmer during the next seven years: the emphasis on demands for lower taxes and higher rice prices. The enemy was identified no longer as the landlords but as monopoly capital and its "executive committee," the conservative government. There remained, however, a certain tension between the logic of their

30. "Shakaitō no Saiken no Tame ni" (For the Rebuilding of the Socialist Party), in *Zenshin, 21* (April 1949), 39.

31. *1951 Nōgyō Nenkan*, p. 374.

appeals (it was to the richer owner-farmer with a large holding that lower taxes and higher prices promised the greatest benefits) and the tradition of the farmers' movement that the appeal to the left must be to the poorer farmer. The prewar oscillation between a *farmers'* movement and a *tenants'* movement appeared in a new guise as a result of the land reform. With tenancy drastically reduced and the remaining tenants protected by laws guaranteeing security of tenure and restricting rents to a low figure, there was no longer a division in the villages between a class of landlords and a class of tenants. Instead, there was a continuous gradation ranging from those who emerged from the land reform as owners of fairly large and viable holdings, to those who emerged as owners of small holdings, forced to rely on subsidiary employment—often with their richer neighbors—for a living. The policy statement adopted at the 1949 convention of the Independence Group revealed the ambiguities resulting from a natural tendency to appeal to the little man conflicting with a realization that the party had more chance of winning over the somewhat more propertied man. One section read:

> Our enemies in the villages are the remaining landlords who try to prevent the completion of the democratic revolution in the villages, the village bosses and the richer farmers insofar as they appear as obstacles to the development of cooperative production. Our central source of strength lies in the cultivating farmers who operate under positive conditions predisposing them to the adoption of cooperative forms of production. In recent struggles against taxes and food requisitions our most active allies have been the full-time farmers in general [i.e., those who have holdings large enough not to depend on subsidiary employment] not necessarily exclusively the poor farmers and the middling farmers. It is these full-time farmers who, suffering an overall economic decline, are unable individually to advance to capitalist farm management, and who form our main source of strength.[32]

In this policy statement the emphasis on taxes and prices as a means of appealing to the economic self-interest of all farmers mingled with three other strains, all hinted at in the paragraph quoted. First, there was the emphasis on cooperative production as the ultimate aim of

32. "Nichinō no 1949-nendo Undō Hōshin" (The 1949 Action Policy of the Japan Farmers Union) in *Zenshin, 24* (July 1949), 90.

policy. This was something which sprang from ideological rather than from tactical considerations. That it was no popular vote-catching device is clear from the statement itself:

> The development of cooperative forms of land use is faced with great obstacles inasmuch as it runs counter to the farmer's desire for private ownership of land. We must, therefore, proceed gradually, beginning with elementary forms of cooperation in such matters as village electrification, food processing, communal ownership of cattle and large machines, land improvement and consolidation and the introduction of new techniques.[33]

Socialists have never felt fully at ease with the petty proprietor aspect of the Japanese farmer, hence their vague prewar declarations about the ultimate "socialization" of the land, and hence also their initial lack of enthusiasm for the land reform. The development of voluntary cooperation represented a solution, interest in which was stimulated in postwar years by the stories of prisoners returned from Russia concerning the operation of Soviet collective farms. Equally ideological and reformist in inspiration has been the emphasis on democratization and "the sweeping away of feudal customs." "The liberalization of farm women and the development of family planning," "cultural activities," and "the improvement of family life" are examples of such policy slogans. This has not been an endeavor in which the Socialist Party has had any monopoly. It has accorded with the well established tradition of reformist modernization movements sponsored by central authority since the beginning of the Meiji period, and, since the war and Occupation, continued by conservative governments in the form of Reformed Living Campaigns and New Life Movements, actively promoted by agricultural extension services.

The third main theme represents the vestiges of the agrarian movement's traditional campaign on behalf of tenants and against landlords. It was expressed as a demand for full completion of the current land reform program, for the enactment of a "third land reform" which would transfer the ownership of the remaining tenanted land to its cultivators and redistribute forest land, and for "the complete elimination of remaining landlord strength and of the reactionary control of bosses." In subsequent years it was to be a cardinal difference between the Socialist Party and the Independence Group on the

33. *1951 Nōgyō Nenkan*, p. 378.

one hand, and the Communists and their Unity Group on the other, that the latter made this the central theme of its campaigns. Until the switch in the Communist line in 1955–56, it was held as axiomatic among Communists that land reform had had no appreciable effect on the situation in the villages.

These, then, were the main features of the Socialist Party's approach to the farmers in the years following the land reform. Agriculture did not, however, figure very prominently in the political issues of the period from 1949 to the end of the Occupation, nor did questions of agricultural policy play any part in the disputes between the left and the right wings of the Socialist Party which occupied an increasing portion of its political energies until the split in 1951.

As might be expected, the period saw a greater integration of party and farmers' union organizations. In 1950, a Committee for Rural Policy Measures was established in the party, and the agrarian Diet members moved the center of their activities from the Farmers' Union to within the party framework. At the same time the Organization Committee's Farmers' Section organizers sought to create farmers' sections within the party prefectural federations. About a dozen prefectures had "Farmers' Section Chiefs" by early 1951.[34] It was from this time, too, that the party began the formulation of full-scale agricultural policies, designed as a comprehensive statement of the intentions of a hypothetical future Socialist government.[35]

Meanwhile, the organizational strength of the farmers' unions themselves declined even further. The fifth national convention of the Independence Group in March 1951 could hardly raise a quorum, and the right-wing All-Japan Farmers' Union, unable to muster a convention, contented itself with a Central Committee meeting which began and ended with a dispute between Socialists among its leaders, who wished to amalgamate with the Independence Group, and the followers of Hirano (now depurged and the leader of his own political party) who objected vociferously to any such move.[36]

That the farmers' unions survived at all is due probably to two things: first, to a sense of loyalty on the part of its leaders and a small number of provincial organizers toward a movement with a long tradition of comradeship and dedication; second, to the fact that the

34. *Jōhō Tsūshin, 28, 29* (March 31, 1951), 52–56.
35. See infra, pp. 401–07.
36. *Jōhō Tsūshin,* 28, 29 (March 31, 1951), pp. 1–4.

unions still provide useful organizational forms and labels within and under which to organize local support for rural Socialist Diet members. From that time on, in fact, the unions became little more than loose federations of electoral support committees for such incumbent, or would-be, members of the Diet or of prefectural assemblies. It was they who preempted the leadership, who directed the unions' policies, and who contributed funds for the upkeep of the unions' skeletal central offices.

THE PERIOD OF SOCIALIST SCHISM

Just how much this was so was clearly revealed when the Socialist Party split in the fall of 1951. Although the dispute concerned foreign policy, labor issues, and ideological problems, and had nothing to do with agricultural matters, the left-wing Socialists who predominated in the Central Committee of the Independence Group lost no time in calling a meeting to expel their former colleagues who had voted with the right. Thereafter the agrarian leaders of the Right Socialist Party formed their own body called the "New Village Construction Group of the Japan Farmers' Union" (Nichinō Shin-nōson Kensetsuha), taking their name from a theme slogan in the party's agricultural policy adopted before the split. Its organization was undertaken as an activity of the Farmers' Section of the right-wing Organization Bureau,[37] and it remained, during the six years of its existence, a head without a body, never once managing to hold a national convention or delegates' conference and producing no regular information bulletin of its own. Later, when Hirano dissolved his own party and merged with the Right Socialists, his All-Japan Farmers' Union and the New Village Construction Group came together to form a loose federation called the General Federation of Farmers' Unions (Nōmin Kumiai Sōdōmei). This also absorbed a number of formerly independent local organizations such as the Farmers' Alliance of Hokkaidō and Nagano, but in only a few prefectures could it claim active local branches.[38]

During the years 1951–55, when the two Socialist parties maintained their separate existence, no really important agricultural issue arose to divide them, or indeed, to divide them collectively from the conservative parties. The deflationary policies of 1949 had resulted in

37. *Jōhō Tsūshin,* 47 (June 7, 1952).

38. Ōhara Shakai Mondai Kenkyūjo, *Nihon Rōdō Nenkan* (The Japan Labor Yearbook), *26,* 522–23.

a depression of agricultural income at the end of that year, but with the beginning of the Korean War, Japanese villages entered on a period of gradual economic improvement. The tax reforms of 1949–50 resulted in a net reduction of taxation on agriculture, though the switch in emphasis from national income tax to less progressive forms of local taxation meant that the richer farmers benefited disproportionately from the change. The growth of industry relieved the employment situation in rural areas, both by providing opportunities for younger sons to move out of farming, and by increasing the opportunities for subsidiary employment of farm household members. The latter have proved to be the main factor in the rise in farm income since 1951.

But the absence of fundamental conflict in matters of agricultural policy derives from another important factor. The conservative parties over these years have shown a realization of the fact that they depend heavily on the electoral support of the farmers, including those who benefited from the land reform, and that this support is by no means automatic and depends on conservative governments' providing concrete benefits. That the conservative parties were no longer simply the parties of landlords and capitalists became clear in 1952 when Yoshida's Liberal government presented a bill designed to freeze the post-land reform status quo, maintaining all the checks against a reversion to widespread tenancy (rent control, land sale control, security of tenure, and landholding maxima) embodied in the original land reform legislation. There was opposition to the measure from sections of the Liberal Party, but it was eventually suppressed by the argument that the land reform, by creating a large class of landholding farmers, had created the ideal basis of support for a conservative party, and that it should be the Liberal policy to foster that support.

Successive conservative governments have taken other measures to that end. Throughout the period 1951–55, the producer price of rice —the chief single determinant of farm income—was slowly but steadily raised relative to the general price level. Until 1953 there was a rapid increase, too, in budgetary appropriations for agricultural subsidies and disaster relief. Promises and actual appropriations of such funds, which are distributed in the form of grants and loans for purposes of agricultural improvement, irrigation works, purchase of equipment and livestock and the like, have been important to conservative politicians in their electioneering activities.

In these circumstances the Socialist parties, in their appeal to the farmers, were able to do little more than call for bigger and better benefits. Thus, in their election programs for the Lower House elections in 1952, both parties stressed the need for increased state funds to develop new farm lands, the abolition of compulsory quotas for rice deliveries, and an increase in the producer's price of rice (the Right, but not the Left, specifying the exact price), the reduction of taxation, and a wide expansion of agricultural credit.[39] These remained the staple themes at the time of the electoral campaign.[40]

The parties sought various means, during this period, for impressing on the farmer their generous championship of his economic interests. The frequent electoral campaigns provided opportunities, though it was noticeable, during the elections of 1955 at least, that even rural Socialist candidates were more inclined to stress their opposition to the government's foreign policy and constitutional reform proposals than agricultural matters. The annual budget enabled them to criticize the government's provision of agricultural funds, but this, in the general context of budget news, was unlikely to filter through abbreviated newspaper reports to the farmer. More important were the annual meetings of the Rice Price Deliberation Commission, charged with recommending to the government the price structure for the following year's requisitioning of staple crops. Both parties adopted the practice of drawing up their own "fair price" calculations, presenting them to the Commission, and issuing protests to the government at the price eventually adopted. The press coverage of these activities was enhanced by mass demonstrations and sit-down strikes of farmers arranged in Tokyo during the Commission's sittings by the parties, the farmers' unions, and the agricultural cooperatives.[41]

Similar demonstrations were arranged in the provinces in the form of prefectural farmers' rallies, called under the auspices of local party branches and farmers' unions and addressed by Socialist Diet members. These often laid special emphasis on particular local interests.

39. *Jōhō Tsūshin,* 52 (Sept. 15, 1952), and *Tōkatsudō* (Sept. 23, 1952).

40. *Jōhō Tsūshin,* 123–124, (Jan. 15, 1955), and *Tōkatsudō* (Dec. 20, 1954).

41. For examples see *Nihon Rōdō Nenkan, 27,* 561, 584; *28,* 641–42; and *Tōkatsudō* (Sept. 20, 1954).

In addition to such "rice price struggles" and continuing "tax struggles"[42] other local issues—demands for natural-disaster relief grants or for the sale to poor farmers of idle reclaimable land—provided opportunities for the dwindling band of left-wing farmer union activists to keep union organizations alive. During this period, also, two new types of "struggle" assumed increasing importance.

The first reflected the revival of landlords' and ex-landlords' organizations. Their activities at the national level, organizing campaigns for state compensation for losses in the land reform and demanding changes in the existing land laws, brought forth hostile statements from the parties but little more. Occasionally, though not as often as one might expect, demonstrations in Tokyo by landlord organizations would be met with counter-demonstrations by farmers' unions.[43] At the local level their impact in some districts was somewhat greater. At the instigation of their organizations landlords sometimes made concerted attempts to pressure tenants into giving the formal consent which the law required before landlords could repossess leased-out land. Such attempts led to the sporadic revival of tenant-centered farmers' unions.

A second major theme in these years was the organization of opposition—in the form of demonstrations and sit-down strikes—to the requisitioning of land for air bases and military installations, particularly for American bases. This tendency for farmers' unions merely to reflect the national political attitudes of particularly the Left SDP—a tendency even more marked in the Communists' Unity Group—is an indication of how much these organizations had lost their roots in the countryside and how much they depended for continued existence on Diet members who hoped to use them for electoral purposes and on a residue of provincial political enthusiasts.

The Independence Group, however, was still closer to having a national organization than the New Village Construction Group, the All-Japan Farmers' Union, or the General Federation of Farmers' Unions. To that extent the Left Socialists probably derived more benefit than the Right from connections with farmers' unions in the

42. For a description of one such very tense struggle, organized by local Independence Group members and precipitated by the local tax office's enforcement of a house search to correct tax returns suspected of under-reporting, see *Nihon Rōdō Nenkan, 27,* 602 and Takeshi Takeuchi, "Yamagata-ken ni okeru Nōmin Undō no Zenshin" (The Advance of the Farmers' Movement in Yamagata Prefecture) in *Shakaishugi, 54* (Feb. 1956).

43. *Tōkatsudō* (Aug. 10, 1955).

elections of 1955. At any rate, whereas 31 of a sample of 48 left-wing candidates said in answer to a questionnaire that they received support from farmers' unions, only seven of a sample of 33 right-wing candidates claimed any such support.[44] Again reservations must be made about the extent and influence of that support.

REUNIFICATION

The same general features which characterized the two Socialist parties' relations with farmers' unions, their activities in matters of agricultural policy, and their tactical approaches to the farmers have remained characteristic of the reunited Socialist Party since 1955, with three main differences.

The first is that, with the greater apparent possibility of an eventual accession to power, there has been some modification of the party's willingness to seize any popular appeal as an excuse to beat the government. This is most notable in its declarations on the rice price issue. In 1957, the party issued a statement supporting the cooperatives' demand for a basic price of ¥1,140 per *koku*.[45] This showed a rather more realistic approach than in the years 1954–55, when both parties had declared for a price of ¥1,250. (Difficulties in framing an alternative budget seem to have been chiefly responsible for this retreat.) A milder approach was also apparent in the party's attitude to agricultural legislation proposed by the government in this period. Two laws were passed during the 24th Diet, one concerning the reorganization of agricultural committees and the other concerning credit provision for settlers on newly reclaimed land. Both received the support of the Socialist Party, the first after prolonged negotiations and amendments in the course of which the government gave up its intention to abolish direct election procedures for agricultural committees and the Socialists gave up their insistence on divided constituencies which would give each economic category of farmers separate representations.[46]

The second difference is that the party itself has made some progress in establishing its own provincial organizations aimed specifically at farmers and their problems. After reunification, the Farmers' Section of the Organization Bureau was staffed with four full-time organizers —men with some experience in the farmers' movement, whose task it

44. Allan B. Cole et al., "Support for Japanese Social Democrats in 1955," p. 8.
45. *Asahi Shimbun* (June 8, 1957, morning).
46. *Shakai Tsūshin, 250* (May 20, 1957).

was to develop these organizations. A report of a series of "block conferences"—meetings of Socialist leaders in blocks of five or six prefectures—which these men organized in the spring of 1956 indicates how difficult this task was.[47] Most prefectural federations by then had a Farmers' Section Chief, but a good many of them had no Farmers' Section to be chief of. In some prefectures, such as Tottori, it was reported that the small remnants of the Japan Farmers' Union *were* the Farmers' Section. In Yamagata, on the other hand, a still flourishing local branch of the Independence Group with ten full-time organizers was the sole framework of activity, outside of the party organization. In others, such as Fukushima, the party took the initiative in prompting the organization of local tenants' and owner-farmers' unions to counter landlords' attempts at repossession, in holding farmers' discussion groups, or in infiltrating the radically inclined Agricultural Cooperatives' Youth Alliance.

Other delegates reported a complete absence of organization of any sort but, like the Aichi delegate, proclaimed their intention of trying to round up men who had once been active in the Farmers' Union and get them into some sort of association. A delegate from Hiroshima said he would like to do this, but since the local Diet member kept a tight hold on the address book (presumably for sending New Year cards and postcards from foreign countries in order to keep up his electoral machine) things were very difficult. In general there was lamentation for the past days of active militancy, relieved occasionally by flashes of optimism, more especially in the northeastern district where the party was planning a three-day hot-springs summer school for a hundred Socialist farmers.

Although the party was in this way taking the initiative in stimulating organizations which could be useful to it for electoral purposes, there was no apparent disposition to press for a formal replacement of farmers' unions by party branches. Rather, the tactics to be adopted—as was more explicitly spelled out in a "Farmers Movement Thesis" drafted by the Farmers' Section a year later[48]—were to seize on any local grievance, any source of resentment shared by farmers in a particular area, to create local ad hoc organizations which could be brought indirectly under the influence of the Socialist Party.

As this indicates, the attachment to the farmers' union tradition on

47. Ibid., *181* (May 20, 1956).
48. *Shakai Tsūshin, 251* (June 30, 1957).

the part of party organizers both at the center and in the provinces was and is strong. In part it has sprung from calculation: farmers, it has frequently been said, are reluctant to join overt party organizations for to do so brands one as a deviant "enthusiast," and, when the party in question is socialist, in many villages as an agitator and a "red" as well.[49] Farmers' unions, however, are said to arouse less suspicion, hence the emphasis on "independence" (from party control) incorporated into the Independence Group's title.

Nostalgia for the militant tradition, involving as it does an attachment to "unity" as such, has partly explained the third main development in the Socialist Party's relations with the farmers in the period since 1955, namely the reunification of the farmers' unions. It is significant, for instance, that the unity movement started with a ceremony held to honor dead leaders of the farmers' movement on the tenth anniversary of the Japan Farmers' Union's postwar inauguration. The move toward reunification, thus launched with solemn pledges to the spirits of the dead, was to receive many setbacks before, two years later, it was eventually brought to success with the formation of the National Japan Farmers' Union (Zenkoku Nihon Nōmin Kumiai) in March 1958. Two particular circumstances favored the advocates of unity. The first was the reunification of the Socialist Party; the second was the change in policy of the Communist Party after its sixth national consultative conference in June 1955.

After the reunification of the SDP near the end of 1955, there were obvious advantages in reuniting all the farmers' unions headed by members of the new party. Moreover, time had already resolved the differences which had led to their original divisions. Hirano's All-Japan Farmers' Union had broken away because it could not work with Communists, but now the Independence Group, after its separation from the Unity Group in 1949, was anti-Communist. The New Village Construction Group was solely a result of the split in the Socialist Party and now the Socialist Party was reunited. If, therefore, the other remaining fraction of the Japan Farmers' Union—the Communists' Unity Group—had continued to maintain the doctrinaire rigidity which characterized JCP policy in the years 1950–55, there would have been no difficulty in organizing a union of the three main Socialist-affiliated groups.

49. See, e.g., *Tokyo Shimbun* (Sept. 11, 1957).

But the Communists had changed. In their period of "left-wing adventurism," Communist theory had held, firstly, that the land reform had only scratched the surface of feudalism in the villages and that, in the words of the Unity Group's General Secretary at a Central Committee meeting in 1952, "the present enemy is the forces of feudal landlordism" against whom the exploited should be organized.[50] Secondly, it held that all farmers' movements were mere tactical skirmishes for eventual revolution. The policy statement of its convention in 1952 mentioned the need for "the working classes to lead the farmers' movement . . . if the farmers' movement is to become truly revolutionary,"[51] and there was talk of "a two-stage revolution—against feudalism and against [American-Japanese] imperialism."[52]

These tactics, which required automatic and vociferous opposition to all governmental authority, however well-intentioned, together with the general discrediting of the Communists in the period after the May Day riots of 1952, had caused the Unity Group an attrition of support even greater than that suffered by the Independence Group. With the reappearance of Nozaka, however, and the reversion of the Communist Party to its earlier postwar policies of mildness, many-roads-to-Socialism, peaceful revolution, and democratic cooperation with all progressive forces, a change took place. It was discovered that feudalism had been all but eliminated by the land reform and that the farmers' movement was properly an independent endeavor designed to improve the lot of the farmer. At its convention in 1956, the Unity Group opened its arms to any farmer who supported any one of its twenty-odd reasonable demands for improvement of the farmer's lot.

This left no overt difference between the Unity Group and any other farmers' union. This group was, moreover, conforming to the general anxiety of the Communist Party to develop popular front associations, willing to go more than halfway to achieve a new unity in the farmers' movement. The left-wing elements in the Independence Group, for their part, had always had for the Communists something of the sneaking regard of the parish priest for the ascetic monk, a feeling that though the Communists might not have quite the right

50. *Nihon Rōdō Nenkan, 27,* 604.

51. Ibid., p. 617.

52. Ibid., p. 605. Yutaka Kubota, the Union's Chairman at the third Central Committee meeting in August 1952.

conception of virtue, they showed an admirable and heroic dedication in the fight against sin. Consequently, as in 1947, they found in themselves more fellow-feeling for the Unity Group than for many of the anti-Marxist Socialists of the New Village Construction Group or the All-Japan Farmers' Union. Thus it happened that, as the discussions on reunification proceeded in 1956 and 1957, it was the right-wing members of the latter two groups who, out of suspicion of the Communists, began to drag their feet.

Eventually the left wing of the Independence Group and the Unity Group decided to go it alone. Despite repeated attempts to block such moves by Suzuki and the "mainstream" faction of the party, the Unity Group and all except a small staunchly anti-Communist rump of the Independence Group came together in a "first-stage amalgamation" in September 1957.[53] The objections of the party leaders were obvious. It was their policy to oppose alliance with the Communists; they were interested in the reunification of the farmers' unions only insofar as it might produce a supporting organization for the Socialist Party. But so strong was the emotional appeal of "farmer unity," and so long-established was the fiction that the farmers' movement should be autonomous and above party, that to have said so openly would have been to invite charges of deceitful ulterior motives and would have been regarded as a "betrayal" of the farmers' cause.

As it was, the "first-stage amalgamation" of the left placed the right-wing Socialists in the unenviable position of being opposed to unity. Moreover, things having gone thus far, and the largest remaining section of the farmers' movement under Socialist influence being already committed to the new merger, there were obvious arguments for the right wing to join it in an effort to counteract Communist influence. Accordingly, in March 1958, the rump of the Independence Group, the All-Japan Farmers' Union, and the New Village Construction Group joined with the new union to form the National Japan Farmers' Union. As is the common pattern in these cases, the inaugural convention was delayed for four hours by backstairs negotiation concerning the distribution of offices, and the chairmanship was left vacant for the time being, its powers to be exercised by a Committee of Three. Occupied as it was with such matters, the convention gave only perfunctory attention to a brief and not very explicit statement

53. *Tokyo Shimbun* (Sept. 11, 1957).

of the new union's policies. Newspaper comment stressed the possibilities of disunity in an organization which sought to unite such men as Rikizō Hirano (attempting a comeback to political life after his recent disgrace), Yutaka Kubota, former Chairman of the Unity Group, and Hisao Kuroda whose left-wing Worker Farmer Party was readmitted to the Socialist fold only in 1957.[54]

No one was disposed to take very seriously the new union's claim to a quarter of a million members, but it is possible that formal unity, in an organization which has deliberately taken a looser federal structure than its predecessors, will reduce competitive bickering in the provinces and make easier the organization of "demand-by-demand struggles" and of ad hoc local bodies to prosecute them. It is unlikely, however, to alter the fact that the main function of the farmers' unions is to provide a front for the mobilization of electoral support for the individual politicians who lead them, nor is it likely much to enhance their effectiveness to this end. Given the inclusion of the Communists, moreover, the new union is even less likely to be effective in increasing support for, or in disseminating an appreciation of the policies of, the Socialist Party as such.

After the elections of November 1960, the party tried to form "agricultural policy research organizations" in villages and to foster exchanges between agricultural producers and "livelihood cooperatives" in urban communities. More important are the recently increased efforts to plan and execute more effective joint labor-farmer actions. Sōhyō since 1957 and Nichinō since 1959 have sent organizers who, by 1961, had helped to launch nearly two dozen prefectural labor-farmer councils. Late in February of the latter year, these two organizations, in alliance with the Socialist Party and the JCP, held a convention attended by delegates from all prefectures except Hokkaidō. It inaugurated a new National Labor-Farmer Congress the declared purposes of which were: organization of farmers (a survey in 1960 showed that less than one per cent were unionized), democratization of agricultural associations (including unionization of their employees), provision of study meetings for farmers, and the organization of nonagricultural workers in rural areas. As in years past, however, many farmers continued to view such efforts as intended to mobilize them primarily in the interests of urban workers.

54. *Asahi Shimbun* (March 24, 1958, morning); *Nihon Nōgyō Shimbun* (March 28, 1958).

After the right-wing Nishio faction of the SDP seceded in 1959–60, there occurred another schism in the briefly unified national farmers' movement. From the more moderate elements in Nichinō came a splinter allied with the DSP, calling itself the All-Japan Farmers' Federation (Zen-Nihon Nōmin Dōmei). At that time it was estimated that there were only about 1,200 active farm members in the main Socialist Party.

AGRICULTURE UNDER A SOCIALIST GOVERNMENT

One sign of an increasingly thoughtful approach to agricultural matters on the part of the Socialist Party has been the increasing concreteness and degree of realism of its long-range agricultural policies (as distinguished from its tactics designed for current agricultural issues). The basic agricultural platform of 1950 represents the party's first attempt to subject itself to the discipline of deciding what it would do with agriculture if it ever formed a government. Of the two statements produced by the two wings of the party during the period of schism, the Left's, a document accepted by the Central Executive Committee a few months before reunification, was in the basic platform tradition in its concentration on basic theoretical principles. Two and one-half pages are devoted to an historical analysis of the development of monopoly capitalism and its effects on agriculture, and only one and one-half to practical policy suggestions. The Right eschewed such philosophical discussions and contented itself with a fairly detailed statement of policy. It will be seen that the policy statement approved at the thirteenth convention in January 1957 owed more to this pragmatic approach of the Right than to the theoretical concerns of the Left. It was, moreover, an earnest of the party's serious intention to have these policies widely considered in the villages that this statement was reprinted in a cheap booklet, and was followed in 1958 by another pamphlet outlining its main principles in a simpler and more popular question-and-answer form.

One feature common to all these proposals, as one might expect, has been the attempt to outbid the conservative parties in the promise of concrete economic benefits to the farmer. There are to be bigger and better subsidies, higher prices, and lower costs. Policy statements have shown an increasing generosity in these matters over the years. The Left wing's statement of 1955, for instance, actually suggested that there should be progressive reductions in the price paid to the farmer for his rice, but in 1958 the gloss on the 1957 policy spelled out a formula which would commit a Socialist government to a price well above the current one and consequently to large food subsidies. (The statement in 1957 was somewhat more cautious.) More recent policies, indeed, have been hardly realistic in the scale of benefits they have envisaged, particularly regarding grants for land reclamation and improvement.

The party's plan for the period 1957–61 provided for investments in agriculture, forestry, and fisheries triple the corresponding amounts in 1954. Two hundred thousand poorer farm families were to be settled on 2.45 million reclaimed acres. The Socialists promised that, once in office, they would increase productivity by developing new irrigation systems, fostering the use of tractors in certain suitable terrains, encouraging the raising of livestock, expanding double-cropping where possible, and stimulating diversification of crops. Recognizing that farmers tend to be conservative and to cling to familial emphases, Japan's Socialists keep advocating a combination of state subsidized programs and regulatory functions, on the one hand, and, on the other, a number of cooperatively organized local centers for improved access to machinery, technological information, credit, and necessities for production. They hope that peasants can thus be induced by stages to accept more collective methods and the reorganization of agrarian labor and management according to larger, more efficient units. Their plan proposed the unionization of farm laborers and inauguration of new "farm village construction councils." In addition to transactions involving land, they advocated strict public control of water rights.

This five-year plan envisioned 4.9 million acres of new forests and afforestation of 612,500 more by 1961. New roads for lumbering were to be built. Local "construction councils" were to promote planning and the cooperative use of forest resources. There should be unions and cooperatives for forest workers, and they should enjoy social security benefits.[55]

Similar advantages were to be provided for fishing families. Socialist programs for this sector have always advocated elimination of the

55. The agricultural policies for the SDP five-year plan for the period 1957–61 may be found in Nihon Shakaitō, *Dai Jūsankai Teiki Taikai Kettei Shū: Seisaku Hen* (Resolutions of the Thirteenth Regular Convention: Policies Section) (Tokyo, Nihon Shakaitō Shuppambu, 1957), pp. 37–45.

small boss system and state regulation of the unevenly competitive large fishing companies. In 1957, they called for an increase of two million tons in annual catches by 1961. This was to be accomplished by revised treaties with Canada and the United States as well as by new agreements with nearby communist countries.

In 1959, the SDP published an eight-year agricultural plan, but it was soon confronted by rapidly changing conditions and by agrarian features of the ruling party's Income-Doubling Plan for the 'sixties. Having the initiative, the Liberal Democrats could and did propose that stress be on agricultural products which enjoyed advantages in domestic markets and that unprofitable commodities be imported rather than be expensively subsidized. They envisaged and—along with economic forces for which they were not entirely responsible—have been achieving a faster shift of surplus agricultural labor into urban occupations. New provincial industrial zones were planned. LDP politicians and governmental agencies were in a better position to promote further agricultural mechanization as well as the use of improved pesticides and management. They also promised greater efforts to rationalize the processing and marketing of farm products, and the stabilization not only of main crop prices but also those of implements and materials which farmers need. Villagers were led by them to expect improvements in education and in public works and facilities. In agricultural as in industrial matters, the post-"great leap" troubles of Communist China tended to weaken the appeal of more doctrinaire socialist approaches to such problems.

Responding to these challenges, the SDP early in 1961 introduced its version (soon superseded by the LDP draft) of a Basic Agricultural Law. Soon they included agricultural programs in their "Long-Term Political and Economic Plan." In commentaries, Socialists averred that the conservatives emphasized the efforts of peasants, while they stressed farmers' rights. Liberal Democrats, they charged, were too limited in the sums they proposed to invest. In addition to other policies mentioned as characteristic, the substitution of genuine cooperatives for the agricultural associations, and *planned* reduction of the agricultural labor force were stipulated. They argued that enforcement of an adequate minimum wage law would create more jobs for underemployed farmers. While demanding more central planning, they denounced the "cruel capitalistic principle of economic rationality."

Still, agricultural prosperity continued to march with general economic growth. The Socialists have insisted, however, that their opponents have not really adopted the aim of equalizing farm incomes with those earned in industry and commerce. To do this would involve vast governmental spending and drastic revisions of the structures of taxation, subsidies, and credit. They also want to see Japanese farmers organized adequately for collective bargaining with the large companies which buy their crops and sell them producers' supplies. The Socialists demand protection of farmers against alleged exploitation by such firms. Long-range agricultural planning with annual reports to the Diet were among their proposals.[56]

In 1961 the SDP called for conversion of various large companies of the sorts just mentioned into governmental enterprises, or alternatively for state regulation by means of licenses and price setting. It promised a series of key measures on behalf of fisheries: a "fundamental law," provisions for stabilizing prices, promotion of coastal fishing, and reform of the industry. The party advocated nationalization of all forests except those related to farms and a systematic program of conservation.

By that year, the SDP had encouraged the development of 16 larger farms with joint management; its aim was to have at least three such models in each prefecture. It also urged the organization of producers' cooperatives comprised of five to ten families. The Socialist "farmers' charter" in October 1963 called for state assistance to such units and to small-scale producers. Party missions were observing agricultural methods in Communist China and in Eastern Europe. The "charter" added that publicly managed wholesale markets should be founded in major cities as well as elsewhere. Without being very specific as to means, it advocated measures which would ensure that the diets and housing of farmers would come to be on a par with those of people in other occupations.[57]

Promises of large-scale agricultural investment are, however, not intended solely, or even chiefly, as bait for farmers' votes. Nor are they based on any rational calculation of the likely economic productivity of investment in agriculture, as distinct from transportation or industry. They are rather a consequence of the party's foreign policy. In 1950, before the peace treaty, the security pact, and the development

56. *Shakaitō no Shin Rosen,* pp. 40–65.
57. *Nihon Keizai Shimbun,* Oct. 14, 1963.

of a stable—and to the Socialists wholly unwelcome—pattern of economic dependence on the United States, the party's basic platform set its face strongly against self-sufficiency in staple food supplies, and insisted on the diversification of the farm economy, a reduction of the emphasis on staples, and the development of trade. Later the situation changed. The party anticipated a serious dollar shortage when it could assume power; it expected to be on uneasy terms with Washington and had to plan for the withdrawal of dollar-spending American forces. Its statement of policy in 1957 further asserted that no Socialist government could seriously contemplate taking American food surpluses under the scheme set up by Public Law 480. Hence its insistence on reducing the country's dependence on food imports. It did not go as far as the Right wing's statement of 1954 in planning for complete self-sufficiency. In the development schemes there has been emphasis on the diversification of agriculture as well as on increased production of staples. But self-sufficiency is the ultimate goal which is to be approached as nearly as possible, almost regardless, it seems, of the cost in economic efficiency.

Two other elements of these programs—the emphasis on cooperation and the frequent mention of state control and ownership—spring more directly from socialist principles than from any intention to win votes. In the Socialist view, as preambles to these policy statements make clear, the farmer's chief enemy is monopoly capitalism. The Socialist aim will be to exclude capitalist operation from agriculture as far as possible, partly by encouraging greater cooperation, but more extensively by increasing the regulative powers of the state which, under a Socialist government, would have the true interests of the farmers, rather than the interests of monopoly capital, at heart. Although the party has begun experimentally to introduce cooperative production on newly reclaimed land, it has been clearly concerned about counter-propaganda to the effect that it has persisted in a doctrinaire desire to nationalize all agricultural land. The first section of the pamphlet published in 1958 was headed, with categorical reassurance: "The Socialist Party will not nationalize land."

Proposals for greater state control are not likely in themselves to prove very attractive to the farmer; he finds it difficult to see the monopoly capitalist wolf in the sheep's clothing of the friendly fertilizer merchant who, as he often says, gives better service than the cooperative. On the other hand, the campaigns led by the agricultural cooperatives in the last few years against the abolition of rice controls (an abolition which would be mortally dangerous to the cooperatives as organizations as well as to the farmers as individuals) have probably created a predisposition to believe that the farmer is better protected with controls than without them. The Socialist contention that a wide extension of controls will be beneficial to the farmer may therefore find considerable support, mitigated somewhat by occasional disclosures, as in the fertilizer scandal of 1957, of corruption in the administration of the controls which already exist.

One clear switch in Socialist thinking over these years has been apparent in the final disappearance of the demand for a third land reform. Until 1955 both parties had been insisting that a new measure was necessary to complete the work of land reform. Since then, however, the SDP has apparently come to the conclusion that, provided the present tenancy regulations are maintained and the tenant is guaranteed low rents and security of tenure, the present degree of tenancy is innocuous and that many tenants would probably prefer to remain tenants under present conditions than secure ownership at purchase prices which in present-day Japan could not feasibly be as near-confiscatory as they were at the time of the postwar land reform.

Second, they have discovered that the ownership of forest land is in fact widely distributed (the 1958 booklet mentioned a round five million as the number of owners of forest land, which compared with a total of less than six million farm households) and that it is rare for farmers to be held in feudalistic subjection to forest owners by virtue of their need for firewood or for the fodder or green fertilizer necessary for agriculture (as opposed to their need for employment in the lumber industry or as free-lance charcoal burners).

Third, the party has apparently found that forests have not been properly maintained by their owners because of fear that a Socialist government would take their land away from them.

Fourth, the Socialists have probably discovered that a good number of their supporters or potential adherents are among the very large class of owners of tiny patches of leased-out land or forest whom it is therefore unwise to alienate. By the early 'sixties, the SDP and Nichinō faced shrinkage in the number of marginal farmers, the rural element which they had considered to provide their natural support. Also, they found that agricultural diversification was hampering the organization of farmers in numerous districts. Under the influence of "structural reform," the party has tried to appeal more broadly by advocating price supports not only for rice but also for wheat, milk, and meats, as well as by stressing the need for improved terms of trade and social security for farmers. Left Socialists have, as tariffs have been lowered, posed as champions of Japanese products against foreign competition.

THE RECENT TACTICAL APPROACH

Some of these trends underline the old dilemma in the party's approach to the tactical problem of gaining farmers' support. Traditionally, as we have seen, the appeal has been to the tenant and the underdog. The demand for a third land reform sprang from that tradition. So did some elements of the program adopted in 1957, such as the insistence on a reversion to more progressive forms of taxation to relieve the burden on the smaller farmer, and the charge that the present government's policy of agricultural benefits is a "thirty per cent policy" designed to profit only the richer thirty per cent of farmers.[58]

In prewar days there was a shift away from this tradition of support for the underdog toward an emphasis on the demands of all the farmers, in part because it was politically less subversive to attack capitalists than to attack landlords. Now the same change has taken place, this time largely because there are hardly any landlords left to attack. Once more it is monopoly capital which is the enemy, and more flexible Socialists draw the moral that this gives them theoretical as well as tactical justification for bidding for the support of *all* the farmers. The abandonment of the third land reform, a move to play down appeals which divide one class of farmers from another, is evidence of this change. It parallels the change already noted in Socialist attitudes to small and medium businesses, where the emphasis has been less on stirring up the hostility of workers toward their small entrepreneur employers than on stirring up the hostility of the small entrepreneurs toward the large corporations and the government.

The change has not been an easy one to make, however, particularly for the rural activists who have had the task of spreading the party's

58. The latter charge, somewhat glossed over in the 1957 policy statement, was reiterated with vigor in the more polemical 1958 pamphlet, but it was not explained how any policy, even a Socialist one, which is designed to improve the competitive position of agriculture largely by price manipulation, can fail to benefit most the largest agriculturalists.

message in the villages. The difficulties were apparent in the drafting of the "Farmers' Movement Thesis," a statement prepared for the fourteenth convention in 1958 as a guide to rural tactics. The original draft[59] contained a confused statement that the farmers' movement, being a fight against monopoly capitalism, could properly be a movement of all the farmers and that, further, it was not the small farmers (many of whom were on the verge of *lumpen* proletariat status) but the middling and larger farmers who exercised most influence in the villages. But these elements, though exerting leadership, were said to lack the economic grievances which could make the small farmers really throw themselves body and soul into "demands" and "struggles." Therefore the emphasis should be placed on the poor farmers. But, on the other hand, if *excessive* emphasis were placed on their needs, this would only succeed in alienating the middle farmers, so due emphasis should be given to their demands, too.

This section was completely rewritten in the later draft. First of all, noncultivating landlords—the few who live off forest land or supplement a salary with the rents from a modicum of leased-out agricultural land—together with those cultivating landlords who had been active in the new landlords' movement, were written off as enemies. But there was to be no nonsense about a major emphasis on the poor farmer this time.

> In the villages, middling or better economic status is a precondition for influence. Even in the old days of tenant unions it was not the pure tenant, but the part-owner–part-tenant who generally held the reins of leadership. Since they are influential and since they economically have most to gain or lose, it is this class which must form the center of gravity of the movement, with those above and those below as supporting echelons.

However, there was a danger that this would lead to an excessive "petty producer emphasis." This was to be guarded against by bringing into the movement wage-earning members of farm families, and more ideologically minded women as well as young men.[60]

In other respects than the definition of friends and enemies, the Farmers' Movement Thesis, taken together with the two previous policy pamphlets, provided an indication of the party's divided approach

59. Published in *Gekkan Shakaitō, 4* (Sept. 1957).
60. *Shakai Tsūshin,* 275 (Dec. 25, 1957), p. 9.

to the farmer. The careful delineation of SDP plans for agriculture (which owed more to the right than to the left) seemed to be an ideal instrument for political education in the villages, designed as it partly was with the tactical aim of winning the farmer's support. But that thesis was the product of a tradition more actively preserved by the Left than by the Right during the period of separation. It did not urge party members to take these policy pamphlets to the villages and preach their contents to the villagers. It mentioned briefly in an introduction the fact that the Socialist Party did have a policy for agriculture. It was concerned rather with the traditional farmers' movement activity of organizing "struggles," channeling "demands," creating organizations, with, as the jargon has it, getting the farmers to "rise." Such activities, dear to the heart of left-wing traditionalists of the farmers' movement, were to be the core of the Socialist Party's approach to the villages. The technique has been the "demand-by-demand struggle." Any resentment shared by a number of farmers in common provides an opportunity for struggles and organization, and an opportunity for the leaders to point out that the real enemy is monopoly capitalism.

FARMER SUPPORT FOR THE SOCIALISTS

Under the much improved economic conditions of the late 'fifties and early 'sixties, Japanese farmers have seemed reluctant to "rise up." It appears, however, that a by no means negligible proportion of them have been prepared to vote for the Socialist Party. This final section will consider some of the factors which determine the size of the Socialist vote in rural areas, and the prospects for its increase or decrease.

The first, and fairly obvious, point to be established is that the Socialists poll a smaller percentage of votes in rural than in urban areas. In the Lower House election of 1955, for instance, the Socialists secured 51 per cent of the seats in the thirteen most urbanized constituencies, but only 28 per cent of those in the 69 most rural constituencies. A further indication of the difference, and one which shows fluctuations over time, may be gleaned from the following figures, based on a sampling of administrative areas, which show the total non-conservative vote in Lower House elections in different types of districts.[61]

61. Alfred B. Clubbock, "Japanese Conservative Politics," in Center for Japanese Studies, University of Michigan, *Occasional Papers*, 7 (1957), pp. 21–59.

TABLE 5. DISTRIBUTION OF NON-CONSERVATIVE VOTES BY TYPE OF DISTRICT, 1947–1955

Type of District	*Non-Conservative percentage of total votes in election of*				
	1947	*1949*	*1952*	*1953*	*1955*
Villages (pop. less than 5,000)	47.5	34.6	28.6	27.6	30.4
Larger villages and small towns (pop. 5,000–30,000)	47.8	36.5	29.4	31.1	31.4
Medium towns (pop. 30,000–150,000)	50.1	40.6	35.0	36.9	39.8
Large towns (pop. more than 150,000)	53.6	46.1	44.1	44.9	44.9

These are, of course, votes for all except the Liberal and Democratic parties or their forerunners, rather than votes for the Socialist Party only. Except for the elections of 1949, however, Socialist votes predominated in the total and it is a safe conclusion that in all elections the village areas produced a considerably smaller proportion of Socialist voters than the large towns.

Opinion polls provide somewhat more detailed evidence of farmers' as distinct from rural votes in general. Polls asking farmers which party they supported showed a consistent pattern during the period 1950–58. Fifty or sixty per cent of the samples gave their support to the conservative parties, while the proportion declaring themselves for the Socialists rose slightly during the late 'fifties from 15 to about 20 per cent.[62] In a survey after the Lower House elections of 1955, 16.2 per cent of a sample of 476 farmers, foresters, and fishermen said that they had voted for one of the Socialist parties.[63]

What sort of people, then, compose this Socialist sixth of the farmers? Some clues may be gained by considering first the types of Socialist candidates who have been elected in rural constituencies. A limited amount of information is available concerning the careers of 81 of the 93 men and women who have been elected to the Lower House as official candidates of one of the Socialist parties at one or more of the three elections held in the years 1952–55,[64] in the 69 most predomi-

62. Allan B. Cole, *Japanese Society and Politics*, p. 132.

63. Senkyōbu Jichichō, *Shōwa Sanjūnen Nigatsu Shikkō Shūgiin Senkyo, Saikō Saibansho Saibankan Kokumin Kansa Kekka Shirabe* (Report on the Results of the Election of House of Representatives of February 1955 and the Referendum on the Members of the Supreme Court) (Tokyo, 1955), p. 175.

64. Data secured from a questionnaire survey of officeholders in the Socialist Party conducted by this research project, and from the *Shūgiin Yōran*.

nantly rural constituencies. They may be broadly classified according to a limited number of dominant career patterns.

First of all, there are 25 men who were active in tenant and farmers' movements before the war. A dozen of them were lawyers who had defended farmers and their leaders in the courts (many of them former sons of poor families who had worked their way through a university). Some had been active in the proletarian parties of the 'thirties and had remained Diet members until the end of the war; others had withdrawn from political activities altogether, or had adapted themselves to modest activity in agricultural or patriotic associations. Most of these, it may be presumed, were well known in their constituencies for their farmers' union activities and still maintained some sort of farmers' union organization which worked for them in elections. Two more with half a foot in this category were younger men who entered the farmers' movement after the war.[65]

The second important category is of men and women with a background in labor union work. It included 28 of the younger men and women, nearly all of whom entered active politics after the war via the union movement. Nine of them were local leaders of the Teachers' Union, two of the Railway Workers' Union, two of the Postal Workers', and two of the Local Government Workers' Unions. Others were leaders of unions in particular industries important in the district—mines, pottery works, pulp factories, and the like.

A third category is composed of what might be called locally prominent people. It includes 18 men and women with no record of prewar left-wing activity, people of middle- or upper-class status who had achieved some eminence in their constituencies as local businessmen, local politicians, bureaucrats, perhaps a doctor or the personnel manager of a mining company, three of them as active leaders of agricultural associations or the postwar cooperatives. A few were members of the local aristocracy—the son of a prewar conservative politician, the descendant of a high-ranking samurai family, and so on. Most were university-trained, and a number of them, doubtless, were drawn into the Socialist Party by the reactivation after the war of left-wing leanings they had entertained in their youth. Others frankly say, in answer to questions concerning their motives for entering the party, that they

65. Twenty-seven, of course, does not represent the total number of Lower House members with this background. A number of other men with farmers' union connections were elected in constituencies which are less exclusively rural than the 69 selected.

wished to get into politics and saw, after the war, that the Socialist Party was the party of the future.[66]

The fourth and similar category is again of men with no record of prewar political activity, and of middle-class origin. They might be called the local boys who made good—eight men who had achieved some position in national life, rather than in their native districts, as journalists, bureaucrats (one as a high-ranking police official), or as officials of large corporations, returning to their native districts with the prestige so acquired to enter politics after the war.

Men of backgrounds as diverse as these obviously attract different types of voters for different reasons. The prewar farmers' union leaders, though many of them today derive a great deal of support from labor organizations in their constituencies, usually have a solid core of support in the villages based on personal links forged in the militant days before the war. Many of their key supporters, formerly tenant leaders in the villages, are now prosperous owner-farmers, and often the same qualities of energetic leadership which made them union leaders before the war have secured them responsible positions in local government or in the agricultural cooperatives. As such they are no longer subject to the resentments and frustrations which prompted their prewar radicalism. They may remain loyal, and they are probably influential in swaying the votes of their fellow-villagers, but the latters' loyalty may be to their former friend and leader rather than to socialism. A village cooperative leader had this to say in a newspaper article:

> You have to go to the left to find the true loyalists. They never forget their "indebtedness" in the days of tenancy disputes, and they rush around collecting votes for their candidate. . . . The relation between these farmers' union members and their candidates is much more of a feudal one than a modern one. In the villages it is the left which is acting as the guardian of "beautiful feudal values."[67]

This may not be the whole story, however. The loyalty of these ex-tenants may be to their own radical past and, if not to socialism, at

66. For data about the proportional strength of agrarian leaders in the left and right Socialist factions in the Diet up to 1958, see Scalapino and Masumi, *Parties and Politics,* pp. 69, 71–72.

67. *Asahi Shimbun* (March 22, 1958, morning).

least to the Socialist Party as the present embodiment of the prewar radical tradition. Many of them, too, being intelligent and thoughtful men, and being brought into contact with Socialist policies through their association with the candidate, may be supporters of the party by conviction rather than merely out of loyalty.

It may be more especially the candidates in the third or fourth groups whose following is personal rather than ideological. Very often their marriage with the Socialist Party is one of convenience. They need the additional union votes guaranteed by the party label, and the party needs a candidate who can win enough votes by his personal prestige to reinforce the core Socialist votes to the point of electoral victory. Their personal votes are mobilized in much the same way—by emphasizing their status claims to leadership, by the granting of favors, and by punctiliously keeping up personal relations with gifts and periodic postcards—as by conservative candidates. Many of them, indeed, maintain support societies on the conservative model. The importance of the person and the irrelevance of the party for many of the voters they attract is well illustrated by the case of Iku Kinoshita and his brother Tetsu. They were sons of a former mayor of the town of Oita, in Kyūshū, which dominates their constituency. Iku became a lawyer and in 1942 was elected to the Diet as one of Tōjō's "recommended" candidates. He reentered politics after his release from purge restrictions and was elected as a Right Socialist in 1952 and 1953. In 1955 he gave up his seat and left the party to run for the prefectural governorship as an independent. At the same time his brother, Tetsu, a local businessman and former member of the prefectural assembly with no apparent Socialist leanings up to that time, entered the SDP to succeed his brother's seat and was handsomely elected.

It is significant of the large and probably growing importance of labor organizations as a means of mobilizing Socialist votes, even in rural constituencies, that the number of former trade union leaders exceeded the number of farmers' union leaders in this group of 81 rural Socialist candidates. This in part reflects the fact that, given a large constituency electing four or five members, it is often possible, even in an overwhelmingly agricultural area, for a single Socialist candidate to be elected by relying chiefly on the votes of a single isolated industrial area. (Sometimes as little as eight or nine per cent of the total votes is enough for election.) But this, as a study of the geographical spread of Socialist votes in such constituencies shows, is not usually the case in practice.

Union organizations can be effective in mobilizing the votes of the farmers too. The large postwar increase in nonagricultural employment of farm-family members has already been mentioned. Japan's six million farm families now derive about 50 per cent of their income from outside sources. This means that many farm families have a son or a daughter, or perhaps the husband himself, in wage or salary employment. Some commute to nearby towns; others are employed in village offices, or in railway, postal, and teaching services in their home villages. It is significant that members of the Teachers', Railway, Postal, and Local Government Workers' Unions make up over half of the rural union-based Diet members. Such unions are often influential in elections, the more effective in that their members are scattered throughout the villages. It is their practice to urge their members not only to vote for the Socialist candidate themselves, but to get "three—or four or five—votes per man." Teachers in particular are often men of influence in their villages who find no difficulty in fulfilling such a norm, and it is no accident that nine of these union men were originally leaders of the local Teachers' Union.

This kind of personal influence radiating from the unions can operate not only in the case of farm commuters and village wage-earners, but also through sons and daughters in small industrial towns separated from their parental farm families. The operational slogan adopted by the Yamaguchi Prefectural Labor Federation for the elections in 1955 was "Three votes per man, and everybody take a day trip home." Unions also help influence farmers' votes in a more impersonal way, by offering their labor and administrative resources for election campaigns in the villages. The same Yamaguchi Federation sent film teams into the villages in 1955 to hold shows of propaganda films for farmers.

So far we have suggested, in discussing types of rural candidates, four kinds of motivation which may be effective in mobilizing Socialist votes in the villages: personal loyalty for a man with a long record of championing the farmers' cause; personal admiration for a candidate who carries local prestige; loyalty to a union which has thrown its weight behind a Socialist candidate; and susceptibility to the suggestion of a relative or neighbor who is a union member. To this must be added a fifth motive, not dissimilar in type: personal loyalty toward a man who himself has a direct loyalty to a Socialist candidate, the loyalty in both cases being of the traditional, personal type, maintained by the exchange of favors. Such networks of personal relations often provide for Socialist candidates as cohesive an electoral machine as conservative candidates enjoy. Very often the key intermediate figures in the network are local politicians, especially members of prefectural assemblies. In one district of Niigata, for instance, it was reported that the Socialist candidate, who had considerable influence among the farmers, came to an understanding with a local businessman who had connections among cottage industry textile workers. The latter used his influence with the workers to swing their votes behind the former in the Diet elections, and the compliment was returned when the businessman stood as candidate in the prefectural assembly elections. Welfare officers, members of village assemblies, officials of agricultural cooperatives or of irrigation unions, agricultural extension workers and the like often occupy such important intermediate positions in the electoral "machines" of Socialist, as of conservative, candidates.

There is another form of "deal," important as a determinant of rural voting, which at present, however, operates chiefly as a reason for not voting Socialist. This involves the promise by Diet members of particular financial benefits for their constituents. At present about one third of the national budget is distributed in the provinces in the form of ad hoc grants and subsidies—for schools, roads, and bridges, and also, more relevantly in this context, for a wide variety of agricultural purposes. More than a hundred different types of subsidies are at the disposal of the Ministry of Agriculture and Forestry: grants to villages or to cooperatives for irrigation works or the building of village installations, or grants which go ultimately to individuals for the purchase of cattle or machines, for soil-dressing, or the building of silos. Diet members, particularly of the government party, have considerable influence over the officials who make the decisions concerning the distribution of these grants. Judiciously used, this power can be an effective instrument for winning votes. Socialist Diet members are not entirely lacking in the power to influence officials with such discretionary powers. A member from Shizuoka, for instance, is said to have had the solid support of the orange exporters for whom he arranged a favorable allocation of foreign exchange. But inevitably it is members of the party in power who are most influential, and this, at present, is a powerful factor in the success of the Liberal-Democratic Party in the villages.

But this by no means exhausts the catalogue of the motives which underlie Socialist support in the villages. It has been stressed before in this chapter that there are a good number of voters in rural districts whose vote is influenced to a greater or less degree by the impressions they receive, from the press, the radio and television, and in conversation with their neighbors, of the relative capacities and records of the two main parties and of their respective policies. Farmers turn out in large numbers to election meetings in the village and listen attentively to the speeches. In a survey after the Lower House elections in 1955, people were asked how they made up their minds whom to vote for. Of the nearly 500 farmers, fishermen, and foresters in the sample, 41 per cent answered: "by reading the candidates' election addresses" or "after hearing their speeches." This was a smaller proportion than the 49 per cent of white-collar workers who gave the same replies, but considerably larger than the corresponding figure of 28 per cent for manual workers.[68] The figures quoted earlier for the non-conservative vote in different types of districts suggest that there are more floating votes in rural than in urban districts. The decline in the Socialist vote in rural areas between 1947 and 1949 was somewhat greater than in urban areas. This may be due in part to the decline in farmers' unions, in part to the satisfaction of the tenant farmers' desire for a land reform, and in part to population movements, but it was doubtless also due to the failure of the Socialist Party to form an effective government.

What, then, are the policies and what are the features of the Socialist Party, *qua* party, which win it support in rural areas? The answer would seem to be much the same policies and features which win it support among the unorganized voters in the towns. After the House of Councillors election in 1956 one newspaper commentator, in analyzing Socialist gains in the predominantly rural prefectures of Kumamoto and Akita, came to the conclusion that the party's reiterated opposition to constitutional revision was the biggest single factor in winning new Socialist votes.[69] It is a sign, too, of the "ideological" nature of Socialist support that, in rural as in urban areas, its supporters appear to be disproportionately numerous among the young

68. Senkyōbu Jichichō, *Shōwa Sanjūnen,* p. 180.
69. *Asahi Shimbun,* July 15, 1956.

and the better educated.[70] The Socialist Party itself is aware of this. A recurrent theme in the post-mortem discussions of the election of 1956 published in the party journal was the effectiveness of support by youths' and women's organizations, and the need to use them even more effectively in the future in order to spread the party's message.[71]

This is not to say, of course, that appeals to the farmer *qua* farmer have had, and are likely to have, no effect. Certainly, in a negative sense, it is widely believed by Socialist organizers that the party suffers in rural districts from being stereotyped as the party of the industrial workers which cannot possibly, therefore, have the interests of the farmer genuinely at heart.[72] Simply in the sense of softening such antipathies, greater efforts to propagandize its latest agricultural programs might pay dividends. So possibly, too, might greater activity in fanning farmers' curent resentments, on the lines of the Farmers' Movement Thesis. But in these terms the Socialist Party in opposition is never likely to be able to compete successfully with conservative politicians able to promise concrete local benefits in the form of agricultural grants and subsidies.

We have already noted that in its rural electioneering, at least in 1955, the Socialist Party was much more inclined to stress matters of constitutional reform, foreign policy, political corruption, and the like than it was to talk of agricultural policies. It is perhaps odd that a Marxist party should, in its casual neglect of the appeal to immediate economic interest, so openly flout the doctrine of economic determinism. But in this it is probable that its practice is better than its theory. To reiterate the point made at the beginning of this chapter, Japanese villages are no longer peopled by unsophisticated yokels who are unaware of the great national issues which are the stuff of modern Japanese politics. It is probably on its general attitude to these issues, on its record and capacities as a party, and especially, perhaps, on the public personalities of its leaders, as these are filtered through the press, radio, and TV to the farmer, that its future will depend. The Socialist Party's electoral prospect in the villages may be slightly less promising than, but is not likely to be much different from, its electoral fate among the unorganized voters in the towns.

70. R. P. Dore, *Land Reform in Japan* (London, Oxford University Press, 1958), pp. 455–59.

71. *Shakai Tsūshin, 192* (July 15, 1956).

72. See the discussion in *Shakai Tsūshin, 181* (May 20, 1956).

12. Socialist Support from Middle and Other Strata

Long before emergence of the two-main-party system, many a Socialist campaigner had become fully aware of the importance of support by voters who belong neither to Japan's most potent elites nor to the industrial working class. Relative to Japanese society and defined in these sweeping terms, people in the middle strata comprise some 60 to 75 per cent of the population. More narrowly and occupationally defined, they constitute about one quarter of the total population and nearly one half of all city dwellers.[1]

Total numbers in various types of occupations usually associated with middle-class status will be mentioned later when we discuss the political tendencies of such groups. As we study the behavior of people in these strata, and in particular view them in relation to the Social

1. In November 1963 the total number of eligible voters was more than 57.6 million. In 1956, it was estimated to be 50.3 million. More than 15 million voters were then non-employed, while as many as 12 million youths with jobs were under age twenty and thus not able to vote.

Among the increasing number of studies of Japan's middle strata are: Ronald P. Dore, *City Life in Japan, A Study of A Tokyo Ward* (Berkeley and Los Angeles, University of California Press, 1963), see esp. Chaps. 13, 17, 19, 23; Ezra F. Vogel, *Japan's New Middle Class, The Salary Man and His Family in a Tokyo Suburb* (Berkeley and Los Angeles, University of California Press, 1963), esp. Chap. 5; Kazuo Ōkōchi, *Nihon-teki Chūsan Kaikyū* (The Japanese Middle Class) (Tokyo, Bungei Shunjū Shinsha, 1960), esp. Chaps. 4, 5.

Democrats, it will be well to have some idea of their occupational (and related stratal) distribution. A survey in 1952 by interviewers of the National Public Opinion Research Institute judged the stratal identifications of a national sample of 2,670 adults to be shown in Table 6, page 420.

Socialists and labor union leaders who frequently talk and write about "confrontation" tend to oversimplify popular impressions of how workers and capitalists behave politically. Table 6 clearly shows an elite of corporate executives, high professionals, and proprietors; and from other sources we know that politically these elements are overwhelmingly conservative. About two thirds of the laborers incline toward the other end of the spectrum, being lower-middle and lower in class status. But at least three quarters of each of these larger groups can be identified with middle strata, though in political outlook they may tend to be assimilated to some other class. The interests of big business and upper bureaucracy, on the one hand, and of much of unionized labor in larger industries and government, on the other, are better organized and often mutually opposed. Though this is reflected in their prevailing political choices, to a lesser extent the larger groups to which they belong also bunch mostly in the middle strata. Thus it is inevitable that the electoral support of major national parties will be cross-stratal, though certain organized interests exert special influence on and within them. Also it is natural that there is keen competition for the support of voters in the mid-middle and lower-middle strata. Though these elements have less economic reserves and weaker traditions of individualism than their counterparts in the West, the diversity of their interests has enabled them in normal times to play somewhat stabilizing roles in politics.

Particularly among Japanese of lower-middle-class status there are indications that significant percentages of those whom experts classify in the middle view themselves as members of the lower or working class. Obviously this might affect their electoral choices. But in reasonably stable or improving economic conditions this does not cause the lower plus lower-middle strata to become a majority. Of course, there are factors other than class membership which influence voting preferences.

Opinion polls confirm what is common knowledge in Japan: that the principal supporters of the Social Democratic Party have been industrial workers, company and governmental employees, students,

TABLE 6. SOCIAL STRATIFICATION OF OCCUPATIONAL CLASSES IN 1952*

Class rating by interviewers	*Executive & Managerial*	*Professional*	*Clerical*	*Individual Manufacturer & Merchant*	*Farmer, Fisher, Forester*	*Labor*	*Other*	*Student*	*Household worker*	*No occupation*	*Number*
Upper	18.2%	18.0%	6.6%	6.2%	7.4%	0.2%	9.3%	8.2%	8.4%	5.0%	161
Middle	77.3	51.3	59.0	53.1	49.7	33.7	39.5	71.8	52.1	40.9	1277
Lower Middle	4.5	25.6	31.1	38.8	32.8	43.9	37.2	16.5	30.9	38.4	920
Lower	0	5.1	3.3	7.9	10.1	22.2	14.0	3.5	8.6	15.7	310

* National Opinion Poll Research Institute, No. 51, "Shakai Kyōiku" (Social Education) (March–April 1952), this part of which was reproduced in Wendell D. Baker, "A Study of Selected Aspects of Japanese Social Stratification: Class Differences in Levels of Aspiration" (Ph.D. dissertation, Columbia University, 1956), p. 52.

teachers, and—especially before the land reform—tenant-farmers. In this chapter we are stressing the urban middle strata, but in some senses there is also a rural middle class. In 101 villages and towns of the Inland Sea area, a sample of 961 predominantly male household heads was interviewed in 1952; 34.5 per cent of them were considered to be of upper-middle-class status, while a slightly larger proportion were identified as lower-middle. Less than one quarter were engaged in occupations usually thought of as middle-class in nature. Among these rural respondents, 14.8 per cent of those of upper and upper-middle-class status had supported the SDP in 1949, while 17.3 per cent of those in the lower-middle and lower strata had done so. Among the minority which supported this main opposition party in the election month of October 1952, young men, the more highly educated, and those with other interests in addition to (or in place of) farming were somewhat more prominent.[2]

The nature of the party did not motivate these rural supporters as much as did its platform and their own personal reasons. In April 1961, a survey of samples in 70 rural communities and 17 medium-size towns found that non-farmers identified with the middle class in rural villages (managers, proprietors, clerks, and the like) were by themselves rather weakly identified with that class; many thought of themselves as members of the working class. In the towns, components of the middle class were more self-conscious. Their status identification was determined chiefly on the basis of occupation. Their levels of formal education were higher than for counterparts in the villages, but that of proprietors was not as high as for some other subgroups.[3]

In an effort to analyze more reliably the kinds of social strata and organizations supporting the Socialist Party and the ways in which candidates accordingly shaped campaign strategies, our research group sent questionnaires to all SDP candidates soon after the elections of February 27, 1955.[4] From other sources we learned that, among the total of 67 Right and 89 Left Socialist Diet members elected, 27 right- and 36 left-wingers had been professional people; 13 and 14, respec-

2. This survey was sponsored by the Okayama Field Station of the Center for Japanese Studies, University of Michigan. Professors and students from a number of universities in the Kansai and Inland Sea regions cooperated.

3. Ibid., pp. 79–81.

4. Fifty Left and 43 Right Socialists (48 and 33 successful candidates, respectively) responded to the questionnaire. Results have been more fully tabulated and interpreted in Cole et al., "Support for Japanese Social Democrats in 1955."

tively, had been or were businessmen; 5 and 6, respectively, had had bureaucratic careers; while one had to be identified as a professional politician.

Right and Left Socialist respondents agreed that labor unions were their chief source of organized support, and that next in order of importance were organized white-collar employees and youths. Next came emphasis on organizations of women (Left) and small business people (Right).[5] Two Right and six Left Socialists had been supported by Kankōrō and affiliated unions of governmental workers; 18 had been supported by organized prefectural and metropolitan office workers. Some of the responding candidates stated that they then were affiliated with a variety of organizations: professional (6), economic development groups (6), trade associations (4), small business groups (5), cultural societies (14), and educational bodies (4).

Regarding support by *unorganized* voters, candidates of both factions stressed the political importance of intellectuals. Of the successful candidates, 12 moderates and six on the Left mentioned specific assistance from such persons. Unorganized youths were mentioned by more leftists but in weighted choices were given more emphasis by the right-wingers. Unorganized women were in an intermediate position. Unorganized office workers and small businessmen were each mentioned by 67 respondents, but they received less prominence. Thus we can conclude that, although the Socialist Party is chiefly based on unionized workers in large enterprises and in governmental offices, many of its leaders and organs have become increasingly aware of the importance of middle strata, both with and without organization.

Having in summary grasped the overall proportions of the middle class and surveyed some patterns of bourgeois political behavior and

5. Of 43 Right and 50 Left SDP candidates who replied that they had received support from middle-class organizations, the following numbers mentioned specific types:

Types of Organizations	*by Right SDP candidates*	*by Left SDP candidates*
Employees (white-collar)	32	43
Youth	26	38
Women	26	37
Small business	18	30
Local public corporations	9	9
Large corporations	6	4

their significance for the SDP, let us turn to specific middle strata: professionals, bureaucrats, white-collar workers, students, women, and small to medium enterprisers. In each case we shall try to assess the importance of the stratum for the Social Democrats, to mention the party organ which is specially designed to provide liaison and cooperation, and—using small business as the main example—to describe pertinent party policies and activities.

PROFESSIONAL AND TECHNICAL WORKERS

In 1953, there were approximately 1.64 million professional and technical workers in Japan, divisible into two main groups: those in higher, more skilled, less populous, in general politically more conservative professions and technical positions; and the lower, more numerous statuses shading into an intermediate group (including public school teachers, for example) on the fringe of the white-collar stratum.[6] On other bases, some observers would subdivide professional and technical people according to whether they earn independent livelihoods usually on a fee basis, are mainly employed by public authorities, are controlled by such national or local authorities, are employed by private corporations, or live in situations where they are largely influenced by social pressures. Higher professionals and technicians tend to feel a strong stake in their skills and to value contacts with the more powerful elites of government and business. However, especially some female specialists, such as nurses, who find promotion difficult may tend to favor parties of protest. Of course, professionals and technicians constitute the best educated (in a formal sense) and therefore one of the most politically conscious strata.

During the Occupation period, polls showed that 42–52 per cent of this stratum of the population samples polled characteristically supported conservative parties; this slumped in 1954 during the scandals and decline of the Yoshida government's popularity, but there was partial recovery by mid-1955.

The same surveys indicated that in the neighborhood of 11–15 per cent of professionals and technicians supported the SDP during the

6. In this chapter, some statistics from the early 1960s are provided, but most of the figures pertain to 1948–57. Most of the patterns which emerged continue to obtain, the main modifications reflecting economic growth and prosperity since 1957. In these terms, the important changes have been the decline of discontent and militancy on the part of workers, and the expansion and strengthening of Japan's middle strata.

Occupation. About one fifth to one fourth supported no party, and, if we add those in the "don't know" columns, the fraction would reach one third. During 1953, the pro-SDP minority seems to have been between 17 and 23 per cent, and during the first half of the next year the Socialists of Left and Right gained at the expense of the troubled conservatives. Socialist support from this stratum evidently declined in the last half of 1954, and probably not more than about one fourth of such people supported the two Social Democratic Parties during 1955. Soon after reunification, a *Yomiuri* sample (which may have been inadvertently skewed in favor of the SDP) showed this group divided 40:44 between the Socialist and the main conservative party. During the SDP schism (1951–55), pro-Socialist people of professional status seemed to favor the Right faction somewhat more than the Left, but some of the *Yomiuri* and Yoron Kagaku Kyōkai polls showed the reverse.[7]

Traditional Confucian morality has conferred high prestige on intellectuals in this society where sharp distinctions are made between desk and manual occupations. The Social Democrats, some as genuine and others as lip-serving Marxists, have a generation-old tradition of intellectualism within their movement. They, like the Communists, give many intellectuals the impression that in the planned society there would be more influential roles for them. The party shares to some extent the wider prestige of professors, writers, actors, and friendly scientists; it recognizes the leftist minority as the most articulate in formulating ideas.

The Left Socialist faction and Sōhyō have loosely affiliated, overlapping circles of "cultured men" (*bunkajin*) which are activated—often in concert—to supply a rationale and help popularize campaigns in favor of peace and against rearmament, advocacy of a "peace economy" and of cultural and economic relations with Communist China, defense of the democratic Constitution, opposition to renewal of the security treaty, and the drafting of five-year economic plans. Some of these intellectuals also connect the faction with the left wing of the

7. This information came from 37 political opinion polls, which gave breakdowns for support by professional and technical workers, between January 1948 and November 1955. These included: 1 by *Jiji* News Service, 1 by *Asahi Shimbun,* 15 by *Yomiuri Shimbun,* 4 by *Mainichi Shimbun,* 1 by the Shimbun Yoron Chōsa Remmei (Newspaper Public Opinion League), and 15 (confined to the Tokyo area) by the Yoron Kagaku Kyōkai (Public Opinion Science Society). See Cole and Nakanishi, *Japanese Opinion Polls, 1.*

Japan Farmers' Union. Somewhat less active are similar circles which have provided an intellectual aura and partial liaison for the Right Socialist faction and its related labor and farmers' organizations.

In the offices of the Ammonium Sulphate Workers' Union the left-oriented Socialist Society has its headquarters. In mid-1950, an editorial split resulted in termination of its organ *Zenshin* (Forward) and initiation of the still current magazine, *Shakaishugi* (Socialism). Foremost members of this society are veterans of the prewar Worker-Farmer faction, young scholars, certain leaders of leftist Sōhyō unions, and some politicos of the Left SDP. Some members of other organizations, such as the Fabian Institute and the National Economic Research Institute, at times cooperate with the Socialists. During the struggle against the Subversive Activities Prevention Bill, the Japan Teachers' Union and Sōhyō jointly fostered a conference which resulted in a loosely organized "Cultured Men's Council." This group cooperated with Sōhyō and the Left Socialists during the elections of 1952 and 1953. There is also a Socialist Lawyers' Association and an Actors' and Writers' Association which assisted the SDP during the campaign for seats in the House of Councillors in 1956.

Some call the Democratic Socialist League (Minshu Shakaishugi Remmei, or Minsharen) the brain-trust of the Right Socialists. It was founded immediately after the schism in 1951 to counter the influence of the Socialist Society. Its monthly publication is entitled *Minshu Shakaishugi* (Democratic Socialism); the order of these names is deliberate. Its programmatic thought is along the moderate, anti-communist lines of policies adopted by the Socialist International during its convention at Frankfurt-am-Main in 1951.

BUREAUCRATIC INFLUENCE AND THE SOCIAL DEMOCRATS

Japan's Socialists are keenly aware that, although sizable proportions of civil servants in middle and clerical ranks prefer their party, upper bureaucrats who wield power are predominantly conservative. And a party which is both chronically in opposition and remote from power has a weak appeal for topflight bureaucrats, whose relative power has increased since 1945 and the temporary purges of militaristic politicians; they have increasingly entered the Diet, parties, and corporations with their administrative skills.

In 1954 there were approximately 1.28 million Japanese employed in national ministries and agencies,[8] another million in governmental corporations and other services, plus 1.5 million in all local levels of administration. These people may be divided into four main groups: the elite; the university graduates (especially in law and economics) who are often promoted to positions just under the elite; graduates of technical colleges who are less preferred; and the army of "little soldiers," i.e., clerical workers. The Japan Council of National and Local Government Workers' Unions (Kankōrō), which usually cooperated with Sōhyō and the left Socialists, was composed on the national level mostly of the latter two groups. Automatic membership prevails, however, so that the figure of 2.27 million members claimed in 1955 by this federation is rather misleading. Dissatisfied, socialist-minded graduates of technical colleges tend to become leaders of many affiliated governmental service unions. Clerical workers usually lack cohesion, and one reason communications workers have been able to deploy more strategically in radical politics is not only that they have superior liaison but also are more homogeneous because of the nature of their duties.

Many youths entering governmental ministries from universities are circumspect during examinations yet really hold progressive if not radical views. They learn, however, that it is unwise to discuss politics at the office and that the Personnel Section would frown on any controversial community activities. From the ninth official grade on, supervision over them shifts to the ministerial administration; and (as in industrial bureaucracy) when they reach the tenth to thirteenth grades they are forbidden to belong to unions. This is the time when they will be climbing to headships of sections and bureaus, and it often coincides in private life with the stage when many men become heads of families and therefore tend to become more conservative. Another moderating influence is their closer association with the top brass of bureaucracy and their aspirations for further promotion.

A 1952 survey of 239 officials of the Ministry of Agriculture in the sixth and seventh grades, levels at which university graduates usually enter, and 250 officials with similar rank in the Ministry of International Trade and Industry showed that 60 per cent in the former supported one of the Social Democratic Parties, while in the latter it

8. Of these, about 456,500 were divided among the 15 civil service grades: 64–69,000 in each of the fourth through seventh ranks; 27–40,000 in each of the eighth through tenth; 3,500 to 1,200 in each of the twelfth through fourteenth.

was 64 per cent. In the MITI sample, choices were two-to-one in favor of the Right Socialists. Support for conservative parties by these young civil servants was only 13 and 17 per cent, respectively. Strong distrust of the Communist Party was expressed.[9]

But without control over officials at the apex of ministries the Socialist Party cannot command the potent state mechanisms. On the basis of its brief and partial tenure of power during 1947–48, only a few leaders with bureaucratic experience joined the national party elite. Since party research staffs are inadequate, bureaucratic officials and experts often aid (especially conservative) party leaders to formulate policies and bills. The Social Democrats began to receive this kind of assistance when they briefly shared power, and a few governmental specialists have continued in their spare time to advise that party. Also middle bureaucrats supply information to the Socialists for their own purposes, hoping that the Socialists will use the information when interpellating the government, especially regarding budgetary allocations for increased social services and the like. Socialist leaders say that when they come to power they will remove senior bureaucrats from high posts and promote more progressive junior officials. It is reasonably conjectured that, if the SDP should return to power, only a few influential officials would sincerely cooperate, but that after two or three more party incumbencies the national bureaucracy might become seriously divided.

COOPERATION WITH THE WHITE-COLLAR SALARIAT

Of the more numerous middle-class components, white-collar workers, being lower in the spectrum, respond most to the features and appeals of the Socialist parties. They constitute what is sometimes called "the new middle class." This stratum can be said to begin with lower professionals such as teachers, and to include clerks, secretaries, bookkeepers, agents, and less skilled specialized workers. In the mid-'fifties, this population was divisible into some three million governmental workers at several levels plus about 737,000 teachers in public, technical, and vocational schools; and, in addition, approximately eight million privately and corporately employed clericals, two million of whom were women.

According to a research survey conducted in January 1960, white-

9. This information was provided by Professors Kiyoaki Tsuji and Tōru Takahashi in 1956.

collar workers can be subdivided into an upper stratum, composed of the employees of large companies and professional workers, and a lower group—mostly employed in small and medium-size enterprises, chiefly wholesale and retail as well as service firms. Significant for the Socialists is the fact that the upper group—especially employed professional specialists—are more class-conscious and "progressive"; they read more and are aware of political issues and platforms. At least in terms of opinion, they give as much support to political strikes as laborers do, and they are more favorable to a national policy of denuclearized neutralism than are blue-collar workers. Young, well educated, white-collar workers tend to think like left-wing intellectuals, but such proclivities may be eroded as they grow older and mount various vocational ladders.[10] Many white-collar workers are influenced by the prevailing political tinge of their unions, and in general the governmental and corporate sectors are highly unionized.

A survey of 57 political support polls which had a salariat category in the breakdown of their samples (1948–57) indicates some tendencies and trends.[11] In mid-March 1948, when the Social Democrats were still part of a coalition with the conservative Democrats, an *Asahi* poll showed that slightly more than one third of the salariat supported the SDP, while nearly half favored conservative parties. Then the failure of a politically motivated strike wave, followed by SCAP-inspired legislation to deprive civil servants of the rights to strike and bargain collectively, apparently led to declining support of the SDP from this stratum. Support seems to have been stronger in the Tokyo area and in certain other cities, such as Kyoto, than in the country at large.

The Socialists recovered part of their support from this stratum by the fall of 1951. All the polls during the SDP schism and until shortly before the elections of February 1955 showed the salariat supporting the Right Socialists by a margin of 2 to 10 per cent over the Left. Thereafter, the polls almost consistently showed greater white-collar support of the Left wing. This would indicate perhaps that these peo-

10. This research was accomplished by the Research Society on Japanese Social Structure and was based on a sample of 3,000 adult males, age 20 and above, living in the 23 administrative wards of Tokyo. See: "Special Traits of White-Collar Workers in Large Urban Areas," *Journal of Social and Political Ideas in Japan, I* (Aug. 1963), 76–78.

11. During the period March 1948 to March 1957, the surveyed polls were distributed as follows: 13 by *Asahi Shimbun*, 8 by *Mainichi Shimbun*, 15 by *Yomiuri Shimbun*, 17 by Yoron Kagaku Kyōkai (in Tokyo area only), 3 by Shimbun Yoron Chōsa Remmei, 1 by *Jiji* News Agency. See *Japanese Opinion Polls, I*.

ple had been impressed by the greater electoral gains by the Left than by Right Socialists in 1952 and 1953. Also the dominant issues of constitutional revision and of rearmament may have led white-collar workers to favor the stronger opposition stand of the leftists.

Since March 1955, polls have indicated that 40 to 45 per cent of the salariat have supported the Socialist parties; this proportion apparently did not increase merely as a result of party reunification in October of that year. After the emergence of the two main parties, a minority of 30 to 39 per cent of white-collar workers supported the Liberal Democratic Party. According to the polls, between one tenth and one quarter were in the "no party" and "don't know" categories.

As mentioned earlier, the Socialist Party doubtless receives considerable support from unorganized clerical workers, but coordinated campaign and struggle activities are usually waged by the main party factions together with their respective labor federations as well as with friendly independent federations and unions. Especially have the Left Socialists, Sōhyō, and the governmental workers' unions federated in and under Kankōrō operated as a formidable alliance.[12] Outstanding in its radical political tendencies is the Japan Teachers' Union (Nihon Kyōshokuin Kumiai, abbreviated Nikkyōso), claiming more than 547,000 members and an active affiliate of Sōhyō.[13] Organized white-collar workers demonstrated vigorously against the revised Police Duties Bill in 1958 and against renewal of the security treaty in 1960.

12. In 1955, Kankōrō claimed 2.27 million members divided into 238,850 in the National Public Servants' Association, 824,800 in the Public Enterprises' Association, and 1,211,000 in the Local Public Servants' Association. Unions for governmental employees included those for teachers, communications workers, post office employees, railway workers, and workers in telecommunications, monopolies, national hospitals, the ministries, tax collectors, and printing. Nongovernmental clerical workers were unionized in such fields as private railways, express delivery, newspapers, broadcasting, movie and theater, banking, department stores, printing and publishing, insurance, hotels and restaurants.

13. The central committee of this union has had pro-Communist leanings; its positions have frequently been to the left of those taken by the Left Socialists. However, since 1950, these Socialists have provided the only effective channel for leftist political action by the JTU on a national level. It has therefore exerted pressure both directly and through Sōhyō on these parties. In 1953–54, the two Social Democratic parties stoutly but in vain opposed laws which placed public school teachers on the payroll of the central government, made them subject to its supervision, and limited their scope in political activities. In the following year, the prevailing leadership of the teachers' union changed from the militant radicalism of Sōhyō's "Unification faction" to somewhat more moderate policies. This trend further improved cooperation between the union and the soon reunified SDP.

Their members have been keenly interested in the Socialist debates over "structural reform."

UNIVERSITY STUDENTS AND OTHER YOUTH GROUPS

Japanese university students, most of whom wear distinctive uniforms, constitute a status group known for its political awareness and activities. In 1955 there were approximately 15.9 million Japanese in their twenties, almost all of them eligible to vote according to the liberalized election law. University and college students numbered 680,000 in 1957, those in national institutions tending to be more radical both because more of them come from humbler backgrounds than do students in private universities, and because more of them aim at governmental careers.

Actually, a résumé of 19 opinion polls showing political support by university students (between 1950 and 1955) indicated that 13 to 27 per cent supported conservative parties, and that one quarter to one third of the samples were in neutral, indecisive, or evasive categories.[14] Student advocates of leftist parties are not only a clear majority but also are better organized and more articulate. What seem to be the factors making for their radicalism?

We have noted the greater readiness of youth in general for change; it has been crudely estimated that perhaps as many as 70 per cent of new voters favor reformist parties, but by the mid-'sixties this proposition has had to be revised downward. We have also mentioned the more progressive tendencies of people with higher educations. From the influence of professors and universities, students tend to become part of a tradition of protest, fearful of state oppression and subscribing to Marxist critiques of capitalism and of feudalistic survivals. The much older Confucian tradition bids men of education to assume responsibilities in government and relates this sphere closely with morality. Youth shares the bitterness of national defeat but, repudiating much that was reactionary in the old order, most young people are unwilling to express nationalism in conventional ways. Alleged American imperialism vis à vis Japan and other parts of Asia is, of course, one of the targets which they share with leftist parties. Although many students are of middle-class status, either by virtue of

14. From 15 polls by the Yoron Kagaku Kyōkai (in the Tokyo area, where 22 universities are situated), 3 by the Shimbun Yoron Chōsa Remmei, and 1 by *Mainichi Shimbun*. See Cole and Nakanishi, *Japanese Opinion Polls, I*.

family background or because of higher education and their intended careers, they strongly sympathize with laborers and poor farmers. This tendency has been reinforced by the poverty and inadequate welfare of many in the lower strata and by the scarcity of suitable employment—conditions which have changed more rapidly than militant student attitudes.[15]

Polls and other interview surveys in 1952 by the National Opinion Research Institute and associated researchers under UNESCO auspices reached conclusions that help to explain youth and student support of leftist parties. They are more sanguine than their elders about the feasibility of reforms and the ability of Japan to avoid war. They are more worried about, and opposed to, rearmament. They are more critical of conservative governments and of the police. Though only a minority of youth is seriously interested in domestic politics and in the labor movement, the concerned students tend to be more vocal about such problems. Youth in general is apparently more interested in international affairs. The opinions of a sample studied by Takao Sofue agreed with the leftist parties in emphasizing government "for the people" more than "by the people."[16]

The previously mentioned 19 polls, which included a student category in their samples, indicated that this kind of support for the Communist and the Worker Farmer parties was usually between 6 and 12 per cent during the period 1950–55. In those years, although the JCP was still a legal party, most of its activities were underground.

A sizable plurality of support by students has evidently been given to Socialist parties, especially after they became the most effective political agencies of protest. Student support for the Left has apparently

15. Among other factors influencing postwar student attitudes have been their lack of integration in the profit-and-loss economy, the isolation of Japanese intellectuals during the long years of militarism, their lack of political experience during this period of repression, the revolt against parental authority directly or by projection against other symbols of authority, frustrations over the impotence of intellectuals to help achieve needed reforms, kindred feelings of inferiority regarding the relative position of the nation and (until recently) of its technology, offense caused by grosser aspects of the behavior of Occupation personnel, and bitter criticism of the Occupation's shift from emphasis on democratization to encouragement of a "reverse course."

16. The NPORI findings have been published independently of the more available UNESCO study: Jean Stoetzel, *Without the Chrysanthemum and the Sword, A Study of the Attitudes of Youth in Post-War Japan* (New York, 1955); see especially pp. 129–34, 144, 146–49, 152, 162–63. See also: Baker, "A Study of Selected Aspects of Japanese Social Stratification," Tables XXV–XXXVII, pp. 76, 81, 82.

been stronger than for the Right Socialists. If these factions are considered together, more than one third of students sampled in the Tokyo area in 1950 supported them. This rose to more than half in 1952. A nationwide sample in July 1953 indicated that one third of students supported the two Socialist parties, but other polls showed over 55 per cent between September 1953 and December 1954. The highest support of this kind was indicated by a national survey conducted in March 1955 by the Newspaper Public Opinion Research Federation in Japan, which found that three quarters of sampled students supported the SDP.

Both organized and unorganized student opinion has shared many causes and demonstrations with the Socialists—not so much from direction of the SDP as from the leadership of Communist fractions and because of prevailing student opinions. Thus, both the student and Social Democratic movements have opposed rearmament and the retention of U.S. military bases after the peace treaty; they have both advocated policies of peace, neutrality, and support for the U.N.; they have opposed Mutual Security Assistance and the testing of thermonuclear bombs; they have clamored for return of Okinawa and the Bōnins to Japanese administration and for economic and national independence in relations with the United States; both of them favor some relations with the U.S.S.R. and with Communist China; they both fought the Anti-Subversive Activities Bill and measures intended to regulate national university administrations, teachers' political activities, and the loci of student voting. Both are ardent defenders of the democratic peace Constitution and the most articulate elements of both opposed renewal of the alliance with the United States. Party and student organizations may give timely assistance to each other in their respective spheres of struggle or they may participate as major elements in ad hoc leagues.

In order to understand the somewhat tenuous relations between the SDP and major student federations, we should first mention student disappointment with the performance of the Katayama Cabinet (1947–48). Even previously, the mainly unfederated student organizations had grown critical of conservative governments and of certain Occupation policies. Some of them had participated in the threat of a general strike set for February 1, 1947, but banned by SCAP. During the Ashida administration, most students resumed antagonism toward conservative governments. In a series of demonstrations, student organizations participated with the Teachers' Union, the SDP, and fractions of the JCP. Goaded by miserable conditions of life for many, and convinced that there would be a conservative resurgence, a number of student organizations in the summer of 1948 formed the All-Japan Federation of Student Self-Government Associations (Zengakuren). From the start it displayed an extremist orientation because of manipulation by Communist fractions; also it cooperated with left Socialists and with certain radical unions, especially the Teachers' Union. There have been variations in Zengakuren's membership; by 1959 its affiliates claimed 300,000 members, but only about 2,000 were real activists. Another 10,000–20,000 could be counted on for demonstrations during crises.

The more conservative federation, Shigakuren, based on student organizations in a few private universities, was founded later in 1948 as a counter-movement. It has had a loose affinity with right Socialist factions. But in membership, organization, and vigor it has been insignificant compared to Zengakuren.

Thus, the Social Democrats, though having more student electoral support than other parties and despite their party Youth Sections, have failed to encourage and assist young members to control and guide the organized activities of by far the largest and most active student federation. More significant, they have not led in showing students that there are means by which student welfare, employment, political autonomy, and free expression can be promoted. Nor has the party consistently and vigorously encouraged more effective organization or found ways to mediate tensions between administrations and student bodies. So, in student pressure group activities, SDP influence has been marginal. Unfavorable public reactions to student participation in the May Day riot in 1952, the truce in Korea, the decline of Stalinism, the Sino-Soviet rift, schisms in the Russian and Japanese Communist party leadership, and the rise and recession of extremism in the labor movement, all have influenced Zengakuren and student opinion.

Particularly the extremist wing of the JCP, together with the Teachers' Union and the Youth Section of Sōhyō, have encouraged such demonstrations as the Japan Student Peace Conference in May 1954, and the Festival for Peace and Friendship sponsored in July 1955 by Zengakuren and the All-Japan Youth and Women's Council (Zen Nihon Seinen Fujin Kyōgikai). This organization was founded under

Left Socialist auspices in 1951 and has been composed chiefly of youth and women from the Left SDP, Sōhyō, and the Japan Farmers' Union. Its leaders and those of the Sōhyō Youth Section are mostly former Zengakuren leaders. Its activities are mainly devoted to cultural causes and to demonstrations such as those for peace and against "imperialism" and use of nuclear bombs.

Former Communists and Zengakuren leaders reorganized the New Men's Society (Shinjinkai), which in 1947 had been revived chiefly by Communists at the University of Tokyo; at the time of the Socialist schism in 1951, these more moderate reformers were encouraged by the Right Socialists. Continuing since then to follow the theories of Kautsky, the revisionist, parliamentary Marxist, the Shinjinkai has shifted favor to the Left Socialists since 1955. The right-wing Socialists have had loose connections with the Kensetsusha Dōmei (Founders' Federation).

During the crises over the revised Police Duties Bill in 1958 and the revised security treaty in 1959–60, the Socialist Party cooperated with difficulty and misgivings in a People's Council with both main wings of Zengakuren, which had emerged since 1957–58. Though the SDP was the main liaison for these ardent, young revolutionaries whenever they sought to exert pressure on the Diet, it was repeatedly alarmed by their extremism and obviously did not have them under adequate party control. The "mainstream" and "anti-mainstream" divisions of Zengakuren were both Communist in orientation. The latter remained loyal to the JCP and agreed that United States imperialism should be the main target of reformist forces; the more radical "mainstream," though passionately committed to Marxism-Leninism, had become disillusioned with Stalin's "socialism in one country" and with Khrushchev's revisionism and coexistence. For these fiery dissidents, Japanese "monopoly capitalism" was the principal enemy. They rejected control over the student movement by the JCP and criticized its attempted united fronts with the Socialists. During the crisis of 1959–60, these so-called "Trotskyites" of Zengakuren's "main current" hoped to shock demonstrating workers into revolutionary action.[17]

The postwar Socialists have been making overtures to youth and students especially since 1951, both in rural and urban communities,

17. See George R. Packard, *Protest in Tokyo,* Chap. 3, for an analysis of components of Zengakuren.

but their success has been modest. After the party schism in the fall of that year, the Right Socialists fostered a Democratic Socialist Youth League, which cooperated with the Democratic Socialist League of older moderate intellectuals. The less well organized Socialist Youth League was allied with the party leftists. Each had an organ for expounding theories and engaging in controversies. The youthful ardor and conflicting views of the memberships made difficult the combination of these organizations after party reunification, but the Youth and Women's Bureau in the reunified party headquarters included a single Student Section. The plan for reorganization adopted in 1961 called also for a youth and student committee under the Organization Bureau, and the Cultural Bureau was to be active in this field. Following the anti-treaty crisis, in October 1960 the SDP founded the Japan Socialist Youth Alliance (Nihon Shakaishugi Seinen Dōmei, or Shaseidō). Its early membership was composed mostly of Sōhyō activists and younger neutral trade unionists. Under party leaders like the popular Saburō Eda and his son, the party with more vigor cultivated relations with students and renewed its call for the reunification of Zengakuren.

WOMEN VOTERS AND THE SOCIAL DEMOCRATS

The Social Democrats have made special efforts to maximize support from the 30 million women eligible to vote, by stressing peace, opposition to rearmament and to retrogressive revision of the Constitution and of the liberalized family law, and support for social insurance and education.[18] Among the sources casting light on the political awareness and degree of interest among adult women are some 39 opinion polls extending from August 1947 to November 1955.[19] The National Institute of Public Opinion Research in March 1951 asked a sample of 700 women in the Tokyo region whether they were interested in politics. Only 6 per cent said yes, and 35 per cent were

18. The figure for the total number of eligible women voters is for 1960. In 1955, the total was 26.5 million; nearly 8 million of these were then in their twenties. Among eligible voters in that year, women outnumbered men by 2.1 million, but the proportion of actual male voters was higher by 7.8% of the sex group. The total number of employed women over age 14 was then 16.5 million—approximately 7 million in predominantly urban occupations, about 8.6 million in agrarian livelihoods.

19. *Jiji* News Agency–4; Yoron Kagaku Kyōkai (Tokyo area)–3; Shimbun Yoron Chōsa Remmei–6; *Mainichi Shimbun*–4; *Asahi Shimbun*–1; *Yomiuri Shimbun*–8; National Opinion Research Institute–3. See Cole and Nakanishi, *Japanese Opinion Polls, I*.

slightly interested. However, in September of the following year, nearly 30 per cent of the women in a *Yomiuri* national sample declared strong interest in the imminent election, while 47 per cent indicated a fair degree of interest. There can be little doubt that since first obtaining the right of suffrage in 1946, Japanese women have been slowly growing in knowledge about and interest in public affairs. Comparison of a poll in 1947 with one in 1955 indicates that women have probably been increasingly independent in reaching political decisions.[20]

Heavier voting seems to characterize employed women, those in the salariat, those in commercial and industrial occupations, those with at least middle school educations, and those with middle- and upper-class standards of living. The views of women in their twenties and early thirties tend to be more reformist; those in their forties are likely to be more conservative, while those older than fifty usually are not only still more conservative but also are more ignorant and apathetic about political issues. Young, urban women vote somewhat more according to party than do other female groups. And as a whole, women are less informed and decisive about party affairs and political processes than about specific issues. Even so, they respond with interest concerning questions which the mass media of communication have emphasized for a considerable span of time. SDP strategists are aware of most of these tendencies but could profitably pay them more heed.

Many commentators have speculated about the degree to which women have supported Socialist parties because of their opposition to rearmament. In general it is clear that this is an issue of strong concern to Japanese women, though emotions are commonly more influential than reasoned arguments. A study of 47 opinion polls between March 1950 and September 1955 indicates that women's views about such matters tend to agree with the contours of male opinion, except that there were more women who "didn't know." Some earlier polls show a small majority of women favoring moderate national defense, but undecided respondents potentially could determine the balance. Women in a national sample late in May 1951 responded as follows in

20. *Jiji* News Agency poll in August 1947 and one by the Labor Ministry's Women's and Minors' Bureau in March 1955. See Cole and Nakanishi, *Japanese Opinion Polls, 2*. For some findings of the latter, see: Shio Nakanishi, "Women's Position and the Family System," *The Annals of the American Academy of Political and Social Science, 308* (Nov. 1956), 130–39.

comparison with SDP supporters of both sexes to the question: "Do you support rearmament after the peace treaty?"[21]

	Yes	*No*	*Don't know*
Women	32.9%	38.8%	28.3%
SDP supporters	37.5	52.0	10.5

From this and other poll results we are probably safe in concluding that women as a whole are less committed than the SDP in opposition to rearmament. In such matters their opinions are closer to those of the Right than the Left Socialists. A poll in September 1951 showed that women respondents strongly favored moderate rearmament *after* economic stabilization—a policy being stressed chiefly by Right Socialists.[22] Two nationwide samples polled in April and August 1952 again provided comparisons of the opinions of women and of SDP supporters of both sexes:[23]

"In case of a plebiscite concerning revision of the Constitution to permit legal rearmament, how would you vote?"

	Favor	*Opposed*	*Don't know*
Women	32.5%	25.1%	42.4%
Supporters of Right SDP	38.8	51.1	10.1
Supporters of Left SDP	8.9	88.9	2.2
SDP supporters (not classified)	42.2	39.4	18.4

"What do you think about rearmament?"

	Must rearm	*Status quo*	*Should stop rearming*	*Don't know*
Women	21.2%	27.9%	26.2%	24.7%
Supporters of Right SDP	30.5	37.9	24.2	7.4
Supporters of Left SDP	16.2	25.7	50.0	8.1

Again we see how much more undecided and less opposed to rearmament women in general seemed to be, and how their patterns were

21. Poll by Shimbun Yoron Chōsa Remmei, May 26–28, 1951; 2,932 actual respondents chosen by systematic random sampling, which is the usual method for such polls. See Cole and Nakanishi, *Japanese Opinion Polls, 3.*

22. Poll by *Mainichi Shimbun,* Sept. 13–14, 1951, in *Japanese Opinion Polls, 3.*

23. Polls by the Shimbun Yoron Chōsa Remmei in April 1952 and during August 10–12, 1952—the first with 2,907 actual respondents, the latter with 2,370—are available in ibid.

more like those of the Right than the Left Socialists. By 1957 not only had opposition to rearmament through constitutional revision increased from 32 per cent to 52 per cent but also the disparity between men and women had grown. Of all men, 5 per cent were opposed compared to 32 per cent for all women. But age, too, was an influential factor, for from 20 to 29, 38 per cent of the young men and 50 per cent of the young women opposed constitutional revision for the sake of rearmament.[24]

A study of 69 polls during the period 1947–56 for indications as to support of the Socialist parties by women yields some conclusions, though based upon samples.[25] During the Katayama and Ashida governments, 12 to 27 per cent of adult female voters seem to have supported the Social Democrats, and, after a recession, this degree of favor seems to have been at least regained since reunification of the party in 1955. Between these periods, the two Social Democratic factions apparently were supported by 10 to 20 per cent of women constituents—more commonly by 15 to 19 per cent. During the party schism, all except two polls showed female preference for the Right over the Left Socialists, by two or even four to one in the earlier part, but this disparity declined during the latter phase of the cleavage. The difference may have been smaller in the Tokyo region.

Apparently women have consistently given more support to conservative parties; during some periods this has been twice the extent of their support for the SDP, but it has varied. For example, scandals and the decline in popularity of the Yoshida Liberals early in 1954 cut deeply into this support. Since emergence of the two main parties, one fifth to one fourth of female respondents usually have been pro-SDP, while one third to somewhat more than one half have favored the Liberal Democrats. Usually two fifths to one half have been in neutral or indecisive categories. More men than women have consistently supported the SDP, judging from these many samples. Hence it is probably safe to conclude that Socialist support by women has been of relatively modest significance and that great opportunities still may exist in this

24. Douglas H. Mendel, Jr., *The Japanese People and Foreign Policy: A Study of Public Opinion in Post-Treaty Japan* (Berkeley and Los Angeles, University of California Press, 1961), pp. 74, 76.

25. Use has been made of 69 polls from February 1947 to August 1956: 3 by *Jiji* News Agency, 23 by the Yoron Kagaku Kyōkai (Tokyo area), 13 by the Shimbun Yoron Chōsa Remmei, 14 by *Asahi Shimbun,* 4 by *Mainichi Shimbun,* and 12 by *Yomiuri Shimbun;* see *Japanese Opinion Polls, 1.*

sector of the population as the political consciousness of women continues to increase.

It has been estimated (1957) that women constitute about 10 per cent of the active membership of the Socialist Party. At that time, eleven Socialist Diet members were women, and two women were members of the CEC. Those under thirty years of age can—since 1960—belong to the party's youth affiliate, Shaseidō; older ones are the concern of the Women's Department in the Youth and Women's Bureau at national headquarters. The party has connections with a number of women's organizations, including a Housewives' Association founded by Sōhyō and labor unions with numerous female members. The White Plum Society, long headed by Mrs. Katayama, is composed mainly of the wives of right-wing Socialist leaders. More active is the Society for the Study of Women's Problems, which is led by Mrs. Shizue Katō and publishes a monthly magazine and newspaper. It has branches in Tokyo, Osaka, Kobe, Nagano, Hiroshima, Yokohama, and Sendai. The leftist Council of Youth and Women is composed principally of trade unionists and intellectuals; its activities are usually conducted as adjuncts to those of unions. It has predominantly favored the Ōta–Iwai "mainstream" in Sōhyō, but a minority of its members have leaned toward the more radical Takano faction.

In addition to issues stressed by the Socialists in bidding for women's votes, there are others: old age pension measures, maintenance of rice rationing, strengthening of the Labor Standards Law, women's rights, prohibition of prostitution, and promotion of the activities of Parent-Teacher Associations. A high point in cooperation with women's organizations was reached during the crisis of 1960, but the party has admitted that most of those organizations subsequently lost touch with its agencies. Efforts have been renewed to attract women into the party, but apparently there is less than wholehearted response from Diet members when headquarters asks that lists of women who have supported Socialist candidates be reported.

PARTY EFFORTS TO ATTRACT SMALL AND MEDIUM ENTERPRISERS

Chronic problems and grievances of these massive strata have caused Social Democrats to view them as actual and potential supporters. Before analyzing socialist attitudes toward small and medium enterprisers, let us briefly describe the characteristics of this group.

At least 16.5 million people—about one third of them proprietors and managers of small industries, stores, and service enterprises—constituted this complex stratum in 1960. If family employees are not counted, the number of small proprietary managers outnumbers hired workers in this sector. All but 2 per cent of Japanese establishments employed less than 30 persons.[26] Though most small businessmen have proprietary attitudes which make for political conservatism or apathy, a large proportion are not genuine capitalists (some call them "industrial and commercial peasants"), for—except in prosperous years like 1959–64—they have merely eked out a livelihood. Their earnings have often been less than those of skilled workers in large industries. Moreover, they cannot cut costs as large corporations can; subcontractors must buy supplies from "parent companies" yet must sell to those companies often at a discount and sometimes wait for payment. Most small businessmen feel that they pay disproportionate taxes, have greater difficulties gaining access to credit, and that conservative administrations at all levels show favoritism to large corporations, which sometimes are formidable competitors.

At the very time when the two-main-party system has given rise to rivalry for middle-class support, small businessmen are becoming better organized for economic and political purposes.[27] More of them are realizing the advantage of an opposition party, in part to offset the proverbial alliance between conservative parties and both big business and farmers. However, even petty capitalists dislike socialism with its connotations of nationalization. Small industrialists fear that the Socialists might try to enforce the Labor Standards Law, which is flagrantly violated throughout this sector. They dread the Socialists' demands for a minimum wage and unionizing offensives by labor federations with their political connections. Owners of tiny shops sometimes feel the competition of left Socialist- and Sōhyō-sponsored consumers' cooperatives, but not as much as that of department stores.

Small plants and shops are apt to be suffused with traditional family influences, and the political significance of small entrepreneurs stems

26. In 1953, 90% of all those in wholesale and retail trade worked in small stores; 60% of those in manufacturing were in plants having fewer than 30 employees. In 1951, three quarters of all retailers worked in stores with fewer than 5 employees. In the same year, less than one third of Japan's workers had jobs in large establishments.

27. For a more detailed treatment of four main federations of small and medium enterprisers, see section VIII of a longer treatment by Allan B. Cole: "Political Tendencies of Japanese in Small Enterprises, with Special Reference to the Social Democratic Party" (New York, Institute of Pacific Relations, mimeo., 1959).

in part from the effects of their paternalism on their largely unorganized employees. The former have been referred to as quasi-intellectuals who often can boss the people in their social microcosms.[28] This mainly lower-middle stratum has lived under great pressures and, as during and after the prewar depression, has shown a disposition to rightist extremism and national expansionism. It has never initiated a major cross-stratal movement, but any program which would obtain such broad acceptance would have to enlist its support.

Only two out of 100 polls from 1947 to 1955 showing sampled political support separated small and medium enterprisers from the general group of merchants and industrialists. One in January 1948 indicated that 12.3 per cent of small-scale businessmen supported the SDP; another in April 1950 showed 14 per cent.[29] A minority of the larger group, varying between 11 and 26 per cent, has supported the Socialist Party or the divided factions. There are reasons, verified by less systematic sources, for thinking that most of these supporters of the opposition party are small business people. Somewhat similar business minorities during 1950–55 opposed constitutional revision and rearmament and advocated Japanese neutralism. Support for the right Socialists by these elements is naturally stronger than for the leftists, although the latter have some advocates, especially among small shopkeepers.

Selective interviewing independent of the polls indicates that support for the SDP by such persons is seldom for ideological reasons but rather because these voters consider that party to be most active on their behalf, and because of personal connections with SDP politicians who may have helped their associations. Leaders of such associations have not overlooked the principle of balance between two major parties. On the national level they try to exert pressure on the policy planning boards of parties; in localities their approaches are usually to their Representatives in the Diet.[30]

Increasingly since the victory of somewhat more moderate elements

28. Masao Maruyama, *Thought and Behaviour in Modern Japanese Politics*, ed. Ivan Morris (London, Oxford University Press, 1963), pp. 62 ff.

29. These polls were made by the *Jiji* News Agency and *Asahi Shimbun*, respectively. See *Japanese Opinion Polls, 1*.

30. It is safe to conjecture that most of the approximately 35% of industrial workers who have supported conservative parties are from nonunion small factories and shops. A fuller interpretation of public opinion polls in this regard is to be found in Cole, "Political Tendencies of Japanese in Small Enterprises," section IV.

in Sōhyō and the formation of two main parties in 1955, the SDP and its related labor federations have tried to drive wedges between small and big business interests instead of exploiting tensions between small-scale employers and workers. This has been more of a change for the left Socialists and Sōhyō than for the right wingers and Sōdōmei. The latter pair are conciliatory rather than militant in either direction. However, they feel challenged by the left and so press mildly for further unionization of workers in small shops. In the fall of 1954, the Right wing encouraged the organization of—and has special connections with—the All-Japan Federation of Labor Unions in Small and Medium Enterprises (Zen Nihon Chūshō Kigyō Rōdō Kumiai Sōrengō). By 1956, it claimed about 100,000 members, which was perhaps half the number belonging to its Sōhyō-sponsored rival. Its president was a member of the Small and Medium Enterprises Section under the Organization Bureau of SDP headquarters.

Before the decline of the radical faction in Sōhyō, and informally consonant with the Communist "national front" line, efforts were concentrated on persuading adults in families to vote in accordance with their labor union members and to weld ententes between worker-patrons and small merchants in localities where workers live or work. Subsequently, tactics more suitable to the survival problems of small enterprises have been employed by Sōhyō organizers (with some left Socialist cooperation) to press offensives for unionization of workers in such establishments. Though nominally independent, the Federation of Small and Medium Enterprise Workers Unions (Chūshō Kigyō Rōdō Kumiai Rengōkai) has been fostered by Sōhyō and, in the manner of its right-wing counterpart, has connections with leftist SDP factions. Its affiliates are chiefly in Osaka, Kyoto, Sakai, Tokyo, Yokohama, Tokushima, and Hokkaidō. Local federations of small unions are typically rallied around neighboring branches of major industrial or governmental service unions which belong to Sōhyō.

Turning now to SDP activities and policies to cope with the problems and to attract the support of small enterprisers, it is significant that, in 1956, 10 right-wing members of the party Central Committee were small businessmen as well as politicians. Members of the Policy Planning Board included 9 right and 5 left Socialist leaders known either as modest entrepreneurs or as champions of such interests.[31] In

31. For a list of many of the 27 SDP Representatives (after the elections of February 1955) identified with these interests, see ibid., section X, n. 3.

the central party headquarters, the section which supervises implementation of current policies in these matters has been headed by Ikkō Kasuga and by Takeo Tanaka, both of whom are small businessmen with wide connections.

Special "policy meetings" of party leaders have been convened, and there is a Small and Medium Enterprises Diet Members League, which at opportune times participates in joint action committees combining the efforts of small business associations, labor unions, and representatives from the comparable sections of Sōhyō and Dōmei Kaigi. In addition, a Special Committee for Formulating Policies for Small and Medium Enterprises was appointed by the Central Committee after reunification of the SDP. More than half of its members have been Representatives in the Diet.[32] It has held meetings with businessmen, economists, and representatives of small enterprise associations and has sponsored two intensive conferences; the second one in the autumn of 1956 assisted the party in drafting the part of its new five-year plan concerned with policies to protect and promote small business interests.[33]

In 1948, when the Socialists shared governmental power, they were chiefly responsible for establishment of the Small and Medium Enterprises Bureau in the ministry which was subsequently renamed International Trade and Industry (MITI).[34] In the following year, they

32. The veteran right Socialist lawyer-politician, Chōzaburō Mizutani, was chairman of this committee until his death. He relied heavily on middle-class support in his Kyoto constituency, and he had special connections with two synthetic or composite enterprise associations. Kasuga was secretary of this group. For a description of Mizutani's connections and electoral support, see ibid., Appendix 1, esp. pp. 113–14, 121–24. See also: Lawrence Olson, *Dimensions of Japan* (New York, American Universities Field Staff, 1963), Chap. 7. In May 1958, there were 14 Socialist members of the House of Representatives who had significant connections with small enterprises.

33. Prefectural and municipal branches of the SDP have been encouraged to form sections to handle small business affairs. These sections are urged to establish "places for consultation" to assist small businessmen with problems and to improve relations between proprietors and workers. In 1956, about 400 persons were working at least part-time to strengthen liaison among small business, labor, and party elements. Trained organizers then began to be sent out from Tokyo. A number of local conferences have been held, and there has been some cooperation with various local struggle fronts. In some areas the party finds ways to mediate between Sōhyō and proprietary managers. Branches are urged to help members or other friendly persons to gain positions in official agencies and regulative committees having to do with small enterprises.

34. Mizutani was then Minister, and Torazō Ninagawa was first chief of the Bureau. The former was long a Representative from Kyoto, the latter has been Governor of Kyoto-fu.

were the main proponents of a Cooperative Associations Law, which sought to improve joint facilities and organization and to strengthen the bargaining position of associated small enterprises. This measure has been partly superseded by a Small and Medium Enterprises Organization Law enacted in 1957 by the conservatives. Of course, the Socialists and small businessmen agreed with many aspects of the Occupation's democratization policies, such as the partial deconcentration of economic combines. They were hurt by the disinflationary policies of 1949–50, however; the party then began to place more emphasis on tax relief and easier credit for small businesses. During the Korean War boom, the opposition party coupled its denunciations of rearmament with complaints that military contracts were not bringing enough "sunshine" to producers and sellers of consumers' goods.

Rivalry during the four-year schism in the SDP stimulated both parties to develop further their policies designed to attract the support of people in the small business sector. It was not until 1953–56 that Socialist policies for this field became fairly comprehensive, though even then not realistically mature in analytical economic terms. During the cleavage, informal alliances were made in a number of cities by the three main leftist parties with campaigns by small business elements, labor unions, and consumer organizations against certain commodity taxes. Out of these movements were born "enterprise associations"—combinations of small mercantile, industrial, and service units which pooled capital and centralized management; in each association all personnel technically became employees of one corporate office, thus greatly reducing what had been separate payments of the corporation tax. Socialist lawyers and politicians, especially right Socialists, helped these infant associations to obtain legal recognition and credit. Thus there developed mutually useful economic ententes with political significance.[35]

During 1954–56, the Socialist parties joined with aroused small business and labor federations to push through bills regulating de-

35. For a brief case study of relations between certain Socialist politicians and "enterprise associations" in Kyoto, see: Cole, "Political Tendencies of Japanese in Small Enterprises," Appendix 1. For Socialist connections with a progressive federation of small businessmen and subcontractors, called the All-Japan Council of Small and Medium Enterprises (Zen Nihon Chūshō Kigyō Kyōgikai, or Zenchūkyō) see: ibid., pp. 75–79.

layed payments to subcontractors and limiting the expansion of department stores. The measures finally enacted were conservative compromises with the interests of large companies, but the regulations were stronger than they would have been if the Social Democrats, especially the right wing, had not been so active in support of rival bills. However, conservative Representatives returned to the Diet in 1956–57 and passed the Small and Medium Enterprises Organization Law, which legalized selective, compulsory cartelization of associated small enterprises, though subject to reservations and governmental regulation. The Socialists were irresolute on the essential issues at stake until very late, and in the end their opposition was determined more by their partisan role than by basic objections. Cartelization, even in certain formerly "destructively competitive" fields, has hampered the Socialist strategy of trying to align small against large business interests.

When talking publicly in terms of principles, Socialists have usually favored noncompulsory associations, whose main policies and controls are from below rather than by bosses above. They refer favorably to the experience and experiments with half a dozen types of functional associations; and they share with many small businessmen the dread of recurrent centralized control by government. If the Socialists could regain power, however, they might use the susceptibility of such circles to subsidies and official contracts to achieve the same trend under their own auspices.

The five-year economic plan adopted in 1957 added further recommendations to the remedies and assistance already suggested for this sector. Certain fields, it averred, should be reserved for small and medium producers and merchants. Fields of merchandising should be better delineated as between wholesalers and retailers, and between large and small retailers. The plan called for a clearer distinction between small enterprises, whose personnel needed relief through social security, and those which needed assistance for growth. Again it advocated reduction of corporation taxes on small firms with low earnings. It would have the government award a guaranteed percentage of public contracts to such companies. Moreover, the SDP has championed enforcement of improved minimum wage legislation and the extension of such standards to the still largely unregulated field of domestic labor. It contended that social security benefits in this sector should be comparable with those available to workers in large establishments.[36]

Both the plan for 1957–62 and the "Long-Term Political and Economic Plan" issued by the party in 1961 insisted that governmental assistance must go beyond relief measures to help improve the technical and managerial efficiency and productivity of small industries and businesses.[37] Considerable modernization and rationalization have been achieved since 1957, both as a result of filtrative prosperity enabling new investment and because the government has taken further steps, including the fostering of more cartel associations. Today there are controversies among socialists as to the future of small and medium enterprises. Orthodox Marxists admit that people in this sector have grown in number, but they insist that pressures on them from larger scale and more efficient firms have been increasing and that in proportion the role of small and medium enterprises has been declining. A more objective analysis of trends would probably show, however, that, although readjustments among small shops are required when any large-scale innovation (like the introduction of supermarkets) gains headway, phenomenal economic growth such as that in recent years has been accompanied by extensive improvements and new vitality among small producers and businessmen.

Japanese Socialists emphasize their special affinity with industrial laborers, especially with those organized into trade unions. But when referring to "the masses" they generally mean most of society other than the "ruling class." With respect to middle strata there is disagreement, yet almost all recognize political opportunities among the many highly educated citizens with a sense of alienation and in the hardships and grievances of the massive petty bourgeoisie. Moreover, they hope for future growth in part because a significant majority of youth are expected to vote for "progressive" parties, and because most of Japan's growing population is being absorbed into the urban labor and lesser middle strata. The chief obstacles for the SDP in this regard are conservatism, apathy, and difficulties in organizing cohesive

36. For a more detailed treatment of SDP policies on behalf of small business interests, see: ibid., section IX. For provisions of the Socialist five-year plan (1957), see: *Chōki Keizai Keikaku,* pp. 50–57 and passim; *Heiwa to Shakaishugi no Tame ni,* p. 199.

37. See: *Shakaitō no Shin Rosen,* pp. 146–50 for a summary of policies to benefit small and medium enterprises.

middle-class groups for political action. Some leftist ideologues have long predicted that much of the weaker middle strata will or should be proletarianized, while most Socialists think that only in the long run, and gradually, could the least economical enterprisers be absorbed into state-operated corporations.

The controversy between left and right in the party over "class party" versus "national party" in essence asks whether SDP gains between 1952 and 1965 have maximized the support available from the more readily organized labor sector and whether, if there is to be continued growth toward a ruling majority, there must be more efforts to attract middle-class votes. Except for the cultivation of the leftist intelligentsia, disproportionate attention has been given to organized labor. This was natural, for during the democratization period there was no great organized surge of middle-class forces comparable to that of the labor movement. White-collar workers, it is true, did organize, but for reasons already explained their unions usually identified themselves with labor. A combination of circumstances in and after 1953 caused leaders and factions of the SDP to pay more attention than before to middle-class interests. As reunification became possible and the two-main-party pattern emerged, strategic imperatives accentuated competition for the support of middle strata. Since 1957, the rapid growth of the Japanese economy has made observers generally more aware of the increased significance of these social elements. However, it is not so easy to interpret the import of this trend for practical politics. "Structural reformers" within the SDP have had such changes in mind in proposing more moderate tactics, but related polemics have impeded development of a concerted strategy to attract middle elements and "break the barrier of one third" strength in the national legislature. One might expect that the Democratic Socialists would make the most effective overtures to the middle strata, but in this they have so far not notably succeeded. Meanwhile, the militant Sōka Gakkai has attained the third largest bloc of seats in the House of Councillors. Its appeal is to economically and psychologically insecure people; it builds, chiefly within Japan's sprawling urban agglomerates, inner communities with apostolic solidarity, voluntary welfare systems, and a sectarian hierarchical ladder for advancement and recognition. There could be no more graphic indication that all of the national parties have been conspicuously remiss in neglecting the needs and latent responses of the petit bourgeois and lowest classes.

Conclusion

13. Prospects and Problems

Reviewing trends in the two decades since World War II and peering into the future, it is safe to conclude that Japan's Social Democratic parties will continue to stress their criticism of "capitalism," "feudalistic" survivals, conservative authoritarianism, and manifestations of a "nationalistic mystique"—in apparent disregard of the decreasing relevance of such slogans to the real world. Conversely, however, their emphasis on peace, on new forms of collective security through the U.N. and regional arrangements, on banning nuclear testing, and on friendlier relations between East and West may have increased in relevance with the intensification of conflict in Southeast Asia, while defensive alliances in both the Communist and Western blocs have loosened. They will, as they have, provide political mechanisms for labor strategy and noncommunist outlets for more and less alienated intellectuals. Though the JCP will doubtless continue barely within, or at times beyond, the pale of legality, the Social Democrats and Democratic Socialists will continue to press for a more equalitarian, planned economy—a gradual socialist revolution, though with great differences on how fundamental the "revolution" should be. Barring severe economic distress or extreme political polarization for some other cause, it is probable that these objectives will be sought by parliamentary and educative means.

These Socialists are among the foremost exponents of Japan's public idealism, of longer range hopes, including pacifist and somewhat nationalist neutralism. Since 1948 they have been waging a rearguard defense of major democratic reforms, most of which are related to preservation of the new Constitution. Some Socialists, especially right wingers, will admit in private that certain well-considered amendments of that basic law are desirable, but they cannot advocate this openly; and most leaders of these parties fear that to open the door a crack might invite a revisionist flood. Some say that constitutional amendment should wait at least until old guard Liberal Democrats have passed from leadership and a younger generation of more progressive conservatives has supplanted them.

In Japan, an Asian society still divided by chasms between the political and economic elites and the governed, where the rural minority is seriously affected by the pace-setting influences of the more dynamic industrial system, the Socialists can and probably are making significant ethical contributions, even though a thorough system of socialist ethics may never predominate. Despite pettiness and opportunism, they insist that human dignity and social justice must be achieved and degradation in a mechanizing culture be overcome.

Even if the Socialists in the foreseeable future continue as a chronic opposition, indications are plentiful that they can exert influence on the majority conservatives toward policies of a welfare state. Witness the somewhat cautious enactments in the late 'fifties under Liberal Democratic auspices of a reduced income tax especially on smaller earnings; expansion of unemployment benefits, pensions, and medical insurance; guarded efforts to protect small enterprisers; a diluted minimum wage law; expansion of state loans and heavier governmental investment in such fields as development of power, communications and transportation, iron and steel, highways and housing. In stealing Socialist thunder the conservatives move slowly toward part of what their rivals advocate. Of course, this process and these indirect achievements do not satisfy the ambitious and more ardently revolutionary Socialists, chiefly in the left wing, who express in Marxist terms scorn for such compromises. Discontent with slow change impels some to harbor reservations about keeping within parliamentary limits; in "certain circumstances," they argue, forms of direct action could be justified.

Between 1952 and 1958, the Socialists as a whole gained in each national election; after reunification and following elections to the

House of Councillors in 1956, some SDP leaders hoped for attainment of power through a Diet majority after two or three more campaigns. Since 1957, however, "relative" Socialist electoral failures have been more impressive than the "relative" victories won by the party. This raises the oft-mentioned problem of how such parties can gain in maturity and responsibility. If power corrupts and absolute power tends to corrupt absolutely, it is also apparent that perennial absence of power has adverse effects. In crises it can lead to exasperation and violence, and in more normal times it conduces to doctrinaire attitudes and "pie in the sky" irresponsibility. Party leftists can be counted on to use this frustration as evidence that socialism cannot be attained by legal means only. Also, realization that power is not readily available tends to encourage recrimination and factionalism.

The future of the Japanese Socialist cause can probably best be discussed in terms of persistent problems which will challenge the SDP (as well as the splinter DSP) and their supporters. One of the chief problems is Socialist unity; obviously this is related to whether there can indeed be a two-main-party system in Japan—even though it must long be unbalanced—or whether there can only be the preponderant conservatives, the religio-traditionalist Komeitō, and a variety of leftist splinters.

The dissidents, led by Nishio in 1959–60 to form the separate Democratic Socialist Party, have endured as a faction and may for some time constitute a viable lesser party, for they attract support from the right wing of organized labor. There are, however, doubts that they can win the adherence of significant additional numbers of small and medium enterprisers, workers, white-collar employees, and "people of culture." In Diet strategy they are selectively cooperating with the main body of Socialists, though it is conjectured that the DSP might be lured into another coalition government with conservative elements predominant, especially if the LDR should splinter.

The secession of the Nishio faction and additional sympathizers, its separate alliance with Zenrō—and since 1962 with the somewhat reorganized moderate labor wing calling itself Dōmei Kaigi—has tended to dissuade the Socialist Party and Sōhyō's "mainstream" from excessive radicalism. Such braking action has been reinforced by the lowered discontent in several social strata and by lessened labor militancy, encouraged by diffused consumer gains from the remarkable economic growth. The moderate Kawakami group within the SDP, rather than being soon overwhelmed by leftist factions (in which case there were conjectures that this group might transfer adherence to the DSP), first gained new leverage and then became a component in a revised party "main current." Thus three blocs have emerged in Japanese noncommunist socialism: the reformers on the right, whose socialism is in doubt and who approximate a centrist minority; the new "mainstream" whose three elements want socialism to remain vigorous but to come to terms with developing realities; and the more leftist, doctrinaire factions. Clearly the prevailing coalition within the main Socialist Party since 1960 has stood to the left of the two right-wing factions in the previously unified party, but the context and inner alignment are changing. Leaders and factions long devoted to socialism are now trying to shed the more dogmatic aspects of Marxism-Leninism and to revitalize a still meaningful, more realistic movement.

Especially since 1955, the two-main-party system has accentuated another major issue as to the fundamental nature of the SDP. Should it be a cross-stratal national party or one based primarily on, and responsive to, the interests of unionized workers? In some respects, such as the recruitment of leaders and dependence on Sōhyō, the SDP has grown into more of a labor-dominated party than its British counterpart. The requirements of parliamentary politics and the actual patterns of support for parties demand that it become a national party, while the greater strength of Sōhyō and of the party's left wing encourages contradictory tendencies. Attempts to gloss over this issue with such policy phrases as "class party with a mass base" have proven to be futile. The resolution of this problem is one prerequisite for continued Socialist growth; it also is fraught with significance for the stability of liberal parliamentarianism, for, if the party seeks to gain the helm of state, the logical implication of the "class party" doctrine is resort to expedient kinds of direct action. In the discernible future the organized workers, even though in Japan they include many in the white-collar stratum, will comprise a minority of relatively modest electoral proportions.

Neutralism in international relations would be insufficient to enable such a minority to advance to power. If the game is to be played according to parliamentary rules in a sovereign state, there is no dodging the necessity of making broad appeals; this involves compromises between the oft-conflicting interests of various groups. It is probably significant that, while the SDP was gaining in successive elections, the hope of attaining power tended to exercise a cohesive influence, but reverses have again contributed to schism. Excessive labor politicism and influence on the party have been among the main grievances of right-wing Socialists. There has been significantly greater realism on the part of Socialist planners of economic policies, though they still have far to go. They are learning how to deal with pressure groups and about the necessity of efforts to compromise between, if not to reconcile, disparate interests.

As long as the Social Democratic bloc epitomizes a minority opposition movement aspiring to power by legal means through multigroup support, the winning of new adherents on the basis of its economic policies will present difficulties. Especially before the phenomenal growth of the national economy from 1957 on, Japan's overall economic limitations and resulting inflexibilities made it hard to assist one type of interest without injuring and antagonizing another. The Socialists have had to reconcile policies of relief, on the one hand, with stress on reconstruction into the mid-'fifties and subsequently on further economic development. At times, notably in early postwar years, they denounced the government's inflationary policies, yet they have been perennial champions of labor's wage offensives and of expanded state credit and investment policies.

As mentioned above, in a populous country with, until recently, limited capital and few natural resources, there is less latitude for the making of choices. Vulnerability to pressures from organized labor tends to warp economic planning away from truly national perspectives. So the SDP, especially its left wing, has been rather nationalistic in regard to recommended foreign policies but less so with respect to domestic affairs. Ultimately and theoretically, however, the collectivism inherent in socialism is internally more nationalistic in an egalitarian sense; it aims at a fusion of social elements so that all can comprise a more unitary and thus a mightier nation. Yet no society can long be wholly proletarianized. New strata persistently emerge with at least some distinct interests. So this paradox between the proletarian emphasis and the actual pluralism of interest groups is inescapable whether socialists operate as a minority critical of a capitalist order or can carry out a socioeconomic transformation. Under current conditions, the more the class character of the party is emphasized, the more difficult it becomes practically to offer economic advantages to strata other than to those workers organized in large industries and in governmental services; as a corollary, the less likely the party is to achieve national power by legal means, unless other issues and policies can be utilized to attract many other kinds of voters. Of course, this is often a major Socialist strategy.

In shaping appeals, the Socialists will have to keep pace with, and even anticipate, many changes both internal and in Japan's foreign relations. Industrialization is mounting to new levels and in some sectors is being greatly affected by technological changes. For example, the development of atomic power generation and, in some fields, the coming of automation are raising a number of complex questions. Improved education, the rising political consciousness of workers, farmers, and women, the interests of people in small enterprises, and further growth of population are all significant for politicians. Changes in the distribution of the employed population are underway. Urbanization has made another spurt; new industrial zones and improved transportation routes are being developed. Certain issues which the SDP has stressed are growing threadbare; others must take their place. Problems of land reform, of economic independence from the United States, and of general unemployment have faded as issues, whereas more attention is being given to measures for vocational retraining, to other dimensions of social security, state credit facilities, relations with Communist neighbors, and Japan's role in economic and technical aid to later-developing countries. Defense of the Constitution and opposition to military alliance with the United States are bound to come to the fore at certain times, and the Socialists can be counted on to continue urging a more diversified pattern of foreign trade.

Another need of the Socialists is to build a much stronger nationwide organization. At present theirs can hardly be called a machine. Small party membership and centralization of controls have led to complaints of elitism out of keeping with democratic, socialist ideals. The condition of the SDP is far different from that of the rather well disciplined British Labour Party, which has had some five to six million members, mostly unionized workers. Writers on economic development are stressing the importance of two-way administrative communication and mobilizing techniques between headquarters and myriad local communities if national programs are to be effectively carried out. The same can be said of party programs, particularly since the SDP must rely less on traditional pyramids of boss-type control. As compared with the more extensive Liberal Democratic machine with its incomparably better financing and its influence on appropriations and patronage, the Socialists must rather emphasize organization, the quality and number of personnel, platforms, propaganda, and ideological conviction. Local SDP branches are being urged to keep trying to involve in their activities key personages linked with other local organizations. The party knows that it should become a force in the "daily struggles" which interest Suzuki-san—the Japanese equivalent of John Q. Public. And, when possible, it must try to be more positive than merely serving as a magnet for the discontented.

The next few years will certainly bring marked changes in the leadership of both major wings—and the mentioned three blocs—of the Social Democratic movement. The prewar generation, composed mainly of Marxist-oriented intellectuals who learned to organize and lead labor and peasant unions—becoming in the course of time politicians—is fading. No longer do their lineages, notably the Socio-Democratic and Japan-Labor cliques and traditions on the right or the Labor-Farmer faction on the left, exert so much influence. Instead, the main supply of younger leaders has come from labor unions and federations, especially those with leftist proclivities. Most of these have absorbed their Marxism indirectly, from their environment in the labor movement, not from a thorough grasp of socialist theory. Already veterans in labor politics, they bring to legislatures on the three main levels a measure of practicality. Their limitations are more likely to be in terms of intellectual training and breadth of perspective. And they tend to perpetuate in politics the attitudes of "confrontation" and "struggle."

But profound challenges and changes are confronting the labor movement in Japan. For years organization has not been keeping pace with growth of the labor force and, since the Socialists reached a plateau in the Diet, the channels for mobility up through unions and federations to the national legislature have become constricted at the top. The lowering of tariffs and changes in industrial technology face unions and their Socialist allies with a choice between resisting imperative readjustments or competing in the search for rational responses. Moreover, there are developing changes in what might be called the mood and orientation of many Japanese workers. These are not all explained by increased, though unevenly distributed, incomes and consequent gains in consumption, education, and welfare. The gulfs between managerial elites and employees, which are reflected in those between political conservatives and socialists, still persist; but Japanese industrialists are gradually becoming less autocratic and paternalistic, more interested in aspects of human relations in their workshops. Younger workers with newer, more needed technical training are forging ahead and are developing more professional attitudes. Thus, while left-wing Socialists would have the party become more specifically the exponent of organized labor, that movement seems to be losing headway as an influence in the national community, as it is in the United States—but more slowly. These are some of the problems which have compelled Sōhyō politicians to become less militantly political, to return in another swing of the pendulum to a stress on economic aims, and to advocate a "Japanese unionism" less sensitive to influences from Communist China and the Soviet Union.

The right-wing Socialists, who feel more acutely the shortage of able and experienced candidates for leadership both in constituencies and in the party, will have to recruit more from sympathizers among professional and small business groups. Their labor allies have been gaining strength in part by cooperating in the processes of economic growth. Both wings are strengthening their coteries of intellectuals and are using them more in the planning of policies, but it is not to be expected that many university experts will become career politicians. Perhaps more recruiting can be done among journalists and lawyers, and gradually from the bureaucracy. We have noted the accentuated tendency of senior bureaucrats to enter conservative politics, and that the largest politically influential reservoir of expertise is to be found in governmental agencies. Although more junior officials are thought to prefer the Socialists, particularly the right wing, they must be circumspect in political activities. Greater efforts will probably be made to enlist their support and contributions, but it is unlikely that they can soon supplement or offset the increment of labor leaders who have invigorated the SDP's left wing.

One of the most interesting challenges to right-wing Socialists—one which may have disproportionately great significance for Japanese politics in general—is whether a rising generation of younger leaders will outgrow the principal limitations of their seniors. Will they be associated with free rather than "kept" unions in the process of collective bargaining? Will their relations with employers become more independent? Will they redefine their view of socialism in relation to parliamentary politics in ways which will appear realistic and theoretically sound? What will be the nature of their factions? Will traditionalism, which has lurked so markedly in the social attitudes of many older right-wing Socialist leaders, be abated so that the younger elite can be regarded as more reliable reformers? These questions may not be answered in uniform patterns.

In addition to the need of these parties for leaders of stature and public experience, it is essential to rethink the Socialist position in the light of the changing evolution of both totalitarian socialism and increasingly regulated capitalism. It has often been pointed out that Japanese Marxists still think in terms of theories worked out before communist-oriented socialism and the dictatorship of the proletariat had been tried in nation-states, and when capitalism was still largely unregulated and more exploitative. In the course of two generations it has been possible to observe that new strata are developing in supposedly classless societies; that the state has not withered away but has become bureaucratically oppressive under proletarian dictatorships; that problems of determining the most efficient investment of state capital and of increasing the efficiency of production exist in socialist economies; that labor unions in such systems become agencies of state policy without independence; and that imperialism is no monopoly of capitalism—rather that capitalist countries are divesting themselves of colonies, while powerful communist states have added satellites. These are but a few facts which can be ignored only at the peril of drifting ever farther from reality.

On the other hand, although capitalism is far from ideal in some of its features, it can be seen that advanced capitalist economies are not likely to collapse from their own inner contradictions, and that regulative means have been developed both to minimize fluctuations in business cycles and to curb serious forms of exploitation. Welfare state concepts are being applied, and graduated income taxes in Japan and other countries exert corrective influences. Moreover, modified capitalist economies have not only recovered from the effects of war but have made possible new gains in levels of popular income and consumption. Especially since the late 'fifties, these trends have become increasingly evident in Japan, and the implications of this prosperity may, more than anything else, induce some Socialists to reconsider. The advance in the resources and public significance of Japan's petty and "mid-"middle strata is posing a great political challenge and opportunity. And now that the state has become financially more capable of extending assistance to weaker and destitute segments of the population, the main parties will compete more avidly for their favor. It is significant that, as the Socialists reached an electoral plateau, the Sōka Gakkai and its political organizations became important vehicles for social criticism and action in public affairs. The young Komeitō (Clean Government Party) competes with both of the principal parties and has behind it a movement probably more solidly organized than either the Labor-Socialist alliance or the LDP machine.

One cannot be very hopeful that more extreme Socialists will readily become more flexible, however, for their emotional attitudes, habits, and prejudices are deeply ingrained. The lower and alienated Japanese strata have lived under great pressures and tend to find in theoretical slogans and "confrontation" outlets for their counter-aggressions. To become more practical and concrete would require compromises, and insofar as alienation seeks expression there is a tendency to prefer theory to practicality.

Social and economic gulfs have not been reduced as much in Japan as in the United Kingdom; welfare facilities and social security are not as adequate. The Japanese Socialists have not been sobered by a period in exclusive possession of power. Their British counterparts were able to achieve part of what workers, the petty middle class, and some of the intelligentsia sought. They found, however, that working conditions did not markedly improve for employees in nationalized enterprises. They also encountered problems of expanded bureaucracy and red tape. Socialist participation in the Katayama and Ashida governments did not involve the SDP, especially its left wing, with sufficient responsibility to have a durably disillusioning effect. If they could hold power and when out of office remain within reach of it, the Socialists might gradually feel less compulsion to demonstrate extreme contrasts between their assumptions and policies and those of the more forward-looking conservative elements. For decades socialists were not allowed freely to promote their ideas in Japan, and they have never had a real opportunity to apply them.

Many Japanese still suffer from aftereffects of severe repression under the legal disabilities and police surveillance which characterized the Meiji system. At least a generation may be required before left-wing Socialists can react less extremely to the past, reassured that the greater freedoms enjoyed since 1945 are likely to continue. Of course, all democratic societies must keep reinterpreting, asserting, and expanding democratic freedoms in new dimensions. Socialist and Communist militants undoubtedly have important, though minority, roles to play in such efforts. It is significant that since 1960 younger leaders in the left wing have propounded "structural reform," thus precipitating an intensified polemic which continues. As compared with some socialist parties in Western Europe, this willingness to rethink socialist theory came tardily in Japan. Its advocates have had to defend their views against more orthodox critics by elaborate rationalizations and by assertions that ultimate revolutionary aims have not been abandoned.

We live in such an unstable world that one cannot be sure that Japan will be permitted a long period of development free from invasion and atomic disaster; but if the economy can grow satisfactorily with only minor recessions, and if liberal parliamentary institutions can be consolidated, the percolative advantages to ordinary Japanese under capitalism further modified will—particularly after population begins to decline in absolute numbers—probably compel Socialists further to reformulate their analysis. The power and influence of Chinese Communism will probably by then have matured, however, and their effects in Eastern Asia are difficult to predict.

For the Socialists to win power gradually and soundly will require more cohesion, more adequate organization and training of personnel, as well as more rational and knowledgeable planning of policies. It will further require the attraction of much more support from rural voters, people connected with small and medium enterprises, professional workers, female voters, and even better discipline among organized workers plus the adherence of adult members of their families.

The Kōmeitō rather than the SDP appears to be the principal beneficiary of declining LDP support. The latter, though commanding majorities in both Houses of the Diet, received less than 45 per cent of the national vote in elections to the House of Councillors in 1965. If this trend—together with acute LDP factionalism—continues, Japan may enter a phase of lessened political stability. Despite their philosophical critique of capitalism, the Sōka Gakkai and its political affiliate are based on traditional values and probably will increasingly reveal nationalistic conservatism. With sagacious leaders and a syncretism that includes a kind of apostolic socialism, however, one cannot quite dismiss the possibility of a future Kōmeitō-DSP-SDP coalition. But none of these parties would ally in this formal way with the JCP. In certain now unforeseen circumstances, the combination seeking to form a government might include some of the more reformist conservative factions if the LDP should suffer schism.

As revolutionaries in chronic opposition, Japan's socialists have often expressed nationalism in negative or inverted forms. But the new identity and world role now sought by the nation require more positive implementation. If Japan is to become more independent of the United States, as Japanese broadly seem to desire and consider more feasible, then its capability to ensure its own security will have to be strengthened. Obviously this would argue for a changed Socialist position concerning deterrent rearmament and other arrangements for defense. It might induce more practical Japanese support of a United Nations police force.

Another political crisis in 1970 over the security treaty and related issues is quite likely. The conservatives should not expect to avoid this by the clause providing for continued validity of the treaty until preannounced abrogation. If the war in Vietnam still rages, and if escalation has advanced further, Japanese—from anxiety about involvement—might respond more broadly and radically than a decade earlier. The Socialists will do their best to reap advantages from such a crisis; their agitation may compel the ruling party to take such an independent stance that it might deny bases in Japan to the United States, augment Japan's defensive power, and perhaps coalesce on a negotiated basis with a party like the Kōmeitō. These steps might well seem to conservatives preferable to yielding decisive initiatives to Socialists and their allies. A negotiated peace in Vietnam might make it easier to weather the probable crisis in 1970.

Whether party, labor, and intellectual leftists can turn the deteriorated world situation into a genuine revolutionary opportunity remains in doubt. Only in such a situation might the SDP be tempted to permit pragmatic cooperation with the JCP. Some moderate Japanese observers fear that, if the war in Southeast Asia still is being waged in 1970, demonstrators may—unlike the pattern in 1960—be joined by masses from the curbs, making critical the preservation of law and order. If necessary, the police could—as leftists have long feared—be buttressed by the National Safety Forces. Such a resort could boomerang politically, however, and the conservatives would probably avoid it except in extremity. Some say such a drastic policy might reveal disaffection in the Safety Forces, too.

That the Socialists can break through "the barrier of one third" Diet strength and mount in electoral support to a majority, thus to governmental mandate in the near future is, as we have seen, doubtful. A real two-party system in Japan—with either main contender within possible reach of governmental power and agreeing sufficiently on the nature of the state and on political procedures—is not on the visible horizon. It is therefore academic to ask what policies the Social Democrats would be likely to invoke if they should come to power, but for purposes of interpretation such an attempt may have some point. Of course, much would depend on the immediate circumstances in which such a change might occur. If it happened in the near future and if the left continued to be the stronger wing, the programmatic gulf between the two main parties would become even more apparent. It might become clearer that they differ on the fundamental nature of the state, on basic values and procedures. The SDP has been promising gradual nationalization and attainment of a socialist revolution, but, as we have seen, there are more radical elements in and supporting the party which might try, in a promising situation, to push on more rapidly. These groups would probably be satisfied neither with policies like those the British Labour Party employed after its victory in 1945, nor with Scandinavian patterns of social democracy.

Any drastic moves would almost certainly encounter stiff opposition from conservative interests, including some sectors of the bureaucracy, and possibly from some units of the police and armed services. Instead of disbanding these services, the new regime might feel obliged to retain and even enlarge them, after reorganization, as protectors of the new government and its reforms. If more moderate leftist factions combined with right-wing Socialist leadership, they might foresee opposition and move more cautiously. In that case, the Socialist government would likely be defeated before it could go far toward a new order.

If more extreme counsels prevailed, resort could be had to authoritarian trends. There have been hints that, if necessary, the Constitution would be amended in order to safeguard such a revolution. The familiar rationalization would be that since the new order would be for all the people—a classless society—ipso facto it would be democratic; and therefore many of the institutions of bourgeois liberalism would become anachronisms. This would be to abandon the principles of liberal social democracy. Such a trend would almost inevitably be accompanied by resurgent militancy.

There is a basic inconsistency between militant "struggle" tactics and attitudes of "confrontation" characteristic of the Socialist left wing and, on the other hand, its professions of peacefulness. As Lincoln Steffens once remarked, many men want peace but on their own terms. There is nothing like a systematic dogma to make them feel righteously intransigent. However, we have been conjecturing about latent possibilities. It is highly doubtful that the right wing would cooperate in such a desertion of parliamentary politics; thus, in such an unlikely crisis, party unity probably could not be maintained.

Moreover, there are less doctrinaire factions on the left which prefer to attain a planned economy by legal methods and by utilizing existing state mechanisms. The structural reformers, including the small nucleus of former bureaucrats led by men like Wada and Katsumata, seem to be of this persuasion. If the party were to attain power and exercise it for two or three years to achieve reforms gradually, many more leaders with administrative experience might rally to it. Also there might be opportunities for the Socialists to expand their following among rural voters and to persuade university-trained experts to play more active roles, even though remaining outside the ministries. They would also be in an excellent position to revise and strengthen legislation on behalf of small and medium enterprises, though—as we have seen—there are financial limitations which would have to be considered.

Such experiences—not only once but if intermittent—would probably have the salutary effects already described as needed. The reforming zeal of these Socialists instead of being frustrated might be practically employed; the party and allied movements could contribute much while Japan continues its quest for social justice and labor-management cooperation in production as the industrial order advances. But in actuality, unable so far to advance beyond the plateau of one third of the seats in both Houses of the Diet, these parties and allied movements must continue uphill with no certainty as to their course and destination.

Index

Italicized page numbers refer to tabular material.